Vocational Guidance and Human Development

Edited by
Edwin L. Herr
The Pennsylvania State University

Vocational Guidance and Human Development

Houghton Mifflin Company · Boston

Atlanta
Dallas
Geneva, Illinois
Hopewell, New Jersey
Palo Alto
London

Printed in the U.S.A.

Library of Congress Catalog Card Number: 73–10231

ISBN: 0–395–17437–6

To All NVGA Members
Past, Present, and Future
and to Those They Serve

Contents

9944

Foreword

In 1964 *Man in a World at Work*, edited by Henry Borow, was published. Representing the profession's best thinking about the role of work in the life of man, this volume was a major contribution to professional literature. Since 1964 our knowledge and understanding about the role of work in the life of man have been greatly extended and expanded. Deeper understanding of man's relationship to work and the many other arenas of life is available. New and innovative guidance practices are now being used by practitioners across the country.

To bring these developments to the attention of the profession and the public on a systematic basis, NVGA has decided to sponsor the decennial volume series, of which *Man in a World at Work* becomes the first book. *Vocational Guidance and Human Development*, the second volume, reports new knowledge and practices in the area of human growth and development that have occurred since 1964, while it also looks at future directions for guidance both nationally and internationally.

This volume was begun under the leadership of President Donald E. Super (1969–70). During his tenure of office a decennial volume committee was selected consisting of Norman C. Gysbers (Chairman), Henry Borow, Edmund W. Gordon, Edwin L. Herr, Esther E. Matthews, and Donald E. Super. Their work provided the basic structure for the volume. Edwin Herr was selected as editor, and under his leadership the outline was developed and implemented. Presidents John G. Odgers (1970–71) and William C. Bingham (1971–72) provided continued support and leadership during their terms of office.

On behalf of the NVGA membership, the Board of Directors is proud to present to the public and the profession this second book in the decennial volume series.

Norman C. Gysbers, *Past President*
National Vocational Guidance Association

Carl McDaniels, *President*
National Vocational Guidance Association

Preface

During the past decade many of the cherished reference points in the American belief system have been assailed. Similar assaults upon the images and values which serve as shapers of human behavior have occurred in other nations of the world. Journalists, philosophers, and theologians have looked in dismay at the growing number of persons figuratively adrift without the moorings of stability in social attitudes or institutions. In these conditions many questions have been raised about the continuing viability of work as a central activity through which to secure meaning for one's life.

In America, as in the other highly industrialized societies of the world, work is undergoing redefinition. The characteristics of work in relation to play or to leisure are subjects for much philosophical and theoretical speculation. The lines of demarcation between education as preparation for work and education as a continuing necessity to cope with the demands of work for rising cognitive abilities are becoming prominent issues in describing the connections between work and other social institutions. Questions about the degree to which work is important to or hinders man's quest for personal identity have grown in intensity among the disaffiliated, the alienated, and the minority groups living in the industrial or postindustrial societies.

Some observers have suggested that as societies become developed (industrial) the concommitant magnitude of opportunities poses a "burden of decision" for the young and the displaced. The resulting situation is one in which questions of "Who am I?" or "What investment of my characteristics do I want to allocate to work?" are not only legitimate but, indeed, required by the multiple possibilities available to the individual. The problem is, however, that the individual choice-making competencies required in such a context are rarely facilitated systematically by the institutions or family to which the individual is exposed. Thus, a crescendo of support has grown in the last decade for vocational guidance to take on an aggressive role in developing such skills rather than reacting only when they have gone awry or failed the individual.

The opportunities available in the most industrialized countries for self-definition or for decisions about the degree to which one wishes to commit oneself to work are not typical of the less industrialized nations of the world. In such societies citizens are likely to be more concerned about whether work is available and about gaining access to it than they are with how much control or psychological commitment they have. In this sense, "having work" or "not having work" are likely to be more economic than psychological issues for the individual than where the range and availability of work is unlimited. Such societies are more likely to be concerned about having enough jobs for the people than about the affective dimensions of work. Thus, the problem tends to be one of fitting people to limited existing opportunities rather than fitting a wide range of opportunities to the characteristics of people.

All of this tends to suggest that the form and focus of vocational guidance will differ from nation to nation because these dimensions are interactive with the social order, political system, and economic structure of the particular society. The pervasiveness of industrialism and the character of its technology have symbiotic relationships to the social order of which they are a part. The more sophisticated the technology, the more the questions which arise are social and psychological questions rather than technical ones and the more the centrality of work compared to alternative life-styles is at issue. In the less industrialized nations of the world work as the dominant factor in personal identity remains powerful and pervasive. As the nations of the world and their citizens are in economic and social flux, so also is vocational guidance as it responds to these changes.

The title of this volume, *Vocational Guidance and Human Development,* reflects an attempt to clarify some of the relationships between vocational guidance and its changing contexts as well as to reinforce its emerging role in human development across national boundaries. The book begins by identifying some of the major social, legislative, and conceptual changes which describe the intervening ten years since the first volume in this decennial series, *Man in a World at Work,* edited by Henry Borow, was published in 1964. Part One examines the status of vocational guidance in America compared with the characteristics of such processes in selected nations of Europe and Asia. Part Two focuses upon the implications for individual choice in such factors as urbanization, the social structure, economic enterprise, work, the family, and the educational structure, as these are descriptive of America in the early 1970s. Part Three describes the current state of theory and research pertinent to career development, life-staging phenomena, and models of vocational maturity. Part Four is concerned with implications for professional practice found in assessment, career planning, planned utilization and change of environments, as well as media and systems technology. This part also describes the interaction of career development and professional practice in relation to women, disadvantaged and minority populations, and the handicapped. It also examines the emerging requirements for competency and the professional preparation of vocational guidance practitioners. Finally, Part Five of the book suggests the growing international requirements for vocational guidance as well as the dimensions of professional practice which are likely to be evident in the decade ahead.

E. L. H.

Acknowledgments

I would feel remiss if I did not make a few personal observations at this juncture. It is important to recognize that books, like people, have personal histories. This one began with the vision of the NVGA Decennial Volume Commission—Henry Borow, Edmund Gordon, Norman Gysbers, Edwin Herr, Esther Mattehws, and Donald Super—who deliberated long and hard about what perspectives vocational guidance specialists needed to consider as they looked to the future. The format for this volume was their collaborative product.

Since assuming the editorship of this volume it has been my task to operationalize the vision of the Decennial Volume Commission by outlining chapters, contacting authors, getting their agreement to write, and providing editorial supervision of the process. After the authors were originally committed two found it necessary to withdraw without completing their chapters and on May 7, 1972 one of the authors and a very personal friend, Joe Impellitteri, was killed in an automobile accident. I continue to miss him and his affectionate insights and good humor. But I was fortunate enough to secure replacements who were willing to work against difficult time lines. They did it, and, although I will not identify them here, they each know of my profound respect for them.

In conclusion, I want to express my appreciation for the continuing support of the Decennial Volume Commission members. Their encouragement is much appreciated. I also want to thank my colleagues in the Department of Counselor Education at The Pennsylvania State University for their insights and their support. They each have the knack of saying the right thing at the right time. I particularly acknowledge the insights of John Horan and Stanley Baker who read and commented on three of the chapters for me.

Finally, to my wife, to my mother, to Amber, and to Christopher—my love and my thanks.

E. L. H.

PART ONE
Perspectives on
Vocational Guidance

Vocational guidance responds to the stimulation and shaping of those to be served and to the social events which define the psychological determinants for choice. In Part One, Super discusses the economic and political determinants of the philosophy and practice of educational and vocational guidance in both the developed and the developing nations of the world. Herr examines the American manpower policies which have evolved in the past ten years, identifying the images of vocational guidance in selected major pieces of legislation as well as the social conditions which spawned this legislation. Borow addresses the dynamic perceptions of life and work in relation to youth, paying special attention to the growing pluralism of life-styles and the implications these hold for defining work in the 1970s.

Throughout Part One evidence is cited which tends to support the importance of the emerging prevocational or developmental role of vocational guidance as well as the refinement of its adjustment or treatment roles. Particularly apparent is a rising expectation that vocational guidance practitioners will be aggressive in seeking appropriate clientele and providing them with educative experiences designed to facilitate their choice-making capability. Super reminds the reader that as emphases in vocational guidance change, several significant issues continue to be in conflict. Among the most important are manpower distribution versus human development as the focus of vocational guidance, a continuing emphasis in practice upon occupational choice while the theoreticians advocate career development, perceptions of vocational guidance as principally concerned with information rather than counseling, and, finally, the importance of professional as contrasted with lay counseling.

Apathy, Unrest, and Change: The Psychology of the 1960s

1

Henry Borow
University of Minnesota

Henry Borow
University of Minnesota

THE PERILS OF PROPHECY

Man's incorrigible penchant for peering over his horizons and speculating at what might lie beyond carries with it the promise of mixed returns. If, as observer, he makes educated guesses about a distant day, he may win the necessary time to plan a smooth and orderly transition between epochs. If, as visionary, he incorrectly gauges the nature, direction, or pace of change, he prepares himself for unreality. The hazards of writing society's biography in advance have not been lost upon skeptics. Horace Walpole once cautioned, "The wisest of prophets makes sure of the event first." "To prophesy is extremely difficult—especially with respect to the future," runs one waggish aphorism.

Yet such admonitions have hardly dampened the ardor of futurists. Indeed, the exponential rate of social and technological change, especially since the middle of the century, would appear to have spurred a sharply expanded interest in what is coming to be known as "futurology," the subscience of knowing about and planning for the future. In *The Shape of Tomorrow*, economist George Soule[1] drafted a provocative yet admirably restrained picture of what life in America would be like during the ensuing quarter-century ending about 1985. Drawing chiefly upon the promise of technology, Soule delineated a culture marked by significant advances in the commercial use of synthetic substances and radioisotopes, in the development of telecommunication systems, mechanized houses, automated factories, solar energy, desert irrigation plans, and policies and techniques for both population control and the management of world poverty.

Soule also addressed the question of how an advancing technology might likely affect man as consumer, man at work, and man at play. Here he is more circumspect and less imaginative. No clear picture is projected of the life-style of late twentieth-century man. We are told that the elimination of unskilled jobs will lead to greater satisfaction of the worker, a promise that has hardly been vindicated by subsequent developments. On balance, Soule, like many futurists, displays a keener ability to foresee the physical and economic form of the new age than to discern the moral and interpersonal issues of the shifting human condition.

An audacious attempt to foretell the form of the sixties was published in 1959 by the editors of *Newsweek*. Seen from the perspective of the middle 1970s, the world they projected furnished an imprecise and, in many

3

respects, deceptive preview of the events and conditions that we have experienced. In the domains of economics (rising inflation), transportation (congested highways, larger proportions of compact cars, government aid to financially troubled railroads), space technology (a timetable for man's first lunar landing), *Newsweek*'s forecasts were close to the mark. But in the arena of human affairs (politics, poverty, race relations, work, religion and general life style) the magazine displayed a limited talent for prescience. Few, if any, intimations are given of major conditions which were soon to emerge—America's anguished preoccupations with a decade-long war in Indochina; profound stirrings among the nation's ethnic and racial minorities; the sexual revolution, far-reaching legislative enactments to redress injustices in housing, employment, and education; mounting concern about air and water pollution and the ravaging of natural resources; and the tormented debates over man's existential plight. A lengthy section of the report devoted to the "America at Work" theme, dealt only with economic and productivity factors and utterly failed to address the problems of work alienation that loomed large in the ensuing decade. Finally, *Newsweek*'s editors joined an ample company of errant educational soothsayers in unhesitatingly forecasting a continuance of the teacher shortage and in concluding that "the over-all value of a college degree will not depreciate—to the class of 1970, it will be more precious than ever."[2]

A PROFILE OF THE SIXTIES

It has been the practice of social historians and popular chroniclers to assign descriptive titles to the passing decades which purportedly capture their thematic essence. Thus we speak of "the gay nineties" and "the roaring twenties," the latter era subsequently renamed "the lawless decade"[3] to signify the Prohibition, bootlegging, and racketeering years beginning about 1925. The 1930s are understandably recalled as "the depression years." Following World War II, "the silent generation" became a widely employed appellation thought by some observers to distill the passive, sullen, and detached ideological mood of uncommitted youth of that period.[4]

How will the 1960s be remembered? It was a time of awakening group conscience; of indignation and outrage fed by a spreading realization of the pervasiveness of social and economic inequality and deprivation; of insurgency among blacks, Chicanos, and native Americans; of sharp challenges by women liberationists, youth countercultures, conservationists, and consumer protection groups; of the championing of the values of the new individualism and "Consciousness III";[5] of the erosion of popular trust in major social institutions—business firms, organized labor, Congress, the executive branch of federal government, the military, the courts, the press, the schools, and the scientific community[6]—and of the antihero in literature and cinema (e.g., *Cool Hand Luke, Butch Cassidy and the Sundance Kid*). Yet, it was also a time of the "silent majority" which, at least tacitly, supported America's deepening involvement in the Vietnam tragedy; of unprecedented personal affluence which saw the real Gross National Product exceed threefold the level of the year 1900; of breathtaking social, economic, and technological change; of confident prophecies about the decline of work and the emergence of the leisure phenomenon; and of the outward thrust of a new hedonism, aptly characterized by Martha Wolfenstein as the "fun morality." Whatever else they may be said to have been, the 1960s were complex and they were polylithic.[7]

When the United States entered the sixties, it had reached midstream in a course of economic expansion that had begun with the termination of World War II and had run apace, interrupted only by a moderate recession in the early fifties. Faith in the power of formal schooling to legitimize upward socioeconomic mobility was a stamp of the great majority of American households. (As we were soon to discover, certain bypassed and then largely invisible subpopulations, trapped by geographic and cultural isolation and a profound sense of powerlessness to share in the promise of an improved life station, were not partners to this vision.) The construction of new plant facilities and programs in secondary and postsecondary academic and technical education moved briskly forward to accommodate the inexorable demands of a sophisticated economy and to qualify both youth and middle careerists for fuller participation in the abundant life. In the new age, one was told, the untrained person was obsolete.

It was not, however, only concern about the prerequisites for individual advancement which motivated the sharply accelerated pace of education; national survival was also felt to be at stake. When the Soviet Union launched Sputnik I, the first artificial earth satellite on October 4, 1957; sent a dog into space on November 3 of the same year; and dispatched the rocket Lunik II to hit the moon on September 12, 1959, United States complacency about its assumed technological superiority over the rest of the world was rudely shattered. Propelling education toward the front ranks of America's priorities was the argument that the schools had been found shockingly wanting and that an urgent and massive thrust toward educational excellence was required. How might a democratic nation's idealistic aspiration to foster individual development and self-betterment through education and guidance be harmonized with the perceived need to employ the same mechanism for more efficient manpower utilization in a world power struggle? It is against the backdrop of these conflicting national aims that the events of the 1960s must be interpreted if one is to attempt to comprehend one major component of the value dilemma confronting the youth of that period. Given the shifting and uncertain mood of the nation and the strident debates over where the primary moral obligations of a free society lay, it may be argued that the identity diffusion and avoidance behavior which appeared to typify many of our young people in that decade were as directly ascribable to a country's inability to find its confident direction as to the "future shock" which Toffler[8] has contended is generated by the forces of rapid cultural and technological change.

Cold wars, small and large, still tormented the world in the early 1960s. The United States was ending its diplomatic relations with Castro's Cuba. East-West tensions on a broader scale existed in many quarters. Two Germanys glared menacingly at each other across the Berlin Wall. The sleeping and mysterious giant, The People's Republic of China, was beginning to move onto the center stage of world politics, although Taiwan, with American help, still maintained active fortifications on Quemoy, a few short miles off the China mainland coast. Unbridled nationalism remained the dominant political mode. Relations between nations still rested heavily on unilateral instruments and bilateral agreements or on coercive shows of strength. The bright post-World War II hopes for the development of a world rule of law and for a strong United Nations capable of resolving international misunderstandings by means of peaceful diplomacy were dimmed.

The United States and Russia continued to practice one-upsmanship for prestige and influence among the other nation states through spaceage exploits. In April 1961 Russian astronaut Yuri Gagarin became the first man to reach outer space, circling the earth once in a flight of 108 minutes. The following month America countered with Alan B. Shepard's 15-minute suborbital flight over the Atlantic ocean in Freedom 7. A year later the United States successfully shot aloft the satellite Telstar and, in doing so, ushered in the age of immediate history in which live events in Europe could be simultaneously monitored in America, and vice versa. Once again technology had shrunk the world. The announcement of each such event was met with a mixture of admiration and anxiety, admiration for the scientific achievement it represented, anxiety over the political and military advantages it appeared to win for the sponsoring nation. In the presence of persistent international tensions, the selective service draft remained an imminent reality for the majority of American male youths and influenced educational and vocational plans in many ways.

Domestic events in the United States during the 1960s more than matched those in the international arena in turbulence and in capacity to effect significant and durable change.[9] Beginning early in the decade with the efforts of the "Freedom Riders" to extend the franchise to numerous Southern blacks to whom it had been denied, the civil rights movement fanned out along many paths and in all parts of the land to challenge harsh inequities in employment opportunities, education, housing, and criminal justice. Numerous confrontations arose out of bitterly contested attempts to implement the 1954 school desegregation decision of the United States Supreme Court. History once again provided a cheerless reminder that social reform, when met by resistance to change, is the conveyor of turmoil and violence. The sixties witnessed a surfeit of both and led H. Rap Brown to react to widespread expressions of revulsion and shocked dismay with the laconic observation that "violence is as American as cherry pie." A riot erupted in the Watts district of Los Angeles in August 1965, and within a two-month period during the "long, hot summer" of 1967, violent racial episodes occurred successively in Boston, Tampa, Cincinnati, Atlanta, Buffalo, Newark, and Detroit. In Detroit alone more than forty lives were lost. It was in the sixties, too, that assassinations claimed the lives of four prominent leaders, President John F. Kennedy, black nationalist Malcolm X, the Reverend Martin Luther King, Jr., and Senator Robert F. Kennedy. And it was during the same decade that countless skirmishes were grimly played out between antiwar protestors and police, national guardsmen, and hard hats.

Even as American embroilment in the Southeast Asia conflict began to intensify, the federal government initiated a series of bold programs in an effort to rectify long-standing economic and educational inequities and to extend civil liberties to those groups to whom they had previously been systematically denied. Social Security provisions were liberalized in 1961, making workers eligible for retirement benefits at the age of sixty-two. The following year saw passage of the Manpower Development and Training Act, which furnished greatly expanded schooling and on-the-job training for the unemployed and underemployed sectors of the labor force. In his 1964 State of the Union message, President Lyndon Johnson announced the Administration's War on Poverty and pledged to broaden the civil rights of the victims of discrimination. Initiating his second term in office before the newly convened Eighty-ninth Congress in January 1965, Johnson reported his sanguine plans for the Great Society. Reminiscent of the New Deal and the Fair Deal programs which Franklin Roosevelt and Harry Truman had earlier pursued to resolve the domestic crises of the 1930s and late 1940s, the Great Society was envisioned as a rich, sophisticated, yet humane nation dedicated to providing all of its citizens with a broad spectrum of services and opportunities for achieving the good life. Bent upon making the boast a reality, the government enacted an ambitious and sweeping succession of measures within the close span of a few years during the middle sixties, many of these expressly designed to extend social justice, raise family incomes, aid the handicapped, and afford a fuller range of educational and job opportunities to the economically and culturally disadvantaged.

In 1964 Congress passed the influential Civil Rights Act, a major piece of legislation, and in 1965 the Voting Rights Act. Economic assistance to youth from low-income families came in varied forms—the Job Corps, the Neighborhood Youth Corps, Youth Opportunity Centers, Community Action Programs, work-study programs, and low-cost student loans. Many of the new programs were legislated under a major omnibus measure, the Economic Opportunity Act, and were administered under authority of a specially created agency, the Office of Economic Opportunity. Judgments about the effectiveness of OEO differed widely, and the agency became an object of intense political partisanship, defended by some attacked by others. In early 1973 the OEO was abruptly abolished by the Nixon administration and most of its programs drastically curtailed or terminated.

THE TRANSFORMING SOCIETY

America in the 1960s was characterized by a discernible reshaping in behavioral standards, both those of implicit values and beliefs and those relating to patterns of overt conduct. It would be an oversimplification to conclude that such social mutations were brought on by some special cataclysm peculiar to the decade. A more reasonable interpretation would hold that the forces of change had been long under way and that their effects were becoming increasingly visible. While it is hazardous to attempt to capture the special quality of the newer ways of feeling, valuing, and acting under a single rubric, concepts like the "open society" and the "new humanism" are helpful approximations of the shifting climate.

Technologically simple cultures, especially those faced with a constant struggle for physical safety and biological survival, typically establish stringent controls over individual behavior and exact severe penalties for deviations from group norms. The self-indulgence of ego motives is frowned upon; self-denial and disciplined asceticism become the chief marks of the person who is strong and moral. Such a life view was hardly foreign to most American settlers who emigrated from Northern and Western Europe or to their progeny. Many of the same people who sought enonomic opportunity and political or religious freedom in a new land espoused a life of piety, rewarded puritanical austerity, and sternly discouraged expressions of individualism. The transcendental movement in New England, which flourished for a relatively brief time in the mid-nineteenth century, was, indeed, mainly a reaction against the ideological and spiritual restraints of Puritanism and its closed social systems. During that era, as in our own, various conditions—urbanization, burgeoning industrialism, progressive national and individual affluence, spreading secularism and the declining influence of the church in defining acceptable personal conduct, the growing power of the mass communication media to shape attitudes, challenges to the dominant role of the conjugal family as the socializer of morals, and the phenomena of increased geographic and occupational mobility—combined and interacted in complex ways to erode traditional ethical imperatives and to elevate notions of "person" and "being."

Curiously, the humanistic surge of the 1960s represented not only a departure from major assumptions and values within conservative forms of institutionalized religion but also, in some ways, from those of behavioristic psychology and orthodox psychoanalysis, which had been seen as the major adversaries of established theistic systems in the 1920s and 1930s. The sin-and-guilt ethic and the stoicism of religious orthodoxy (e.g., one must endure hardship and one's natural lot without unseemly display of passion) were antithetical to the new humanism; but so, too, were the controlled behavior and preset human goals that most contemporary existentialists, rightly or wrongly, have seen as the unacceptable perils of behavior modification methods and societies in the age of Skinner's *Walden Two*.[10] The demeaning sexual duality of classic Freudianism (e.g., penis envy) has also been rejected by many.

At the heart of the reformed attitudes toward individualism, now embraced by large numbers of American youth, but by no means limited to the young, are several interdependent prescriptive principles—recognize your uniqueness, tune in to your own feelings, learn to think well of yourself, and discard masks and charades in favor of authenticity and of mutual sharing of inner experience with others. In his ardent advocacy of "Consciousness III," which he offers as the distinguishing mark of the new generation, Reich observes that it is a life view which begins with selfhood and with the axiom, "What I am I am." Logically extended, this position argues that each person must "do his own thing," a conclusion which troubles traditionalists and which brings philosophical individualism into inescapable conflict with notions of a neatly ordered society. Fretful preoccupation in the 1960s and early 1970s with the law-and-order issue and with alleged societal permissiveness is partly traceable to the standoff between these two positions.

The fabric of emerging life-styles has been woven from the strands of many movements and positions on the nature of man. The existential philosophy of Jean-Paul Sartre is clearly relevant. So, too, are the humanistic psychologies of Carl Rogers, Abraham Maslow, and Rollo May, which stress fully functioning man's need for the examined life and self-actualization. Contemporary systems of interpersonal problem solving and group psycho-therapy, such as sensitivity training and encounter groups, appear to derive much of their appeal from their vigorous endorsement of individualism, openness of expression, and the free sharing of feelings. (Paradoxically, such structured group experiences, while proclaiming the uniqueness of personal-ity, are frequently guilty of compelling participants to conform to the strict rule of intimate self-disclosure or risk the candidly expressed wrath of the group.) The quest for understanding the reaches of the mind that range beyond the mundane and for liberation from the pain and cares of the external world is akin to the search for the state of nirvana in Hinduism and that of satori in Zen Buddhism. On the periphery of experiments with new forms of augmented selfhood and selftranscendence are the arcane systems whose adherents, impatient with slower, more analytical methods, choose hallucinogens and the occult allures of astrology, tarot cards, and Satanism. In the 1960s and early 1970s such diverse beliefs and practices as all the foregoing formed the complex *modus vivendi* of numerous subcultures and cults, marking the period as one of energetic social challenge and change.

Wrenn has succinctly summarized the assumptions about life and society which have long been embedded in the value system of the dominant culture and which are now being critically questioned. His list includes assumptions about the need for implicit respect for authority, the virtues of war and patriotism, the place of women, the worth of work, the need to justify time spent in leisure, the major functions of sex, the use of drugs, and, finally, the meaning of life itself. Wrenn draws on the analysis of Paul Nash in identify-ing the nation's principal value shifts from "(1) puritanism to enjoyment, (2) self-righteousness to openness, (3) violence to creativity, (4) politeness to honesty, (5) bureaucratic efficiency to human relationships, (6) 'objec-tive truth' to personal knowledge, (7) ideology to existential decision-making and action, (8) authority to participation, and (9) tradition to change."[11]

How widespread is the new wave? Toffler writes of the life-style factories which propagate the doctrines of the counterculture and of the many youth ghettos with their distinctive patterns of housing, mobility, "fads, fashions, heroes, and villains."[12] Yet although the memberships of such new-style subcultures with their divergent value sets appear to be rising, dependable population estimates are unavailable. It is necessary to remind ourselves that it may be more the dramatic, the novel, and the patently iconoclastic character of these belief systems, rather than the sheer numbers of their con-verts, which have made them the object of constant popular attention and of copious news reports.

Whatever the size of the movement, it is clear enough that society in the 1960s became less rigidly structured and more open than formerly. The cultural diversity of an earlier period, which consisted largely of immigrant groups trying to learn *the* American way, had been replaced by the multi-fariousness of indigenous groups, each doubtful about the worth of estab-lished institutions and traditional ways, each seeking to discover a unifying identity and to redefine a code of acceptable beliefs and behavior norms for its constituency. The discussion which follows briefly examines the nature of this changing social order as it applies to significant subpopulations—youth, women, and ethnic and disadvantaged minorities.

THE DILEMMAS OF ADOLESCENCE

The classical picture of adolescence is one of struggle for emotional and economic independence. G. Stanley Hall, a pioneer of the child study movement in the latter part of the nineteenth century, characterized the age as one of *Sturm und Drang* (storm and stress). Adolescence was understood to be, for most individuals, an uncertain psychological no-man's land between childhood and adulthood. In its Latin origin the term carries the literal meaning, "to lead to maturity," but the idea of adolescence as a life stage of intensive and deliberate preparation for the assumption of adult responsibilities is waning.[13]

Adolescence has traditionally been viewed as a stage in which parents who have loved, succored, and taught the child to explore his expanding life space, but who have also inculcated impulse control and set limits on behavior during this apprenticeship for adulthood, come to be perceived by the developing youth as constricting growth and denying rightfully earned freedom. It is questionable whether this active clash of wills between loving, anxious, and constraining parents and ambivalent, restive youth is any longer the cardinal feature of the intergenerational problem in most families. A number of observers have challenged the idea that this alleged crucible of conflict continues to have functional utility in allowing the child to sever a second umbilical cord, to synthesize a new self-identity, and to learn to "become his own man."[14] The conditions of a post-World War II, urban-centered, technological, mobile, value-diffused, and role-segregated society have drastically diminished both the family's and the community's capacity to socialize children for adulthood and have driven the young to search for role models and behavior standards within their own ranks and beyond the established order. A powerful feature of the social order of recent years has been the rise of a distinct and conspicuous youth culture, or, more precisely, of an age-separated series of youthful subcultures—preteens, teens, postteens, and young marrieds.[15]

The inability of the young to feel a sense of serviceability, a unity of purpose with the adult world, stems in significant measure from the changing organization of the household and a radically altered occupational structure. Previous generations of youth may have complained about family chores, but they knew that their grudgingly given ministrations were needed and tacitly valued. However, the current trends toward smaller families, a plenitude of labor-saving appliances, the purchasability of public utilities, and repair services for home maintenance have rendered the home-related work of children trivial or unneeded.

In earlier years able-bodied children were regarded as distinct economic assets, and they typically worked at the side of other members of the household in home, field, or shop to help the family earn its livelihood. During the industrial expansion of the pre-Depression years, older children were able to move out into a job market which was eager to exploit their energies and which placed few obstacles to employment in their path. On the other hand, with its stress on academic degrees, vocational certification, and occupational specialization, and with power machines, servomechanisms, telecommunications, and electronic data processors available to speedily perform myriad tasks previously assigned to human workers, contemporary society devalues the occupational potential of youth and holds it at bay through the imposition of age, education, and experience barriers. The remoteness and inaccessibility of the world of work may severely impair the ability of the family to equip its younger members for autonomous adult status. Adelson concludes, "Given the long preparation required for advanced technical training, given the uselessness of the adolescent in the labor market, parent and child settle down for a long, long period of time during which the child will . . . remain a dependent being."[16] Ironically, the blunting of family effectiveness in facilitating vocational development is occurring at a time in history when the rate of biological maturation has been accelerating. During the period between 1840 and 1960 the onset of menses in girls is estimated to have advanced about four months every ten years.[17] This finding, when coupled with evidence of the steadily improving size, health, education, and general knowledge status of adolescents, points to the disturbing discontinuity between the potential readiness of youth to assume full partnership in the work, decisions, and benefits of community life and the reluctance or incapacity of society to prepare and allow them to do so.

Dissent among the Young

The sixties witnessed a mounting dissatisfaction among high school and college students, much of it openly and boldly expressed, with prevailing institutionalized beliefs and practices and with what they perceived as the limited life options made available to them by a morally insensitive and unresponsive society. While the rebelliousness of the young against the adult world is a drama which is acted out anew with each passing generation, the dynamisms of the youth-versus-establishment conflict which seethed during the 1960s appeared to set it apart from earlier versions in several important respects. Among these were the large number who participated, the broad and complex socioeconomic, racial, and age mixture of the dissenters, the sweeping diversity of issues in controversy, the frequency and intensity of direct confrontations with campus authorities and public officials, and, above all, the extent to which protestors translated slogans into organized programs for action in the peace movement and in the realms of ecology, conservation, education, consumerism, and politics.

Wrenn has identified some of the generative factors and salient characteristics of the youth revolt, presented here in slightly abbreviated form.

1. A rejection of many of their parents' goals of life as superficial, unrealistic, and materialistic.
2. The irrelevance of much formal education in comparison with the relevance of the informal education inherent in television, travel abroad, etc.
3. An awareness that youth today are much older in knowledge and experience than were their peers of a generation ago.
4. The power of numbers possessed by youth, who are feeling that power.

In 1970 the median age of the United States population dropped to its lowest point since 1940—27.9 years of age.

5. The desire of youth for quick results in social and educational change because rapid change is the order of the day in many other dimensions of our culture.

6. The triggering effect of outspoken . . . minority groups, with their sense of social injustice, upon the white majority group disaffections.

7. A willingness of youth to take more risks in demonstrating their resistance to the status quo—they worry less about jobs than youth of previous generations.

8. The uncertainty and disagreement among adults about what is "right," despite their seeming dogmatism.[18]

Much of youth's disenchantment with the established social order centers on the institution of work. Elsewhere this writer has reviewed studies which suggest that the unplanned process of occupational socialization in children produces age-related shifts from predominantly positive images and attitudes of work to negative and rejecting ones.[19] By the time they have reached senior high school, many students have unconsciously assimilated unfavorable stereotypes and preconceptions of many broad occupational groupings, and they tend to exclude consideration of these fields from their planning without, however, being able to articulate such decisions in an acceptably realistic manner.

In the youth counterculture the repudiation of institutionalized work is both more conscious and more highly generalized. What David Riesman termed the "withdrawal of emotional allegiance to work" among such students appears to have its roots in moral repugnance and discordant values. They censure society for its failure to make available to the young challenging and socially useful opportunities which are commensurate with their ability and training. They charge that the vast preponderance of jobs in the economy reflect the avarice and competitiveness of the corporate system with its exaggerated emphasis upon the profit motive. To accept such jobs, they argue, is to run the grave risk of loss of one's individuality and personal freedom. Moreover, these jobs are exploitative of both human and natural resources. Rather than prepare for positions which are unfulfilling and dehumanizing, these youth opt for *vocations for social change,* examples of which include operating organic food shops, providing paraprofessional counseling and legal aid services to the disadvantaged, working at crisis intervention centers, creating and selling homemade craft products, such as jewelry, teaching in the free school movement, and serving in the ACTION Corps (VISTA/Peace Corps).[20]

Those who are alienated from the world of work and from the work morality of the major culture understand that such new-style vocations as the foregoing are not highly remunerative, but they claim that they are not interested in employment chiefly for material gain and that work which is altruistic and which contributes to social reform is to be greatly preferred over work which has as its hallmarks prestige, power, pay, and the loss of personal integrity. At the extreme of the anti-work movement are the self-styled flower children who reject virtually all work and who, by choice, live a spare, ghetto-type, or nomadic existence, soliciting or accepting donations of food, shelter, transportation, and goods almost in the manner of a nonworking holy man receiving alms. John Ciardi's[21] wistfully amusing little essay records his sympathetic, yet frustrating and unsuccessful, attempt to come to terms with the logic of one such flower child.

The Extent of Youth Estrangement

There is danger in painting the outlook of contemporary youth in single hues and with too broad a brush. The college generation of the 1950s was generally depicted as a student mass resistant to involvement with social change, ideologically superficial, anxious about its own future economic security, and resigned to the rules of conformity, depersonalizing competition, and getting ahead. The alienation of this generation was interpreted mainly as an alienation from self, one marked by the motivational poverty of diffused and vaguely articulated personal values. Keniston described a significant deviation from this generational mood of "the uncommitted."[22] His sample consisted of a small, select group of Harvard male undergraduates who turned their disaffection with prevailing beliefs and practices into an uncompromising individualism, a devotion to the sentience of the immediate presence, and a studied unwillingness to stake out and pursue long-range goals. Their rebelliousness, however, was more covert than militantly acted out in frontal attacks on society and, in this sense, they are more accurately seen as the percursors of the more passive "hippies" of the 1960s rather than of the confrontative campus radicals and political activists of that decade. Keniston recently[23] has attempted a differentiation between these two youth alienation types, both culturally disaffected and rejecting the societal *status quo*, but the former marked by passive aggressiveness and cultural withdrawal behavior while the latter by direct, overt revolt against a system which it feels must and can be changed.

Keniston's analysis helps sharpen our understanding of the nature of youth dissent in an emotionally charged climate in which, as Block, Haan, and Smith have noted, "important differences are obscured when such labels as *alienation, lack of commitment, passivity, disaffiliation,* and *resignation* are used interchangeably."[24] Yet, all typologies of the value frameworks and preferred life-styles of youth groups, including Keniston's, are oversimplifications of actuality in that they postulate the existence of discrete subcultures and fail to allow for the many shadings within the spectrum. Barber,[25] for example, faults Keniston's forced polarization of a broad range of dissonant youth postures into the two categories of alienated privatists and alienated radicals. Moreover, there is probably considerable instability of group membership and more than occasional reluctance to support by action a political or ideological position to which one has previously given strong verbal endorsement. At Princeton University, where the conviction was widely shared that students should try to influence public policy by constructive participation in the political process, classes were suspended early in the fall semester of 1972 in order that students might be free to campaign for acceptable candidates for office. Among liberal idealists it was the bright hope that, by such means, the case for peace and a new set of national priorities could be effectively laid before the electorate. Yet, by the admission of student leaders themselves, very few students acted energetically to carry out the objectives of the school moratorium. The course of youthful dis-affection and protest is thus uneven, and often it is unpredictable.

Granting the existence of ideological and other forms of dissent among the young and acknowledging, as was done earlier in the chapter, the pervasive and many-sided character of unrest in the 1960s and early 1970s, we must still admit a lack of hard evidence concerning the actual extent and depth of the alienation. There appears to be support for Barber's claim that most of the young are not greatly alienated from well-established beliefs and institutions. A national survey of nearly 189,000 freshmen in postsecon-dary institutions, conducted by the American Council on Education, found two-thirds of the subjects classifying themselves as politically middle-of-the-road or conservative, fewer than one-third as liberal, and only 2.4 percent as falling on the political far left. While the great majority supported the need for action on the issues of pollution and consumer protection, concerns over student rights, criminal justice, and the rate of school desegregation were hardly universally shared.[26] Such findings, of course, must be in-terpreted in the light of our knowledge that freshmen are typically more con-servative than upperclassmen in their social and political views.

The Yankelovich[27] national survey of the attitudes of college students produced a two-thirds majority acceptance of established social views and a strong belief in the importance of work as a human activity. Despite the abundant claims that students have grown more challenging and critical of social norms, Gottlieb's[28] questionnaire of nearly two thousand 1972 graduates of five Pennsylvania universities found students to be strikingly similar in their attitudes to those of students in a national survey taken eleven years earlier. Few students in either Gottlieb's study or the earlier one reported that they were alienated, rebellious, or cynical, and the work attitudes of the two student generations were in close correspondence. Yet, there were some important changes. Gottlieb's 1972 students described themselves as "more independent . . . from formal religious affiliation, more concerned with their fellow man, less concerned with money and material possessions, more inclined to seek a bridge between work and family, and in general pursuing a lifestyle quite different from that of their parents." The avowed work values of Gottlieb's students appear to match closely those describing young workers on the job in the *Work in America* report.[29] The latter group was found to place more importance than did older workers on interesting work and on the ability to grow on the 'job. Correspondingly, the younger workers attached less importance to job security.

WOMEN IN THE SIXTIES

The view of woman as inferior to man and subservient to his requirements has had a long and tenacious history. In the Western world the influences of Judeo-Christian morality and the code of chivalry rooted in European feudalism of the Middle Ages account for vestigial customs in contemporary American sex-role relationships which, even as they weaken, remain clearly discernible. The idealized portrayal of female sanctity and fragile beauty, drawn by English writers of the Romantic period (e.g., Lord Byron's "She Walks in Beauty Like the Night") and read by virtually all American school children, has been tied to the sharply delimited and subordinate station accorded to women in the real world.

The Women's Rights Movement

In the early 1960s John F. Kennedy created the President's Commission on the Status of Women. The women's rights movement, however, is hardly an exclusive phenomenon of the mid-twentieth century. Over a period of time expanding industrialism, the trend toward secularism, the spread of democratic ideas, and the attendant loosening of lines in a hitherto rigidly stratified society brought about a gradual liberalization of attitudes toward women and an elevation in their social status. Susan B. Anthony's achievements on behalf of women's suffrage were recorded before 1900, and one of America's legendary social reformers, Jane Addams, established Hull House in 1889 and had become a powerful spokesman for women and for the peace movement long before the war-peace issue commanded the energies of American campus ideologues in the 1930s. And yet, even while acknowledging the evolutionary nature of the movement, one must distinguish the 1960s as a decade of unusually vigorous activity and of dramatic gains in the realm of women's rights and opportunities.

Margaret Mead's[30] assessment helps us to understand why the exhortations of Betty Friedan[31] and other feminine protest writers have galvanized the dissatisfactions and restiveness of numerous bright and well-educated young women. Despite many evidences of progress, Mead asserts that the traditionally biased division of labor between men and women still persists. American women are envied by their sisters in other countries for their comparative freedom and affluence, and they are, admittedly, more mobile, less home-bound, and less tied to the immediate and the extended family group than was true of their mothers and grandmothers; yet they are among the hardest working women in the world, carrying, in addition to whatever new interests and jobs they have acquired, a heavy burden of home managerial duties. With a large capital investment in household equipment, their chores are less physical in nature than formerly, but they have taken on a formidable assortment of consumer and money management functions as well as planning and decision-making activities which cannot be easily delegated to young children and for which they receive little. Furthermore, in an age of mass communication and externally imposed social role modeling, it is difficult for a woman to be complacent about her success and efficiency as a homemaker since she must now compare herself, not with her real life neighbors, but, as Mead reminds us, with the annoyingly competent and slickly attractive women she sees on television "whose kitchens are always spotless and whose children are well-fed and well-behaved."[32]

Nor does volunteer service in community and philanthropic organizations provide as large a proportion of women as it once did with a sense of worth and meaningful identity outside the home. Both the time demands of increased paid employment and the apparently lessened prestige attached to voluntary service have reduced the effectiveness of this option for many women who seek to add a significant and useful dimension of experience to their lives. The *America's Young Workers* study, directed by Levine and Herman[33] warns that a major adjustment problem of young women workers is likely to take place when economic circumstances require that they resume interrupted careers with less skill, seniority, and bargaining power than their competitors, while their children also demand their attention and energy.

Women in the Work World

The drive during the 1960s to reduce sex discrimination practices and strengthen women's rights extended to the areas of welfare, child care, legal aid, equity in the courts, birth control assistance, abortion counseling and abortion law reform, sponsorship of women candidates for political office, and employment opportunities. Because most of those problem areas are related to family and personal economics and because job discrimination is known to be a major source of differential economic power between men and women, such feminine liberation groups as the National Organization for Women attacked employment bias with special vigor. For similar reasons considerable legislation aimed at improving the status of women dealt with the enlargement of employment opportunities. The 1963 Equal Pay Amendment to the Federal Fair Labor Standards Act insured equal compensation for substantially equal work without regard to sex. By 1972, acting on adjudicated violations of this law, the courts had directed that $44.5 billions in back wages be paid to more than 108,000 women.[34] Title VII of the 1964 Civil Rights Act outlawed sex discrimination practices in hiring and work dismissals, pay, employment privileges, employee training and promotion, labor union membership, and in other areas of employment. Several presidential orders have expressly prohibited sex discrimination in employment by federal contractors and in the hiring practices of federal agencies.

Such developments represent a sharp departure from past employment policies. Although women have long made up a substantial part of the nation's labor force, previous generations of married women who worked, especially those with preschool and school-age children, suffered opprobrium at the hands of coworkers and neighbors. In blue-color communities, where sex-role distinctions tend to be most clearly drawn, working wives and mothers were regarded with particular disapproval since they were thought to be neglecting their domestic obligations. Moreover, their role as worker posed an embarrassment for the adult males in the household, who were judged by neighbors to be poor providers. Such attitudes still prevail to some extent in the blue-collar subculture.

During the economic depression of the 1930s industrially employed women were criticized on the grounds that they were taking jobs from men, and it was not uncommon for firms to dismiss women employees openly on the basis of their sex. Married women teachers sometimes chose to use the title "Miss" out of fear of hostility and possible loss of job. While sex discrimination in employment has persisted in many quarters, it has assumed less blatant and more subtle forms with the passing years. For example, women are channeled into occupations sex-typed as female, like teaching, secretarial work, and nursing, although there are few empirical grounds on which to base such practices since some of these fields, such as teaching, were once almost exclusively male employment preserves. It is against such subtle restrictive practices that the women's rights movement was vigorously directed during the 1960s.

A durable myth shared by many employers holds that the occupational career motives of young women are transitory inasmuch as the great majority look forward to early marriage and family. Yet, of all employed women in America, one-half have attained the age of forty or beyond. Between 1960 and 1969 the number of working women rose from 23 million to 30 million. During the same decade the number of married women at work increased by half, from 12 million to 18 million, and in 1970 about 60 percent of the female work force was married.[35]

In noting similar gains in the occupational status of European women, Kievit cites the following trends contained in a report from the International Labor Office.

1. The average duration of women's occupational life will increase; thus greater attention should be given to choosing a satisfying occupation with opportunities for advancement than has been given by many expecting a short work life.
2. With larger proportions of women reentering the labor force in the 40–45 years of age period, there is need for counseling and training for reentry.
3. The proportion of married women workers is increasing; thus more workers are combining domestic and work obligations.
4. Decrease of proportion of workers in the lower age categories reflects the fact that girls are continuing their education, which is in keeping with the increased need for skilled workers.[36]

Despite impressive increases in labor force participation by women, serious evidence of employment inequality between the sexes remains to be dealt with. Although the report on the 1960 national census revealed women workers to be represented in all 479 Bureau of the Census occupational categories, females were still absurdly underrepresented in many fields. At the close of the decade only 7 percent of the nation's physicians were women, despite the heavily publicized doctor shortage, and only 3 percent of the lawyers were women, the same percentage as in 1955. Students assimilate the sex-typing of occupations as part of a powerful socialization process and tend to plan their careers accordingly. Surveying the occupational aspirations of large samples of two-year and four-year college students who had taken the ACT Assessment in the late 1960's, Carmody, Fenske, and Scott concluded that the women students in both types of institutions "only rarely thought of themselves as future scientists, sales or business women, or technologists. Rather, they ended their undergraduate college careers with occupational expectations traditionally held to be appropriate for women, such as elementary or secondary school teaching."[37] It is yet unclear to what extent the gathering momentum of the women's rights movement will continue to reverse the deeply entrenched attitudes which militate against a more versatile and prominent participative role for women in the nation's work.

PROBLEMS OF THE POOR AND THE MINORITIES

A stirring of the nation's conscience in the 1960s illuminated and dramatized the plight of several groups—the economically disenfranchised of Appalachia, the widely dispersed rural poor, blacks, Indians, Spanish-Americans, the mentally and physically handicapped—who had long been effectively excluded from partnership in the nation's expanding affluence. Largely separated from these minorities by conditions of geography, a comfortable cultural parochialism, and an abiding belief in the melting-pot myth, the great mass of middle-class Americans possessed only a dim awareness of the way of life and of the awesome problems of these disadvantaged groups. They were, in many respects, invisible citizens who seldom intruded upon the group consciousness of the majority culture or who, at best, evoked tragically quaint and stereotypic images. When, finally, books like *The Other America*[38] and *Black Rage*[39] began to appear, relating the story of disadvantaged Americans in unvarnished detail and with passionate indignation, the revelations and charges they contained shocked many who read them. (Of course, many earlier notable books had been published on the predicament of America's minorities, for example, Myrdal's *An American Dilemma*[40] and Richard Wright's powerful novel *Native Son*.[41] However, the prevailing climate of the times found the country less prepared psychologically to frame a new conscience and to be moved to concerted action by these literary tours de force.) Since the early 1960s countless books and innumerable newspaper and magazine articles have been published about bypassed populations in the United States, their characteristics and their problems. The discussion which follows makes no attempt at a comprehensive analysis of the topic but, instead, deals with some of the significant work-related perceptions and career-adjustment problems of those who have been disadvantaged through socioeconomic and ethnic positions.

Conditions of poverty and employment status are, of course, closely related. Among the poor are disproportionately large numbers who are unemployed and underemployed, who are trapped in unskilled jobs and casual day labor or on welfare rolls, and who exhibit the typical marginal workers' history of disorderly careers. Such dreary and interrupted career patterns also identify many members of minority nationality and ethnic groups. In the past these subpopulations have been overrepresented in the ranks of the jobless and in entry-level occupations, while underrepresented in high-status fields. Starting the 1960s the unemployment rate of blacks with high school diplomas was almost double that of white secondary school graduates according to the Department of Labor study of 1970. Among school dropouts, in itself a condition far more common among blacks than whites (at least in the past), the black-white unemployment gap was even wider. For young, black, female dropouts, the unemployment rate has often reached alarming levels, variously estimated at 35 to 50 percent. As will be indicated below, recent changes have resulted in a sharp reduction in these imbalances; nevertheless, blacks and other minorities, in proportion to their numbers in the population, still hold fewer white collar and skilled jobs than whites, and they frequently face difficult problems of career planning and adjustment.

Work-related Behavior of Disadvantaged Youth

It is hazardous to attempt to draw too sharp a picture of the vocational self-concepts, occupational aspirations, and job adjustment problems of the poor and of disadvantaged minorities. The range of individual differences on such characteristics within these subpopulations far exceeds the difference in group averages between themselves and majority culture subjects. Furthermore, broad population attributes, such as race and social class origin, are probably less accurate as indicators of occupational perceptions and work-relevant behavior than are the individual's experiences and interaction with significant others during his formative years. Yet, when psychosocial deprivation is severe and protracted, the stunting and disorganizing effects are generally predictable. Elsewhere the author has enumerated some of the typical consequences that prolonged human deprivation may produce in the adolescent victim.

> (1) persistent feelings of personal inadequacy as worker-to-be; (2) lack of a sense of agency whereby one simply does not believe in the efficacy of rational planning for one's future; (3) disturbing disparity between one's verbalized occupational aspirations and one's sober expectations; (4) subjective occupational foreclosure whereby one prematurely and unconsciously rejects many broad categories from consideration on vague grounds; (5) lack of realism evidenced by poor understanding of the sequence of preparatory steps leading to the announced vocational goal.[42]

The general outlook of disadvantaged youth on work is likely to be marked by low self-confidence and weak expectations of success. Inner-city ninth-grade boys tend to express their work needs and values in terms of situational concerns (e.g., work location, type of coworkers, and ability requirements), while suburban ninth graders tend to be oriented toward work values which are related to interpersonal satisfactions and the psychological fulfillments of self-expression.[43] A number of studies have reported only negligible differences between high-income and low-income subjects in educational and occupational aspirations. The goal levels of both economic classes are high. However, when asked to state their expectations of reaching their objectives, the low-income students and their parents are distinctly less confident; and even the more modest expectations of the disadvantaged students often appear unrealistic when judged against their inappropriate planning and striving. Such findings furnish a persuasive argument in support of opportunity programs such as Upward Bound.

The effects of psychosocial deprivation extend beyond the poor vocational self-concepts and immature career planning of the school years. As the following description makes clear, they continue to be felt after the disadvantaged individual has entered the labor force.

> Transitory and extrinsic motivation attaches to the work of such an individual. He looks chiefly for short-term, tangible returns from his job. Intrinsic rewards and the prospect of long-term advancement do not occupy a significant place in his perception of the work he performs. Self-actualization through work is at best a remote possibility for him, partly because of the demeaning jobs he normally occupies but also because his work imagery and anticipations cannot accommodate the notion that occupational experience may be self-fulfilling.[44]

Gains for Minorities

During the 1960s educational opportunities for the culturally disadvantaged improved steadily, although slowly in some places, and their attitudes toward postsecondary schooling as a means to socioeconomic advancement grew more favorable. Between 1960 and 1968 the number of blacks and other minorities leaving school as high school graduates had risen from 50 percent to about 70 percent, while the school completion rate of white students, rising more slowly, had shifted from 75 percent to 80 percent. By the end of the decade little difference remained between the percentages of white and black high school girls who stated that they were planning to enter college. Among blacks eighteen to twenty-four years of age, 18 percent were in college in 1971, a sharp rise over the 10 percent figure for 1965.

Some progress also occurred in the trend toward equalization of earnings, although a wide gap still remained to be closed. For full-time male workers in 1968 the average annual earnings of blacks with high school diplomas had reached 73 percent of the level of whites. Blacks with four or more years of college had attained average annual earnings which were 77 percent of those of whites with comparable education. The income picture was brightest for blacks who were young, well educated, and residing in favored regions. For example, among young, black married couples in 1970, the heads of household who were under age thirty-five and living in the northern and western United States attained a median income which had reached 96 percent of that for a comparable population of whites.[45]

Despite intimations in the foregoing discussion that many who have experienced severe and extensive psychosocial deprivation harbor negative feelings and expectations about work and may exhibit a limited vocational maturity, the devaluation of the idea of work cannot be said to describe the poor or disadvantaged minorities as a whole. Indeed, Goodwin's work[46] has shown that poor people in many categories—youth and adults, male and female, white and black—appear to see work as being as important to their preferred way of life as do those of higher socioeconomic status. They see a meaningful job as enhancing their self-esteem and avow a willingness to continue working even if it were no longer necessary for them to do so for economic reasons. Goodwin concludes that female welfare recipients have essentially the same work ethic as middle-class individuals but are unsure of their ability to achieve job success. Similarly, blacks share the majority group belief in the personal significance of work, but many of them lack a sustaining conviction of their ability to make the grade in the world of work as it is. Like whites, blacks report dissatisfaction with routine and meaningless work, especially when performed in an authoritarian climate; but while whites are more disposed to seek intrinsic rewards from work, untrained blacks are more likely to be motivated by security and survival needs in what they perceive as a hostile and rejecting world. For many blacks concerns about job discrimination supersede all others, and it is among the young, educated, white-collar blacks that charges of discrimination are most frequent.[47] Again, all such differences are to be understood as applying to group averages. One must remember that there are a great many blacks, and the number is probably increasing, who share the work values and expectations of middle-class whites as well as lower-class whites whose perceptions of work closely match those of disadvantaged ethnic minority group members.

REVALUING WORK VALUES

Swiftly moving social and economic changes following World War II, particularly those generated by spreading industrial technology, transformed the nature of work for millions of Americans and led many observers to ponder the worth and meaning of the work experience.[48] In the late 1950s and early 1960s a dominant theme of those who were troubled about the issue was mass unemployment, which, it was ominously predicted, our automated factories and offices would soon create. What could be done about the countless workers who would be rendered economically obsolete by the new technology? Might constructive leisure be designed to gratify psychological motives and provide the sense of purpose and usefulness eroded through the decline of work?[49] Although unemployment remains a national problem, since the middle sixties the emphasis appears to have shifted from concerns about the specter of a workless society to the alleged depersonalization and meaninglessness of many of today's jobs.[50] Whatever disagreements may appear in the interpretation of analysts, there is virtually unanimous accord that, in a sophisticated and affluent America, the meanings of work and the work ethic itself have been undergoing significant change.[51]

Roots of the Work Dilemma

While work in its generic sense continues to be valued, it seems clear that many Americans, youth and adults alike, no longer embrace the axiom that work for its own sake is rewarding and ennobling. The Puritan spirit referred to earlier in the chapter had at one time furnished an atmosphere which engendered and fortified a belief in the intrinsic merit of labor. But work has lost its religious meaning for most citizens, and even the valuing of work as a social duty is gravely challenged. In an earlier age economic scarcity and privation supplied the motive power for a work-or-perish ethos. Few today recall the Depression of the 1930s so vividly that they are driven by the fear of hunger, and, as Morrison[52] suggests, many young adults may now be too well educated and too antiauthoritarian to submit to dull, routine jobs which fail to serve personal values and, in particular, the need for self-esteem. During the 1960s absenteeism in business and industry rose sharply, and job turnovers, early retirement, and the reluctance of employees to work overtime, even at extra pay, were common problems. Such conditions have generally been regarded as evidence of the low commitment of substantial numbers of workers to their jobs, and, indeed, of strong job dissatisfaction.

Sheppard and Herrick's[53] survey of white, male, blue-collar workers found only a minority who claimed to be satisfied with their jobs most of the time, and other studies have reported a majority of even white-collar workers admitting that they would not voluntarily choose the same work again. An intractable form of alienation is bred by work which denies the individual any opportunity for expression of autonomy, which excludes him from decision-making processes that affect his welfare, which binds him to job and company through an unrewarding relationship with impersonal supervision, and which fails to allow identification with and pride in the finished work product. It is ironic that improvements in fundamental economic and physical conditions of employment have, over the years, elevated the job expectations of workers and led them to demand even greater returns from their work in the form of self-regard and a sense of meaningful effort. The core of man's quarrel with his labor may lie in the relatively static nature of most occupations, that is, in their incapacity to change rapidly enough in content and person-centeredness to meet his rising aspirations and nonmonetary work values.

The *Work in America* Special Task Force has drawn on the writings of Robert Blauner to analyze the work alienation phenomenon. Four components of the experience are identified:

> (1) powerlessness (regarding ownership of the enterprise, general management policies, employment conditions and the immediate work process), (2) meaninglessness (with respect to the character of the product worked on as well as the scope of the product or the production process), (3) isolation (the social aspect of work), and (4) self-estrangement ('depersonalized detachment,' including boredom, which can lead to 'absence of personal growth')[54]

Work as a Durable Value

That society is in obvious value conflict with its work has led to a widely shared belief that many adults and most youth categorically reject work as without human merit. Available evidence refutes such a conclusion. Whatever arguments may be marshaled against *homo faber,* there are very few prospective bridges to personal power, status, meaningful existence, and self-worth totally apart from occupation. By their overt choices and planning, if not by verbal affirmation, the vast majority of Americans demonstrate that they comprehend this rule of life. Thus, Katz[55] asserts that the potential efficacy of work in mediating one's socioeconomic advancement makes it "a major tenet of the American ethic." (p. 99) The *Work in America* Special Task Force (1973) is in agreement with this view in concluding that work still holds a central position in the lives of most adults and brings order and meaning to life. The Yankelovich report, previously cited, found nearly four out of five college students declaring that they regarded career commitments as an essential way of life. We have already noted that poor people state that they would work even if their financial circumstances made it unnecessary to do so. When the same hypothetical question is put to a cross-section of Americans, 80 percent give the same response, although only a small number say they feel this way because they like the job they hold. When asked how they would spend the additional two hours if they had a 26-hour day, many respondents, including two-thirds of college professors and one-quarter of lawyers, reported that they would devote this time to work-related activities. Only a small proportion of nonprofessional workers, however, gave this response. Available evidence suggests that workers do not tend to reduce the time effort they invest in their jobs as their earnings and affluence increase.

Despite changing work meanings, ambivalent attitudes, and even the active dislike that many workers hold for their jobs, it seems clear that work fills significant needs that people see no other means of satisfying. As seen by a large majority of Americans, work is, indeed, a necessary way of life. The nation's task is to learn to balance the economic outcome of occupational experience with the self-fulfillment outcome, particularly as the latter contributes to a sense of social purposefulness and to heightened self-respect.

AMERICA'S YOUNG AND THE WORK ETHIC: A REASSESSMENT

The incompatibility between human values and the limited psychological rewards that most occupations are able to return is seen most dramatically in the postures of youth. The restlessness and rebelliousness of so many young Americans during the sixties were stirred not only by the Indochina involvement but also by the major, established social institutions thought to reflect the nation's inverted priorities. A chief target of youth in this period was the economic system, particularly the rigidity, materialism, authoritarianism, and meaninglessness which, it was charged, infected most occupations. The intensity and pervasiveness of the attack led many observers to conclude falsely that adolescents and young adults, as a class, uncompromisingly repudiated work as an obligation and as a redeeming human experience. This chapter has already noted the error of assuming that a sameness exists for the attitudes and beliefs of all youth, and survey findings have been presented to show that the so-called counterculture, then and now, has embraced only a relatively small number of individuals. More importantly, while youthful views on work were undoubtedly undergoing change in the 1960s and early 1970s, the rejection of the world of work as they saw it hardly signified that young Americans were disavowing the *idea* of work as necessary and good. A brief examination of their evolving occupational aspirations and values may help to sharpen this distinction.

Work Aspirations of Youth

High school students who are college bound consistently attach considerable importance to the occupational needs of their postsecondary training. In overwhelming numbers they aspire to high-level positions. While many are vocationally undecided and others have made vague and unstable choices, well over half of those who are able to specify occupational goals name careers in the professions and sciences. Because students feel persistent pressure from their parents and colleges to state a vocational objective, as freshmen and sophomores they frequently choose curriculums and occupations to which they are only superficially committed and from which they later retreat. For some this maneuver is an attempt to win additional time during which they may assess possible career alternatives;

for others it is a decision-avoidance stratagem, often unconscious, which allows them to hold off for awhile the confusions and uncertainties of the external world. In fact, remaining in school as long as is feasible becomes for some students a goal in itself.

The American College Testing Program has studied the consistency of curricular goals among high school students who entered two-year and four-year colleges in the late sixties. At the end of the sophomore year two-fifths of the junior college men and women students had retained the same major fields as their precollege choices. Instability of choice was most frequent among men students who had originally named a major in one of the medical fields. For four-year college students consistency between precollege and senior-year curriculum choices was slightly under 40 percent, although stability of choice was somewhat higher for the women students.[57] Socioeconomic class status has been examined by Brue[58] and shown to be correlated with the levels of collegiate aspiration among junior college students. Those from higher socioeconomic backgrounds are more likely to enroll in programs preparatory to transfer to baccalaureate institutions, while students of lower socioeconomic status enroll with greater frequency in terminal occupational programs. Moreover, male high school students who enroll in transfer programs typically make their decision to enter college at an earlier date than do those who enroll in occupational programs, probably owing to family expectations and peer influences.

Associated with these findings are revealing differences in the self-concepts and work values of transfer program and occupational program students. Members of the former group have greater self-confidence in their ability to succeed in college and they specify opportunities for service to others (altruism) as an important condition of satisfying work. Students in occupational programs have less academic self-confidence and tend to rate job security and financial return as the conditions they would chiefly value in a job.[58] Baird's[59] study of over 21,000 prospective college students is among the most recent to show that the level of educational aspiration is significantly related to family income. It was during the 1960s that candid recognition of this long-standing condition of inequality of college opportunity helped spur the establishment of programs of recruitment, financial aid, guidance, and compensatory education for the previously bypassed children of economically disadvantaged families.

Toward the close of the 1960s the democratization of college admissions policies gave rise to a national situation that had not been clearly anticipated and the implications of which are still somewhat obscure. College attendance not only reflects a high aspiration level, but for substantial numbers of students it also boosts the level further. Thus, both educational and vocational hopes and goals are raised as a consequence of the collegiate experience. Among junior and community college students, an increase in educational aspiration level commonly occurs for both those who enter transfer programs and terminal occupational programs. Relatively few transfer program students change to occupational curricula, but many of those in occupational programs as well as those originally undecided about curriculum upgrade their objectives to transfer programs which, they hope, will allow them to move into four-year institutions. A study involving about 36,000 students in 246 accredited four-year colleges and universities found that nearly three-fourths of the subjects planned to earn graduate degrees. Of this group, over one-fourth aspired to the doctoral degree.[60]

Academic degree plans not only bear a strong relationship to socioeconomic background but to scholastic achievement as well. In Baird's[61] study a majority of the most academically able students anticipated pursuing academic degrees beyond the baccalaureate. At midcentury Seymour Harris,[62] an economist, predicted changing supply-and-demand ratios for college graduates by extrapolating the growth curves for college enrollments and employment opportunities in the professions and related higher-level fields. He warned that the precipitous rise in college-trained applicants, outstripping the expansion of professional and technical positions, would create a serious oversupply of college graduates for the job market by 1968. His concern proved well founded. By the end of the sixties graduates faced diminishing opportunities for employment at the levels for which they were trained, a sobering experience which increased the disillusionment of many youths. It is not known at this writing whether the imbalance between the numbers of college graduates and the numbers of job opportunities is a transient condition; but, given the prestige with which the professional, technical, and managerial positions are endowed, the millions of dreary, lower-level jobs that youth scorns, and the enormous pressures upon students to maximize their chances for upward social mobility and the good life through lengthy investments in postsecondary education, it is necessary to consider the possibility that the United States may be becoming, in occupational terms, an overtrained nation.[63]

We have already seen that the mass of young Americans do not disdain the idea of work as a necessary and at least potentially meaningful and rewarding life activity. Their attack is upon the character of available jobs and the overly conforming and depersonalizing conditions under which most individuals must labor. Because the socialization processes operating in the dominant culture are potent shapers of attitudes and expectations, it should not be surprising to learn that the work ideals of most high school students do not differ radically from those of their parents' generation.[64] We are often misled by flamboyant in-mode behavior styles of adolescents and young adults and mistake them for underlying attitudes. However, most of today's youth do seem to be less driven by job security and income needs and appear to place more importance than their elders on such conditions of employment as interesting work and the chance to use their abilities, expand their skills, and advance with increased competence. On the job young workers frequently report their impression that management stresses the quantity of work more than the quality, and this feeling tends to diminish their job satisfaction. For these and other reasons, young workers more often than their older coworkers see their jobs as failing to yield the outcomes they had most looked for in work, and for these same reasons they appear to have weaker ego involvement with their specific job than older work colleagues.[65]

During the 1960s greater education, more affluence, and growing intolerance of institutional authoritarianism were factors in young people's rising expectations of work and their challenges to jobs and employers. In general, they now appear to take their work more seriously, not less so. It is no longer sufficient that a job be steady and provide a liveable income. What is demanded is that the job be useful, allow a reasonable degree of self-expression, nourish self-esteem, and contribute to a preferred life-style. The Survey of Working Conditions conducted at the University of Michigan indicates that when such high expectations are not met, disillusionment with the job follows. When young workers in the Michigan study were asked, "How often do you feel you leave your work with a good feeling that you've done something particularly well?" fewer than 25 percent replied "very often."[66] There is little evidence that those who design the strategies and shape the policies governing the climate of the work place have come directly to grips with the issue.

Wanted: A New Work Morality

Some of the elements of recently changing attitudes that have been identified in this chapter, particularly those related to work, may now be recapitulated, and others added. The American occupational structure grew in response to the nation's firm goal of a high standard of living, not as a conscious effort to provide varied and humanizing work for men and women. The tradeoff for the attainment of an immense Gross National Product has been the loss of intrinsically satisfying jobs for many citizens. A sharp divergence now exists between the personal needs and values of unnumbered workers and of young people planning for careers and the impersonal, ritualized, and fragmented nature of the positions available to them. Technological and social advances have brought a gradual proliferation of professional and related occupations, but the rapid growth of the college-trained population has produced more candidates for high-level jobs than can presently be absorbed. One result has been young people's mounting disaffection with work as it actually exists and, to some extent, with higher education itself. More schooling is a less certain means to coveted jobs than formerly. Efficiently run households and adult-managed businesses have steadily narrowed the economic utility of children, adolescents, and even young adults in America. Age, education, and experience requirements delay their early participation in the work of their community and promote a sense of remoteness from the world of work. Unemployment rates among youthful workers, ages 16 to 19, are several times higher than those of the 25-and-over age group, and the gap between the two steadily widened during the 1960s.[67] The inevitable concomitants of such conditions in the psychological makeup of the young are feelings of powerlessness within the dominant social order, unstable vocational self-concepts, a distaste for many forms of work as they are perceived to exist, and the substitution of vocational fantasies and avoidance behavior for realistic planning and exploration.

The contrast between the economic role of youth as described above and that which is frequently found in revolutionary and developing societies can be startling. While it is reported that a growing proportion of

Soviet youth may now share the work discontents of young Americans, for many years following the 1917 Revolution and, again, during the intensive rebuilding years following the devastation wrought by World War II, the boys and girls of the Russian communes occupied an indispensable and valued place in the work force. Esteem for the needed work skills of youth is also evident today, although in different ways, in the kibbutzim of Israel and in the burgeoning, labor-short economy of industrial Japan.

Perhaps the most impressive illustration of a nation which husbands its youthful resources and assiduously cultivates those assets in a sustained climate of proud and purposeful work is that offered by the People's Republic of China. The report of the Committee of Concerned Asian Scholars[68] describes the instruction of fourth-grade children in the use of metal files to cut grids on metal treads for bus steps. Older children are being taught to electroplate small metal parts to be used in making oil filters. Adults everywhere work purposefully and contentedly, though often in menial jobs that most Americans would abhor. The conditions of work— clean shops, health and safety measures, small medical clinics in all factories—contrast sharply with the long working days and the crowded, uncomfortable, and hazardous work environments of the past. Among the Chinese there is a sense of national mission. One works not for individual gain or fame but, in a pioneering spirit, for the needs of the Revolution and the glories of nationhood. Some observers view this enthusiastic devotion to hard work as the new Chinese version of the American Puritan ethic.

A lack of unifying national vision has deeply affected the work attitudes of young Americans today, although as we have repeatedly acknowledged, it is not work in itself, or even hard work, that most of them deride. Rather, it is dull, demeaning work that they reject and, above all perhaps, the jaded moral (or immoral) principles of their grandparents' past— "Work hard for work's sake and be thankful for the opportunity" and "Subordinate your individuality to the cause of the system." To the first of these commandments many youths would respond that unless work is significant, it is pointless. To the second they would protest that submitting cheerfully and unquestioningly to authority and, in the bargain, forfeiting one's individuality is hardly a virtue to be emulated. The compassion once quickly aroused by the vision of a dutiful Bob Cratchit, groveling servilely before Scrooge's orders and threats, would be displaced today with a mixture of scorn, ridicule, and amusement. For contemporary youth Cratchit is incomprehensible as a suitable model of probity in the work setting.

By the same token, today's youth has devalued the Horatio Alger success myth—the notion that industriousness and patience, if steadfastly pursued, will bring merited rewards in a just social system. In a provocative collection of essays by de Tocqueville and others,[69] William James savagely attacks American adoration of the "bitch-goddess SUCCESS," which he perceives as a vulgar pursuit of material and monetary ends. *The American Gospel of Success* anthology, edited by Rischin,[70] explores variations of the powerful success motif and the ideology of personal achievement, in America. It would be difficult to know to what extent conforming and striving behavior among America's young has, in past years, been defined and inexorably shaped by the ideology of success. It is much easier to propose that a not insubstantial part of today's youth, in its uncertain quest for a humane individualism, wishes to be tested by a different touchstone.

NOTES

1. G. Soule, *The Shape of Tomorrow* (New York: Signet Key Books, 1958).
2. "America at Work," *Newsweek*, 14 December 1959, pp. 86–100.
3. P. Sann, *The Lawless Decade* (New York: Crown, 1957).
4. K. Keniston, *The Uncommitted: Alienated Youth in American Society* (New York: Delta, 1965).
5. C. A. Reich, *The Greening of America* (New York: Random House, 1970).
6. L. Harris, "Trust of Institutions Falls," The Harris Survey, *Minneapolis Star*, 25 October 1971.
7. R. Berman, *America in the Sixties* (New York: Free Press, 1968).
8. A. Toffler, *Future Shock* (New York: Random House, 1970).
9. *The World Book Yearbook*, 1960–1970 (Chicago: Field Enterprises).
10. B. F. Skinner, *Walden Two* (New York: Macmillan, 1948).
11. C. G. Wrenn, *The World of the Contemporary Counselor* (Houghton Mifflin, 1973), p. 11.
12. Toffler, *op. cit.*, p. 292.
13. E. Z. Friedenberg, *The Vanishing Adolescent* (New York: Dell, 1959).
14. J. Adelson, "The Mystique of Adolescence, *The Young Adult: Identity and Awareness*, G. D. Winter and E. M. Nuss, eds. (Glenview, Ill.: Scott, Foresman, 1969), pp. 2–7; E. H. Erikson, ed., *The Challenge of Youth* (Garden City, N.Y.: Anchor Books, 1963); F. Musgrove, *Youth and the Social Order* (London: Routledge and Kegan Paul, 1964).
15. D. H. Blocher, "Social Change and the Future of Vocational Guidance," *Career Guidance for a New Age*, H. Borow, ed. (Boston: Houghton Mifflin, 1973); J. S. Coleman, *The Adolescent Society* (Glencoe, Ill.: Free Press, 1961); Toffler, *op. cit.*
16. Adelson, *op. cit.*, p. 7.
17. Musgrove, *op. cit.*
18. Wrenn, *op. cit.*, pp. 18–19.
19. H. Borow, "The Development of Occupational Motives and Roles," *Review of Child Development Research: Volume 2*, L. W. Hoffman and M. L. Hoffman, eds. (New York: Russell Sage Foundation, 1966).
20. H. Borow, "Career Development in Adolescence," *Understanding Adolescence*, 2nd ed., J. F. Adams, ed. (Boston: Allyn and Bacon, 1973); "Graduates and Jobs: A Grave New World," *Time*, 24 May 1971, pp. 49–59.
21. J. Ciardi, "Manner of Speaking," *Saturday Review*, 24 October 1970, pp. 10–11.
22. Keniston, *op. cit.*
23. K. Keniston, *Youth and Dissent: The Rise of a New Opposition* (New York: Harcourt, Brace, Jovanovich, 1971).
24. J. H. Block, N. Haan, and M. B. Smith, "Activism and Apathy in Contemporary Adolescents," *Understanding Adolescence*, 2nd ed., p. 312.
25. S. R. Barber, "Review of K. Keniston's *Youth and Dissent: The Rise of New Opposition*, *The Progressive*, March 1972, pp. 54–58.
26. *New York Times* Service, "Survey Reveals College Freshmen Turning Away From Liberal Attitudes," *Minneapolis Tribune*, 25 February 1973.

27. D. Yankelovich, *The Changing Values on Campus: Political and Personal Attitudes on Campus* (New York: Washington Square Press, 1972).
28. D. Gottlieb, "Youth and the Meaning of Work," study conducted for U.S. Department of Labor, reported in *Penn State Review,* Winter 1973.
29. Special Task Force, Health, Education, and Welfare, *Work in America* (Cambridge, Mass.: M.I.T. Press, 1973).
30. M. Mead, "The American Woman Today," *World Book Yearbook* (Chicago: Field Enterprises, 1969), pp. 78–95.
31. B. Friedan, *The Feminine Mystique* (New York: W. W. Norton, 1963).
32. Mead, *op. cit.,* p. 81.
33. I. M. Levine and J. Herman, "America's Young Workers: Interim Background Report of the National Project on Ethnic America," submitted to U.S. Department of Labor, Office of Policy, Evaluation, and Research, Washington, D.C.: 1972.
34. Special Task Force, *op. cit.*
35. United States Department of Labor, *U.S. Manpower in the 1970s: Opportunity and Challenge* (Washington, D.C.: Government Printing Office, 1970).
36. M. B. Kievit, *Review and Synthesis of Women in the World of Work* (Columbus, Ohio: ERIC Clearinghouse of Vocational and Technical Education, The Center for Vocational and Technical Education, 1972).
37. J. F. Carmody, R. H. Fenske, and C. S. Scott, *Changes in Goals, Plans, and Background Characteristics of College-bound High School Students,* ACT Research Report No. 52 (Iowa City: American College Testing Program, 1972), p. 13.
38. M. Harrington, *The Other America* (New York: Macmillan, 1963).
39. W. H. Grier and P. M. Cobbs, *Black Rage* (New York: Basic Books, 1968).
40. G. Myrdal, *An American Dilemma* (New York: Harper and Brothers, 1944).
41. R. Wright, *Native Son* (New York: Harper and Brothers, 1940).
42. H. Borow et al., "Effective Task or Work Orientation," *Perspectives on Human Deprivation: Biological, Psychological, and Sociological* (Bethesda, Md.: National Institute of Child Health and Human Development, 1968).
43. D. L. Shappell, L. G. Hall, and R. B. Tarrier, "Perception of the World of Work: Inner-city versus Suburbia," *Journal of Counseling Psychology* 18 (1971):55–59.
44. Borow et al., *op. cit.,* p. 24.
45. U.S. Department of Labor, *U.S. Manpower in the 1970s, op. cit.,* B. Wattenberg and R. Scammon, "Black Progress and Liberal Rhetoric," *Commentary,* April 1973, p. 35.
46. L. Goodwin, *A Study of the Work Orientations of Welfare Recipients Participating in the Work Incentive Program* (Washington, D.C.: Brookings Institution, 1971).
47. Special Task Force, *op. cit.*
48. S. DeGrazia, *Of Time, Work and Leisure* (New York: Twentieth Century Fund, 1962); C. G. Wrenn, "Human Values and Work in American Life," *Man in a World at Work,* H. Borow, ed. (Boston: Houghton Mifflin, 1964), Ch. 2.
49. G. Piel, "The Future of Work," *Vocational Guidance Quarterly* 10(1961): 4–10; Wrenn, "Human Values and Work"; G. B. Childs, "Is the Work Ethic Realistic in an Age of Automation?" *Phi Delta Kappan* 46(1965):370–75.
50. H. Swados, "Work as a Public Issue," *Saturday Review,* 12 December 1959, pp. 13–15 and 45; A. Levenstein, "Work and Its Meaning in an Age of Affluence" *Career Guidance for a New Age.*
51. D. M. Morrison, "Is the Work Ethic Going Out of Style?" *Time,* 30 October 1972, pp. 96–97; H. Borow, "Shifting Postures Toward Work: A Tracing," *American Vocational Journal,* January 1973, pp. 28–29 and 108; Special Task Force, *op. cit.*

52. Morrison, *op. cit.*
53. H. L. Sheppard and N. Herrick, *Where Have All the Robots Gone?* (New York: Free Press, 1972).
54. Special Task Force, *op. cit.*, p. 22.
55. M. R. Katz, "The Name and Nature of Vocational Guidance," *Career Guidance for a New Age, op. cit.*
56. Carmody, Fenske, and Scott, *op. cit.*
57. E. J. Brue, "Characteristics of Transfer and Occupational Students in Community Colleges" (Ph.D. thesis, University of Iowa, 1969).
58. H. Borow and V. L. Hendrix, "Environmental Differentials of Occupational Programs and Education Career Roles in Public Junior Colleges," Research Project No. 5-0120, submitted to U.S. Office of Education, Washington, D.C. 1973.
59. L. L. Baird, *Patterns of Educational Aspiration*, ACT Research Report No. 32 (Iowa City: American College Testing Program, 1969).
60. A. W. Astin and R. J. Panos, *The Educational and Vocational Development of College Students* (Washington, D.C.: American Council on Education, 1969).
61. Baird, *op. cit.*
62. S. Harris, *The Market for College Graduates* (Cambridge, Mass.: Harvard University Press, 1949).
63. H. Borow, "Student Decision Making: When and How," *College/Career Choice: Right Student, Right Time, Right Place*, K. J. McCaffrey and E. King, eds. (Iowa City: American College Testing Program, 1973), pp. 33–43.
64. Measurement and Research Center, *Vocational Plans and Preferences of Adolescents*, Report of Poll No. 94 (Lafayette, Ind.: Purdue Opinion Panel, Purdue University, 1972).
65. Special Task Force, *op. cit.*
66. H. E. Striner, *Survey of Working Conditions* (Ann Arbor: Survey Research Center, University of Michigan, 1970).
67. U.S. Department of Labor, *U.S. Manpower in the 1970s, op. cit.*
68. Committee of Concerned Asian Scholars, *China! Inside the People's Republic* (New York: Bantam Books, 1972).
69. A. de Tocqueville et al., *The Bitch-Goddess Success* (New York: Eakins Press, 1968).
70. M. Rischin, ed., *The American Gospel of Success* (Chicago: Quadrangle Books, 1965).

SUGGESTED READING

Berman, R. *America in the Sixties.* New York: The Free Press, 1968. An intellectual history of some of the dominant ideas and major sociocultural forces at work during the decade of the 1960s. Discusses the position of the intellectual in America, the civil rights movement and the changing status of blacks, political and social activism, and culture heroes of the times. While the book does not directly treat the problems of youth and work, it attempts to capture the prevailing climate of the 1960s in which significant changes in social and personal values were occurring.

Dunnette, M. D. (ed.) *Work and Nonwork in the Year 2001.* Monterey, Calif.: Brooks/Cole, 1973. A compilation of critical essays on past, present, and future meanings and functions of work and productive leisure.

Treats the problem of synthesizing individual and social needs through work and nonwork activities, explores the common psychological ground of work and leisure, and proposes future ways of redesigning formal work systems to accommodate important human motives.

Musgrove, F. *Youth and the Social Order.* London: Routledge and Kegan Paul, 1964. A searching interdisciplinary analysis by a British writer of the changing position of young people and of the causes and consequences of their new status. Stress is placed on the problem created by contemporary society's exclusion of youth from the adult world and on the diminished function of adolescence as a training ground for responsible adulthood.

Special Task Force, Health, Education, and Welfare. *Work in America.* Cambridge, Mass.: M.I.T. Press, 1973. A comprehensive report by a blue-ribbon task force on the contemporary status of work, with special emphasis on conditions contributing to the dehumanization of work. Discusses changing meanings and attitudes of work, identifies sources of job dissatisfaction among various classes of workers, and sets forth specific proposals for the redesign of the occupational enviroment and the humanization of work.

Winter, G. D. and Nuss, E. M. (eds.) *The Young Adult.* Glenview, Ill.: Scott, Foresman, 1969. A collection of readings drawn from the published literature on "adolescenthood," a psychosocial stage which the editors assert is at least equal in significance to other stages of human development. Selections are organized around the major themes of the adolescent's representative characteristics, personal dilemma, and antisocial problems (dropouts, delinquency, drugs). The final sections of the book treat the adolescent in cross-cultural perspective and offer approaches to fostering hygienic adolescence in a changing social order.

Wrenn, C. G. *The World of the Contemporary Counselor.* Boston: Houghton Mifflin, 1973. An intimate and broad-ranging interpretation by one of the counseling movement's most influential exponents of changing American attitudes, values, and life-styles, and of the significance of such changes for the work of counselors. The concluding chapters summarize the author's views of emerging priorities, roles, and practices in counseling.

2 Manpower Policies, Vocational Guidance, and Career Development

Edwin L. Herr
The Pennsylvania State University

As Borow suggests in Chapter 1, each decade or so seems to be characterized by different emphases or themes which give it a distinctive quality. This phenomenon seems to be operable regardless of the domain under examination, whether politics, religion, economics, the quality of human life, or manpower policies. In part this is true because of the interaction between historical events, social policies, and the institutions or programs which respond to these events and policies.

In discussing the pluralistic nature of inputs to manpower policies, Ginzberg suggested that human behavior is too complex to be captured by the substance of any single academic discipline. He contended that manpower policy represented an interaction across knowledge bases which could be explained by the fact that most economic theory has an implicit or explicit psychological foundation. Psychology, he maintains, has provided the following five major contributions to manpower policy:

1. The public has been encouraged to adopt a more humane attitude toward people who are ineffective.
2. The public has acquired a positive stance toward the amelioration of social and human ills, particularly through reliance on education, but also through other approaches, including supportive services.
3. Psychology's study of the distribution of human attributes has contributed substantially to the decline in discrimination against women, Negroes, and others who were formerly "beyond the pale."
4. Psychology has led to more constructive views and behavior with regard to the rearing of children and the development of young people.
5. Psychology has thrown a searchlight on the critical importance of work for individual and social integration.[1]

The contributions to manpower policy of emerging knowledge beyond academic disciplines is evident in viewing the evolution of vocational guidance. Ehrle, for example, has suggested that the 1930s and 1940s were characterized by a great deal of testing and research in the trait-and-factor tradition of matching men and jobs, while the 1950s were characterized by a great surge of theory building relating to occupational choice and career development. But "it was not until the 1960s that the prospect of vast numbers of out-of-school, out-of-work youth was recognized as a national problem of major proportions."[2] This theme echoed and reechoed throughout the decade. In 1968, and again in 1969, the factors of unemployment and underemployment were linked directly to the problems of civil disorder in the country by a prestigious Presidential Advisory Committee on Vocational Education and by a National Advisory Council on Vocational Education.[3] Throughout this period of time the national responses suggested that the 1960s represented the base for a manpower policy revolution[4] in the United States unprecedented in size and comprehensiveness.

To a degree unparalleled in previous American history, vocational guidance and counseling became identified consistently in federal or in state legislation as a vital part of the manpower policies designed to respond to human needs in the occupational and economic arenas. Program after program, regardless of its target population—occupationally displaced adults, out-of-school youth, school children, women reentering the labor force, military veterans returning to civilian life, migrant workers, the physically handicapped, minority group members, or economically disadvantaged persons— included an emphasis on providing vocational counseling or guidance. (It is imperative here to distinguish between the demand for guidance or counseling services and the demand for counselors *per se*. The latter were not necessarily consistently identified as the group to provide the former.)

The continuing concern for maximizing the personalization of manpower programs during the 1960s probably came from sources that were at once idealistic, pragmatic and politically viable. Ginzberg's observations about the influence of psychology on manpower policy represent one level of input. In addition, Chapter 1 indicates some of the changes in minority group identity and consequent demands for action, as well as shifts in social values which stimulated political responses to personal needs. But these were not the only factors stimulating a need for manpower programs to take into account individual differences and the emotionality surrounding occupational retraining, job placement, securing vocational identity, and converting unemployables into productive citizens. Experience and knowledge were expanding, which indicated that dealing with individuals only in terms of skill training was ineffective without concurrently helping them develop improved self-images, perspectives of personal competence, and ego strength. Manpower policies took on an affective quality as well as a cognitive or manipulative one. Emphases in legislation and in program operations began to shift from a sole concern on developing a competent person to a greater accentuation on developing a sense of personal competence.[5]

The effects of the fallout from growing speculation and research about career development were evident not only in a shift from placing manpower planning priority on needs of the labor market to the needs of individuals, but also in the timing and character of the services offered. Since the beginnings of the twentieth century, vocational guidance or counseling had been essentially problem focused and treatment oriented. In other words, the implementation of these services was essentially remedial or *post hoc* to a problem rather than anticipatory of or *a priori* to a problem. Vocational guidance and counseling were seen as services to be implemented after persons experienced an emotional crisis or trauma in their occupational adjustment. However, explanatory approaches to career development began to infuse a concept that some of these crises could be avoided by the provision of prevocational information and experiences designed to facilitate individual coping with choice or adjustment—to build strength rather than to repair weakness.

The manpower policies of the 1960s and their extensions and refinements in the 1970s have continued to reflect awareness of systems or networks of interdependence. The legislation and its accompanying programmatic implementation has acknowledged the interactive contributions of government, education, commerce and industry, labor and management, professional organizations, and the private sector in meeting the personal, socioeconomic, and vocational needs of the population.[6] As a result, it has become obvious that no group of specialists or specific social institution can attend to the manpower needs of the nation alone. The needs are too complex, and they require the multidimensional responses found in cooperative effort, rather than the unilateral outcomes associated with responses proffered only by a rigidly compartmentalized structure.

The remainder of this chapter will focus upon a selected inventory of the principal manpower legislation since 1962, its incorporation of vocational guidance and counseling, the events and populations to which responses were being made, and the influence of career development.

MANPOWER LEGISLATION IN NONEDUCATIONAL SETTINGS

The United States entered the 1960s in a climate of unemployment. Unemployment in the third post-Korean War recession exceeded 8.1 percent (unadjusted for seasonality in February 1961), causing it to become a key public issue for the first time since the 1930s. The focus of intensive debate was whether the cause of unemployment was slow economic growth and a deficient rate of job creation or inadequate skills in an economy of abundant but high level employment opportunities.[7]

When President Kennedy entered office in January 1961, he was apparently convinced that he had to face the high level of unemployment and poverty,[8] which he believed to be one of the most serious domestic problems facing the nation. Apparently influenced by Harrington's *The Other America*,[9] which dramatically portrayed the plight of the poverty stricken in the midst of affluent America, one of Kennedy's initial actions, designed to alleviate unemployment, was to direct the Secretary of Health, Education, and Welfare to appoint a panel of consultants on vocational education. He also instituted the process of creating a variety of laws which came to be known as "antipoverty" in their focus upon the severe socioeconomic problems of large segments of the population.

In 1961 Congress passed the Area Redevelopment Act (ARA), which was concerned with the concentration of unemployment in economically depressed areas and the importance of attracting new sources of jobs to such areas. It also pioneered the use of direct federal funds for the occupational training of eligible unemployed persons residing in economically distressed areas meeting specific criteria. In 1962 the Manpower Development and Training Act (MDTA) was passed in an effort to provide assistance to those who were actually or potentially victimized by automation. Initially this legislation was directly targeted on the needs of semiskilled workers who, while still part of the labor force, were in danger of experiencing skill obsolescence. Originally this legislation did not address the special needs of drop-outs, out-of-school youth, or older unskilled workers from economically disadvantaged backgrounds. However, as experiences with implementing the Act unfolded, it became clear that each of these groups experienced some difficulties peculiar to their characteristics and that planners needed to incorporate such differences in their programs.[10] Perhaps more importantly for the topical area to which this chapter is addressed, amendments to the MDTA of 1962 attended to the needs of special problem groups in the society and also introduced the importance of providing counseling and placement activities as major components of programs. It had become obvious that people being retrained or being taught occupational skills needed the opportunity to relate these to their self-attitudes, changes in personal habits, emotional responses to life situations, attitudes toward work, experiences in planning, and transition to new jobs.[11] These were conceived as areas to which vocational guidance and counseling, including evaluation and placement, could respond. Manpower Development and Training Act amendments also supported an outreach dimension as part of counseling services. While principally focused upon recruitment of eligible persons for participation in training programs, this legislation stimulated awareness that vocational guidance and counseling services needed to be active and mobile in seeking appropriate clientele, rather than passively awaiting clientele to come for services. Thus, though manpower training was initially conceived as a relatively simple solution to an immediate and presumably correctable problem, neither the problem nor the solution has been simple.[12]

Aligned with the objectives of the MDTA was the Economic Opportunity Act (EOA) of 1964. While the MDTA had focused on the occupational training needs of family heads by providing classroom drill or on-the-job training in the immediate geographic area of the participants, EOA took a different stance. Focusing on both the young and the old from impoverished backgrounds, it created programs tailored to the rather different needs of these two groups. Under its aegis, programs implemented for the young included the Job Corps, the Neighborhood Youth Corps, VISTA, the Special Impact Program, and the Head Start Program. These programs dealt with such problem areas as the preschool child who needed basic language and academic enrichment as well as nutritional supplement, the adolescent who needed part-time work opportunities to provide sufficient remuneration so that he could remain in school, and the out-of-school youth who needed to break out of the habits and attitudinal patterns of his neighborhood while being trained for occupational opportunities. For older unskilled or illiterate workers the EOA supported adult basic education classes, work experience programs and various forms of special training; these latter opportunities were included first in the Community Work and Training Program and later in the Community Action Program. The EOA of 1964 clearly considered education in all its forms as a first-line weapon against poverty.[13] The 1966 Amendments to the EOA added Operation Mainstream, which stimulated jobs on behalf of rural conservation and beautification efforts, as well as the New Careers Program, which stimulated national thinking about the creation of certain types of subprofessional jobs, career ladders, and differentiated staffing. The EOA has given attention to direct aid for migrant and seasonal farm workers. By 1970 Adult Basic Education (ABE) programs were available in thirty-six states, providing assistance in language skills, mathematics, consumer education, and prevocational training. Also available are the Migrant Compensatory Education Program (MCEP), combining education and social services for school age students and their families, and the High School Equivalency Program (HEP), conducted at colleges and universities for migrant youth.[14]

Guidance concepts pertinent to such areas as planning and the development of a positive self-concept permeated many of the programs sponsored under the EOA. Indeed, following close upon the experience of the MDTA programs, programs were planned to deal with both the affective and the skill development dimensions requisite to employability. Using the Job Corps as an example, the following selected recommendations were outcomes of a study designed to examine the characteristics of effective counseling procedures with disadvantaged students:

> Counselors in Job Corps settings should render equal time to self-concept development and not concentrate solely on vocational decision-making skills. Counselors in Job Corps settings must create stability for their clients by adhering to time limits in counseling interviews, being prompt for their meetings, and respecting the confidential aspect of each client's problem. Above all, counselors must be consistent in their relationship with Job Corps trainees.[15]

These observations, while limited, represent attempts to tailor existing vocational guidance and counseling approaches to the specific characteristics of "special needs" groups being served. Other attempts pervade MDTA programs.[16] In addressing the experiences gained from EOA and MDTA programs, Levine has indicated that:

> As a minimum for the culturally deprived, educationally deficient youth, living in penurious circumstances, the first step, once rapport has been established, is intensive counseling involving *diagnosis* of his problems. . . . An important implication growing out of the Economic Opportunity Act, therefore, is the need to provide highly individualized, customized service, specifically shaped and related to the needs of each youth.[17]

Another part of the manpower legislation evolving in the early and middle 1960s was the Social Security Act (SSA) of 1967, which initiated training programs for welfare clients who wished and were able to become economically self-sufficient. Called the Work Incentive Program (WIN), this program, which was a partial extension of aspects of the EOA, also included funds for training, education, day care for children of participants, and a variety of supportive services, including counseling.

BROADENED DEFINITIONS OF CLIENTS APPROPRIATE FOR SERVICE

Simultaneous with the creation and expansion of the programs thus far identified there were spin-offs which focused more directly on specific counseling agencies. For example, by 1965 the definitions of the clientele to whom the Employment Service had historically been responsible had been broadened. As a function of different aspects of the Area Development Act of 1961, the Manpower Development and Training Act of 1962, and the Economic Opportunity Act of 1964, Employment Service counselors were given responsibilities for testing and counseling all eighteen-year-old boys unable to meet the "mental" standards for induction into the Armed Forces; for identifying those persons of all ages to be recruited, trained, and guided into available manpower training programs; and for interviewing and counseling youth specifically involved with the Job Corps and the Youth Opportunity Centers. The responsibilities of the Employment Service were subsequently broadened again in the Vocational Education Act Amendments of 1968 and in other legislation to be discussed later.

The basic point is that the United States Employment Service, as the federal manpower agency most directly identified with vocational guidance, counseling, and testing, had experienced a rather dramatic shift in expectation from the rather static matter of matching jobs with those persons who came for assistance to a much more active involvement in manpower development. The increasing concern with referring clients for training as well as for jobs and the expectation that Employment Service counselors would take on a job development role was reflected in the agency's name change to United States Employment and Training Service. In order to respond to such expectations, Employment Service personnel were required to identify, recruit, counsel, and make available appropriate training experiences for wider classifications of persons than had been true previously in the history of this agency. Required was a greater emphasis on professional counseling than on job advising, as well as an emphasis on communication between Employment Service counselors, school counselors, teachers, and representatives of business and industry.

By 1964 the *Manpower Report of the President,* under the title "Impact of Government Programs on Personnel Requirements in the Counseling Profession," was forecasting unprecedented demands for well-qualified counselors in educational and vocational guidance, employment service, and occupational training settings to meet the increasingly critical needs of youth and adults in preparing for the rapidly changing social and occupational world. The speculation at that time was that 32,000 new counselors— more than 90 percent above the existing full time equivalent counselors— would be needed in public education, vocational training, and employment services for youth and adults.[18] This was, of course, before the impact of many of the other legislative activities described here had taken hold in program development.

During this period it was being contended vigorously that employment counseling had to be considered an integral part of an active labor market policy.[19] Reinforcing such a point of view, Ehrle maintained that the major impact of counseling as an integral part of an active labor market policy occurs in three areas: (1) prevention of long-term unemployment, (2) adjustment to rapidly changing labor market conditions, and (3) occupational rehabilitation of the marginally employable.[20]

In 1965 new legislation also authorized increasing by 300 percent the federal support for the Vocational Rehabilitation Administration. In the process the charge of this agency was transformed from that which had prevailed since the 1920s—to qualify the physically and mentally handicapped for productive employment—to a broader concern with impairments to effective vocational life caused by educational, cultural, social, or environmental factors. For example, in 1968 Congress enacted legislation providing for a special program of vocational evaluation and work adjustment services for disadvantaged individuals both physically disabled and without such impairment.

Throughout this process of redefining an appropriate clientele for rehabilitation counselors, the term habilitation has become increasingly prominent. While rehabilitation is fundamentally concerned with restoring or reeducating individuals to productive lives, vocational habilitation is an educational process concerned with the development of the vocationally unsophisticated (persons with little or no previous contact with the work world).[21] Impetus for the latter is growing through the upsurge of job training programs for the handicapped and the disadvantaged as well as state cooperative programs between special education and vocational rehabilitation.

By the spring of 1966 the unfolding of a Federal-state Manpower Development System had been launched with the cooperation of the Manpower Administration, the United States Office of Education, and the Community Action Programs of the Office of Economic Opportunity. Less than a year later, this interagency cooperative activity was restructured, other participating agencies were added—including the Welfare Administration, the Vocational Rehabilitation Administration, the Economic Development Administration, and the Department of Housing and Urban Development—and the Cooperative Area Manpower Planning System (CAMPS) came into being under the coordinating responsibility of the Department of Labor. In essence, this structure was to facilitate the planning and development of responses to manpower needs at state, regional, and local levels, with particular emphasis on reducing unemployment and underemployment.[22]

MANPOWER LEGISLATION PERTINENT TO EDUCATIONAL SETTINGS

At this point, then, it must be recognized that much of the legislation enacted during the early and middle 1960s, while oriented to needs for vocational counseling, upgrading employment skills, and positive attitude formulation, was focused on nonschool agencies. In a sense, these legislative foci were symbolic of feelings that schools and school counselors had not prepared students to cope with the expectations and requirements of the labor market. These pieces of legislation cast doubts that the formal educational structure and school counselors were able to function effectively with other than college-bound academic students. Yet throughout this period there was a pervasive awareness that the occupational structure was changing in such a way as to require more dependence upon formal education, not less, an awareness that manpower supply and its quality is intimately linked with the character of education provided.[23]

Veblen had predicted in 1914 that the time was coming when preparation for work would be acquired more effectively in the school classroom than through on-the-job training in industry.[24] By 1968 Drucker had indicated that such a prophecy had become fact. He pointed out that the shift to a knowledge economy in the United States and the concurrent need

> . . . to gain advanced skills through programmed acquisition of knowledge makes traditional craft structure untenable . . . The way to teach a skill today is by putting it on a knowledge foundation and teaching it through a systematic course of studies, that is through a program . . . With everybody going to school till adulthood, school has become the place for learning whatever one needs in order to be both a human being and effective.[25]

In 1967 Galbraith contended that:

> With the rise of the technostructure, (which he portrayed as descriptive of the American Society in the 1960's), relations between those associated with economic enterprise and the educational and scientific estate undergo a radical transformation. There is no longer an abrupt conflict in motivation. . . . Both see themselves as identified with social goals, or with organizations serving social purposes. And both it may be assumed, seek to adapt social goals to their own. . . . Meanwhile the technostructure has become deeply dependent on the educational and scientific estate for its supply of trained manpower. . . . The question remains as to how closely the educational and scientific estate, which owes its modern expansion and eminence to the requirements of the industrial system, will identify itself with the goals of the latter.[26]

The point of these observations seems to be that while much of the legislation of the 1960s reflected awareness that changes in manpower requirements suggested a need for improvements at all levels of the educational system, the role of education was expanding as *a*, if not *the*, vital mode for responding to manpower distribution and upgrading. Indeed, education and training were increasingly being recognized as elements directly tied to the process of economic growth, particularly in a situation (1961) when less than one-half of the noncollege trained labor force had any formal training for their jobs.

One of the major responses in the early 1960s directly focused on the schools was the Vocational Education Act of 1963. As indicated earlier in this chapter, President Kennedy had appointed a panel of consultants on vocational education soon after he took office in January 1961. The report of the panel in 1962 emphasized two broad factors: (1) vocational education's lack of sensitivity to changes in the labor market and (2) its lack of sensitivity to the needs of various segments of the population. In addition, the panel stressed the need for school counselors who "have exceptional understanding of the world of work and its complexities. What is obviously needed is a counselor who meets all the requirements of a professional background in pupil personnel services and who at the same time is a specialist in occupational information, vocational guidance, and counseling."[27] Most of the specific recommendations for change in vocational education and its ancillary dimensions were incorporated into the Vocational Education Act of 1963.

The Vocational Education Act of 1963 continued the support of agricultural subjects, home economics, distributive occupations, trade and industrial occupations, business and office education, as well as practical nursing as these had been defined by the Morrill Act of 1862, the Smith-Hughes Act of 1916, and the George-Barden Act of 1946. In addition, the Vocational Education Act of 1963 gave a significant push to work-study programs, residential schools, area vocational education programs, and general education as it could be tied vaguely to specific needs in vocational education. Further, the Act specifically stated that vocational guidance and counseling were to be provided to students enrolled in vocational courses and those planning to enroll. In a fairly dramatic extension of the clientele typically served by vocational education, the 1963 Act explicitly identified four groups for whom federal funds could be expended. They included: (1) persons who attend secondary schools, (2) persons who want to extend their vocational education beyond the high school level and such persons who have left high school before completion but are available for full time vocational education before entering the labor market, (3) persons already in the labor market and needing further training to hold their jobs, to advance in their jobs, or to find suitable and meaningful employment, and (4) for the first time, persons who have academic, socioeconomic, or other handicaps that prevent them from succeeding in the regular vocational education program. Of further significance was the Act's expectation that resources of vocational educators and of the state employment services were to be combined in determining labor market needs and placing vocational graduates.

The emphasis in this legislation upon vocational education's responses to the needs of people was reflected in the observations of a national vocational education review task force which stated that, "the most important change between 1917 and 1963 was the conceptual shift of emphasis from the needs of employers for skilled labor (The Smith-Hughes Act) to skills needed by people to assure their own welfare (The Vocational Education Act of 1963)."[28] The notion that this legislation also reflected dramatic shifts in social and occupational characteristics was identified by another national group, which put its observations in the following fashion:

> In 1963 Congress gave fundamental and philosophical attention to vocational education for the first time since 1917. The immediate motivation was high unemployment among untrained and inexperienced youth. However, a long run impetus was provided by the growing importance of formal preparation for employment in an increasing technical and sophisticated economy.[29]

During essentially the same time span as the creation of the Vocational Education Act of 1963 other significant legislative events also were occurring. In 1964 Title V-A of the National Defense Education Act (NDEA) of 1958 was amended. Originally this legislation responded to the general miasma attending the Soviet launching of Sputnik in 1957, which generated serious questions about the focus and the quality of American education. With an emphasis on strengthening science education and identifying gifted students who might be encouraged to pursue careers in that field the NDEA legislation provided funds for establishing and maintaining testing programs, as well as for training and employing school counselors. However, by 1964 the initial, fairly restrictive interpretation of NDEA, V-A, as serving only the identification, recruitment, and encouragement of able students had been dampened and the impact of the legislation broadened. Specifically, the 1964 Amendments encouraged funding of counseling and guidance activities not only in the secondary schools but also in the elementary schools, public junior colleges, and technical institutes.

Such modifications in legislative intent and funding created several possibilities. One was that, for the first time, effective models of guidance programs which could be developmentally focused from kindergarten to grade twelve or beyond seemed to be stimulated. Secondly, such structural possibilities provided encouragement to guidance services being seen as comprehensive in the range of services they provided. Thirdly, with increasing numbers of school counselors being trained and available at the different educational levels, it was possible to plan for counselor-pupil ratios at a level which permitted counselors to serve not just remedial and adjustive needs but developmental needs as well. Indeed, by 1969 the counselor-pupil ratio at the secondary level had changed from 1 counselor for every 960 students in 1958 to 1 counselor for every 450 students. These certainly did not represent ideal ratios (defined by many spokesmen as 1 to 250 or 300), but significant progress had occurred in this area. With the implementation of elementary school counselors and other changes made possible by 1964, initial attempts to inform and advise elementary school children about future educational and occupational opportunities available to them were begun— an area to which little thought had been given in 1958.[30] While not all of these possible ramifications of the amendments of 1964 have become realities generally distributed across the country, they stimulated model building and theory generation in many forms. The 1964 amendments to NDEA also reaffirmed that in the original legislation the phrase "identification and encouragement of able students" was not meant to be a categorical distinction pertinent only to college-bound students. Rather, it was emphasized that a major intent of the NDEA legislation was for guidance and counseling programs, "(1) to help students, directly and through their parents and teachers, to achieve educational and *career development* commensurate with their abilities, aptitudes, interests, and opportunities."[31]

In 1969 the federal funding support provided for guidance and counseling was incorporated into the amendments to the Elementary and Secondary Education Act (ESEA) of 1965. Under the title "Supplementary Educational Centers and Services; Guidance, Counseling, and Testing," guidance support from Title III, ESEA, and Title V-A, NDEA, were combined into a single authorization. The original legislation, the Elementary and Secondary Education Act of 1965, was probably the most comprehensive piece of education legislation conceived to that time. Under its five titles, aid was included for disadvantaged children in schools in poverty areas, for library resources, for supplementary educational centers, for a national network of educational laboratories, and for the improvement of state education agencies. In Title I (disadvantaged children) and Title III (supplementary educational centers), the provision of counseling and guidance services, while not the emphasis of the titles, were designated as areas for support. The effects of including guidance and counseling in these titles was a spur to elementary school counseling, particularly in terms of outreach, parental contacts, and work with inner-city children. At the secondary level several demonstration centers provided, among other emphases, guidance services related to vocational counseling, career exploration programs in conjunction with the community, and tentative steps toward planning programs of career development. The latter guidance activities reflected the intent of Title III of the ESEA legislation, which was to demonstrate the feasibility of innovations in a local context. In this sense, Title III represented educational "risk capital" for facilitating pilot projects, establishing or expanding innovative and exemplary guidance and counseling programs and projects for the purpose of stimulating the adoption of new programs, as well as establishing, maintaining, and improving programs of guidance and counseling services and activities, especially through new and improved approaches.[32] Prior to combining Title V-A, NDEA, with Title III, ESEA, in the Amendments of 1970 (PL 91-230), projects under Title III dealing with guidance and other pupil personnel services were funded to the extent of over $6,000,000.[33] Many of the locally developed ESEA III projects had foci pertinent to vocational guidance and career development, but since these were not the specific intent of this portion of the Act, the number and comprehensiveness of them was restricted. Even so, they represented thrusts to be expanded upon or used as important reference points following passage of the Vocational Education Act Amendments of 1968, which will be discussed shortly.

As indicated previously, Title V-B of NDEA had supported directly the preservice preparation of school counselors while Title V-A had provided for support in the development and maintenance of local programs of guidance, counseling, and testing. When NDEA, Title V-A, and ESEA, Title III, were combined, the continued funding emphasis on preparing counselors was covered principally by the Higher Education Act Amendments of 1968. Title V of this Act was entitled Education Professions Development. Fundamentally, the intent of these legislative actions was to improve the "qualifications of persons who are serving or preparing to serve in educational programs in elementary and secondary schools (including preschool and adult and vocational programs) or postsecondary vocational schools or to supervise or train persons so serving."[34] Part D (Improving Training Opportunities for Personnel Serving in Programs of Education other than Higher Education) provided for "programs or projects to train or retrain other educational personnel in such fields as guidance and counseling (*including occupational counseling*). In terms of these laws guidance and counseling personnel were considered part of the critical shortage of adequately trained educational personnel and representative of a career in a field directly related to teaching in elementary and secondary schools. (A full analysis of counselor preparation will be found in Chapter 20 by Kenneth Hoyt.)

At this point it is necessary to return to the legislation more explicitly focused on the vocational aspects of education or guidance. Even though the Vocational Education Act was passed in 1963, it did not become operational until two years later. In 1967 a second panel of consultants (after the first established by President Kennedy in 1961) was formed to examine the current status of vocational education and in particular the impact of the 1963 Act to that time. Among other things, the panel of consultants observed that "vocational education still appears to suffer most in quantity and quality for those who need it most." They identified inadequacies in vocational education in both inner-city and suburban schools, noted its inadequacies for women and for out-of-school youth, and emphasized that too few occupationally oriented public school courses or programs were available for adults.

According to the panel, those least well served by the education and training system were individuals out of school and under age twenty. In particular, they observed that:

> Graduates of the general high school curriculum, graduates of the college preparatory curriculum who did not attend college, and graduates of the many vocational curriculums which have lost touch with the world of employment have nearly as many problems as the people labeled "dropouts."[35]

The report of the panel evidenced strong concern that counseling and guidance needed to place greater emphasis on the world of work and its requirements. These observations were consistent with other reports which were casting intense scrutiny upon counseling emphases immediately prior to the panel's formation.[36] It was strongly proposed that the school program needed to be modified to include as a part of the course work of all students, instruction designed to acquaint them with today's world of work. Finally, it was argued that it was no longer possible to compartmentalize education into separate aspects labeled general, academic, and vocational.

Specifically, the Report of the Advisory Council outlined a series of recommendations focused upon creating what was described as "a unified system of vocational education." The recommendations included the following:

1. Occupational preparation should begin in the elementary schools with a realistic picture of the world of work . . .
2. In junior high school economic orientation and occupational preparation should reach a more sophisticated stage with study by all students of the economic and industrial system by which goods and services are produced and distributed . . .
3. Occupational preparation should become more specific in the high school, though preparation should not be limited to a specific occupation . . .
4. Occupational education should be based on a spiral curriculum which treats concepts at higher and higher levels of complexity as the student moves through the program . . .
5. Some formal post-secondary occupational preparation for all should be a goal for the near future.
6. Beyond initial preparation for employment, many, out of choice or necessity, will want to bolster an upward occupational climb with part-time and sometimes full-time courses and programs as adults . . .
7. Any occupation which contributes to the good of society is a fit subject for vocational education. In the allocation of scarce resources, first attention must be paid to those occupations which offer expanding opportunities for employment . . .
8. Occupational preparation need not and should not be limited to the classroom, to the school shop, or to the laboratory. Many arguments favor training on the job . . .
9. Effective occupational preparation is impossible if the school feels that its obligation ends when the student graduates . . .

10. No matter how good the system of initial preparation and the opportunities for upgrading on the job, there will always be need for remedial programs . . .
11. At every level from the elementary school through the post-secondary, adult and remedial programs there will be those with special needs as defined by the 1963 Act. For both humanitarian and economic reasons, persons with special needs deserve special help . . .
12. Many communities are too small to muster sufficient students for a range of occupational offerings broad enough to provide realistic freedom of occupational choice . . . residential schools may be appropriate in these situations . . .
13. The public system for occupational preparation must be supported by adequate facilities and equipment, buttressed by research and innovation, and by the preparation and upgrading of competent teachers, counselors, and administrators . . .
14. The system of occupational preparation cannot operate in a vacuum. Data must be made available on public and private training opportunities to eliminate undesirable duplication.[37]

In essence, these recommendations were translated into legislation in the Vocational Education Act Amendments of 1968, which in turn provided the foundation for "career education," as it will be discussed later.

Fundamentally, the 1968 Amendments to the Vocational Education Act significantly expanded those portions of the 1963 Act which charted new directions for vocational education and the populations which it should serve. More significantly, the 1968 Amendments began the process of converting into programs the many concepts that had been generated from the 1962 panel through the subsequent panels and reports up to 1968.

The 1968 Amendments to the Vocational Education Act reasserted the importance of expanded efforts in research and training with emphasis on the development of new career programs, residential schools, rehabilitation of special needs groups, particularly the disadvantaged and the physically handicapped, cooperative programs, and work-study programs. The amendments strongly advocated curriculum development and the initiation of exemplary projects pertinent to vocational education and its many ancillary components, including guidance and counseling. In this latter thrust, it was emphasized that new ways of conceptualizing vocational education needed to be found beyond the traditional lines of identification: agriculture, trade and industrial education, distributive, office occupations, and the health areas.

The 1968 Amendments also supported an expanded concept of guidance and counseling to include services which facilitate job choices and job placement. Inherent in both of these conceptions was an emphasis on needs for prevocational activity extending into the elementary school. These perceptions were clearly congruent with and influenced by career development as it will be discussed later. Burkett has indicated that a key word in the Act's statement of purpose is "access" in the sense that all persons "will have ready access to vocational training or retraining which is of quality, which is realistic in light of actual or anticipated opportunities for gainful employment, and which is suited to their needs, interests, and ability to benefit from such training." In addition, he indicated that this concept of "access" also has social implications because it extends and creates avenues of opportunity "for all who seek to become productive workers—without regard to race, creed, class, or national origin . . . A basic precept of vocational education is that man gives dignity to the job. No job can, of itself, bring dignity to the man." Burkett contended further that the provisions of the 1968 Amendments address themselves to the task of bringing about fundamental educational change.

> The act provides that exemplary and innovative programs may begin at the elementary level thus bringing the relevancy of vocational education to the entire system. Early exposure to career models can help students aim higher in their occupational aspirations and provide them experiences that will give them a basis for making realistic occupational choices when the time comes.[38]

There have been many implications of this expanded view of guidance and counseling. Perhaps the most important was a reaffirmation that vocational education and guidance have reciprocal needs, one for the other. Stephens[39] contended that until World War I such a relationship did exist since both vocational guidance and vocational education were seen as parallel responses to the social needs extant at that time. However, this relationship deteriorated, in part, because the National Education Association (NEA) in 1918 accepted a craft rather than a technical training emphasis in vocational education and a guidance-for-education rather than for jobs conception of vocational guidance. Because of the ensuing identity split between vocational education and vocational guidance, each took increasingly independent pathways and pursued professional emphases unrelated to their earlier symbiotic relationships. Outlining the necessities for interrelations between vocational guidance and vocational education spurred by the 1968 VEA Amendments, Law suggested three propositions:

1. Career guidance and orientation is needed by everyone.
2. Vocational guidance needs a regular place in the school curriculum.
3. There can be no satisfactory program of vocational guidance without vocational education.

He contended further:

> If the vocational guidance program were longitudinal, a continuing process, as it has been described in career development theory, there would be an ample opportunity for an individualized program. From a common core of group activity, individual students would move toward the development of occupational knowledge, concept of self, and vocational competence in any variety of ways, largely determined by each person's qualities and drives.[40]

Law's succinct summary captured the essence espoused by a rising crescendo of voices in the ranks of vocational education, vocational guidance, and manpower agencies during the late 1960s.

One of the components of the Vocational Education Act Amendments of 1968 which provided a stimulus to moving toward such goals as are implicit in Law's observations was Part D, the Exemplary Programs and Projects section. Analogous to the intent and function of ESEA, III, Part D of the Amendments provided risk capital to finance innovative practices pertinent to those outlined in the 1968 report of the Advisory Council on Vocational Education. Funding from this section of the legislation supported a national conference as well as a number of projects designed to plumb the options for implementing its focus. The national conference provided a forum for invited papers by persons representing vocational education, research, school administration, and vocational guidance.[41] Among the concepts developed by the papers was advocacy of using developmental tasks and current knowledge about career development to provide the organizing structure for a systems approach to education from kindergarten into higher education. In the paper presenting this position it was strongly emphasized that education needed to develop directly and systematically student attitudes and knowledge about themselves, their occupational and educational alternatives, and the decision-making alternatives which are central to vocational identity and choice.[42] This emphasis was complemented by others analyzing ways to promote career development in elementary and junior high school;[43] the possibilities of developing work experience and cooperative education programs;[44] and, among others, ways of implementing change.[45]

The Exemplary Program and Services Branch of the U.S.O.E. recommended these papers as useful background references on the design of vocational exemplary projects. While it is not possible to gauge the direct influence of such materials on programs implemented under the aegis of Part D of the Vocational Education Act Amendments of 1968, it is possible to analyze some of the characteristics of such projects. In one review of selected projects associated with funding under either the Vocational Education Act of 1963 or the Amendments of 1968, the following observations were made.

> On balance, the project objectives and assumptions reported are comprehensive in their response to local conditions as these are defined by characteristics such as the inner-city, the rural small school, community resource availability or the needs of specific target groups—Mexican-Americans, blacks, rural-poor, out-of-school youth and adults or a total student population. In addition, it is apparent that most projects are more than simple additions to ongoing programs. They often represent efforts to articulate program elements across disciplines or professional specialties as well as longitudinally. There are also efforts to link up with community agencies in establishing mutual objectives.

> It is fairly obvious but worth noting that the majority of current and completed career program efforts have been at the elementary and junior high school levels; and, these efforts generally deal with pupil's self and occupational awareness. Relatively speaking, little has been done at the senior high school level in terms of developing career development programs which infuse the total curriculum . . .

> Finally, there is in most of the projects reported, a significant emphasis on individual self-awareness, developing personal preference, and planfulness, understanding and being able to relate one's own characteristics to occupational and educational alternatives. Such emphases have seemed to find their roots in the growing body of theory and research about career development and in the apparent demands upon self-definition which is a characteristic of our current levels of social and technological complexity. While career development has been considered by many as the domain of vocational guid-

ance, its implications have also affected evolving conceptions of vocational education.[46]

While it seems clear that the Vocational Education Act Amendments of 1968, and earlier the basic Act of 1963, had identified the importance of vocational guidance in meeting the goals of the legislation, Hoyt, for one, did not see this fact as an unmixed blessing. Indeed, he contended that, "The Vocational Education Amendments of 1968 contain both hope and headaches for the guidance movement."[47] He indicated that analysis of the different sections of the Act in which reference was made to vocational guidance or to guidance and counseling suggested that the image of the role of vocational guidance could be described as follows (presented here in outline form with discussion added):

Goals in the Regular Ongoing Program

1. *To provide opportunities for choosing vocational education to secondary school students, out-of-school youth, and adults.* Interestingly enough, while the Act talked about promoting prevocational activities extending into the elementary school, there are clearly no funds made available in the regular program for vocational aspects of guidance in the elementary school or for the support of elementary school counselors.

2. *To provide vocational guidance and counseling services to students in vocational education programs.* Hoyt's interpretation of the legislation is that Congress intended that comprehensive guidance programs be provided for vocational education students. Specifically, he quotes, for support of this position, Title I, Part D, of the Act, which states "The Congress finds . . . it . . . necessary . . . (to give . . . the same kind of attention as is now given to . . . those young persons who go on to college, to . . . (those who do not)."

3. *To develop and maintain cooperative relationships with Employment Service Counselors.* This represents a goal for the sharing of information from the employment service to school counselors about occupations and the labor market and from school counselors to employment service counselors about the occupational qualifications of vocational education students for placement purposes.

4. *To develop effective working relationships with a wide variety of professional personnel concerned with manpower problems.*

Goals in the Exemplary Programs

5. *To define, develop, operate, and test the effectiveness of vocational aspects of guidance in the elementary school.* It is apparent that the Congress recognizes the need for the development of comprehensive programs of vocational development beginning in the elementary school and is encouraging guidance personnel to undertake such programs and evaluate their effectiveness, even though the legislation does not provide funding for elementary school counselors *per se.*

6. *To define, develop, operate, and test the effectiveness of vocational aspects of guidance related to the transition from school to work.* Essen-

tially, the legislation strongly encouraged the school to include a job placement and followup service as part of its regular guidance program

Other Goals

7. *To include a clear emphasis on vocational aspects of guidance in regular counselor education programs and to provide inservice education to counselors who need such an emphasis.*

8. *To vigorously attack our current areas of ignorances by sound research studies concerning the differential efficacy of various counseling approaches with various populations, the need for drastic change in the nature and dissemination of occupational and educational information, improving the process of transition from school to work, and the evaluation of guidance.*[48]

While Hoyt's analysis suggests that the eight goals for vocational guidance supported by the Act are exciting, he also expresses concern that they be implemented in such a way that they will not violate other basic philosophical goals of guidance, which he describes as follows:

1. We must retain the concept of unity of guidance as a program of services for all.

2. We must retain a reasoned and reasonable balance between cognitive and affective emphases in guidance and counseling.

3. We must uphold and promulgate the basic value anchors on which the personnel and guidance field is based:
   a. Worth of the individual.
   b. Freedom of choice for each individual.
   c. Expansion of both the basis for decision-making and the variety of choices made available to the individual.
   d. The value of personalized and individualized assistance in the decision-making process.[49]

Hoyt's concerns stand as one of several points on a historical continuum which periodically reminds counselors that while they clearly have manpower responsibilities, their first reference point must be the welfare of the individual. One does not preclude the other, but the rights and the needs of the individual must be the overriding concern in counseling.[50]

CAREER DEVELOPMENT AND CAREER EDUCATION IN THE 1970s

In this analysis of legislation the influence of career development theory and research has been inferred at several points. It seems apparent that the major influence has been less visible in the nonschool oriented legislation than in the school legislation. The latter is a probable result of the fact that most of the nonschool agencies dealing with manpower needs work with clients in restricted time frameworks while career development speculation and thought has, by definition, a longitudinal character. Given such a premise, the school is the social institution which deals with the most persons at the times in their lives when their behavior is most malleable for the most sustained period of time. Systematic recognition of the implications of this fact began to appear in the Vocational Education Act of 1963, were intensely magnified in the Vocational Education Amendments of 1968, and had their clearest national expression in the model building and program development associated with efforts described as "career education," which have been in process since January 1971. Confirmation of this trend is evident in statements emanating from the United States Office of Education. For example, the Exemplary Programs and Services Branch, Division of Vocational and Technical Education, has indicated that Part D, Section 142(c), of the Vocational Education Act Amendments of 1968 actually represents "early attempts to structure operating models of what is now coming to be referred to as K through 12 'career education system.' The roots for such a system go back into many years of basic research on career development theory."[51]

Such an observation seems to be validated in another document from the United States Office of Education, which, in addressing vocational education for the 1970s, indicates that:

> Vocational education in this decade must be conceptualized as lifelong career development for every person who can profit from such a program . . . Vocational education must now provide the framework for a career education system that will: (1) introduce the elementary school child to the world of careers; (2) provide exploration, guidance and counselling for career choices throughout elementary and secondary education; (3) provide specific skills training, job clusters skills, or pretechnical education at the secondary level; (4) provide pretechnical and significantly more technical education at the secondary and post-secondary levels; and (5) provide upgrading and retraining opportunities throughout adulthood.[52]

Actually, as career education concepts have been translated into models or programs, they have been extended beyond the traditional kindergarten to twelfth grades, reaching into higher education, the community, and places of employment.[53] Beginning in late 1971, four models were under development and being implemented under the aegis of the United States Office of Education: The "school-based comprehensive career education model," the "employer-based career education model," the "home/community-based career education model," and the "residential-based career education model." Refinements or variations of these national models are occurring in virtually all states, thus extending significantly the potential power of the concepts underlying career education. Collectively, these models represent attempts to direct the force of the substance of career education to all segments of the population at those points in their lives and in the contexts which promise the most impact. While research and evaluation pertinent to career education has not yet been accomplished because of the short period of time which has elapsed from mustering support for the concepts on which career education is based, to model building, to site selection and implementation, to program operation, it is useful to consider the gross objectives to which the four national models of career education were initially addressed.[54]

The school-based model will seek to develop within students:

1. A concept of self which is in keeping with a work oriented society.
2. Positive attitudes about work, school, and society, and a sense of satisfaction resulting from successful experiences in these areas.

3. Personal characteristics of self-respect, self-reliance, perseverance, initiative, and resourcefulness.
4. A realistic understanding of the relationships between the world of work and education.
5. A comprehensive awareness of career options in the world of work.
6. The ability to enter employment in an appropriate occupation at a productive level and/or to pursue further education.

In translating these objectives into a school-based model, the Ohio State Center for Vocational and Technical Education (the agency granted the U.S.O.E. contract to develop this model) indicated that it would be necessary to:

1. Restructure the entire educational program around real life.
2. Integrate academic knowledge and skills with occupational training.
3. Assure that each exiting student will be prepared for further career education or for entry into an occupation.
4. Provide for each student a program relevant for his becoming a self-fulfilled, productive, and contributing citizen.
5. Incorporate into the program community resources and nonschool educational opportunities.[55]

The center further concluded, "In developing the detailed conceptualization of career education, it is imperative to determine the elements of career development that provide for the self-actualization of the student."[56] After examining essentially the same body of knowledge described in Chapter 10 of this volume, it was determined that the elements of career education to which the school-based model would be directed and the outcomes sought would include:

Element	*Outcome*
Career awareness ⟶	Career identity
Self-awareness ⟶	Self-identity
Appreciations, attitudes ⟶	Self-social fulfillment
Decision-making skills ⟶	Career decisions
Economic awareness ⟶	Economic understanding
Skill awareness and beginning competence ⟶	Employment skills
Employability skills ⟶	Career placement
Educational awareness ⟶	Educational identity

While the brief description of the school-based model provided here does not begin to capture the substance of each of the elements identified, it suffices to indicate the importance of career development and a vocational guidance point of view permeating the model (although, as Super contends in Chapter 3, much of what falls under the rubric of career education is not related to career but to occupation). It further indicates that the intent is to provide an articulated educational system incorporating emphases on behavioral outcomes related to decision making and employability skills, individualizing approaches to such outcomes, a greater use of technology and simulation as developmental media, and a general redefinition of the purpose of education.

The employer-based career education model is designed to provide an alternative to current formal educational structures for young people ages thirteen to eighteen. More specifically, it is intended to demonstrate the relevance of the educational process through "intimate student involvement in professional and industrial operations." The program emphasizes educational experiences that are available on a twelve month basis within a variety of nontraditional settings, such as scientific and medical laboratories, warehouses, construction and housing projects, parks, museums, banks, insurance companies, hospitals, factories, and prisons. Thus the classroom will be one with community occupational opportunities. It is intended that the guidance system will mediate actively between students and their work-education-community environments. It will assist directly in the mapping of an individualized learning program for each student and in his achievement of the learning objectives inherent in his plan. Specifically, it is intended that the learning experiences integral to the employer-based model include attention to:

1. Review and reinforce students' educational competencies and interests.
2. Provide opportunities for a variety of activities with a variety of people other than the limited peer group and teacher associations available in the public school.
3. Develop a strong self-concept through participation in an individualized and self-directed learning program.
4. Provide multiple opportunities for obtaining directly relevant information concerning career opportunities and requirements, and advantages and disadvantages of a variety of career options.[57]

The home-based career education model is designed for adult populations including those which are homebound for a variety of reasons. In this sense, the home itself is to be used as a career education center in conjunction with three components: (1) a career-oriented educational motivation program, focused upon building motivation to study for a career, providing information about career opportunities, and some occupational competency instruction; (2) a home and community education system, using television correspondence programs, as well as radio and instructional aids; and (3) career clinics in the community to provide career guidance and counseling, referral services and information on relevant institution-based education programs. The initial objectives for the model include:

1. To develop educational delivery systems into the home and community.
2. To provide new career education programs for adults.
3. To establish a guidance and career placement system to assist individuals in occupational and related life roles.
4. To develop more competent workers for the world of work.
5. To enhance the quality of the home as a learning center.[58]

The residential-based career education model is, at the time of this writing, the least well-defined of the four models sponsored under the aegis of the U.S.O.E. The major target groups for this effort appear to be disadvantaged and rural families. The major expectation is that total family units will be brought to residential training sites where they will be housed. During the residence period each member of the family will be involved in that aspect of a comprehensive career education program most applicable to him. The assumption is that different members of a family might be undergoing simultaneously activities which are prevocational, or motivational or skill and competency based depending upon their age or employment history. It can also be assumed that such family units will be provided medical care, psychological services, consumer education, and such other assistance as is likely to enhance their viability as a self-reliant and economically independent group.

As the four models briefly described suggest, career education is comprehensive in the concepts it employs, the contexts in which it will be operational, and in the segments of the population to which it is addressed. Nevertheless, the major thrust seems to be focused in the school-based model. Swanson would likely contend that this is as it should be since it is his judgment that career education is the responsibility of the school primarily. His reasons include the following.

1. It is the only place where individuals can discover self in relation to the world of work.
2. It is the only institution to provide the multiple delivery systems needed for career education, i.e., instruction, guidance, placement, community interaction.
3. It can implement the concept of decision making.
4. It has interchangeable parts needed for statewide emphasis.
5. It cannot accept the obligations of career education without expanding programs, particularly in training for job entry skills and in adult education.[59]

In a general sense, analyses of the current rhetoric and writing about career education tend to support Swanson's observations, although the goals which have been identified as appropriate to career education go beyond the capabilities of the school alone. In analyzing the various speeches, papers, and models descriptive of career education, Herr concluded that the term can be used to mean at least the following:

1. An effort to diminish the separateness of academic and vocational education.
2. An area of concern which has some operational implications for every educational level or grade from kindergarten through graduate school.
3. A process of insuring that every person exiting from the formal educational structure has job employability skills of some type.
4. A direct response to the importance of facilitating individual choice making so that occupational preparation and the acquisition of basic academic skills can be coordinated with developing individual preference.
5. A way of increasing the relevance or meaningfulness of education for greater numbers of students than is currently true.
6. A design to make education an open system so that school leavers, school dropouts, and adults can reaffiliate with it when their personal circumstances or job requirements make this feasible.
7. A structure whose desired outcomes necessitate cooperation among all elements of education as well as among the school, industry, and community.
8. An enterprise requiring new technologies and materials of education (i.e., individualized programming, simulations).
9. A form of education for all students.[60]

Career education, then, can be seen as a process of facilitating career development in all students by modifying in-school educational experiences, as well as experiences in the business/industrial sector and the home. The institutionalization of career development encompasses both emphasis on skill preparation, whether conceived in a cluster concept or a more narrow focus, and the preparation to choose wisely. It has evolved from an emphasis on matching men and jobs to one of commitment to the clarification of those aspects of life, such as interests, capacities, values, which need development for a lifelong process of planning and decision making.

An interesting fact in the escalating momentum of career education in the early 1970s is that such movement occurred without benefit of national legislation or direct funding support. The original models of career education were funded through exemplary project funds provided by the Vocational Educational Act Amendments of 1968 and the United States Commissioner of Education's discretionary monies within that legislation, as well as from the Cooperative Research Act and the Education Professions Development Act.[61] Almost simultaneous with Commissioner Marland's initial assertions that Career Education was a national priority, there was a great flood of support for such a concept across the nation. Among the first state legislatures to give legislative support to career education on a statewide level was Arizona. In Arizona's Senate Bill #5, that state declared its support of career education and defined it in terms of emphasizing orientation to work, preparation for work, retraining of those educational personnel to be involved with the program, guidance and counseling, curriculum changes, on-the-job training, and linkages to the state manpower and labor systems through apprenticeships. Other states, as well as large city systems, implemented legislative or other types of planning committees to examine the implications of career education for state aid formulas or special program development.[62] The National Association of State Directors of Vocational Education[63] published a position paper on career education and other representatives of educational components undertook similar tasks. Professional publications devoted entire issues to defining and applying career education concepts to the specialties which their readership represented.

OTHER LEGISLATIVE EMPHASES IN THE EARLY 1970s

At the national level a number of pieces of legislation potentially affecting manpower distribution, career education, vocational rehabilitation, and other areas discussed in this chapter continue to be at the center of congressional consideration. Among them are the amendments to the Higher Education Act of 1965, which were passed in July 1972. The higher education portion of the bill extended all titles of the Higher Education Act of 1965 enabling the continuation of community service and continuing education programs, college library programs, developing institutions programs, student financial aid, international education, and public service education. In addition, the amendments included provisions for:

1. The Higher Education Opportunity Act, which provides (a) a combination of grants, work-study, and subsidized loans for low- to middle-income full time undergraduate students and (b) the creation of a National Student Loan Association.

2. The National Institute of Education to support and conduct educational research, dissemination, and training. The Institute will also include a National Council on Educational Research, a National Center for Educational Communication as well as the functions for a National Foundation for Higher Education (not yet created) to encourage excellence, innovation, and reform in postsecondary education.

3. The Emergency School Aid Act, which provides grants to districts to improve desegregation and prevent segregation. Authorizations were to be used for remedial services, additional staff and training of staff, *counseling and guidance,* shared facilities and interracial educational programs.

4. A major title in the legislation concerned with "Improving of Community Colleges and Occupation Education." This title requires the development of statewide plans for establishing and expanding community colleges and for *occupational education programs.* Also of particular interest in this title is *the creation within the United States Office of Education of a Bureau of Occupation and Adult Education which is responsible for career education.*

5. Under the Cooperative Research Act, $14 million for *demonstration models of career education.*

6. Extension of funding for the Vocational Education Act Amendments of 1968 through 1975.

Thus, the Higher Education Act of 1972 is a comprehensive piece of legislation dealing with a broad range of educational funding and organizational change within the United States Office of Education. Of prime concern for this chapter is the first direct affirmation of and funding for career education.

Another pertinent piece of legislation was the Education Revenue Sharing Act, which would provide federal money to be shared with state and local education officials for purposes of education of the disadvantaged and handicapped, innovations and development of new educational programs and practices, and vocational and career education as well as supporting educational materials and services. Also under consideration were the Economic Opportunity Act Amendments of 1971, which would authorize a comprehensive program to provide health, nutrition, and education services to disadvantaged children and children of working mothers. A partial response to the continuing allegations of sex typing and sexual discrimination in occupational opportunities was the Equal Employment Opportunity Bill. The Emergency Employment Act of 1971 provided programs of public service employment designed to develop new careers, career advancement, and continued training when unemployment is 4.5 percent or above.

Perhaps more pertinent to the substance of this chapter is the Occupational Education Act of 1971 (not passed at the time of this writing), which had as its purpose: to assure an opportunity for occupational education (other than that resulting in a baccalaureate or advanced degree) to every American who needs and desires such education by providing financial assistance for postsecondary occupational education programs, and to strengthen the concept of occupational preparation, counseling, and placement in elementary and secondary schools, and for other purposes.

This Act, along with some of the others just mentioned but not yet passed, seem to be stymied because they represent fragments of a comprehensive manpower act which, while not yet formulated, seems to have conceptual support. It would likely incorporate the current provisions of the MDTA as well as separate components of certain of the education acts bearing upon career education, vocational education, placement, and, possibly, guidance and counseling. Such possibilities seem inherent in President Nixon's Message to Congress in March 1972, transmitting the Manpower Report of the President.

> The second decade of an active manpower policy, which begins in March of this year, is dedicated to attaining full opportunity for all American workers.
>
> Our tactics for pursuing this objective are twofold: First, to accomplish much needed and long overdue reform of the manpower programs set up under the Manpower Development and Training Act and subsequent legislation and thus increase their effectiveness in enhancing the employability of jobless workers; and, second, to move toward a broader national manpower policy which will be an important adjunct of economic policy in achieving our Nation's economic and social objectives.[64]

The *Manpower Report of the President* for 1972 outlined a variety of responses to providing manpower services in the years directly ahead. In that sense, they provide some points of reference for speculating about the future characteristics of manpower programs, the importance of guidance and counseling in such efforts, and the needs of special groups to be served. Among the data on the preceding are:

1. A fiscal and programmatic strengthening of the employment service system which separated the U.S. Training and Employment Service into the U.S. Employment Service and the Office of Employment Development Programs. These organizational changes are intended to reemphasize services to employers, employment counseling, and job placement.

2. The expansion of the computerization and creation of national job banks.

3. The development of comprehensive models for the delivery of employment services tailored to three levels:

   a. A streamlined, self-help service for job-ready applicants.

   b. Job development and assistance in planning a personal job search for applicants needing somewhat more help.

   c. Intensive counseling, placement, and supportive services for the most disadvantaged—with continuity of service assured by assigning applicants to employability development teams having limited caseloads. These latter essentially will package and facilitate individual acquisition of career development.

4. The expansion of Manpower Training Skills Centers.

5. The continuous restructuring and strengthening of state and local planning and management responsibilities for manpower programs to insure cooperation among all pertinent agencies, a diminution of duplicated services, and linkages across regions rather than simply towns or cities.

6. The unfolding of programs increasingly refined in terms of the needs of special groups. While the definitions of which are special groups change because of social conditions, in 1972 major concerns were focused on:

a. Veterans and servicemen
b. Welfare recipients
c. Migrant workers
d. American Indians
e. Spanish-speaking Americans
f. Public offenders
g. Youth.

IMPLICATIONS FOR VOCATIONAL GUIDANCE

The analyses of legislation, manpower policy, and needs of different groups of persons within the American society presented in this chapter confirm the central importance of vocational guidance to each of these. While the image of vocational guidance and, by extrapolation, the role of the practitioner, varies across these domains, several implications pertinent to the profession and its representatives seem to be clear:

1. The forces which support the viability of vocational guidance as a major factor in responding to the manpower needs of persons of all ages and characteristics also indicate that it cannot stand alone in meeting these needs. Rather, its practitioners must be in cooperative relationship with teachers and with employers, as well as with their counseling counterparts in other settings.

2. Vocational guidance has both a prevocational or developmental role and an adjustment role.[66] Current legislation, rhetoric, and literature seem to combine in promoting the counselor's developmental and prevocational role as a priority one which has not received sufficient emphasis.

3. In response to their role in vocational guidance, counselors must be more active in identifying their clients, in working with them directly at their training, educational or employment sites, and in emphasizing their job development and placement roles.

4. The narrow definition of vocational guidance as pertinent to job choice only is being replaced by terms such as career guidance. More than semantic in its implications, the latter term refers to the necessity that vocational guidance be concerned about the implications of providing assistance in such areas as educational as well as vocational choice, in the development of the personal attitudes which underlie acquisition of vocational identity, the formulation of personal values in relation to different life-style alternatives, job development, job placement, and identification of avocational or leisure pursuits as well as the traditional concerns. Unfortunately, the idea of a career for other than professionals is fairly novel any place in the world. Production jobs have usually been considered entities in themselves without a sense of the possible movement of an individual from one stage of development to another. However, today in job design and restructuring concepts of career development and career progression are influencing such tasks. Persons prominent in such tasks are advocating clearly articulated jobs as stages in a chain through which individuals can progress to find one which has dignity

and meaning for them. Counselors must begin to internalize such conceptual models as ways of helping the client think beyond the immediate as his sense of career is stimulated.[67]

5. The delivery of vocational guidance services must be increasingly individualized, not just individual in implementation. The characteristics of different groups whether described by sex, age, or economic factors require that services be provided on a continuous basis throughout the formal processes of education and into community settings attuned to diverse types of need. While the school is a major setting for providing vocational guidance services, as is the employment service office, the needs of adults who are under utilized, unemployed, disadvantaged, or anticipating retirement require that vocational guidance be provided in locations and circumstances most encouraging and convenient for them.

6. While some observers may reject on philosophical grounds the notion that counselors or vocational guidance services should be or can be described as part of the manpower development network of the nation, federal legislation seems not to share that ambivalence. Indeed, it is likely that if counseling is to continue to receive legislative support that such support will occur within the parameters of a comprehensive manpower act or some modification thereof.

7. Much of the legislation speaks to the need for vocational guidance and counseling but does not equate this with a need for counselors. It seems apparent that unless counselors more effectively include such an emphasis within the services provided to clients, persons other than counselors may provide such services. Unless counselors remain open to ways of realigning their time allocations to various types of services to clients through the use of such possibilities as differentiated staffing, group work, technological augmentations for information retrieval, etc., they will be limited in their response capabilities.

This latter is penetratingly summarized in the Sixth Report of the National Advisory Council on Vocational Education. In its letter of transmittal to the Secretary of Health, Education, and Welfare, the Council made the following statements:

> The Council has discovered that the general quality of counseling and guidance services today is greatly in need of improvement. The counseling and guidance profession is not keeping up with the latest developments in our educational system . . . Little attention is given by counselors to vocational and technical education, and the expanding variety of new career opportunities which do not require a four-year college degree . . . Counseling and guidance is a useful tool for providing young people with the information and advice they need to make intelligent career choices in today's modern society. If the information offered is restrictive and out-of-date, however, the guidance role could do more harm than good. We are interested in seeing the necessary improvements made in counseling and guidance to make it a truly beneficial and constructive part of our educational and social service system.

It is therefore clear that vocational guidance continues to represent promise for many and has been so considered by national observers over the past fifteen years in manpower policies and legislation. But it is also evident that being seen in these ways brings with it very great responsibilities for the profession and for individual counselors. We must not falter at either level in the decade ahead.

NOTES

1. E. Ginzberg, "Psychology and Manpower Policy," *American Psychologist*, 21(1966):549–554.
2. R. Ehrle, I., "Counseling for Vocational Training and Employment," *The Encyclopedia of Education*, vol. 2 (New York: Macmillan Co. and Free Press, 1971), pp. 516–22.
3. National Advisory Committee on Civil Disorders, "Manpower Proposals of the President's Commission on Civil Disorders," *Monthly Labor Review*, 91 (1968):37–41; National Advisory Committee on Vocational Education, *Annual Report, Vocational Education Amendments of 1968*, P.L. 90–576 (Washington: The Committee, July 15, 1969).
4. "Nation's Manpower Revolution," Hearings before the Subcommittee on Employment and Manpower of the Committee on Labor and Public Welfare, United States Senate, Relating to the Training and Utilization of the Manpower Resources of the Nation, 1936–1965.
5. W. W. Tennyson, "The Psychology of Developing Competent Personnel," *American Vocational Journal*, 42(1967):27–29.
6. L. Levine, "Implications of the Anti-poverty Program for Education and Employment," *Vocational Guidance Quarterly*, 13(1965):8–15.
7. Advisory Council on Vocational Education, *Vocational Education: The Bridge Between Man and His Work* (Washington: The Council, 1968).
8. *Ibid.*
9. M. Harrington, *The Other America: Poverty in the United States* (New York: The Macmillan Company, 1962).
10. U.S. Department of Labor, *The Manpower Report of the President* (Washington: Government Printing Office, 1966).
11. U.S. Department of Health, Education, and Welfare, "Manpower Development and Training Program," *Prevocational Exploratory Programs in Manpower Development and Training* (Washington: Government Printing Office, 1970).
12. *Ibid.*, p. 3.
13. Chronicle Guidance Professional Service, *Education: Weapon Against Poverty* (Moravia, N.Y.: Chronicle Guidance Publication, Inc., 1964).
14. P. Scarth, "Migrants, Education of Adults," *The Encyclopedia of Education*, vol. 6 (New York: Macmillan Co. and Free Press, 1971), pp. 364–8.
15. C. W. Ryan, "The Poland Springs Story," *Job Corps: Guidance Training for Today* (Washington: American Association of Colleges for Teacher Education, 1970), pp. 7–8.
16. U.S. Department of Labor, Manpower Administration, *Orientation, Counseling, and Assessment in Manpower Programs* (Washington: Government Printing Office, 1969), Chapter 10 particularly; ————, *Project Build* (Washington: Government Printing Office, 1970); ————, *Breakthrough for Disadvantaged Youth* (Washington: Government Printing Office, 1969).
17. Levine, *op. cit.*

18. U.S. Department of Labor, *The Manpower Report of the President* (Washington: Government Printing Office, 1964); see also D. H. Pritchard, "Impact of Government Programs on the Development and Employment of Counselors," *Vocational Guidance Quarterly,* 13(1965):36–40.

19. E. W. Baake, "Employment Service Role in an Active Labor Market Policy," *Employment Service Review,* 1(1964):1–8.

20. R. A. Ehrle, "Employment Counseling as an Integral Part of an Active Labor Market Policy," *Vocational Guidance Quarterly,* 13(1965):270–274.

21. J. A. Bitter, "The Training Counselor: An Emerging Professional," *Vocational Guidance Quarterly,* 15(1967):294–296.

22. U.S. Department of Labor, *The Manpower Report of the President* (Washington: Government Printing Office, 1968).

23. G. Venn, *Man, Education, and Work* (Washington: American Council on Education, 1964), Chapter 1 particularly.

24. T. Veblen, *The Instinct of Workmanship and the State of Industrial Arts* (New York: W. W. Norton Co., 1964). This piece was originally published in 1914.

25. P. Drucker, *The Age of Discontinuity: Guidelines to Our Changing Society* (New York: Harper and Row, 1969).

26. J. K. Galbraith, *The New Industrial State,* 2nd ed. (Boston: Houghton Mifflin, 1971) p. 289f.

27. U.S. Department of Health, Education, and Welfare. Panel of Consultants on Vocational Education, *Education for a Changing World of Work* (Washington: Government Printing Office, 1963), pp. 206–214.

28. U.S. Department of Health, Education, and Welfare, Vocational Education Review Task Force, *Report of the Analysis Group* (Washington: Government Printing Office, September 1970).

29. U.S. Senate Committee on Labor and Public Welfare, *Notes and Working Papers Concerning the Administration of Programs Authorized Under Vocational Education Act of 1963, P.L. 88–210, as Amended* (Washington: The Committee, March 1968).

30. U.S. Office of Education, Bureau of Elementary and Secondary Education, *Review of Progress under Title V-A, National Defense Education Act of 1958, as Amended* (Washington: The Office, 1969) p. 19; also see S. L. Wolfbein, "The Role of Counseling and Training in the War on Unemployment and Poverty," *Vocational Guidance Quarterly,* 12(1964):50–2.

31. U.S. Office of Education, Bureau of Elementary and Secondary Education, *Review of Progress under Title V-A, National Defense Education Act of 1958, as Amended* (Washington: The Office, 1969), pp. 10 and 19.

32. U.S. Office of Education, *State Plan Administrator's Manual, Title III, Elementary and Secondary Education Act* (Washington: The Office, 1971), p. 49.

33. Personal Communication from Dr. Donald D. Twiford, June 1972.

34. U.S. Office of Education, Bureau of Educational Personnel Development, *The Preparation of Proposals for Educational Personnel Development Grants 1968, 1969, 1970* (Parts C and D, Educations Professions Development Act of 1967) (Washington: The Office, 1967); also see U.S. Congress, The Higher Education Act of 1965, P.L. 89–329.

35. Advisory Council on Vocational Education, *Vocational Education: The Bridge Between Man and His Work* (Washington: The Council, 1968).

36. U.S. Department of Labor, The Subcommittee on Career Guidance, *Career Guidance* (Washington: Government Printing Office, 1966).

37. Advisory Council on Vocational Education, *op. cit.*

38. L. A. Burkett, "New Routes in Vocational Education" (Washington: Government Printing Office, 1970), pp. 2–3. Originally published as "Access to a Future," *American Education,* March 1969.

39. W. R. Stephens, *Social Reforms and the Origins of Vocational Guidance* (Washington: The National Vocational Guidance Association, 1970).

40. G. F. Law, "Vocational Curriculum: A Regular Place for Guidance," *American Vocational Journal,* 44(1969):27–28, 60.

41. G. Bottoms and K. B. Matheny, *A Guide for the Development, Implementation, and Administration of Exemplary Programs and Projects in Vocational Education* (Atlanta: Georgia State Department of Education, September 1969).

42. E. L. Herr, "Unifying an Entire System of Education Around a Career Development Theme," paper presented at National Conference on Exemplary Programs and Projects—1968 Amendments to Vocational Education Act, Atlanta, Georgia, March 1969.

43. N. C. Gysbers, "Elements of a Model for Promoting Career Development in Elementary and Junior High School," paper presented at National Conference on Exemplary Programs and Projects–1968 Amendments to the Vocational Education Act, Atlanta, Georgia, March 1969.

44. G. Burchill, "Work Experience Educational Programs for Secondary Youth," paper presented at National Conference on Exemplary Programs and Projects–1968 Amendments to the Vocational Education Act, Atlanta, Georgia, March 1969.

45. S. Moore, "Strategies for Change in the School," paper presented at National Conference on Exemplary Programs and Projects–1968 Amendments to the Vocational Education Act, Atlanta, Georgia, 1969.

46. E. L. Herr, *Review and Synthesis of Foundations for Career Education* (Washington: Government Printing Office, 1972).

47. K. Hoyt, "Operational Goals, Policies and Functions for Guidance as seen from the Vocational Education Amendments of 1968," *Proceedings of the National Conference on Guidance, Counseling, and Placement in Career Development and Educational-occupational Decision-making,* N. C. Gysbers and D. H. Pritchard, eds. (Columbia, Mo.: University of Missouri, October 1969).

48. *Ibid.*

49. *Ibid.*

50. R. F. Berdie, "The Counselor and his Manpower Responsibilities," *Personnel and Guidance Journal,* 38(1960):458–463.

51. U.S. Office of Education, Exemplary Programs and Services Branch, Division of Vocational and Technical Education, "Background in the Design, Development, and Implementation of Vocational Education Amendments of 1968" (Washington: The Office, 1971). (Mimeo.)

52. U.S. Office of Education, Division of Vocational and Technical Education, *Vocational Education for the 1970s.* Conference Discussion Paper (Washington: The Office, March 1971). (Mimeo.)

53. Robert M. Worthington, "The Need for Career Education," keynote address at the Invitational Workshop on Career Education, Washington, D.C., March 1, 1972.

54. U.S. Office of Education, "The Career Education Status Report–July 30, 1971" (Washington: National Center for Research and Development, The Office, July 1971).

55. The Center for Vocational and Technical Education, *Requirements of the Comprehensive Career Education Model* (Columbus, Ohio: Ohio State University, September 1971).

56. *Ibid.*, p. 2.
57. U.S. Office of Education, "The Career Education Status Report–July 30, 1971" (Washington: National Center for Research and Development, The Office, July 1971).
58. *Ibid.*
59. G. I. Swanson, "Concepts in Career Education." Paper presented to American Vocational Association Task Force on Career Education, Portland, Oregon, December 2, 1971.
60. E. L. Herr, *Review and Synthesis of Foundations for Career Education* (Washington: Government Printing Office, 1972).
61. Robert M. Worthington, "Provisions for Research and Development Programs in Vocational Education for FY 1972, under the supplemental $9 million allocation from the U.S. Commissioner's Discretionary Funds." POLICY PAPER—AVTE-V-7Z-1, U.S. Office of Education, Bureau of Adult, Vocational and Technical Education, September 9, 1971.
62. U.S. Office of Education, Bureau of Adult, Vocational and Technical Education, *State and Local Developments in Career Education* (Washington: U.S. Office of Education, November 1, 1971). (Mimeo.)
63. National Association of State Directors of Vocational Education, position paper on career education, adopted at Las Vegas, Nevada, September 1971.
64. R. Nixon, Foreword to *The Manpower Report of the President* (Washington: Government Printing Office, 1972).
65. U.S. Department of Labor, *The Manpower Report of the President* for 1972 (Washington: Government Printing Office, 1972).
66. E. L. Herr and S. H. Cramer, *Vocational Guidance and Career Development in the Schools: Toward a Systems Approach* (Boston: Houghton Mifflin, 1972).
67. L. E. Davis, "Restructuring Jobs for Social Goals," *Manpower*, 2(1970):3–6.
68. National Advisory Council on Vocational Education, *Counseling and Guidance: A Call for Change*, 6th Report (Washington: The Council, June 1, 1972).

SUGGESTED READING

U.S. Department of Labor, *Annual Manpower Report of The President.* Washington: U.S. Government Printing Office. A comprehensive summary of manpower problems, planned federal responses to these problems, and some glimpses of pertinent history. Typically reviews current or pending legislation relevant to manpower issues.

Drucker, P. *The Age of Discontinuity: Guidelines to Our Changing Society.* New York: Harper and Row, 1969. Detailed discussion of factors in the technological and economic areas which suggest a movement to a knowledge economy in America and in some other "developed nations." Considers implications for assisting the developing nations economically, educationally, and in the uses of human resources.

Advisory Council on Vocational Education, *Vocational Education: The Bridge Between Man and His Work.* Washington: The Council, 1968. Outlines factors which supported the need for major shifts in vocational education, the groups to be served by vocational education, the interrelationships between vocational education and guidance.

Herr, E. L. *Review and Synthesis of Foundations for Career Education.* Washington: Government Printing Office, 1972. Analyzes historical, legislative, and theoretical factors underlying recent emphases on career education.

Stephens, W. R. *Social Reforms and the Origins of Vocational Guidance.* Washington: National Vocational Guidance Association, 1970. Reviews in depth the social movements, professional and trade organizations, and people who gave impetus to the vocational movement in the late nineteenth and early twentieth centuries.

The Broader Context of Career Development and Vocational Guidance: American Trends in World Perspective   3

Donald E. Super
Teachers College, Columbia University

Throughout the highly developed countries there are certain common reasons for the emergence of vocational guidance, but the solutions adopted have varied greatly from one country to another. We thus have, in effect, most of the elements of good experiments with different policies and practices, with various organizational structures and staffing patterns, with a number of types of counselor education, and with many differing techniques of guidance and counseling. Yet surprisingly little use has been made of these opportunities for cross-cultural experimentation and evaluation.

SIMILARITIES AND DIFFERENCES IN AMERICA AND EUROPE

This is true despite the large numbers of international visitors entertained each year by vocational guidance experts in cities such as Amsterdam, Geneva, Brussels, Copenhagen, London, Madrid, New Delhi, New York, Paris, Rome, Tokyo and Vienna. Most such visitors travel with Blue Guides, Fodor, Michelin, or Muirhead and not with Lytton and Craft,[3] Pal,[4] or Reuchlin.[5] Reuchlin's scholarly survey of policies and problems in Western European countries should be part of the stock-in-trade of everyone engaged in the administration of pupil personnel services or in the preparation of counselors, but it is not known even to leading American counselor educators who are planning trips to Europe for themselves and for conducted tours. An older classic by two eminent American specialists in vocational guidance[6] which covers also Asian countries is now completely forgotten, even though in its day it received far more public recognition than has Reuchlin's more intensive study, and even though its now retired authors are still active in the guidance and counseling fields. Thirty-five years ago they wrote:

> Occupational adjustment is interwoven with political and social philosophies, circumstanced by economics, circumscribed by tradition, and circumvented by politicians. Amid this welter of social forces, individual attributes—personality, culture, intellect, physique, all the characteristics that

This paper is based in part on papers read at an international seminar in Rome, Italy,[1] at Harvard University in 1969,[2] and at a workshop at the University of Louisville in 1972.

contribute to the making of morally excellent and dynamically effective human beings—must somehow be adapted to the realities of day-to-day existence. If possible, the human beings embodying these attributes must attain not only the good life, but the happy life. Vocational guidance is the instrumentality through which these forces may become operative.[7]

The statement seems almost timeless, although today most experts on career development and vocational guidance would write that "individual attributes . . . must somehow adapt . . . ," making the individual an active rather than a passive agent; and they would more modestly claim that "vocational guidance is *one* instrumentality . . ."

Common Origins of Interest in Career Development

The similar origins of interest in career development and vocational guidance in Europe and America, and more recently in Asia and Africa, become apparent in a reading of the histories of vocational guidance[8] and of the international surveys.[9]

In America, Brewer played up the concern with out-of-school youth which launched the work of Frank Parsons and of the Boston Vocation Bureau in 1908. Stephens stressed the work of associations of manufacturers, trade unions, and educators concerned with manpower needs and vocational education, and he showed how Parsons and others perceived vocational education and guidance as ways of modifying the public schools in order to assimilate the large numbers of immigrants who floundered in the slums. This made them, in their day, social reformers. But both Brewer[10] and Stephens[11] make it clear that the planning and the action began with voluntary social agencies and then moved quickly to the schools.

The movement started at about the same time in Europe as in the United States. Parsons' work in the U.S. in 1908, Lahy's in personnel selection in France in 1910, Gemelli's in personnel selection in Italy in 1912, Christiaens' in vocational guidance in Belgium in 1912, were followed by further pioneer work in Geneva and London in 1914 and 1915.[12] In Europe Keller and Viteles pointed out that vocational guidance developed out of placement work in the ministries of labor, but that "consideration of individual characteristics has led these bureaus back to the school, first for information, then for active cooperation."[13] Had their book been written ten years later, they would probably have supported the need for transferring programs to the schools and to the ministries of education. Reuchlin brought the picture up to the middle 1960s:

> In the most selective and exclusive school systems the choice of employment seems a problem which scarcely arises before the end of school life. In such systems it is an extraschool service that is called upon to provide vocational guidance. Such services were established between the two world wars in most European countries. These services continue to function, but *their role is changing in countries where educational reforms have taken place . . .* (editor's italics).
>
> Everywhere these services have the duty of providing the adolescent about to finish his studies information about the various opportunities of employment open to him. They often have the further duty of placing him

in employment and possibly of keeping in touch with him during the first years of apprenticeship or of his working life.

They give advice to individuals, and are consequently concerned to know the young people they have to inform, advise, or place in employment. But their techniques may vary greatly.[14]

Diverse Approaches to Vocational Guidance

The organization of career development work and of vocational guidance, unlike their origins, differ considerably from one country to another. Although there is some unity of purpose, there is great diversity of method. What Reuchlin pointed out ten years ago is still true:

> If it is considered that the choice of employment is not a question that directly concerns the schools, there is a tendency to attach the guidance services to the Ministry of Labour rather than to the Ministry of Education. The opposite solution is adopted where it is held that as a result of changes in the economic world today the vital choices for a vocational future are taken at school. It is also possible to combine both answers, as is done in the United Kingdom with the Youth Employment Service, and attach guidance services to both Ministries jointly . . .

> In France . . . the first 'Guidance Offices' were set up by professional (sic, meaning 'occupational') organizations: employment bureaus, chambers of commerce, trade councils, and apprenticeship committees. A decree of . . . 1922 officially recognized the existence of vocational guidance and placed it under the aegis of the Undersecretary of State for Technical Education. In 1938 vocational guidance tests became compulsory for all pupils at the end of their elementary education (i.e., school leavers). The range of guidance services expanded rapidly after the second world war to help pupils with difficulties of any kind and at every level of education, and this expansion was recognized by the decree of 10th October, 1955. The Vocational Guidance Centers became associated at this time with what may properly be called school guidance . . . the educational reforms of 1959 . . . renamed them 'Centers for School and Vocational Guidance,' and gave them as their principal task the guidance of pupils during attendance at school, particularly at the moment of entry to secondary education . . .

> From these examples it seems that in countries where there have been changes in the administration of extra-school guidance services these changes have tended to increase the responsibility of education authorities for them, and even in some cases to place them completely in their hands. Within educational institutions the role of these services, which was originally limited in practice to the guidance of pupils leaving primary schools for certain lower-level technical courses, subsequently tended to become a more general one, for all types of secondary education.[15]

The training of those who do the counseling varies from one country to another as much as does the organization for guidance.

> Sometimes the officers of these services have never had any psychological training and rely essentially on school reports or on interviews with the family and the adolescent himself. Psychological tests are only contemplated in special cases and are then carried out by a psychologist outside of the service. In other cases, however, the guidance counselor is primarily a psychologist, and psychological tests are an intrinsic part of the system. The techniques

employed in Germany and in the United Kingdom [by Youth Employment Officers and Careers Masters] are a good illustration of the first approach while the methods used in Belgium and France correspond more closely to the second.[16]

In the rapidly changing cultures of Western Europe what was written about solutions in 1964 is already in need of updating, for the training provided and the techniques used have changed in response to the pressures that Reuchlin described so well.

In England Youth Employment Officers still rely on group lectures and brief interviews to tell school drop-outs about employment opportunities, but they feel increasingly the need to do more than that and to have more training to equip them to do it. In the schools "careers masters" play an increasingly important role in disseminating educational information. Increasingly, school counselors trained at English universities following the American model (often with the assistance of American counseling psychologists active in counselor education and supported in England by Fulbright lecturerships) provide services of individual assessment and individual counseling and consult with pupils, careers masters, teachers, and parents concerning the career decisions and career development of pupils in school.

In France the school-related but center-based guidance counselors continue to be given two years of largely psychological but partly economic training in several special institutes for school and vocational guidance, and their role has been redefined to include the work of school psychologists, which many of them have been doing for some years. But there has been constant pressure to place more responsibility on teachers in the schools, more pressure for school-based as contrasted with center-based services, and, as in England and the United States, there has been increasing professionalization of counseling accompanied by growing suspicion of professionalism in guidance.

Other countries could be cited as evidence of the conflicting patterns of organization, types of service, and education of counselors. But the United States, England, and France well illustrate the differences in organization, type of service, and type of counselor education in these and in other developed countries, such as Japan and India. When launching guidance programs, the developing countries tend to copy one of these models with minor variations. These models also illustrate the conflicts which exist even within a system.

THE CONFLICTED STATE OF VOCATIONAL GUIDANCE
Conflicting Trends in the United States

While for half a century vocational guidance was conceived of as helping individuals in the selection of an occupation at some clear point in time such as entry into the labor market, we now recognize that it should really be a developmental process beginning in early childhood and continuing until after retirement. As Zaccaria puts it, "Although theories of occupational choice continued to thrive, in recent years the theories of vocational development have constituted the main stream of thought and research in American vocational psychology."[17] In practice personal data, school grades, work experience, and test results still provide a means of helping an individual to make a specific decision at a particular point in time, rather than serving as a truly cumulative record which is extrapolated into the future[18] to project the sequence of probable career experiences of an individual.

Career education, stressed by President Nixon in his 1972 State of the Union Message, by Education Commissioner Marland, and by many contemporary American educators as the key to educational improvement, still deals with occupations rather than with careers, with a variety of types of occupations and with the choice of one for which preparation is to be provided, rather than to a sequence of positions and occupations which a person may occupy and pursue during the course of a significant part of his or her lifetime. Exponents of career education do not explicitly define the term "career," despite the fact that long before the current programs were conceived, and two years after the Career Pattern Study[19] first defined the word for vocational psychology and vocational guidance, Shartle[20] added it to the definitions of the terms *occupation, job,* and *position* which he had included in the earlier editions of *Occupational Information.* Thus, although Worthington states that career education is "*not* a high-sounding new name for what we have always called vocational education," he maintains that it is "a way to provide career awareness and career preparation in the upper grades that continues at an ever-increasing level until every student is equipped to enter the occupation of his choice—limited only by his personal ability."[21] *But career education is not career development,* for career awareness in this and other Office of Education documents is implicitly defined as awareness of a variety of occupations, and, similarly, career preparation is implicitly defined as preparation for an occupation. Furthermore, in the various Comprehensive Career Education Model (CCEM) programs a career is always operationally defined as an occupation, not as a sequence of positions including those of student, worker, and pensioner, and not as a career pattern.

In Hackensack, New Jersey, for example, one of the six school systems implementing the CCEM on subcontract with the Center for Vocational and Technical Education of the Ohio State University (itself the major contractor with the U.S. Office of Education for career education), the concepts of career awareness, orientation, and exploration have in the first stages of the program resulted in exposure to a variety of occupations in innovative as well as traditional ways, through the regular curriculum in the elementary schools, the science curriculum in the middle school, and the English curriculum in the high school. But teachers and curriculum specialists developing instructional materials concentrate on teaching about occupations as static sets of tasks performed and as static ways of life. The only variation is in the depth of orientation, exploration, and training as the pupil becomes aware of occupations, explores some of them, prepares for one of them, and enters it; the concept of life stages is usually not considered after one is established occupationally, although much is made of the fact that an individual may be forced, by technological change, to change occupations several times during his lifetime. The career education perspective may change in due course to include career development concepts, the curriculum may in due course provide experiences which help students to understand how their own development as well as the development of society may lead them to seek and pursue, at one stage in life, an occupation which differs in type from that in which they engage at some other stage of life.

This is not to deny the importance of occupational awareness and exploration. Occupational psychology was for many years the foundation of vocational guidance in the United States.[22] Personal data, and especially test results, provided the means of comparing a person with men or women in various occupations, so that each one might be helped to choose an occupation for which he or she was well qualified. Since the early 1950s a new approach has emerged in which the focus is on the careers of individuals rather than on occupations; there is an emphasis on helping people to think in terms of the span of the working life and of the sequence of occupations which they may pursue as they mature and as the economy develops.[23] This conflict of theories has as yet had no divisive effects. Theorists tend toward a synthesis of views, but the theoretical and methodological issues are real; unfortunately, practitioners still tend to think and work mostly in terms of occupational orientation.

A second area of conflict concerning guidance in the United States is the issue of *professionalization,* meaning the development of a special body of knowledge, a code of ethics, and a virtual monopoly of the right to do a certain kind of work by the members of an occupation, who have the special knowledge and ethical standards.

The conflict concerning professionalization is not one of whether or not to professionalize, for that issue was settled some thirty years ago in the United States and in France, even though it is still an issue in England and may become one in Germany. The question is one of how much professionalization (one, two, or four years of advanced study), and of the amount of emphasis on psychology as the basic discipline drawn upon by the profession. Consequently, we have two professional associations concerned with educational and vocational guidance, one the National Vocational Guidance Association of the American Personnel and Guidance Association[24] and the other the Division of Counseling Psychology of the American Psychological Association.[25] Some school counselors complain that psychology tends, to too great a degree, to dominate the field of guidance; some psychologists active in both fields feel that they dominate because they help to fill a vacuum.

Conflicting Trends in France

In France the same conflicts also have become clear, although of course in somewhat different forms. Professionalization became an issue through the work of the Institut National d'Orientation Professionnelle and the Centres d'Orientation Scolaire et Professionnelle of which it is the model. For many years the emphasis was on occupational choice, particularly through the testing of aptitudes and through occupational information, but during the past twenty years there has been an increasing emphasis upon occupational choice as a developmental process.[26] The educational reforms of 1959 recognized this, and there was a professional revival among the counselors of France as the scope of their work was broadened. The increasing professionalization of the status of French counselors, as shown in admission requirements for programs leading to the diploma of educational and vocational counselor and in the concept of the *conseiller-psychologue,* was one immediate result. Guidance was to become the function of psychologists with special training for this work, rather than of classroom teachers or placement officers. But the conflict between the two theories, and between professionals and laymen in France, has been aggravated by two other trends in other areas of conflicting ideologies and theories.

The question of guidance for manpower distribution or guidance for human development is the most fundamental of these conflicts. Governments, both national and state, tend to view vocational guidance as a means of assuring the nationally desired flow of manpower from schools to work. Counselors and many other educators tend, however, to consider it a means for furthering the development of human talents for the facilitation of self-fulfillment.[27] The educational reforms of the last decade were designed to democratize education, to increase the opportunity of youth to find appropriate educational and occupational outlets for its latent and actual capacities and interests. As in career education's occupational awareness programs in the USA, the *cycle d'orientation* might have become a process of self-discovery and of broadening perspectives for many young people. But the official function of educational and vocational guidance in France, in contrast to the views of many counselors, is the proper flow of manpower, not the furthering of individual human development. Economic planning concepts tend to dominate education, but, nevertheless, French counselors still insist on guiding human development. They demonstrated this in the Declaration of the Guidance Counselors of the Academie de Clermont-Ferrand, as reported in the February 1968 issue of the *Bulletin de Liaison de l'Association des Conseillers d'Orientation de France.* In that declaration they expressed their dismay

1. That guidance is conceived as a simple administrative process of the distribution of pupils;
2. That the adolescent is considered an unchangeable, completed, being;
3. That economic factors are stressed to the detriment of human factors;
4. That instead of guidance tailored to individual needs there will be authoritarian pupil assignments;
5. That such a conception is opposed to the development of the individual and multiplies cases of occupational and social maladjustment and will in the long run be proved less effective for our country.[28]

When educational and vocational guidance are seen as a matter of sending the proper numbers of people to different types of education and of employment, they are involved in distributing information rather than counseling. The careful study of abilities and interests is thus made to seem unnecessary; instead, one sees as sufficient the dissemination of information as to the types and numbers of opportunities available and the limiting of admissions to those numbers by the schools, institutes, or universities.

The phenomenon of guidance by classroom teachers rather than by counselors is a result of this viewpoint, one which produces additional conflict in France. If the dissemination of information is called for rather than counseling, and if the information needed is conceived of as largely that of numbers and types of openings for people completing a given kind of education, then professionally trained and qualified counselors are hardly needed. Guidance can, instead, be provided by untrained classroom teachers who are supplied with information by a central bureau which compiles and distributes it to students in appropriate schools. This is the system discarded by the Americans in the 1930s and that which broke down in England in the 1950s. It is the system of which Williamson wrote: "This observational preparation for choosing is still widely used today, but little is known, through hardheaded research, about its role in making valid choices and about its limitations."[29]

Conflicting Trends in England

In England (specifically England, rather than the United Kingdom) only three of the four conflicts of theory and practice so far identified are to be observed. These are in the realms of occupational choice as contrasted with vocational or career development, of information rather than counseling, and of professional versus lay counseling. Although occupational psychology dominated the work of the National Institute of Industrial Psychology, long virtually the sole locus of professional vocational guidance in England, elsewhere in that country guidance has been seen as information-giving, which essentially non-professional counselors could handle, whether briefly trained youth employment officers or untrained careers masters.

In recent years, however, there has been considerable interest in career development theory and methods[30] of counseling, which takes into account individual differences and requires knowledge of the psychology of occupations and of vocational development, and in the preparation and employment of counselors equipped to use this technical knowledge and the related methods.[31] Universities such as those at Keele, Exeter, and Reading have led in the professional education of school counselors after the American model, while Leeds has led in theory and research.

Conflicts still arise due to the suspicion that teachers, untrained in educational and vocational guidance, often have concerning this specialty. Counselors, who profess to know something about people, about schools, and about occupations which teachers do not know, are something of a threat to those who have long worked in schools and who have long dealt, whether well or badly, with people. The fact that France, which has been so much more highly developed than England in its theory and practice of vocational guidance, recently considered regressing to a more primitive system in the name of "planification" is another indication of the general educator's suspicion regarding the specialist and of the domination of educational administration by economic planners.

Causes of the Present Conflicts

Neither professional jealousy nor the zeal of economic planners is the main cause of our present conflicts. The principal causes are more fundamental.[32] One is the increase in knowledge and the concomitant increase in the number and complexity of methods and instruments available for use in educational and vocational guidance. Hence the visions of planning manpower distribution and of guiding human development; hence the emergence of occupational psychology and of career psychology; hence the importance of both information and counseling; and hence the confrontation of professional and of lay counselors. Another cause is the rapid democratization of education, which requires a much greater variety of educational opportunities to meet individual differences in abilities and interests, which calls for much better guidance of youth in choosing between these varied types of education and training, and which taxes both the understanding and the time of those who must help youth to make these choices. Differences of viewpoint as to ways in which these needs can best be met are brought out and magnified by the knowledge explosion, the population explosion, and what might be called the opportunity explosion.

THE FOUR FOCI OF CONFLICT

Four conflicting trends in educational and vocational guidance have been identified: 1) guidance for manpower utilization versus individual human development, 2) occupational choice versus vocational or career development, 3) information dissemination versus counseling, and 4) professional versus lay guidance. Let us look at the main issues involved in these four areas.

Manpower Utilization versus Individual Human Development

As long ago as 1954, in a presidential address to the American Personnel and Guidance Association,[33] I analyzed a sample of documents on educational and vocational guidance from a number of countries in terms of their emphases on manpower utilization and on individual development. Differences in philosophy were clear then, some countries viewing guidance as an instrument of national policy for the meeting of manpower needs, others stressing the importance of identifying whatever talents and interests each person has, of helping him to develop them to their maximum potential, and of assisting him in finding appropriate ways of using them for his benefit and for that of society. One of the conclusions which I then drew was that, when economic and political pressures are great, those who formulate guidance policies tend to stress the importance of directing and training manpower to meet these economic and social needs. When, on the other hand, the economy is healthy and the international situation is peaceful, those who formulate guidance policy tend to emphasize the importance of self-fulfillment and the contribution which educational and vocational guidance can make to social welfare and to personal happiness.

Nothing during the last two decades, during which I have spent a great deal of time in Western and Central Europe and some time in Canada, in Eastern Europe, and in Asia, leads me to change this evaluation of the economic and political determinants of the philosophy and practice of educational and vocational guidance. If anything, the conflict of the two philosophies seems more acute now than it was twenty years ago, although it is not as acute as in 1937 when Keller and Viteles wrote.

Perhaps the conflict of philosophies is not as important today as here implied, although it has been important in the past. Philosophers have debated the issue of the individual versus society since the time of Hobbes and Locke, some contending that the individual achieves self-fulfillment only in subordinating himself to society, and others arguing that society exists only to meet the needs of individuals. That the issue has been so long debated suggests that it is important. Certainly, guidance practices vary according to the dominance of one or the other of these contrasting philosophies, as is well illustrated by a leading European applied psychologist who, discussing American vocational guidance practices, summarized his views by saying: "You know what these young people should do, why don't you tell them?" That most counselors consider it important for people to find out for themselves, through whatever experiences they can be helped to use and to evaluate, is incomprehensible to those who are preoccupied with national economic and political needs.

Two fundamental questions are suggested by these observations. First, are the theorists and practitioners of educational and vocational guidance merely the tools of national politics? Or are there values which transcend economic conditions and political considerations, humanistic values which are permanent and paramount regardless of particular situations? Second, if guidance theory and national policy appear to conflict, which should be questioned, and how should the conflict be resolved?

Occupational Choice versus Vocational Development

The classical problem in vocational guidance has been that of predicting occupational choice or occupational success, an occupation being an organized set of tasks; the classical method, as developed to the fullest by Paterson and Darley,[34] has been that of relating test scores prior to entry into the labor market to occupational status at some later time. In this model the researcher and the counselor deal with status at two points in time. Intermediate and subsequent statuses are typically disregarded. Despite the fact that the counselor is aware of the problems of training and entry, and despite widespread recognition of the facts of occupational mobility, this model matches youth and jobs and implicitly assumes that, once the match is made, the lucky pair lives happily ever after. This is the *occupational model*.

Interest in vocational or career development has led to activity among theorists and researchers in the construction and use of a different type of model, a *career model*.[35] A *career* is the sequence of occupations, jobs, and positions occupied during the course of a person's working life.[36] The definition of a career may be extended beyond either end of the actual working life to include prevocational and postvocational positions such as those of students preparing for work and annuitants playing a substitute-work role in retirement. In the psychology and sociology of occupations the emphasis is on the characteristics of the occupation with considerations of time and sequence disregarded,[37] whereas the emphasis in the study of careers is on the continuity or discontinuity in the lives of individuals and on the patterns of continuity in the lives of groups.[38]

The career model called for in developmental vocational counseling is one in which the individual is viewed as moving along one of a number of possible pathways through the educational system and into and through the world of work. The starting point is usually one's father's socioeconomic status; one climbs a certain distance up the educational ladder at a speed determined by psychological and social characteristics and by the situation into which one is born; one enters the world of work at a point which is determined in part by the rung he has reached on the educational ladder at the time of leaving education for work. The individual progresses through an entry job into one or more other jobs which may or may not be related to each other as elements in a career field. Understanding, predicting, and modifying these career patterns, which many vocational counselors actually do attempt to do, is the essence of true career counseling. Counselors need to consider more than simply a decision about a specific school or a specific job, but they have so far had little in the way of data and instruments to help with this work. The methods available fit the occupational but not the career model, although new methods are being studied.[39]

In a realm such as this the conflict is not so much one of formal policies as it is one of commitment to a theoretical model, of unthinking habituation to a way of conceptualizing career decisions and to a method of work. It is the conflict between established and emerging conceptions of the nature of guidance and of ways in which to guide individual development.

Again two pertinent issues emerge. First, that of the nature of the steps to be taken to insure a more rapid spread of the understanding of career development. Second, that of the more rapid formulation and adoption of methods of guiding such development. These are issues which the current pressures for career education and the limited interpretation given it by its advocates make crucial.

Information Dissemination versus Counseling

The pendulum of professional and of official opinion has been swinging back and forth for two generations, from virtually complete dependence on guidance by the dissemination of educational and vocational information to an equally extreme emphasis on the interaction of counselor and student or client in the discussion of affectively-laden personal interests, values, and needs.[40] Many university counseling centers at first functioned as centers for the collection and dissemination of information on educational and occupational opportunities. They then became well-rounded counseling centers which for some years combined the informational and the counseling functions. In due course many evolved into personal counseling or psychotherapeutic centers. With the neglect of their information function, some then found their support withdrawn or their role changed by administrative fiat for the purpose of restoring the dissemination of information to its central place in their work. At the same time some centers, such as those at the Pennsylvania State University and the University of California at Berkeley, have succeeded in maintaining a balance between these functions, while others, such as that at Columbia College, retain the psychotherapeutic function to which they shifted some years after having been founded for the purpose of balanced vocational and personal counseling, as well as information dissemination.

It is important to recognize the external and internal pressures which cause these changes in conceptions of the role and function of counseling. They arise from the personal needs and misconceptions, and from the over-simplifications, of laymen and of professionals alike. One major misconception involves the creation of a false dichotomy between information and personal counseling. Information is too often viewed as strictly impersonal and objective, and man is conceived of as a rational creature capable of accepting and using information which is presented to him. Personal, affective matters are too often considered to be divorced, or at least divorceable, from facts; they are viewed as irrational feelings to be dealt with only as feelings. But things human are rarely if ever dichotomous: facts have emotional significance, and feelings both arise from and attach themselves to facts.

This interaction has been demonstrated by a number of research projects in which the effectiveness of supplying educational and occupational information, counseling, and a combination of information and counseling have been compared.[41] Effectiveness has been judged by various criteria, ranging from the realism of educational and vocational aspirations and plans to client satisfaction with the pertinent experience. The evidence is overwhelmingly in favor of group dissemination and discussion of information combined with personal counseling.

The false information-counseling dichotomy is created by the professional's desire for mastery and status and by the layman's fear of self-revelation. The professional counselor has a commendable desire for professional competence. Recognizing the importance of affective matters in human aspirations and plans, he seeks understanding of and skill in personal counseling and psychotherapy. Counselors have tended to turn to the field of psychotherapy for improvement in professional skills, and during the decade from 1945 to 1955 most of the progress made in counseling was in the understanding of how one person works with another in such a way that one of them develops self-understanding. When they become absorbed in psychotherapeutic concerns, it is easy for counselors to lose sight of the normal problems of human development and to wish to devote their energies to working with problems of maladjustment. It is easy to become thus absorbed if one works in a university counseling center because of the demanding nature of these problems, the freedom of university staffs to structure their own work, and the greater prestige typically attached to being a psychotherapist as compared to being a counselor. School counselors tend to develop similar aspirations and role concepts while graduate students, although the role expectations of the secondary school and the case loads which their counselors carry preclude this possibility.

The nonprofessional counselor and layman often view personal dynamics as private, almost indecent, topics, as less mentionable even than the dynamics of gastrointestinal systems. To seek to understand human behavior is often seen as an invasion of privacy, and to seek to influence it, even by freeing it from inhibition, is seen as an infringement of personal freedom. When the mind is viewed as an indecent mystery, those who work with it tend to be considered guilty of voyeurism or black magic. The anxious layman therefore takes refuge in conceptions of man as strictly rational and of guidance as simply the supplying of information.

There are, then, two pertinent issues. First, how can those who are responsible for the practice of guidance, whether through administration, through work with students and clients, through the training of counselors, or through the conduct of the research which is essential to its improvement, help counselors to achieve competence in the use of the interpersonal relationship in career guidance? How can this be done without converting counselors into psychotherapists and thus neglecting educational and vocational guidance?

Second, how can teachers with whom counselors work, the administrators to whom they are immediately responsible, and the parents and public to whom they are eventually responsible, be helped to understand the inseparable connections between the information and the counseling processes?

Professional Guidance versus Lay Guidance

The fourth and final area of conflicting trends is that of the professionalization of guidance. Forty years ago many American educators liked the slogan "Every teacher a counselor," but today those words are rarely heard, despite the teacher's major role in career education. Instead, there seems to be a well-established recognition of the fact that if a teacher is to teach well, keeping up with the subject, planning instruction and actual teaching must take up the bulk of his or her time. Counseling students and consulting with parents and colleagues is itself a full-time job.[42] As pointed out earlier, and as Reuchlin[43] showed a decade ago, in a number of countries the issue is still one of how much professionalization, while in others it is still one of whether or not to professionalize.

Professionalism is closely related to the other issues. Information giving does not require training beyond that of a teacher; it requires only the provision of appropriate materials. However, if it is recognized that information which affects one's career is *ipso facto* emotion laden, then it becomes clear that career guidance necessarily involves counseling, which requires professional skill.

The issue then becomes basically one of how much professionalization. Some countries now expect little training in educational and vocational guidance, others require one year beyond the first university degree, still others consider two essential, and in some circles there is pressure for three or four years of special training, at least for those responsible for the supervision of guidance.[44] At the same time the democratization of education brings such numbers of students to counselors and to guidance centers that there are not enough well-trained counselors to meet the current, much less the emergent, needs. The result is a renewed interest in the possibilities of short-term training for counselor aids or technicians who might work under the supervision of more highly trained counselors, together with a new interest in the possibilities of computer-assisted counseling.[45]

Three pertinent issues are clear. First, how can educators and administrators, parents and public, be helped to recognize the fact that the provision of guidance for youth and adults requires the availability of professionally prepared counselors? Second, can educational and vocational guidance be made more readily available to more people by the training of two levels of professional counselors? If so, what should be the content and duration of these programs, and what should be the division of labor between the two levels of professional competence? Third, how can the potential of computer-assisted counseling and of other devices and procedures designed to supplement the work of the counselor be exploited more fully and more rapidly?

SUMMARY

At least four areas of conflicting trends in career development theory and vocational guidance practice are observable in several countries. In some instances these trends appear to represent a regression toward older and less adequate philosophies and methods of guidance, while in others they seem to be the result of the emergence of newer and perhaps superior theories and methods. Each of these conflicts suggests issues or questions with which educators, counselors, and psychologists must deal. They must deal with them objectively, in terms of human and social values elucidated by relevant facts and research results, and with the best wisdom and judgment of professionals and of laymen. The four issues may be summarized as follows.

I. *Is guidance to be for manpower utilization or for individual development?*
   A. Are educational and vocational guidance simply the instruments of national policy, or do they have values which transcend economic and political considerations?
   B. If guidance theory and national policy conflict, how is the conflict to be resolved?

II. *Is guidance to be for occupational choice or for career development?*
   A. How can a more widespread understanding of the developmental nature of careers be promoted?
   B. What can be done to make available a body of knowledge and an armamentarium of methods suitable for career as contrasted with occupational guidance?

III. *Is guidance to consist of information dissemination or of counseling?*
   A. How can counselors be better prepared for a balanced use of the information and counseling processes in guidance?
   B. How can administrators, teachers, and the public be helped to see the inseparability of the information and counseling processes?

IV. *Is guidance to be a service of laymen or of professional counselors?*
   A. How can support be developed for professional guidance?
   B. Can guidance be made available to more people by the preparation of counselors at more than one level, and, if so, what would constitute these levels of training and the division of labor?

    C.   What prospects for assistance are available in computers and other devices and procedures for supplementing the work of counselors?

NOTES

1. D. E. Super, "Conflicting Trends in Guidance," *Bulletin of the International Association for Educational and Vocational Guidance,* 20(1969):2–6.
2. D. E. Super, "The Changing Nature of Vocational Guidance," *Issues in American Education,* A. M. Kroll, ed. (New York: Oxford University Press, 1970).
3. H. Lytton and M. Craft, *Guidance and Counseling in British Schools* (Whitstable, England: Edward Arnold, 1969).
4. S. K. Pal, *Guidance in Many Lands* (Allahabad, India: Central Book Depot, 1968).
5. M. Reuchlin, *Pupil Guidance: Facts and Problems* (Strasbourg: Council of Europe, 1964).
6. F. J. Keller and M. S. Viteles, *Vocational Guidance Throughout the World* (New York: Norton, 1937).
7. *Ibid.,* p. 17.
8. J. M. Brewer, *The Vocational Guidance Movement* (New York: Macmillan Co., 1918); J. M. Brewer, *History of Vocational Guidance* (New York: Harper & Brothers, 1942); W. R. Stephens, *Social Reform and the Origins of Vocational Guidance* (Washington: American Personnel and Guidance Association (NVGA), 1970).
9. Keller and Viteles, *op. cit.;* Reuchlin, *op. cit.*
10. Brewer, *History of Vocational Guidance, op. cit.*
11. Stephens, *op. cit.,* pp. xiv–xv.
12. Keller and Viteles, *op. cit.,* p. 293.
13. *Ibid.,* p. 21.
14. Reuchlin, *op. cit.,* pp. 122–123.
15. *Ibid.,* pp. 123–126.
16. *Ibid.,* p. 123.
17. J. Zaccaria, *Theories of Occupational Choice and Vocational Development* (Boston: Houghton Mifflin, 1970), p. 55.
18. D. E. Super, *The Psychology of Careers* (New York: Harper, 1957).
19. D. E. Super, J. O. Crites, R. C. Hummel, H. P. Moser, P. L. Overstreet, and C. F. Warnath, *Vocational Development: A Framework for Research* (New York: Bureau of Publications, Teachers College, Columbia University, 1957), p. 131.
20. C. L. Shartle, *Occupational Information,* 3rd ed. (Englewood Cliffs, N.J.: Prentice Hall, 1959), p. 23.
21. R. M. Worthington, "The Need for Career Education" (Washington: Keynote address, International Workshop on Career Education, 1972).
22. D. E. Super, "Some Unresolved Issues in Vocational Development Research," *Personnel and Guidance Journal,* 40(1961):11–25; D. E. Super, "L'Orientation Vers Une Profession ou Une Carriere," *Bulletin de l'Institute National d'Orientation Professionnelle,* 21(1965):239–248; D. E. Super, "Vocational Development: Persons, Positions, and Processes," *Perspectives on Vocational Development,* J. M. Whiteley and A. Resnikoff, eds. (Washington: American Personnel and Guidance Association, 1972).
23. Super, *The Psychology of Careers, op. cit.;* Zaccaria, *op. cit.*
24. C. G. Wrenn, *The Counselor in a Changing World* (Washington: American Personnel and Guidance Association, 1962).

25. A. S. Thompson and D. E. Super, eds., *The Professional Preparation of Counseling Psychologists* (New York: Teachers College Press, 1964).
26. A. Leon, "Variations de Choix de Metiers," *Bulletin de l'Institut National d'Orientation Professionnelle,* 9(1953):213–215.
27. M. Reuchlin, "Orientation et Marche du Travail," *Bulletin de l'Institut National d'Orientation Professionnelle,* 23(1967):147–164.
28. Association des Conseillers d'Orientation Scolaire et Professionnelle de France, *Bulletins,* Fevrier, Mars, 1968.
29. E. G. Williamson, *Vocational Counseling* (New York: McGraw-Hill, 1965), p. 132.
30. J. Hayes and B. Hopson, *Career Guidance* (London: Heinemann, 1971).
31. C. J. Gill, "Counseling," *Youth Employment,* 19(1966–67):13–15.
32. Wrenn, *op. cit.;* Reuchlin, *Pupil Guidance: Facts and Problems;* D. E. Super, "Guidance in American Education: Its Status and Its Future," in E. Landy and P. A. Perry, eds., *Guidance in American Education: Backgrounds and Prospects* (Cambridge: Harvard University Press, 1964).
33. D. E. Super, "Guidance: Manpower Utilization or Human Development?", *Personnel and Guidance Journal,* 33(1954):8–14.
34. D. G. Paterson and J. G. Darley, *Men, Women, and Jobs* (Minneapolis: University of Minnesota Press, 1936).
35. Super, "Some Unresolved Issues in Vocational Development Research"; Super, "L'Orientation Vers Une Profession ou Une Carriere."
36. Super *et al., Vocational Development: A Framework for Research, op. cit.*
37. A. Roe, *The Psychology of Occupations* (New York: Wiley, 1956).
38. Super, "Guidance: Manpower Utilization or Human Development?"; D. V. Tiedeman, "Decision and Vocational Development: A Paradigm and Its Implications," *Personnel and Guidance Journal,* 40(1961):15–20; R. LoCascio, "Delayed and Impaired Vocational Development: A Neglected Aspect of Vocational Development Theory," *Personnel and Guidance Journal,* 17(1964): 885–887.
39. Super, "Some Unresolved Issues in Vocational Development Research"; J. C. Flanagan and W. W. Cooley, *Project Talent: One-year Follow-up Studies* (Pittsburgh: University of Pittsburgh, 1966); P. R. Lohnes, "Markov Models for Human Development Research," *Journal of Counseling Psychology,* 12 (1965):332–337; W. D. Gribbons and P. R. Lohnes, *Emerging Careers: A Study of 111 Adolescents* (New York: Teachers College Press, 1968).
40. Wrenn, *op. cit.;* E. Ginzberg, *Career Guidance* (New York: McGraw-Hill, 1971).
41. M. E. Bennett, "Strategies of Vocational Guidance in Groups," *Man in a World at Work,* H. Borow, ed. (Boston: Houghton Mifflin, 1964).
42. Wrenn, *op. cit.*
43. Reuchlin, *op. cit.,* Ch. 4.
44. Thompson and Super, *op. cit.;* Wrenn, *op. cit.*
45. W. W. Cooley, "A Computer-Measurement System for Guidance," *Harvard Educational Review,* 34(1964):559–572; D. E. Super, ed., *Computer-assisted Counseling* (New York: Teachers College Press, 1970).

SUGGESTED READING

Keller, F. J., and Viteles, M. S. *Vocational Guidance throughout the World.* New York: W. W. Norton, 1937. Provides a historical perspective.

Reuchlin, M. *Pupil Guidance: Facts and Problems.* Strasbourg: Council of

Europe, 1964. Provides a detailed and comprehensive study of vocational guidance in Western Europe about 1960.

Pal, S. K., ed. *Guidance in Many Lands.* Allahabad: Central Book Depot, 1968. Presents the work of a world-wide symposium.

For a discussion of issues on British schools: Lytton, H., and Craft, M., eds. *Guidance and Counseling in British Schools.* London: Edward Arnold, 1969. Discusses current issues in British schools.

International Association for Educational and Vocational Guidance. *Educational Documentation and Information.* Paris: UNESCO, 1971. Provides a comprehensive, annotated bibliography.

PART TWO
The Human Environment

Much of human behavior is a product of the individual's interactions with his or her environment. In this sense, the environment is a fabric of many possibilities and impediments which operate uniquely to shape one's personal history, including his orientation to the past, present, and future, his approach to risk taking, and his attitudes toward personal competence. The environment or life space of any particular person defines the range of alternatives available as well as the value complex which he is likely to apply in his ranking of those choices. Environments have geographic, social, political, and economic components. These, in turn, are refined and mediated through one's interaction with family, education, and work. This section examines the status of these factors in the American society and extrapolates from the implications for individual choice and for counseling.

In his examination of the growing urbanization in America, Yamamoto reminds the reader that it is easy but inaccurate to stereotype the effects of this process. He discusses the growing interdependence and similarity between urban and rural Americans. Suggesting that the availability of resources in urban areas is no guarantee of their utilization, he speaks of the rising need for persons (counselors) to help others through the maze of opportunities so that they may come to terms with the fact that autonomy resides not in where one lives but in individual power to shape one's own character.

Darcy extends Yamamoto's observations about the rise of bureaucratic or corporate organizations in highly industrialized societies in his analysis of the economic power of giant corporations. He describes the characteristics of mixed capitalism as contrasted with socialism and communism and draws implication for the world of work, dealing with differences among the developed, developing, and least developed nations. Like Wolfbein in Chapter 21 and Herr in Chapter 22, he addresses the matter of investments in human capital versus other manpower policy. Finally, he identifies for counselors, the relationship between economics and individual choice.

Hansen addresses the interdependence of political and social issues which are caught up in the American society's evolution through a technology of technology, a technology of management, and, an emerging technology of institutions. He analyzes changing priorities at the center of the American society and relates them to the effects of science, rationality, and functionalism upon humanistic ideals, democracy, and capitalism. Like Borow, in Chapter 1, he identifies the effects of clashes among special interest groups and the social messages embedded in contemporary discontent and collective violence. He sees them as responses to America's current status as a "transforming society," the potential precursor of a "planned society" or, indeed, an "international society." Finally, he speaks to the elements of the confusion about rational humanism, applied behavioral science, and the nature of man which is apparent in the attempts of counseling to respond to the social transition now underway.

Neff speaks of perceptions of work historically and cross-culturally, indicating that even though the meanings of work have changed in the past there is nothing to suggest that it is in the process of disappearing. However, partially as an affect of the counterculture and of the cultural change, work may be in the process of coming to be seen as somewhat less of a driving personal necessity. In this light Neff outlines a theory of work behavior and relates its implications to child development, particularly during middle childhood and early adolescence.

Lathrop discusses his view of schooling in America. He identifies the need for a reexamination of educational priorities since he believes that the programs which exist in most schools are so out of balance with the total needs of youth that many aspects of the child's life are given only token attention or are ignored completely. He suggests that in the schools' attempts to meet the needs of all people they only approximately satisfy the needs of any individual. Finally, he identifies the special responsibility which guidance workers have for correcting the meager attention which schools have paid to orientation to and preparation for occupations and to vocational counseling. He suggests that the lack of emphasis in vocational guidance is not based upon a lack of knowledge but upon a distorted sense of priorities.

Luckey ends Part Two with a discussion of the impact of the family on vocational identity and choice. She indicates that the association between family and occupation tends to be lifelong, even though it may be far from stable. She links the development of self-image, the climate and practices of childbearing, and the formation of attitudes, values, and behaviors through the process of parental modeling. In a comprehensive analysis of the biological and attitudinal impact of the family on self-concept and choice, she indicates that it is not only what the parents *do* that helps to shape the child's world, it is also who they are and *who* the others *are* on the ancestral tree. Among the insights to which counselors will be particularly responsive is her discussion of decision making, identity formation, and commitment.

Man in Urban America 4

Kaoru Yamamoto
Arizona State University

Man's dilemma may lie in the fact that, while trying to be what he is, he cannot help attempting to become what he is not. He senses that he can no more return to the bucolic life of yore than leap into the third millennium free of bygones. Inescapably, his time is now and his place is here. Yet he still finds solace in reliving the past and finds hope in dreaming of the future. Out of the misty visions of yesterday and tomorrow a backdrop is woven for today's drama. He is both a playwright and an actor. Mythologies of man are continuously created or recreated, and various *personae* (masks) are worn to fit different characters. While he is acting, he becomes one with his part; he feels and thinks as the character, and, indeed, he is the character. To any spectators, therefore, D. W. Brogan's query remains an intriguing one: Are we really watching "a new American," or are we merely witnessing "a new myth about the new American?"[1] To find out, let us follow the protagonist as he plays out his repertoire on the diverse stages of contemporary America.

MEN OF SOIL, MEN OF TOIL

The 1970 Census revealed that 73.5 percent of the 204 million resident Americans lived in urban areas—that is to say, in aggregates of 2,500 people or more. Among the rural population of about 54 million only 10 million were actually classified as living on farms, the rest largely staying in small communities of under 2,500 or in nonfarm open country. Of the 150 million urban dwellers, on the other hand, approximately a third resided in the ten largest metropolitan areas.[2] The trend for lessening dependence upon extractive agricultural activities and increasing concentration of urban populations seems to have persisted over the decade of the sixties.

The development of urban centers is not a phenomenon which necessarily presupposes technological advances.[3] Nevertheless, at least in the United States, industrialization has played a critical role in transforming the face of the once agrarian American society. The collective energy output of men and work animals in the United States was not exceeded by that of fossil fuels (coal, petroleum, and natural gas) and hydraulic power (electricity) until 1910. At that time human workers provided 8.4 percent of the

I wish to thank Beverly Hardcastle Lewis (Mrs. Clayton W.) of Holcomb Campus School, State University of New York, Genesco, and David H. Bauer of California State University, Chico, for their helpful comments on an earlier version of this chapter.

total output of 131 billion horsepower-hours, animals 34.7 percent, and the inanimate energy sources 56.9 percent. In comparison, the corresponding figures for 1960, when the output was 490 billion horsepower-hours, were: humans, 2.4 percent; animals, 1.3 percent; and the inanimate sources, 96.3 percent.[4] The surge in the total output itself makes the effects of the shift in distribution all the more remarkable. The energy surplus thus made available allows, as well as demands, the development of an elaborate culture.

Industrialization of agriculture was established during the 1920s, and one estimate today has it that "a Kansas wheat farmer, with his much greater technological efficiency, produces about three hundred calories for each one spent in raising wheat."[5] Another states that "fifty years ago, one farmer grew enough food and fibre for seven people; today he provides for twenty-four."[6] The increase in the production and capitalization per farm has been impressive, while the decrease in the proportion of farmworkers in the population has been drastic. Large mechanized farms, strongly oriented toward systematic management and mass marketing, have forced many people to shift to other occupations. In 1900 nearly 40 percent of the nation's labor force worked on farms; the proportion in 1970 was down to about 5.5 percent. Of the 1970 farm employment of 4.5 million, almost 74 percent came from farming families themselves. This arrangement insures ready manpower replacement for its declining demands but, at the same time, provides less than ideal training for those who (need to) seek jobs elsewhere.[7]

In the Web

Overall, however, life-styles of farm and urban families have rapidly come to resemble each other. In fact, there are probably more intragroup (i.e., within the farm or urban category itself) variations than intergroup differences in the patterns of marriage, childbearing, child rearing, education, kinship interaction, religious practice, or financial management.[8] Modern devices of transportation and mass communication have undoubtedly played an important role in this narrowing of the urban-rural gap, but possibly of equal influence has been the whole network of "agri-business," which incorporates farmers as an integral part of a large unit of the national economy.[9]

The agri-business network subsumes (a) the suppliers of manufactured goods and services for farm consumption, (b) the growers and producers, and finally (c) the processors and distributors of raised food and fibre. Though relatively new, the first and third component groups of agri-business have developed into major industries, centralized and city-based. Feed, seeds, fertilizer, insecticides, implements, equipment, power, fuel, and other commodities are fed into farms; the operations traditionally closely related to farming, such as milling, freezing, canning, weaving, and dyeing, have been transformed into large corporate businesses in their right. The processing and distributing functions are becoming very crucial correlates of the remarkable success of farmers and the resultant pressing problems of agricultural overproduction.

Farmers are no longer mythically self-sufficient individuals who depend only upon their own hard work, prudence, thrift, and family solidarity to face their daily tasks. Now they are a link in the complex chain of industrial manufacturing and services, and they recognize their own stake in technological progress and national-international economics. The whole enterprise involves about one-third of the total American labor force, and its mode of operation is clearly not one of agrarian America but that of a modern corporation with a high premium on efficiency, productivity, and profit. The language of business is spoken in rural communities not only by the representatives of suppliers, processors, and distributors, but also by agents of such nationwide organizations as the Cooperative Experiment Station, Agricultural Extension Service, Soil Conservation Service, Forest Service, Farmers Home Administration, Food and Drug Administration, Home and Farm Bureaus, 4-H Clubs, land grant colleges, high school programs in vocational agriculture and home economics, and church denominations.

Like the city-based media of mass communication, all these people act as mediators of cultural transmission of rural and urban life. Symbols are shared, acts are mutually understood, indigenous cultures are diffused, and an awareness of interdependence is heightened. Farmers may resent the intrusion of transient outsiders who allegedly carry some of the worst features of city life (crime, vice, pollution, anti-Americanism, etc.) into their ostensibly idyllic rural communities. They may not really trust these agents whose institutions can, and often do, put into effect major policy decisions which affect them deeply, without any seeming concern for farmers and often without consistent patterns at all. Nevertheless, they must acknowledge the fact of their technological, economic, and political dependence upon their urban neighbors. Ambivalence persists, but the process of cultural leveling continues relentlessly.[10] "Urbanism as a way of life" indeed permeates the whole society of America, regardless of where one lives.[11]

Forgotten Brothers

Having said this, however, we must hasten to add that the effects of industrial urbanization have been felt differently by various rural regions and communities. Some have made the transition rather painlessly, while others have suffered miserably. It was earlier suggested that the fast dwindling farm employment has been posing a serious problem to the children of farmers themselves. The threat is particularly serious because small, low-producing farms are far more numerous than prospering ones. "There are 312,000 big farms in the United States that produce half of all agricultural sales. The 1,600,000 at the poor end, each earning less than $1,000 a year, produce only 5 percent of sales."[12] The operators of these marginal farms are by definition self-employed; thus they are never "jobless," even though theirs is a life of barest subsistence. They do not have anyone or any organization to speak for them, and their children do not have a place on their own farms. Many of these property-owning poor, and most of their young, quit and flee to the cities only to "discover that they are almost completely unprepared for the complexity of metropolitan life. They are part of the selective service of poverty; they are sent from one culture of the poor to another."[13]

Historically, the largest concentration of these farms has been in the most rural of the nation's four major regions, the South.[14] From the beginning days of the transformation of American agriculture, through the Depression, New Deal, and post-World War II prosperity, to the present, urbanization has progressed very unevenly in the South, and much of that region has remained a vast belt of misery. The Bureau of the Census classifies families as poor if their annual income does not reach a certain specified level. For instance, in 1969 the poverty level was at about $2,000 to $2,400 for a family of two, $3,200 to $3,700 for a family of four, and $5,200 to $6,100 for a family of seven or more, the larger figures applying to nonfarm families and the smaller ones to farm families. On this basis, slightly more than 24 million individuals (69 percent white; 30 percent black; 1 percent other) were found in poor families all across the country. Approximately 11 million were in the South, and of these only about 36 percent lived in metropolitan areas, that is, cities of 50,000 or more, including their surrounding complexes.

That leaves 7 million people in nonmetropolitan settings of southern states, and 45 percent of them are black. Life for all these Americans is bleak, particularly for the members of the long persecuted minority group. Their status may vary from farm owners, tenants, sharecroppers, farm laborers, to casual farm hands, but their plight seems as dismal now as in the depression years of the 1930s. As touchingly expressed by Charles C. Johnson in his 1934 work *The Shadow of the Plantation,* they "ain't make nothing, don't speck nothing no more till [they] die."[15]

Another major group of impoverished Americans are those lost figures we call seasonal workers, who, by definition, work as farm employees less than 150 days a year. For the three main migratory routes of the Atlantic Coast, Pacific Coast, and old Louisiana Territory, most estimates range from 300,000 to 500,000, consisting largely of black and Spanish-speaking Americans from southern states.[16] In addition, a group of about the same size used to come in from our neighboring country across the Rio Grande under the Mexican Contract Labor (Bracero) Program, originally started in 1951. Although this legitimate source of influx was closed in 1964 by a Congressional act, many migrants continue to enter unlawfully from Mexico. For example, one recent report states that in 1970 the U.S. Border Patrol caught more than 200,000 would-be workers, or the so-called "wetbacks," attempting to enter this country without appropriate legal documents.[17]

Migrant workers toil in the earth, but they have practically no earthly possessions of any sort. In fact, their life seems defined almost totally in negative terms. Their functions are always threatened by the continuing mechanization of agriculture, and their presence counts only when machines cannot do the job more inexpensively. In our history, unfortunately, cheap labor has been a stranger neither to the profit-conscious employers nor to the desperate workers themselves (as in the plantations of the South, the stockyards of the Midwest, or the railroad building in the West). No minimum wages apply to the majority of migrant workers, and their constant moving precludes them from receiving welfare benefits and from exercising voting rights.[18] No workman's compensation covers their injuries or deaths on the job, and no unemployment compensation is open to them, even though they engage in activities vulnerable to every whim of the elements and fraught with serious accidents. Health standards are not maintained, housing is less than marginal, and decent medical and legal services are unavailable in their life of squalor.[19] Unionization and self-help efforts are found here and there—for instance in California, Texas, Wisconsin, and New Jersey—but the road ahead is long and hard.[20] Education of children cannot help being neglected under such circumstances, while community schooling efforts, when offered at all, have typically been haphazard and grossly misdirected.[21] Our regular curriculum, anchored in the urban life-style of middle class families, offers little which is meaningful to the life and work of these children.

A Long Procession

The list of our brothers and sisters forgotten in hopelessness and helplessness seems almost endless. There is a group of several million on the outskirts of hope in the southern Appalachian range from West Virginia to northern Georgia and Alabama. Typifying the plight of these once proud, individualistic people of early American stock are the residents of the Cumberland Plateau of Kentucky. When the fifteen golden years of coal mining, which thoughtlessly drained both the men and the land of their vitality, came to an abrupt end with the great flash flood of May 1927, nothing but sterile, eroded hillsides remained to curse the region to this day. Moonshine wars, the Depression, abortive efforts at moving from the doomed hillside corn farming to livestock raising, a brief wartime rebirth of coal industry whose strip mining further ravaged the Plateau, and the final postwar bust— all these events led to the formation of a resigned style of life. After all, why break one's back tilling the eroded soil or raising livestock to compete in vain against the big, rich farms of the Midwest? By keeping their land in the federal soil bank and staying on welfare, they can often make more for idling than for working. The price, however, of such forced leisure becomes much too high. "The cloak of idleness, defeat, dejection, and surrender has fallen so heavily as to leave them scarcely more than half alive. Their communities are turning into graveyards peopled with the living dead and strewn with the impediments of a civilization which once needed them but does so no longer."[22]

Then there is, of course, that other group that our civilization never really "needed," save their precious land! American Indians numbered 792,000 in 1970, about one and one-half times that of their 1960 population, and approximately 53 percent of them lived in Oklahoma, Arizona, California, and North Carolina. The story of two centuries of mistreatment and expropriation is too well known to be retold,[23] but the central value conflict persists. "The Oriental contemplated nature; the white man conquered nature; but the Indian lived in nature."[24] To the victor land was (and still is) an object for manipulation, something to be aggressively acted upon. It had to be subdued so that a living might be wrested from it.[25] To the vanquished, however, the earth was (is) a mother who gave life to all and sustained them side by side. Land was not an individual property but a communal estate for fishing, hunting, gathering wild plants, and horticultural activities. The land's resources were for men and women to cherish and partake of, never to exploit or destroy.[26] What whites did was consistent with their view of nature and man.

> The Allotment Act of 1887 divided and distributed tribal land among the Indians, attempting to remake them in the white man's image—a homesteader tilling the soil—a rugged individual. But its effect was to break up the tribes, fragment the land and make 'surplus land available for white purchase and occupancy.' By 1934, two-thirds of the land held by Indians at the time of the Allotment Act has passed into the hands of the white man.[27]

Even the remaining reservation land is not for Indians to manage at their discretion. They have practically all the components necessary for economic development to attain self-sufficiency, but they are not free to run their own business. They are the U.S. Government's wards, and every action must be cleared through federal agencies, such as the Bureau of Indian Affairs and the Public Health Service. Not surprisingly, things have not worked out under this arrangement. "History, if it has taught anything, should demonstrate that unless the Indians can shape their own policies and priorities and have the opportunity to participate—an opportunity which is, after all, integral to American democracy—the solutions will fail."[28] The message has been repeated in one scholarly study after another and one Congressional committee report after another,[29] but still it hasn't really reached the ears of urban America. The latter's efforts to relocate and remold the Indian into city settings have typically failed, only to degrade and alienate them further. For the long-suffering Indians this is still not an open society.

TOOLS OF THE PAST, TOOLS FOR THE FUTURE

For those who have been left by the wayside, the process of change from agrarian to urban ways of life is slow and painful.[30] Many have been forced to move from farms, mines, forests, or reservations to cities, merely to find themselves displaced from the fringes of one world to those of another. So long as the process of industrialization depended heavily upon unskilled and semiskilled labor, emigrants from rural hinterlands here or elsewhere were not hopelessly handicapped in their struggle to become established in the urban world of America. Unfortunately, the recent changes in occupational requirements tend to deprive latecomers of even a fighting chance.

One of the most remarkable correlates of the transition from exclusive dependence upon preindustrial agriculture has been the lengthening of the life span and the accompanying extension of working-life span. Men and women no longer become unemployable at the prime age of forty-five, and their working life can now last from their middle teens to beyond seventy. At first sight this gives everyone a better chance to join the urban order; there are, however, other conditions which militate against the young and/or the uninitiated.

Of nonfarm industries, goods-producing occupations, such as manufacturing, construction, and mining, are growing at a much lower rate than service-producing occupations, such as recreation, health services, business services, government, public utilities, communications, and transportation. By 1980 nearly 70 percent of all nonfarm workers are expected to be employed in these people-oriented industries. Furthermore, the fastest gaining categories of service-producing workers are professional, managerial, and technical, including such groups as systems analysts, computer programmers, urban planners, medical technologists, stenographers, and office machine servicemen. These jobs presume, at the minimum, high school graduation. Indeed, more than a quarter of the projected 1975 civilian labor force twenty-five years or older, and more than a third of those in the twenty-five to thirty-four age bracket, will have had some college experience. The median number of years spent in school will be 12.4.[31]

Able-bodied and willing young men and women have no direct access to the job market except via the route of longer and longer formal education. The poorly schooled are as unneeded in the industrialized urban milieu as on mechanized farms,[32] and the rising educational threshold puts a severe strain upon rural youngsters who have been found to lag behind their urban brethren in their educational aspirations and achievements. This ecological difference applies to all socioeconomic strata, while the restricted range of available opportunities and role models seem to handicap rural boys more than girls.[33] Irrespective of the place of residence, moreover, educational avenues are less open to those in lower social classes, no matter what their ability, sex, or ethnicity may be.[34]

New Trails, New Traps

It is a peculiar fact that the extension of schooling years does not directly correspond with a rise in complexity of required skills, an improvement in performance, or an increase in productivity. What it has done, rather, is to raise the entry age into work force, and to enhance people's expectations for white-collar jobs. Most important of all, however, it has perpetuated knowledge, instead of muscle or experience, as the most potent basis for employment.[35] Application of systematic knowledge to work is the realm of technology and, needless to say, that is what underlies an industrialized society such as the contemporary United States. One spends many years in school, not to accumulate inert knowledge as such, but to learn how to use it in many different situations, how to apply it to new tasks, how to derive still newer knowledge from it. These are the *skills* expected of a "knowledgeable" worker of today, and these are precisely the sorts of skills denied to the unlearned, that is, to those who have not learned how to learn.

Some of the dangers associated with exclusive dependence upon formal education as the royal road to skill development are obvious. A "diploma curtain," or discriminatory practices on the basis solely of an individual's schooling experience, can be devastating in its effects. If opportunities for more and more jobs are refused to those who cannot produce a proper diploma and other formal academic credentials, and if systematic means for identification of talents through direct performance are not developed, a large portion of human resources will be left untapped and the society will turn sterile after draining its small corps of elite.[36]

Skills based upon knowledge are typically abstract in nature. People work not so much with tangible things as with symbols which stand for these things. Abstracting is a necessary and convenient process to enable us to condense information, generalize across contexts, and engage in communication. However, the trouble is that we are inclined to forget its extractive character (leaving out the details and individual configurations), and begin to reify the abstract. Moreover, symbols, be they figural, numerical, linguistic, or otherwise, tend to be confused with whatever they stand for.[37] It is relatively easy to sort out 25,000 IBM cards, but to interview the same number of individuals for employment is another story. It is, likewise, much simpler to design a supersonic plane on a drawing board, than to build and fly it. By disregarding the fact that symbols may be readily manipulated when things and people may not, school practices risk the trap of irrelevance, and many social policies suffer from insensitivity to individual needs.

A related pitfall is that of an overemphasis on a limited range of human capabilities. Even within the cognitive domain, formal education often stops short of synthetic modes of functioning, and the conative and affective domains, encompassing such modes as perceiving, feeling, and valuing, have been largely ignored.[38] Whether fortunately or unfortunately, men and women are not collections of disparate, closed systems, and their challenges cannot be met one domain at a time. In each person's total life situation the aesthetic and the spiritual are at least as important as the intellectual. The realization seems crucial that negative side effects of technological advances may not be resolved by another application of the same, narrowly analytical perspective which could not foresee the overall impact to begin with.[39]

Its shortcomings and excesses notwithstanding, schooling in the application of knowledge certainly helps a worker to be flexible and mobile. He or she may be unfamiliar with a particular job, but may already have the principal tool necessary for acquiring what the job requires. With some additional systematic preparation (or knowledge training), a person can prepare for any new tasks in no time, a far cry from the long apprenticeship system of yore. This transferability of basic learning is very important in a fluid society in which the occupational world undergoes frequent and largely unpredictable changes, both in its structure and contents.[40] New materials, processes, and techniques emerge to make those of today obsolete almost overnight; novel patterns of skills come into being as old ones are dropped or incorporated into different combinations; and lateral worker relationships become increasingly crucial, while the classic management-labor dichotomy loses much of its significance.

To Have and To Develop

For those with knowledge and training the urban society offers much. Given many options on, as well as off, the job, they can no longer follow the rigid but safe ways of tradition; they must try to choose rationally and must suffer the consequences themselves.[41] Alternatives are numerous in the choice of occupations, locations, commodities, services, or leisure activities, and the individual patterns of selection can be very heterogeneous. Metropolitan areas, in particular, represent an immense concentration of talent, information, energy, and facilities. The resultant cultural inventory is rich, comparisons of different ideas and practices are inevitable, much competitive stimulation is in evidence, and cooperative efforts make functional specialization feasible. With such a combination it is no accident that modern inventions have typically originated in cities or market places to be disseminated later to the countryside.[42]

Availability of resources are nevertheless no guarantee for their full utilization. For instance, fragmentation of various urban services and the enormous complexity in their organization often have prevented ordinary citizens from getting the needed help with ease. Just think of the nightmarish process of selecting the right medical specialist, or that of identifying the necessary procedures for obtaining a license, legal assistance, repair service, or credit review! The *Yellow Pages* is a meager aid in coping with the abundance of possibilities which simply overwhelm and confuse the consumer. One is not in control of the situation and, under these circumstances, one's choices tend to be blind and restricted. As the service system itself becomes more and more complex, there is a greater need for provision of unspecialized facilitators to guide people through the network.[43] These are the trouble shooters, ministers without portfolio, or police officers, whose function is helping individuals to reach their destinations in the maze and keeping institutions responsive and flexible. Unfortunately, such an instrumental mechanism has not yet been successfully developed in most systems. To be efficient intervention probably needs to be routinized, but once so institutionalized, it loses its very effectiveness. This is a familiar dilemma in our society, whether speaking of technological advances, social welfare, or the quest for identity.[44]

In the absence of helpful guides, many people starve in the midst of cultural plenitude. Given the scope of the educational task, it is obvious that no single institution can handle it alone. The total urban environment itself must be planned for this purpose, and some even argue that cities should be designed in the tradition of a good museum, emphasizing both easy accessibility to its diverse resources and responsiveness to individual initiative and control.[45] Though such an environment may not necessarily be safe, predictable, or efficient, it is bound to challenge man to continue to learn and grow.

No single design appears to satisfy the need for such a development, even though different approaches have their own groups of proponents and ardent supporters.[46] Some argue for new towns or experimental cities, communities totally planned for a certain optimum population size, for conservation of such increasingly precious urban resources as land, sunshine, air, water, green, and quiet, for coordination of living, working, and recreation activities, and in general for an environment which works for people.[47] The advocates argue that urban dispersal. not urban renewal, is the direction in which to go.

Others interpret the idea of dispersal to mean ultimately nonplace urban realms, or community without propinquity.[48] In this view "cityness" is no longer space-bound: new communications and transportation systems allow urban functions which are cultural rather than territorial in nature;

social organizations need not coincide with any particular spatial arrangement; and urban relationships do not require a special locale or shape.

> If currently anticipated technological improvements prove workable, each of the metropolitan settlements will spread out in low-density patterns over far more extensive areas than even the most frightened futuremongers have yet predicted. The new settlement-form will little resemble the nineteenth century city so firmly fixed in our images and ideologies. We can also expect that the large junction points will no longer have the communications advantage they now enjoy . . . .[49]

However, the vision of urban sprawl, especially if unplanned, alarms many observers. Some deplore the megalopolitan expansion as lacking in form and focus, condemning it as inhuman because of its violation of the human scale.[50] Others, while acknowledging the inevitability of the development of huge universal cities or ecumenopolises, believe that these cities of extrahuman dimension can be kept human by deliberate plans for building smaller cells of perhaps 30,000 to 60,000. These units or communities satisfy most immediate human needs within the human scale.[51] Instead of calling for decentralization, they argue for "new centralization," that is, for the creation of new centers of this size as the need arises. (The Model Cities or other small-scale demonstration redevelopment programs may be kindred in spirit if not in fact.) Already existing small cities and suburbs must be encouraged to retain their human scope and unique features.[52]

Does the Center Hold?

Those who read the trend to run against urban dispersion urge us to prepare ourselves for greater centralization and higher density. Rather than a fragmentation, a further build-up of the core cities should be anticipated so as to operate the metropolitan areas closer to their full capacity. After all, "concentration is the genius of the city, its reason for being."[53] We cannot wipe the slate clean to begin at the beginning. We can, however, make the presently available space, both occupied and unoccupied, much more functional so that a larger number of people may be accommodated and better services provided.

> Concentration provides efficiency; for the same reason it provides maximum access to what people want. This is what cities are all about. People come together in cities because this is the best way to make the most of opportunities there are, the more access to skills, specialized services and goods, and to jobs.[54]

This school of thought reminds us that, some timely warning notwithstanding,[55] the matter of urban crowding has not been sufficiently clarified to warrant any definite conclusions. First of all, high density is not synonymous with overcrowding, and the number of people per area does not correlate simply with the number of people per room. "When towers are spaced out in rows, as in the conventional urban project, the density figures for the overall project can be surprisingly low."[56] The overall pattern and manner of land use are more important to consider than residential units in isolation.

Second, crowding in a closed environment, that is, crowding with confinement, is not the same as that in an open environment, or crowding without confinement.[57] As they are now, metropolitan areas are not really closed in this sense. Moreover, further developments in the systems of transportation and communications, coupled with better spatial and social arrangements, can improve the situation.

Third, openness is not merely a function of physical structure and movement. If one has to live continuously exposed without any sense of privacy, or perpetually withdrawn without any interpersonal concerns and actions, he will not long stand the stress without developing some extreme and dysfunctional forms of defense. Luckily, however, man has a capacity to create and maintain an open psychological (or, perhaps more properly, existential) sphere, even under very adverse circumstances.[58]

For instance, the immense significance of the way sidewalks are incorporated into the life space of center-city residents was perceptively described by Jacobs.[59] Sidewalks are the stage for casual social contacts which intervene between their closely guarded private spheres and those of formalized institutions. In other words, sidewalks are an arena for people to establish their informal identity as compared with their private identity, as well as formal public identity. Sidewalks are also the place for collective socialization of children in the daily, working world of diverse neighborhood women and men.

The importance of these socialization functions, and of the underlying sense of community (which implies nonanonymity and mutual responsibility), has been repeatedly shown in many ill-fated urban renewal projects. What tends to be overlooked in these redevelopment efforts is "the kind of social warmth and the sense of place and belonging"[60] which people find where they are now. The whole local area beyond their individual dwelling units constitutes an integral part of home and cannot thus be simply disassembled, relocated, and reassembled without losing its vital, subcultural functions.[61]

Blighted city blocks are indeed unsatisfactory in many regards,[62] but thoughtless interventions are bound to destroy the intricate and well-organized mechanisms of mutual support among the residents.[63] The strongly space-bound and peer-oriented style of life in these areas may defy the accepted middle-class understanding, but it is no less genuine and no less viable for that.[64] Simple association of city living with depersonalization, kinship disorganization, and social disorder does not, in most instances, hold up under scrutiny.[65]

Nevertheless, any arguments on dispersal or renewal of the urban core, with or without enrichment and/or integration efforts, must be tempered with the recognition that the population under discussion and its culture are far from homogeneous, and also that no single-dimensional programs will in themselves solve the interrelated problems of education, employment, housing, health, safety, and welfare.[66] At the same time, there is a need for an overall strategy to coordinate various actions. Priorities must be assigned to feasible alternatives and a choice made, lest the limited available resources be squandered on too many fronts.[67]

WORLD WITHIN, WORLD WITHOUT

Diversity and complexity, it appears, are both a blessing and a curse in urban life, vitalizing it and confounding it at one and the same time. Extreme conditions in any single dimension—for example, very poor housing or prolonged unemployment—doubtless contribute much to the stress experienced by a city dweller, or, for that matter, by anyone else. Any arrangements which isolate an individual for an extended period of time, either physically or mentally, which rigidly restrain activities and movements, again physically or mentally, or which force one into excessively close contact with others, would impair radically one's chances for maintaining constructive patterns of life. Under less extreme conditions, various factors interact with each other to overdetermine the life-style, and it is not easy to identify the influence of any particular variable.[68]

Major crimes (murder, forcible rape, robbery, aggravated assault, burglary, etc.) have consistently been found concentrated in the inner cities of large metropolises.[69] These are the areas typically characterized by physical deterioration, poverty, anonymity, low educational level, unemployment, overcrowding, and high rates of diseases and infant mortality. Due to the current residential distributions, the aged poor whites, the blacks, the Puerto Ricans, and the Mexican-Americans tend to bear the brunt of the combined misery and, in spite of the overall prosperity, the gap in living standards between the inner and outer cities appears to be widening.[70] Crime rates for blacks, based on such conventional statistics as arrests and prison commitment, are currently three to four times higher than those for whites, the figures being comparable to those compiled earlier by other ethnic groups under similar unfortunate circumstances.

Within the same metropolitan area, crime rates decrease more or less monotonically from the central to outlying regions. Among different areas, the larger the population size, the higher the rate for all serious crimes combined. Youth crimes follow a parallel trend, concentrating in inner cities and tapering off into suburbs and then further into rural areas. While juvenile delinquency is a grave matter anywhere,

> . . . it is well to remember that many aspects of American ethos—like this freedom, or our benevolent attitude toward rapid social change, our heritage of revolution, our encouragement of massive migrations that uproot families and shift friends, our desire to be in or near large urban centers, our wish to travel fast and in our own vehicles—and many other values that we cherish may produce the delinquency we deplore as well as many things we desire.[71]

Shadows Cast

Although the temptation is strong for us to explain every form of deviance in terms of social instability, material deprivation, cultural exclusion, and other alleged concomitants of city life, a clear association of the sort found in crime statistics is an exception rather than a rule between community characteristics (size, urbanization, locale, etc.) and human behaviors. For instance, only small and inconsistent relationships have been found between an individual's place of residence and his or her subjective feelings of distress. The only variable consistently found to correlate with indices of mental health is socioeconomic status.[72]

In the famed Midtown Study, it was reported that of the 1,660 adults of ages 20 through 59, representing some 110,000 East Side Manhattan residents, 23.4 percent were classified as psychiatrically "impaired" (the "marked symptom formation," "severe symptom formation," and "incapacitated" categories combined), while 58.1 percent were "subclinically disturbed" (the "moderate symptom formation" and "mild symptom formation" categories), and only 18.5 percent were identified as "well" (free of any symptoms other than inconsequential ones).[73] The middle group was functioning more or less adequately to perform their adult responsibilities passably or better, even with some signs and symptoms of mental disturbance present.[74] The proportion of subjects falling in the mild and moderate symptom categories did not vary greatly as a function of socioeconomic status.

For the well-functioning and impaired groups, however, the status differences were very clearly drawn. Thus, when respondents were classified into twelve strata based on their socioeconomic standing, the symptom-free category included 30.0 percent of the top group, while only 4.6 percent of the bottom group. Still more striking was the observation that 47.3 percent of the lowest socioeconomic stratum were found in the impaired categories, while a mere 12.5 percent of the highest stratum fell in these malfunctioning-to-incapacitated categories. Trying to recast the percentage figures in a simple, comparable index, the investigators further reported that the sick-well ratio (the number of impaired cases per every 100 well-functioning ones) increased from 40–60 for the upper four socioeconomic strata to 125–130 for the next six, then jumped to 360 for the second to the last stratum, finally to climb steeply to 1,020 in the bottom stratum. Parallel, though less marked, contrasts were found when paternal socioeconomic status, instead of their own, was used to group the subjects.

Given the scope of the whole project, it should be expected that various aspects of this Midtown Study have been scrutinized and questioned.[75] For our immediate purposes, it suffices to recall that only 18.5 percent of the subjects (and, by generalizing, of the resident population) were judged to be free of psychiatric symptoms and to experience no difficulties in daily living. In other words, more than four-fifths of the urban population revealed some debilitating symptom, so that "freedom from psychiatric symptoms would then be abnormal behavior."[76] On the basis of extensive records obtained by highly trained, though nonmedical, interviewers, clinicians classified the majority as either actually or subliminally sick, and only a marginal group as healthy.

Although the Midtown Study serves as only an example here, the issue itself deserves the careful attention of psychiatrists and anyone else interested in *helping* others. The strange state of affairs observed above stems from our familiar, negative approach to the phenomenon under study. If a mere absence of sickness means health, and if the existence of disorders in the individual means sickness, a healthy person is rare indeed. Actually, however, any living organism, including humans, reveals a dynamic state of disequilibrium, and disturbances and tensions are natural to our open system.[77] Human beings are not passive, reactive automatons; rather, they are dreamers and actors, carving out and controlling their own niche in life, and simultaneously seeking further challenges and new goals.

In this process one not only adjusts affectively, though largely unconsciously, to the stresses and strains, but also cognitively copes with the social demands of the world as perceived. Each person mobilizes his or her knowledge, skills, and techniques to face multitudinous tasks and resolve them as effectively as he or she knows how. By concentrating on the defensive efforts of a person, psychiatry has been inclined to ignore the coping side of adaptation.[78] Severe symptom formation, incapacitation, or psychiatric impairment may not actually be a matter of self-preserving defenses, but rather one of underdevelopment of instrumental capabilities. In other words, these "unwell" urban residents may not be mentally ill from some underlying psychological or developmental problems; they may simply be not well-learned and well-exercised in the kind of social coping skills that they need in their particular environments.

The distinction is not trivial in view of the powerful condemning effects of diagnostic classification.[79] Labeling typically leads to the processes of social degradation, stigmatization, rejection, and isolation.[80] The accompanying patterns of stereotyped expectations and actions affect all, namely, the deviant minority (allegedly sick), those who directly work with them in the name of the majority, and the normal majority themselves (allegedly healthy).[81] The dominant culture applies its outlook and practices to the deviant, and the interaction tends to be interpreted in such terms as to reinforce the existing myths about mental illness, delinquency, retardation, poverty, and other so-called pathologies of the minority group. Stereotypes persist on both sides of the fence, and, meanwhile, the professionals themselves remain captives of their own prejudices and cults.[82]

Greener Pastures

Naturally, myths are not confined to the urban core. During the 1950s many critics painted a very unflattering picture of another part of the metropolis, characterizing suburban life as synthetic, anonymous, monotonous, conforming, shallow, and provincial.[83] One of the works influential in propagating this nightmarish image focused on those who resided in the New York "exurbs"—Bucks County, Pennsylvania; Fairfield County, Connecticut; Rockland and Westchester Counties, New York; and the like—and commuted to New York City to work in the communications industry.[84] The picture was that of talented, well-to-do men and women who, by design or by accident, emigrated in groups to the promised environment of rustic comforts, only to find another rat race waiting for them.

The highly competitive business world seemed to carry itself over into the exurban life of these executive elite whose career goals were inseparably enmeshed with social activities at home. They were always reaching beyond their means, and their hyperactivity on and off the job brought them nothing but a sense of futility and cynicism. Women were equally frustrated by their clock-controlled, isolated life, and, unable to find constructive means to express themselves, many turned to their children, liquor, or extramarital relationships without finding any genuine fulfillment. Uncertainties, boredom, and disillusionment appeared to be pervasive among these entrapped exurbanites, and their children obviously did not have a broad spectrum of adult life to model after.

Another study described the planned community development in Park Forest, Illinois, a suburb of Chicago, where a group of upwardly mobile junior executives housed themselves.[85] This was not a single industry arrangement as in the New York exurbs, and the population was very transient, the annual turnover rate being about 35 percent. Incomes were comparatively modest, and excessive consumption was frowned upon. Here, the whole style of life was centered upon the idea of looking happy and fitting into the group, a good training ground for corporate adjustment necessary for a success as organization men. Community participation was frenetic, in part as overcompensation for the residents' rootlessness, and the theme of togetherness was throughout their activities. Individuality was suspect, and even acceptable ways of being different were carefully specified. One learned to get along with others, so long as it helped to get ahead of them.

Still another work concerned itself with Forest Hill (or Crestwood Heights), a long established, wealthy suburb of Toronto.[86] This is the sort of residential area about which those in Park Forest may dream, a community populated by successful businessmen, senior executives, and professionals. Some of the career struggles observed in exurbia are also found here, and the family life is governed by a demanding schedule of punctuality and regularity. Busy with housework, social entertainment, cultural interests, and philanthropic activities, women gave as small a portion of their time to children as their spouses, and the balance was made up by strong parental faith in, and frequent uses of, professional human relations expertise and guidance. These could come from magazine articles and books on child rearing, practicing pediatricians and psychiatrists, school counselors, or adult education courses.

Career success was emphasized, and the attendant prestige was expressed in properly displayed property. No hard and fast guidelines for children seemed to exist, except the expectation that expectations continue to change. Flexibility was a virtue, and children were controlled more by subtle techniques of withholding pleasure than by direct verbal or physical control. Youngsters were rushed into experience (e.g., nursery school at two, hairdressing at four, dating at ten, and formal prom at twelve), and childhood was transformed into a mock replica of adulthood. By thus compressing distinctive stages of the life cycle into a continuous sameness, the cultural system of Crestwood Heights tended to induce pervasive ambiguity about one's identity and peculiar emotional immaturity in both children and adults.

These depressing pictures of upper-middle class suburban life need to be contrasted with others which do not share the same characteristics. For example, Milpitas, a blue-collar San Jose suburb, was found to cover a wide income range and many different jobs within the manufacturing industry.[87] The residents were stable, 94 percent regarding their jobs to be permanent and 73 percent expecting to stay in their present homes for a long, long time. Social participation was low, with 70 percent belonging to no organizations of any sort and a mere 13 percent evidencing frequent visits with their neighbors. Few revealed any signs of upward status mobility. One cannot draw a sharper contrast with the largely upper-middle class suburbs described above. The comparison suggests that people conduct their own lives more or less in the same way wherever they happen to reside, whether urban or suburban areas. In other words, they transform their environment to suit their respective life-styles, rather than being passively molded by the environment to fit a uniform suburban frame.

This suggestion was reinforced by another investigation which studied Levittown,[88] a New Jersey suburb in which three distinct subgroups— working class, upper-middle class, and lower-middle class—coexisted side by side in a reasonably harmonious relationship with each other. First, there was the working class group with strong, tightly knit family life. The roles of spouses were clearly differentiated, and the parent-child relationships were more adult centered. Social entertainment was less frequent than in the other groups, and so was participation in political and community organizations. In the small upper-middle class group, consisting of business managers and professionals, participation in philanthropic associations and community activities was extensive, and their home life centered around children more or less in the manner of Crestwood Heights. The largest group (about three-fourths) of Levittowners belonged in the lower-middle socioeconomic class. Children were raised strictly, but they were allowed to be children. Every child was an individual, but not any exceptional one as in the upper-middle class tradition. As can be imagined, the differential expectations held of children and their future often brought confrontations between the upper-middle class group and the working and lower-middle class groups, particularly on school issues. Many in the lower-middle class group were active in church-related and other voluntary activities, while they shared the working class distrust of government and politics.

Analogous results were reported in another Levittown, this one on Long Island.[89] Beginning around 1950 as a planned suburb of middle-class homogeneity, the community gradually changed its character to a bimodal one by 1960. Working-class families moved in to create their own social world in coexistence with that of older middle-class residents. Their values were different, and their life-styles were different. As time went by, Levittown became more heterogeneous and less isolated a part of the metropolis. Both suburbanites and city dwellers, in other words, were joined by common bonds of social class, with some variations naturally, to face common problems of urban America.

The Lingering Specter

To recapitulate, then, mass-produced suburban housing did not necessarily lead to mass-produced lives. By moving into the same community developed by upper-middle class planners, different groups retained their own patterns of social life, maintained their identity, and availed themselves of the advantages of the overall heterogeneity. Most were much happier there than in their previous communities closer to the center of the metropolitan area, and they were fulfilling their aspirations, however imperfectly. Opportunities for social contacts were real among different groups, no matter how rare or transient, and compatibility was learned by all.

These suburbanites were certainly not mindless, anxious, copying conformers. They brought varying class values and social conceptions to the same residential development to arrive at different goals. It was true that they lived in similar houses, drove similar cars, shopped at similar stores, watched similar television programs, and engaged in similar recreations. Nevertheless, they did not think alike or feel alike, and, most certainly, they were not the feared mass men and women who could not strike an individual balance between personal desires and social demands.[90]

Identification of hypothetical social characters with live individuals is an easily misleading operation. Autonomy is based upon "the power of individuals to shape their own character by their selection among models and experiences,"[91] and it is not personified simplistically in either "the well-heeled organization man (other directed)" or "the well-shod cowboy (inner directed)."[92] Those at the bottom, whose work routines are rigidly structured to provide little variety, interaction, intrinsic gratification, prestige symbols, status mobility, or occupational stability, will mold their life around the family, local kin and friends, and nonwork activities. Understandably, their identity is not anchored in their careers or the larger communal scene, and their work attitudes may be apathetic if reliable. In other words, they are not the model organization men of, say, Riesman and Whyte.

At the other end of the hierarchy, a small number of top executives also defies easy incorporation into the lonely crowd, due to the requirements of broad perspectives, ultimate decision making, clearer responsibility, and inventiveness on the job.[93] This leaves the middle ranks of bureaucracy as the most likely breeding ground for compulsively social, yet highly competitive, functionaries. They show much anxiety and little initiative, and their stereotyped behaviors give rise to the familiar characterization of impersonality and technicism (red tape).[94]

Yet a recent interview study of a representative national sample of civilian men reported something unexpected. When the number of formal levels of supervision within an organization was used as the index of bureaucratization, this variable showed a small but revealing association with various indices of worker values and attitudes.

> Men who work in bureaucratic firms or organizations tend to value, not conformity, but self-direction. They are more open-minded, have more personally responsible standards of morality, and are more receptive to change than are men who work in nonbureaucratic organizations. They show greater flexibility in dealing both with perceptual and with ideational problems. They spend their leisure time in more intellectually demanding activities. In short, the findings belie critics' assertions.[95]

The findings, based on about 2,750 subjects, apply to entrepreneurs as well as employees, to private as well as public sectors of the economy, and to blue-collar as well as white-collar workers; the canonical correlations for the said association ranged in size from .16 to .24. Controlling for discrepancies in educational level, which favored those who work in bureaucratic organizations, still left the same sort of differences between bureaucrats and nonbureaucrats. Of the numerous occupational concomitants of bureaucracy, job protection, income, and substantive complexity significantly and individually contributed to the social-psychological impact of hierarchical organization of authority. Higher job income tended to add to the feeling of self-direction. Job protection seemed to give workers, especially those in blue-collar categories, more openness to change and a keener sense of personal responsibility. Substantive complexity of work appeared to provide them, particularly those in white-collar occupations, with an opportunity to exercise higher ideational flexibility on the job and to make more intellectually demanding use of leisure time.

Bureaucratic employees were supervised more closely than were other men of the same educational level in less bureaucratic firms, but any constricting effects this arrangement might have had seemed to be amply offset by the protective functions it performed against capricious actions of superiors. "What is notable about bureaucratic practice is not how closely authority is exercised but how effectively it is circumscribed."[96]

Although a share of such circumscription is built into the bureaucratic structure, probably a larger share stems from secondary adjustments people make to any task-oriented formal organizations. In a primary adjustment, individuals accept the formal view of themselves as members of a given organization to perform their roles within the narrowly defined world. Secondary adjustments, in contrast, allow them to carve out their own backstages within the institutional context in order to maintain some individual uniqueness. While some secondary adjustments can be disruptive, most help to maintain smooth operation of the organization and, at the same time, allow crucial individual adaptations.

> Without something to belong to, we have no stable self, and yet total commitment and attachment to any social unit implies a kind of selflessness. Our sense of being a person can come from being drawn into a wider social unit; our sense of selfhood can arise through the little ways in which we resist the pull. Our status is backed by the solid buildings of the world, while our sense of personal identity often resides in the cracks.[97]

Man in Urban America

It may indeed be that to seek an alternative to being an organization man or woman is not a viable quest in a highly industrialized and urbanized society like contemporary America. The question to be raised may in fact be, "What kind?" rather than, "Whether or not?"[98] The collective resources and potential flexibility within an organization are very large for anyone who knows how to find them and utilize them. If, however, one does not have the basic security, skills, and outlook necessary for handling the task, one may be so frightened and overwhelmed as to reduce oneself to the spectral organization man.[99] One may isolate oneself in a tiny enclave with few models, narrow perspectives, and limited opportunities; or, without knowing how to utilize the immense potential that large system provides him for individual development, one may frantically strike back at the organization or technology as evil incarnate. To prepare and assist individuals for full participation in the life of urban America at its best thus becomes the challenge for education, be it through schooling, counseling, or any other means.

While what lies ahead may be difficult to foresee on the basis of the partially known past and the uncertain present, it seems definitely the case that a bright future cannot be built upon negative and constricted images of man and his society.[100] Great visions of the future must be seen before a few can be chosen. People should be educated for the emergent, both as dreamers and actors. They can be helped then in clarifying their values for themselves, and they can be assisted in formulating their unique goals and in reaching their individual decisions. They can be encouraged to shape their own lives, and they can be aided in their goal-directed movements with continuous adjustments and changes. These future-oriented functions, rather than the past- or present-anchored remedial activities, ought to come to characterize the guidance profession in the coming years.

Gloomy assessments and forecasts abound, and there are many real problems. Nevertheless, if they so choose, man will remain autonomous to create his world and to maintain his dignity. His existence will stay rooted in love, hope, and faith and he will be "free to the extent that he makes choices, that he consciously strives to design his life, that he accepts personal responsibility for his behavior."[101]

Is there, then, a new American after all? Or is it just a new myth about the new American?

NOTES

1. D. W. Brogan, *The American Character* (New York: Random House, 1956), p. xii.
2. George H. Brown, "United States Population," *The 1972 World Almanac and Book of Facts*, Luman H. Long, ed. (New York: Newspaper Enterprise Association, 1972), pp. 145–212. (In the following discussion population statistics come from this source, unless otherwise specified.)
3. Gideon Sjoberg, *The Preindustrial City* (New York: The Free Press, 1960); ————, "The Rural-Urban Dimension in Preindustrial, Transitional, and Industrial Societies," *Handbook of Modern Sociology*, Robert E. L. Faris, ed. (Chicago: Rand McNally, 1964), pp. 127–59; ————, "Comparative Urban Sociology," *Sociology Today*, Robert K. Merton, Leonard Broom, and Leonard S. Cottrell, Jr., eds. (New York: Harper & Row, 1965) pp. 334–59.
4. William R. Burch, Jr., "Resources and Social Structures: Some Conditions of Stability and Change," *Annals of the American Academy of Political and Social Science* 389(May 1970):27–34.
5. Peter Farb, *Man's Rise to Civilization* (New York: Avon Books, 1969), p. 51.
6. Ben H. Bagdikian, *In the Midst of Plenty* (New York: The New American Library, 1964), p. 76.
7. David Allee, "American Agriculture—Its Resource Issues for the Coming Years," *Daedalus* 96(Fall 1967):1071–81; see also a contrast in the complexity of life spaces of rural vs. urban children, documented in Roger C. Barker and Herbert F. Wright, *Midwest and Its Children* (New York: Harper & Row, 1955).
8. Ruth S. Cavan, *The American Family*, 3rd ed. (New York: Thomas Y. Crowell, 1963).

9. Lee Taylor and Arthur R. Jones, Jr., *Rural Life and Urbanized Society* (New York: Oxford University Press, 1964).

10. Art Gallaher, *Plainville Fifteen Years Later* (New York: Columbia University Press, 1961); Arthur J. Vidich and Joseph Bensman, *Small Town in Mass Society* (Princeton, N.J.: Princeton University Press, 1958).

11. Louis Wirth, "Urbanism as a Way of Life," *American Journal of Sociology* 44(July 1938):1–24.

12. Bagdikian, *op. cit.*

13. Michael Harrington, *The Other America* (Baltimore: Penguin Books, 1963), p. 61.

14. It is true that this is also the area which is becoming urbanized at a faster rate than the other three. Nevertheless, the proportion of urban population there in 1970 was still 64.6 percent, and many other indices suggest that the South is still lagging far behind. For example, the region showed, in 1970 as in 1960, the highest proportion of housing units lacking basic plumbing. See a recent analysis in John C. McKinney and Linda B. Bourque, "The Changing South: National Incorporation of a Region," *American Sociological Review* 36(June 1971):399–412.

15. Milton Meltzer, ed., *In Their Own Words*, vol. III (New York: Thomas Y. Crowell, 1967), p. 127.

16. "The Migratory Farm Worker," *Monthly Labor Review* 91, 6(June 1968): 10–12; National Planning Association, Agriculture Committee, "Ending the Misery of Migratory Farm Labor," *Looking Ahead* 17, 10(Jan 1970):1–4; U.S. Senate, Committee on Labor and Public Welfare, Subcommittee on Migratory Labor, *The Migratory Farm Labor Problem in the United States* (Washington: U.S. Government Printing Office, 1969).

17. William A. Allard, "Two Wheels along the Mexican Border," *National Geographic* 139(May 1971):591–635.

18. Karen E. Kuntz, "New York Minimum Wage Act for Migrant Workers," *Prospectus* 3(Dec 1969):249–256; Manpower Evaluation and Development Institute, *Migrant Research Project* (Washington: The Institute, 1970).

19. Truman E. Moore, *The Slaves We Rent* (New York: Random House, 1965); Lee P. Reno, *Pieces and Scraps* (Washington: Rural Housing Alliance, 1970); Myrtle R. Reul, "The Many Faces of the Migrant," *Manpower* 2, 8(Aug 1970):13–17; Philip Trupp, "The Migrant Worker," *VISTA Volunteer* 5, 4(April 1969):12–17.

20. Mark Erenburg, "Obreros Unidos in Wisconsin," *Monthly Labor Review* 91, 6(June 1968):17–23; Armando Rendon, "How Much Longer . . . The Long Road?" *Civil Rights Digest*, Summer 1968, pp. 34–44.

21. Robert Coles, *Uprooted Children* (New York: Harper & Row, 1971); Sylvia Sunderlin, ed., *Migrant Children* (Washington: Association for Childhood Education International, 1971).

22. Harry M. Caudill, *Night Comes to the Cumberlands* (Boston: Little, Brown, and Co., 1963), p. 346; also see Jack E. Weller, *Yesterday's People* (Lexington: University of Kentucky Press, 1965), and Mary W. Wright, "Public Assistance in the Appalachian South," *Journal of Marriage and the Family* 26 (Nov 1964):406–409.

23. Cf., e.g., Angie Debo, *A History of the Indians of the United States* (Norman, Oklahoma: University of Oklahoma Press, 1970); Vine Deloria, Jr., *Custer Died for Your Sins* (New York: Avon Books, 1970); Helen H. Jackson, *A Century of Dishonor* (New York: Harper & Row, 1965); and Dale Van Every, *Disinherited* (New York: Avon Books, 1967).

24. Stan Steiner, *The New Indians* (New York: Dell Publishing Co., 1968), p. 166.

25. David Lowenthal, "The American Scene," *Geographical Review* 58(Jan 1968):61–88.

26. Vine Deloria, Jr., *We Talk, You Listen: New Tribes, New Turf* (New York: Macmillan, 1970).

27. Edgar S. Cahn, ed., *Our Brother's Keeper: The Indian in White America* (Washington: New Community Press, 1969), p. 94.

28. *Ibid.*, pp. 191–92.

29. See, for example, the highly repetitive document by the U.S. Senate, Committee on Labor and Public Welfare, Special Subcommittee on Indian Education, *Indian Education: A National Tragedy—A National Challenge* (Washington: U.S. Government Printing Office, 1969).

30. Cf., e.g., St. Clair Drake and Horace R. Cayton, *Black Metropolis* (New York: Harper & Row, 1962); Varden Fuller, *Rural Worker Adjustment to Urban Life* (Ann Arbor, Michigan: University of Michigan, Institute of Labor and Industrial Relations, 1970); and Mark Nagler, *Indians in the City* (Ottawa: Canadian Research Center for Anthropology, 1970).

31. Joseph W. Duncan, "The Impact of Technology on Employment Opportunities for Young People," *Battelle Technical Review* 13(Jan 1964):9–15; Russell B. Flanders, "Employment Patterns for the 1970s," *Occupational Outlook Quarterly* 14, 2(Summer 1970):2–6; Denis F. Johnston, "Education of Adult Workers in 1975," *Monthly Labor Review* 91, 4(April 1968):10–13.

32. Irene B. Taeuber and Conrad Taeuber, *People of the United States in the Twentieth Century* (Washington: U.S. Government Printing Office, 1971); Sidney M. Willhelm, *Who Needs the Negro* (Cambridge, Mass.: Schenkman, 1970).

33. Glen H. Elder, Jr., "Achievement Orientations and Career Patterns of Rural Youth," *Sociology of Education* 37(Fall 1963):30–58; William H. Sewell, "Community of Residence and College Plans," *American Sociological Review* 29(Feb 1964):24–38.

34. Aaron V. Cicourel and John I. Kitsuse, *The Educational Decision-Makers* (Indianapolis: Bobbs-Merrill, 1963); Robert J. Havighurst, *et al.*, *Growing Up in River City* (New York: John Wiley & Sons, 1962); William H. Sewell, "Inequality of Opportunity for Higher Education," *American Sociological Review* 36(Oct 1971):793–809.

35. Ewan Clague, "Effects of Technological Change on Occupational Employment Patterns of the United States," *Manpower Implications of Automation*, U.S. Department of Labor, Office of Manpower, Automation and Training (Washington: U.S. Government Printing Office, 1965), pp. 29–38; Peter F. Drucker, "Worker and Work in the Metropolis," *Daedalus* 97(Fall 1968):1243–62.

36. Peter Drucker aptly cites the China of the Mandarins as a striking example of the deleterious effects of a "diploma curtain" in his "Education in the New Technology," *Think Magazine* 28(June 1962):2–5; for some details of the state of affairs in Imperial China, consult Frederic Wakeman, Jr., "The Price of Autonomy: Intellectuals in Ming and Ch'ing Politics," *Daedalus* 101(Spring 1972):35–70; also see John W. Gardner, *Excellence* (New York: Harper & Row, 1961).

37. S. I. Hayakawa, *Language in Thought and Action*, 2nd ed. (New York: Harcourt, Brace & World, 1964);Wendell Johnson, *People in Quandaries* (New York: Harper & Row, 1946).

38. Aldous Huxley, "Education on the Nonverbal Level," *Daedalus* 91(Spring 1962):279–293; Richard M. Jones, *Fantasy and Feeling in Education* (New York: New York University Press, 1968).

39. David B. Hertz, "The Technological Imperative—Social Implications of Pro-

fessional Technology," *Annals of the American Academy of Political and Social Science* 389(May 1970):95–106.

40. Louis Levine, "Effects of Technological Change on the Nature of Jobs," *Manpower Implications of Automation*, U.S. Department of Labor, Office of Manpower, Automation and Training (Washington: U.S. Government Printing Office, 1965), pp. 39–51; Jerry M. Rosenberg, *Automation, Manpower, and Education* (New York: Random House, 1966).

41. Scott Greer, "Urbanization and Social Character: Notes on the American as Citizen," *The Quality of Urban Life*, Henry J. Schmandt and Warner Bloomberg, eds. (Beverly Hills, Calif.: Sage Publications, 1969), pp. 95–127; Philip M. Hauser, "On the Impact of Urbanism on Society," *Confluence: An International Forum* 7(Spring 1958):57–69.

42. H. G. Barnett, *Innovation: The Basis of Cultural Change* (New York: McGraw-Hill, 1953); Harry L. Shapiro, ed., *Man, Culture, and Society* (New York: Oxford University Press, 1960).

43. Adam Yarmolinsky, "The Service Society," *Daedalus* 97(Fall 1968):1263–76.

44. Allen Wheelis, *The Quest for Identity* (New York: W. W. Norton, 1958).

45. Stephen Carr, "The City of the Mind," *Environment for Man*, William R. Ewald, Jr., ed. (Bloomington, Ind.: Indiana University Press, 1967), pp. 197–231; Stephen Carr and Kevin Lynch, "Where Learning Happens," *Daedalus* 97(Fall 1968):1277–91; also see Abbott Kaplan, "Non-School Cultural Agencies of a Metropolitan Area," *Metropolitanism, Its Challenge to Education*, Robert J. Havighurst, ed. (Chicago: University of Chicago Press, 1968), pp. 268–86.

46. Carlos C. Campbell, "Insights on the City of Man from Isles of the Gods," *City* 5(Winter 1971):16–19; Peter J. O. Self, "Urban Systems and the Quality of Life," *The Quality of Urban Life*, pp. 165–186.

47. Harvey S. Perloff, "Modernizing Urban Environment," *Daedalus* 96(Summer 1967):789–800; James W. Rouse, "Cities That Work for Man," *Man in the City of the Future*, Richard Eells and Clarence Walton, eds. (Toronto: Collier-Macmillan Canada, 1968), pp. 147–61; Athelstan Spilhaus, "The Experimental City," *Daedalus* 96(Fall 1967):1129–1141.

48. Melvin M. Webber, "Order in Diversity: Community without Propinquity," *Cities and Space: The Future Use of Urban Land*, Lowdon Wingo, Jr., ed. (Baltimore: Johns Hopkins University Press, 1963), pp. 23–54.

49. ————, "The Post-City Age," *Daedalus* 97(Fall 1968):1091–1110, quoted from p. 1098.

50. Lewis Mumford, *The City in History* (New York: Harcourt, Brace & World, 1961).

51. Constantinos A. Doxiadis, "How to Build the City of the Future," *Man in the City of the Future*, pp. 163–188.

52. The importance of keeping small, specialized cities viable is emphasized not only by Doxiadis, but also by Margaret Mead in "The Crucial Role of the Small City in Meeting the Urban Crisis," *Man in the City of the Future*, pp. 29–57.

53. William H. Whyte, *The Last Landscape* (Garden City, N.Y.: Doubleday, 1968), p. 384.

54. *Ibid.*, p. 378.

55. Edward T. Hall, *The Hidden Dimension* (Garden City, N.Y.: Doubleday, 1966).

56. Whyte, *op. cit.*, p. 381.

57. John W. Dyckman, "Some Conditions of Civic Order in an Urbanized World," *Daedalus* 95(Summer 1966):797–812; Robert Sommer, "Man's Proximate Environment," *Journal of Social Issues* 22(Oct 1966):59–70.

58. One of the most moving examples of this was told by Viktor E. Frankl in *Man's Search for Meaning* (New York: Washington Square Press, 1963).

59. Jane Jacobs, *Death and Life of Great American Cities* (New York: Random House, 1961).

60. Max Lerner, "The Negro American and His City: Person in Place and Culture," *Daedalus* 97(Fall 1968):1390–1408, quoted from p. 1402.

61. Marc Fried, "Grieving for a Lost Home," *The Urban Condition*, Leonard J. Duhl, ed. (New York: Basic Books, 1963), pp. 151–171; Marc Fried and Peggy Gleicher, "Some Sources of Residential Satisfaction in an Urban Slum," *Journal of the American Institute of Planners* 27(Nov 1961):305–315; Albert E. Parr, "Psychological Aspects of Urbanology," *Journal of Social Issues* 22(Oct 1966):39–58.

62. National Commission on Urban Problems, *Building the American City* (New York: Praeger, 1969); Lee Rainwater, "Fear and the House-as-Haven in the Lower Class," *Journal of the American Institute of Planners* 32(Jan 1966): 23–31.

63. Peter Marris, "The Social Implications of Urban Redevelopment," *Journal of the American Institute of Planners* 28(Aug 1962):180–186; Patricia C. Sexton, *Spanish Harlem: Anatomy of Poverty* (New York: Harper & Row, 1965), especially Ch. 4, "Urban Renewal: The Bulldozer and the Bulldozed."

64. Herbert J. Gans, *The Urban Villagers* (New York: The Free Press, 1962); Elliot Liebow, *Tally's Corner* (Boston: Little, Brown, and Co., 1967); William F. Whyte, *Street Corner Society* (Chicago: University of Chicago Press, 1943).

65. The classical idea of degeneration was cogently presented by Wirth, *op. cit.*

66. Anthony Downs, "Alternative Futures for the American Ghetto," *Daedalus* 97(Fall 1968):1331–78 [Chapter 16, "The Future of the Cities," *Report of the National Advisory Commission on Civil Disorders* (Washington: U.S. Government Printing Office, 1968) borrows heavily from this author and the article]; John R. Seeley, "The Slum: Its Nature, Use, and Users," *Journal of the American Institute of Planners* 25(Feb 1959):7–14.

67. Michael Young, "The Liberal Approach: Its Weaknesses and Its Strengths," *Daedalus* 97(Fall 1968):1379–89.

68. Kenneth B. Clark, *Dark Ghetto* (New York: Harper & Row, 1965); Leo Levy and Harold M. Visotsky, "The Quality of Urban Life: An Analysis from the Perspective of Mental Health," *The Quality of Urban Life*, Henry J. Schmandt and Warner Bloomberg, Jr., eds. (Beverly Hills, Calif.: Sage Publications, 1969), pp. 255–268; Alvin L. Schorr, *Slums and Social Insecurity* (Washington: U.S. Government Printing Office, 1963).

69. The President's Commission on Law Enforcement and Administration of Justice, *The Challenge of Crime in a Free Society* (New York: Avon Books, 1968); Marvin E. Wolfgang, "Urban Crime," *The Metropolitan Enigma*, James Q. Wilson, ed. (Garden City, N.Y.: Doubleday, 1970), pp. 270–311.

70. Daniel P. Moynihan, "Poverty in Cities," *The Metropolitan Enigma*, pp. 367–85.

71. Wolfgang, *op. cit.*, p. 292.

72. John A. Clausen, "The Sociology of Mental Illness," *Sociology Today*, pp. 485–508; James A. Davis, *Education for Positive Mental Health* (Chicago: Aldine, 1965); Arnold M. Rose and Holger R. Stub, "Summary of Studies on the Incidence of Mental Disorders," *Mental Health and Mental Disorders*, Arnold M. Rose, ed. (New York: W. W. Norton, 1955).

73. Leo Srole *et al.*, *Mental Health in the Metropolis: The Midtown Manhattan Study* (New York: McGraw-Hill, 1962).

74. The characterization is essentially the authors' (*Ibid.*, p. 138, p. 213, etc.).

75. Davis, *op. cit.;* August B. Hollinghead, "Review of *Mental Health in the Metropolis* by Leo Srole et al.," *American Sociological Review* 27(Dec 1962): 864–866; Ernest M. Gruenberg, "A Review of 'Mental Health in the Metropolis: Midtown Manhattan Study,'" *The Study of Abnormal Behavior,* Melvin Zax and George Stricker, eds. (New York: Macmillan, 1964), pp. 80–91; Gardner Murphy, "Roles, Nomos, and Midtown Misery," *Contemporary Psychology* 8(Jan 1963):35–37.

76. Stephan P. Spitzer and Norman K. Denzin, "Issues and Problems in the Sociology of Mental Illness," *The Mental Patient,* Stephan P. Spitzer and Norman K. Denzin, eds. (New York: McGraw-Hill, 1968), p. 464.

77. Ludwig Von Bertalanffy, *General System Theory* (New York: George Braziller, 1968), especially Chapter 9, "General System Theory in Psychology and Psychiatry."

78. David Mechanic, "Community Psychiatry: Some Sociological Perspectives and Implications," *Community Psychiatry,* Leigh M. Roberts, Seymour Halleck, and Martin B. Loeb, eds. (Garden City, N.Y.: Doubleday, 1969), pp. 211–234.

79. Thomas S. Szasz, *Ideology and Insanity* (Garden City, N.Y.: Doubleday, 1970).

80. Gordon W. Allport, *The Nature of Prejudice,* abridged ed. (Garden City, N.Y.: Doubleday, 1958); Howard S. Becker, *Outsiders* (New York: The Free Press, 1963).

81. Benjamin M. Braginsky, Dorothea D. Braginsky, and Kenneth Ring, *Methods of Madness* (New York: Holt, Rinehart and Winston, 1969); Dorothea D. Braginsky and Benjamin M. Braginsky, *Hansels and Gretels* (New York: Holt, Rinehart, and Winston, 1971); Thomas J. Scheff, *Being Mentally Ill* (Chicago: Aldine, 1966).

82. John B. Enright, "Synanon: A Challenge to Middle-Class Views of Mental Health," *Community Psychology and Mental Health,* Daniel Adelson and Betty L. Kalis, eds. (Scranton, Pa.: Chandler Publishing Co., 1970), pp. 238–61; Jerome D. Frank, *Persuasion and Healing* (New York: Schocken Books, 1963); Everett C. Hughes, "Mistakes at Work," *Canadian Journal of Economics and Political Science* 17(Aug 1951):320–27; Milton Rokeach, Martin G. Miller, and John A. Snyder, "The Value Gap between Police and Policed," *Journal of Social Issues* 27(Spring 1971):155–171; Sam D. Sieber and David E. Wilder, "Teaching Styles: Parental Preferences and Professional Role Definitions," *Sociology of Education* 40(Fall 1967):302–15; James Q. Wilson, "Planning and Politics: Citizen Participation in Urban Renewal," *Journal of the American Institute of Planners* 29(Nov 1963): 242–49.

83. William Alonso, "Cities and City Planners," *Daedalus* 92(Fall 1963):824–839; Maurice R. Stein, *The Eclipse of Community* (Princeton, N.J.: Princeton University Press, 1960).

84. A. C. Spectorsky, *The Exurbanites* (Philadelphia: J. B. Lippincott, 1955).

85. William H. Whyte, *The Organization Man* (Garden City, N.Y.: Doubleday, 1956).

86. John R. Seeley, R. Alexander Sim, and E. W. Loosley, *Crestwood Heights* (New York: Basic Books, 1956).

87. Bennett M. Berger, *Working Class Suburb* (Berkeley, Calif.: University of California Press, 1960).

88. Herbert J. Gans, *The Levittowners* (New York: Pantheon, 1967).

89. William M. Dobriner, *Class in Suburbia* (Englewood Cliffs, N.J.: Prentice-Hall, 1963).

90. Daniel Bell, *The End of Ideology* (New York: The Free Press, 1960).

91. David Riesman, "Preface," *The Lonely Crowd,* abridged ed. (New Haven, Conn.: Yale University Press, 1961), pp. xi–xlviii, quoted from p. xlviii.
92. *Ibid.,* p. xliv; also see David Riesman, "Some Questions about the Study of American Character in the Twentieth Century," *Annals of the American Academy of Political and Social Science* 370(March 1967):36–47.
93. Harold L. Wilensky, "Work, Careers, and Social Integration," *International Social Science Journal* 12(Fall 1960):543–560; of course, this characterization of top executives may not apply to those at the very, very top depicted, e.g., in C. Wright Mills, *The Power Elite* (New York: Oxford University Press, 1959).
94. Joseph Bensman and Bernard Rosenberg, "The Meaning of Work in Bureaucratic Society," *Identity and Anxiety,* Maurice Stein, Arthur J. Vidich, and David M. White, eds. (New York: The Free Press, 1960), pp. 181–97; Robert K. Merton, "Bureaucratic Structure and Personality," *Social Theory and Social Structure,* enlarged ed. (New York: The Free Press, 1968), pp. 249–60.
95. Melvin L. Kohn, "Bureaucratic Man: A Portrait and an Interpretation," *American Sociological Review* 36(June 1971):461–474, quoted from p. 465.
96. *Ibid.,* p. 473.
97. Erving Goffman, *Asylums* (Garden City, N.Y.: Doubleday, 1961), p. 320; also see Chris Argyris, *Personality and Organization* (New York: Harper & Brothers, 1957).
98. Solon T. Kimball and James E. McClellan, Jr., *Education and the New America.* (New York: Random House, 1962), particularly Chapter 14, "Moral Commitment and the Individual."
99. Drucker, "Worker and Work in the Metropolis"; Edward Gross, "A Sociological Approach to the Analysis of Preparation for Work Life," *Personnel and Guidance Journal* 45(Jan 1967):416–23; Victor A. Thompson, *Modern Organization* (New York: Alfred A. Knopf, 1961).
100. Bettina J. Huber and Wendell Bell, "Sociology and the Emergent Study of the Future," *American Sociologist* 6(Nov 1971):287–295; also see Alvin Toffler, *Future Shock* (New York: Bantam Books, 1970).
101. Chris Argyris, "Essay Review of B. F. Skinner, *Beyond Freedom and Dignity,*" *Harvard Educational Review* 41(Nov 1971):550–67, quoted from p. 561.

SUGGESTED READING

Drucker, Peter F. *The Age of Discontinuity.* New York: Harper & Row, 1969. Subtitled *Guidelines to Our Changing Society,* this book examines four major social discontinuities as the real molders of tomorrow. Projections based upon the assumption of continuity of the present trends will be of little use, it is argued, when these hidden forces of technology, world economy, large organizations, and knowledge are changing the total configuration of our life and its meaning.

Jacobs, Jane. *Death and Life of Great American Cities.* New York: Random House, 1961. The author presents an ardent plea for better understanding, conservation, and refinement of what is good about American cities. In her perceptive analysis of various facets of the structure and dynamics of city life, readers will find much that has been overlooked and ignored by citizens, planners, politicians, and scholars alike.

Whyte, William H. *The Last Landscape.* Garden City, N.Y.: Doubleday, 1968. Whyte discusses some of the controversies on urban and suburban development and presents his own ideas on how better to proceed. His sphere of concern is a little larger than that of Jacobs, while smaller than that of Drucker's. It will be a good exercise to try to place these different treatises in a proper relationship with each other.

The Nature of Economic Enterprise 5

Robert L. Darcy
Colorado State University

From the traditional economic viewpoint, work is human effort devoted
to production—something that is done by a "factor of production" variously
called *labor, manpower, or human resources.*[1] The theory of a market
economy assumes that men and women are motivated to perform their
human resource function in order to earn money income (termed wages),
which is the payment they receive in exchange for work.

When we recognize that two of the primary functions of work are *producing goods* and *earning income,* it is obvious that work is part of the
economic process. What may not be equally clear is that even the so-
called noneconomic functions of work—*satisfying psychological* and *social
needs* and *contributing to human development*—are also inseparable from
the economic process. There are two reasons why this is so: (1) all four
functions of work are jointly performed[2] and (2) the work is done within
a distinctive social environment dominated by technological processes, institutional patterns, and human values that we acknowledge to be essentially economic in nature.

Because work and the economic process of production are so inextricably bound together, it would seem that a strong case might be made
for studying the nature of economic enterprise in order to develop a functional understanding of the world of work. Such a study could provide
perspective and orientation to help productive men and women know
themselves, the world around them, and the multi-faceted nature of work
in our complex, highly specialized, interdependent industrial society.

While this perception of the relationship between work and economics
seems plausible to an economist, especially a nontraditional human resource economist, the sober fact is that many specialists in world-of-work
or career education seem not to feel terribly deprived by their limited exposure to the discipline of economics. This attitude suggests that the case
for economic education has not yet been convincingly made. What follows
is an attempt to help repair that shortcoming.

THE STRUCTURE OF ECONOMICS

Although it is true that economists talk about many things—including
shoes, ships, sealing wax, cabbages, and kings (to recall Lewis Carroll's

For their critical reading of a draft of this manuscript I am grateful to three Colorado State University colleagues: Jacque Suzanne Darcy, Edward F. Dash, and
Rodney D. Peterson.

line from "The Walrus and the Carpenter")—it is not very useful to define the nature and scope of economics by drawing up a vast list of all the specific topics included within its purview, such as money, coal mining, stocks and bonds, work, taxes, foreign trade, profits, unemployment, inflation, and virtually the entire universe of human interests and activities. The social science of economics essentially studies *how society organizes to develop and use its productive resources to satisfy human wants.*

The basic subject matter of economics includes *resources* (manpower, capital, and natural resources); *technology* (toolmaking and toolusing knowledge); and *institutions* (coordinating mechanisms or established patterns of social behavior that influence the development and use of resources and technology). The human community is interested in resources (both quality and quantity) because this is the stuff from which goods and services are produced. More advanced technology makes it possible to increase productivity, that is, to increase the ratio of output per unit of resource inputs. Better institutions not only enable the economic community to make full use of its existing resources (avoiding waste and inefficiency), but they also contribute to the development of qualitatively superior resources. For example, better systems of vocational guidance and career planning result in more productive and satisfied workers.

One of the fundamental principles of economics is stated in the functional relationship $GNP = \langle R,T,I \rangle$, which simply means that our Gross National Product (total output of goods and services produced in any given year) is a function of the quantity and quality of resources available, the level of technology, and the nature and functioning of our economic institutions. This is semitechnical jargon for the familiar proposition that "There is no such thing as a free lunch," or "You can't make a silk purse out of a sow's ear." It takes inputs of resources to get outputs of goods and services, and the amount and type of output is determined by the productive resources we have available and how we use them.

Basic Questions Facing the Economic System

Economists analyze the production function of a system from two perspectives, "macroeconomics" and "microeconomics," and they organize theoretical inquiry around three basic questions:

1. What determines the overall level of economic activity (employment, production, and income)?
2. What determines the composition of the nation's output (i.e., the specific types of goods and services produced, such as consumer durable and nondurable goods, consumer services, capital goods in the form of plant and equipment, government services such as public education)?
3. What determines the distribution of the nation's income (i.e., how the money income and real goods and services are shared among members of the economic community)?

The first question encompasses macroeconomics, which is the study of economic aggregates such as the total level of GNP, the rate of unemployment for the nation's labor force, and changes in the general level of consumer prices. To explain how the overall level of economic activity is determined we start with the available quantity and quality of resources (e.g., 90 million workers and $3 trillion of capital goods); add the current level of technology (for which we have no convenient quantitative measure); and observe how well our institutions are functioning (e.g., effectiveness of the manpower market, price and wage policies of large corporations and labor unions, government fiscal policies).

Economists may frequently be wrong in their predictions about employment, GNP, and prices, but they are seldom in doubt about the basic forces which interact to determine actual outcomes. If there is just enough, but not too much, "total spending" in the market (by consumers, business, government, and foreigners), and if our institutions are functioning smoothly, then the U.S. economy will be operating at full employment (typically defined in terms of providing jobs for 96 percent or more of the labor force at any given time), producing goods and services at full capacity, and making this output available to buyers at prices no more than one or two percent higher than the previous year. When the system performs badly, as it began to do in the late 1960s, the reason(s) why can be traced to specific imbalances and malfunctions in the way our economic institutions direct the use of available resources and technology: for example, inappropriate fiscal and monetary policies, inefficient manpower markets, excessive price increases by powerful corporations, and the familiar price-wage inflationary spiral with business and labor unions passing burdens on to consumers in the form of higher costs of living.

The second basic question that we posed about the functioning of an economic system referred to the composition of the nation's output, or the "product mix." This subject falls under the heading of microeconomics, which studies the particular parts of the economy, such as the price of pinto beans in Denver and the going wage for carpenters in Chicago. The process by which this mix is determined depends to a great extent on the institutions that make up the economic system; indeed, economic systems are compared chiefly in terms of their distinctive institutional features. The institutions of capitalism, a market-regulated economy where the consumer is alleged to be sovereign, are described in the next section. Under socialism the composition of the nation's income is determined largely through a system of comprehensive economic planning. In less developed, subsistence economies, market transactions and comprehensive planning have less influence than custom, tradition, and the exigencies of nature.

The economic concept of "opportunity cost" is useful in clarifying choices that must be made within an economic system with respect to the kinds of goods and services to be produced. Shall we have more guns and less butter, or vice versa? The Russians choose more capital goods (increasing future productivity) and less consumer (present) goods. The British prefer more civilian goods and fewer armaments. The Swedes take more social goods (for collective consumption) through the government sector, leaving less private goods. The concept of opportunity cost helps us to see the real costs of choosing one package of goods as opposed to some other.

If all the resources of a nation are fully and efficiently employed, the only way to increase the production of guns is to divert some manpower, capital, and natural resources from producing butter and make them available to the guns industry. Bearing in mind the "principle of production"—that it requires resource inputs in order to produce goods and services—the reallocation of resources has the effect of reducing the output of butter. If we can calculate the quantity of butter that must be sacrificed (say, twenty-five units) in order to produce, say, ten additional guns, and if we are able to compare the value or benefit of twenty-five units of butter with ten guns, we are then able to make a rational choice about the preferred composition of output. This is the meaning of opportunity cost and an illustration of how it is applied in the choice-making process.

At a personal level, if we know that it takes two years of postsecondary education to qualify for occupation X, whereas a high school graduate is eligible for occupation Y, then a calculation of the cost of tuition, books, miscellaneous private costs, and the sacrifice of income that could have been earned if the individual were employed instead of going ahead with his schooling can be compared with the monetary and nonmonetary benefits associated with occupation X, and a more rational choice can then be made between the two career paths.

This hypothetical application of the "principle of choice" leads to the third basic question that every economic system must answer: how to divide up the total income among the various members of the economic community. Economic theory has less to say about this problem than the macroeconomic question of how much total production, or the microeconomic question of what kind of production. There is, however, a strong tradition in economics that suggests that in general whatever income a member of the economic community (e.g., a physician, migrant farm worker, business executive, plumber, professional baseball player, or heiress) obtains legally, it may be presumed that he or she (or the estate, in the case of the heiress) has made a productive contribution to society commensurate with the income received. This marginal productivity theory of income distribution suggests that the various shares of income flow to workers, landowners, enterprisers, and capital owners according to the economic value of their contribution to production. Hence, low-income people receive low incomes because their productivity is low, whereas high-income people get their "just due" on the basis of their high productivity. The "productivity principle of income distribution" in a sense wears two hats: it purports to be a description of how income actually is distributed in a market economy, and it does double duty as an ethical precept, suggesting that it is fair and just that one should receive as his share of income an amount equal to what he produced.

Economic Goals

Thus far in our discussion of the structure of economics we have defined its essential focus, identified the basic subject matter, described the basic questions that every economic system must answer, and introduced several principles of economics that shed light on the functioning of the economic enterprise. To round out this simplified structure, we turn now to the "principle of goal pursuit."

Webster's Seventh New Collegiate Dictionary defines *enterprise* as "a project or undertaking that is difficult, complicated, or risky; a systematic purposeful activity." In speaking of an individual business enterprise (some of which are indeed difficult, complicated, and risky), the acknowledged purpose is the pursuit of private profit. But what is the purpose of the systematic economic activity of the nation as a whole? Not profit, certainly. Probably "the general welfare," however defined, or enhancement of the quality of life for the nation's people. Usually we think not of the goal of the economic system, but rather of the more specific goals of "full production"; reasonable stability of the price level; growth; freedom of choice for consumers, workers, and business enterprisers; security; distributive justice; and international harmony. These are the standards by which we typically judge the performance of the American economic enterprise.[3]

A Method of Economic Policy Analysis

The naming of goals demonstrates the relevance of those elements of structure previously described and also identifies the need for a method of policy analysis which can be utilized in searching for the best means of achieving stated goals. A method of rational problem solving known to us for some time is described here under the rather formal label of "the rational-empirical-comprehensive methodology of economic policy analysis." This method consists of five steps.

1. *Define the problem* by examining the most important facts and clarifying key issues, making effective use of economic statistics, theory, and history.
2. *Identify the goal(s)* or end to be achieved, expressing it as clearly and objectively as possible, including recognition of the underlying values that led to its adoption.
3. *Consider alternative courses of action,* or *means,* for reaching the goal, again making effective use of economic theory and history to discover the full range of logical possibilities.
4. *Analyze the probable consequences* of following the alternative courses of action, using statistics, history, and theory to estimate the likely benefits, costs, and other effects.
5. *Choose the best course of action* in light of the goal that has been set, implement the policy, study actual outcomes, and make appropriate revisions in both the means and the goals as the changing situation warrants.

This "principle of rational-empirical decision making" was emphasized a decade ago by a task force of economists and educators as being the most important element in economic literacy,[4] and its applicability to both social policy and personal decision making is evident.[5] As a method of policy analysis, it provides a framework for asking fruitful questions; acknowledges the value content of the problem; demonstrates the essential role of logic, theory, and empirical data in searching for answers; provides a measure of assurance that all possible solutions will receive a reasonable hearing; and puts into practice the rational prescription that "a value judgment is as good as the reasons for it, and as weak as the reasons that support alternative views."[6]

NATURE AND FUNCTIONING OF A CAPITALISTIC ECONOMY

The theoretical structure of economics sketched in the preceding section is largely cross-cultural, not limited by a particular set of economic institutions. It purports to identify central concepts, problems, relationships, principles, and practices that can prove useful in interpreting the "real world" economic enterprise wherever modern industrial technology prevails. It provides a framework for closer examination of the U.S. economy, which for a century and a half was characterized as "capitalistic"—a free enterprise, private enterprise, profit, market, competitive, price system.

Few economists today would be comfortable using those terms, except in a rather special context. The American economy today is better labeled a "mixed economy" or "mixed capitalism"—a blend of private enterprise (not necessarily "competitive" or "free") and government control, of competition and market power (in the hands of large corporations and labor unions). But even today enough remains of the institutions and ideology of pure capitalism to justify describing such a system in order to gain a deeper understanding, to paraphrase Abraham Lincoln, of where we have been and "whither we are tending."

First, let us recognize that all advanced economies today use money, credit, capital equipment, and industrial technology. They practice a high degree of specialization in producing certain goods and services (according to the concept of comparative advantage), and they engage in rather sophisticated patterns of exchange. Economic activity is coordinated by means of competitive markets, cartels, government planning, or variations on those themes; little is left to custom, tradition, or chance.

Significantly, however, not all economies are organized in the same way to make use of their resources, technology, and technically efficient structural organizations such as money, credit, and markets. The essential and distinctive institutional features of capitalism, to be discussed presently, do not prevail under socialism or communism—and, in fact, that is what makes the systems different. The Soviet economy, for example, makes abundant use of industrial technology, money and credit, market exchange, and certainly capital (i.e., plant, equipment, and other goods that have been produced for use in further production), but it is by no means a capitalistic system because its institutions (coordinating mechanisms) are quite different.

Circular Flow Model of a Market Economy

What are the basic and distinctive institutional features of capitalism, and what relevance do they have for understanding America's contemporary world of work? Figure 5.1, which depicts the circular flow of economic activity in a private enterprise economy, helps identify these features and illustrate how they interact in a functioning system.[7]

The solid lines pointing counterclockwise represent real flows of productive resources (in the input market) and goods and services (in the output market). The broken lines pointing clockwise indicate monetary flows of consumer spending (to purchases output) and business spending (to pay for productive resource services which firms employ in the process of turning out a flow of final goods and services). At the top of the model we have

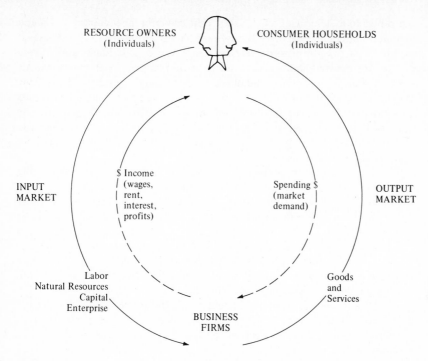

RESOURCE OWNERS
(Individuals)

CONSUMER HOUSEHOLDS
(Individuals)

INPUT
MARKET

OUTPUT
MARKET

$ Income
(wages,
rent,
interest,
profits)

Spending $
(market
demand)

Labor
Natural Resources
Capital
Enterprise

Goods
and
Services

BUSINESS
FIRMS

Figure 5.1 The Circular Flow of Economic Activity in a Private Enterprise Economy

pictured the two economic roles played by individuals in a market system: all persons in our economy are consumers (mouths to feed) and belong to *consumer households,* while nearly half of the American people at any given time are economically active as *resource owners.* At the bottom of the diagram are *business firms,* which purchase resource services in the input market, convert them into marketable products, and offer them for sale to consumers in the output market.[8] The circular flow model depicts a pattern of exchange relations involving three *decision-making units* (resource owners, business firms, and consumer households); two kinds of *markets* (input and output); *flows of money* (consumer spending and income payments to the suppliers of manpower, natural resources, capital, and enterprise); and *flows of real services and goods* for which the money payments are made.

What, then, are the ground rules, incentives, and safeguards on which this system of market exchange is based, and what implications are there for understanding a world of work that operates as a subsystem within the broader capitalistic economic enterprise?

Institutional Features of Capitalism

Of the five essential and distinctive institutional features of capitalism, the most basic and pervasive is *private property.* Contrary to popular thinking, the term does not refer to "things" such as factory buildings and coal mines, but rather to a "bundle of legal rights" that prescribe how capital goods and natural resources may be used. Because we have a constitutionally guaranteed institution of private property in the United States, individuals and private groups are allowed and encouraged to own factories, coal mines, banks, farms, railroads, and other nonhuman resources, and they can decide how they will be used in production subject to only broad and general constraints imposed by society. The institution of private property entails not only the right to buy, hold, use, and dispose of the means of production, but also implies that the police powers of government will be used to protect these rights and to enforce the laws of contract.

Given the institution of private property—the rejection and outlawing of which is the core feature that distinguishes the economic systems of China and the Soviet Union from that of the United States—what are people to do with the means of production? How, for example, should the coal mines be used? The answer given under a private enterprise system is that they should be used in whatever way individual owners want them to be used, and the presumption is that the owners will want to use them in a way that will bring in the most profits. Since the sixteenth or seventeenth century in Western Europe, the desire for monetary gain has been at the heart of the economic incentive system. Thus *the profit motive,* the second distinctive feature of capitalism, has occupied a central place both in theoretical explanations of decision making in a market economy and in actual economic life.

According to the theory of rational behavior, buyers and sellers in both the input market and the output market will try to maximize their own pecuniary self-interest: to "buy cheap and sell dear." Indeed, this pervasive power of money to motivate and regulate economic behavior is counted on to perform the functions of both stick and carrot. If a business firm is earning 10 percent by manufacturing hats but could turn 15 percent by switching to the production of shoes, it is predicted that under a free-enterprise market system the firm will make the conversion just as quickly as circumstances permit, to the benefit of both the individual firm and the economy as a whole. Similarly, if a carpenter is earning $5 per hour working for employer X, but could get $6 by going to work for employer Y, then according to the pecuniary capitalist ethic and the postulate of rationality, he would naturally make the move, thereby increasing his productivity and earnings. The outcome for society, according to the "invisible hand" hypothesis, would be more efficient allocation of resources and greater national production.[9]

Free enterprise, the third distinctive feature of capitalism, is really a corollary of private property conjoined with the profit motive. It is simply the freedom of individuals or groups to start their own business enterprises, to avail themselves of the opportunity to use the means of production to enhance their own pecuniary self-interest. In economic jargon this means, ideally, that there must not be obstacles to entry, such as franchises or inimical market practices on the part of monopolistic or oligopolistic firms already operating in the industry.

A fourth characteristic of capitalism is *competition,* the real meaning of which is not simply rivalry among producers or "trying harder," but the absence of market power. Pure competition requires that there be enough sellers and buyers of a particular good to insure that no individual has sufficient power to significantly affect supply or demand and thereby impose his or her will on other traders in the market. The function of competition is to prevent sellers from charging excessively high prices, selling shoddy merchandise, or offering consumers no more than a Hobson's choice ("you can have any color Ford you want, as long as it's black")—practices that are not altogether inconceivable under a system of private property and individual self-interest.

The fifth institutional feature of pure capitalism is that *prices and wages* are set by the interaction of buyers and sellers in competitive markets, as discussed above, and not by government, powerful business firms, and labor unions. The method by which prices and wages are determined is crucial in any economy that makes use of market transactions—whether capitalistic or socialistic—because these values are important criteria of choice for buyers and sellers, and they basically determine the pattern of resource allocation.

Implications of Capitalism for the World of Work

What are the implications of pure capitalism, or even a mixed capitalistic system such as the contemporary U.S. economy, for the world of work? First, remembering the functions of work identified earlier, it can be seen in Figure 5.1 that workers (and other resource owners) are valued in the economic process because they perform the basic function of helping to produce goods and services. It is the worker's productivity, both physical and monetary, that induces an enterprise to provide remunerative employment. If a worker has valuable labor service to offer in the market, he qualifies for employment. If the resource that he owns is of low quality (e.g., raw, unskilled labor), then the market will offer a worker unattractive employment at low wages or reject him altogether.

To qualify for wage employment in a market system, the worker must have something valuable to exchange and must be willing to respond to monetary incentives in terms of what, where, when, and how he works. The prospective employer looks to the output market to determine whether sufficient demand exists to justify hiring more manpower to produce goods for sale. The demand for labor is thus a derived demand, dependent on the volume of sales to final customers. Since the wage that an employer offers to his workers is a cost of production, it must not exceed the expected revenues from selling the worker's output; otherwise there would be no monetary incentive to hire, produce, and sell. Moreover, if the firm can reduce its costs of production by substituting machines for workers, it will naturally tend to do so, thereby depriving workers of their jobs.

In a market economy, based on specialization and exchange, the individual worker is in a precarious position: the resource he owns is highly perishable, his manpower services will command a money wage only when an employer is willing to hire, and the employer is willing to hire only when he anticipates being able to sell at profitable prices the output that the worker helps to produce. A breakdown at any point in the system can leave the worker jobless, deprived of an income, and denied an opportunity to meet social and psychological needs through employment.

THE MIXED ECONOMY OF THE UNITED STATES

By the third decade of the present century it was clear that the economy of the United States did not conform to the model of pure capitalism depicted above, and by the 1970s the divergence was even more apparent. The rise of giant, quasi-public corporations has blurred the institution of private property. Nonpecuniary values have eroded the power and predictability of the profit motive. Obstacles to entry have severely limited the exercise of free enterprise. The old competition has given way to great blocs of "countervailing powers," with questionable effects for consumers and resource owners. Prices and wages are influenced, if not "administered," by billion-dollar corporations, million-member labor unions, and powerful governmental agencies. No longer is the capitalistic price system relied upon for final determination of the overall level, composition, and distribution of the nation's income. The economy's quest for full production, growth, price stability, freedom of choice, distributive justice, security, and international balance has come to involve an active partnership between the private (market) sector and the public (government) sector. As a result, the *mixed economy* of the United States today is a blend of decentralized decision making in the market (heavily influenced by concentrations of private economic power) and centralized government policies. The United States has modified its economic institutions in such manner as to transform fundamentally the way we organize to develop and use our resources and technology, with far-reaching consequences for consumers, businessmen, citizens, and men and women who participate in the world of work.

Economic Power of Giant Corporations

Some statistical data will help provide perspective. In 1970, for example, when the GNP was approaching the trillion-dollar level and employment averaged 80 million, the 500 largest industrial corporations (a tiny fraction of one percent of the nation's eight and one-half million nonagricultural business firms) accounted for $464 billion of sales, $22 billion of profits after tax, and employment of 14.6 million workers. One company alone, the General Motors Corporation, had sales of $18.8 billion and employed nearly 700,000 workers. More than 100 corporations reported annual sales of over a billion dollars.[10]

The impact of such concentration of economic power, described in numerous books and articles,[11] has been enormous, and the question is raised whether the giant, quasi-public corporation has so completely undermined the institutions of private capitalism that what we have today is really "collective capitalism." How do thousands of stockholders effectively exercise the rights of private property in a giant industrial corporation? How does the profit motive express itself when the owners of an enterprise are different from the managers? How much is left of free enterprise when a newcomer to the industry must battle with multi-billion dollar rivals to gain a share of the market? What is the nature of competition when four firms control two-thirds or more of the output of the entire industry?[12] And to what extent are resources allocated on the basis of competitively determined prices and wages when, in fact, large corporations, labor unions, and the federal government all have administrative power to influence or establish outright these criteria of market choice?

Growth of Labor Unions

Since the 1930s the trend toward collectivism has also transformed many segments of the manpower market. By 1968, nearly 20 million American workers belonged to labor unions, accounting for 23 percent of the total labor force and 28 percent of all employees in nonagricultural establishments. The three largest unions (Teamsters, Auto Workers, and Steelworkers) each reported over one million members; and organized labor's chief lobbyist and spokesman on public issues, the AFL-CIO, had a 1968 membership consisting of 126 affiliated unions representing nearly 16 million workers. In such basic industries as transportation, construction, manufacturing, and mining, wages typically are determined not by the interaction of supply and demand among competitive buyers and sellers of manpower services, but through a system of collective bargaining.[13]

Government as an Active Economic Force

Along with business and labor, government has emerged as one of the economy's active countervailing powers, intervening in the economic process not merely to protect the rights of private property and promote market competition, but also to influence directly and deliberately the overall level, composition, and distribution of the nation's income. The methods of economic intervention used by federal, state, and local government include: 1) making rules (prescribing and enforcing the laws of contract and incorporation, prohibiting pollution, etc.); 2) producing goods and services (e.g., operating schools and constructing highways); 3) transferring income (taxing, borrowing, subsidizing, paying social security benefits, and providing public assistance payments to needy families); and 4) stabilizing the economy (raising or lowering taxes to regulate total market demand, controlling the supply of money and credit, administering an "incomes policy" such as the 1971 wage-price freeze and its aftermath). In 1969 local, state, and federal government agencies employed more than 12 million workers (nearly one-sixth of the employed civilian labor force) and spent $308 billion to carry out their economic and other responsibilities.[14]

In addition to economic statistics, historical-institutional data can also help document the transformation of American capitalism and clarify the responsibilities of government in the contemporary mixed economy of the United States.[15] Noting again the three fundamental questions facing every economic system, we see that reliance on the market mechanism for determination of the overall level, composition, and distribution of income has steadily diminished over the years.

Responsibility for promoting the overall level of economic activity—"maximum employment, production, and purchasing power"—is ascribed to the federal government under Section 2 of the Employment Act of 1946. Hailed as the economist's Magna Charta at the time of its bipartisan passage, this legislation is the basis for presidential and congressional manipulation of federal taxes, expenditures, and the public debt, as well as for Federal Reserve Board control of the supply of money and credit in such a way as to assure that total spending in the economy (market sector plus government sector) is at the appropriate level to assure full employment without price inflation.[16]

The steady growth of government spending in recent decades is another indication of general loss of confidence in the price system to meet our goals.[17] Dissatisfaction with the composition of the nation's output of goods and services (i.e., insufficient output of educational services) is what led to enactment of the National Defense Education Act of 1958, the Vocational Education Act of 1963, the Higher Education Act of 1965, and the whole spate of federal-aid-to-education legislation of the sixties. Since choices expressed in the marketplace resulted in apparent underproduction in the education industry, an alternative to the market mechanism was sought for channeling more resources into education.[18]

Increasing influence on the pattern of income distribution has been exerted by government through Social Security legislation, the Manpower Development and Training Act, the Economic Opportunity Act, and other programs designed to raise low incomes and assure a greater measure of economic security either through direct transfer payments or enhanced employment opportunities.

Despite government's growing interest in direct income transfers, it is significant that in 1971 only a little over one-tenth of total personal income came from "transfer payments" such as Social Security insurance and public assistance, while seven-tenths came from "wage and salary disbursements and other labor income." The remaining two-tenths was accounted for by "personal interest income" and other sources of proprietors' and property income.[19] Payment for work remains by far the most important source of purchasing power for American consumers.

In concluding this discussion of the contemporary mixed economy of the United States, it is necessary to underscore our earlier reference to the role of technology in the economic process. As observed by the National Commission on Technology, Automation, and Economic Progress, "If there is one predominant factor underlying current social change, it is surely the advancement of technology . . . new methods of production, new designs of products and services, and new products and new services."[20] There is no doubt that technology has been the strategic factor in generating our trillion-dollar GNP, triggering the manpower revolution, and transforming the economic enterprise of the United States into the dynamic and sometimes frenetic mixed economy we know today. Yet little attention is given in our schools and colleges to a study of the processes and consequences of technological change.[21] Whether this gap will be filled by existing disciplines is uncertain, but the socioeconomic impact of technology clearly qualifies for inclusion as an essential component of the world of economics and work.

NEW DIRECTIONS IN THE ECONOMICS OF WORK

The decade of the sixties was a watershed in what might generally be termed the economics of work.[22] Simultaneous but separate developments in theory and policy heightened interest in human resources and raised new questions for research and public policy.

Investment in Human Capital

Theoretical developments centered around the concept of human capital,[23] a term which refers to acquired capabilities of man that can be used in his capacity as a factor of production. Schooling, on-the-job training, medical care, expenditures on internal migration, and vocational counseling are examples of investments in human capital that enhance the quality of human resources. Successful investments result in the accumulation of "stocks" of human capital (such as knowledge, skills, good health, geographic mobility, and career motivation) embodied in people who function as human resources. Such investments can be expected to improve employability, productivity, and earnings.

Empirical research has generated a substantial amount of evidence in support of these expectations. Statistics on the incidence of poverty, for example, show a consistent negative correlation between years of school completed and percent of the population below the official low-income level.[24] Sample surveys similarly indicate lower unemployment rates for persons with higher educational attainment,[25] and studies of "the cash value of education" show that persons with more schooling, as a group, earn higher incomes.[26] Rates of return on investments in education are seen to compare favorably with returns on investments in conventional (physical, nonhuman) capital.[27] Estimates of the contributions to economic growth made by various factors in recent decades assign approximately one and one-half times as much credit to the increased educational attainment of the labor force as is given to the accumulation of new plant, equipment, and other conventional capital.[28] Despite their methodological shortcomings, these studies have apparently convinced many economists, educators, and the general public that education—one form of investment in human capital—does indeed pay off for both the individual and society. Research on the returns for geographic mobility, medical care, manpower training, and other kinds of investment in human capital has attracted growing interest in recent years.[29]

Manpower Policy

The 1960s also witnessed the beginnings of a comprehensive national manpower policy aimed at developing workers' abilities, creating jobs, matching workers and jobs, and demonstrating sensitivity to what the U.S. Department of Labor has termed "the quality of employment."[30] At the *macroeconomic* level, manpower policy requires a full-employment, noninflationary level of aggregate demand. At the *microorganizational* level it requires particular job opportunities[31] where, when, and of the type that can be filled by available workers; it also requires career development paths and manpower market processes that provide maximum information on job vacancies and available workers, preclude discriminatory practices, and assure supportive services (such as child care, transportation, counseling) that enable people to find and hold jobs. At the *microindividual* level, manpower policy requires such investments in human resource development as career education (including work-world orientation, occupational exploration, and vocational education), work experience, vocational counseling, job information and placement, postplacement support (especially for disadvantaged workers), and career guidance.

The outcome of a successful manpower policy designed to meet the needs of all the people will be full employment with high productivity and a labor force made up of men and women who are employable, motivated to work, capable of finding and holding jobs, productive, earning an adequate income, and who derive a measure of satisfaction, enjoyment, and fulfillment from work itself.

ECONOMICS AND INDIVIDUAL CHOICE

Given the nature of economic enterprise in the contemporary United States, what choices do young people face (and older workers too) relative to participation in the world of work? In one sense, of course, technological progress and economic growth expand the range of choice and make us more free.[32] The decade of the seventies will bring new products, new industries, new occupations, new jobs, expanded educational opportunities, and a much broader range of career paths than were available to past generations.[33]

On the other hand, certain options are no longer open. The individual who approaches career planning according to the principle of rational-empirical decision making will find that his or her chances of success in the manpower market are greatly diminished in the fields of farming, mining, certain manufacturing industries, and low-productivity, less essential service industries. Entry jobs in blue-collar occupations are shrinking, and for workers without a functional education, some work experience, and job skills, the world of work will be a cold, hard one indeed. With the development of our sophisticated "skill economy" (in this postindustrial "human resource era"), men and women face the growing threat of unemployability and subemployability whereby their productivity, unless enhanced by substantial investments in human capital, is too low to justify employment, or employment at a socially acceptable wage. Avoidance of the harsh demands of the manpower market, through self-employment, is not a reasonable alternative for many.

Realistic career choice will demand that a sharp eye be kept on economic constraints and manpower trends, and that careful attention be paid to the costs and benefits of alternative means for achieving occupational goals. As workers, union members, managers, and citizens, there will also be choices relative to the quality of employment and the uses of our growing affluence. Traditionally the tradeoff has been viewed in terms of income versus leisure, but increased concern for the quality of life suggests that we may choose to modify the work environment and job practices, *even at the cost of reduced productivity,* in order to satisfy social, psychological, and physical needs of the individual worker, who, after all, should not have to be merely a means to an end—consumption or leisure—but is a sensitive, unfragmentable human being twenty-four hours a day, including time on the job.

The ultimate problems of choice will be value judgments—knowing the good—skillfully reconciling the sometimes conflicting activities of "making a living" and "knowing how to live."

If one accepts the notion that knowing what *is* (and how and why it is) can help in judging what *ought to be,* then it follows that a better understanding of the world of work, including the socioeconomic environment within which work takes place, can lead to better strategies for improving the quality of life.[34]

NOTES

1. Economists classify resources (defined as all things that can be used in production) into four groups: labor, land, capital, and enterprise. Labor has been defined above. Land is a synonym for "natural resources": anything existing in nature that can be used in production. Capital includes all man-made goods used in further production. Enterprise, or entrepreneurship, is a special kind of resource defined as the policy-making, risk-bearing, and profit-receiving function performed in a business firm. These are the familiar "factors of production"—inputs into the productive process and recipients of "factor income" —around which much of economic theory is built.

2. The white-collar worker employed as a technician in a manufacturing enterprise simultaneously helps produce goods, earns a salary, collaborates with a group of co-workers, and in varying degrees experiences satisfaction from performing tasks competently, creatively, and with a sense of personal usefulness and human fulfillment. It is not implied that this sort of arrangement is immutable. We may easily conceive of circumstances in the future when a sizeable proportion of our potential labor force will no longer be working for the purpose of earning an income, perhaps not even to help produce socially valuable goods and services, but "merely" to satisfy social and psychological needs and to acquire skills, competencies, and insights that contribute to self-actualization.

3. Growing citizen concern for such goals has influenced the development of economic science in recent decades and vastly increased its importance as a guide to public policy. Well in advance of "the new economics," Frank H. Knight, a distinguished past president of the American Economic Association, urged that unless economists are to make their living by providing pure entertainment or teaching individuals to take advantage of each other, economics must have some kind of relevance to social policy. *Risk, Uncertainty, and Profit* (Boston: Houghton Mifflin, 1921, reissue 1933), p. xxv.

4. Report of the National Task Force on Economic Education, *Economic Education in the Schools* (New York: Committee for Economic Development, September 1961), pp. 14f.

5. Robert L. Darcy and Phillip E. Powell, *Manpower and Economic Education* (Denver: Love Publishing Co., 1973), pp. 278f, 297–301.

6. Michael Scriven, "Values in the Curriculum," *Social Science Education Consortium Newsletter,* 2,1(1966):3.

7. Darcy and Powell, *op. cit.,* pp. 95–99.

8. In the more complex process of real economic life, firms sell their output not only to consumers but also to government (federal, state, and local) and to other firms (domestic and for export abroad).

9. "Every individual endeavors to employ his capital so that its produce may be

of greatest value. He generally neither intends to promote the public interest, nor knows how much he is promoting it. He intends only his own security, only his own gain. And he is in this led by an INVISIBLE HAND to promote an end which was no part of his intention. By pursuing his own interest he frequently promotes that of society more effectually than when he really intends to promote it." Adam Smith, *The Wealth of Nations* (1776), quoted in Paul A. Samuelson. *Economics,* 8th ed. (New York: McGraw-Hill, 1970), p. 37. Samuelson discusses (pp. 39, 609–11) the conditions under which this "invisible hand" hypothesis is and is not valid, depending on the degree of market competition, optimality of income distribution, accuracy of market prices in measuring full benefits and costs, and the extent to which the demands of people in the market place express what is truly consistent with their own well-being.

10. The sales figure of $464 billion should not be interpreted to mean that the 500 firms account for almost half our GNP. Aggregate business receipts, which include intermediate transactions, amount to more than double the GNP, which reflects only final sales. It is interesting, however, that receipts of the 500 largest industrial corporations greatly exceed combined receipts of all 10 million of the nation's farm and nonfarm unincorporated enterprises. See *Fortune,* LXXXIII, 5(1971):170–191; also see U.S. Department of Commerce, Bureau of the Census, *Statistical Abstract of the United States 1971* (Washington: U.S. Government Printing Office, 1971), p. 459.

11. John Kenneth Galbraith, *The New Industrial State* (Boston: Houghton Mifflin, 1967); Richard Caves, *American Industry: Structure, Conduct, Performance,* 3rd ed., paperbound (Englewood Cliffs, N.J.: Prentice-Hall, 1972); Adolf A. Berle, Jr., and Gardner C. Means, *The Modern Corporation and Private Property* (New York: Macmillan, 1934). In a widely quoted pamphlet entitled *Economic Power and the Free Society* (Santa Barbara, California: Center for the Study of Democratic Institutions, 1957), Berle reported (p. 14) that "about two-thirds of the economically productive assets of the United States, excluding agriculture, are owned by a group of not more than 500 corporations . . . (and) . . . within each of that 500 a still smaller group has the ultimate decisionmaking power." Describing this situation as "the highest concentration of economic power in recorded history," he went on to observe that "Since the United States carries on not quite half of the manufacturing production of the entire world today, these 500 groupings—each with its own little dominating pyramid within it—represent a concentration of power over economics which makes the medieval feudal system look like a Sunday School party." In *The New Industrial State,* Galbraith points out (p. 71) that not only have modern technology and the rise of the giant corporation blurred the decisionmaking function in business enterprise relative to the separation of ownership (by stockholders) and control (by management), but now the "guiding intelligence" function in many corporations is actually performed by a still different group, which he terms the "Technostructure."

12. This was true in 1963 for passenger cars, locomotives and parts, primary aluminum, electric lamps, cigarettes, household laundry equipment, typewriters, metal cans, soap and detergents, and tires and inner tubes, among other industries. See F. M. Scherer, *Industrial Market Structure and Economic Performance* (Chicago: Rand McNally & Co., 1970), p. 55. Scherer reports (p. 85) that "for all but a few industries, the degree of national market concentration was substantially in excess of what was needed merely to take advantage of production and physical distribution economies at the plant level."

13. Union membership grew from less than 3 million in 1933 to nearly 9 million

in 1939, then jumped to more than 14 million by the end of World War II. U.S. Department of Labor, Bureau of Labor Statistics, *Handbook of Labor Statistics* (Washington: U.S. Government Printing Office, 1971), p. 307; and Lloyd G. Reynolds, *Labor Economics and Labor Relations*, 5th ed. (Englewood Cliffs, N.J.: Prentice-Hall, 1970), pp. 343f.

14. The economic functions of government are discussed in Darcy and Powell, *op. cit.*, pp. 137ff. Data on government employment and spending for 1969 are from *Statistical Abstract of the United States 1971, op. cit.*, pp. 217, 399. "Incomes policy" refers to arrangements that will prevent money incomes in all forms—wages, profits, interest, dividends, rental payments—from increasing at rates that are inflationary.

15. Use of economic theory, statistics, and historical-institutional data to analyze the American economy follows the tradition of one of the great teachers of economics, the late Joseph A. Schumpeter. In his *History of Economic Analysis* (New York: Oxford University Press, 1954), he suggested (p. 12) that "What distinguishes the 'scientific' economist from all the other people who think, talk, and write about economic topics is a command of techniques that we class under three heads: history, statistics, and 'theory.'"

16. As indicated in our earlier discussion of basic questions facing the economic system, both aggregate employment and national product are determined by the rate of total spending in the market (subject to upper limits set by technology and the quantity and quality of available resources). Spending to purchase newly produced final goods and services is done by consumer households, business firms, units of government, and foreigners. The "principle of aggregate demand" is expressed in the equation $GNP = C + I + G + X_n$, which states that total spending for the Gross National Product is equal to consumer expenditures, investment spending, purchases of goods and services by the various levels of government, and net exports. If the *actual* level of aggregate demand is equal to the *potential* level of GNP, frictions and bottlenecks aside, the economy will achieve full utilization of its resources without inflation; and actual GNP will equal potential GNP. This simple "principle of aggregate demand" is the theoretical basis for the once shocking notion that it is possible for a depressed economy literally to spend its way to prosperity. An interesting discussion and graphic illustration of potential and actual GNP is presented in the *Economic Report of the President 1969* (Washington: U.S. Government Printing Office, 1969), pp. 61–67.

17. As a percentage of GNP, government expenditure rose from 10.0% in 1929 (three-fourths of which was accounted for by state and local government) to 31.1% in 1969 (with federal government accounting for two-thirds of the total). On a *per capita* basis, not adjusted for inflation, government spending rose from $95 in 1927 to $821 in the war year of 1944, fell to $380 in 1948, then began a steady climb to $1,647 in 1970. The nation's tax bill increased from $9.5 billion in 1927 to $108 billion in 1957, rising to $274 billion in 1970. Apart from national defense (which accounts for three-quarters of the federal government's purchases of goods and services), the chief functions absorbing government funds are education, highways, public welfare, health and hospitals, and natural resources. *Facts and Figures on Government Finance*, 16th Biennial Edition (New York: Tax Foundation, Inc., 1971), pp. 16, 18, 20, 30, 37.

18. Underinvestment in education might have resulted from insufficient purchasing power in the hands of individuals (or local and state educational agencies) desiring more education, or possibly from their unwillingness to incur private expenditures on a product whose benefits cannot be appropriated by the purchaser for his own exclusive use. In the latter case, where substantial

social benefits exist, it may pay society to subsidize production in order to bring the level of resource use up to a point where marginal social benefits equal marginal social costs. This illustrates the "principle of social effects," which asserts that costs or benefits associated with a particular economic activity (consumption or investment) sometimes spill over to third parties, or to society at large. For an accurate calculation of total costs and total benefits, it is necessary to add these social effects (externalities) to the private costs and benefits. Only then can a socially rational decision be made about the allocation of resources.

19. *Economic Report of the President 1972* (Washington: U.S. Government Printing Office, 1972), pp. 214f. Given the total amount of personal income and its classification by source, how is income distributed among the 60-odd million households in the nation? For the past thirty years, the data have changed very little. Families and individuals in the lowest 20 percent of the scale receive 5 percent of total income, while households in the highest quintile get more than eight times that amount (both before and after taxes). Herman P. Miller, *Rich Man Poor Man,* 2nd ed. (New York: Thomas Y. Crowell, 1971), pp. 16, 49.

20. National Commission on Technology, Automation, and Economic Progress, *Technology and the American Economy,* Vol. 1, February 1966 (Washington: U.S. Government Printing Office, 1966), p. xi.

21. For a discussion of technology in the context of a world-of-work economic education program for secondary school students, see Darcy and Powell, *op. cit.,* pp. 309–317, 113–116.

22. The term is used here to include, among other topics, human capital theory, the economics of education, labor force analysis, employment and wage theory, labor mobility, manpower policy, human resource development, and the quality of employment.

23. Theodore W. Schultz of the University of Chicago stimulated a great deal of professional interest with his presidential address, "Investment in Human Capital," delivered at the 1960 annual meeting of the American Economic Association. Subsequently the paper was published in *The American Economic Review,* LI(1961):1–17.

24. A March 1971 Current Population Survey by the Census Bureau disclosed a poverty rate of more than 35 percent for persons (fourteen years and over, both sexes, all races) with less than six years of schooling; an incidence of poverty of 12.5 percent for persons with one to three years of high school; 6.3 percent for high school graduates; and only 5.3 percent for persons with one year or more of college. U.S. Bureau of the Census, "Characteristics of the Low-Income Population, 1970," *Current Population Reports,* Series P–60, No. 81 (U.S. Government Printing Office, Washington, D.C., 1971), p. 51.

25. For young workers (eighteen to twenty-four years old), unemployment rates in March 1968 ranged from more than 10 percent for those with less than four years of high school to 7 percent for high school graduates, 4 percent for persons with one to three years of college, and 2 percent for college graduates. For workers in the twenty-five to fifty-four age group, unemployment rates were lower at all levels of educational attainment but still showed a consistent inverse relationship between years of schooling and unemployment. U.S. Department of Labor, Bureau of Labor Statistics, *Occupational Outlook Handbook,* 1970–71 edition (Washington, D.C.: U.S. Government Printing Office, 1970), p. 19. The seasonally adjusted unemployment rate for the civilian labor force as a whole in March 1968 was 3.6 percent. *Economic Report of the President 1969,* p. 253.

26. Mean annual income in 1968 for men aged twenty-five and over was $3,333

for those having less than eight years of school; $5,096 with eight years; $6,569 for one to three years of high school; $7,731 for high school graduates; $8,618 for men with one to three years of college; and $11,257 for those with four years or more of college. Based on 1966 dollars, expected lifetime earnings were estimated at $189,000 for men with less than eight years of schooling, $341,000 for high school graduates, and $508,000 for men with four years of college. Miller, *op. cit.,* pp. 166–94.

27. A widely quoted study by W. Lee Hansen ("Total and Private Rates of Return to Investment in Schooling," *Journal of Political Economy,* 71(1963): 128–140) indicated returns of 29.2 percent on investment in the eighth year of schooling, 13.7 percent on the twelfth year, and 15.6 percent on the completion of college. For a concise summary of methodology, findings, and bibliography, see Jon T. Innes, Paul B. Jacobson, and Roland J. Pellegrin, *The Economic Returns to Education* (Eugene: Center for Advanced Study of Educational Administration, University of Oregon, 1965). A more recent and comprehensive survey is provided in Martin O'Donoghue, *Economic Dimensions in Education* (Chicago: Aldine-Atherton, 1971).

28. According to estimates by Edward F. Denison, improvement in the quality of labor because of more education contributed 23 percent of the total growth of U.S. national product between 1929 and 1957, whereas increased capital input contributed only 15 percent. See *Sources of Economic Growth in the United States and the Alternatives Before Us,* Supplementary Paper No. 13 (New York: Committee for Economic Development, Jan. 1962), pp. 267f.

29. A valuable reference on human capital research is *The Journal of Human Resources,* an interdisciplinary quarterly emphasizing "the role of education and training . . . in enhancing productive skills, employment opportunities, and income," but also including articles on health, mobility, and other topics related to manpower. *The Journal of Human Resources,* I(1966):2.

30. The 1969 *Manpower Report of the President* (Washington: U.S. Government Printing Office, 1969) summarizes major developments in "An Active Manpower Policy—Its Genesis and Implementation" (pp. 1–17). The 1968 *Manpower Report of the President* (Washington: U.S. Government Printing Office, 1968) discusses the importance of understanding and evaluating "not only how well the economic system absorbs individuals into employment and meets their financial needs, but also . . . the adequacy with which it satisfies quite different kinds of needs—physical, psychological, and social" (pp. 47–58, "The Quality of Employment").

31. Increasingly these job opportunities may lie outside the "regular" productivity-oriented private and public sectors, perhaps through subsidized private employment or an expanded public service employment program that operates as a system of government-as-employer-of-last-resort. See Sar A. Levitan, Garth L. Mangum, and Ray Marshall, *Human Resources and Labor Markets* (New York: Harper & Row, 1972), pp. 356–359; and Garth L. Mangum, "Government as Employer of Last Resort," *Toward Freedom From Want,* Sar A. Levitan *et al.,* eds. (Madison: Industrial Relations Research Association, 1968), pp. 135–61.

32. In *The Recovery of Confidence* (New York: W. W. Norton, 1970), John W. Gardner quotes Edmund Burke (p. 5): "The effect of liberty to individuals is that they may do what they please. We ought to see what it will please them to do before we risk congratulations." Economist Moses Abramovitz acknowledged both the importance and the difficulty of choice by asserting that "The most important economic problem in any age is to know what we want, to define useful and worthy ends, and to balance our efforts among them in due proportion." Committee for Economic Development, *Problems*

of U.S. Economic Development, Vol. I (New York: Committee for Economic Development, 1958), p. 191.

33. By 1980 employment in the U.S. economy will approach 100 million. More than two-thirds of the labor force will be employed in the service-producing industries, with the remaining one-third working in manufacturing, construction, agriculture, and mining. Over half the labor force will be in white-collar occupations, one-third in blue-collar jobs, 13 percent in service occupations, and less than 3 percent in farm employment. "The U.S. Economy in 1980: A Preview of BLS Projections," *Monthly Labor Review,* 93,4(1970):3–34.

34. For a discussion of the relevance of economics to values and valuing, see Robert L. Darcy, "Economic Education, Human Values, and the Quality of Life," *Humanistic Frontiers in Education,* Roy P. Fairfield, ed. (Englewood Cliffs, N.J.: Prentice-Hall, 1971), pp. 102–11.

SUGGESTED READING

Economic Report of the President. Washington: U.S. Government Printing Office. Published annually in January. Annual report from the President to the Congress, as required by the Employment Act of 1946, together with the annual report of the President's Council of Economic Advisers. Review of the U.S. economy's recent performance, expectations for the future, and policies recommended to achieve maximum employment, production, and purchasing power. Statistical appendix includes more than 100 pages of current and historical data on national income, employment, prices, government finance, etc.

Galbraith, John Kenneth. *The New Industrial State.* New York: Houghton Mifflin, 1967. Stimulating and controversial treatise by a past president of the American Economic Association describing the transformation of the U.S. economy from a competitive enterprise system to the industrial system dominated by modern technology and the giant corporation.

Heilbroner, Robert L. *The Making of Economic Society,* 3rd ed. Englewood Cliffs, N.J.: Prentice-Hall, 1970. Nature and evolution of the economic process from theoretical and historical viewpoints. Readable and insightful analysis of the rise of the market society, evolution of "guided capitalism," and problems of the underdeveloped world.

Levitan, Sar S., Garth L. Mangum, and Ray Marshall. *Human Resources and Labor Markets.* New York: Harper & Row, 1972. A policy-oriented text that integrates economic theory, human resource development, and labor market analysis.

Manpower Report of the President. Washington: U.S. Government Printing Office. Published annually in the spring. Annual message from the President to the Congress on manpower issues, along with a report by the U.S. Department of Labor on manpower requirements, resources, utilization, and training. Statistical appendix includes more than 100 pages of current and historical data on the labor force, employment, unemployment, productivity, earnings, etc.

Miller, Herman P. *Rich Man Poor Man,* 2nd ed. New York: Thomas Y. Crowell, 1971. Income distribution in the United States, with special emphasis on problems of the poor. Authoritative analysis of employment, earnings, and the cash value of education by a top economic statistician in the U.S. Bureau of the Census.

Samuelson, Paul A. *Economics,* 9th ed. New York: McGraw-Hill, 1973. Widely used introductory college text by the world's first Nobel laureate in economics. Encyclopedic and authoritative.

Technology and the American Economy, Vol. 1. Report of the National Commission on Technology, Automation, and Economic Progress, February 1966. Washington: U.S. Government Printing Office, 1966. Analysis of the pace of technological change and its impact on employment, productivity, community development, and human needs. Conclusions and recommendations stress the need for public and private policies that will facilitate adjustment to change.

6 Social Change and Humanistic Confusion: Considerations for a Politics of Counseling

Donald A. Hansen
University of California, Berkeley

Through the past decade we have been told to the point of tedium that we are living in revolutionary times. Though weary of such claims, we must nevertheless recognize that a massive transformation is under way in America today, a transformation as profound as that surrounding the French revolution in the late eighteenth century.

The contemporary transformation is not born of the energies of the young Marxists, Maoists, and self-proclaimed revolutionaries, nor of the struggles of Blacks, Chicanos, and other aroused minorities. Their movements against modern injustice and despotism may help bring important reforms in our communities, and even to our systems of decision making and governance; but while their battles are being fought, other changes are taking place on such a wide scale and so deeply within our society that the "political revolutions" pale by comparison. Nor is the massive transformation originating in the grass roots; it is no "greening of America," no rebirth of society by a "new consciousness." Surely something important is happening in the ways we think, value, choose and act—but these changes, too, are less pervasive, less profound, less generative than the real "revolution" of our times.

For the massive transformation is being generated not in the desperate and privileged peripheries of our society, but in its centers—in business and industry, in government and international relations, in military organization, in the largest universities and research institutes, in the new organizations of information processing and control, and in other parts of the exploding knowledge industry. The transformation was born of cybernetics, out of a bureaucratic culture. It has been developing for over a half century, in the decline of early, individualistic capitalism and the rise of organizational capitalism, and many decades yet will pass before it is complete.

This transformation provides a context for this essay, but not its focus; rather, what follows will be directed toward themes that hover around one aspect of the transformation: changes in socially effective ideas about the nature of the individual and of society and of their relationship to one another—changes in what might be called "images of man." Indeed, the

For a less sketchy treatment of various themes in the first two sections of this essay, see Donald A. Hansen, *Consciousness, Conflict, and Society* and *Marx, Weber, and Mead: An Invitation to Social Theory* (both forthcoming). I am indebted to Lawrence H. Stewart, Vicky A. Johnson, Thomas Livingston, and Edwin L. Herr for their critical readings of an earlier draft of this essay.

themes will be even more narrow, focusing on those images of man and society that we know as "rational humanism."

The implications of these themes are, I believe, especially relevant to those who work within the traditions of guidance and counseling. For the ideals of these professions, more than most, remain rooted in the traditional images of rational humanism, images that appear to have grown irrelevant to the political and economic life of modern society. This essay will argue that the appearance of irrelevance is in part valid, but in part rests on a confusion of two contemporary forms of rational humanism that, for want of better terms, I have labeled "individualistic" and "functional." Always, it should be remembered, the discussion is meant not to be definitive, but interpretive and suggestive.

INSTITUTIONAL TRANSFORMATION AND DISCONTENT

If there could be a specific date of birth, a point at which the social transformation emerged from its organizational womb and into the institutions of the larger society, it would be about a quarter of a century ago, some time in the wake of World War II. It was then that the rapidly advancing social change of the twentieth century made a quantum leap. The war had aggrandized automation, which, in turn, injected the already accelerating specialization of modern times. As computers joined that automation, our industrial, political, and social lives felt the impact of cybernation—automated systems that could correct their own errors, even detect them before they occurred, and discover possibilities unrecognized by the men who fed them.

Today cybernetic industrialism is bringing profound changes in economic and political leadership, new arrangements of our centers of power and influence, new forms of our supporting institutions, and even of our peripheral institutions and of our private lives. In this era of cybernation—often called "postindustrialism" or the "postmodern society"—new priorities are emerging in the centers of our society, heralding the end of traditional capitalism and altering the established forms of power, economics, and status.

Transformation and Functional Rationality

The transformation is not without precedent, even in the short history of the modern world. In feudal societies of the seventeenth century power, economy, and status were organized around the central concept of land. But with the growth of industry and trade through the eighteenth and early nineteenth centuries, the primacy of land gave way to capital. To be sure, property remained important in the lives of men and was still useful to success in economics and politics, but it was no longer the most critical thing. Now surplus monies, not real property, became the most scarce necessity, the most productive, and the most coveted. With the transition, the centers of power shifted, new routes to success opened, new breeds of men gained honor and influence. Still old patterns persisted; the landed aristocracy and nobility did not vanish but simply gave way, virtually moving from the centers of society to privileged positions on the peripheries, where they retained their old ways and appearances of life, though not their power.[1]

As property gave way to capital as the central value in Western societies of the eighteenth and early nineteenth centuries, so today capital appears to be giving way to functional coordination and control, planning and organization. Both investable funds and property remain important, but evermore the new "capital," the scarce and critical element of societal success, is information and expertise.

The movement towards a cybernetic, rational society may be seen in the organization in this century. Functional rationality—the evaluation of each task and role for its contribution to the functioning of the larger group or organization—was first applied broadly at the "lowest" levels of organization, to the technical activities that directly contributed to the organization's goals: the roles of station agents of a railway, the production lines of a factory, the teachers of a school. As functional rationality was applied to such jobs, a "technology of technology" developed, most clearly seen in the production lines pioneered by Henry Ford and vividly satirized by Charlie Chaplin in *Modern Times.*

In the wake of World War I, Ford's system worked out brilliantly, but in short order new troubles developed. The new technologies required new levels of supervision and coordination: new men of "middle management," whose jobs, in turn, required coordination and technical efficiency. Thus, the "technology of technology" was followed by the application of functional rationality to management, by the rise of a "technology of management"— the "scientific" management of business, governmental, and educational administration. The new kind of rational management was pioneered in the thirties by General Motors and has dominated organizational thinking for the past half century. Once exciting in its possibilities, it is today commonplace and familiar, dull even to those who most fully believe in it.[2]

Today, however, we are moving into something new and strange, exciting and worrisome: The application of functional rationality to the "institutional representatives" of the organization, to the networks of executives, boards of directors, and others whose primary jobs concern the relations of their organizations to other organizations and other parts of society. Today a "technology of institutions" is emerging. Not only are technical and managerial jobs planned, but now, evermore, the operations of our central, most important institutions are being rationally planned and coordinated.

In this mutation at the very centers of society we are coming to recognize more fully the power of symbols and communication. Not long ago techniques fairly well determined the symbols that men used to plan their organizations; if a technique worked, it was retained and written into the organizational plan or institutional symbol. Today, however, the relation is being reversed: in the technology of institutions the plans are the thing; the technologies, the organizations, even the institutions are manipulated to meet the symbolized requirements of an anticipated future.

We are, in short, rapidly moving toward a "planned" society, perhaps even toward the "intentional society" that Harvey Wheeler[3] calls for. As we move in this direction, the lines that have divided the centers of society from one another—government, industry, military, education—are blurring.

Rather than a separation of state and economy, we are moving to a corporate state, marked by a scale of planning that is already influencing the quality of life throughout society.

With the change in our institutions comes changes in access to the centers of power and new leadership. As the twenties and thirties saw the rise of the managerial elite, now new elites are emerging to serve and challenge managerial leadership, diploma elites of specialized professionals whose scientific and technological expertise is indispensable in the control and direction of a cybernetic society.

Some believe that the new experts will steadily gain control over the new society. A few see the ascendance of the experts as man's hope; others see it as the coming of a new decadence.[4] One suspects, however, that both the fears and hopes are unfounded, for, as Max Weber[5] suggested long ago, the indispensable technician is rewarded by an organization, but he is not given its control. Almost certainly, experts are becoming a new elite, but I suspect they will remain an elite in service of tomorrow's Princes—those new leaders who master the "technology of institutions" much as Alfred Sloan and his successors in the management of General Motors have mastered the "technology of organizations" for the past three decades. The new men of power will be those who are able to manage and manipulate information and planning in ways that effectively control massive organizations and massive collectivities of persons in the new corporate state.[6]

Perhaps I am wrong about the nature of the transformation taking place today, but clearly something is decaying in the fields of American life that even a few decades ago made up the stable centers of our society. It is also clear that something is emerging, the new centers are developing to vie with the old and with one another for dominance. These new centers seem to evermore intertwine with one another in intricacies of planning and coordination, intricacies made possible and necessary by modern networks of communication and information storage, retrieval, and transmission.

In this process of transformation we run the enormous risk of being so mesmerized by the challenges of new technologies that we fail to see the new forms of life that are emerging, even while we scramble in frantic efforts to save the institutions that are decaying. Of all the indications that we are succumbing to these risks, none is more compelling than our tendency to ignore the social messages in contemporary discontent and collective violence. Once again, we might gain insight into our own times by considering the earlier transformation from feudalism to capitalism.

Transformation and Status Discontent

The eighteenth century transformation was far from abrupt; it had begun over a century earlier, and its effects were still emerging a century later. It was also far from smooth. The French revolution was only the most dramatic eruption of the pervasive discontent and confusion that attended the transition. Throughout Europe, and even in America, the developing systems brought widespread insecurity and discontent. Old men of power burned with resentment as they gave way to the challenges to their "rightful authority" and privilege. For most of the poor and powerless, the great

majority of whom had little to lose with the decline of feudalism, the transformation was catastrophic. Even if under feudalism they were little better
than slaves, still they were secure, economically and socially. Industrial
capitalism freed them from their slavery, but for most it was a cruel freedom,
ever threatening hunger, offering little assurance in the present and little
hope for the future. So, too, were businessmen thrust into insecurity. Free
enterprise meant a chance at great wealth, but it also meant a great chance
at failure. Discontent mounted rapidly in all parts of society, and with it
came the outbursts of collective violence that are so familiar a part of nineteenth-century history in Europe and America.

This relationship between violence and social change is often neglected,
even by persons who live within changing and violent times. In our century
collective violence is usually seen as irrational, even as "un-American." Thus
many are shocked at bank burnings, at the waves of rioting that sweep
through the urban ghettos, at the brash speeches of young activists, at the
"trashings" and "take-overs" and the battles between students and police.
But underlying this shock, as Michael Wallace[7] puts it, is an "historical
amnesia": we have for so long believed in the Horatio Alger myth—that
any man can rise from rags to riches—that only the most controlled and
tasteful conflict seems justified.

It is true that much collective violence is ill-conceived, offering little
chance of success to its authors. Some is certainly little more than a howl,
a violent exasperation, an acting out of deep despair. Yet even this violence
may not be so irrational as it seems, for it may spring from a desperate
discontent that can find no effective voice in the established and changing
society. Collective violence seems often to be a response to the demands and
deprivations that develop as new forms of society replace older ones.
Indeed, the history of modern western societies shows undulating fevers of
collective violence at those times when political and economic structures
are in flux, when old forms of organization show signs of weakness or
inadequacy, when new kinds of men gain influence and wealth but are
denied power, when others are displaced or held in a disadvantage grown
obvious.[8] This perspective on change and discontent suggests that the
violence and confusions in the second half of the twentieth century are but
contemporary examples of historically common reactions to the breakdown
of old forms of power, economics, and status.

Nor are radical youth the only ones who seem to struggle for a better
life in a changing society. Discontent with one's roles and opportunities
may arise among those who have been underprivileged, generating the
"revolutionary" and "reforming" violence that is often urged by those who
rally the oppressed, especially the Blacks, Chicanos, Indians, and Orientals,
but also women, gays, and even the elderly.

Discontent and violence may also be "reactionary" in its thrust, arising
from those who see their privileges, real or imagined, vanishing—expressed
in the demands of small business persons and of men and women in blue-
collar and small town communities for a return to old ways and a stop to
the frantic confusions of both big government and reform movements.

"Revolutionary" and "reactionary" violence are familiar to most who observe the social landscape today, but a third type of discontent and violence

often escapes unrecognized. Discontent may also arise among those who have been and continue to be privileged, but who are threatened by the actions and words of those who oppose the way things are currently going. This "status-maintaining violence" is often unrecognized because the discontent is so widespread and familiar in all but the most desperate subcultures. Yet there is another reason as well: status-maintaining violence usually appears as a legitimate effort to maintain law and order and to safeguard society.

This perspective on change and violence helps us to understand not only the discontent of youth and minorities, but also the violent response it so often elicits from those in the "establishment." Today radical youth tend to express a reforming discontent, while adults tend to counter with status-maintaining discontent and, in lesser numbers, with reactionary discontent. In this clash discontent is deepened on all sides: established ways of doing things are called into question and fail to work; old practices lose their potence; the authority of one person over another is challenged; the right to dissent is attacked; stances that differ from one's own are mocked, rejected, and ignored. The crisis of legitimacy that seems to threaten men and women in times of massive transformations lies in the failure of society's conflict-resolving institutions and the striking evidence that old forms of social organizations are decaying. The evidence is so striking that we usually see only its surface appearance and conclude that the discontented are simply selfish, spoiled, or undersocialized.

If we look beneath those surfaces, however, we see that the violence and discontent of recent years point to far greater depths of social crisis in the changing worlds that surround and infuse contemporary counseling.

Transformation and Cultural Discontent

It may be that most radical movements involve a desire for reform that will bring their supporters better positions in their society. Such motivation is clearly present in their attacks against constraints that the dissidents feel weigh unfairly on themselves and others, but such observations should not lure us to conclude that rebellious youths are simply acting out their frustrations or challenging the organizations of their society in the hope that they will win a more fortunate status. This perspective is, at best, only a partial explanation.

Something else is also involved in youthful discontent, something akin to the utopian dreams of the Wobblies and other idealistic labor movements in the nineteenth and early twentieth centuries. Whatever other themes might be discovered in the dissent of recent years, it is clear that more than a few among the young rebel not simply because they lack privilege within the emerging system, but that in some ways they also seek a livable alternative to that system, an alternative in which they and others will be able to live with more human meaning. What we are witnessing is not only a transformation of the social order, but a breakdown of the social bond, an erosion of the old myths and images of man that have for generations given coherence to human life and made the structures and processes of the social order seem reasonable. Today's discontent points not only to organizational and to institutional mutations of our society; its indictment goes deeper, into the culture of our society, into the assumptions that we make about the nature of man, his relation to his communities, and his relation to the economics and politics of his society. In the depths of that discontent lie clues to the confusions of contemporary counseling and guidance.

CULTURAL DISCONTENT AND THE CRISIS OF HUMANISM

The contemporary spectrum of discontent is suggested in the art and literature that flowered between the two World Wars, most strikingly in the works of the Cubists, the New York abstractionists and the "beat" writers. From their vantage point on the political peripheries of society, these artists perceived the early signs of the decline of individualistic capitalism and the rise of organizational technology and planning. By the fifties, when the spectrum first became visible in the everyday lives of the middle class, the messages of change had grown lusty and confusing. Not surprisingly, it was most often youth who were most attuned to these messages, and who expressed their confusion and discontent most dramatically.

The Spectrum of Discontent

Most of the generation of the fifties, born in the years of the Depression and maturing in fermenting abundance, saw hope and high promise in the new signs of leisure and in other possibilities of their society. But for a few, including those who were to be labeled as "beatniks," the demands of industry, commerce, government, and other modern organizations were seen as debasing and demeaning, and the life of the consuming middle class seen as debilitating and immoral. In their eyes the illusions of capitalism and liberalism had shattered, revealing the exploitation and emptiness of modern life.

The "beat generation" sent up a howl of protest, a harsh condemnation of their society and of themselves. For many perceptive poets and writers the howl was something akin to the infant's inarticulate cry; some looked to Marx and saw the roots of their discontent in inequality; others read more closely and saw the roots spreading down into the ways industrial society is organized, into the roles men and women are forced to accept. A few looked even deeper, following Camus, Sartre, and other existentialists in recognizing a poverty of culture, an emptiness of belief and values, a societal confusion about the very meaning of human existence. There was a validity in all these perceptions and expressions, yet throughout this spectrum of organizational, institutional, and cultural discontent there was little hope, little vision. It was the discontent of anticulture, negative and profound.

Like the labor unions in earlier decades, the beats saw problems in the way society was organized and cried out for an end to the injustices and the inequities. But the howl of the beats also spoke of things far beyond *organizational* problems; they saw a need for institutional change. The problems of American society could not be solved simply by rearranging the positions of people in the existing system. To be sure, rearrangement was necessary and organizational problems were involved, but those problems demanded *institutional* solutions. The entire system had to be changed, for it was mutilating modern man. They embraced the rebellious sociology of C. Wright Mills, condemning the self-serving purposes of the "power elite," the blindness of bureaucracy, the military-industrial-governmental complex, the inhumanness of technology. They were antiwar, antiorganization, anticonsumption, and antibusiness. Nor did their rejection stop at institutional dissent, for the beats saw that the problems of American society were also *cultural:* men were enslaved to this wayward system, not only by false religions and political ideologies, but also by other fundamental values. Thus the beats decried the normative view of work, property, and propriety.

The argument in the last paragraph is so important to those who try to understand contemporary discontent that it bears repeating, though in slightly different form. In the howl of the beats, three waves of discontent can be heard.

1. An indignation focused in the question "Who does what?" This is a discontent with the organizational structures of society and the roles it allocates. Why do some people live well, others in poverty? Why do some work hard for nothing, while others reap the rewards?

2. A rejection focused in the question "What is done?" This is a discontent with the institutions of society, not only with their immediate effects, but with their latent and long-range consequences. Why have the government, the military, and industry taken such power in contemporary society? Why do we follow the dictates of technology, ever expanding our production and consumption, making human lives secondary to economic growth?

3. A frustrating anxiety, focused in the question "Why is all this done?" This is a cultural discontent, a concern over the meanings, values, and goals of society; a rejection not only of the institutional structures and organizational relations, but of the entire social fabric. Even the most basic and honored values and beliefs are questioned and found wanting.

The beats' condemnation of their society seemed to resonate in a hollowness of their parent culture. But they found no vision of a better world, and no purpose, no inspiration, no unifying mission, no believable and workable image of man and society. Within a few years their energies gave way to retreat, but the spectrum of discontent that some among them had struggled to articulate was to gain in coherence and energy through the following decade, as the disenchantment with modern society heightened to a radical attack.

It is difficult for many of us to find anything other than nihilism and irrationality in the words and actions of recent radicalism. For radicals often justify their actions in Marxist and other ideological terms that seem meaningless, even traitorous, in our political arenas. Yet, ironically, it seems that many, even the majority, of the youthful white activists in the sixties and early seventies rebelled in the name of the ideals of their elders, the humanistic ideals that underlay the fundamental images of liberal democracy. In the light of those ideals the activists seemed to see something profoundly wrong in their society, they seemed to feel violated in their sense of justice and humanity. If this sense of violation was not the mainspring of their discontent, it became the justification and inspiration of their dissent.

It is more than instructive to at least briefly look at our society through their eyes, or through a "prototypical" radical lens. Just as we can now see that much in the beat movement of the fifties was not simply deviant but was a cogent expression of their society's troubles, it is possible that through contemporary radicalism we may discover fundamental problems in the commonsense "truths" of our times. It is this that makes contemporary radicalism so important to contemporary society, for whatever the inadequacies of the radicals' own images of man and society, from their unusual perspective it is possible that they can discover telling flaws in the social fabric and suggest possibilities otherwise undreamed.

This is not to say that the radical, or the less political communitarian, speaks only truth and points the way to certain improvement. Nor is it to say that the messages of discontent offered by other groups—of blacks, of Third World movements, of blue-collar workers, of small businesspersons and corporation executives, of women, of gays, and of the elderly—are not also revealing. Nor is it to say that those who voice satisfaction and hope should be neglected. All of these messages can help us to understand our times and to recognize possibilities that might otherwise go unnoticed. But it is the radical whose words are most easily ignored and whose message is most easily lost.

Today's radicalism is different from that of earlier decades in twentieth-century America, for the recent radicals have virtually redefined politics. To them it is not simply the business of taxes, tariffs, and treaties—the "organizational" and "institutional" concerns of western government for centuries.[9] The radicals have restated the messages of the beats in political terms, thus bringing the substance of American culture to political debate.

If in their quest they have failed to find a workable image of man and society, they have found at least one touchstone, the conviction that politics are useless unless they improve the quality of human life. Thus they rest their hopes on a humanistic legacy that has been part of the political images of man through the history of our nation, a legacy that took form in the uncertainties and discontent that came with the decline of feudalism. But to today's radical, that legacy of rational humanism has become a cover for repression and exploitation.

The Rise of Rational Humanism

The roots of liberal humanism are deeply imbedded in eighteenth-century discontent. With the growth of commerce, cities grew rapidly in size and vibrancy, bringing changes in the ways people related to one another. In the ambiance of the new cities human satisfactions could no longer be found in the passive pleasures that feudalism had offered. The meanings of kinship and community were changing, and old meanings and ways of life that had provided coherence were vanishing. More fluid, more open, and more diverse ways of living were emerging. With greater freedom to express themselves, men and women discovered exciting possibilities, opportunities unimagined by their parents and grandparents; but with those possibilities they also discovered the uncertainty and terror of a newly found freedom.

We have earlier seen how this instability contributed to violence, as men and women struggled to win or maintain satisfying positions in the new society. But the discontent also found another important kind of expression: a search for new images of man and society that might lend coherence to the disturbed times. The old images that their parents had simply assumed as the truths of everyday life no longer seemed adequate. For centuries men had accepted the idea that God was the author of human institutions and of the king's authority. As the old social order crumbled, the poverty of images of a social order authored by God and ruled in his name became painfully clear. New images of man and society slowly began to take form. They centered on a revolutionary idea, the idea that man is rational and that human rationality is the basis of society and of authority. This meant that institutions were not to be seen as God-given and unchangeable but as created by men and therefore to be changed by men.

Today this rational humanism is so deeply embedded in our traditions of thought that it seems commonsensical, simply a "truth" of human progress. The basic beliefs in this image of man and society are familiar: that individual personality is the paramount value in human society; that only the power of reason can secure and protect this and other humanistic values; that human freedom is absolutely essential, for without it, there can be no individual growth, no exercise of reason, no justification for society; that policies are as good or bad as their effects on human beings; that organizations are to be judged according to their effects on the individuals they serve and according to the qualities of human meaning they encourage and allow; that political and social institutions are made by men and hence can be perfected by men. In short, man is the measure of all things, and reason is his hope.

In the context of the politics and traditions of thought in the eighteenth century, the new images of rational humanism were compelling advances in man's awareness of himself and his society. Still, new traditions build from the old, and the values of feudalism infused the new images of humanistic rationality. As they did, the classic images of freedom, equality, and brotherhood somehow became entangled with the unquestioned value of "private property." From this tangle of concepts, a myth emerged that continues to confuse us even today—an image of "economic man."

In the political philosophy of the enlightenment the idea of property became a key to social order. Rousseau believed the social order of free men can rest only on a "general will" that emerges as each individual acts in ways that will best serve the entire community. But a man will do this only if he recognizes that his "rights" are contingent on their acceptance by others; each man supports the rights of others so that others will support his.

As George Herbert Mead[10] pointed out a half century ago, this leads to an interesting conclusion: to have a social order of free men, all men must be *equal*, so Rousseau's "reciprocity of rights" is possible only when there is equality of men, and, as feudal traditions held, the most fundamental equality of all is found in the equal rights of property. Unless men respect the rights of others to hold property, they will fall into a Hobbesian war of all against all, and man's hopes of developing a society of freedom and brotherhood will be lost. Thus, in this image, freedom and equality are impossible without the concept of private property.

There is, then, a tension between freedom and equality, for if there were total freedom for everyone, equality would be impossible. Thus emerges a concept of "equality of freedom": if there is to be equality for all, freedom must be rationed. But who should do the rationing? To answer that question the concept of "liberal democracy" arises: if we are to be equally free, we must be equal in decision making about how to ration freedom and equality and about all other political matters. Hence, the liberal image of democracy —of a government resting on consent by a free and equal people—has become firmly interlinked in our political traditions with the idea of private property. If we fail to uphold private property, our traditions tell us, we lose all hopes of democracy, equality, liberty, and brotherhood.

Rational Humanism and Free Enterprise

In the nineteenth century liberal humanism intersected with the idea of "laissez faire" economics, affirming free enterprise as the route to human progress. From the conflict of individual interests would come social harmony, not only bringing economic growth but also serving the needs and even desires of the great majority. In business and commerce the will of the people would be expressed through their market behavior, meaning that economics must be free from governmental and other interference. The state and the economy had to be kept separate or chaos would result.[11]

The idea endured through the nineteenth century, though not exactly in its original form. The sanctity of free enterprise—still based, in theory and in politics, on private property—became moderated into a social Darwinism. Now it was argued that in the economic world there was a "survival of the fittest," that human progress required the freedom to compete naturally, that inequality is inevitable and therefore good. Success testifies to ability, and the whole system will work only if the lure of success, wealth, privilege, and power encourages the able to compete and triumph.

The attitude remains popular today, especially among those in corporation management. Ironically, it rests in a fundamental Marxian image of man, although where Marx saw in it reason for fiery anger, men of management find optimistic satisfaction. Inequality may be unpleasant for some, but all benefit from the necessary leadership of the able. If this elitism makes one uncomfortable, he can ignore it, pleading that there is no real elitism as long as there is an equality of opportunity. Since all have an equal chance to success, each person should be left alone to make his or her own life.

From this perspective develops one of the most compelling arguments of industrial leaders against government intervention in the affairs of private corporations. Yet in today's society the only viable institutions that might offer the means for preserving freedom are those of industry, of government, and of the military. Others, especially the unions and the mass media, but also the political parties, universities, and other centers of research and development, are influential; but it is the industrial, military, and governmental centers that are crucial. They offer the real alternatives and they must be kept separate.

But the separation of government and industry has long ceased. Indeed, the separation of state and economy was a modern invention, tailored to the emergence of industrial capitalism in the late eighteenth and nineteenth centuries. It freed business from governmental constraints in a way never seen before in history, and as it did, Western societies reorganized around "free enterprise." Ironically, however, almost as soon as free enterprise was invented, it began to disappear. Especially in America—where mercantilism, an older form of economy carefully controlled by government, lasted well into the nineteenth century—the idea of free enterprise was barely established when businessmen began to capitalize on their new freedom by setting up monopolies, trusts, and other methods of controlling market prices. Thus "free enterprise" quickly became "unfree," though now it was the businessman, rather than the government, who managed the controls.

Despite decades of growing governmental involvement in the economy, the belief in the separation of state and government today remains widespread in America. So, too, does its basic justification that only with such separation can there be the free enterprise necessary to a healthy economy. To the radical, however, what remains of the argument is mostly myth, and that myth is dangerous and destructive. It supports corporations in their resistance to price controls and labor arbitration. It justifies the failure of "private" industry to consider their "public" responsibility. It blinds well-meaning men to the political realities of their times.

Rational Humanism and Images of Democracy

In the nineteenth century liberal humanism—again influenced by social Darwinism—encouraged a sort of "town meeting" concept of democracy. The "wisdom of the people" will emerge from the competition of ideas, and as long as men are free to speak their minds, the best ideas will survive. The idea seemed to work in the early nineteenth century, but as society, politics, and economics grew even more complex and dynamic, the hypothesis seemed to be in trouble. World War I pushed home the message that rational men could be manipulated by propaganda and passions of nationalism, and it was brutally clear that the government was willing to do so. Where, then, is the wisdom of the people?

The "town meeting" concept faded through the twentieth century, yet the basic political images persisted. Even among liberals this humanism today is popularly expressed in a vague image of an ideal democracy that is essentially equalitarian, an image of society in which the power to make rules is exercised by all for the good of all, with only occasional and limited reforms needed to keep the balance stable. Today few Americans would deny that the image remains more an ideal than a reality, but many, even most, would argue that the United States has come closer to the ideal than other societies, and, despite occasional setbacks, it is ever coming nearer.

To the radical, however, that image is also myth. It is not so much the basic values of classic humanism that are questioned as it is the uses to which those values have been put, and especially the social injustices that they have helped to uphold. In the twentieth century the ideals have been used even by liberals to support the existing and emerging institutions of our bureaucratic centers—the industrial, commercial, governmental, military, educational, and scientific centers. The institutions of a corporate economy themselves have become the real values for which they work. Indeed, so deep and so blind is the faith in humanistic ideals that those who act in their name fail to see the reality of their lives, the reality that those institutions are worlds apart from the ideals of liberal humanism—for the institutions of our bureaucratic centers stress the primary importance not of the individual but of the organization itself. In the face of evidence that the classic image of democracy is unworkable, a revised version of democracy emerged, presenting the view that the best possible solution for the greatest number of people will result from a "pluralism" of competing interest groups.

Even though each organization grows oligarchic, their competition with one another creates a condition of freedom for the average citizen, a variety of choices—choices of political representatives, of commodities, even of ways of life. Most importantly, the competition gives the average man a political voice. Given a number of autonomous centers of power—of independent groups of men of power and influence—elites may often seek the support of the people as they struggle against one another. The result may not be democracy, but it is a safeguard against arbitrary exploitation.

Urged today by many liberals as well as conservatives, this "rugged pluralism" assumes that the centers of society are effectively independent of one another. Not only political parties compete with one another, but so, too, does one industry compete with another and one business with another; unions compete with corporations, the government competes with and constrains industries and the military, and universities work independently to influence other parts of the system. Thus, the hope of democracy and freedom is found as individuals align themselves with organizations, especially those at the centers of our society, and work to influence them.

To the radical, this liberal argument is blind: True humanistic pluralism is based on "grass roots" coalitions of individuals who have joined in a common struggle for their own individual ends. If large and powerful organizations can carry the struggle, all the better, but to do so an organization must be truly responsive to its own membership and independent from its opponents. In our corporate world, the radical asks, what groups can effectively compete? The central organizations in our society are far from independent of one another, far from responsive to their own members. Today's liberal pluralism is therefore based on an assumption that is a myth, and so the liberals who urge "pluralism" help destroy the possibilities of the democracy they believe they are supporting. Through the nineteenth and twentieth centuries, and dramatically in the past few decades, the social, political, and economic structures of American society have changed strikingly, altering the relationship of private property to social order and revealing how the traditional beliefs of today's liberals contradict the humanistic ideals on which they are supposedly based.

This is the charge of radicals against "liberal humanism": that those who hold rigidly to images of rational man and to a humanism that is grafted to an unbending belief in the sanctity of private property have gone blind, unaware of the political, economic, and social world in which they live, and insensitive to its outrages, its injustices, and the dangerous paths it is following. Their humanistic ideals remain inspiring, and the society is rich with potentials for moving towards them, but the most important of these potentials will not be won as long as they remain indifferent to the conditions in which they and other human beings live.

It is not necessary to endorse any of the radicals' alternatives to ask whether their criticism adds anything useful to our understanding of our times, whether anything in their charges might help us to redirect our efforts. Obviously, I believe that contemporary radical criticism does offer much that is valid and suggestive—that, above all, it has suggested dramatically the confusion and inadequacy of contemporary humanistic images of man, society, and change.

Perhaps not surprisingly, the radical critique often goes too far but never far enough. It goes too far when, armed with evidence and argument that the political images of liberal humanism are inadequate to our times, it encourages the dismissal not only of liberal humanism, but of all rational humanism; it fails to go far enough when, as the rest of our society, it ignores a basic confusion that has grown in our images of rational humanism.

Technology and Humanistic Confusion

As the humanistic ideals of brotherhood, equality, and freedom moved through the thought of the past century and a half linked to faith in rationality, they underwent an intriguing mutation and gave birth to the new belief that in America today the humanistic ideals have become a reality for most and are quickly becoming reality for all through the greatest accomplishments of man's rationality: science and technology. As faith in the humanistic powers of science and technology grew, new confusions crept into humanistic images of the individual and society, confusions that have plagued counseling and guidance, and American society in general, through the decades of the twentieth century.

With each decade science and technology came to be seen increasingly as man's greatest hope. They would give man the power to bring order to his own world; poverty and hunger would be ended, natural disaster and man's wars would be controlled; and in new contexts of abundance and security, iron hard guarantees of justice and humanity would be forged. With freedom and reason scarcity would be conquered, and then brotherhood would flower, as men of good will created a society of democracy and equality.

The image is inspiring, but by the middle of the twentieth century, and then increasingly in the following years, it came under attack. Somehow, doubters charged, the image had failed to materialize. Reason was to be the key to the new humanism, science and technology the tools, but it seemed that when they were employed by men, rationality grew irrational. For a century and a half industrial democracies had operated in the name of rationality, science, and technology, but as they did humanistic goals seemed to recede even farther into the distance. Science and technology had made wars more barbarous, and World War II made it brutally clear that man's new abilities to create large-scale, rational organizations could be turned to inhuman purposes, even to the systematic extermination of millions of men, women, and children on the grounds that they were "racially inferior."

Again liberal humanism seemed to point in the wrong directions, or even nowhere at all. Our humanistic traditions told us that in a free market of ideas truth emerges, and this came to mean that science and technology must be "free and private." Yet modern history showed free and private science generating monopolies of laboratories and even opinions; it also showed that science can thrive under totalitarianism.

In the fifties new doubts grew about the human costs of pursuing full production and the relentless application of new technologies. In the sixties and seventies these were joined by fears that science, technology, and the habits of consumption and waste they nurtured within our economy were making the world unsuitable for human satisfaction, even for human life. Somehow human reason seemed to work on everything except man; as the world grew more rational, human life grew less humanistic and more confusing.

Yet many continued to accept the old vision of rational humanism. The convinced insisted that the rationality of science and technology had not yet been given a full chance. If science and technology brought new problems, the problems could be solved by more technology and research; if the organizations that had grown around the industries of a technological society were imperfect, they could be improved by more organization; if the products of technology were threatening our ecology, then ecology could be saved by new products of technology. In such arguments rational humanism had been transformed. Once it had offered an image of humanity perfectable by reason, but somewhere along the line, the liberal utopia had become a conservative ideology. Now it seemed that human reason was to be used not for the perfection of the existing order but for its protection, not to improve society to better meet the needs of the individual but to mold the individual to fit the needs of the society.

A new humanism had developed to challenge the "individualistic humanism" of Rousseau, Thoreau, Emerson, and modern existential psychology. That individualistic humanism was linked to rationality, a "substantive" rationality in which reason was to serve the ends of the individual human, in which man—not society, nor the organization, nor the "system"—was the justification of all action. At the same time, however, the new humanism emphasized the "functional rationality" of technology and organization, stressing the vital importance of social order and progress and the contribution of each individual to that dynamic order.

For want of a better term, this paradoxical humanism might be labeled "functional humanism," "collective humanism," or "instrumental humanism." Some label is needed today, for the continuing practice of lumping together all forms of rational humanism lends only further confusion to these confused times and blinds us to the potentials and problems faced in living out the transformations of modern society.

To gain at least a preliminary feeling for these confusions and their costs, few subjects are more fertile than the uniquely twentieth-century profession of guidance.

CONSIDERATIONS FOR A POLITICS OF COUNSELING

In recent years serious doubts have surfaced about the future of guidance and counseling. In the early sixties Gilbert Wrenn[12] had urged counselors to come to grips with a changing world, but in the years that followed the challenge went virtually unmet. Although a few studied efforts appeared,[13] for the most part, rather than stimulating more penetrating analyses of counseling in society, Wrenn's suggestive effort suffered the fate of so many other difficult challenges: it simply set a standard to be imitated by those who aspired to social and cultural awareness. In the emulation the challenge was all but lost.

Among those perhaps best equipped by training, habit and disposition to pick up the challenge—those critical sociologists, anthropologists and other critics of social behavior whose particular joy is to "debunk" and search beneath surface appearances—there was also little concern for the kind of challenge Wrenn offered. In a decade of turmoil and rapid change, the social critics had more seductive and exciting places to look than in the offices and journals of counselors. Their rare excursions into counseling and guidance, as in the works of Corwin and Clarke,[14] Cremin[15] and Bernard,[16] seemed to generate little interest, and their suggestive leads, like Wrenn's, went undeveloped.

Still the uneasiness was growing, and in 1972 Ralph Berdie, following his tenure as president of APGA, picked up one of Wrenn's diverse themes and projected it into the near future. His argument was built on the failure of counseling to find a useful and accepted place in the emerging society and to effectively ally itself with the extraordinary potentials of social psychology and other behavioral sciences. From the vantage point of the seventies, he saw that counseling had developed as a response to the social problems of the twentieth century, but that it was a response not carefully thought out or planned, its rationale devised after, rather than before, the practices were established.

> Unlike the oldest profession, this younger one has failed to incorporate itself into the fabric of society or to demonstrate that it satisfies basic continuing needs of individuals. Counselors have done much good and have helped many individuals, but their occupation has not been widely acknowledged as a profession, nor have its roots extended deep into our supporting economic and social strata. The survival of counseling as it now exists is doubtful.[17]

Berdie proposed and predicted that counseling will be replaced by "applied behavioral science." Counselors in schools, colleges, rehabilitation and employment agencies will give way to concerned and altruistic behavioral scientists who are dedicated to working with others "in order to provide experiences that will facilitate individual development most efficiently." If behavioral theory is now inadequate to such a task, if today's behavioral scientists lack altruism, he suggested, perhaps things will change, "perhaps a new kind of scientist will emerge, a new pattern of motives, and a greater chance of discovery." But whatever the prospects, he concluded, "the present and current profession of counseling is not sufficient to the challenges. Something new is needed. Are applied behavioral scientists a realistic alternative? Will they be by 1980?"[18]

Other doubts about the future of counseling also came to the fore, none more irritatingly than those of youthful radical activists. It may be useful to briefly compare Berdie's argument with that of our imaginary activist, the prototypical radical who has already done service earlier in this essay. Had he come across Berdie's parting question, the radical might have suggested that counseling was already well on the way there. The problem of counseling, the radical might charge, is not that it has failed to become incorporated into twentieth-century economics and social strata, for, if anything, it has been too closely, too reactively, a part of its society; if counseling has failed to be accepted as a profession it is not because counselors have been out of touch with the needs of their society, but because they have responded to those needs so willingly that they have not projected the kind of image of distinctive service and "professional autonomy" that characterizes the more prestigious vocations.

Nor, according to the radical, is the hope of counseling simply that it will give way to more effective and efficient means of guiding and influencing individual choice, behavior and growth. This is a solution only in terms of means; like his problem, Berdie's solution ignores basic questions of the relation of means, ends, and contexts. Effort to what end, the radical asks; decision in terms of what?

At first glance Berdie's hopes for an applied behavioral science and the radical perspective seem worlds apart. In many important ways they are, yet we can see that both Berdie and the young radical represent searches for alternatives in times that have grown strange. True, the alternatives for which they grope are widely divergent, but alternatives do not emerge from a vacuum; they emerge from the rejection, extension, and reflection of traditions already established, traditions that almost always continue in some form, to some degree, in the new alternatives that are found.

It is not surprising, then, that a basic commonality joins Berdie and the radical: a commitment to humanism, to the fundamental value of individual life and experience. But here contrast again grows insistent, for in the name of humanism the two embrace different images of the alternatives open to society and of the roles for individuals supporting and changing the social order. The contrast—little noticed—has plagued counseling all this century.

The Two Humanisms of Counseling

Themes of rational humanism have played through guidance and counseling from their beginnings. But rational humanism is a mutable belief: from the start it took a variety of forms in counseling and guidance. From Frank Parsons on many of the leaders of guidance have been social workers and reformers critical of many social problems and deeply humanistic in their commitment. In the first decades of this century modern theories of individual development and self-realization had not yet appeared in the literature of guidance and counseling, but an individualistic humanism could be seen in Parsons' ideas on social reform. He called these "mutualism," a kind of gradual socialism in which individuals, finding fulfillment in their vocations, would contribute actively to the creation of a more humane and efficient industrial system.

Themes of more pronounced social adjustment also came into play early and quickly dominated emerging images of guidance. Jesse B. Davis was deeply embued with the Protestant ethic, preaching the moral value of hard work, ambition, honesty, and the development of character as the vehicles of success in the business world. Anna Y. Reed and Eli W. Weaver were more taken with a conservative form of social Darwinism which preached the importance of fitting into the competitive business world in which the most able would rise to the top. David Hill saw science as man's hope for adapting to a changing social world and for helping guide men toward a more perfect society.[19]

Critics, especially from the thirties on, have rebelled against such themes of adjustment, seeing in them "antihumanist" calls for a march toward Aldous Huxley's *Brave New World* or C. Wright Mills' society of "cheerful robots." Humanism, they argue, requires commitment to individual development, to self-actualization or some other expression of autonomy and growth; without individuality there can be no humanly meaningful society. But these critics often miss an important point: that humanistic assumptions can be used to support pleas for closer adjustment of the individual to societal "needs" or "realities"; indeed, it can be argued that unless a coherent societal matrix is ensured the individual cannot effectively develop and function. Thus, seemingly similar ideals—humanistic images of the individual in a "humanly meaningful society"—are used to justify seemingly incompatible images of guidance and counseling.

From the days of Parsons, Davis, the Weavers, and Hill, these two general images of counseling—"functional" and "individualistic"—have often appeared to fuse within a seemingly shared commitment to "humanism," but at times they have emerged as distinct, revealing contradictions beneath their apparent compatibilities.

Stated most simply, the two images are, on the one hand, to further the collective good (for instance, aiding in manpower utilization), and on the other hand, to further the individual good (for instance, aiding in development of autonomy). The first image in essence presents the functional question: given a particular, specific social structure, where will the individual fit best? To adequately answer the question requires not only a breadth and depth of knowledge about society but also about the individual; however, if a choice must be made the image prescribes commitment to the "functional needs" of the society. The second image presents the individualistic question: how might the capacities and resources of the individual be developed most fully; how might he be helped to develop his capacities for, say, autonomous responsibility? To adequately answer this question, too, the counselor must consider both community contexts as well as the essential qualities of the individual; but always, in a choice situation, the image requires the counselor to opt in favor of the individual.

Many counselors today are articulate in their defense of one or the other of these images. Represented as clear cut alternatives, however, the two views are disarming, for the relation of the individual and society is not one of opposition. Rather, they are interdependent: one cannot be understood without understanding the other, and neither can change unless the other changes in some way. The question, then, of whether counseling serves national programs or serves individual growth invites attack, for it is obvious that it can and does serve both, even that any action of a single counselor can serve both at the same time.

From this argument it is a journey of only a few steps to the idea that there need be no real tension between the individual and society and, hence, that the distinction between the two images is artificial. But that short journey must be made over a dizzying chasm for which no secure bridges are available, for although functional and individual needs may often be compatible, they remain far from identical. However effectively the two can, ideally, coexist, they must by nature coexist in some tension. Individual needs do clash with functional needs, at times overtly, more often subtly, the conflict imperceptible, unarticulated, yet profound.

In this perspective the two images of counseling are seen as less polar than popular argument would have it. On the one hand, the counseling literature evidences "functional" humanism—themes of improving the abilities of counseling to maximize effectiveness of societal programs in ways that involve the fewest unnecessary restraints on individual development—while, on the other hand, it also reveals a more "individualistic humanism"—themes of improving counselors' abilities to maximize individual development in ways that involve the fewest unnecessary costs to society. Each of the two general images that play through the literature suggests some sort of "balancing" of potential service against potential disservice, but the balances suggested in the two lean toward strikingly different images of man and society.

In the middle 1950s functional perspectives seem to have reached a zenith in calls for manpower utilization. Represented in extreme by the argument that "What is good for General Motors is good for the nation" and by the implicit commitments in a "search for talent," this phenomenon allowed for little more than token regard for problems of individual development and choice. Within guidance, however, the assumptions of rational humanism continued to weave into the foundations of the arguments. One of the more eloquent spokesmen of this functional humanism was Ralph Berdie.

> Thus manpower is this country's most valuable natural resource. Classifying men as a resource to be used has unpleasant connotations for some people, but such a concept is not necessarily degrading since manpower, along with timber, or metallic ores, or animal products, is used for man's own betterment.
>
> Just as other natural resources have to be processed and subjected to various degrees of refinement, so does manpower. . . . The degree of refinement of petroleum depends upon the purposes for which the final product is to be used. Manpower must also be refined progressively as more exacting demands are placed upon the final product.[20]

By contrast, consider Stewart and Warner's effort to find a balance, starting from individualistic assumptions.

We have insisted on the right of the individual to freedom of choice—within, of course, the limitations imposed by his own ability and effort and by society. How, then, can such freedom serve the needs of society: In other words, how can the distributive needs of society be met if the individual is not urged in his choice to consider his obligations to that society? As we envisage the program of guidance services, one of the relevant types of information to which youth would be exposed is that dealing with man-power needs. The counselor should make the student aware of the social consequences of any decision he makes. This is a part of the confrontation process in which the counselor engages the student. Information about the needs of society would be evaluated by the student along with other relevant information. In the long run, we believe the needs of society will be met best in this fashion without the counselor's becoming a recruiter for special interest groups.[21]

These two excerpts illustrate the fundamental tension that exists in the literature of the counseling profession, a tension of "individualistic" and "functionalistic" images of man and society, a tension obscured by appearances of a shared commitment to rational humanism. To those who believe in them each of the images might appear basically "scientific"; to those who reject them each might appear "political." Both are at once political and theoretical statements; both can be used to promote special images of man and society and prompt men to act in ways through which the images may be realized. The dual nature of our scientific and political images of man, including those that underlie theories of counseling and guidance, is not new. What is somewhat new, or perhaps renewed, is our recognition of the duality, for in times of confusion, when meaning and authority are in question, we once again realize what Plato told us long ago—that all social issues are political issues, that human society is political through and through.

That lesson can be seen in the brief history of Progressivism, a history closely linked to the humanistic confusion of guidance and counseling.

The Lesson of Progressivism

In the movements of thought that dominated Progressivism through the first half of this century, "functional" values fused with individual humanism. With John Dewey in the fore, Progressives spoke glowingly of a Darwinian "adjustment" of the individual to his environment, an idea that, even as shaped with Dewey's brilliance and compassion, turned into political weaponry in the hands of others. The biological metaphor, as Joseph Featherstone[22] argues, was misleading in its picture of a cooperative struggle: men may cooperate to some extent in building bridges or fighting epidemics, but most social situations lack such unity, and many reveal the exploitation of some people by others. The metaphor was also ambiguous, vacillating from images of the individual as passively adapting to his social environment, to images of the individual as the master of his environment.

The misconception was dangerous, allowing the idealist to believe he was encouraging one thing, while ignoring any facts that might have helped him recognize that his words were used to justify something quite different. Thus, calls for "social reform" came to cover familiar practices of discrimination, and reform was seen as the effort to assimilate immigrants and other hapless creatures into a society that despised them. The words of the Progressives were inspiring, but, even apart from their misconceptions, they were politically manipulable. Given the class and ethnic situation of the times, they were readily turned into political weapons used by the powerful and ascendant against the discontent of the disadvantaged.

Ironically, despite the political disinterest of those who rallied to Progressivism, the movement itself was in large part a political phenomenon. This perspective, as Cremin[23] has pointed out, helps explain both its rise and fall. The movement brought together the energies of the social reformers of urban settlement work, the pedagogues who preached Rousseau's individualism and the scientism of the university psychologists. Woven into a reasonably consistent image of education, it promised to meet the challenges of urbanization; it would show the way to a humanistic system of education that would give birth to a new society, functionally potent, yet individualistically humanistic.

However, with the functional success of the schools, the humanistic promise failed. As Corwin and Clarke note:

> The needs of industry for specialized skills created unprecedented demands on existing public school facilities, and urban schools were accommodating the diverse interests of lower-class children, who were swelling the cities and classrooms. The schools were forced to adjust their curriculums and procedures to this new clientele. However, it was not only the *schools* that had to adjust, for it was apparent that students too would have to learn to reconcile themselves to the new society. Eventually, in fact, social adjustment became the guiding principle and the progressivism which had promised to redirect the spirit of education in the interests of the socially deprived turned into an adaptive philosophy in defense of the *status quo*.[24]

By the fifties the cloak of Progressivism had grown tattered, torn by dissension and worn thread-bare with age. The alliance fell apart. Nevertheless, although Progressivism was finished as an organized movement, its ideals and ideas lived on, and, as Cremin points out, its effects are still seen in the architecture of school buildings and classrooms, in the programs of students, and in the attitudes of teachers.

> Nowhere are the effects more apparent, however, than in the work of the guidance counselor. Beyond any other individual in today's educational system, he incarnates the aims and ideals of progressivism. He is the most characteristic child of the progressive movement, and as such is heir to all of its diversity and contradiction.[25]

Progressivism had joined functional images of societal needs to images of individualistic humanism, unwittingly forming a cloak that helped cover the political character of life and effort in contemporary society. Beneath this cover the tensions in counseling between individual-humanist and functional-humanist images of man and society could go unnoticed. But in the wake of World War II, the cloak of Progressivism began to come apart at the seams, and the tensions that it had helped cover surfaced—on the one extreme in individualistic images of a search for existential meaning and self-realization, on the other extreme in calls for manpower utilization, a search for talent and the national pursuit of excellence.

The Political Thrust of Counseling

The fact that both individual and functional images could be seen in the literature of guidance and counseling gives the impression that, at least in recent decades, each was a viable and energetic alternative. The appearance is not entirely misleading.

Surely, at least, functional perspectives abound. If Berdie's call in 1955 for the progressive refinement of manpower today seems extreme, it may be less due to a contemporary distaste for functional values in American society than to the lessened urgency of manpower utilization throughout the past decade and to the responses of rational humanists to the widespread cultural discontent of our times. Yet, as we have seen in the call for an "applied behavioral science," the themes of functional humanism have not vanished from counseling; rather, they have grown less abrasive, more powerful, and more appealing. Moreover, as we see even more dramatically in the tantalizing efforts of B. F. Skinner to apply behavioral psychology to cultural diagnoses and prescriptions, such themes are vitally alive in the general intellectual ferment of our transforming society.

So, too, there is evidence that themes of individual humanism remain professionally popular. As Burgess and Borrowman[26] point out, even though the general trend of education through the fifties and into the sixties was toward functional efficiency, themes of counseling literature have continued to stress themes of "self-realization" and the reconstruction of schools and society in more human terms. These authors suggest that the counter-direction of counseling to the dominant trends of education—a counter-direction that first began to surface in the thirties, expressing the discontent and forced leisure brought about by the limited opportunities of the Depression—was in part a response to the intrapersonal conflicts of students that required some form of therapy or near-therapy.

In actual practice, however, it seems that individualistic themes were, and still are, far less pronounced than the literature would suggest, while functional practices are far more common. Even today in the more sheltered of college settings, where individual counselors are comparatively free to work closely with moderately small numbers of students, "counseling in depth" is unwieldy, often unyielding, and generally uncommon. Indeed, if we are to listen to radical critics, there is little if any relation between the ideals of individual humanism and what actually goes on in counseling offices; for, fair or not, even in the more favorable settings of college campuses, counseling suffers from an image that belies its often repeated ideals of individual humanism. National leaders in the counseling movement have continued to stress their role in helping students "discover themselves," but, as Burgess and Borrowman note, "the student radicals perceive even the counseling centers as engaged in a near conspiracy to sell them out to the establishment, i.e., to find a calling consistent with national purpose."[27]

Just as the confusions of humanistic images are not new to contemporary guidance and counseling, neither is the discrepancy between ideal and practice. Right from the beginning the individualistic ideals and hopes for reform found little support from private and public benefactors, and the activities of even the early counselors seemed to contradict their ideals. The problem was not simply one of vision, dedication, and energy; rather, throughout the history of guidance the goals and ideals of counselors have been constrained and changed by the communities and organizations in which they worked, and even by the professions that they themselves developed.

Ideally, the tension between the two general images that play through guidance and counseling literature, like the tension between political liberalism and conservatism, not only protects both individual and society from dysfunctional demands of the other, but also allows and even stimulates development of both. Theoretically, the proponents of each image might accept the other as legitimate, though of different perspective, and each might recognize that the two can contribute to the effectiveness of both. If there were this kind of basic agreement in the profession, or if the movement broke into two distinct professions, the tension between the two images might become productive, finding expression in a competition of ideas and programs.

But theory and practice are different things; there is no such agreement, and today even most educational counselors must work in ambiguous and constrained situations. Even if the images were clearly and consistently identified in academic discussions—and they are not—in practical settings the competition of images is not waged between organizations or between groups of practicing professionals. Rather, it takes the form of tensions maintained within the individual counselor who has been encouraged by professional literature and training to value individual experience and development, but who is constrained by his or her organizational responsibilities and duties to emphasize societal "needs" and "opportunities." If the counselor is sensitive to the potential conflicts of the images, the result may be role conflict, perplexity, and vacillation. In dealing with a difficult case, even the most aware "humanistic" counselor working within a school or agency may not succeed in serving the individual to the degree he or she desires. The functional humanist is unable to effectively work against even needless restraints on the individual, and the individual humanist finds herself unable to keep the individual's needs and growth at the center of her attention. Thus the practice of each grows more functional, as the counselor's actions belie humanistic ideals.

Meanwhile, those who continue to speak of the "role of the counselor" as if he were removed from the constraints and pressures of the organizations and society in which he works—those who continue to ignore what Joseph Stubbins has called "the politics of counseling"[28]—encourage the continued isolation of the working counselor from the potentials of his situation and help blind him to the effects of his actions. For most counselors, those I have grossly labeled functional humanists and those whose humanism is more individualistic—just as the Progressives and other liberal humanists, as well as our society in general—have neglected a profound lesson of life in a transforming society: so most counselors have failed to recognize that they are political actors in a political world. They are not simply working with individuals, they are building bureaucracies; wittingly or not, they are contributing to the changing structures and processes of the society in which they work. And what they help build in turn helps shape and constrain them.

NOTES

1. This transition is brilliantly described and linked to the collapse of "nineteenth century civilization" in K. Polanyi, *The Great Transformation* (Boston: Beacon, 1957; originally published in 1944).
2. For a suggestive description of these two levels of organizational rationalization see F. W. Howton, *Functionaries* (Chicago: Quadrangle, 1969).
3. H. Wheeler, *The Politics of Revolution* (Berkeley: Glendessary, 1971).
4. A cogent and readable summary of these positions and many others is found in V. Ferkiss, *Technological Man: The Myth and the Reality* (New York: Braziller, 1969).
5. M. Weber, "Bureaucracy," *From Max Weber: Essays in Sociology,* H. Gerth and C. W. Mills, translators and eds. (New York: Oxford, 1958) p. 232.
6. For a discussion of the modern "Prince" and his experts, see G. Benveniste, *The Politics of Expertise* (Berkeley: Glendessary, 1972).
7. M. Wallace, "The Uses of Violence in American History," *The American Scholar,* 1971, pp. 81–102.
8. This categorization was stimulated by C. Tilly, "Collective Violence in European Perspective," *Violence in America: Historical and Comparative Perspectives,* H. Graham and T. Gurr, eds. (Washington: Government Printing Office, 1969), pp. 5–34.
9. Christopher Lasch, *The New Radicalism in America, 1889–1963: The Intellectual as a Social Type* (New York: Knopf, 1965), p. 90.
10. G. H. Mead, *Movements of Thought in the Nineteenth Century* (Chicago: University of Chicago Press, 1936), p. 17.
11. For stimulating discussions of this and other aspects of the rise and fall of liberal humanism, see H. Wheeler, *op. cit.*
12. C. G. Wrenn, *The Counselor in a Changing World* (Washington: American Personnel and Guidance Association, Commission on Guidance in American Schools, 1962).
13. For example, see L. H. Stewart and C. F. Warnath, *The Counselor and Society: A Cultural Approach* (Boston: Houghton Mifflin, 1965); C. Weinberg, *Social Foundations of Educational Guidance* (New York: The Free Press, 1969); D. H. Blocher, E. R. Dustin, and W. E. Dugan, *Guidance Systems: An Introduction to Student Personnel Work* (New York: Ronald Press, 1971).
14. R. G. Corwin and A. C. Clarke, "Organizational Contexts and Constraints; Reflections on the Counseling Movement," and "Social Change and Social Values: Further Reflections on the Counseling Movement," *Explorations in Sociology and Counseling,* D. A. Hansen, ed. (Boston: Houghton Mifflin, 1969), pp. 200–36; 294–328.
15. L. A. Cremin, "The Progressive Heritage of the Guidance Movement," *Guidance—An Examination,* R. L. Mosher, R. F. Carle, and C. D. Kehas, eds. (New York: Harcourt, 1965), pp. 3–12.
16. J. Bernard, "Functions and Limitations in Counseling and Psychotherapy," and "Counseling, Psychotherapy and Social Problems in Value Contexts," in Hansen, *Explorations in Sociology and Counseling,* pp. 348–77; 378–414.
17. R. F. Berdie, "The 1980 Counselor: Applied Behavioral Scientist," *Personnel and Guidance Journal,* 50(1972):451–56.
18. *Ibid.*
19. P. J. Rockwell and J. W. M. Rothey, "Some Social Ideas of Pioneers in the Guidance Movement," *Personnel and Guidance Journal,* 40(1961):349–354.
20. R. Berdie, *After High School—What?* (Minneapolis: University of Minnesota Press, 1954), pp. 3–4.

21. L. H. Stewart and C. F. Warnath, *op. cit.*, p. 46.
22. J. Featherstone, "Reconsideration: John Dewey," *The New Republic*, July 8, 1972, pp. 27–32.
23. L. A. Cremin, *op. cit.*
24. R. G. Corwin and A. C. Clarke, *op. cit.*, p. 317.
25. L. A. Cremin, *op. cit.*, p. 5.
26. C. O. Burgess and M. Borrowman, *What Doctrines to Embrace?* (Englewood Cliffs, N.J.: Prentice Hall, 1969), p. 136.
27. *Ibid.*, p. 136.
28. J. Stubbins, "The Politics of Counseling," *Personnel and Guidance Journal*, 48(1970):611–618.

SUGGESTED READING

Benveniste, Guy. *The Politics of Expertise*. Berkeley: The Glendessary Press, 1972. A suggestive and somewhat Machiavellian examination of the new social roles of the "Prince's Pundits," with emphasis on the political uses and values of expertise, knowledge, and information.

Ferkiss, Victor C. *Technological Man: The Myth and the Reality*. New York: Mentor Books, 1969. A concerned and optimistic overview of the varied visions and prognoses for the cybernetic society.

Hansen, Donald A., ed. *Explorations in Sociology and Counseling*. Boston: Houghton-Mifflin, 1969. A collection of original essays on the sociology and social psychology of counseling. Most relevant to the themes in this chapter are the works of Joel Gerstl, Ronald Corwin and Alfred Clarke, Jessie Bernard, and David Ricks.

Harrington, Michael. *The Accidental Century*. Baltimore: Penguin Books, 1966. A lucid sketch of the ways in which the contemporary revolution is radically reshaping the human environment. Although Harrington has elaborated these themes in later works, this remains the most stimulating of his statements.

Lasch, Christopher. *The New Radicalism in America, 1889–1963: The Intellectual as a Social Type*. New York: Alfred A. Knopf, 1965. An examination of the radical effort of Jane Addams, John Dewey, and others to see society from the bottom up, and the price paid in estrangement. See especially Chapter Five, "Politics as Social Control."

Mills, C. Wright. *The Sociological Imagination*. New York: Oxford University Press, 1959. A now classic examination of contemporary social inquiry, centering on the argument that "no one is 'outside society'; the question is where each stands within it." Thus, to be aware of what one is doing is to be explicitly a political man.

Polanyi, Karl. *The Great Transformation: The Political and Economic Origins of Our Time*. Boston: Beacon Press, 1957. A profound and deeply probing interpretation of the political and economic origins of the collapse of nineteenth-century civilization and its continuing influence on the consciousness of Western man, especially on our knowledge of freedom, of death, and of society.

Wheeler, Harvey. *The Politics of Revolution.* Berkeley: The Glendessary Press, 1971. A discussion of the possibilities of gaining control over our cybernetic age, emphasizing constitutional re-creation as a foundation for an "intentional society."

7 The World of Work

Walter S. Neff
New York University

WORK AS A SPHERE OF BEHAVIOR

Even the most superficial reflection on human work appears to raise a number of tantalizing questions. Why do we work at all? What is it that transforms the playing child into the working adult? Do nonhuman animals also perform work, or is work a distinctively human activity? What is work, anyway?

We might start looking for answers in the dictionary. *Webster's International* (3rd Edition) provides a score of different meanings for the noun *work* and over thirty separate meanings for verb forms. Intrinsic to all of these definitions is some sort of active process through which one object or entity influences another, although the activities described are not always carried on by human beings, or even by living beings. Thus, in physics, the term "work" is used to specify the transfer of energy from one body or system to another. In the same way, wine or cider are described as "working" when the process of fermentation is going on. Although these usages are essentially analogies or metaphors which crept into the language when the distinctions between animate and inanimate events were less strongly maintained than today, they do, nevertheless, tell us something about the meaning of the term. Whatever its subject, the word work is always being used to refer to some active process, the outcome of which is some sort of change or alteration. If the inanimate usages are metaphors, then the original model is an activity of living beings. But what kind cf activity and of what beings?

Some Definitions of Work

The first definition Webster presents for the noun *work* is:

> Exertion of strength or faculties for the accomplishment of something; physical or mental effort directed to an end.

Among the numerous definitions given for the intransitive verb *work* is the following:

> To exert oneself physically or mentally for a purpose, esp., in common speech, to exert oneself thus in doing something undertaken for gain, for improvement in one's material, intellectual, or physical condition, or under compulsion of any kind, as distinct from something undertaken for pleasure, sport, or immediate gratification . . .

Thus, in English usage, work is clearly conceived of as an *instrumental* activity; that is to say, it is not something that is performed spontaneously or for its own sake, but as a means for the procurement of other ends. The implication is clear. To work is not merely to "do something"; it is to do something "for a purpose." This implication already begins to distinguish work from other great spheres of human activity, such as play and love. The latter areas of human behavior appear to require no special motivation, since they are themselves either pleasurable or, perhaps, are responses to certain biologically based needs. In contrast, there is no requirement that work be pleasurable and no real evidence that it fulfills some deep instinctual or biological need. It is generally seen as something that we engage in to "get" something else. If we ask what this "something else" is, we hear talk about gain or improvement in one's material, intellectual, or physical condition. When we come right down to it, however, it appears that work is the instrumentality that man has evolved to guarantee his means of subsistence so that he can continue to exist in an inimical or indifferent environment.

It may be noted that we appear to be implying that work is a distinctively human activity, that although nonhuman animals certainly appear to carry on goal-directed activities designed to procure the means of subsistence, they do not work at it. To maintain this position we shall now have to go somewhat beyond the kinds of popular understandings that are summarized in dictionaries. In seeking a reasonably clear distinction between human behavior and the behavior of other animals, we at once become confronted with numerous semantic and scientific difficulties. After all, man is an animal in most respects like any other animal. There are impressive evolutionary continuities as well as discontinuities. Like any other animal, man must certainly obey the letter of certain fundamental biological laws. One of these laws dictates that man, like all living things, is an open system which must constantly incorporate substances from its environment to replace substances that are broken down or used up by the normal process of living. This point is, however, that it is only the human species that has managed to erect such an immense structure of social and cultural phenomena that the basic biological substratum sinks under their weight and almost vanishes from sight.

We are prepared to concede, of course, that all animals learn to various extents and that some display social learning. If work is defined simply as a goal-directed activity designed to secure the means of subsistence, then it would appear that the food-procuring activities of many infrahuman animals seem very much like work. Modern ethological studies have produced many instances of what looks very much like foresight, learning, and teamwork among the higher predatory mammals. Nevertheless, we are prepared to maintain here that *Homo sapiens* is the working animal and that penetration of this distinction will tell us something important about the nature of work.

A key principle here is that work involves a planned alteration of the environment, whether the latter is conceived as physical, social, or cognitive. While it cannot be denied that many nonhuman animals make certain changes in the world about them—insects and birds build nests, beavers build dams, etc.—virtually all animals other than man generally must live in the world as they find it. Because of certain evolutionary assets not available to other species—upright posture, opposing thumbs, the huge cerebrum—only man can and does massively intervene to change the structure and relationships of the world about him. Archeologists certainly accept this distinction when, in deciding whether a particular fossilized bone fragment is anthropoid or hominoid, they are happy to find accompanying artifacts (worked stones) which are seen as exclusively human products. One can speculate that there was survival necessity involved, for man's evolutionary assets are also accompanied by evolutionary deficits. Compared to the other predatory animals with which, in the dawn of his species, he must have had to compete both for life and game, man's nails, teeth, general physical strength and speed are relatively meager instrumentalities with which to seize and kill. Very early in his career on earth man must have been able to use his unique brain and manual ability to alter nature and thereby supplement his meager bodily resources. Early human technology seems to have been comprised of various prosthetic devices for extending and improving the body. What man could not run down or seize by sheer excess of agility or speed, he learned to trap or snare; what he could not kill by sheer strength or by the sharpness of fang and claw, he learned to club, or spear, or transfix with arrows. Thus, man has not only been capable of making massive changes in his physical environment, but also, in the process, he has "made" himself.[2] By this we mean that the social life of other animals appears to be largely a function of their biology and has remained largely unchanged during the millions of years they have existed as distinct species. Men, on the other hand, have invented a bewildering variety of social and cultural norms in the course of their long struggle to maintain themselves as individuals and as a species.

As we see it, therefore, work is a distinctively human enterprise, for which analogies and precursors cannot easily be found through a comparative study of other living things. Other animals may expend a great deal of directed energy in staying alive, but it is only men who work. Second, work is, as we have said above, an *instrumental* activity, performed not for its own sake but for other aims. Third, and perhaps most important, it is an *alterative* activity, performed in order to alter some aspect of man's environment—whether physical, cognitive, or social—so that staying alive will be made more certain and more efficient. As at least a preliminary definition of our subject matter, we are now prepared to say the following. *As a sphere of behavior, work is an instrumental activity carried out by human beings, the object of which is to preserve and maintain life, and which is directed at a planned alteration of certain features of man's environment.*

Work, Love and Play

Our tentative definition of work has the disadvantage of being rather abstract. Perhaps we can clothe it with concrete meanings if we compare work with two other major spheres of human behavior, the activities of play and of love.

A number of writers have suggested analogies between the play of children and the work of adults.[3] It can hardly be denied that both involve efforts to master the environment and to develop one's personal skills in doing so, and it is also true that both forms of activity may call upon all of the physical and intellectual resources of the organism and may involve very considerable expenditures of energy. Both work and play involve practice and the acquisition of skills. But work and play also differ in some very important respects, the chief difference being that play is fundamentally not an instrumental activity at all, although certain instrumental goals may be attached to it by the society in which it takes place. As Huizinga, one of play's chief analysts, has pointed out, play is essentially a free activity. There is nothing forced or compelled about it, either by biological nature or social necessity; it is never a task but is performed at leisure, during "free time." A second important characteristic of play is that it is not "real life." There is a strong element of pretending in play, through which other important life activities may be simulated (e.g., war, competition, "things that grown-ups do"), but play's objectives and aims always remain clearly different. Although many of the games of children are elaborate efforts to simulate the nonplay activities of adults, we are all aware, as are the children, that they are "only pretending." It is also clear that the rules of play are designed to maintain its "unreal" and simulative character. When a violently competitive contact sport spills over into a free fight among the players, the game is stopped. Similarly, the terminology and rules of chess are military in origin, but the outcome of the game does not decide the fate of nations. It is in this basic fact—that people play as an end in itself—that there lies the principal distinction between work and play. Given that play is aimless or, more exactly, that the aim of play is the play activity itself, given also that work is both phylogenetically and ontogenetically later than play, how is the playing child transformed into the working adult? To answer this question we need to look at human development, and we shall return to this question at a later point.

The relations between love and work appear to be more complex than those between play and work. Like adult love, adult work appears to be the outcome of a long process of individual development, starting in childhood and passing through many phases. As we shall attempt to specify later, the developmental conditions of our ability to work are by no means identical with those which influence our ability to love, but the manner in which we cope as children with certain demands is important nonetheless. Another interesting similarity between work and love is the degree to which the former, as is certainly true of the latter, may be influenced by all sorts of hidden motives of which the individual worker may not be aware or which he does not acknowledge. If we asked people why they work, the most ready reply would be that they work for money. Seldom acknowledged—perhaps not even known to most—is the degree to which given persons may work to maintain their self-esteem, to avoid boredom, to acquire an identity, or even simply to feel that they are responsible and worthwhile human beings.[5] It is also true that we cannot understand human work, no more than we can understand human love, merely from examination of its cognitive and motor components. Work also engages the affects; like love, it becomes enmeshed with all kinds of human emotions and these entanglements may promote a variety of forms of psychopathology.

Nevertheless, as in the case of play, there are some quite fundamental differences between the world of love and the world of work. Like play, love is not basically an instrumental activity; its gratifications are intrinsic, while those of work are basically extrinsic. Although they both require a long period of individual development to come to fruition, it seems likely that they constitute responses to different kinds of developmental experiences. Whether we accept Freud's biologically tinged notions of the stages of libidinal development or are inclined toward more culturally oriented theories of development, it is probable that the emotional patterns which play a part in adult love begin to be formed during very early interactions between the child and his parents. On the other hand, to anticipate a later discussion, the habitual modes of responses which later coalesce into adult work patterns do not appear in infancy but are molded by certain events in a much later period of childhood, perhaps not until the child (in modern societies, at least) is first confronted with formal schooling. To the degree that the conditions which form the ability to work are not identical with those that form the ability to love, then it may follow that disturbances in either sphere are not necessarily traceable to the same causes. This distinction will become particularly important when we consider the issues involved in giving therapeutic assistance to people who find themselves unable to work. As a general rule, it may turn out to be quite inappropriate to attempt to solve difficulties in working simply by giving deeper therapy in the areas of the inability to love.[6]

WORK AND CULTURE

There is abundant evidence that work is an essentially cultural phenomenon. The kinds of work people do, the motives they have for performing it, the reward and constraint system in which it is embedded, the personal and social meanings attached to it—all these are functions of cultural norms, beliefs, and practices that can be shown to differ markedly from society to society and at different points in historical time.[7] Many of both the positive and negative meanings attached to work are matters of cultural history rather than necessarily intrinsic to the nature of the work performed. In the hunting and gathering type of tribal society, the exigencies of procuring the means of subsistence are so pressing that everyone must work, including small children. Even the shaman or war leader is primarily a hunter or food gatherer like everyone else and carries out his special duties extracurricularly, so to speak.[8] Under these conditions neither a division of labor (except between "men's work" and "women's work," which itself varies from tribe to tribe), nor a hierarchy of values attached to kinds of work, is likely to appear to any extent. On the other hand, work begins to take on ignoble meanings once settled agriculture makes it possible to compel conquered or enslaved populations to work for masters. From the time of the classical Greeks through much of the history of feudal Europe, work acquired a servile character because it was essentially performed by slaves or serfs and carried the clear implication of being unfree.[9]

In contrast, the United States can be regarded as virtually the classical example of a heavily work-oriented society. It has been customary in some quarters to attribute this to the force of the so-called Protestant ethic, but the latter is only one factor among a number of others. Although the idea that work was a virtue was brought to the New World from Europe, the special conditions of life in the United States greatly accentuated it. The white settlers of the United States were principally people with no claims to wealth because of lineage or aristocratic tradition. The abundance of open land and natural resources, the extreme scarcity of labor, the comparative ease with which the aboriginal population could be exterminated or driven off, the early preoccupation with manufacturing and trade—all these factors helped to establish North America as the land where the path to success and security was through hard work. Moreover, in the industrializing countries of Europe, there remained strong aristocratic traditions which made for a sharp distinction between intellectual and manual work. For several generations the American of all classes was expected to be "good with his hands," even though manual work was to be seen as merely a hobby or sideline for the intellectual elite. It should be noted, however, that in no other country has the inventive mechanic and the practical engineer reached as high status as in the United States and, in instances, as much monetary reward. The other side of this coin, however, has been, until recently, a strong tendency to depreciate theoretical education as compared to practical experience "on the job."

There can be little doubt that these traditions have somewhat weakened in present day America, but the past has not been forgotten. The idler still tends to be derogated as a drone or parasite. If he is poor, he is regarded with contempt and anger as someone who doesn't want to work and is a public burden on those who do; if he is rich, he is, at best, merely tolerated but not really respected. The enormous development of industrial technology in the United States has, however, brought about a major shift in the evaluation of different kinds of work. While it is still clearly more virtuous to work than to be idle, people are evaluated in accordance with a very elaborate occupational hierarchy. However, even the most exalted occupations in the United States are still regarded as work, and it is argued that the top leaders of industry, government, and science work harder than anyone else.[10] The meaning of work in the contemporary United States, therefore, is manifestly different from its negative aura in ancient Greece and medieval Europe. Counteracting cultural trends, through which work is again acquiring certain negative connotations, will be discussed in a concluding section of this chapter.

A THEORY OF WORK BEHAVIOR

The Characteristics of Work Environments

From the point of view of a general theory of human work, it seems evident that work behavior is a function of two interlocking and intertwined sets of variables. One set is made up of the more or less enduring *personal characteristics* of the working person: abilities, skills, and aptitudes on one level and certain habitual patterns of both cognitive and emotional responsiveness on another. The other set arises from what may be described as the demand characteristics of work situations, to the degree that they comprise a special kind of environment. Industrial and counseling psychologists have generally concerned themselves with the first set of variables and have tended to slight the second set. In this section we shall try to correct this imbalance somewhat by concentrating on the *input factors* that influence work behavior. These features will be presented in outline form, classified under three main dimensions which comprise the *subculture of work:* I. Structural Features, II. Interpersonal Features, III. Customs and Traditions. We shall limit our discussion here to features common to most kinds of work in our own society.

I.   *Structural Features of Work Settings*

A. *Locale*

With minor exceptions, work is carried on in special places which are separated from our homes and to which we have to travel. De Grazia[11] has estimated that the problems of urban sprawl have added approximately two hours to the working day of the typical worker in our major metropolitan areas. Even more seriously, the location of the work place is becoming as significant a feature as its nature.

B. *The public character of work*

Most kinds of work are performed under conditions in which the worker is under the more or less continuous observation of supervisors, peers, or the general public. This feature demands that the worker must cope with a rather rigid set of demands concerning appearance, deportment, and manner. In other words, the worker must meet certain culturally defined stereotypes of the role of a worker—differing from job to job and differing also according to one's status in the occupational hierarchy. This constitutes a general constraint no matter what skills or aptitudes a given individual may possess.

C. *The impersonal character of work*

The persons to be interacted with in the work place typically constitute an aggregate of relative strangers. Thus, the work place is quite unlike the settings of love or play, in which intimacy is both possible and necessary. At work, however, intimacy is at a low premium and may invite negative sanctions. People with strong and insistent needs for intimacy often find this feature of work settings to be among the most difficult to handle appropriately.

D. *Time*

Nothing so firmly binds one to the clock as the conditions of work in modern industry. Work begins and ends at designated times, and specific periods are set aside for eating and rest. Production is often rated on a temporal basis and turns on the amount of work produced per hour or per day. An inability to discipline oneself by the clock is one of the most severe barriers to an adjustment to work, whatever useful abilities a person may display. For a considerable number of persons adherence to rigid temporal requirements is one of the most onerous demands of work environments, one that most sharply distinguishes the work place from the environments of home or play.

II. *Interpersonal Features of Work Settings*

While it is certainly possible to work alone or on one's own, most work situations are peopled by other human beings to whom the worker is required to react in prescribed and conventional ways. Adaptation to work is therefore an aspect of social behavior that makes a variety of interpersonal demands. The most crucial of these demands have to do with authority and with peer relationships.

A. *Relations to authority*

Although some kinds of work escape it, work generally is carried out under some type of supervision, whether direct or indirect, simple or complex. No matter how democratic the society, the organization of work tends to be hierarchical in character, and much of the literature on industrial organization is concerned with such issues as how to supervise and how to accept supervision. In reality considerable flexibility is also required. The individual worker is expected to be able to maintain some balance between dependence and independence. He cannot depend on supervision to the degree that his work deteriorates unless he is continuously watched over. On the other hand, there are usually definite limits to the degree to which he can work "on his own" or assume responsibility. Failures in job performance are at least as often related to inappropriate reactions to supervision as they are to lack of some skill or aptitude.

B. *Relations to peers*

Work settings not only involve the worker in both autonomy and compliance with respect to authority but also in finding his way through the complexities of cooperation and competition. Even where formal contracts do not exist, many work settings have unwritten rules through which work peers jointly regulate their mutual productivity. One can neither be a blatant "rate buster" nor so poor and indifferent a worker that others must take up the slack. Beyond all this there are also more subtle matters of personal interaction. The limited, immature, or disturbed person may demand from his fellows more than they wish to give, or he may find them more indifferent to his personal problems than he can tolerate. Again, there is an array of expected behaviors, without which an adaptation to work becomes difficult or impossible.

III. *Customs and Traditions*

Like all subcultures, that of work has its own special customs and traditions, makes role assignments in special ways, and develops unique kinds of private language, even a set of private mystiques. In this sense, a person must become encultured to work in the same sense that he or she becomes encultured to a particular tribe or society. The following are some of the chief "culture traits" common to modern work settings.

A. *Language and demeanor*

Both speech and dress, as well as more subtle tags of demeanor and general behavior, are identifying signs of various sectors of the work subculture. In some of the older trades and in most of the learned professions, conversation among habitues ("shop talk") is almost unintelligible to the outsider. A new entrant must learn the lingo or remain excluded. In the same way, styles of dress become the badges of certain occupations, or of status positions in a work hierarchy. Thus, we have the "hard hat", the "business suit", the work shirt vs. the dress shirt, the "neat-but-not-gaudy" clothing required of the female in the business world. While there are current trends toward greater permissiveness in dress and, perhaps, more homogeneity in speech, these occupational badges still prevail to a very considerable extent.

B. *Gender*

Quite sharp distinctions still persist between "men's work" and "women's work," despite the fact that these distinctions are largely, if not entirely, social in origin. Although one-third of the U.S. labor force is female, a great many occupations are exclusively or almost entirely peopled by one or the other sex.[12] Women workers are largely to be found in light manufacturing (although the foremen and executives are usually men), in the lower levels of white-collar work, and in such traditional female occupations as nursing, teaching, and social work. It is no accident that many "female" jobs have the character of extensions of the home. The proponents of Women's Liberation can hardly be faulted when they argue that these dispositions of work by sex have little to do with ability or aptitude. The rapid development of technology has abolished muscle power from most industrial tasks, and there is really nothing in such occupations as the ministry or medicine which requires that only men should perform them. The fact that these distinctions are "man-made," however, does not make them any the less real or less resistant to change.

C. *Status and role*

One of the most significant features of highly industrialized societies is the degree to which a person's status is derived less from one's lineage or group affiliation than from the kind of work one does. We have noted that most work settings are hierarchical in organization and have clearly marked pecking orders. Part of the process of becoming a worker involves mastering the intricacies of interacting with one's peers, superiors, and subordinates. Students of industrial organization have paid a great deal of attention to roles and statuses on the job, giving special attention to the frequent clash between formal and informal structures. A distinction is often made between the "office" and the "person" who fills the office; the former is defined by a rationally derived set of rules, but the latter involves a maze of folkways, norms, and values. Roethlisberger and Dickson[13] were among the first to report on the important role of the informal work group in the underground life of the modern factory, a finding which later studies have merely amplified.

The Ontogeny of Work Behavior

In the preceding section we have attempted to sketch in some of the determinants of work behavior that arise from certain features of the work setting itself. A theory of work behavior cannot be indifferent to the views of such environmental psychologists as Kurt Lewin[14] and Roger Barker,[15] who have argued that behavior cannot be understood, at any given point, without taking into account the structural features and demand characteristics of the settings in which it takes place. To the extent that these input variables have tended to be underplayed in theories of human work, further study of the effects of work environments is a dire necessity. But the most exhaustive study of work environments will tell us only part of the story, for the individual worker also brings with him to the job a variety of psychological baggage. How does he or she acquire it?

To answer this question satisfactorily we need much more information about the secrets of human development than we now have available, but this is not to say that nothing is known. From the work of such child development theorists as Heinz Werner,[16] Jean Piaget,[17] and Erik Erikson[18] we have derived the very important concept of "stages" of human development, imposed in part by traditional ways in which societies have institutionalized the care and training of their children. Central to the concept of stages of development is the notion that at different life periods the individual is confronted with somewhat differing life tasks, concerning which he or she must develop appropriate coping abilities. From the work of such counseling psychologists as Donald Super,[19] Eli Ginsberg,[20] and Anne Roe[21] we also have acquired much useful information about the development of those abilities, aptitudes, interests, and attitudes which bear upon work and career. However, there are certain major gaps in these accounts which will require much further research to fill.

In seeking a theory of work development, we also cannot ignore certain ideas advanced by certain psychoanalytically oriented theorists, although we have elsewhere criticized psychoanalysis for its meager attention to work behavior and the degree to which whatever attention has been paid has been largely schematic.[22] Nevertheless, the ideas of such psychoanalysts as Ives Hendrick,[23] Barbara Lantos,[24] Erik Erikson,[25] and Robert White[26] point us in some interesting directions. Hendricks, for example, has argued that from earliest infancy the child commits an enormous amount of energy to the exploration and mastery of his environment and appears to derive a great deal of "primary" pleasure from doing so. For Hendricks this appears so early in the life of the child and is so insistent that he assumes the existence of a "mastery instinct" to account for it. That we need not follow him to a speculative instinctual source is indicated by the later ideas of White, who coined the term "effectance motivation" to describe what he thinks of as an independent ego energy in human beings, observed from birth onwards. In a different vein, Lantos has suggested that the transition from pleasure-in-activity to pleasure-in-achievement takes place during what Freud called the "latency period" (from approximately age five or six to the onset of puberty). She argues that this occurs because the instinctual response networks are "broken" in man, with the interposition of intellectual activity between the instinctual need and the gratifying act. In this sense, Lantos argues, the objects of human gratification are usually not directly and immediately available (as in lower animals) but must be "worked for."

Finally, Erikson's theory of the life cycle may be very useful for us. Among other things, he notes that early childhood (prelatency) is largely dominated by the problems of nutrition and elimination, by play, by early mastery of the workings of the body, and by the working out of the child's basic relationships to his immediate family. When the child enters the latency period, he is ready for new developmental tasks. Erikson calls the latency period the "industry stage," observing that only then does the child begin to internalize the fundamentals of instrumental technology. For Erikson early schooling provides the arena in which the child begins to move out of the womb of the family into the larger world of work.

To assemble all of these fragmentary ideas into a coherent theory of work development is not easy, but we shall make a modest attempt. We will start with the explicit proposition that the events of early childhood are less critical for the formation of work behavior than are those of middle childhood. This is not to say that we can be indifferent to very early child development, for, obviously, a child may be so traumatized by transactions in the early family setting that later inputs may be entirely or partially ineffective. However, we will maintain, as a hypothesis at least, that the prelatency period is largely taken up with the vicissitudes of nurturance, love, and play, all of which are almost entirely perceived as ends in themselves. The child is not yet being faced with life demands that are primarily instrumental in nature.

This hypothesis leads us to the view that the critical components of work-related behaviors are probably laid down during the periods of middle childhood and early adolescence. The child, who must now leave his family for hours at a time to go to school, is faced with a new set of demands and is called on to make a new set of adaptations. Many of the requirements of the work role are first encountered in the school environment. The child receives his first serious conditioning to the clock; he must learn to be at school on time and stay a fixed number of hours. He is compelled to adapt to the requirements and peculiarities of a whole series of strangers—to a set of authorities and peers who are not at all members of his immediate family. In effect, he must begin to lead a "public" life. Above all, he is now confronted with the demand to achieve something, to acquire a set of instrumental skills.

Thus, the distinctions between love and work and between play and work only begin to take shape in the behavior of the child when he is compelled to leave the shelter of the family for the vicissitudes of schooling. School thus provides the early set of environmental pressures which end by transforming the child into an adult worker. In this sense, a great deal more is learned in school than a particular set of cognitive skills. Distressed by certain deficiencies of mass education, modern educational theorists strive to develop techniques which may make the acquisition of such skills both more personally enjoyable and more meaningful to the child. But we should understand that this is a technical problem and is not the main aim of the process of education. It may be desirable, even more efficient, that the child enjoy schoolwork, but enjoyment is *not* its basic purpose. What school requires of the child is that he begin the process of being productive, of meeting tasks, of distinguishing play from work.

We are not saying that the schoolchild yet knows what work means in the sense of career or vocation. The developmental studies of Super and Ginzberg suggest that the world of work does not begin to take on concrete meanings until the child is at least eleven or twelve years of age. What we are saying, however, is that certain habitual modes of response appear to be laid down fairly early. These habitual patterns of response to authority and achievement tend to be self-fulfilling. Reactions to success and failure, patterns of relations to work peers, and responses to supervision are early precursors of many important adult behaviors. Even though adult occupations may remain largely unknown or be perceived only in fantasy, toward the end of middle childhood children already differ in how industrious they are, in their demeanor toward impulse gratification, in the affects mobilized by alien authorities and peers. Although later experiences provide concrete contents and serve to consolidate these early patterns, it is unlikely that they will greatly change them.

It seems unnecessary to add the caveat that we are dealing here largely with theory, even with speculation. We know a great deal more concerning how the child's cognitive skills develop than about the more vague issues we have been discussing. Our evidence for the importance of middle childhood as the critical area for the origin of many work-related dispositions is obviously fragmentary. In fact, it is hardly in existence at all. We have advanced these ideas largely because we think they point to some vital areas of needed research, research which is yet even to be formulated, let alone carried out. Hopefully, a new generation of researchers can follow up some of these leads. If our suspicions about the developmental origins of work behavior can be verified, some interesting mysteries may be clarified. We may then have some explanations for the intriguing fact that there are people who seem badly damaged in the ability to love or play but who yet are able to work, and that, conversely, there also appear to be people who are unable to adapt to work but whose capabilities in the worlds of love and play seem relatively unimpaired.

SOME CONTEMPORARY PROBLEMS

Throughout our discussion we have insisted that human work cannot be understood unless it is seen to be a heavily enculturated activity. By this we mean, of course, that the kinds of work done, the motives for performing it, the meanings attached to it, and the reward system in which it is embedded, are all functions of the kind of society in which it takes place. It should follow, then, that work may have changed its meanings many times in the history of the human race and that, at any given period, the prestige and identity attached to the roles of work must vary considerably across different types of societies. At the same time, we have tacitly assumed that work is an instrinsic aspect of human culture, that no human group could exist for very long without the investment of substantial resources and ingenuity in insuring that required portions of successive generations grow up to assume the expected productive roles.

But if the necessity to work—and many of the both positive and negative values thereby imputed to it—is conceded to be an essential feature of man's historical past, is it true today? We are currently in the midst of a hot controversy among social scientists as to whether the enormous pace of technological progress and of the managerial routinization of work tasks is being achieved at the cost of making the worker redundant or, at best, of transforming him into a mere appendage of the machine. Such writers as Harvey Swados,[27] Paul Goodman,[28] B. B. Seligman,[29] and Daniel Bell[30] argue that a machine-centered society ends by transforming man himself into a sort of automaton, thereby stripping from work whatever elements of human dignity, gratification, and identity formation it had hitherto possessed. If these arguments have merit, then we are witnessing the paradoxical phenomenon that an explosion of interest in work is taking place at the very moment we seem to be abolishing the need for it. This issue is so important that we need to give it more than cursory attention.

Work and Technology

It is very difficult to make an objective appraisal of the effects of technological change on the conditions and meanings attached to work. In the first place, written history is silent concerning the meaning of work for the productive persons of previous societies—whether the workers in question were free hunters, slaves, serfs, peasant farmers, or skilled craftsmen. Second, many historical writers tend to romanticize the past, to assume that there was a "golden age" in which things were better than they are now. Both of these circumstances should make us very cautious in arriving at specified generalizations concerning major changes in the meaning of work.

At the same time, the Industrial Revolution brought about very substantial changes both in the manner in which work is organized and in its associated meanings. Before the rise of the factory system work was largely performed with the use of hand tools, the available sources of energy being the forces of nature—human muscle power, draft animals, wind, water, and fire. It has been theorized that these conditions permitted a very close relationship between the worker and his work, a closeness which encouraged the worker to express in his product—whether produced for his own use or for exchange—his own personality, individuality, and creativity. The most widely cited examples are the products of the skilled artisan or handicraft worker, who seemed to be able to incorporate in his product some of the qualities of the work of art. Our contemporary museums are crowded with ancient objects and implements that were once fabricated for useful purposes, but are characterized, in our eyes at least, by considerable beauty and individuality. In this sense, premodern work, insofar as it was not simply limited to agriculture, can accurately be called *manufactured,* that is to say, it was essentially the work of the human hand.

Whatever, in fact, was the meaning of work for the artisan—and it is certainly possible for us today to exaggerate its positive qualities—one can hardly doubt that the Industrial Revolution brought in its train the virtual disappearance of the individual handicraft worker. Whereas the artisan may have been capable of expressing his individuality in his product with whatever satisfactions this brought, the modern factory worker is engaged with thousands of others in serving powered machinery which turns out an anonymous product. As Karl Marx[31] and many writers since have argued, the organization of work in the modern industrialized society appears to face man with a double kind of alienation. Not only is he alienated from the means of production, which no longer belong to him but to his employer, but he is also alienated from the product. It is no longer his product to enjoy or dispose of. If anyone can claim to have produced it, it is the entrepreneur, since he controls, organizes, and plans all the processes by which it comes into existence. Seligman speaks of the consequences for the worker in quite moving and evocative language:

> In the historic process of transferring his energy into a commodity and control of which rested in other hands, however, man really lost control of himself . . . Work was freed from tools, craft, and community and was metamorphised into a commodity with a price tag attached to it. The significance of work was twisted: man became a laborer, without a sense of engagement in the meaningful. As a laborer, he engaged in uniform activity, mere expenditure of energy. Yet work was once a diverse phenomenon, gathering esteem by its very particularity and providing joy in the articles produced. There was a human delight too in its structure and organization and in the comradeship gained from other workers. There was a sense of dignity in work. Unfortunately, the elements of craft—spontaneity, exuberance, and the freedom to perform—which made work, play and culture virtually identical have been irretrievably lost.[32]

Seligman's comments are fairly typical of a number of current writings on work alienation. Yet an objection to this sort of general attack on technology is that it constitutes an unpalatable aggregate of both fact and myth. It can hardly be doubted that the factory system—and indeed virtually the entire organization of work in modern society—has had the ultimate effect of transforming work from an essentially individual and personal activity into something both public and impersonal. On the other hand, Seligman harks back to a "golden age" when work was a joy, when it enhanced human dignity, when work, play and culture were virtually the same thing. Here we are in a dangerous area of myth-making, for there seems to be no evidence at all that human work ever had the qualities for which some of the opponents of technology appear to yearn. Earlier we were at some pains to point out that every society of which we have knowledge has been perfectly capable of distinguishing play from work and does not look with approval on any of its members who confuse the two. It also seems difficult to maintain that work was ever an unalloyed "joy." Certainly it seems to have been true for several millennia that whenever individuals or groups managed to become militarily or politically powerful, they divested themselves of any necessity to labor and forced that duty on others.

The point is that man is a very adaptable animal and usually manages to find something good in anything he is required to do. The factory system also made work a social activity in that it brought masses of workers together in a joint work site. This inevitably led to social interactions among them, even if the initial consequence was simply shared knowledge of their mutual misfortunes. The long-run result, however, was the organization of formal and informal work groupings and the eventual rise of trade unions. While this sort of development was certainly not intended by the entrepreneur and was resisted with all of the very considerable forces he could mobilize, the widespread development and recognition of labor unions has undoubtedly restored to the worker some elements of human dignity. But there are also other social consequences of the factory system. Many workers increasingly found their friends, their acquaintances, and even their spouses within the work site itself. This has become so much the case that one of the negative consequences of retirement is that many stable social relations are thereby disrupted.[33] Thus, the high level of organization required for modern industry has added certain social features to work at the same time as it has tended, as certain of its critics correctly point out, to depersonalize the work activity itself.

But what of "automation"? This term refers to the development of the fully automatic machine which is not served and controlled by a human worker but by an electronic computing system. The possibility is now arising of the fully automated factory in which the entire process of production is carried out by machine and electronic control systems, making the human worker almost entirely redundant. The implications of this development appear so vast that it has induced some writers (e.g., Wiener[34]; Friedmann[35]) to speak of a "second Industrial Revolution." Despite the vast dislocations which accompanied the first Industrial Revolution, the prior effects of industrial technology did not threaten to make work a superfluous activity. If anything, in the most highly industrialized countries work increasingly came to be regarded as both a necessary and desirable way of life, to which all sorts of positive social and economic values were imputed. But if we assume that automation will eventually swallow up the entire economy—something that it is very far from doing as yet—does this mean that work will no longer be a primary human activity?

Here we are in the uncharted realm of economic and social prophecy. Technology has never existed in a social vacuum! Technological advances have frequently instigated men to invent new types of social arrangements, although their installation, it must be conceded, has often been the occasion for widespread and intense social conflict. How will society react to vastly increased rates of man-hour productivity? By equally vast increases in institutional employment? By shortened hours of work? By permitting entry into the work force at later ages than is now customary? By earlier retirement? By vast expansion in the resources available for education, recreation, and culture? Clearly all of these options are at least thinkable, and some may become areas for vast social changes in the future.

We can only reinforce certain arguments we have offered in earlier sections of this paper. Both technology and culture are uniquely human products. Work may have no intrinsic meaning in itself, but only those imputed to it by the society in which it is embedded and with which it is intertwined. Human history is characterized not only by major technological changes, but also by equally massive social changes. We can make hardly more than a few educated guesses. If technological progress ultimately has the effect of greatly reducing the present large share of our lives that we devote to work, then some meanings it now has may suffer major changes. The entire content and goal of the educational system may need to be modified to place less of a concentration on work and career than is now the case. There may be changes in our traditional methods of child rearing, which place heavy and subtle emphasis on the internalization of work-related attitudes. Indeed, the whole of society may have a very different shape and carry with it a very different set of social norms. The meanings attached to work may then be very different from what they are today. But this should hardly be surprising! After all, the meanings attached to work *now* would be hardly recognizable by a citizen of classical Greece or medieval Europe.

Work and the Counterculture

In a book to be published in the early 1970s we cannot close without at least attempting to take account of certain phenomena which appear to run counter to the major cultural forces that we have been at some pains to describe. These phenomena have become visible only during the past decade and are perhaps best exemplified by the books of such writers as Charles Reich[36] and Theodore Rozcak,[37] who observe that a significant portion of American youth are becoming disaffected with the "work ethic," that (in the language of the drug subculture) they are "turning on and dropping out," abandoning the pressures of higher education and stable careers for simpler and less "processed" lives. In short, the powerful cultural forces that transform most of us into workers are being rejected or undermined by new cultural forces that stand opposed to the old ones. It is argued that the very successes of industrial technology have brought certain major negative consequences: pollution, the development of wholly artificial and man-made environments, the abandonment of nature, exploitation of man by man, dehumanization (the gradual transformation of man into a machine or an appendage to a machine). For many young people the real devil in the woodwork is the centrality of man's commitment to work, for which they would substitute the expressive, aesthetic, emotional, "play and love" aspects of human behavior. Describing the "greening of America," Reich[38] argues that our society is in process of giving up its singleminded concentration on the conquest of nature (and correspondingly its commitment to the work ethic) for a program which will place the development of the individual human personality at the center of life.

It is very difficult to make any kind of sober estimate as to whether these arguments have any merit at all. Assuming that we are dealing here with genuine social trends, these trends are so recent that the evidence for them is fragmentary at best. We are told about the "hippie" and commune movements of the past few years; we hear that increasing numbers of college youth in the more prestigious universities are not completing their required courses of study; we have anecdotal reports that at least some individuals have given up lucrative corporate positions to eke out a relatively meager existence as a handicraft worker or a small farmer. That these reports are not limited to the sons and daughters of the affluent is attested to in a recent collection of studies of the blue-collar worker,[39] in which it is argued that even the young factory worker in the mass production industries is no longer so easily disciplined to unremitting labor as he once apparently was. However, the major question at issue still remains unresolved. Are we dealing here with relatively minor frictions and difficulties in a work-oriented society that has never been free from imperfections, or is something new appearing on the horizon? Are we witnessing the first signs of what will ultimately be a major shift in man's orientation to work, a shift that is one of the consequences of the very success of work itself?

It is too early to tell. In the United States, at least, it seems more likely that we are observing some of the consequences of important shifts in the mix of the labor force, as major groups hitherto largely excluded from access to the opportunity structure are finding somewhat easier entry. These changes are taking place in the midst of fairly sharp social conflicts, in which the values imputed to work are perhaps beginning to take on different meanings in different sectors of the population. It is also quite probable that the major changes in the relative weights of such areas of the economy as agriculture, industry, service, and the professions are bringing in their wake a number of shifts in the values imputed to different specific occupations.

There is, however, one feature of the modern social scene that may have very important consequences for work behavior. This is the degree to which egalitarianism appears to be becoming an increasingly important social force within all levels of society. It is easy to overlook the fact that much of human work behavior—certainly as it takes place in the more complex societies—has a fairly prominent component of social compulsion. This negative side of work should be surprising or uncomfortable only to those theorists of work behavior who have chosen to describe work as wholly noble and gratifying. But very few kinds of human behavior are unalloyedly pleasurable, and work is very far from being an exception. Our reading of human history suggests that there has always been a prominent component of necessity attached to work, whether the compulsion comes from the driving forces of imminent starvation or natural disaster, or whether the pressure to work has its source in the demands of other human beings. There appear always to have been a fairly large number of human beings who were quite ready to arrange things in such a way that they themselves are divested of the need to labor so long as other human beings were forced to labor for them. Freud was perhaps too pessimistic when he argued that men would not work at all unless compelled to, either by direct force or by early threats of loss of love. His association of work with renunciation of pleasure is too simple a description of such a complex activity. Robert White is undoubtedly closer to the mark when he suggests that there may be a primary pleasure in successful mastery of the environment. Moreover, this has never prevented some people from enjoying the fruits of environmental mastery under conditions where the real work is performed by someone else. One does not have to be either a cynic or a Marxist to observe that virtually all societies, except perhaps the most primitive, have developed very elaborate arrangements (including provisions for direct and indirect punishment) to ensure themselves of a labor force. All this is not to deny that all sorts of pleasures and gratifications have become imputed to work during the course of cultural development.

But to the extent that we concede an element of compulsion to work, the spread of egalitarian ideas may tend to weaken this force. It may no longer be quite so simple to compel people to work or to arrange the cultural institutions so that these compulsions are easily internalized. Among the consequences of a high technology are the abolition of the necessity to labor unremittingly from dawn to dusk, the increasingly heavy reliance on machinery to carry through the heaviest and most unpleasant kinds of labor, the spread of education, the undermining of aristocratic beliefs that one's lineage entitles one to be freed from any kind of work. Perhaps in the more affluent sectors of modern society there is no longer the strong determination to raise children to become productive persons. Even in the less affluent sectors, work may be in process of coming to be seen as somewhat less of a driving personal necessity. In societies of high technology the required commodities appear on hand as if by impersonal magic. This illusion is dispelled, however, in instances of individual unemployment or when a mass labor struggle causes the hands and brains that really run the machines to grind to a halt. Work or starve is an extremely powerful compulsion when it is both enforceable and enforced. It becomes less so when an advanced technology permits a people to tolerate increased measures of democracy and to institutionalize concerns for the welfare of others.

The increasing democratization of contemporary social arrangements may weaken some of the compulsions to work. These are the positive sides of a high technology, just as its negative sides have been industrial pollution and the progressive exhaustion of certain natural resources. But we may have to change some of our culturally derived notions concerning the values and rewards attached to human labor, and perhaps some of these ideological shifts are already beginning to operate. Work may have to become less of a compelled necessity and more of a voluntarily assumed social obligation. To achieve this, much of the hierarchy of differential reward and prestige attached to different kinds of occupations may have to be modified or stripped away. Work may then become something rather different from what it is today—still not a joy, but at least a more easily accepted condition of human existence.

It is possible that the prophets of the counterculture are responding to this sort of anticipation, although they are wildly misperceiving its nature and are offering remedies that are, at best, utopian and, at worst, require that the clock of human progress be turned backwards. Work is the sword that mankind evolved to master nature and preserve itself as a species. It is obviously a two-edged sword, but there is nothing that requires that it remain so. We have stressed that work is a primary human activity, an activity that is probably unique to the human species, but we have also stressed that the values and meanings imputed to work are very much a consequence of the particular cultural setting in which it takes place. The onrush of science and technology appears to be bringing about massive shifts in the kinds of work that society requires and perhaps also in the meanings imputed to it. Although the world of work is not in imminent danger of disappearing—at least not in the foreseeable future—it is obvious that certain of the values, rewards, and meanings imputed to work by our culture may undergo important shifts.

From this standpoint work can be regarded as neither a blessing nor a curse; it is simply one of the major conditions of our existence as a species. Without the ability to work, it is likely that *Homo sapiens* could not have survived and that the queries now being raised about this unique ability could not be asked. Through work a naked but clever animal, devoid of either fang or claw, has been able to compete with stronger and better armed animals with such effectiveness that the latter are in danger of vanishing as species. Through work our species has harnessed and controlled the indifferent and dangerous forces of nature, invented and perpetuated norms of behavior and rules to govern social relationships, and created art and literature. Through work also, it must be admitted, we have developed the most efficient means of stripping the land of its natural resources and also of subjugating and killing our fellow men. Obviously, there have been darker sides to the accomplishments of work, and it would be senseless to disregard them. Nevertheless, it is fair to say that the entire aggregate of human culture, for better or worse, is a product of work. Without the ability to work, it is difficult to say how we could have become human at all.

The world of work, therefore, is properly described as exceedingly complex, but it is also exceedingly flexible. The meanings associated with work have changed greatly in the past and, presumably, will continue to change in the future. There is nothing in the nature of work as a primary human activity which suggests that it is in process of liquidating itself. On the contrary, if work is, as we believe, the ability of human beings to bring about alterations in their conditions of existence, then it is a set of functions which are inseparable from being human. The world of work may have different features in the future than it possesses today, but so long as there are human beings, this is the world they will inhabit.

NOTES

1. Ludwig von Bertalanffy, *General Systems Theory* (New York: Braziller, 1968). A basic requirement of systems theory, as applied to living things, is that the functioning and behavior of the living unit must be understood in terms of a complex set of interactions between the unit and its surroundings. In this sense the characteristics of the environment are at least as important determiners of the behavior of the unit as the intraintegumental features of the unit. As applied to psychology, this theory has come to be called the *transactional* viewpoint. For further reading, see John Dewey and A. F. Bentley, *Knowing and the Known* (Boston: Beacon Press, 1949). The writer's theory of work is based on this notion. A brief account will be found in

Walter S. Neff, *Work and Human Behavior* (Chicago: Aldine-Atherton Press, 1968), pp. 71–74.

2. V. Gordon Childe, *Man Makes Himself* (London: Watts & Co., 1936). An instructive account of the manner in which the human race, through its invention and development of culture, has changed both its own nature and that of the world in which it lives.

3. Sigmund Freud, "The poet and day-dreaming," *Collected Papers*, Vol. IV (London: Hogarth Press, 1948). As is well known, Freud argued that artistic production is more analogous to the play of children and more dependent upon the operation of the "pleasure principle" than is true of adult work.

4. Johan Huizinga, *Homo Ludens: A Study of the Play-element in Culture* (New York: Beacon Press, 1955).

5. Neff, *op. cit.*, pp. 141–149. This section is based on research reported in Neff, W. S., *The Meaning of Work* (Final Report under Grant #1603-p, Rehabilitation Services Administration, the U.S. Department of Health, Education, and Welfare; Washington, D.C., 1968).

6. Cf. various studies reported in the proceedings of a recent national conference on the psychological aspects of disability. The proceedings have been published under the title *Rehabilitation Psychology,* ed. Walter S. Neff (Washington, D.C.: The American Psychological Association, 1971).

7. W. S. Neff, *Work and Human Behavior;* see especially Chapters 3 and 4, pp. 43–68.

8. Most ethnologists have called attention to the fact that in the relatively small band that constitutes the basic economic unit of hunting and gathering society the social division of labor is at a minimum. Cf. M. J. Herskovitz, *Economic Anthropology* (New York: Knopf, 1952). Also see M. E. Opler, *An Apache Life-Way* (Chicago: University of Chicago Press, 1941) and C. D. Forde, *Habitat, Economy and Society* (London: Methuen, 1934).

9. Hannah Arendt, *The Human Condition* (Chicago, The University of Chicago Press, 1958). In this important book Arendt argues that raw labor is itself demeaning and that ancient slaves were derogated because they were compelled to perform it "as animals do." The present writer believes that it is just as plausible to argue that labor began to acquire ignoble meanings when it became possible for the powerful to relegate it to others to perform. It then became a sign of prestige and status to be freed from the necessity to work, and labor then began to take on clear associations with the status of being unfree.

10. S. de Grazia, *Of Time, Work and Leisure* (New York: Twentieth Century Fund, 1962). One of de Grazia's major points is that the shortening of the working day is something of a myth in modern urban society, since the official data do not take into account the greatly increased time required to get to and from the work place.

11. de Grazia, *Ibid.*

12. R. W. Smuts, *Woman and Work in America* (New York: Columbia University Press, 1959). That the situation described has changed little in the current period is attested to by a series of publications by the U.S. Department of Labor Statistics for the years 1967–70.

13. F. J. Roethlisberger and W. J. Dickson, *Management and the Worker* (Cambridge, Mass.: Harvard University Press, 1939). For a more contemporary account see C. Argyris, *Integrating the Individual and the Organization* (New York: Wiley, 1964). Compare also Chapter 5, in Abraham K. Korman, *Industrial and Organizational Psychology* (Englewood Cliffs, New Jersey: Prentice-Hall, 1971).

14. Kurt Lewin, *Field Theory in the Social Sciences* (New York: Harper and

Row, 1951). A leading member of the Gestalt psychology group in Berlin, Lewin became in the United States probably the most influential force in modern social psychology. His chief interest was in analysis of the "topology" of the social structures which govern behavior and through which individuals must move.

15. Roger Barker, *Ecological Psychology* (Stanford, Calif.: Stanford University Press, 1968). This most recent book by Barker, a student and associate of Lewin, is committed to the thesis that there are instances in which the behavior of persons is almost entirely determined by the social settings in which they find themselves embedded. He also attempts to develop a metric and language through which the features of settings can be described. See also a recent collection by H. M. Proshansky, W. H. Ittleson and L. G. Rivlin, *Environmental Psychology* (New York: Holt, Rinehart and Winston, 1970). This work is cross-disciplinary and includes contributions by architects, urban sociologists, city planners, etc., as well as the work of a few psychologists who have begun to interest themselves in problems of environmental analysis.

16. Heinz Werner, *The Comparative Psychology of Mental Development* (Chicago: Follet, 1948).

17. Among Jean Piaget's voluminous writings, see particularly *The Construction of Reality in the Mind of the Child* (New York: Basic Books, 1954), *The Language and Thought of the Child* (New York: World Publishing Co., 1955) and his very stimulating *Play, Dreams and Imitation in Childhood* (New York: W. W. Norton, 1951).

18. Erik H. Erikson, *Childhood and Society*, 2nd ed. (New York: Norton, 1963); also see his "Identity and the Life Cycle," *Psychological Issues*, I,1(1959).

19. Donald E. Super has written a number of important books on vocational development. See particularly his *Psychology of Careers: An Introduction to Vocational Development* (New York: Harper, 1957). In later books he describes an extensive research on the vocational development of teenage boys: D. E. Super and M. J. Bohn, Jr., *Occupational Psychology* (Belmont, Calif.: Wadsworth Publishing Co., 1970); D. E. Super and P. L. Overstreet, *The Vocational Maturity of Ninth Grade Boys* (New York: Bureau of Publications, Teachers College, Columbia University, 1960).

20. Eli Ginzberg *et al.*, *The Development of Human Resources* (New York: McGraw-Hill, 1966); also see Ginzberg, *Occupational Choice: An Approach to a General Theory* (New York: Columbia University Press, 1951).

21. Anne Roe, *The Psychology of Occupations* (New York: John Wiley, 1956). See also Roe and M. Siegelman, *The Origin of Interests* (Washington, D.C.: American Personnel and Guidance Association, 1964). Roe presents an interesting and self-critical appraisal of her theoretical outlook and research findings (or lack of them) in "Personality Structure and Occupational Behavior," *Man in a World at Work*, Chapter 9, Henry Borow, ed. (Boston: Houghton Mifflin, 1964).

22. Walter S. Neff, "Psychoanalytic Conceptions of the Meaning of Work," *Psychiatry*, 28(1965):324–33.

23. Ives Hendrick is one of the very few psychoanalysts who have written specifically on work and its dynamics. See two papers in particular: "Work and the Pleasure Principle," *Psychoanalytic Quarterly*, 12(1943):311–29, and "The Discussion of the Instinct to Master," *Psychoanalytic Quarterly*, 12 (1943):561–65.

24. A psychoanalyst interested in ego psychology, Barbara Lantos has also written two very interesting papers on work: "Work and the Instincts," *International Journal of Psychoanalysis*, 24(1943):114–19, and "Metapsychological

Considerations on the Concept of Work," *International Journal of Psychoanalysis,* 33(1952):439–43.

25. Erik H. Erikson, *op. cit.*

26. Robert W. White caused something of a stir in American psychology when he launched an attack on reductionist theories of motivation, including classical psychoanalysis and much of modern learning theory. See his carefully reasoned paper "Motivation Reconsidered: the Concept of Competence," *Psychological Review,* 60(1959):297–333. White has developed his ideas still further in a more recent monograph "Ego and Reality in Psychoanalytic Theory," *Psychological Issues,* Monograph #11, 3(1963).

27. Harvey Swados has written novels on this theme and also discussed it in essay form. See "Work as a Public Issue," *Saturday Review,* 12 Dec. 1959.

28. Paul Goodman is, of course, well known for the force of his objections to the "processing of people" by the familiar institutions of modern society. See "Youth in Organized Society," *Commentary,* 29(1960):95–107, and *People or Personnel* (New York: Random House, 1965).

29. B. B. Seligman, *Most Notorious Victory: Man in an Age of Automation* (New York: The Free Press, 1966). Seligman, a labor economist, has attempted here a major assault on what he regards as the victimization of man by the machine.

30. Daniel Bell, *Work and its Discontents* (Boston: Beacon Press, 1956), a widely quoted essay which argues that the increasing division of labor and its managerial routinization have stripped most kinds of work of both meaningfulness and dignity.

31. Karl Marx, *Capital,* Vol. I (Chicago: Chas. H. Kerr, 1887). Marx's theory of work alienation has, of course, been enormously influential but is not always understood. Marx was less concerned with the feeling side of the process than he was with analyzing the structural features of the capitalist system of production. According to Marx, the transformation of both labor and its product into commodities and the appropriation by the entrepreneur of both the means of production and their product, have reduced what was once a "natural" relation of man to his environment to so many quanta of undifferentiated human energy at the command of the employer. Alienation is thus presented as an objective fact of a particular system of production, not merely a psychological aspect of individual workers, which might appear in any system of production.

32. Seligman, p. 368.

33. B. Kutner, D. Fanshell, A. M. Togo and T. M. Langer, *Five Hundred over Sixty* (New York: Russell Sage Foundation, 1956). In speaking of the attitudes of male workers toward retirement, these writers report that for some the demand that they give up their work is psychologically equivalent to a demand that they change their sex.

34. Norbert Wiener, *Cybernetics,* 2nd ed. (Cambridge, Mass.: MIT Press, 1961).

35. George Friedmann, *Industrial Society* (New York: The Free Press, 1955). Friedmann, a French industrial sociologist, is noted for his detailed studies of the life habits of blue-collar workers.

36. Charles A. Reich, *The Greening of America* (New York: Random House, 1970). A Professor of Law at Yale, Reich has written a book which has become something of a scandal among the *cognoscenti* and a popular best seller. It is frankly addressed to that sector of affluent youth whom Kenneth Kenniston has described as the uncommitted. On the basis of an historical and predictive analysis of industrialized societies, Reich argues that work and production are on their way out as important and necessary human

activities. His book has been sharply attacked as both frivolous speculation and unsupported by any real evidence.

37. Theodor Rozcak, *The Making of a Counter-Culture* (New York: Anchor-Doubleday, 1969). Rozcak must be counted as antitechnologist, attributing the bulk of our contemporary social problems to the victory of scientific world outlook. In effect, he argues that science is antihuman and ends by dividing the person from his own emotions and his "true" inner self. In doing so he calls for a return to mystical experience.
38. Reich, *ibid.*
39. The winter 1972 issue of *Dissent,* titled the "World of the Blue Collar Worker," consists predominently of interviews and statements by workers currently employed in the mass production industries. For a sociological study of considerable merit, see A. Kornhauser, *Mental Health of the Industrial Worker* (New York: Wiley, 1965), which presents very vivid descriptions of the aspirations and discontents of assembly workers in the automotive industry.

SUGGESTED READING

Arendt, Hannah. *The Human Condition.* Chicago: The University of Chicago Press, 1958. An analysis of the meaning of work and the social regulations that govern it, from ancient times to the present. The point of view is that of the political philosopher; work is studied in relation to the power structures of organized societies. The book is particularly interesting when discussing political philosophies that purport to justify slavery and serfdom.

de Grazia, S. *Of Time, Work, and Leisure.* New York: Twentieth Century Fund, 1962. A sociological study of changes in hours of work, the relation of work to leisure, and changes in the meanings of both work and nonwork. This is a major contribution to a topic that is apparently becoming of increasing concern to labor sociologists and behavior scientists.

Friedmann, G. *Industrial Society.* New York: The Free Press, 1955. A major work in the tradition of European industrial sociology. Is concerned with the relations of the human worker and industrial technology. It is a very balanced work, managing to avoid the opposite errors of either arguing for an end to technology or being so enamored of the machine that the human being is lost sight of.

Neff, W. S. *Work and Human Behavior.* Chicago: Aldine-Atherton Press, 1968. Attempts both to survey changes in the conceptualization of work and to develop a comprehensive theory of work behavior. An elaboration of some of the ideas suggested in this chapter.

Nisbet, R. A. *The Sociological Tradition.* New York: Basic Books, 1966. Very comprehensive account of the seminal sociological theories. It is useful for those unacquainted with the chief approaches to sociological analysis.

Vroom, V. H. *Work and Motivation.* New York: Wiley, 1964. The best current account of the types of research which interest the industrial psychologist.

Wright, B. A. *Physical Disability—A Psychological Approach.* New York: Harper and Row, 1960. Still the best current treatment of the meaning of work for the handicapped and disabled person. The viewpoint is essentially that of the social psychologist with an interest in vocational rehabilitation.

8 The American Educational Structure

Robert Lathrop
The Florida State University

The title of this chapter seems far too ambitious, for the term "education" in its fullest sense would include all human experiences, many aspects of which are dealt with by the other contributors to this volume. This chapter, therefore, will limit the use of the term "education" to those activities which take place in formally organized schools.

THE SCHOOL IN AMERICAN SOCIETY

In a very real sense, the school in America is a societal institution which is simultaneously responsible to everyone and to no one. Like the church, government, and most other social inventions, schools attempt to meet the needs of all people and thereby only approximately satisfy the needs of any individual.

If one thinks of any large or small community in the United States and considers the range of educational services that schools are expected to provide to the varied individuals in that community, the enormity of the task assigned to schools in this country begins to become apparent. In earlier days, when society itself was less complex, social expectations of schools also were much simpler. Formal schooling was a luxury enjoyed by only a few, and children were more often found at work than in the classroom. Those few children who were able to attend formal schooling expected and received a very limited curriculum, consisting of the classics and the "three r's"—"reading, 'riting, and 'rithmetic." There was no expectation that schooling had any utilitarian value other than to teach children how to keep simple accounts and how to read the Bible. The Nation's economy was largely agricultural, and, in fact, the current school calendar is still a vestige of an earlier time when children needed to have the active summer months for planting, tending, and harvesting crops.

As society gradually became more industrialized and urbanized, laws were passed by social reformers to protect children from economic exploitation, primarily by their parents. Children were required (allowed) by law to attend school until the legal age when parents could put them to work to help supplement the family income. Curriculums tended to remain largely academic, and in only a few highly industrialized sections of the country were there programs provided for children interested in learning skilled trades or technical subjects.

It was not until the turn of the twentieth century that the high school as we know it came into being. Before that time secondary schools were,

180

in fact, college preparatory institutions. In 1870, for example, eight out of ten high school graduates entered college, but only a small fraction of the population entered high school. For the generation growing up during the early 1900s attending high school was the exception rather than the norm, and it is well to remember that only during the past forty or fifty years has a high school education been the norm, rather than the exception.

As schools have grown in the proportion of the society they serve, they have also been faced with the reality that society is not of one mind with regard to the purposes of formal schooling. For example, a sizeable segment of the American population believes that the primary purpose of schools is to transmit the accumulated knowledge and experience of previous generations. In the minds of such people, to be educated means to have at one's command the vast store of information about the evolution of man's understanding of his place in the "total scheme of things," to stand, as it were, upon the "shoulders of past generations." Another point of view, of somewhat more contemporary origin, stresses the importance of developing students' problem-solving abilities. Advocates of this more "forward-looking" philosophy argue that past knowledge is only important if it contributes to the ability of students to develop strategies and techniques for solving new problems and challenges that they will inevitably face in their future lives. Still others believe that the primary purpose of schools is to develop attitudes and values which will make students aware of their obligations and responsibilities as citizens of the community, the state, and the Nation.

The list of expectations and priorities could go on, and, indeed, every few years a national commission is established to define the goals of education, presumably reflecting society's expectations of schools. One of the most recent attempts to define the goals of education was published in 1966 by the American Association of School Administrators. According to the school administrators, there are nine imperatives to be considered when curriculums are modified, instructional methods revised, and organizational patterns reshaped. These imperatives are

1. To make urban life rewarding and satisfying;
2. To prepare people for the world of work;
3. To discover and nurture creative talent;
4. To strengthen the moral fabric of society;
5. To deal constructively with psychological tensions;
6. To keep democracy working;
7. To make intelligent use of natural resources;
8. To make the best use of leisure time;
9. To work with other people of the world for human betterment.[1]

It is obvious from examining such a list that the role of the school in American society has evolved a long way from simply teaching the "three r's." There is, in fact, no aspect of contemporary society that could not be included in such a list.

Unfortunately, however, as a result of accepting responsibility for such broad social missions, educators have created for themselves an undoable task. Over a long period of years they have successfully "educated" the American public to believe that the school is the principal agent of social evolution and that education is the key to individual advancement and success. Although few would deny that education is a necessary condition to societal and personal improvement, it is not in-and-of itself *sufficient,* and it is this subtle but critical distinction that educators, in their enthusiasm, have failed to convey. For sizeable segments of American society education has not led to personal advancement, employment, equal rights, freedom from hunger, or adequate health care. For many it has not led to anything other than disappointment and cynicism.

Education in this country has been "over-sold," and it is therefore at a critical turning point in its relation to society. Either it must admit that it is only prepared to assume a limited role, or it must reorganize its emphases to deliver the results that it has long claimed. It cannot much longer expect to be supported on one basis and deliver on another.

ORGANIZATION OF SCHOOLING

It is reasonably safe to assert that, somewhere in this country, it is possible to find an example of virtually every educational plan which has ever been devised by human intellect: publicly supported, privately supported; secular, nonsecular; day schools, night schools; preschool programs, postgraduate programs; vocational programs, academic programs; full-time, part-time; degree-granting, nondegree; the list of descriptive vectors could go on almost infinitely, with any particular school or program located in n-dimensional space, depending on its particular combination of descriptive coordinates. A simple description of the structure of education in the United States is no longer possible (if indeed it ever was) and educational planners are constantly at the task of shuffling the pieces of this enormously complex jig-saw puzzle that we call schooling in America.

The point in a child's life when he or she first leaves the exclusive care and supervision of the family and is physically placed under the care and the supervision of a nonrelated adult, such a point might be thought of as the child's first school experience. The agency might be described as a nursery school, a day-care center, a preschool program, or any of a number of similar titles. In a majority of instances preschools are privately managed, and they vary in purpose from routine care (child-sitting) to intellectual acceleration (enrichment). However, although increasing attention has been given to the early admission of children to planned educational experiences, the great majority of children do not attend preschool programs and have no real continuing contact with schools before enrollment in kindergarten, usually at the age of five. Even here there are wide regional and local customs regarding attendance in kindergartens, with only about two-thirds of the five-year-old population enrolled in schools.[2]

In the age group of six to thirteen years, the proportion of children in school reaches 99 percent. If one assumes the normal relationship of grade placement and age (grade one, six-year-old children; grade two, seven-year-old children, etc.), we may conclude that virtually every child (not otherwise institutionalized) attends at least eight grades of formal schooling. Within these first eight years of formal education there are almost endless organizational patterns, including a recent emphasis on ungraded schooling which eliminates the classification of students by grade level (first grader, second grader, etc.) and, in principle, groups children according to levels of performance. Ungradedness, however, is only the most recent of many structural plans for the first few years of formal education.

Most typically we find the first eight or so years divided into primary grades kindergarten (K) through three, intermediate grades four through six, and junior high school grades seven, eight, and sometimes nine. The rationale for this organizational pattern has been largely based on developmental or maturational similarities of children within these grade groupings. A recent variation on this general pattern of organization is the middle school, which includes grades five, six, and seven and occasionally grades four and/or eight and/or nine. There is little uniformity across communities concerning middle-school organization, and some critics have suggested that the middle school has emerged as much out of a desire for better physical plant utilization as out of educational or maturational considerations.

The great majority, about 85 percent of the kindergarten through eighth-grade children attend publicly supported schools, although in certain regions and selected communities the proportions of children attending private and secular schools are substantially greater. Almost without exception, private elementary schools are more oriented to intensive development of basic academic skills than to the somewhat broader objectives professed for the public elementary school. Beyond the age of thirteen the proportion of individuals enrolled in formal educational programs drops progressively from the high 90s to about 70 percent graduation from grade twelve. In most states there are compulsory attendance laws requiring school enrollment of students up to age sixteen. However, communities are not equally diligent about enforcement of such laws, and, consequently, there is a self-selected attrition of students beyond age fourteen.

Within the ninth, tenth, eleventh, and twelfth years of schooling there is a clear trend toward compartmentalizing or tracking of students. Secondary schools attempt to identify early the some 40 or 50 percent who are expected to enter college and place them in an "academic" program. The remaining students are placed in the "general" program and, if they so indicate, may be further identified as "vocational" students. In many large communities the separation of academic, general, and vocational students may be so complete as to enroll them in different schools.

In most secondary schools curriculums are designed around subject matter lines. Within disciplines courses are further organized sequentially so that English II follows English I, etc. To support the curriculum organization schools often place students into "tracks" based upon previous achievement records and test results. Although tracking is promulgated as a means of adjusting the difficulty of course material to the level of student ability, the long history of research evidence suggests that its principal virtue is to suit the predispositions of teachers and that it is generally detrimental to the academic and personal development of students placed in the lower tracks. Teachers often resent being assigned students in low tracks, and they convey their resentment and lowered expectations to such students in many overt ways. Students adjust their expectations and respond accordingly, so that those in lower tracks fall further and further behind and can never pull themselves up. The assignment of a student to a higher track is virtually impossible once he has fallen behind. Thus, tracking is a unidirectional filter opening downward.

The years of secondary school (high school) are clearly a time of selective retention and specialization. Choices are made, knowingly or unknowingly, and those choices open some doors and close others. Directions are set which become increasingly constrictive, narrowing rather than broadening the student's options. In most instances by the time the student reaches the tenth grade the course of his or her remaining formal education is irreversibly set, and he can rarely exert more than minor redirection on the course that has wisely or unwisely been set for him. By and large, students are not encouraged or prepared to consider the major decisions they will ultimately make about their lives but are instead led into a series of short-range decisions which cumulatively determine, *de facto*, the student's educational experiences and ultimately his or her preparation for adult society.

For all practical purposes, the elementary school child is insulated from society by parents and teachers. His social contacts are monitored and filtered and his educational experiences are largely prescribed.

Emerging from this educational and social cocoon, the seventh-, eighth-, or ninth-grade student finds himself in a world that is vastly broader than he has known before. Suddenly he is asked to make certain educational choices about which he knows very little. "Should I take general math or algebra I; should I take general science or biology; should I begin a foreign language (and if so which one) or should I elect industrial arts (or home economics); should I begin typing or go out for football (or music)?" Although teachers, counselors, and parents all attempt to "help" the student understand *their* perceptions of the consequences of these many choices, such adult guidance tends to be focused on short-term consequences inherent in a particular school's programming ("If you don't take French I this year you can't begin it until you are in the tenth grade," etc.) or on parental aspirations ("If you want to go to college, wouldn't it be better to take another course in science than to take industrial arts?"). Administratively, still other "decisions" are made for students by placing them in ability or achievement tracks based upon their previous academic performances and test results. ("Johnny did well in ninth grade math, so he should go into the top algebra class; Suzy didn't do very well, so she should be put in general math," etc.)

Out of this interplay of personal, parental, and administrative decisions a schedule of school experiences is built, year by year, from required courses for graduation (usually four years of English, three years of social studies, two or more years of science and mathematics) and, hopefully, a personally meaningful choice of elective courses and extracurricular experiences.

Although generalizations are risky, it is reasonably safe to assert that most decisions made by students are made against a criterion of high school graduation rather than any life-oriented goal. Since the majority of youth do complete their formal educations at grade twelve and then enter adult society, the orientation to making educational decisions and choices in terms of the short-range criterion of graduation seems significantly in-adequate. Many believe that the school experience ought to lead to more than graduation as an end in itself. The more valid goal for education, and the frame of reference for individual choice points, should be a focus on readiness to enter adult society, which may involve twelve years of education but, more importantly, should mean a continuing commitment to intellectual and vocational self-renewal. The high school diploma as we have known it would then fall into perspective as a vestige of an era when the singular purpose of secondary education was preparation for college and the diploma a certificate marking completion of a specified set of pre-college courses.

In large part, the constraints on student exploration in the secondary school arise out of a questionable but widely held premise that high school programs should be limited to a period of three or four years, regardless of individual needs or ability to profit from additional secondary school experiences. A more enlightened view of secondary school programming would avoid the "direction" of students into choices which are not in their long-range best interests.

Of the students who do complete their high school programs and gradu-ate, one-half to two-thirds end their formal education and enter the world of gainful employment, perform military service, or assume domestic responsibilities. A small percentage of these individuals will have available short-term programs of on-the-job or military training courses. For the most part, however, this one-half to two-thirds of high school graduates will have no further contact with institutionalized education.

Of the one-third to one-half of the high school graduates who do con-tinue their formal education beyond high school, about 20 percent will enter two-year institutions (junior colleges, community colleges, etc.) and the remaining 80 percent will enter four-year colleges, universities, seminaries, or technological institutes. Of the 20 percent who enter two-year institutions, about three out of four will take courses leading to baccalaureate credit and only one out of four will complete an associate degree or other terminal program. Virtually all of the four-year students are enrolled in bachelor's degree or preprofessional programs. Approximately one-half of those who enter college will complete a four-year program leading to a bachelor's degree. Approximately one-fourth of the bachelor's degree recipients will complete a master's degree, and about one out of seven master's graduates will eventually earn the doctor of philosophy degree (or other advanced professional degree).

Aside from a very small number of postdoctoral fellowships, the foregoing comprises the population of students who flow through the American edu-cational system, public and private.

FINANCING AND STAFFING OF EDUCATION IN AMERICA

For the reader who has not made a study of the financing of education in the United States, a brief review of the financial base upon which this very large social institution rests may be appropriate.

Considering first public elementary and secondary education, almost 42 billion dollars were spent for these schools during the 1970–1971 school year. Of this total expenditure slightly over half, or approximately 22 billion dollars, was raised at the local level, largely through property taxes. Over 98 percent of the revenues raised by independent school districts comes from the property tax.

In addition to the public school revenues raised through local property taxes, states made contributions to local school districts in the amount of about 17 billion dollars, approximately another 40 percent of the public elementary and secondary school budgets. State contributions to local school operation are based on fixed amounts for each student in attendance within a given district. Often states develop formulas designed to offset local inequalities in property values. Although well-intentioned, equalization formulas have been shown by recent studies to be largely ineffective with affluent districts often having twice the revenue to spend on education compared to districts having less taxable property or property assessed to be less valuable. Furthermore, most equalization formulas do not recognize the peculiar problems of large urban areas, and state-aid formulas provide proportionally less aid to urban areas than they do to rural and suburban school systems.

Although much attention has been focused on the Federal contributions to elementary and secondary education, in relative terms its financial impact is minor. Slightly less than 3 billion of the 42 billion dollars total revenue collected for elementary and secondary schools in 1970–1971 was obtained from federal sources. This amounts to slightly less than 7 percent of public school budgets. Although an attempt has been made to allocate this relatively small amount of Federal money to special programs for communities having large numbers of low income families and/or minority groups, the total amount expended is just too small to relieve the special financial problems faced by such districts.

Public elementary and secondary schools are currently in serious financial difficulty. The problem is even more acute, however, for private education. Historically, private educational institutions have supported themselves largely through tuition charged to parents and through subsidies and endowments provided by religious institutions or other philanthropic organizations. Although such private elementary and secondary schools enroll a relatively small portion (15 percent) of the total school population in this country, many segments of society feel that private institutions should have the opportunity to survive and are anxiously trying to find ways by which the private institution may be subsidized without violating the constitutional separation of church and state. Such efforts have not met with notable success, however, and there is real question about the long-range survival of privately supported elementary and secondary education in this country.

With the exception of the "white academy" which has sprung up in certain southern states as a reaction to the enforced desegregation of the public schools, private school enrollment has continued to decrease relatively over the past few years, and it will undoubtably continue in that direction unless new plans for its financial support can be conceived and implemented.

At the postsecondary level there have been a number of important trends which have occurred during the past few years. In many parts of the country there has been a dramatic increase in the number of two-year institutions providing postsecondary education and training. Such institutions are partly supported through tuitions, but the major cost for most public community colleges is borne at the local level, in much the same way as public elementary and secondary schools are financed. Four-year institutions, on the other hand, are ordinarily governed and financed separately through a combination of state and federal appropriations along with tuition charged to the individual student. At the postsecondary level, private institutions do share in state and federal governmental support, mainly in the form of monies for capital outlay (such as buildings and land) and for student scholarships and loan guarantees.

Although there has been a gradual growth in the number of students enrolled in private, four-year institutions from just over 1 million in 1950 to close to 2 million in 1970, the growth in private institutions has in no way approached the growth in public postsecondary education during the same period of time. From 1950 to 1970 public higher educational institutions increased their enrollments from just over 1 million in 1950 to 5.6 million in 1970. To a large extent the differential rate of growth for the two types of institutions has been the result of economic factors which have forced the private institutions to keep tuitions high. Even with state and federal subsidies, annual expenditures for students enrolled in private institutions are typically two or more times expenditures for students enrolled in public institutions.

For similar reasons the pattern of growth for two-year colleges parallels that of four-year institutions. In 1950 there was a total of 528 two-year institutions, approximately 300 of which were public and 229 private. By 1968 the number of public institutions had almost doubled, whereas the number of private two-year institutions had only increased to 254. Perhaps, of even greater significance were the ratios of students enrolled in public and private two-year institutions. In 1968, for example, there were just over 120 thousand students enrolled in private two-year institutions, compared with well over a million students enrolled in public junior colleges.

Taken as a whole, the estimated expenditure for public and private education in this country was 73.6 billion dollars for the 1970–1971 academic year. This was divided between public and private elementary and secondary schools (42.5 billion and 5 billion, respectively) and between public and private higher education (17 billion and 9.1 billion, respectively). These estimates were based on a projected enrollment of 59.2 million students at the elementary and secondary levels and approximately 7.9 million students enrolled in higher education.

Because public schools are largely financed at the local level through property taxes, and because of the present state of economy, taxpayers all across the country are in open revolt against requests of school boards for increases in property taxes. In California, for example, thirty school districts went bankrupt during the 1970–1971 school year, and 60 percent of the proposed increases in school taxes and new bond issues were rejected by the voters. Similar pictures, although perhaps less extreme, can be found all across the country with a widespread unwillingness to approve increased tax revenues. Teachers and administrators are not being rehired, or they are being paid in script while major cities go increasingly into debt. Although exact amounts are difficult to verify, major cities such as New York and Philadelphia are reporting that they ended the 1970–1971 school year between 40 and 70 million dollars in debt.

If one were to set out to conceive of a completely inequitable and irrational tax by which to support public services, he could do no better than the property tax. It is regressive and is inequitably applied to various types of property, invariably striking the poor property owner more directly than the more wealthy. In all instances families with low incomes must devote a proportionately higher amount of their expenditures to housing than do the more affluent, and property taxes tend to take a larger percentage of their income. The tax is felt particularly strongly by home owners whose incomes are fixed and rise more slowly than individuals whose incomes are not so constrained.

Because school expenditures are tied to enrollments rather than to economic conditions, the recent "slow down" in the economy has caused expenditures to overtake revenues. As long as the general state of the economy increases sufficiently to match the growth in educational demands, there is no problem. In recent years, however, the increased financial demands required for schools have caught up with lagging revenues, and public school expenditures are putting heavier and heavier burdens upon local property taxpayers. When the increasing press for financial support is coupled with the general lack of confidence in public schools, the result has been a taxpayer revolt in the area of financing public education.

There is no question that schools are in a state of financial crisis and are rapidly being brought to a condition of immobility without any obvious relief at hand. Unfortunately, prospects for increased Federal spending for education or taxation reform are extremely unlikely in the foreseeable future, and it is probable that schools cannot expect any immediate relief from the serious financial crises they are now facing. Because the major portion of educational budgets is devoted to instructional salaries, one of the first and obvious ways in which school and college administrators have attempted to curb rising costs has been to eliminate or collapse instructional positions. This trend of eliminating teaching positions and its concomitant effect of discouraging teacher mobility, plus the inability of training institutions to rapidly adjust their output of graduates, has created a highly unfavorable ratio between teacher supply and demand in many fields.[3] Although the problem is frequently described as a "teacher surplus," this term is something of a misnomer. The matter is not so much a surplus of teachers as a financially imposed shortage of jobs. If schools were not being staffed on a financial austerity basis, there would be jobs for most, if not all, of the teachers who have been and are being trained.

Given the fact that there will be more teachers available for employment than the schools will be able to absorb, one would expect that schools would take advantage of this opportunity to select from the teachers that are available, those teachers who display the highest potential for effectively serving the needs of children. Unfortunately, however, there is little indication at the present time that schools are being more selective. Instead, many communities seem to be taking the financially expeditious view that those few positions which become available should be filled with beginning teachers who can generally be obtained at a lower starting salary than teachers with more experience and training. At the same time, because of tenure and other perceived constraints, administrators frequently refuse to purge the teaching ranks of teachers known to be incompetent. Although the teaching profession probably has no larger proportion of incompetent practitioners than any other profession, the teacher, unlike other professionals, does not operate on the "open market." Even though the present job market would permit administrators to take a more assertive stance with regard to the improvement of instruction, there is little evidence that school officials will take advantage of this opportunity.

In spite of the fact that schools are financially unable to employ the number of teachers who are available and should be employed, there continue to be large unmet needs for school personnel in such areas of emerging concern as early childhood education, habilitative sciences, health education, industrial arts, mathematics education, and physical science, reading, recreation education, vocational and adult education, and vocational guidance.

Of particular relevance to this discussion are the projected demand figures for teachers of vocational subjects and vocational guidance workers. The report of the Advisory Council on Vocational Education[4] projects that by 1975 the number of vocational teachers will be approximately 350 thousand, an increase of 150 percent during the decade following the implementation of the Vocational Education Act. This demand far exceeds the numbers of students now in preparation to teach vocational subjects.

Because of the recentness of the career education movement, numerical estimates of the demand for vocational guidance workers are sheer speculation. It is clear, however, that the demand will continue to be high for many years. During the interim it is probable that vocational guidance will emerge as a distinct specialty and will include within its ranks many paraprofessionals recruited from fields other than counselor education.

SCHOOLS AND SOCIAL UNREST

As if the financial and staffing problems were not serious enough, they are only two of the critical circumstances which face our nation's schools. For the past eight to ten years schools also have become the major battleground of groups struggling for equal rights. Unfortunately, both social reformers and reactionaries have used schools as arenas for testing the constitutional limits of equal rights. Plan after plan has been devised by groups wishing to resist the spirit of the Supreme Court decisions affirming equal educational opportunity for all children. One by one such plans have been ruled unconstitutional, but social change comes grudgingly and the recent controversy over "busing" is only the most recent in a long chain of attempts to preserve the *status quo*.

Similarly, reformers have used the schools, particularly the colleges and universities, as a springboard to launch their programs of social change. Regardless of who uses the schools as a lever, it is the schools that suffer. When parents demonstrated against busing their ire was focused on the local school administration, not on the courts that had ordered the plan.

When disruptions occurred on college campuses it was the universities that were criticized for failing to keep order, rather than the social and political conditions that the students were attempting to dramatize. No matter how one assesses the virtue (or lack thereof) of a particular cause, over the past ten years the net effect of social unrest on the schools has been to weaken public confidence and support.

Due to the continuing social turmoil and partly to the ineptitude of educational leaders at all levels, there has arisen the widely held belief that schools have abdicated their responsibility for maintaining order, discipline, and control. In a recent Gallup poll concerning problems in education lack of discipline headed the list.[5] Although specific problems cited and proposed solutions varied widely, the common theme underlying the comments was that schools have been too permissive, resulting in a weakening of public confidence.

Current concerns about drug abuse have also been focused on the schools since the majority of potential users are of school age. Although more education about drugs is frequently posed as a solution, lack of information about the effects of drugs is usually not the problem. It would be difficult to find a school age child who could not recite the standard arguments against "hard" drugs, and the disquieting fact for educators is that the current research on "soft" drugs indicates that their effects are no more habituating or harmful than the alcohol consumed by the majority of adults in this society. Unless, and until, research provides clear evidence concerning the long- and short-term effects of drugs such as marijuana, educators will find it very difficult to engage in programs of drug education which do more than compromise their lagging credibility with students. With regard to "hard" drugs, there is, of course, no ambiguity about the long-term deleterious effects. However, current research evidence regarding the propensity toward hard drug addiction indicates that it is an outgrowth of medical or societal problems which are well beyond the control of most schools to change.

One could go on elaborating problems of teacher militancy, sexual permissiveness, local control, and a host of other maladies which in one way or another are being faced by schools today. To recite such a list, however, would only serve to underline the point already made. Schools in this country are no longer observers or reporters of social unrest, but, rather they have been drawn willingly and unwillingly into the fray of every significant social problem. Schools, moreover, are completely defenseless in dealing with contemporary social problems since they are entirely dependent upon a consensus of society for their support. At any time a segment of society, including the federal government, is allowed to push the schools into a partisan role in a significant issue, the school will always suffer regardless of the ultimate worth of the cause.

EDUCATIONAL PROGRAMMING

If one takes the premise that schools ought to reflect the priorities of the communities that are asked to provide the financial support for those institutions, then one might reasonably ask how it happens that such a wide gulf exists between the expectations of parents and communities and the existing curriculums. The obvious answer is that the control of schools does not rest within the hands of the community; it rests within the hands of the institutions which train teachers and the administrators who are responsible for the educational leadership within the community. Although school boards are appointed or elected to represent the interests of the community and to provide a liaison between the professional educator and the community, school boards are notoriously ineffective in serving this function. In most communities school board members are unprepared to deal with the complex issues on which they are called to make decisions, and so they depend unquestioningly on the recommendations of their chief school officer. In most communities there is no effective way for the public to represent its point of view to the school board members, and school boards typically end up conducting their business in executive session, "rubber stamping" the recommendations of the administration. It is not surprising, therefore, that most taxpayers and parents feel that they are impotent in their ability to influence local educational policy and, as a consequence, abstain from any real attempt to influence the direction of their local schools.

Even at a more personal level, it is difficult for those parents who are sufficiently interested in the details of the educational programs to interact with teachers or advisors in an effort to learn something about their children's programs, progress, or educational objectives. The gulf, in fact, has grown so wide that neither teachers nor parents feel comfortable in relating to each other, and, consequently, both avoid interactions except in cases where situations have become completely intolerable.

The disquieting fact is that schools are run to suit the convenience of educators, rather than the social, vocational, or emotional needs of children or the expectations of their parents. This state of affairs is not a new one, for one can find a long history of the inappropriateness or unresponsiveness of educational programs to the needs of children. The unhappy fact is that educators traditionally have oriented curriculums around the fragmented discipline-oriented concepts of the nature of knowledge. One merely needs to look at the scheduling of the school day to realize that curriculum is organized around discrete discipline areas with little or no attempt to relate information to the lives of children. Information is taught simply because it exists. Although educational innovators have been arguing for at least seventy-five years that education must recognize the pluralistic needs of children, school curriculums have remained monolithic in character, based on the premise that a general education best suits the needs of everyone and the implicit assumption that each student should go as far as he can in an essentially precollege curriculum. Attempts to provide alternative programs for those who are obviously not college-bound have been relegated to second-class status within the school system, both educationally and sociologically. The ethic is to encourage students to stay in a general education program, and only when it becomes obvious that the student can not succeed in that track is any serious attempt made to provide an educational alternative. This point of view has prevailed in spite of the fact that 60 percent of the high school graduates do not even attempt to enter college programs. Curriculums that are not college preparatory have historically held low prestige in the minds of educators and parents; and they regard children who are shunted into nonacademic programs as in some sense having failed.[6]

The reality is, however, that the majority of students cannot and perhaps should not attend college, both in the terms of the possibility of admission to postsecondary education and, perhaps more importantly, in terms of the types of occupations which the majority of individuals now in school are likely to enter. Projections from the United States Department of Labor indicate that by 1975 about one out of seven employed persons will be in a position of professional or technical responsibility. Another 10 percent will be involved in business or in management, bringing to about 25 percent the total number of individuals who will be in occupations which have traditionally required college preparation. The remaining 75 percent will be in clerical positions, sales, skilled or semiskilled crafts, and service occupations. Since three-fourths of the present school population can look forward to occupations which are nonacademic in their orientation, often requiring specialized training which is not now available in the typical public school program, the inescapable conclusion is that the majority of American youth are now in educational programs which are only incidentally related to their probable employment—if related at all.

Although schools have regularly admitted a responsibility to prepare individuals for subsequent employment, it is clear that the present emphasis upon general education in our public schools makes little or no attempt to provide occupational preparation for the majority of the students, in spite of the stated goals of education and the expectations of parents and of society at large. In the face of the clear unresponsiveness of the education establishment to giving greater attention to the preparation of youth for occupations, the Congress passed the Vocational Education Act of 1963 and subsequently strengthened it with a series of broadening amendments in 1968. More recently, the appointment of Dr. Sidney Marland, Jr., as Assistant Secretary of Education has added further impetus to federal commitment to career and occupational education. Now, for the first time, at the level of the Commissioner and above, there is an apparent and serious commitment to encouraging and supporting a program of education which will meet the needs of the majority of American youth.[7] At this writing it is too early to know what the long term effects of this movement will be on the direction of schooling in this country. It does appear, however, that the federal government, through the U.S. Office of Education, has recognized the dimension of work as important in the preparation of youth; it now remains for local and state level administrators to accept and develop the challenge laid down by Congress.

THE DYNAMICS OF EDUCATIONAL CHANGE

Given this significant mandate to change, what appear to be the prospects? In an attempt to describe the dynamics of educational change Orlosky and Smith summarized the impact and focus of a number of ideas which have influenced education during the past seventy-five years.[8] As an outgrowth of their analysis, Orlosky and Smith set forth several points of which those who wish to promote educational change should be aware. These points are paraphrased below.

1. Changes in methods of instruction are apparently more difficult to make than changes in curriculum.
2. A change that requires teachers to abandon existing instructional practices and replace them with new practices is particularly difficult to implement.
3. If new practices require teachers to be retrained in order to effect the change, chances for success are reduced unless a strong incentive to engage in retraining is provided.
4. Effort to change curriculum involving displacement of the existing curriculum patterns is not likely to be permanent, even if the faculty initially supports the change.
5. Changes in the curriculum that represent additions, such as new subjects, can be made more securely if they are supported by legislation or well-organized interest groups. Conversely, additions to the curriculum made in the face of active social opposition are not likely to survive.
6. Efforts to alter the total administrative structure, or any considerable part of it, are unlikely to be successful.
7. Changes that represent additions or extensions to the existing educational ladder are more likely to be lasting than changes which involve modifications of the existing administrative organization, such as flexible scheduling.
8. Changes initiated in a particular school are not likely to become widespread or permanently intrenched in the absence of a carefully worked out plan for diffusing them throughout the entire system.
9. Changes that have the support of more than one critical element are more likely to succeed. Changes supported only by educators without legal, social, and other kinds of support are not likely to survive.
10. Changes will be resisted if they require educational personnel to relinquish power.
11. Changes which do not require people to learn substantial new bodies of content and procedures are more likely to persist than if the cognitive load is heavy.

The historical evidence regarding change in education seems to be fairly clear. Changes which involve "tinkering" with the system, particularly the curriculum, are relatively easy to implement, especially if the change does not involve extensive retraining of teachers and has the support, both moral and financial, of governmental and other social agencies. On the other hand, changes in the organization of schools involving administrative realignments, shifts of the power base, and major new directions have been infrequent and usually of short-term duration.

Efforts to move education in significantly new directions have been notably unsuccessful and will probably continue to be so without massive and continued societal and governmental intervention. To believe that the educational establishment has within itself a capacity for significant self-renewal has been demonstrated to be unrealistic. Although educational innovators tend to be optimistic that the educational establishment can respond in a self-correcting way to the needs of society, the historical evidence belies this optimism. Though perhaps too critical, the following quotation from William Congrieve seems appropriate.

> How reverend is the face of this tall pile,
> Whose ancient pillars rear their marble heads,
> To bear aloft its arched and ponderous roof,
> By its own weight made steadfast and immovable . . .[9]

THE RECENT EMERGENCE OF VOCATIONAL EDUCATION

One of the major difficulties in promoting educational change has been the fluctuating federal commitment to educational problems which require long and sustained encouragement and study. One does not need to look far for documentation of the "in again-out again" posture of the government with regard to support of solutions to important, educational problems. With each new change in leadership at the federal level there has been a new "horse to ride," with a great many "races" started, but few run to the finish line. As a case in point, for almost fifty years the federal commitment to vocational education has been tied to national crises—war, depression, or unemployment. Note the following acts and their dates: Smith-Hughes (1917), George-Reed (1929), George-Ellzey (1934), George-Dean (1936), Vocational Education for Defense (1940), George-Barden (1946), National Defense Education Act (1958), Area Redevelopment Act (1961), Manpower Development and Training Act (1962), and the Vocational Education Act of 1963 (and the supporting amendments of 1968). Except for the last, every one has coincided with or followed a time of national crisis. Although the historical contexts for these legislated programs is beyond the scope of this discussion,[10] it suffices to say that vocational education has only prospered during times of national crisis.

Now, for the first time, the motivation for support of vocational education appears to arise not out of immediate social crisis but out of a growing awareness of the real needs of people in American society. The 1963 Act, for example, was focused on services to people, in contrast with prior acts which had only provided for training personnel in special occupational categories. The intent of this shift was to remove the artificial barriers of occupational categories and to provide services to people without respect to predetermined occupational groupings or national needs. (For a complete analysis of this Act, see Herr, Chapter 2.) The Act specified that there were several purposes for which Federal funds were to be used.

1. Vocational education for persons attending high school.
2. Vocational education for persons who have completed (or have left high school) and who are available for full-time study in preparation for entering the labor market.
3. Vocational education for persons who have already entered the labor market and who need training or retraining to achieve stability or advancement in employment.
4. Vocational education for persons who have academic, socioeconomic, or

other handicaps that prevent them from succeeding in a regular vocational education program.

5. Construction of area vocational and technical school facilities.

6. Services and activities to assure quality in all vocational education programs (teacher training and supervision, program evaluation, special demonstration or experimental programs, development of instructional materials, and state administration and leadership, including periodic evaluation of state and local vocational education programs and services).

Although the Act authorizes a number of new areas of responsibility in vocational education, two of its most prominent features are the provisions for the area vocational school and the increased commitment to postsecondary and adult education.

Recognizing the low prestige of vocational programs existing prior to 1963, the decision was made to authorize the establishment and funding of a new series of schools to serve the vocational needs of adjacent independent school districts. Known as Area Vocational and Technical Schools (AVTS), these institutions were to be adjuncts to the regular high school programs, emphasizing the training of youth for post-high school employment, but would be administratively and physically separate from the existing secondary schools. Consequently, during the period from 1965 to 1970 there was a massive program of building new area vocational schools with an accompanying jump from 3 million to 4 million students in federally aided vocational education programs at the secondary level.

Although the development of the area vocational school has presented a windfall for school systems and communities alike, this movement has not been without its problems. The attitudes of school administrators and teachers, and for that matter the community at large, toward vocational education has not been changed overnight. In many communities the low status of vocational programs has discouraged parents and students from proper consideration of the opportunities available in the area vocational school. Similarly, counselors and guidance personnel, historically oriented to precollege counseling, have not embraced the concept of vocational education simply by the existence of the area vocational school. The emergence of the area vocational school from the "womb" has not been without its "birth pangs" and it remains to be seen whether it will be adopted or rejected by its educational "foster parents."

In many ways the action of the Congress in 1963 caught the educational community napping. Even the vocational educators were unprepared for the extensiveness of the federal legislation, and they found themselves without programs, staff, or leadership to fully utilize their new-found authorization. Directors of programs were appointed to build new buildings with only the time-worn programs to go in them; staff had to be recruited and often put before classes without any pedagogical training; no adequate criteria for student selection existed, and few trained guidance personnel were available; scheduling, student transportation, and problems with participating high schools were only dimly foreseen. These and many more difficulties accompanied the emergence of this new "school" and continue to face it as it struggles to earn its place in the total system of American education.

In addition to the secondary program, many area vocational schools and most two-year community colleges have expanded their programs for occupational preparation. Although the number of students involved is relatively smaller (about 750 thousand students in 1970), it is this area of vocational preparation which has shown the most dramatic growth as a result of the 1963 legislation. As has already been mentioned, the two-year college enrollment has grown dramatically during recent years. In the period from 1950 to 1970 enrollments mushroomed from approximately 200 thousand students in 1950 to almost 1.5 million students in 1970, many of whom have been attracted recently to such institutions because of their emerging emphases in vocational education.

A REEXAMINATION OF PRIORITIES

In a somewhat simplistic way, education has always been regarded by society as preparation for assuming an adult role. It is the composite of those experiences which allow an individual to move from a position of societal dependence to a position of societal independence (or perhaps even more optimistically, contribution). If one takes for a moment this admittedly oversimplified definition of the role of education, a number of interesting implications come to light. First, the definition recognizes that education is culture-bound, that it varies from culture to culture and from time to time within a given culture. Second, the definition recognizes that education is undertaken by society to encourage the individual to become independent of the need for continuing societal support; education is thus a social investment whereby expenditures for education are weighed against the cost of continued social dependence (welfare, unemployment, incarceration). Third, the definition implicitly recognizes that although society has an interest in providing a basic education for all citizens, education beyond the point of social independence is the option of the individual.

Alternative definitions, of course, are possible, particularly definitions which describe society's obligation to satisfy the internal motivations of the individual learner. Although such definitions are perhaps more idealistic, it is this writer's contention that education is supported by society for its social utility and that the by-products which accrue to the individual beyond social independence, however desirable they may be, are not the primary basis for its existence or support.

Given, then, that education is a societal activity undertaken to prepare people to assume an independent role in society, the expectations for institutions such as schools become somewhat easier to define and assess. What, for example, are this society's expectations of an independent and/or contributing member? Unquestionably, one dimension of the expectation of social independence would be an awareness of the contemporary norms of society with respect to personal behavior. Unfortunately, however, social norms have a very fluid quality, and definitions have been particularly elusive during the past few years. The notion of acceptable social behavior is no longer an absolute, or even a matter of consensus, but is seemingly redefined day by day. But in spite of the transitory nature of society's judgement about acceptable behavior, there is still the expectation that schools will assist the individual in developing a mode of behavior which falls within the bounds of contemporary acceptability. A second dimension of the definition of social independence is the ability of the individual to become economically self-sufficient. Obviously, the definition of economic self-sufficiency also varies widely and is intimately tied to the general state of the economy. Again, in overly simplistic terms, economic self-sufficiency means having a legal source of income which allows the individual to provide for his basic needs without specialty subsidy. A third dimension of societal independence is an awareness of the conditions which promote personal and public health and safety.

Within these three major goals or expectations of education—an adherence to acceptable social behavior, economic self-sufficiency, and a commitment to standards of personal and public health—all other statements describing the goals of education may be subsumed. All other goals for education are elaborations of the expectation that through the process of education the individual will understand society's norms of acceptable behavior, will prepare himself to be economically independent, and will take proper steps to insure the health and safety of himself and other persons.

Given, then, these admittedly utilitarian expectations of education, what educational experiences might serve the end of making the individual an independent contributing member of society?

First, one might propose that schools have the responsibility for acquainting the individual with the various mediums of communication with which he (or she) will come in contact in his society—oral, written, and nonverbal communication involving all of his sensory modalities. Broadly speaking, in order for the individual to be an independent member of society, he must be able to recognize and interpret all of the means of communication with which his senses put him in contact, not simply the arbitrary language systems of written words or the base-ten mathematical notation. In contrast with the apparent attitude of many educators, the training of individuals to use their various sensory modalities is not intended as an end unto itself but should be regarded as a tool, a means of helping individuals deal with the complex environment which constitutes contemporary society.

The second responsibility of education should be to help the individual understand his or her own behavior, the behavior of others and the complex interactions which occur within social groups. No individual can be a truly independent member of any society until he has some understanding of his own behavior and that of other persons with whom he comes in contact, and until he is able to interpret the interactions that occur with him or between other persons. In particular, it is important for the individual to become aware of those forces which have influenced and are influencing his behavior and to recognize his own unique strengths and limitations.

All individuals should recognize that the worth of particular attributes is societally determined and is constantly redefined throughout an individual's life. It is important, therefore, that education allow the individual to explore all of his abilities in a setting which is relatively free from premature judgement about the worth of any of them. Educational programs which place premature judgemental values on such skills as intellectual or physical development thereby condition individual attitudes and values toward personal and social worth which are often irrelevant to the individual's later life. One's concept of personal worth, or lack of worth, develops very early and tends to persist with great resistance to change. No individual can become socially independent if he does not have a sense of personal worth and accomplishment.

A third dimension of educational programs should concern the development of a capacity for economic independence through an appropriate meshing of one's abilities, one's economic expectations, one's knowledge of available occupations, and a realistic understanding of occupational requirements. In this society economic independence is primarily obtained through employment, either through the efforts of oneself or secondarily through the personal relationship with another person who is employed (as, for example, in the case of the housewife). Because of the centrality of economic independence through employment, education has a prime responsibility to help individuals prepare for their eventual entry into the world of work.

Although the preparation of youth for employment is often mentioned as a major goal of education, schools have historically not dealt with this objective in any realistic way. In the early days of this country preparation of youth for employment was not a problem; in fact, quite the opposite was the case, and one of the major problems was to free children from employment so that they could attend school. Today the principal occupation of children between the ages of six and sixteen is schooling which has, in the opinion of many, become an end in itself rather than a preparation for the individual to assume an independent role in society.

During the early years of a child's education virtually no attention is given to the reality that eventually each individual is expected to become economically independent. Indeed, in many situations there seems to be unconscious, but nevertheless real, development of attitudes and perceptions toward work which are debilitating when the individual eventually enters the world of employment. Education seems to be presented as an alternative to work, and the limited attention given to occupational information is in a superficial and unrealistic light. Occupations which demand intellectually related skills are aggrandized, while those which require manipulative or other physical skills are implicitly, and in some cases are overtly, demeaned. Although many educators would reject this analysis, the evidence is incontrovertible that schools present a distorted and devaluating view of the world of work.

A more constructive posture for education would be to recognize that work is a significant aspect of the total lives of adults in this society and that it is society's right to expect that the schools they support will help individuals develop realistic and satisfying attitudes toward this aspect of their lives, regardless of the particular occupation they choose. Not withstanding the sophist's argument that occupations are becoming technologically more sophisticated, the fact remains that the majority of students who are in today's schools will enter occupations which are of a service, clerical, skilled or semiskilled trade nature. Furthermore, there is no inherent conflict between technological advancement and the requirement that an individual have some basic occupational skills upon which to build his continuing education.

THE SPECIAL RESPONSIBILITY OF GUIDANCE WORKERS

For a long period, institutionalized education in this country has been allowed to argue that its primary responsibility has been to provide a general education, leaving the responsibility for obtaining nonacademically oriented employment skills largely to the individual. The recent legislation by the Congress and the action of the Commissioner of Education have made it clear that society expects more of its public schools than a general, academic education, and it remains for the next few years to tell whether or not the educational establishment will rise to the challenge.

In a very real sense, education has hoisted itself upon its own petard. The problem with today's schools is not that Johnny can't read, for the evidence is clear that children are reading better now than at any time in the history of American education. The problem is, rather, that schools are failing to meet other social expectations. It is unfortunately the case that, because of the way schools are oriented, if Johnny doesn't learn to read he also doesn't get a number of the other opportunities which schools could provide. However, teaching reading would fall into perspective if schools could point to other skills, equally important in the total development of children, which they were providing. This broader responsibility of schools to society is perhaps best represented in Disraeli's statement that

> all power is a trust—that we are accountable for its exercise—that from the people, and for the people, all springs, and all must exist.[11]

If one accepts the view that the education establishment has not met its entire responsibility to society, it is the inescapable conclusion that counselors and guidance workers must share a portion of the blame for this neglect. One might excuse the academic teacher for an exaggerated view of the importance of his discipline, but one has more difficulty understanding the meager attention given to occupations and vocational counseling by workers in the field of counseling and guidance. In Borow's *Man in the World at Work,* Super mentions that vocational guidance is a function for which counselors in varied settings have increasing support. However, since they are responsible for other services, they have tended to lose sight of vocational guidance as one of their expected responsibilities.[12] Putting the matter even more bluntly, the report of the Advisory Council in Vocational Education made the following statement.

> The need for vocational guidance appears as an urgent and critical problem in vocational education. Although, nine out of 10 American high schools provide counseling services, only about 50 percent of the high schools provide any form of vocational guidance.
>
> Because realistic occupational selection is a problem of top priority in American education and because a person's occupation is so much a part of his total life, some form of vocational guidance, including actual work experience, must have continuous emphasis during a large part of a person's educational career.

Despite the demonstrated importance of vocational guidance, schools have not moved ahead rapidly in establishing such services for students. It is evident that improvements in both quality and quantity of vocational guidance have been made in recent years, yet at least half of the youth in high school have been denied vocational guidance on an organized basis as a part of their educational career.

Although research in vocational guidance has increased substantially as the result of the financial support available for this activity through the Vocational Education Act of 1963 and its amendments in 1968, the implementation of research findings in the schools of America has been disappointingly limited. The lack of emphasis in vocational guidance is not based upon a lack of knowledge but upon a distorted sense of priorities. Although Gelatt may be correct that school guidance programs are confused about their purposes and objectives, the demand for vocational guidance services will not wait for the resolution of the debate regarding role, functions, status, and training of guidance workers.[13] The demand is here now and will be met by specialists trained in other disciplines if counselors and guidance workers can not respond. The challenge is clear, and it can be met.

A CONCLUDING COMMENT

If the reader has been left with a very somber feeling about the status of schooling in America, the impression was intentional. Schooling has always had its problems and its challenges, but never have its concerns been more insistently pressed by its critics, nor has the nature of the concerns been more mortal in its implications. Schools are not being asked to "tinker" with new ideas about organization, curriculum, or teaching methods; they are being asked to completely redirect their focus, away from an academically oriented emphasis to a program which places academic and intellectual skills on a parity with the individual's total needs for becoming an independent and well-adjusted member of society. Such reexamination of priorities goes against the long tradition of educational thinking in this country and the evidence of previous educational change does not warrant a high degree of optimism.

Contrary to the opinions of many contemporary critics of American education, schools in this country have done an excellent job of what they set out to do—provide a general academic education for the majority of American children. Evidence from national testing programs supports the premise that the general level of achievement continues to rise, in spite of the pockets of educational disadvantagement that continue to exist. If schools are to be criticized, then, the charge should not be that they don't emphasize academic learning enough; rather, the more valid complaint should be that the programs that exist in most schools are so out of balance with the total needs of youth that other aspects of the child's life are given only token attention or are ignored completely.

Ideally there should be no conflict between the development of intellectual skills and the development of all other personal attributes. Just as these various attributes should be integrated within the "being" of the child, so should they be integrated within the school program meant to serve children. Society needs a variety of talents, not just intellectual skills, and it is the challenge to schools in the 1970s to develop the whole child.

NOTES

1. American Association of School Administrators, *Imperatives in Education* (Washington: American Association of School Administrators, 1966).
2. U.S. Department of Health, Education and Welfare, *Digest of Educational Statistics* (Washington: Government Printing Office, 1970).
3. W. S. Graybeal, "Teacher Surplus and Teacher Shortage," *Phi Delta Kappan,* 1971, LIII:82–85; A. H. Halsey *et al.*, *Education, Economy and Society* (New York: The Free Press, 1961); E. L. Herr, *Review and Synthesis of Foundations for Career Education* (Washington: Government Printing Office, 1972); E. L. Herr and S. H. Cramer, *Vocational Guidance and Career Development in the Schools: Toward a Systems Approach* (Boston: Houghton Mifflin, 1972); K. B. Hoyt, "Operational Goals, Policies and Functions for Guidance as Seen from the Vocational Education Amendments of 1968," *Proceedings of the National Conference on Guidance, Counseling, and Placement in Career Development and Educational-Occupational Decision-making,* N. C. Gysbers and D. H. Pritchard, eds. (Columbia, Missouri: University of Missouri, October, 1969), pp. 52–67.
4. Advisory Council on Vocational Education, *Vocational Education: The Bridge Between Man and His Work* (Washington: The Council, 1968) p. 266; K. E. Boulding, "The Schooling Industry as a Possible Pathological Section of the American Economy," *Review of Educational Research,* 42(1972):125–143; R. Corwin, *A Sociology of Education* (New York: Appleton-Century-Crofts, 1965); L. A. Cremin, *The Transformation of the School* (New York: Alfred A. Knopf, 1961); W. Vantil, ed., *Curriculum Quest for Relevance* (Boston: Houghton Mifflin, 1971).
5. George Gallup, "The Fourth Annual Survey of the Public's Attitudes Toward the Public Schools, 1972," *Phi Delta Kappan,* LIV(1972):33–46.
6. J. J. Kaufman *et al.*, *The Role of the Secondary Schools in the Preparation of Youth for Employment* (University Park, Pennsylvania: Institute for Research on Human Resources, 1967).
7. S. J. Marland, "Marland on Career Education," *American Education,* 7 (1971):25–28; H. L. Miller and R. R. Woock, *Social Foundations of Urban Education* (Hinsdale, Illinois: Dryden Press, Inc., 1970).
8. D. Orlosky and B. O. Smith, "Educational Change: Its Origins and Characteristics," *Phi Delta Kappan,* LIII(1972):412–414; S. A. Rippa, *Education in a Free Society* (New York: David McKay, 1971); M. B. Katz, ed., *School Reform: Past and Present* (Boston: Little, Brown and Co., 1971); W. R. Stephens, *Social Reform and the Origins of Vocational Guidance* (Washington: National Vocational Guidance Association, 1970).
9. William Congreve, "The Mourning Bride," *The British Theater,* XIII:B4 (London: Longman, Hurst, Rees, and Orme, 1808).
10. G. Venn, *Man Education and Work* (Washington: American Council on Education, 1964); U.S. House of Representatives, Committee on Education and Labor, *A Compilation of Federal Education Laws* (Washington: Government Printing Office, 1971).
11. Benjamin Disraeli, *Vivian Grey* (London: Longmans, Green, and Co., 1892), p. 361
12. D. E. Super, "The Professional Status and Affiliations of Vocational Counselors," *Man In a World at Work,* H. Borow, ed. (Boston: Houghton Mifflin, 1964), p. 581.

13. H. B. Gelatt, "School Guidance Programs," *Review of Educational Research,* 39(1969):141–151.

SUGGESTED READING

Haubrich, Vernon F., ed. *Freedom, Bureaucracy, and Schooling.* Washington: Association for Supervision and Curriculum Development, N.E.A., 1971. This work is a collection of papers describing the size, complexity, and bureaucratic structure of contemporary schooling. The volume goes on to examine the elements which constitute the educational system of this society and finally makes some projections about the future of the "common" school. This is a useful, first overview of the education "industry" as it now exists.

Herr, Edwin L. and Cramer, Stanley H. *Vocational Guidance And Career Development in the Schools: Toward A Systems Approach.* Boston: Houghton Mifflin Co., 1972. A thorough examination of the historical and theoretical bases for vocational guidance as it now exists and a suggested procedure providing realistic guidance services to students at all levels. This volume should be carefully examined by every counselor and administrator. It is a highly comprehensive and constructive statement of objectives for vocational guidance.

Hurwitz, Emanuel, Jr., and Tesconi, Charles, Jr., eds. *Challenges To Education.* New York: Dodd, Mead & Co., 1972. A collection of articles and chapters focused on the social forces acting on American schools, particularly urban schools. An excellent overview of the major problems influencing the direction of schooling.

Reich, Charles A. *The Greening of America,* New York: Random House, Inc., 1970. A discomforting but revealing explanation of where American social values have been and where contemporary American youth are trying to take them. The book should be required reading for every "over-thirty" educator who wants to know what is troubling todays' youth.

Stone, Shelley C., and Shertzer, Bruce, eds. *Guidance Monograph Series: IV Career Information and Development.* Boston: Houghton Mifflin Co., 1970. A collection of eight monographs dealing with topics ranging from theories of occupational choice to practical techniques for providing occupational information. A valuable reference work for every vocational guidance worker.

The Family: Perspectives on Its Role in Development and Choice 9

Eleanore Braun Luckey
The University of Connecticut

"Family" is a term that is increasingly difficult to define with any sense of certainty and without a multitude of exceptions to almost any definition. In this chapter we will avoid a finite definition and be as vague and ambiguous in our terms as today's family unit itself is in structure and function. In the broadest sense of the word, a family is still that social unit which is responsible for parenting the world's children; but the nuclear family is undergoing so many modifications that some social scientists see these changes as either a major redefinition of the institution or a prelude to its extinction. The stereotype of "the American Family" is disintegrating as racial, ethnic, and socioeconomic descriptions are blurred by the mobility of our society. Families don't stay put: they go up and down the social scale; they move from state to state; they change husbands and wives; they experiment with alternate life-styles that include group marriages, one-parent families, communal groups, marriages on renewable contracts, and no marriages; and they often contain siblings, half-siblings, step-siblings, and visitors.

The major function of the family has traditionally been reproduction of the human race. Today the predominant function is *survival,* and because of this the family is perhaps more closely linked with the technostructure—the organized means by which society produces goods and services to sustain itself—than it ever has been. In spite of much speculation, it is not clear how this linkage will develop but it is certain that one of the family's primary functions will be the transmission of those values, skills, and disciplines that individuals need in order to operate an effective technostructure.

Even so, the family is recognized as the institution which provides the primary setting for personality development. While the family mediates and transmits the influence of the larger society to individuals within it, it also exerts pressures on the larger society. Each member makes an impact on every other member, and each normally makes forays back and forth into the larger society. Often the most meaningful venture one makes is into the world of work, so that the association between family and occupation tends to be lifelong even though it may be far from stable.

Each family creates a structure of roles in keeping with the functions it assumes, and each creates an atmosphere for its members in which all find their ways of existing and growing. The relationships that exist among family members depend largely on the roles and the atmosphere, and these are made clear (or ambiguous) by the quality of the communication that takes place. Individual needs are met or left unmet, values are transmitted or are rejected, attitudes developed or neglected, skills prized or ignored. Members have powerful influences over each other because of their long-term, intimate associations. This is true for all the family members, but it is most especially true for children whose personalities grow or wither in the climate created by those who parent them.

Inevitably, then, the family exerts a significant influence on vocational interest, occupational choice, and career development, a link that has been observed by many theorists and researchers (e.g., Bordin, Ginzberg *et al.*, Holland, Roe, Super, Tiedeman, Tyler, and Winch[1]). However, seeking out such relationships and identifying the nature of them have been tasks so difficult as to discourage continuing investigation. Theories relating the family to vocational behavior have been built primarily by those in the field of vocational psychology rather than those in family studies, and the results of supporting research have most often been confusing or inconsistent, more suggestive than conclusive. However, the lack of definitive conclusions speaks more to the complex nature of the investigation and the inadequacies of evaluative instruments than to the lack of creative conceptualization. Vocational research, like research in the field of the family and in child development, has been plagued by the problems of pursuing longitudinal research, selecting representative samples that can be defined well enough for predictive value, and developing valid and reliable measuring instruments. Therefore, in attempting to understand some aspects of interdependence between family and occupational choice, we will have to rely on assumption and speculation as much as on scientific research, for antecedent variables of behavior do not sort out in neat, orderly relationships. Recent research in the area of family and child development, as in vocational behavior, suggests that any understanding "of developmental processes will be the systematic study of multiple interactions among an assortment of heterogeneous variables."[2]

The aim of this chapter is to demonstrate the importance for counselors of bridging the gap between and an understanding of family development and practice and the application of career development theory. Our pattern of organization, suggested by Roe's statement of theory in *The Origin of Interests*[3] and Kroll's *Career Development*,[4] will be to consider four major aspects of the subject: 1) genetic inheritance and aspects of the general cultural background; 2) the pattern of development of interests, attitudes, and other personality variables determined primarily by individual experiences through which involuntary attention becomes channeled; 3) consciously directed experience emerging in adolescence; and 4) maturity in job and family.

GENETIC INHERITANCE: THE FOUNDATIONS OF DEVELOPMENT[5]

Human personality is the central organization on which career choice and satisfaction are dependent, and genetic inheritance provides the foundation for personality development. An individual's inherited potentials, although modifiable throughout his life span, evolve from the interaction of chromosomal makeup and intrauterine environment. Genetic research is only beginning to unravel the complex of processes by which environmental forces influence the selection and development of an individual's characteristics and by which these characteristics in turn modify their environment so that still other modifications take place. Environmental conditions may set into motion certain organizing patterns which influence the maturation process, but heredity and environment, even in embryo, must be considered inextricably interwoven.[6]

The wide range of factors that play upon human beings and make for significant differences in their adult lives even extends back to prenatal existence. Thompson,[7] for example, has demonstrated through animal studies that prenatal maternal anxiety increases the emotional constitution of the offspring. In other experiments hormones administered to guinea pigs during the fetal period have been found to have an organizing effect on the neural tissues, which are destined to mediate the mating behavior of the animals, even after they have become adults.[8] Dubos developed colonies of experimental animals in which he found that when the mothers were manipulated in some way during gestation or lactation the life spans of their offspring were either shortened or lengthened. He also found that the offspring were resistant to certain forms of stresses and susceptible to others.[9]

Cattell[10] and others[11] have demonstrated that intellectual capacity is genetically determined, at least to some degree. Creativity, talent, and special aptitudes, also a part of the human being's inheritance, may, when combined with the "right" set of environmental and experiential circumstances, determine the main course of the individual's life—what he does for a livelihood, where he lives, with whom, and even for how long.

Studies of human infants also make it clear that each one is born with his own unique patterns of behavior. Kagan[12] has observed five dimensions on which infants differ: vigor of activity, irritability, stimulus satiability, threshold for attention change, and social responsivity. Most psychologists believe that an infant's innate temperamental disposition is related to what is later called his personality. A longitudinal study by Shirley[13] and Neilon[14] gave support to this supposition, pointing out that for unaccountable reasons some persons seem to change less than others. Escolona's[15] studies supported these findings, as did those of Thomas, Chess, and Birch.[16]

Finally, physiological factors such as race characteristics, body build, metabolic rhythms, and a multitude of others also are inextricably linked with personality development and expression at practically every point in the life cycle.

Genetic determinants and the ways in which these are modified by environmental manipulation must be considered in the family *inheritance* of the child. Characteristics handed down from generation to generation are often directly related to career choices and the satisfaction found in these choices. Although children of this generation are much less likely to take up the same vocation as their parents and are less likely to think of themselves as having "inherited" their jobs, if our information were more complete, it may be, nevertheless, that the link between what a child inherits through his genes and what he does with that inheritance in adulthood is more closely associated than casual observation leads us to believe. Without discounting psychological factors, it may well be that the techniques and materials of the neurologist and the biochemist will be those that will increasingly throw light on human personality, choices, and behavior.

Contributing as much to the personality development of the child as the traits and potentials with which he is born are the cultural influences of the society, into which he is born, especially those that are interpreted to him and impressed upon him by his family. Some of these are racial, religious, and socioeconomic class distinctions with their specific attitudes and values. Life-styles in the family, including both occupational and leisure activities, are related to education and salary of the breadwinner, to the characteristics of the neighborhood, and to the size of the family's living quarters. Various combinations of these factors comprise a broad spectrum, for every family is a member of several groups, and this variability is reflected in parental expectations and child-rearing practices.

GENERAL CULTURAL BACKGROUND: PATTERNS OF GROWTH [17]

Biological influences determine the individual's general pattern of maturation, and there is no way of separating factors of skeletal age, motor development, and nerve growth from those of cognition, emotion, and social behavior. As Rheingold has succinctly put it, ". . . the human infant is social by biological origin."[18] The social and cultural environment serves as the mediator of the infant's psychological growth and social adjustment and provides a general schedule of stages through which he passes. Inasmuch as it is the family that is responsible primarily for the physical, social, and cultural conditions under which a child lives and has most of the experiences of his early life, the family is a critical determinant of the personality of the individual and the course of his adult interests and activities.

Primary Needs and Early Learning

Much of every family's interaction with a newly born infant is guided by the infant's viscerogenic needs and by the parents' desire and ability to meet them. Parental attitudes toward these needs and the demands put on the child in meeting them may be crucial in shaping the child-parent relationship, which in turn affects the personality development of the child. It is through the process of experiencing need and recognizing either the frustration or the gratification of that need that the infant begins to develop a concept of the world, of others, and of himself as separate from others. The infant is usually dependent on a parent for the satisfaction of most basic needs. Communication between mother and child in their many intimate contacts may either threaten or enhance the child's sense of safety and trust, depending on the gratification or frustration experienced. Feeding patterns are important in the development of the child's behavior, and this recurrent event is frequently used to instruct the child in what is expected of him in many related instances. Food holds a most important place in the reward and punishment system of many families, and it is used to reinforce behaviors in a gamut of social situations.

Urination and defecation would probably have little significance in the development of human personality were it not for the demands that adults put on infants in regard to the "rightness" and "wrongness" of why, when, and where a child eliminates. Social customs and values imposed on a child at this point help him learn impulse control and the desirability of his taking responsibility for his acts. Toilet training also offers the opportunity for the child to learn how to manipulate powerful adults and to defy their control. Feelings of guilt, shame, and "dirtiness" are often associated with elimination, and they may be taken into the child's self-image to form the nucleus of self-depreciation.

Undoubtedly, the most neglected need of infants and children in our society is that which Murray has called the sentient and has defined as the inclination for sensuous gratification.[19] Pleasure is not the only product of rich sensuous experiences, for severe sensory deprivation results in intellectual and emotional retardation. Adult sexual experience is undoubtedly linked with the richness or sparseness of earlier stimulation of erogenous body areas and may thus relate very directly to the quality of intimate sexual and personal relationships with others.

Other primary needs such as breathing and those needs grouped together under a general term of "avoidance" (avoidance of pain, excessive cold or heat) do not ordinarily play a very important part in personality development because parental interference or stimulation is at a minimum.

There has been less speculation and less investigation about the critical periods of development during which the individual is more likely to be affected by particular events than he would be at other times. It is logical to suppose that there are critical periods before birth as well as after, just as there is prenatal as well as postnatal learning. It is unclear to what extent personality development is affected by either of these factors, but Kagan[20] has suggested that language ability, the capacity for guilt, and the proclivity for heterosexual behavior each have their own critical age span for openness to environmental influences. Other behavior patterns, when more thoroughly investigated, also will doubtlessly be identified with periods of development specifically linked to environmental conditions.

The Role of Parental Personalities and Practices

The most persevering environmental conditions are the personalities of parents, their particular techniques in responding to the child, and their habitual mode of patterned life. As the variety of acceptable life-styles and marriage forms increases, the variety of child-care styles also will increase. The baby born into a nuclear family will be cared for differently than the child born into a commune or a group marriage. The demands of women for equal opportunity in the labor and professional worlds and the increasing number of androgynous marriages certainly mean that more men are personally involved in feeding, bathing, and clothing infants who will find their needs being met by two different people and in different ways. It may be that they find their needs being met by several people in several ways, for the era of the day care center is upon us.

In the past thirty years the number of women working outside the home has almost doubled, and the number of working mothers has increased nearly eightfold. The trend is expected to continue until by 1975, five million mothers with children under five will be a part of the labor market. The day-care center as an auxiliary to parental care has become a national institution with services including everything from the most meager kind of custodial care to elaborate programs for child development. Many centers offer a full array of social services, including parent education, designed to enrich the child's environment at home.

It is usually agreed that the kibbutz movement in Israel demonstrates the ability of children to tolerate a great deal of away-from-parent care if it is of the right sort. However, research on kibbutz-reared children is not without ambiguous results. "Groupiness" seems not to have prevented individuals from growing into decisive, confident men and women. Moreover, although at the inception of the kibbutz movement many predicted that the family would soon cease to exist, today it is still at the center of Israel's social system and is stronger in its influence than twenty years ago.[21]

It has been suggested that a professional group of "imprinters"[22] may eventually aid in the early period of child care, and Toffler[23] believes that "professional parents" may take over the child-rearing function for society. Regardless of whether or not it is the natural parents who have the responsibility of infant care, it will be important for the caretakers to have certain characteristics including: 1) emotional and physiological maturity, 2) energy, 3) emotional investment in the child, 4) high expectations for the child, 5) training and skill in child care. The number of adults who care for the child and the degree of consistency with which they do it are also of critical importance.

INDIVIDUAL EXPERIENCES: INVOLUNTARY ATTENTION[24]

The assumptions of this section cannot be better stated than they already have been: "The pattern of development of interests, attitudes, and other personality variables with relatively little or non-specific genetic control is primarily determined by individual experiences through which involuntary attention becomes channeled in particular directions."[25] Roe and Siegelman point out that the important word is *involuntary*, for "the elements in any situation to which one gives automatic or effortless attention are keys to the dynamics of behavior."

So intertwined that one cannot possibly separate them from each other are the aspects of individual experience that are discussed in this section: the development of the image of self; the climate and practices of childrearing; and the formation of attitudes, values, and behaviors through the process of modeling. All of these link behavior and perception—perception of self, of environment, and of others—and all are imbedded in family experience.

The Development of Self-concept

Basic to understanding any relationship between personality development and occupational behavior is the consideration of the self-concept. Super's careful, long-term studies have best established the association.[26] Research that clarifies the origins of self-image is understandably scant, but it is generally accepted—at least, by those who study the family—that an individual's concept of himself originates in the perceptions and expectations of his parents, and often of their parents and grandparents. Although parents usually do not set out to mold the child's self-concept in the image of any specific vocational role model, the process is subtle and pervasive. Parents have expectations not only for their children but for themselves as parents. These are partially social and cultural expectations, but they are also highly individual expressions of the specific personality needs of the parent. It is not surprising that each parent may perceive the same child quite differently, but it is often confusing for the child, who must seek some way to resolve the conflicts among differing perceptions. These expectations must be incorporated at every stage of his development and in keeping with the needs that he, too, seeks to satisfy.[27]

In a rapidly changing society the notions of what is "good" and what is "bad" in parenting are often unclear. Such confusion may be reflected in the child through inconsistent self-images and uncertainty about what or who he is.[28] Moreover, it may delay or interfere with the patterning of his vocational interests. As the rate of social change accelerates and mobility increases, a child will be dealing with many more adults than those in his immediate family and will thus become acquainted with more occupations, both because his parents may themselves be changing jobs more frequently and because there are more people in his life. The increased number of influences, options, expectations, and demands on the individual may delay the resolutions of conflicts and the emergence of interest patterns into adulthood.

There is always question about which personality characteristics will best serve individuals in their world, but there is even more question when the world itself is in rapid flux. Today's parents are responsible for socializing children in a manner that will equip them to live in an adult world that is constantly changing. Montagu[29] accuses the Western Christian family of being an organization designed for training its members in self-centeredness. The nuclear family, he believes, perpetuates a perverted version of self by which children come to a realization of who they are mainly through satisfying what their culture and their families tell them are their needs rather than through experience with other children in a broader social context. When parental attention is thus concentrated on the child, he learns to expect the same attention from others and emerges into the rest of society feeling the world owes him a good deal. If this is the case, the decline of the influence of the nuclear family and the increase of day-care and other forms of group care would be positive forces toward the incorporation of the concepts of productivity, cooperation, and social participation into the self-concept.

Clearly a child's sense of value and worth is established by the response he receives from the significant persons who people his world. In his adult life the individual's feeling of confidence or lack of it has much to do with the occupations he chooses and the manner in which he applies himself. In an earlier period of American history the work roles of children at home or on the farm were much easier to specify and to evaluate than they are today. Parents needed the labor input and valued it, and often they seemed to value the child in relation to how well he performed his tasks and con- tributed to family productivity. With the family's change from producer to consumer, it has been increasingly difficult for children to contribute meaningfully to family function. Children have had the more complex task of establishing self-images without the props of early work roles, and parents have had the difficulty of learning how to appreciate children on the basis of what they "are" rather than on the basis of what they "do." This being the case, we would expect more children to have vague or negative images of themselves than formerly. The process of building the image of one's self is, then, clearly an amorphous process that emerges from the facts and fancies primarily held by family members,[30] and these are dependent on current societal pressures as well as on the pressures of individual need.

Not only one's self-image but also one's feeling are formed within the family. Out of the special interactions between parent and child emotions are generated, expressed, labeled, and taken in as a part of the child's own feeling and concept of self. The child becomes aware not only of the emo- tions themselves but of the categories to which they belong—good and bad. Thus, inseparably linked with self are one's emotions and their association with significant others within a framework of wider social values that are promulgated by his family.

The Effects of Child Rearing

Although Roe[31] and those who followed her in linking child rearing to occupational choice have not always found definitive pictures of the relation- ship, they have successfully established "the broad proposition that early satisfactions and frustrations in interpersonal relations are crucial factors in general orientation towards persons in later life."[32]

Roe has pointed out that her original hypothesis that early parent-child relations would in themselves materially affect occupational choice (in terms of the major groups of occupations in her classification) was too specific in its application;[33] but other studies have consistently indicated associations between early childhood factors and occupational involvement. For instance, Switzer, Grigg, Miller, and Young found that ministerial students reported greater interparental differences than chemistry majors, and Roe reports that social workers had had more stress in their early relationships with parents than had the engineers. Of special interest was the finding that the farther from the cultural sex stereotype the occupational choice was, the more likely it was that there had been particular pressures in the early histories which influenced that choice.

Reward and Punishment.   Most of the modes of socialization discussed so far have been largely unconscious. The method that parents are most fre- quently aware of using is some system of rewards and punishments. The balance of reward and punishment varies, but in most American homes punishment is probably more prevalent than reward even though controlled studies indicate that it is less effective in bringing about learning.

The effectiveness of reward depends on its amount, consistency, and im- mediacy[34] and on a system of partial reinforcement which encourages the child to hope for reward.[35] Psychological rewards are more frequently "useful" to the child than physical ones. Psychological punishment usually involves temporary withdrawal of love from the child and is a potent influence in the development of the conscience.[36] Rewards are frequently used to motivate and sustain learning and to recognize achievement. Punishment, on the other hand, is used to restrict or inhibit behavior or to discourage undesirable qualities such as inattention, aggression, and anger. There are social class differences and sex differences in the use of punishment; for example, lower-class families use more physical punishment, and boys are more often punished physically than girls.

Related to the practice of rewards and punishments is the whole complex of training practices which are markedly different from subgroup to subgroup and which have recently seen rapid change over a comparatively short period. Bronfenbrenner's[37] study of child-rearing practices in the United States between 1932 and 1957 demonstrated that mothers had become more flexible and permissive and had become more aware of the individual needs of their children. One would expect that these more relaxed methods of child rearing would be reflected in children who may make less rigorous demands on themselves and on those around them.

Use of Authority. Associated with the rewards and punishment that children receive is the degree of authority invested in the parent and the use made of that authority. Studies are numerous and inconclusive, but, in general, they demonstrate a linkage between strict authority and prejudice that persists from one generation to the next and has implications for the conduct of society. After an extensive review of research, McCandless predicts: "It will be more difficult to change the behavior of an authoritarian than an equalitarian child; authoritarian children, like their parents, will be intolerant of ambiguity; authoritarian children will have more latent hostility than equalitarian and will be less trusting; the authoritarian child, in familiar, well-charted situations, will behave at least as efficiently as, and perhaps more efficiently than, the equalitarian child."[38]

Family Patterns and Siblings. Many studies have gathered data regarding the effects of the broken home on the child, and most of the results support findings that the more severe the disruption in the home, the more severe the adjustment problems of the child. Investigations into maternal employment and child adjustment have resulted in conflicting data, but the weight of evidence[39] indicates that where there is disruption, factors other than the employment of the mother have accounted for it. Studies of the importance of father absence from the home have not been able to assess the degree of influence that the lack of a male model may have on boys. However, Mussen and Distler,[40] in investigating the role of rewards and punishment, found that boys are most likely to make a strong masculine identification if they have fathers whom they perceive as a powerful source of both rewards and punishments. Lynn and Sawrey[41] found that the only significant difference in the girls whose fathers were absent was that they were more dependent than girls who had fathers at home. Boys with absent fathers, however, were affected in more respects: they were not as well-adjusted in their peer group relationships, were less certain of sex roles, and were socially more immature. The bulk of information that is available seems to indicate that if the family feels disrupted, the children are likely to show behavioral symptoms; if one of the parents is absent over a long period of time, modeling and training functions are likely to be weakened.

Studies attempting to assess the influence on the children coming from "good" or "poor" marital relationships have generally failed to be conclusive. Hoffman[42] found, however, that the father may act as a catalyst in affecting the mother's behavior toward the child. Subtle factors that show up only when the family as a constellation is studied may be the most potently reflected in behavior. Such examples are numerous in studies of the families of schizophrenic patients.

The child's ordinal position within his family has been found to be associated with his personality development. Schachter[43] reports that first-born subjects exhibit more anxiety under stress than later-born subjects, that when under stress they prefer the company of others, that in nursery school they are more dependent on the teacher, and that they have a lower tolerance for physical pain. First-born children are less likely to become alcoholics than later-borns; when emotionally disturbed they were more likely to seek psychotherapy; and they were not as effective fighter pilots as were later-born subjects. Although these findings are concerned primarily with first-borns, Kagan has pointed out that "each position in the family has its own set of advantages and disadvantages."[44] Other factors in combination with ordinal factors undoubtedly make for differences among siblings; Koch's research[45] demonstrates the interdependence of ordinal position, amount of time in spacing, and sex.

Family size, too, is a variable in personality development, although it is so enmeshed with other variables such as race, economic status, and religion that no direct relationship has been consistently indicated. Both the quantity and the quality of sibling relationships has an impact on personality. "Much of what goes into an early self image is the result of interaction with a sibling. One of the strongest and most constant pressures that children have is the rivalry that exists between them, especially when they are members of the same family."[46] Sharing and cooperating do not come naturally, coercion often is used, and anger and hostility result. Learning to deal with hostility is a very basic part of personality formation and depends largely on how parents permit it to be dealt with.[47]

The importance of sibling relationships in relating positively to others has been emphasized by Harlow, who believes that "It is primarily through the age-mate affectional system, expressed in peer play, that social and cultural patterns are learned, control of aggression is accomplished, and the foundations are laid for later sex-appropriate behavior."[48] The surrogate-reared monkeys in Harlow's laboratory have made it dramatically clear that the mother plays a crucial role in the socialization of the young but that a rhesus can surmount her absence if it can associate with its peers. The Harlows[49] believe that there is an advantage in having two independent sources of affection, mother and peers, so that each may compensate for the deficiencies of the other.

Lack of Conclusive Research.   Child rearing practices are probably more closely related to the parents' own needs and the satisfaction of these needs than to purposefully learned and practiced methods of child rearing based on a rational philosophic approach. The treatment of children will undoubtedly be influenced by the frustrations and joys of individual family members. These will reflect the changes in family patterns as society moves from the patriarchal family through the companionate and colleague marriages to the androgynous, from the four-child family to the single-child family, from the family hearth to the day-care nursery. Bettelheim[50] believes that one's deepest and most permanent attachments, which traditionally have been family centered, will become peer directed. The influence of one's peer group has recently been emphasized by Harlow's[51] findings that monkeys with a peer group and no mother did better than any other group except those with both. Female monkeys that had been badly mothered were not interested in being mothers themselves, and when they were, they were poor ones. It is true that generalizations from animal data to human situations cannot be made with security,[52] but the Harlow studies offer good evidence on which to base a closer look at the human family and infant care as these relate to personality performance and social interaction in adult years. Toffler[53] suggests that the pattern of nonpermanent relationships may lead to the development of the capacity to make instant relationships which can be as easily terminated as created.

Critics[54] have challenged the almost universally held professional assumptions that family life, particularly in the preschool years, is crucial in shaping later development, charging that there have never been any conclusive findings from studies of how child-rearing practices, parental attitudes, etc., affect the personalities of children. Frank, in reviewing the literature (primarily of pathological studies) of the past forty years, sees no consistent and firm evidence that family practices affect child personality, let alone have a carry-over to adulthood. Nevertheless, McCandless[55] defends the assumptions on the basis of practical knowledge held by both professionals and parents, saying that "in our hearts" we know that how children are treated and the conditions to which they are subjected do make a difference in their behavior.

Modeling

In addition to being the source of the child's affection, regard, acceptance, and recognition, and being the authoritarian and disciplinarian in his life, the parent is also his model.[56] The Krumboltzes[57] point out that children follow prestigeful models and that prestigeful models are those who dispense reinforcement. Siblings, then, also serve as models,[58] as do others who demonstrate competencies which the child has been taught to admire and would like to have for himself. Models also come from such places as history, literature, and television, but they are dependent, at least in the early years, on the selection and exposure provided primarily by the family. Children imitate many kinds of behavior that they see parents and others demonstrating, including such simple things as ways of pronouncing words, making gestures, expressing aggression, and venting frustration and also more complex behaviors such as problem solving and acting on a system of values. Examples of modeling behavior are evidenced in sex-typing, moral development, attitudes and values, and communication patterns.

Sex-typing. Probably the most distinguishing feature of human beings is that of sex. Genetic and physical endowment place most individuals in their sexual categories, but the matter is not that simple, for sex-role behavior must be learned. Social learning theory holds that appropriate sex responses are rewarded by parents and so are repeated, while inappropriate behavior is likely to be punished and eventually to become extinguished.[59] Freudian theory bases sex identification primarily on the resolution of the Oedipal complex. Parsons[60] has advanced a theory that the boy identifies with the father and other males because they are powerful or "instrumental." Whiting suggests from cross-cultural studies that a person will identify with "any person who is a successful rival with respect to resources which he covets but cannot control."[61] Thus, if the father's relationship with the mother is envied by the son, then the boy will identify with the father. Kohlberg[62] contends that as a part of the child's cognitive development he learns to label himself either a boy or a girl and then sorts behaviors that are consistent with the label and follows them. Although the emphasis in this theory is on the child's ability to perceive and understand rather than on his relationship to other family members, in all other theories some kind of modeling or imitation has been noted. "The fortunate child," says McCandless,[63] "is the one who has so adequate a father (male model) and mother (female model) that he comes early to prefer the sex role dictated by his physiology, moves naturally into its rehearsal, and eventually identifies easily with it."

Cross-cultural research demonstrates that societies define masculinity and femininity differently and that the example of the parent conveys the concept to the same-sexed offspring. Although much of this is automatic and habitual, there are also deliberate attempts of parents to develop what they consider appropriate sex roles for their children.[64] Direct encouragement to be representative of one's sex and to engage in typical boy or girl activities is ingrained in child-training practices. For example, Bronfenbrenner[65] believes that parents try to instill in the child the attitudes and behaviors which have proved important for holding and succeeding in the kind of job in which the father is engaged and suggests three occupational orientations: relationship, skill, and production, which are used as specific models.

Studies of identification emphasized the importance of modeling aspects from the standpoint of personality characteristics associated with child-rearing practices. Gray[66] found that children who scored high in anxiety showed significantly more sex-appropriate behavior. Studies by Lynn[67] gave evidence that with increasing age males become relatively more identified with the masculine role and females relatively less identified with the feminine role; that a larger proportion of females than males adopts aspects of the opposite sex role; that males tend to identify with a cultural stereotype of the male role but females identify with aspects of their own mother's role specifically. Although the evidence is neither systematic nor consistent, Winch[68] believes that the bulk of studies point to familial functions and structure as relating reliably and positively to sex-role identification of the offspring.

One of the most obvious changes in the American family is that female and male behavior is becoming less well-defined, less separate, and more blurred. Andreas,[69] pointing out the mechanisms by which little girls learn "feminine" behavior, makes it clear that modern mothers are more direct and more conscious in teaching sex-roles which counteract the traditional stereotyped role behavior; she therefore believes that traditional barriers between the sexes will tumble.

Although more husbands and wives are assuming more nearly equal responsibility for the care of the children and household, motherhood will continue to be an important occupation for women for some time to come. However, Janeway[70] believes that because our society does not train for the "job" of motherhood and because mothers are expected to know how to "mother" by instinct, women will continue to feel that their parenting is not valued. On the other hand, a new emphasis on training both parents for parenthood may elevate parenthood to a higher occupational status than before.

In the work world, too, new vocations are less riveted in traditional sex roles, and the traditional ones are moving toward sex equality in such a way that sex modeling by occupation will be blurred increasingly in the future. Men of this generation, however, will continue to look on career opportunities differently from women, for men expect to pursue a career throughout their lifetime, and women are more likely to have careers interrupted by reproduction and home responsibilities.[71] It will take considerable time for expressions of emotion and intimate behavior that are traditionally connected with sex roles to be modified appreciably. Women may rapidly take more jobs in fields that have been dominated by men, but they will be slower to exchange the quality of nurturance for aggression.

Morality, Values, and Attitudes. A sense of morality is dependent upon how well one is socialized. Most people find it necessary to fit their vocational life into a moral framework that provides a socially acceptable status, and some persons actively seek to further or to reinforce the values and the morality of their society by choosing occupations which are involved primarily in reaching such desired goals as teaching, preaching, ministering to the poor or the sick. Learning to live in a group, first accepting one's dependence on others and then being able to achieve independence of others, so that a mutual sense of interdependence and responsibility develops in a complex learning function which is not taught so much as it is demonstrated.

Although research demonstrating the moral development of the child is scant, the little we do have adds cumulative evidence that the family is centrally involved. Hoffman[72] found that mothers of children who had "conventional consciences" based on absolutist morality more often used "ego attack" methods of punishment. Mothers of children with "humanistic consciences" were more likely to use psychological techniques which conveyed both disappointment and the expectation that the child could do better. And in this way Hoffman has linked practices of child rearing, love-oriented techniques of control and identification to a consistency of moral development which grows more pronounced as the child gets older. Piaget's three stages of morality progress from behavior dominated by fear of punishment to behavior based on the individual's internalized sense of moral guidelines.

Kagan and Freeman[73] found that conformity to adult demands and dependence upon mothers were associated with different maternal practices for girls than for boys. For adolescent boys conformity and dependence were preceded by acceptance, affection, and protection in the early school years, but for girls conformity and dependence were predicted by severe discipline and restrictiveness.

Although it is hard to demonstrate the association between parental example and moral development, it has been demonstrated that attitudes such as those toward achievement, success, fairness, honesty, and regard for others relate directly to those held by parents.[74] American middle-class and lower-class values, undoubtedly mediated through parents, can be contrasted in the areas of self-control and inhibition, ambition and "getting by," cleanliness and slovenliness, sexual inhibition and aggression.

In a society in which the younger generation is disowning the values of their parents a conscious effort is made to deny the power of parental modeling and to take on more of the characteristics of prestigious peers. This is fairly easily accomplished in matters of dress, language, and some kinds of transitory behaviors; however, the effects of parental modeling of long-term life-styles, attitudes, and value systems are more difficult to eradicate and may leave residual feelings of guilt and anxiety. Departures from the models that are reinforced by new social norms, however, will be more readily incorporated into the personality and be passed on to the following generation as a model of "flexibility"—a necessary quality in a rapidly changing life.

It is expected that attitudes and values will change in the direction of greater tolerance for differences from anything that might resemble a norm. There will be less value put on "hard work and steady determination" and more on leisure time and creativity in seeking satisfaction on the job. There may be somewhat less emphasis on the importance of earning power and on the possession of material goods and status. Scientific attitudes will be less emphasized, humanitarian ones more emphasized. Those values treasured by middle-class parents of this generation may become the values of the lower-class youth who are upwardly mobile and who are not as eager as their middle-class contemporaries to let go of the "good things" that affluence can provide.

Communication.   The earliest communication between persons is within the family, and in the early years the young often imitate their parents or siblings who are more expressive than they. Communication is intricately linked with the learning of values, with the expression of emotion, and with cognition. Relationships between people, between races, between sexes, between those in authority and those who are not, and between intimates and strangers—all are expressed in the ways persons communicate with each other.

The advent of television has affected the quantity and quality of familial communication. Television has brought into the home new models—both real and imaginary—new values, and new worlds. It has supplanted much family communication and has modified parental influence. The fact that television has brought international happenings to the dinner table creates a world awareness that did not exist to any great extent before 1950. As society moves toward world dimensions, it becomes increasingly important that persons learn to communicate openly and directly with a variety of people, many of whom will be very unlike their families and will have different values and customs; children raised in a society that is expending its family forms and extending its relationships in unpatterned ways can be expected to have this kind of adaptability.

The models of communication that children adopt probably determine more than any other single factor how their own interpersonal relationships develop. These patterns of interpersonal relationships are important in job effectiveness now and will continue to be as long as people work with people.

Conclusion.   This section has pointed to some of the experiences of the early years of life that continue through childhood and into adulthood and that are believed to be associated with occupational choice and career development. Through these experiences within the family a certain "molding" of the developing personality is accomplished by external events and the influence and circumstances of other family members, but there is also a constant active weeding out and evaluating process going on. This process of selecting and incorporating experience contributes to the formation of the concept of one's self and one's interests, aptitudes, and satisfactions. Many factors at which we have only hinted are also importantly linked to personality development and career, factors such as regard for self and others, degree of social participation, ways of recreating, and ways of making decisions and commitments.

As American family life changes, one of the most important influences that will probably be felt in the early years of a child's life is the increased number of persons to whom he will be exposed. Bronfenbrenner[75] proposes the idea that the school, the neighborhood, and the larger community itself must be able to share more of the family's responsibilities for the child-rearing process. Greater breadth and social involvement may mean a more firm sense of autonomy, identity, and responsibility; or it may mean relinquishing more individuality to social organization, for the prospect of selecting and rearing children for specific adult roles and stations in life is being considered as a part of future social engineering.

Historically, most of the family's energy and direction in child rearing has gone into providing for the child's physical needs, but recently we have been increasingly concerned about his psychic needs—security, love, recognition. Even so, however, we have not appreciably attended to the conditions which encourage his growth toward self-actualization. The world in which today's children will live as adults will require persons who are capable of decision making, of living in a very mobile world which may lack permanency, of tolerating uncertainty, of protecting their own freedom and assuming responsibility for themselves, of building new and effective social institutions to serve humanity, and, perhaps above all else, of caring profoundly for other human beings and finding meaning in their own lives.

ADOLESCENCE

One might ask whether adolescence is a period of human development different from childhood and adulthood or whether it is simply a self-fulfilling prophecy[76] created by people who started to believe that there was such a stage of life. The fact is that, since the exclusion of youth from adult employment statuses, there has been a recognizable "youth culture" with its particular phases and problems. During the period of involvement in youth culture familial influences decrease and peer pressures increase. If our family and educational systems continue to assemble teenagers together during this period, peer influences will continue to escalate in importance, and the characteristics of the total society will reflect youth's thinking. If, on the other hand, families begin living in groups, if adults spend more time working and playing with adolescents, and if education leads the way to youth's general incorporation into the adult social structure, the character of adolescence will be tempered by adult sharing and experience. The way our society deals with current adolescent problems will most certainly determine to a large extent the occupations, the work roles, and values of the future adult generation.

In the early years, primarily at home, the child has learned who he is, what he expects of himself, what he values, how he learns, how he relates to others, and how he uses them in meeting his needs. He has envisioned himself in adult roles, learned the social rules, and has laid the foundation for extending himself into larger segments of his society. His adolescent development is consistent with his past, and new family input is limited largely to the events, and circumstances, and the situations of the family's living.

Factors such as a family member's death, a divorce, a move to another geographical area, or a change of social status may present opportunities or obstacles which directly and immediately influence where or how the adolescent enters the labor market. Particularly potent determiners are educational opportunities and exposure to the world of work, for these contribute to the process of self-evaluation as the adolescent collects more data about himself, about others, and about skills that are requirements of vocations.[77]

Achievement

The teen years are those in which the individual usually begins to verbalize, clarify, and share ideas about himself and his place in the world. Young people who have developed negative self-concepts will be less able to assess their own competencies and more dependent on external evaluations. Recent research[78] has generally found that parental encouragement is positively related to the occupational and educational plans of high school students and is considered the critical factor in the child's performance. High socio-economic status of parents is related to certain socialization practices such as providing enriching activities and pressuring children into achieving, so that adolescents of the higher socioeconomic class are more oriented toward goals of excellence.[79] The value placed on work, the development of effective study habits, the preference for mental work over physical work, and preferences for professional occupations have all been found to relate to parents' education.[80] Jacobson's study indicated that, in general, parents make attempts to immerse sons in the occupational arena either by abstractly verbalizing encouragement for jobs, by discussion and example, or by suggesting courses of study, observing work sites, and actually participating in the job. He believed it is this factor of encouragement that accounts for the positive correlation so frequently found between social class and occupational aspiration. However, Sandis[81] found that mothers' educational ambitions for their children were strongly and positively related to the students' own educational plans and also that the association held regardless of the specific socialization methods used, and she concluded that parental values are transmitted in *many* alternative ways and not only by specific instrumental behavior.

When parents have been found to have their doubts about the value of education,[82] students, too, have been disinterested and often drop out of school. Other family conditions that have specifically been related to lack of achievement and low occupational aspiration are[83] broken or emotionally inadequate homes; low socioeconomic status; home environment that limits horizons and fails to stimulate; home environment that fails to instill drive or need for achievement; school and home that fail to instill an intrinsic love of learning. The atmosphere of family interpersonal relationships has been found to influence ambition and achievement levels; Dynes[84] suggests that unsatisfactory interpersonal relationships in the family are significantly related to high aspirational levels of achievement and that the reverse is also true. Rushing's[85] findings indicated that family relationships should be studied according to sex differences, for fathers who were seen as depriving agents exerted a stronger influence on daughters than on sons. Turner's[86] investigations indicated that ambition is likely to be high when the father's education was high relative to his occupation and when the education of the mother exceeded that of the father. Larger families produced less educationally ambitious adolescents than smaller ones, and characteristics of the total family as compared to objective sibling positions were found to account for the character of the child's ambition. Turner suggests that in cases where a child's ambitions are atypical according to his class background, the family has conveyed atypical values or created atypical life situations. In explaining her findings that a child's educational values, aspirations, and achievement are only partially related to parental conduct, Kriesberg[87] is careful to point out that this may be attributed to the fact that the nature of the children themselves is an important factor. The young person with high ability and interest will spur his parents' hopes and may thus invoke parental behavior that encourages the child to achieve.

A recent Purdue study[88] found generally that poor parental education seems to influence the work values of children in that they desire more job security and higher wages or salary. Work preferences appeared more closely associated with father's education than with mother's. "Mental" work rather than "physical" was preferred by children of college educated fathers, as was working alone; children of poorly educated fathers were more interested in working with things rather than ideas and in working indoors. Depending on the level of parental education, more females than males indicated interest in the opportunity to increase skills and abilities in a job: as the level of parents' education increased, the frequencies of girls interested in growth opportunities increased.

The experience that teenagers have with jobs sparks some ambitions and cools others; that which brings the greatest sense of accomplishment and meets psychic needs most satisfactorily will be that which has the greatest drawing power. The value systems and models that have been internalized are reflected in adolescent goals.

Decision Making, Identity, and Commitment

For the most part the family has been responsible for the opportunities that the adolescent has had to internalize decision making as a process. The ability (or lack of it) that parents have exercised in letting their children make decisions and assume the responsibility for their successes or failures has been important in the rate and degree of maturity that the child has developed. How well or how poorly a youngster has internalized the decision-making process is related to the strength of his self-image, his self-knowledge and self-evaluation, his set of values, his information about his world, and his ability to acquire and use such information. The process of making career decisions is probably no different from making any other kind, but during adolescence these assume greater importance because they are directly related to "what he does for a living." "It is through 'good' (personally valuable and socially relevant) decision making that an adolescent forms some identity of his own unique individuality and gains some sense of competence in dealing with his life situations."[89]

Although parents have a good deal invested in these early decisions, the bulk of family literature indicates that any actual "guidance" function seems to have been almost entirely delegated to the schools. Parents feel especially limited in a wide knowledge of vocations and may be ignorant of new career developments, opportunities, and labor trends. Parents may also feel that they "do not understand" their child; they may feel less able to assess his aptitudes or interests and find that they do not share his values and life goals. Aware of the lack of communication, parents become more dependent on the school as a resource to influence their offspring.

If in the future, as the nuclear family form is modified and parental responsibility is shared by more persons, one would expect the adolescent to have more independence in making career decisions, unless, of course, some social mechanism is established for putting him into a given category and training him for an appropriately relevant social slot.

The adolescent task of establishing one's identity has been discussed at length by Erikson,[90] who sees this task as directly dependent upon the individual's opportunities for developing a sense of trust, of autonomy, of initiative, and of accomplishment. Occupational interests begin to be a part of the answer to "Who am I?" and although the facets of any one response are too numerous to explore, membership in a given socioeconomic class, race, and sex group are especially important. In a period of social mobility and more nearly equal opportunity for individuals these factors *per se* will be less determining and more confusing. Personal sexual identification may become less clear during a period in which masculinity and femininity are being redefined socially. Young women are defining themselves less exclusively and less strongly by the wife-mother role, for they also expect to hold jobs. The Purdue study[91] indicated that girls more than boys expect to take special training after high school rather than go to college, and more than half of the students who indicated that they expected to go to work immediately after high school were girls, primarily from homes where the parents were not well-educated. Sex differences still were found in the traditional areas: girls preferred "safe" work without competition and preferred to be guided; they were more strongly oriented toward work with people than ideas or things, and more preferred to work with others rather than alone; and also expressed continued interest in the traditional "female" occupations of nursing and secretarial work. Males expressed greater interest in outdoor, competitive, and risky work. However, the breadth of vocational opportunities that are available to both men and women has been expanded, and sex role will be less identified with occupation than it has been.

Kroll[92] links sense of identity to the dimensions and development of commitment but believes that it is not necessary to have established a firm sense of identity before one makes a tentative commitment. One's identity and one's sense of commitment, although established in adolescence, continue to interact with each other in a "spiraling movement of growth, throughout life."[93] In a period of rapid social change, long-term commitment to individuals, to a specific job, to an organization, or to a locale may be maladaptive. This issue causes youth and parents a good deal of conflict and is of considerable concern to adolescents who are attempting to emerge from one value framework to create a new one. Parents generally want their children to have a sense of direction and to "settle" on a path that will lead to permanent association and involvement. Parents of this generation for the most part have themselves been "committed" to a spouse, a job, and a way of life, and they urge their children in this direction. Whether or not an individual is able to commit himself is probably related to how free he is from parental expectations and how firmly his selfhood is established.

Although it has been traditionally thought that choice of vocation determines life-style, in future generations it is more likely to be the other way around. Choosing whether to marry, to have children, to travel, to live in a group situation, to opt for minimal income, or to accumulate money and property are factors that help to decide one's way of earning a living. In an age where options of all kinds are increasing rapidly and the exposure to peer influences are extremely broad, it is reasonable to assume that the role of the family of orientation will be minimized by the time the child reaches adolescence.[94]

During adolescence young people become consciously engaged in sorting out the factors which influence their individual career choice; like gathering the pieces of a great jig-saw puzzle, they begin to fit their life situation and their attitudes, knowledge, and values into a whole that gives their lives a sense of personal meaning. The present generation, coming from families that in general are better educated and more affluent than previous generations, may well seek jobs which give them opportunities for the development of personhood rather than those which give them places as well-oiled cogs in the world of work. The efficiency model and its attending attributes is not as valued as self-actualization.

MATURITY

Family structure and function is inextricably interwoven with the economics and the vocational pursuits of the adult members of every society. History documents the relationship of the herb-gathering tribes, the hunters, the warriors, the producers, and the consumers to family roles, patterns of authority, power, dependency, subservience, and individual autonomy. The provision of food, clothing, and shelter has been the factor determining how man organized his society, his family, and his personal life. Much of the current generation in the United States has had, for the first time in the history of mankind, a degree of relative freedom from the needs of existence. With this freedom, he may choose to shape a style of personal living which will determine his vocation rather than the other way around, but at the present time family form and structure continue to be dependent on the economy.

Relationships between family structure and occupations *per se* have never been studied to any great extent. Investigations have dealt mainly in broad social and cultural terms with the economic structure, family forms, patterns of child rearing,[95] patterns of task allocation, and power structure.[96] Cavan[97] observed that personal and economic roles of husbands and wives differ greatly among a variety of cultures and subcultures but not in haphazard fashion. The variations are related to the special features of the particular culture and to the position of the couple in the social-class hierarchy. Family power, prestige, and authority have traditionally been linked with the breadwinner's role and with the perception and evaluation of family members as to how well the breadwinner has served this function. The low-skill jobs of housekeeping and mothering have had little leverage, and those occupying these roles have generally been dependent and in subordinate positions. Current research,[98] however, demonstrates that in the United States husbands who have taken on an increasing number of domestic duties do not necessarily lose family authority and wives who work do not necessarily have increased power in family decision making.

Today's family generally wants more equality between its members, more autonomy for each, more personal satisfaction in the relationships, and there is generally a greater emphasis on the quality of living, more humanism, less emphasis on the importance of work itself and more on creativity, leisure time, and self-actualization. These same emphases are found in industry, and just as there is much less willingness for today's children to accept family authority, so this is true at work and in the community.[99] Young people are seeking more variety, more participation, more self-determination, more responsibility at home and on the job. Money and material goods are less important when compared with the richness of life experience. Commitments both to family and career are less binding. People are valued over things, and often "the process" has become more important than the "product" in both the world of the family and of work.

Even considering this kind of congruity in society, Koprowski[100] has pointed out that the family is no longer producing the types of people who readily adjust to the demands of the world of work and that our society becomes more schizophrenic as its citizens attempt to play two incompatible roles—the impulsive, style-conscious, dissatisfied consumer (the family member) and the long-suffering, predictable, hardworking producer (the worker). It is obvious that cities which are the central places for merchandising are not created to serve families. As the family has become increasingly less important as an economic unit, the conflict between the protection and care of the family and the advance of commerce and industry has resulted in a conflict of social values that is reflected in personal confusion and in a search for more flexible family forms that are more responsive to a wide variety of personal needs. Students of the family believe that if human values become predominant over production values, parents will place more emphasis on the humane in socializing their children. This would mean that economic gains and career choices would become secondary to those of lifestyle and family form; only an affluent economy and the recognition of the fact that the skills for survival in the superindustrial society of tomorrow are intrapersonal and interpersonal will support such a hierarchy of values.

It is not only at the level of the social mass that family and vocation are so vitally intertwined, but at the level of the individual life as well. Just as an individual's attitudes and concept of self help to determine his career, so does one's career help to determine his attitude toward self, family, and the world. The kind of family in which one lives, its values and its view of the world, affects the world one works in; and the world in which one works tends, in its turn, to shape family function and structure. Discontent with vocation carries discontent to the family, just as family troubles are reflected on the job in a high accident rate, high turnover, and high absenteeism.

Many personal values are undergoing sharp renovation as a result of industrial policies. Perhaps the most obvious example of this is the effect of the four-day work week, which may provide family benefits but plays havoc with the gospel of work. The meaning of leisure and attitudes toward it are being reshaped, as is our attitude toward work, which itself is judged more and more in terms of leisure values. More leisure time may enrich family relationships or may put more stress on them.

SEX-ROLE TRENDS

An obvious recent familial and occupational trend is the employment of the wife-mother outside the home. This trend is expected to force modifications of policy on industry and the professions so that men's working hours will be reduced, provisions for husband-wife shared jobs will be created, child care provided, health policies and working conditions improved, etc. These changes necessitate others in government and education, and eventually every institution within society takes on new tasks and drops old ones.

In such a transition what happens to the family? Are changes likely to be "good" or "bad" for its members? When both spouses are working the equilibrium of the husband-wife relationship is different, and the parental care system is modified. These changes do not bring stability to the nuclear family, but whether or not this is a social loss is questionable. Some form of group family living more nearly approximating the style of the extended family may serve a rapidly changing society better and form a stronger, broader base of human contacts, love and concern. Grouped families could provide the sense of community that has been lost as the nuclear family has permitted the dispersion and alienation of its members.

Studies of the wife-mother's employment outside the home indicate that the most central factor in terms of the family's welfare is degree of agreement between husband and wife regarding employment and role changes. Essentially it is from the "contract" that marriage derives its meaning and provides the assumptions of parenthood. If these terms are not violated, if they are modified by mutual consent, and if communication is good, then family function is not disrupted. Employment of the wife can be a source of needed additional income, of social contacts, of mental stimulation, and of improved self-image—all of which may reduce tension in the family and improve the interpersonal relationships. On the other hand, it may signal the wife's abandonment of the contract and be a first step toward divorce. Thus, it is not the sheer absence or presence of the wife in the home that determines the effects on the family; the important variable is the source of the wife's motivation, the impact her employment has on her self-image and on that of her husband, the amount of guilt, fatigue, and anxiety she may carry as contrasted with the degree of stimulation and sense of achievement.[101] Sex-role changes that include more freedom for both men and women in their work and in their families will continue to introduce variety and complications into both vocational and familial scenes and will, at the same time, provide more opportunities for fulfilling experience.

Mobility

The increasing industrialization of the United States has made moving the family necessary and easy; twenty percent of American families change their residence every year; the average American moves about fourteen times in his lifetime. A number of studies have investigated the relationship of moving to both career development and family functioning.[102] For example, we have learned that, contrary to general belief, marital stability is associated with upward mobility,[103] that whether or not the husband's employment transfer is successful depends on the wife's adjustment,[104] and that families who have the strongest internal relationships seem to experience the most successful job relocations.[105]

For the nuclear family it has been comparatively simple to move from one part of the country to another in order for the wage earner or earners to take advantage of job promotions. Packard contends that such mobility is related to a loss of identity and sense of direction, that it is associated with "nomadic values" and mental and physical illness. Toffler,[106] on the other hand, considers mobility good training for the rapid physical and social life of our immediate future—disposable jobs, disposable marriages, disposable families. If the future family structure includes more "groupiness," individual mobility will obviously be a threat to group membership and stability. Are the needs of a productive society and stable family relationships incompatible? Can they exist side by side or must one or the other be sacrificed? What kind of social planning is necessary to provide for both or, at least, for human survival?

CONCLUSION

Because vocational choice and career development have their roots in the early years of a child's life, partially determined genetically by physical and temperamental endowment and partially determined by the experiences of the child in its early physical and social environment, much stress is laid in this chapter on the emerging developmental pattern of the human personality within the family. Life experiences that include both knowledge of self and the world of work begin to take on more concrete meaning for the individual in adolescence. On the basis of personal and social values that one has established, one leaves his family of orientation, establishes himself in a world of work and begins a new family. In a time where social patterns of parenting and vocation are both rapidly changing, it is hard to make predictions as to how they will mesh in the near future. Perhaps the most basic problem that must be considered is to what extent the family in either its present form or in any of the proposed alternate styles is able to contribute to the development, the actualization, and fulfillment of persons who must also be a part of the technostructure? To assure survival each generation must learn to parent and socialize the next.

Projecting meaningfully into the future, making speculations on the nature of society and the abilities and skills that individuals will need in order to cope with its circumstances has produced an array of serious books and essays as well as "science fiction." To envision the conditions within the family that will prepare today's children to live in tomorrow's world, one must confine one's self to the broadest of terms. Parents and educators can no longer concern themselves with fostering specific skills in their young, but must devote their energies to developing broad abilities, such as the understanding of self and others, the resolving of conflicts and making of decisions, the recognizing of value positions and living with a strong sense of social consciousness and concern for others. Perhaps the abilities most essential for survival will be the flexibility of character that permits the individual to tolerate the gamut of differences and a dogged belief that life is meaningful both for humanity *en masse* and for the person as an individual.

NOTES

1. E. S. Bordin, "A Theory of Vocational Interests as Dynamic Phenomena," *Educational Psychological Measurement* 3(1943):49–66; E. S. Bordin, B. Nachmann, and S. J. Segal, "An Articulated Framework for Vocational Development," *Journal of Counseling Psychology* 10(1963):107–117; E. Ginzberg *et al.*, *Occupational Choice* (New York: Columbia University Press, 1951); J. L. Holland, "A Theory of Vocational Choice," *Journal of Counsel-*

ing Psychology 6(1959):35–44; A. Roe, *The Psychology of Occupations* (New York: John Wiley and Sons, 1956); A. Roe and M. Siegelman, *The Origin of Interests* (Washington, D.C.: American Personnel and Guidance Association, 1964); D. E. Super, *The Psychology of Careers* (New York: Harper and Brothers, 1957); D. V. Tiedeman, "Decision and Vocational Development: A Paradigm and Its Implications," *Personnel and Guidance Journal* 40(1961):15–20; D. V. Tiedeman, R. P. O'Hara, and E. Matthews, "Position Choices and Careers: Elements of a Theory," *Harvard Studies in Career Development,* No. 8 (Cambridge, Mass.: Harvard Graduate School of Education, 1958); L. Tyler, *The Psychology of Human Differences,* 2nd ed. (New York: Appleton-Century Crofts, 1956); R. F. Winch, *Identification and its Familial Determinants* (Indianapolis: Bobbs-Merrill, 1962).

2. S. K. Escalona, *The Roots of Individuality* (Chicago: Aldine, 1968).
3. Roe and Siegelman, *op. cit.*
4. A. M. Kroll, *et al., Career Development* (New York: John Wiley and Sons, 1970).
5. Roe and Siegelman, *op. cit.,* p. 5.
6. W. R. Thompson, "Development and the Biophysical Bases of Personality," *Handbook of Personality Theory and Research,* E. F. Borgatta and W. W. Lambert, eds. (Skokie, Ill.: Rand McNally, 1968), pp. 149–214.
7. W. R. Thompson, "Influence of Prenatal Maternal Anxiety on Emotionality in Young Rats," *Science* 125(1957):698–699.
8. W. Young, R. W. Gey, and C. H. Phoenix, "Hormones and Sexual Behavior," *Sex Research: New Developments,* J. Money, ed. (New York: Holt, Rinehart, and Winston, 1965).
9. R. J. Dubos, ed., "Environmental Determinants of Human Individuality," V. C. Vaughan, III, *Issues in Human Development* (Washington, D.C.: National Institute of Child Health and Human Development, 1967), p. 8.
10. R. B. Cattell, *The Scientific Analysis of Personality* (Baltimore: Penguin, 1965).
11. R. C. Tryon, "Genetic Differences in Maze-Learning Ability in Rats," *National Society for the Study of Education, The Thirty-Ninth Yearbook* (Bloomington, Ill.: Public School Publishing, 1940).
12. J. Kagan, "Personality Development," *Personality: Dynamics, Development, and Assessment,* I. L. Janis, *et al.,* eds. (New York: Harcourt Brace Jovanovich, 1969), pp. 403–572.
13. M. Shirley, *The First Two Years. Vol. III. Personality Manifestations* (Minneapolis: University of Minnesota Press, 1933).
14. P. Neilon, "Shirley's Babies after 15 Years: A Personality Study," *Journal of Genetic Psychology* 73(1948):175–186.
15. S. Escalona, M. E. Leitch, *et al.,* "Earliest Phases of Personality Development," *Monographs of the Society for Research in Child Development,* No. 17, 1952; S. Escalona and G. M. Heider, *Prediction and Outcome: A Study in Child Development* (New York: Basic Books, 1959).
16. Thomas, Chess and Birch, *Temperament and Behavior Disorders in Children* (New York: New York University Press, 1968).
17. Taken from Roe and Siegelman, *op. cit.*
18. H. L. Rheingold, "The Social and Socializing Infant," *Handbook of Socialization Theory and Research,* D. A. Goslin, ed. (Skokie, Ill.: Rand McNally, 1969), p. 781.
19. H. A. Murray, *et al., Explorations in Personality: A Clinical and Experimental Study of Fifty Men of College Age* (New York: Oxford University Press, 1938), pp. 77–78.
20. Kagan, *op. cit.*

21. K. Whitehorn, "The Open-Plan Family," *Observer Review*, London 30 July 1972.

22. E. B. Luckey, "Education for Family Living in the Twentieth Century," *Journal of Home Economics* 57, 9(1965):685–690.

23. A. Toffler, *Future Shock* (New York: Random House, 1970), p. 215.

24. Taken from Roe and Siegelman, *op. cit.*

25. *Ibid.*, p. 5.

26. Super, *op. cit.*; D. E. Super *et al.*, *Career Development: Self-Concept Theory* (Princeton: College Entrance Examination Board, 1963).

27. G. E. Hill and E. B. Luckey, *Guidance for Children in Elementary Schools.* (New York: Appleton-Century Crofts, 1969) pp. 277–289.

28. S. Ambrosino, "Parents' Expectations," *Childhood Education* 43(March 1967):397–400.

29. A. Montagu, "Quest for Self," *Childhood Education* 41(September 1964): 3–9.

30. H. G. Morgan, "Building Self Esteem at Home and School," *Childhood Education* 38(1962):278–81.

31. A. Roe, *The Psychology of Occupations* (New York: John Wiley and Sons, 1956); A. Roe, "Early Determinants of Vocational Choice," *Journal of Counseling Psychology* 4(1957):212–17; A. Roe and M. Siegelman, op. cit.; R. J. Brunken, "Perceived Parental Attitudes and Parental Identification in Relation to Field of Vocational Choice," *Journal of Counseling Psychology* 12(1965):39–47; L. B. Green and H. J. Parker, "Parental Influence upon Adolescents' Occupational Choice: A Test of an Aspect of Roe's Theory," *Journal of Counseling Psychology* 12(1965):369–383; A. E. Grigg, "Childhood Experiences with Parental Attitudes: A Test of Roe's Hypothesis," *Journal of Counseling Psychology* 6(1959):153–55; D. Hagen, "Careers and Family Atmospheres: An Empirical Test of Roe's Theory," *Journal of Counseling Psychology* 7(1960):251–56; D. K. Switzer, A. E. Grigg, J. S. Miller and R. K. Young, "Early Experiences and Occupational Choice: A Test of Roe's Hypothesis," *Journal of Counseling Psychology* 9(1962):45–48; A. C. Utton, "Recalled Parent-Child Relations as Determinants of Vocational Choice," *Journal of Counseling Psychology* 9(1962):49–53.

32. Roe and Siegelman, *op. cit.*, p. 59.

33. A. E. Grigg, *op. cit.*; D. Hagen, *op. cit.*; D. A. Switzer *et al.*, *op. cit.*; A. C. Utton, *op. cit.*

34. P. H. Mussen and J. Conger, *Child Development and Personality* (New York: Harper and Brothers, 1956).

35. S. W. Bijou, "Patterns of Reinforcement and Resistance to Extinction in Young Children," *Child Development* 28(1957):47–54; S. Rosenblum, "The Effects of Differential Reinforcement and Motivation on Prediction Responses of Children," *Child Development* 27(1956):99–108.

36. R. R. Sears, E. E. Maccoby, and H. Levin, *Patterns of Child Rearing* (Evanston, Ill.: Row-Peterson, 1957); W. C. Becker, "Consequences of Different Kinds of Parental Discipline," in *Review of Child Development Research,* Vol. I, M. L. Hoffman and L. W. Hoffman, eds. (New York: Russell Sage Foundation, 1964), pp. 169–208.

37. U. Bronfenbrenner, "Socialization and Social Class through Time and Space," *Readings in Social Psychology,* 3rd ed., E. E. Maccoby, T. M. Newcomb, and E. L. Hartley, eds. (New York: Holt, Rinehart and Winston, 1958).

38. B. R. McCandless, *Children, Behavior and Development,* 2nd ed. (New York: Holt, Rinehart and Winston, 1967), p. 522.

39. F. I. Nye and Lois W. Hoffman, *The Employed Mother in America* (Chicago: Rand McNally, 1963).

40. P. H. Mussen and L. Distler, "Masculinity, Identification, and Father-Son Relationships," *Journal of Abnormal and Social Psychology* 59(1959):350–356.
41. D. B. Lynn and W. L. Sawrey, "The Effects of Father-Absence on Norwegian Boys and Girls," *Journal of Abnormal and Social Psychology* 59(1959): 258–262.
42. M. L. Hoffman, "Child Rearing Practices and Moral Development: Generalizations From Empirical Research," *Child Development* 34(1963):295–318.
43. S. Schachter, *The Psychology of Affiliation: Experimental Studies of the Sources of Gregariousness* (Stanford, Calif.: Stanford University Press, 1959).
44. Kagan, *op. cit.,* p. 550.
45. H. L. Koch, "Attitudes of Children Toward Their Peers as Related to Certain Characteristics of Their Siblings," *Psychological Monographs* 70, 426 (1965); H. L. Koch, "Some Emotional Attitudes of the Young Child in Relation to Characteristics of His Siblings," *Child Development* 27(1965): 393–426.
46. Hill and Luckey, *op. cit.,* pp. 287–288.
47. D. M. Levy, "Studies in Sibling Rivalry," *American Orthopsychiatric Association Research Monographs,* No. 2 (1937).
48. Harlow, *Learning to Love* (San Francisco: Albion, 1971), p. 64.
49. H. F. Harlow and M. Harlow, "The Young Monkeys," *Psychology Today* 1(1967):40–47.
50. B. Bettelheim, *Communal Child-rearing and American Education* (New York: MacMillan, 1969).
51. H. F. Harlow, *Learning to Love* (San Francisco: Albion, 1971).
52. H. F. Harlow, J. P. Gluck, and S. J. Suomi, "Generalization of Behavioral Data Between Nonhuman and Human Animals," *American Psychologist* 27, 8 (1972):709–16.
53. Toffler, *op. cit.*
54. G. H. Frank, "The Role of the Family in the Development of Psychopathology," *Psychological Bulletin,* 65(1965):191–205.
55. McCandless, *op. cit.,* pp. 102–03.
56. A. Bandura and R. H. Walters, *Social Learning and Personality Development* (New York: Holt, Rinehart and Winston, 1963).
57. J. D. Krumboltz and H. G. Krumboltz, *Changing Children's Behavior* (Englewood Cliffs, N.J.: Prentice-Hall, 1972).
58. H. L. Koch, "Attitudes of Children Toward Their Peers," *op. cit.;* H. L. Koch, "Some Emotional Attitudes of the Young Child," *op. cit.*
59. P. H. Mussen, "Early Sex Role Development," *Handbook of Socialization Theory and Research, op. cit.*
60. T. Parsons, "Small Family Structure and the Socialization of the Child," *Family, Socialization, and Interaction Process,* T. Parsons and R. F. Bales, eds. (Glencoe, Ill.: Free Press, 1955.)
61. J. W. M. Whiting, "Sorcery, Sin and the Superego: A Cross-cultural Study of Some Mechanisms of Social Control," *Nebraska Symposium on Motivation,* M. R. Jones, ed. (Lincoln, Neb.: University of Nebraska Press, 1959), pp. 174–197, quoted from p. 188.
62. L. A. Kohlberg, "A Cognitive-Developmental Analysis of Children's Sex-Role Concepts and Attitudes," *The Development of Sex Differences,* E. E. Maccoby, ed. (Stanford, Calif.: Stanford University Press, 1966).
63. McCandless, *op. cit.,* p. 449.

64. Levin and Fleischmann, "Childhood Socialization," *Handbook of Personality Theory and Research,* E. F. Borgatta and W. W. Lambert, eds. (Skokie, Ill.: Rand McNally, 1968), pp. 215–38.

65. U. Bronfenbrenner, *Toward a Typology of Occupational Orientations* (Unpublished manuscript: Cornell University, 1959).

66. S. W. Gray, "Perceived Similarity to Parents and Adjustment," *Child Development* 30(1959):91–108.

67. D. Lynn, "A Note on Sex Differences in the Development of Masculine and Feminine Identification," *Psychological Review* 66(1959):126–135; D. Lynn, "Sex Differences in Identification Development," *Sociometry* 24(1961): 372–383.

68. Winch, *op. cit.*

69. C. Andreas, *Sex and Caste in America* (Englewood Cliffs, New Jersey: Prentice-Hall, 1971).

70. E. Janeway, *Man's World, Woman's Place: A Study in Social Mythology* (New York: William Morrow, 1971).

71. C. G. Wrenn, C. Gilbert, and S. Schwarzrock, *Changing Roles of Men and Women* (Minnesota: American Guidance Service, 1970).

72. M. L. Hoffman, "Child Rearing Practices and Moral Development: Generalizations from Empirical Research," *Child Development* 34(1963):295–318.

73. J. Kagan and M. Freeman, "Relation of Childhood Intelligence, Maternal Behaviors During Adolescence," *Child Development* 34(1963):899–911.

74. R. Peck and R. Havighurst, *The Psychology of Character Development* (New York: Wiley and Sons, 1960).

75. U. Bronfenbrenner, *Two Worlds of Childhood* (New York: Russell Sage Foundation, 1970).

76. Frank Musgrove, *Youth and the Social Order* (Bloomington: Indiana University Press, 1964).

77. For the development of this assumption see A. M. Kroll *et al., Career Development, Growth and Crisis* (New York: John Wiley and Sons, 1970).

78. D. J. Bordua, "Educational Aspirations and Parental Stress on College," *Social Forces* 38(March 1960):262–269; R. B. Jacobsen, "An Exploration of Parental Encouragement as an Intervening Variable in Occupational-educational Learning of Children," *Journal of Marriage and the Family* (Decade Review) Pt. 2, 33(February 1971):1 174–182; J. A. Kahl, Educational and Occupational Aspirations of 'Commonman' Boys," *Harvard Educational Review* 23 (Summer 1953):1860–203; W. H. Sewell and V. P. Shah, "Socioeconomic Status, Intelligence, and the Attainment of Higher Education," *Sociology of Education* 40(Winter 1967):1–23; W. H. Sewell and V. P. Shah, "Social Class, Parental Encouragement and Educational Aspirations," *American Journal of Sociology* 73(March 1968):559–572; W. H. Sewell and V. P. Shah, "Parents' Education and Children's Educational Aspirations and Achievements," *American Sociological Review* 33(April 1968):191–209; Richard L. Simpson, "Parental Influence, Anticipatory Socialization, and Social Mobility," *American Sociological Review* 27(August 1962):362–74.

79. G. Elder, *Adolescent Achievement and Mobility Aspirations* (Chapel Hill, N.C.: University of North Carolina, Institute for Research in Social Science, 1962); B. C. Rosen, "Family Structure and Value Transmission," *Merrill-Palmer Quarterly* 10:59–76.

80. *Vocational Plans and Preferences in Adolescents* (Lafayette, Indiana: Measurement and Research Center, Purdue University, 1972).

81. E. E. Sandis, "The Transmission of Mothers' Educational Ambitions as Re-

lated to Specific Socialization Techniques," *Journal of Marriage and The Family* 32(May 1970):2 204–11.

82. W. R. Morrow and R. R. Wilson, "Family Relations of Bright High-achieving and Under-achieving High School Boys," *Child Development* 32(September 1961):501–10.

83. R. J. Havighurst, "Conditions Productive of Superior Children," *Teachers College Record* 62(1961):524–531; F. Reissman, *The Culturally Deprived Child* (New York: Harper and Row, 1964).

84. R. R. Dynes, A. C. Clarke, and S. Dinitz, "Levels of Occupational Aspiration: Some Aspects of Family Experience as a Variable," *American Sociological Review* 21(April 1956):212–15.

85. W. A. Rushing, "Adolescent-parent Relationship and Mobility Aspirations," *Social Forces* 43(December 1964):157–166.

86. R. H. Turner, "Some Family Determinants of Ambition," *Sociology and Social Research* 4(July 1962):6 397–411.

87. L. Kriesberg, *Mothers in Poverty. A Study of Fatherless Families* (Chicago: Aldine, 1970).

88. *Vocational Plans and Preferences of Adolescents* (Lafayette, Ind.: Measurement and Research Center, Purdue University, 1972).

89. For an extended treatment of the adolescent decision-making process see A. M. Kroll *et al., op. cit.*

90. E. H. Erikson, *Childhood and Society* (New York: W. W. Norton, 1950); E. H. Erikson, "Identity and the Life Cycle" *Psychological Issues* 1 (1959):1; E. H. Erikson, *Insight and Responsibility* (New York: W. W. Norton, 1950).

91. *Vocational Plans and Preferences of Adolescents, op. cit.*

92. A. M. Kroll, *et al., op. cit.*

93. A. M. Kroll, *Ibid.*, p. 89.

94. *Vocational Plans and Preferences of Adolescents, op. cit.*

95. D. R. Miller and G. E. Swanson, *The Changing American Parent* (New York: John Wiley and Sons, 1958).

96. M. Gold and C. Slater, "Office, Factory, Store—and Family: A Study of Integration Setting," *American Sociological Review* 23(1958):64–74.

97. R. S. Cavan, "Subcultural Variations and Mobility," *Handbook of Marriage and the Family*, H. T. Christensen (Chicago: Rand McNally & Co., 1974).

98. R. O. Blood and R. L. Hamblin, "The Effect of the Wife's Employment on the Family Power Structure," *Social Forces* 36(1958):347–352. L. W. Hoffman, "Parental Power Relations and the Division of Household Tasks," *Marriage and Family Living* 22(1960):299–311; R. Middleton and S. Putney, "Dominance in Decisions in the Family: Race and Class Differences," *American Journal of Sociology* 65(1960):605–09; R. O. Blood and D. M. Wolf, *Husbands and Wives: The Dynamics of Married Living* (Glencoe, Ill.: Free Press, 1960).

99. C. B. Price, *New Directions in the World of Work* (Kalamazoo, Mich.: W. E. Upjohn Institute for Employment Research, 1972).

100. E. J. Koprowski, "Business Technology and the American Family," Address. National Council on Family Relations Annual Meeting, Boulder, Col., 1971.

101. For a more complete treatment see F. I. Nye and L. W. Hoffman, *op. cit.*

102. V. Packard, *A Nation of Strangers* (New York: David McKay, Inc. 1972).

103. J. E. Tropman, "Social Mobility and Marital Stability," *Applied Social Studies* 3(1971):165–173.

104. S. B. Jones, "When Women Move: Family Migratory Patterns as They Affect and are Affected by the Wife," *The Effects of Mobility on the Wife: A Symposium* (Indianapolis: University of Indiana, 1972).

105. J. L. McKain, Ph.D. Dissertation, Catholic University of America School of Social Work, 1969.
106. Toffler, *op. cit.*

SUGGESTED READING

Cox, Frank D. *American Marriage: A Changing Scene?* Dubuque, Iowa: William C. Brown Co., 1972. A collection of articles and papers which consider the family of the future in the American culture, tomorrow's morality, and the romantic ideal.

Erikson, Erik H. *Insight and Responsibility.* New York: W. W. Norton, 1964. Analyzes personality development as related to commitment, identity, and the adolescent processes, stressing the eventual expression in maturity of diversity and fidelity as social contribution.

Hobart, C. W. "Commitment, Value Conflict, and the Future of the American Family." *Marriage and Family Living* 25(August 1963):405–12. A discussion of functions lost by the family and those that may be retained in the future.

Kroll, Arthur M.; Lillian B. Dinklage; Jennifer Lee; Eileen D. Morley; and Eugene H. Wilson. *Career Development Growth and Crisis.* New York: John Wiley and Sons, 1970. Discusses the interrelation and interdependence of the concepts of self and career; especially valuable in the areas of choice, decision making, and commitment as these pertain to adolescence.

Krumbolts, J. D., and Helen B. Krumbolts. *Changing Children's Behavior.* Englewood Cliffs, N.J.: Prentice-Hall, 1972. A behavioral approach to the practical problems of child rearing and a realistic picture of life in today's family.

Otto, Herbert A. *The Family in Search of A Future.* New York: Appleton-Century-Crofts, 1970. A collection of papers from many disciplines, all of which explore the future of the American family and the variety of forms it may take; primarily concerned with the search for viable forms of marriage and family that are uniquely suited to our time, place, and situation.

Skolnick, A. S., and J. H. Skolnick. *Family In Transition.* Boston: Little, Brown and Co., 1971. Articles brought together from many varied sources but all concerned with the structure and function of the family from early times to the present; looks toward future varieties of family styles and socialization.

Sussman, Marvin B., guest ed. "Variant Marriage Styles and Family Form." *The Family Coordinator* 21(1972):4. A collection of articles whose themes include the future of the family, the structural and functional inadequacies of today's nuclear families, and the growing pluralism in family forms.

PART THREE
Concepts of Career Development

To a significant degree the distinction between a professional and a technician resides in the extent to which conceptual frames of reference rather than procedural ritual guides his behavior. Professionals in vocational guidance operate from a growing base of research and theory pertinent to career development and choice behavior. This reservoir of insights provides the practitioner with the analytic materials by which he can assist those whom he serves to generate and test hypotheses about their characteristics in relation to the opportunities which lie immediately and distantly before them.

Miller speaks comprehensively of the conceptual heritage available to counselors under the rubric "career development." He addresses the changing concepts of careers and the influences upon them. He brings forward from the 1950s the evolution of those emphases in the trait and factor, psychodynamic, and situational approaches which have become the major classifications of explanation about career development in the 1970s. In particular, he identifies the rising influence of phenomenological and existential perspectives as viewed through several lenses focused on decision making. In his analysis of the concept of stages of development he sets the stage for Jordaan in the following chapter.

Jordaan focuses rather specifically upon the current concepts of developmental tasks as applied to the understanding of career development at different life periods. He describes in depth the ingredients of life-staging phenomena in relationship to both environmental and individual variables. He describes in some depth the specific research now available and the major research projects bearing upon life staging in vocational or career development. He weaves through his presentation the implications flowing from staging phenomena for individual choice and for counseling.

In his analysis of model building for vocational maturity Crites brings together many of the elements of career development elaborated by Miller and Jordaan. He contends that such model building organizes and explicates what is known about career development and also suggests new lines of inquiry; perhaps, more importantly, it ultimately suggests novel modes of practice. This latter seems to be upheld as one examines the chapters on professional practice constituting Part Four. Crites takes the reader with him through the phases of constructing a model, testing it, and bringing forth its implications for research and for practice. In the process, he describes the components or elements comprising vocational maturity as these are found in attitudes and in choice competencies. Finally, like Miller and Jordaan, Crites identifies the research questions still to be answered in career development and some of the modes by which such inquiries might be effectively mounted.

Career Development Theory in Perspective 10

Carroll H. Miller
Northern Illinois University

If we ask a group of high school seniors what plans they have for careers, we must be prepared for a wide variety of answers. Partly this may be due to difficulties of communication. First of all, the very word "career" may cause trouble, for while some have considered careers, many are thinking simply in terms of jobs. If now we ask what kind of careers or jobs they would like to enter, and what kind they actually expect to find themselves in a few years after high school, we may expect somewhat different answers from the same individuals. If in our curiosity about the paths of career development we probe further and ask the seniors to tell us what influences led to the decisions they made, we shall again receive a variety of answers; the literature is full of reports of such surveys. But we may well have the uncomfortable feeling that many of the answers given are not the "real" reasons for choice and that perhaps in many cases the students are not able to verbalize the "real" reasons.

If now we turn from such general inquiries and seek to understand the career development of some one individual—say, for example, a senior high school boy eighteen years of age—we must realize that the world he has known is very different from our own, even when we were eighteen. If our questioning took place in 1972, then the boy was born in 1954. He knew nothing from firsthand experience of either the Depression or World War II, although his father may be a veteran of that conflict, or perhaps the Korean War. He was born in the year of the Supreme Court decision on integration and is living in an age of protest. He questions, much more than most of us did at his age, the validity of the work ethic. Yet, probably because of the values of his family, he accepts the belief that work and career or job must somehow be related.

CHANGING CONCEPTS OF CAREER

It seems self-evident that if this chapter is to be concerned with career development we must attempt to define or at least clarify the concept of career and to struggle with the relationship between work and career. What is the meaning of work? The answer is clearly different for various groups of people at different times in history. The materials for the ensuing brief discussion on early meanings of work are drawn from the classic study "Work through the Ages" by Tilgher, unless otherwise specified.

To the Greeks work was a curse, imposed by the gods and not worthy of a citizen. They might, however, reluctantly make an exception in the case of agriculture, which provided a livelihood while allowing the farmer to

235

enjoy much of the independence so highly prized by Greeks. To the Hebrews also work was a curse, but a curse imposed because of the sins of their ancestors, and accepted as a means of expiation for this sin. Primitive Christianity accepted much of the Hebrew tradition that work was a punishment for original sin, but to this was added the idea that one must earn one's living and that goods beyond this requirement could and should be shared with needy brothers. But work and life itself was a temporary, interim thing, to be ended with Christ's Second Coming. Early Catholicism did something to dignify work, for in many of the monastaries all were expected to work. Yet work was not a value in itself, but, rather, a necessary activity for maintaining the monastery and, of course, attaining expiation. As the years went on, however, much of the manual work was shifted to the lay brethren. During the feudal period work took on a social status meaning. In the words of Wrenn, "The 'common man' in the feudal society of western Europe had *only* work as a basis of dignity. At a time when blood and land were the qualifications offered by the nobility, work and the product of work became an unopposed virtue. It was available to all who had nothing but brain and muscle. If a man produced—worked—he had dignity even if his blood, possessions, culture, and morals were at a low ebb."[1]

With the breakdown of feudalism and the beginnings of the modern world, some major changes occurred in the meaning of work. During the Reformation Luther held that all who can work should work (one is reminded of the dictum of Captain John Smith at Jamestown many years later); that idleness, begging, and lending at interest are unnatural; that charity is for only those who cannot work; and that monks in the cloister are simply avoiding their duty to their neighbors. In addition, it was held that work is a service to God and that all kinds of work have equal spiritual dignity if done in a spirit of obedience to God and love of neighbor. To these teachings Calvinism added that all men, even the rich, must work, not for the fruits of their labor but so that profits may be reinvested to produce new enterprises, *ad infinitum.* And so we have the Protestant ethic, as well as an early justification of capitalism.

The story should be continued to include something of the impact of the Industrial Revolution, of the growth of socialism, and of many other events and ideas important to the modern world, for some of these ideas and attitudes are those about which our imaginary group of seniors was unable to verbalize. But it is not only high school seniors who are seldom and only dimly aware of the impact of our heritage upon contemporary concepts of work. There seems to be something in the present temper which, even for adults, demands attitudes and ideas reflecting only the contemporary. College-age youth especially, whether in or out of college, seem to regard only the concrete here and now as "relevant." Any detailed consideration of such views is clearly not possible within the necessary limitations of this chapter, so we must be highly selective as we undertake a brief glimpse of contemporary elements.

Two major influences upon careers at the present time are the complex of changes resulting from the development of technology and the impact of the sheer size of business and industrial organizations. The rapidity of technological change, superimposed upon an already highly developed division of labor, has produced a situation in which only a relatively small minority of the working population will be able to choose, prepare for, enter into, and continue in a single occupation during their working lives. We frequently hear estimates that the average worker may expect to engage in five or six or seven different occupations during his working life. New jobs are created by technological change (as in electronic data processing), and old jobs disappear. We shall resist the temptation to enter into a discussion of the whole matter of the effects of automation, real, anticipated, and feared; but in general, it does seem clear that whatever lifelong stability of occupational pursuit still persists is most apt to be limited to professional occupations, to some kinds of management positions, to skilled crafts, and to some white-collar work (particularly some clerical jobs), while the majority of workers can anticipate some change from occupation to occupation, and a number of changes of jobs within an occupation. For the majority of workers in the present world, then, the classic notion of vocational guidance with its assumption that a person chooses and remains in a single occupation seems curiously antiquated.

The second major influence upon careers results from large scale business and industrial organization. Slocum estimates that, "The vast majority, perhaps 85 percent, of American workers are employed by organizations."[2] The day of the independent skilled craftsman operating outside an organization is virtually ended, and the time of day for the small family owned and operated farm is at least late afternoon. Even traditionally independent professionals, such as lawyers and physicians, find themselves increasingly involved in organizations. In view of such conditions, Gross suggests that, "In sociological terms, preparation of an individual for the world of work means four different kinds of participation. He is being prepared for a life in an organization, for a set of role relationships, for a level and kind of consumption, and for an occupational history."[3]

So what is a career? There is no single answer. Wilensky[4] thinks of a career as an orderly work history in which each job is preparatory for the next. Slocum[5] also suggests that such a concept has been the ideal model. Gross regards such a concept as unduly restrictive and thinks that a career may be regarded as "a succession of positions that have a pattern that is, to some extent, predictable and controllable."[6] Workers in a more psychological frame of reference often do not define career as such but devote considerable attention to concepts of career development (including stages and developmental tasks) and of career as a means of self actualization. Although Herr notes that the notion of career as an orderly sequence of positions leading to higher and higher status positions is considered in public terms as good and virtuous, he also makes the important point

> . . . that most theories of vocational development and decision making are based upon limited samples of rather privileged persons. . . . They are addressed to the middle class rather than to those who depart from this classification in either direction. They tend to emphasize continuous, uninterrupted, and progressive aspects of vocational behavior which seem possible in a segment of the population whose limits upon choice are minimal, for whom the resources both psychological and economic are available to facilitate pur-

poseful development, and where a high correspondence between self concept and career concept is probable. Such criteria do not fit all persons about whom guidance practitioners must be concerned.[7]

From this realistic statement it is important to stress the point and the classic model of vocational guidance, resting as it does on the onward and upward value assumption, is not only badly outmoded but is also both a product of and a server of middle class orientations. At present there simply is no broadly adequate concept of career that cuts across values and classes, unless one is willing to apply the term in a nonjudgmental way to the simple sequence of work activities which comprise the work history of the individual. If this is done, however, there seems to be something lost in the translation.

THE HERITAGE FROM THE FIFTIES

Seldom if ever does a theory appear suddenly as a completed intellectual achievement; rather, it emerges from a long and sometimes baffling struggle to integrate a wide range of accumulated data into a meaningful whole. Theory development certainly is not delimited by the calendar, so we should not expect that vocational development theories of the 1960s will represent a pattern of thinking independent of earlier decades; rather, we must expect that many elements of theory characteristic of the 1950s or earlier will be found again in the 1960s, though perhaps with different emphases and modified interpretations.

Matching Men and Jobs

In the 1950s the classic approach of matching individuals and jobs, inherited from the days of Frank Parsons and resting upon a trait-and-factor analysis, still retained considerable vigor. Trait-and-factor theory was not the only kind of theory to be found in the decade, but was perhaps the most characteristic. Revisions of interest inventories, such as the Strong and Kuder, also appeared. Fewer instruments for the measurement of values appeared, although the Work Values Inventory[8] emerged from the Career Pattern Study of Super and associates, and interest in the original Study of Values continued. Looking back, one can say that the decade of the fifties produced a number of appraisal instruments, many of which are still useful. It was a decade of pragmatic enterprise rather than of theory formation.

The concept of matching people and jobs is persuasively simple, if not actually simplistic. In their revision and updating of the Jones text, Stefflre and Stewart[9] give a particularly succinct statement (here paraphrased) of assumptions underlying this approach.

1. Vocational development is largely a cognitive process; decisions are to be reached by reasoning.
2. Occupational choice is a single event. In the spirit of Parsons, choice is stressed greatly and development very little.
3. There is a single "right" goal for everyone in the choice of vocation. There is little or no recognition that a worker might fit well into a number of occupations.

4. A single type of person works in each job. This is the other side of the coin of the third assumption. Taken together, these two notions amount to a one-man, one-job relationship—a concept congenial to the trait factor approach.

5. There is an occupational choice available to each individual. The complete acceptance of this assumption would deny that the social and economic circumstances have any effects upon the opportunities available to the individual. Stated in more theoretical terms, the "social systems" approach has no real meaning. Such an assumption, although it did exist, seems curiously out of tune with the spirit of Parsons, who was at heart bent upon bringing about social and economic reforms which, presumably, would increase the range of options open to individuals.

For all its shortcomings, the theory of matching people and jobs, supported by a trait and factor style of research, made important contributions, but the adequacy of the approach as a theoretical formulation is another question. Osipow notes that this approach has been absorbed into other formulations, so that "few practitioners of vocational counseling today are pure trait-factor adherents." The strongly empirical nature of the trait and factor approach creates a scientific halo about itself, but this very characteristic leads Osipow to remark that, "The trait-factor approach . . . is almost a nontheory since it is basically empirical in nature."[10]

Psychodynamic Theories

There are a number of theories which, although derived from rather different historical roots, have enough in common that they may be placed in one cluster and called the psychodynamic theories. This group includes four identifiable theories: (1) the psychoanalytic, (2) those placing major emphasis on needs and values, (3) those based on the relations between parents and children (especially in early childhood), and (4) self theories. All of these had achieved a considerable stage of development before 1960.

Psychoanalytic Theory. As soon as one undertakes even the most limited discussion of psychoanalytic ideas, there is a danger of becoming entangled in semantics. Surely there are differences in the thought of the early and orthodox psychoanalysts and the later theorists. It is also true that elements of psychoanalysis can be found in the thinking of others who would disavow any complete allegiance to Freud or other orthodox figures. In this discussion the focus is upon only aspects of psychoanalysis as applied to vocational choice, and within this limited framework the fundamental tenet seems to be that vocational activity represents a sublimation of biological desires and impulses; that is, the individual expresses libido in a socially acceptable manner through vocation. Among the more articulate spokesmen for this point of view are Brill,[11] Meadow,[12] Forer,[13] and Bordin, Nachmann and Segal.[14] Psychoanalytic thinking as related to vocational choice is primarily centered about the relation of personality type to occupation. Osipow comments, "The psychoanalytic conceptualization of career choice emphasizes the techniques of impulse gratification and anxiety reduction which a field offers rather than the interests and abilities a career requires."[15] Also relevant is the psychoanalytic concept of developmental stages. Forer offered five stages which he regarded as "roughly sequential"—vocational choice, acquisition of vocational knowledge or skill, utilization of the vocational situation, performance dynamics, and vocational maturation—and the "dimensions"— nurturant, oral, sensual, anal, and genital—set forth by Bordin, Nachmann, and Segal also might well be regarded as stages. This combination view which explicitly stressed need gratification, and more implicitly the developmental stages concept, was carried forward into the 1960s.

Need-and-value Theories.   Another theoretical approach prominent in the fifties and carried on into recent years is that based on needs, sometimes called the "needs-drive theory." Since needs may be regarded as an aspect of personality, needs theories fall within the psychodynamic classification. Vocational choice is generated as the individual seeks a vocation which will permit him to satisfy at least some of his basic needs, and it is not necessary that the person be conscious of all the needs he seeks to satisfy. When needs are broadly defined as both conscious and unconscious, then the concept of unconscious needs reflects a strain of psychoanalytic influence. The most influential single theory of needs in counseling literature is probably that proposed by Maslow.[16]

The earlier studies by Maslow were concerned with dominance. His subjects were at first primates and later adult women, but then, as Poelling[17] points out, World War II "had a dramatic effect upon Maslow." This opinion is based upon a 1968 mimeographed paper, not widely available,[18] in which Maslow shifted his research efforts to studies of aggression. Such studies led to interest in security and insecurity and then to a quest for a theory of motivation. It is against this background that Maslow formulated his often quoted "hierarchy of needs" in which physiological and safety needs are regarded as most basic, followed by needs for belongingness and love, for self-respect and esteem, and for self-actualization as the final need, found among some but by no means all people.

Maslow's needs concept had a definite influence upon Roe's theory of vocational interests. Roe developed propositions which, in their revised form, included five statements: four of these were concerned with limits set by genetic factors—a recognition of factors in the general cultural background of the pattern of psychic energies as the major determinants of interests—and the final proposition was concerned with the intensity of needs, their satisfaction, and their organization are major determinants of motivation. The proposition most clearly reflecting the influence of Maslow was the third: "The pattern of development of interests, attitudes, and other personality variables with relatively little or nonspecific genetic control is primarily determined by individual experiences through which involuntary attention becomes channeled into particular directions." From this general statement are derived two subpropositions: (1) that directions are at first determined by "the patterning of early satisfactions and frustrations" and (2) that "the modes and degrees of need satisfaction will determine which needs will become the strongest motivators."[19]

There are ever present semantic difficulties in any discussion of needs and values. What really is the difference in the constructs represented by these two terms, or are the terms really synonyms? Perhaps the simplest concept of needs is that of a deficit; a need is something one doesn't have. Needs are thus related to values to the extent that one places high value on what one doesn't have. Another concept of values is that of a basic personality orientation. A classic example of this conception is derived from the typology of Spranger,[20] who proposed that it is possible to categorize men into six value types: the theoretical, economic, social, political, aesthetic, and religious. An instrument for measuring the relative strength of these values was developed at first by Allport and Vernon and later revised by the two original authors and Lindzey. A third view, developed in anthropological studies, is that values are concepts of the desirable which influence selection among available modes, means, and ends of action.[21] This view might be called the normative, the norm being derived either from a cultural standard, the code of the immediate group with which one interacts, a reference group, or a personal standard (the ideal self) that the individual has acquired in his or her idiosyncratic experience. The value might be an idea, an object, or an activity. Finally, perhaps the most currently influential concept of values is that given by Katz:

> Values may be regarded as characteristic outer expressions and culturally influenced manifestations of needs. They are teleologically described in terms of the goal or satisfaction that is sought rather than the motivating drive. They are often stated on different levels of complexity and abstraction.[22]

Parent-child Relations.   The very title of this subsection suggests that we shall be dealing with a topic which is not a kind of theory in itself but which involves the application of various theoretical considerations to a particular area of experience—relations between children and parents in the home. The best known of such proposals is that by Roe, whose approach might be regarded as a needs theory, and Crites[23] so treats it. Certainly Roe's theory draws heavily from Maslow's concept of needs, although other interpreters, such as Osipow[24] and Zaccaria,[25] do not see it as exclusively a theory of needs. Such differences suggest the difficulty of assigning Roe to any one section of the filing cabinet, but of one thing there can be no doubt—the theory is psychodynamic, taking its start from within the personality and relating personality to various aspects of the world of work. At this point it is necessary to note for historical purposes that the theory was largely developed (though not fully tested) during the late forties and fifties.

Roe described three patterns of early relationship between parent and child:[26] (1) emotional concentration on the child, manifested as either over-protective or overdemanding behavior on the part of the parent; (2) a loving but casual acceptance of the child; and (3) an avoidance of the child, evidenced as neglect or rejection by the parent. These various types of parent-child relations have sometimes been described in terms of characteristics of parents, and sometimes as different "psychological climates." In this discussion we shall use the psychological climates terminology. In the case of emotional concentration on the child, the basic needs of the child would be readily satisfied, but the satisfaction of higher needs (as Maslow used the term) would depend upon compliance with parental expectations. Thus a child in such a climate would tend to become dependent upon others.

A second kind of psychological climate is one in which a child and his needs would be neglected, or the child would be rejected. The general atmosphere could be described as cold, with the child left relatively on his own. The third psychological climate is one of acceptance of the child, but in a more casual way than that characterizing the climate of emotional concentration. Although basic needs of the child would be satisfied, he would be relatively free to seek his own gratification of needs at all levels.

Fortunately, Roe herself has furnished a review and summary of her work in relation to vocational choice in a very recent publication.[27] She found that although biologists respected their fathers, there was an impressive lack of close family ties, while psychologists and anthropologists reacted with marked rebelliousness to overprotection and firm control. Thus was posed the problem of directional influence of early family experiences upon later vocational development. Differences in early family experiences, Roe thought, came to be translated into differing vocational preferences. In her earlier classification of occupations she had used eight (later reduced to six) levels vertically arranged, and eight fields of primary focus of activity horizontally arranged. In her 1972 paper a model of concentric circles combine level and field, suggesting (1) that there is less differentiation of field at the lower levels represented by the innermost circles and (2) that activity fields represent a closed continuum suggested by the circles, with rather arbitrary divisions between the fields.

Particularly pertinent to a theory of vocational development is Roe's report of her efforts to construct a general formula, and her report of difficulties encountered are most instructive. The descriptive formula developed is intended to apply to one individual at a given point in time, although it would be possible to compare a given individual at two points in time under different circumstances if factor weights could be determined. For those focusing upon a developmental approach, the necessity of repeated assessments at different points in time and under different circumstances becomes important.

Self-Theories.   By 1950 interest in the self as an important construct in psychology was well established, although often criticized. Much less frequent was the application of the self-concept to problems of vocational choice and development, but there had been beginnings. Super[28] notes some contributions made during the 1940s by Carter in his theory of the development of attitudes of adolescents, by Bordin in his theory of vocational interests as reflections of the self concept, by Lecky in his self-consistency concept, by Allport's "rediscovery of the ego in psychology," and by others. In counseling literature of the 1950s there was an upsurge of interest in the self-concept that can scarcely be traced to any one person. It seems as though a number of persons had come to appreciate the implications of the self-concept in counseling within the span of a few years—almost suddenly as such things go. But the most systematic application of self-concept theory during the fifties was in the Career Pattern Study by Super and associates.[29]

In 1951 Super proposed a redefinition of vocational guidance and adjustment: "Vocational guidance is the process of helping a person to develop and accept an integrated and adequate picture of himself and of his role in the world of work, to test this concept against reality, and to convert it into a reality, with satisfaction to himself and benefit to society."[30] Two years later he published his ten propositions for a theory of vocational development, one of which stated, in part, "The process of vocational development is essentially that of developing and implementing a self concept . . ."[31] These quotations are so familiar as to need little or no amplification, but we have here what is probably the most basic element in Super's theory. As Zacarria observes, "The cutting edge of Super's theory . . . has continued to be phenomenology (self-concept theory)."[32]

Developmental Theories

As in the case of the self-concept theory, developmental theory has a number of roots. Among writers who have reviewed the literature (e.g., Crites,[33] Osipow,[34] and Zaccaria)[35] the names of Lazersfeld and Buehler are commonly mentioned as probably the earliest. Super gives particular credit to these two early sources for his developmental stages. Carter[36] adopted a developmental approach to vocational choice, but did not propose specific stages. From the early 1950s the names of Ginzberg and associates,[37] and Dysinger[38] should be mentioned, and later Erikson[39] and Havighurst.[40] Erikson developed a schema of eight life stages with corresponding psycho-social crises and general tasks to be accomplished. Like Buehler, Erikson did not present his theory in a vocational development framework, but Tiedeman[41] and Tiedeman and O'Hara[42] modified and utilized Erikson's stages in their own vocational theory. Akin to Erikson's theory stages and corresponding tasks is Havighurst's statement of developmental tasks first presented in 1950,[43] but later placed in a specifically vocational context.[44]

And so by 1960 a number of variations on the theme of developmental stages could be heard, and the time was ripe for a synthesis. We shall not consider further the matter of life stages since the next chapter by Jean Pierre Jordaan will deal more fully with the topic.

Situational Theories

We turn now to a different kind of theoretical approach, one which accepts as the starting point the reality of things as they exist in the environment surrounding the individual. This area has often been the happy hunting ground of sociologically oriented investigators, and yet it is not fair to label the situational approach as only sociological. Other elements are involved, as, for example, the ideas of culture and acculturation found in anthropology and the idea of historical accidents which can influence vocational development of the individual by limiting or expanding the options open to him. Crites[45] makes a useful distinction between chance factors, which are fortuitous, unplanned, and unpredicted, and contingency factors, which are predictable and can be considered in the individual's vocational planning. In his discussion of accident theories Crites[46] reviews some of the classical economic theories of Adam Smith and others. These will not be discussed here.

In *Industrial Sociology*, the first edition of which appeared in 1951, Miller and Form distinguished six periods in the social adjustment of the worker: the preparatory and initial work periods, the transition from school to work, and the trial, stable, and retired periods. In their discussion of the extensive case history data gathered for the trial work period, they point out that the period involves a vast amount of floundering and that no single motivating influence was found to underlie the majority of choices made. Thus they say flatly, "Chance experiences undoubtedly explain the process by which most occupational choices are made."[47] In their study of the stable work period Miller and Form review a number of factors thought to be related to occupational placement: father's occupation, intelligence, family status in education and income, financial aid and influential contacts, and social and economic conditions.[48] Distinguishing between the individual and social theories of causation, they comment:

> [An accurate weighting of the facts will demonstrate that the social background of the worker is a base of opportunities and limitations. As opportunities are enlarged, the *possibilities* of occupational mobility are increased. Personal motivation and work are necessary components to an enlarging career pattern. However, there is good evidence that the social backgrounds of workers are the crucial determiners in the *number* who are able to come into various occupational levels.[49]]

It will be noted, however, that some of the factors described by Miller and Form are "contingency" factors, as the word was used by Crites (e.g., occupation of father and social status of family), rather than completely unpredictable chance factors. In any event, the study by Miller and Form had the impact of stressing the importance of situational factors in career development, but it should also be noted that the emphasis on the word *number* by Miller and Form seems to suggest that although social factors may be crucial determiners for groups, they may not be so for a given individual. There seem to be two implications contained here: (1) that contingency factors may provide an adequate basis for group prediction, in the manner that a life insurance actuary can predict the average life expectancy for a defined group, and (2) that contingency factors common to a group may not provide an adequate basis for predicting for the individual. There are, after all, many contingency factors which are unique to the individual's life history.

Some of the most important situational factors are those of the culture (and subculture) in which one lives, for cultures carry with them life-styles which become important in vocational development. Various social classes and ethnic groups have their own subcultures, and often rather distinctive life styles and systems of values.

THE FIFTIES IN RETROSPECT

The decade of the fifties was prolific, though rather more in the accumulation of empirical data than in theory formulation. Some of the ideas which emerged from the decade to be passed on to the sixties may be summarized as follows.

1. The theory of matching persons and jobs was on the wane, largely because of its static nature; yet the trait and factor mode of analysis retained

vitality as a means of empirical research. As Zaccaria remarked in 1970, "To date, this simplistic and pragmatic mode of thought has provided the essential framework for the application of the refined methods of psychometric assessment, the development and utilization of occupational information, and the use of various counseling systems."[50]

2. Psychoanalytic views had been found wanting as a basis for building a complete self-contained theory of career development, and this approach claimed relatively few adherents. However, elements of psychoanalytic thought sometimes helped to produce interesting hypotheses such as those developed by Roe, whose proposals nevertheless remained only partially substantiated hypotheses by 1960. The "ego" of psychoanalysis often survived as essentially the same concept, but modified and separated from the classic framework and renamed the "self."

3. Phenomenological thinking had experienced a robust growth and increased acceptance, especially in the form of self-concept theory. Considerable effort was being devoted, and with increasing success, to the use of the self-concept construct to generate testable hypotheses related to career development.

4. Other dynamic elements such as needs and values were accorded increased attention. However, the concept of values, and the relationship of needs to values remained unclear.

5. The concepts of developmental stages and developmental tasks were firmly established, at least on a descriptive if not on an explanatory level. Here was at least one case in which concepts from different disciplines seemed to be converging in essential agreement: the concept of life stages from psychology and psychiatry; the concept of developmental tasks, largely from education; and the concept of work periods from sociology.

6. The situational approach was probably the last to achieve a position of recognition and importance in theory development, although the ideas of accidental factors and of limits imposed by contingencies are old indeed. If contingency factors are taken in the broad sense to include social and economic situations of individuals and of the cultures and subcultures in which individuals participate, then contingency factors seemed to have been gaining recognition in the late 1950s as the spotlight of emphasis shifted away from the classical pattern of psychometric appraisal, the giving of information, and relating the two through counseling.

SHIFTING EMPHASES IN THE SIXTIES

It is difficult to discern any major changes in the social scene of the 1950s which might have laid a basis for an interest in theory development during the 1960s. Perhaps the preparation for a new attack on theory came from within professional groups, since by the late fifties programs of counselor education were beginning to make themselves felt on college and university campuses, and a rising interest in research in counseling became evident. In any event, it is difficult to account for the increased emphasis on one aspect of theory, that of career decision making, but focus on this topic became one of the most characteristic emphases in the sixties. We now turn to this matter.

Decision Making in Vocational Development

More than two hundred years ago the backgrounds for decision theory were being developed from studies of utility in economics. Edwards has pointed out that by 1738 theories of decision making became static, concerned with a single choice among possible courses of action rather than with a sequence of choices. Edwards articulated the problem of a sequence of vocational choices leading to a commitment.

> Since any choice is embedded in a sequence of other choices, any static model can be, at best, only a first approximation. Nevertheless, in 1960, as in 1954, most theoretical and experimental work centers on a single static model. Why? The static models work, at least to some extent, and the theoretical and experimental difficulties become unmanageably complex in most dynamic cases.[51]

In 1953 Bross[52] argued that classic theory had entirely ignored the problem of nonmonetary values and their conflicts. He distinguished between a predictive system and a value system into which data are fed. It is the past which furnishes data upon which decisions must be made in the present. The process becomes a chain of events rather than a causal chain in which outcomes are fixed and known, and so decision making is in itself a predictive act. The first step is making an analysis of past experiences; the second is estimating the possible outcomes according to the individual's own value system in relation to his goals; and so Bross provided a model which, on the one hand, made room for the individual's value system, and on the other took cognizance of his expectations of possible outcomes.

In 1955 Edwards[53] examined four models of decision making in gambling situations.

1. The first of these is expected value (EV) viewed objectively, in which EV is the product of probability and value, with value expressed in dollars.
2. The second (EU) is the expected utility model. In this model subjective utility may be substituted for an amount of money.
3. The third model (SEM) is sometimes called the maximization model. Value is expressed in money but may be the subjectively expected money return; hence this model is sometimes called the subjectively expected money value model. The object of the bet is to combine probability and money value in such a way as to yield the largest product.
4. The fourth (SEU) is a truly subjective model; both probabilities and utility rest on subjective estimates. This model does not assume that the subject actually knows the SEU values of different bets and deliberately chooses on the basis of knowledge, but only that the hypothesis of SEU maximization permits one to predict choices.

Models or combinations of models such as these are still very much alive. Two examples will be noted briefly. In 1967 Thoresen and Mehrens combined the ideas of Bross and the SEU model as formulated by Edwards.[54] Starting from the definition of Bross' approach as "the process of selecting one action from a number of alternative courses of action," Thoresen and Mehrens postulated that, "Two properties of any decision situation that are generally said to influence behavior are: (1) the *utility* values, i.e., the desirability of the possible outcomes of a course of action, and (2) the

probability of these outcomes. Utilities can also be thought of as the anticipated reward value of an outcome." In 1969 Kaldor and Zytowski reasoned,
"If occupational choice represents at least an approximate case of maximizing
behavior, it is useful to recast the problem in an input-output or means-ends
framework in which the person's characteristics conducive to generating
preferred consequences can be viewed as inputs, resources, or means."[55]
They developed a "hypothetical preference map" showing the relationship
between beginning earnings and occupational status. We might say that
the person making an occupational choice is seeking the particular combination of beginning salary and ultimate occupation which will yield the
greatest total satisfaction (utility), when both salary and status are subjectively estimated.

Five Possible Models. Hilton has described five categories of models for
career decision making, here abbreviated and paraphrased from his original
presentation of them.

1. The attribute-matching model implicit in the trait and factor approach.
2. Needs theory. Although Hilton does not actually use this name, his description seems to justify the use.
3. The rational man model. Again Hilton does not actually use the name but
   notes that this approach is that of various models of rational behavior in
   economics. The individual is expected to choose among alternatives in
   such a way as to maximize expected value.
4. The social man approach "which emphasizes the mobility provided and
   the limits imposed by the various social structures through which an individual's career carries him."
5. The complex information processing approach, "a major premise of which
   is that the individual is faced with multitudinous behavioral alternatives
   and information about them and that it is his limited capacity to handle
   information which limits the rationality of decision-making."[56]

Dynamic Models. One of the most promising developments in the 1960s
was the increasing application to vocational development theory of stochastic
models. Although Edwards was not writing in the context of vocational
development as such, what he has to say is highly pertinent:

> In 1954 the theories of choice were mostly deterministic. . . . That is, they
> asserted that whenever A was higher in SEU than B, A would be preferred
> to B. The major recent theoretical development is a shift from deterministic
> to stochastic models, which do not generally assert that A will be preferred
> to B but only indicate a probability of choice between A and B. Two kinds
> of empirical findings, both of which were quite clear in 1954, underlie and
> motivate the development of stochastic models. One is the finding that a sub-
> ject, required to make a choice from the same set of courses of action under
> the same conditions as a previous choice, may not repeat the previous choice;
> this is called inconsistency. The other is that sets of choices are often intran-
> sitive—that is, a subject may prefer A to B, B to C, and C to A. Nonsto-
> chastic models formally exclude both of these empirical facts.[57]

As a single example of the use of a stochastic model, we can look at the
Gribbons and Lohnes study of Readiness for Vocational Planning. The specific type of stochastic model used was the Markov chain.

The fitted Markov chains represent formal probability models for aspects of career development over a seven-year span in adolescence. These models possess a very high degree of abstractness and parsimony, yet they can reproduce the data rather well. It is believed that this mathematical approach to longitudinal data can usefully supplement the established statistical mode of analysis. Besides their theoretical value, the Markov chains provide compact and easily understood tabulations of trends which can support school counseling programs if they are exposed to students as part of the information environment of guidance.[58]

In general, and in an overly simplified statement, stochastic models appear better able to cope with two kinds of phenomena than do static models. These phenomena are inconsistency and intransivity. (We shall make no attempt to deal with the mathematical questions involved, nor to review particular studies; for these matters the reader is referred to Edwards.) By inconsistency we mean the kind of situation in which a subject is required to choose from a set of courses of action a second time and does not repeat his or her previous choice. Intransivity refers to the situation in which a subject may choose A over B, B over C, and yet C over A. Placed in vocational context, we might imagine the boy who prefers being a mechanical engineer over being an electrician (A over B), electrician over auto mechanic (B over C), and yet chooses auto mechanic over mechanical engineer (C over A). As Edwards points out, nonstochastic models formally exclude both inconsistency and intransivity.[59] Even to a nonmathematical reviewer, both these concepts seem remarkably pertinent to considerations of personality variables in vocational choice.

The Phenomenological Approach. Harris[60] has suggested adding to Hilton's five categories a sixth that she calls the "phenomenological-existential." An example of this would be Tiedeman's view that for the individual reality consists of the perceived life space and that decisions are made within these perceptions. There are two phases of the process: anticipation, which is subdivided into exploration, crystallization, choice, and exploration; and implementation, which includes the stages of induction, transition, and maintenance.[61] The developmental process is one of "epigenesis," a term adopted from the field of biology and used by Tiedeman to denote the "concept of successive differentiation from an originally undifferentiated structure . . ."[62] The mechanism of differentiation, however, is accompanied by a second mechanism of integration. Differentiation typically leads to integration, but if not the individual may need to abandon the tentatively achieved integration and start again from some earlier point along the path to integration. There are definite phenomenological elements in the theory of Tiedeman, as Harris recognized, but his approach is not a narrowly conceived phenomenological one. In a 1972 statement Tiedeman reviewed five stages in the development of his thought and remarked

> Finally, around 1963 I found myself with the realization that the processes of exploration and commitment are specific manifestations of general processes in cognitive development as well as in career development. This permitted me in turn to become more explicit about the development and application of those general cognitive processes in the realm of career.[63]

Self-concept Theories. A special case of the phenomenological approach is represented in self-concept theories which have been most conspicuously presented in the cluster of studies growing out of Super's Career Pattern Study. As noted earlier, these were well underway in the 1950s but have continued their development in the 1960s and 1970s. A refinement was introduced by Super in the distinction drawn between the *self-percept,* the *self-concept,* and the *self-concept system.* The self-percept exists at two levels (1) the primary self-percept, the "unmodified or raw impression of an aspect of the self," and (2) the secondary self-percept, a "simple self-percept which has come to function as a percept." The self-concept may also be defined at two levels: (1) simple self-concept which is organized, characterized by "related percepts with accrued meaning," and (2) the complex self-concept, resulting from "abstraction from and generalization of simple self-concepts, generally organized in a role framework." At the highest level of complexity stands the self-concept system, which is a "constellation, more or less well organized, of all of the self-concepts."[64] Super went on to consider the problem of the dimensions of dimensions, or meta-dimensions. This discussion will not be reviewed here.

Starishevsky and Matlin dealt with the problem of translation of self-concept into vocational terms, pointing out that the maturing individual is constantly reacting to his environment in a way characteristic of his own formulation of the nature of the environment and himself.

> [One can, then, view vocational choice as an expression of self-concepts formulated and reformulated throughout life stages. People differ in both their self-concepts and in ways in which they translate self-concepts into occupational terms. Hence, people choose different occupations.][65]

But we must not leave the impression that the Career Pattern Study dealt *only* with the self-concept. As Herr notes, Super is concerned with increasingly complex tasks of vocational development, and he has formulated his statement of stages within which there are "factors internal as well as external which influence the choices made. These factors continue to filter down and narrow the array of options the individual considers. There is an emphasis then on vocational convergence and greater specificity of behavior."[66]

Values in Vocational Decisions. Perhaps the clearest statements to be found in guidance literature in support of the importance of values in decision making are those by Katz.[67] In 1954 he proposed an outline of decision making which is here much abbreviated and paraphrased. In his view career decision making process is:

1. *Prompted* by a disequilibrium by the educational-occupational system which requires a decision and yet establishes or maintains some discrepancy;
2. *Motivated* by the individual's needs and drives and his anticipation of satisfaction;
3. *Mediated* by symbols which permit the individual to evaluate past experience and project expectations for the future, and enable him to try out a role without final commitment;
4. *Shaped* by differentiated characteristics of individuals (including effects of subcultures) and by options available.
5. *Resolved* when a new equilibrium is established.

Katz recognized later that while such a model suggests the interplay of social and psychological forces, it does not delineate the dynamics involved. Thus he proposes:

> [If there is a single synthesizing element that orders, arranges, and unifies such interactions, that ties together an individual's perceptions of cultural promptings, motivating needs, mediating symbols, differentiating characteristics, and sense of resolution, that relates perceptions to self-concepts, and that accounts most directly for a particular decision or mode of choosing, it is here suggested that element is the individual's value system.][68]

The acceptance of values systems as a basic integrating principle is clearly phenomenological in flavor but certainly not completely subjective; as Katz puts it, "Clearly, an individual's vocationally oriented choices are social as well as psychological events—they always involve some transaction with the environment."[69] Moreover, such a model is more general than one limited to some one aspect of the phenomenological world, such as the self-concept.

The Impact of Computers on Decision Making Theory

So long as computers were used simply for storage and retrieval of information, no theoretical issue arose; this was simply a superior method of performing a traditional activity. But when computer applications became interactive systems, things changed rapidly. In an "interactive" system the student himself is in control of the situation to the extent of seeking the kind of information he wishes, and the computer will respond to his individualized questions. For example, the Computerized Vocational Information System (CVIS),[70] used in Willowbrook High School and the College of DuPage, provides for a moderate degree of interaction. Another, the Information System for Vocational Decisions (ISVD),[71] provides for a greater degree of interaction and probably rests on the most developed theoretical base, but, though given a field trial, its completion has been slowed down by funding difficulties. Myers[72] indicates that there are probably about eighteen such systems in use or in some stage of development. Our present purpose is not to survey systems—other chapters will deal with such a focus—but, rather, to identify the relationship of computer-assisted counseling to developmental theory.

In the CVIS system occupations are classified according to Roe's categories of field-and-level, used in conjunction with the occupational information stored in the computer. Also stored in the computer is information from the student's permanent record, such as cumulative class rank, scores on standard tests of educational development, and Kuder Preference Record scores. The student carries on a "conversation" with the computer in which he answers multiple choice questions flashed to him on a screen—e.g., "Do your grades in school place you in the top, second, third, or fourth quarter?" The computer checks the response against its stored information and replies, "You're right," or points out a discrepancy in answer and record.

It is very difficult, if not impossible, to summarize in a few words the complex ISVD system developed by Tiedeman and associates, and no attempt will be made to offer a complete description. One basic concept is that of "epigenesis," noted earlier. The term "facts/data" is used to refer to material directly recoverable from computer storage without mediation and data which must be processed through some numeric and linguistic mediation system. We shall pass over the details of the files, noting only that material in the primary file is so organized that, in exploring, the inquirer (student) is not expected to maintain preference for any one choice (a departure from the classic models of decision making noted earlier) but is expected to be forming his or her own personal basis for preference. In the clarification stage the student may either maintain his or her preference or return to the exploration stage. Data in the secondary file concern the student himself, including summaries generated by the person after previous use of the system. "The inquirer thus *himself* engages in abstracting his life circumstances while creating these data for his life."[73] It is the inquirer who converts facts/data into information in the context of decision making, but this occurs when decision making is subject to "Monitor," which refers "to the computer control functions associated with self-awareness during the decision making practiced while using primary data files."[74] Inadequate as such a sketch must be, it may serve to indicate that the ISVD system provides for a high degree of interaction of student ("inquirer") with the computer and has gone far beyond a simple matching of characteristics of student and occupation as stored in the machine. It is also evident that the system implements the developmental career decision-making theory developed by Tiedeman[75] and by Tiedeman and O'Hara.[76]

What, then, has been the impact of computer systems upon decision-making theory? There seems to be an aspect of computerized systems which might be described as a return to the cognitive, and one wonders if it is really possible to reduce to computerized numerical and verbal symbols the aspirations, the feelings, the idiosyncratic perceptions, the values, and the unconscious elements of motivation which may be very real elements in vocational preference and choice. It is possible to teach decision making through simulation, games, and so on in such a way that the activities can be computer assisted. But will the learnings remain essentially on a cognitive level, even though a part of the ISVD, for example, is intended to move the inquirer toward a level of self-involvement?

THE TYPOLOGIES OF HOLLAND

Although Holland's proposed theory reflects some earlier roots, as do most theories, much of its development took place in the 1960s, and the development is still continuing. Holland has provided a very useful summary of his work and theories,[77] and so there would be little point in offering here a secondhand version. Holland himself regards his 1959 classification of occupational environments—realistic, intellectual, social, conventional, enterprising, and artistic—and of modal personal orientations—motoric, intellectual, supportive, conforming, persuasive, and esthetic—as the first formal presentation, as modified somewhat in later statements.[78] Holland notes that his personality types are in some ways analogous to those suggested by Adler, Fromm, Jung, Sheldon, Spranger, and others, but that they most closely resemble the interest factors derived by Guilford from a factor analysis study.[79]

Two basic assumptions were stated in 1966: (1) that "people search for environments and vocations that will permit them to exercise their skills and abilities, to express their attitudes and values, to take on agreeable problems and roles, and to avoid disagreeable ones"; and (2) that "a person's behavior can be explained by the interaction of his personality pattern and his environment."[80] It was recognized that a given individual's personality may not be described adequately by one modal type since there are moderate positive intercorrelations found between the types. Therefore, a coding system was devised to indicate a primary and one or more secondary types; a person, for example, might be described as intellectual-realistic or intellectual-social.[81] The second assumption regarding interaction of personality and environment was investigated in two studies in 1961 and 1963. In the first of these Astin and Holland[82] devised the Environmental Assessment Technique and used it to study college environments. They found that a college environment could be described by making a census of the kinds of people in that environment. In 1963 Astin conducted another study which supported this general finding.

Probably the most theoretically significant concept to emerge in Holland's recent work is the hexagonal model for representing the relationship between types. As reported by Holland,[83] he and Whitney were searching for a better classification for occupations of women. They were aware of the circular model used by Roe (noted in the earlier discussion of Roe's theory), but that didn't seem to work. A hexagon rather than a circle seemed to be needed. Let the reader visualize a hexagon with the variables placed at each of the angles: realistic, intellectual, artistic, and so on around the figure. On lines drawn between the angles are placed the coefficients of correlation —e.g., between realistic and intellectual .39 for men and .50 for women. Lines are then drawn across the hexagon from each angle to the three opposite angles, and the appropriate coefficient inserted—e.g., between intellectual and conventional .10 for men. The result is a diagram which displays the types having the highest positive correlations arranged around the outside of the figure, while those with the smallest correlations are farthest apart on the diagram. It may be noted also that correlations of types adjacent to each other tend to be higher than those not adjacent—e.g., between realistic and intellectual .50 for women, as compared with only .17 between intellectual and enterprising (which is on the opposite side of the hexagon). Roe also suggested this in working with her circular model.

There remained an important question: do the six types really have independent variance? On the basis of a study by Richards, the answer was yes. However, Holland comments that Richards' analysis "did not demonstrate that there were only six types, but it did suggest that there were at least six, perhaps more."[84]

It is difficult to place Holland's theory in any one of the categories used earlier in this discussion, such as self-concept, developmental, or situational. It may be called psychodynamic since it gives major attention to personality factors, specifically as they operate at a given point in time. The door seems open to tracing patterns of development (Holland prefers the term life history), but thus far most of the data have come from college students and adults. Tiedeman's concept of epigenesis as development of the structured from the originally unstructured seems to contrast sharply with Holland's emphasis in starting with the individual as he or she is. Here we have, then, a theory in its own right, with impressive empirical support, which is a rather distinctive product of the 1960s and still very much alive.

SITUATIONAL THEORIES IN THE SIXTIES

During the 1950s a mass of data was accumulated regarding various situational factors such as social class, and examples of such studies have been noted earlier. If there is one general change which has occurred during the 1960s it is the manner of interpreting such data. But here a semantic consideration intrudes. We shall follow the suggestion made by Crites that it is important to distinguish between chance and contingency factors. If, following this distinction, the meaning of chance is delimited to factors which are fortuitous, unplanned, and unpredicted, there is not much left to say about chance factors except to study the effect of accidents upon the individuals *ex post facto*. Such studies may be extremely important in a context of vocational rehabilitation, but they do not seem to contribute much to understanding preaccident development and choice. On the other hand, contingency factors may have a continuing effect upon development. Predictions from such factors, however, are apt to be much more valid for groups than for individuals. Among the 1960 studies of situational factors there seems to be a tentative emergence of two directions not yet well enough developed to be called trends. One is the examination of the relative importance of situational and personality factors. The other is a change in interpretation with emphasis shifting away from a strictly structural one toward the individual's perception of the situational—a phenomenological interpretation.

The Relative Importance of Situational Factors. Mierzwa[85] studied the relative importance of five systems of data for predicting science and nonscience career choices. The systems were ability, interest, environment, temperament, and personality. The subjects were 192 eleventh grade boys in public schools who were above the 50th percentile on group intelligence test scores and who were in the college preparatory curriculum. Data were gathered a second time two years later. When the various systems were examined for "hits" in classifying the subjects, ability, environment, and temperament systems did not differ significantly, but interest produced more "hits" than any of the other three. Although limited to the discrimination between science and nonscience career choices, this study indicates a kind of study which might well be productive if applied to a wider range of career choices and which would offer help in evaluating the relative importance of environmental as against other data systems.

The Phenomenological Interpretation of Situational Factors. If the frequency of appearance of articles is any basis for judgment, then the interpretation of situational factors on a phenomenological basis is more of a trend than the evaluation of the relative importance of such factors. Here we shall note only selected examples intended to illustrate different approaches to the problem. Zito and Bardon[86] studied the responses of 150 Negro junior high school pupils to two thematic apperception cards, one showing two men at work, and the other a boy sitting at a school desk. The work picture elicited mostly imagery of hope of success, but the school picture most frequently elicited responses of fear of failure. Cosby and Picou[87] studied the vocational expectations of adolescents in four states of the Deep South, hypothesizing that if an individual perceives various blocks or obstacles as formidable, he may lower his vocational plans. The pattern of responses was what previous work would lead one to expect: high expectations were found more frequently among those whose fathers were in high-level occupations and had better education. Several studies by Glick[88] examined the aspirations, expectations, and perceived obstacles of undergraduate students in agriculture. The most frequently mentioned obstacle was lack of money, and the next three, much less frequently mentioned, were lack of aptitude, lack of graduate degree, and lack of grades necessary for admission to graduate school. Only one of these (lack of money) is clearly a situational factor.

EXISTENTIAL THEORY

In spite of the wide ranging array of articles and books given to existentialism in relation to counseling, very seldom is attention specifically directed to this point of view as related to vocational development (or choice) theory. One exception is the article by Simons.[89] Relying heavily on Sartre as a source of existential thinking, he addresses himself to four theories of vocational development.

In consideration of Holland, Simons maintains that if the categories had been limited to the intellectual, social, enterprising, and artistic, there would be no clash. But a clash does occur because Holland's theory fails to recognize that a person of intellectual bent may accept a conventional job, not because he is conventionally oriented but because he finds objectification too painful. The concept of objectification is a rather elusive one for those not of existential persuasion. The concept derives from Sartre, who sees the life process as one of moving from self-centeredness toward altruistic love and each step in the process as upsetting. Although it is only by revealing his true or objective self to others can a man see himself as he truly is, man is basically ashamed of his identity, and so objectification is a painful experience which requires great courage.

Simons cannot accept Roe's idea of job selections as a primary source of need satisfaction. He feels that difficulty occurs because of Roe's acceptance of the Maslow hierarchy, while existentialism does not attempt to analyze the basic need for self-fulfillment.

Super's ideas of vocational development and its stages are compatible with the existential view, but Simons states that this view of vocational development as a specific aspect of personal development does not go far enough. From the existential point of view, decisions leading to vocational choice actually form the personality.

Looking at the theories of Tiedeman and O'Hara, Simons observes that a "marriage" between existentialism and the concept of vocational decision as a series of small decisions seems possible. However, there is need to recognize that in every decision the individual has the option of objectifying himself before others or conforming in order to escape the pain of having others see him as he is.

It is exceedingly difficult for one who is not a committed existentialist (such as the present writer) to discuss objectively the relation of existentialism to vocational development. Existentialism starts from a philosophy, and in a sense represents a revolt against the analytic methods of science, while down through the years vocational guidance has sought to become scientific, at least in its methods. In the matter of goals and purposes, guidance has sought to achieve its own philosophy, but growing out of the results of applied science rather than as a starting point. In recent years nonexistentialist theorists have often used the concept of self-realization which at first glance seems compatible with existentialism. But the meaning is seldom the same as the "I-thou" meaning which existentialists give it. And for the nonexistentialist the related concepts of "shame" and "objectification" are simply not needed. And so comparing existentialist and nonexistentialist approaches to vocational development is a little like comparing a philosophical belief held in the eleventh or twelfth centuries of the age of faith with the kind of philosophy which has emerged in the scientifically oriented twentieth century.

SOME PARTIAL CONVERGENCES IN THE SIXTIES

The most obvious common ground which has gained considerable recognition is the concept of stages of development, originally popularized by Ginzberg and his associates. Although there are differences among various theorists as to details and interpretations, the general concept is accepted and used by a number of theorists representing rather divergent general views: Super; Tiedeman and O'Hara; Havighurst; Bordin, Nachmann, and Segal; and Forer. Katz, though not rejecting the concept of development, prefers to focus on "career" guidance, "with career represented as a sequence of choices," in which case "the concept of sequence suggests that any single choice bears some relationship both to antecedent and to subsequent choices."[90] He does not think of values as needing a genetic base and disclaims any seeming conflict with Ginzberg's theory of stages during the period of tentative choices. Rather, the apparent conflict may be resolved by regarding the dominance of interests at ages eleven and twelve as another way of saying that interests are valued at this age.[91] Holland seems to find little use for the idea of stages and, in fact, has thus far given little attention to the process of development, but he is concerned with the life history or changes in behavior over time as representing a particular pattern of living or lifestyle. The existentialists, to the degree that Simons[92] may be accepted as a spokesman for this view, do use the concept of stages (the I stage, the Thou stage, and the I-Thou stage), but the interpretation of these stages gives a meaning clearly apart from the usual meaning of the term. For the existentialist objectification is the life process by which one moves from self-centeredness toward altruistic love. In this process man comes to see himself as he truly is, and the experience is painful because man is basically ashamed of his identity. Thus, although the concept of stages finds a number of supporters, its acceptance with any uniform meaning is certainly not unanimous.

The thrust of phenomenological views has been strong during the sixties, although varied terminology is used. Super builds much around the "self-concept" idea, but Tiedeman speaks of "self-identity." The difference in preference for terms seems to reflect, in part, a difference in background sources used. Super drew heavily from developmental psychology (particularly Buehler); from self-concept interpretations of interests by Carter and Bordin; from Lecky's "self-consistence" concept; and from Allport's ego psychology. Tiedeman made Erikson's life stages and crises his starting point. Katz has made values the major synthesizing element in decision making, but his values seem no less phenomenological than the self-concept of Super or the self-identity of Tiedeman. Holland, primarily interested in the relationship between personality and environmental types, sees people searching for congenial environments. Surely this is a phenomenological approach, though perhaps with a more hedonistic flavor than suggested by the terms self-concept, self-identity, or values. The psychoanalytic view is clearly phenomenological, though with more emphasis on unconscious motivations and less recognition of the outside world than that accorded by Super or Tiedeman, and certainly less than is suggested by Holland's matching of personality and environmental types. Need theorists are clearly on the road to the land of phenomenology. Existentialists seem to go all the way, but with the inner world conceived according to their own special philosophy.

A third tentative convergence is more a matter of awareness of the problem than of actual incorporation of elements into a theory. The problem is that much of the data used to support existing theories has been gathered from restricted groups, and the theory so developed cannot be generalized to a total population. This criticism has been made of the early work of Ginzberg and associates and, to a lesser degree, the work of Super and Holland. It should be noted, however, that the last two have recognized the difficulty. Super has discussed the career patterns of the semiskilled and called for "an all-class theory of vocational guidance."[93] Holland's early work was done with highly selected groups of college students in the national talent search of the National Merit Scholarship program, but he recognized the need for more representative samples. Borow recognized the problem in his comment that many of the studies which have supplied normative data have been marred by biased sampling. "For many investigators, college students offer a convenient, built-in pool of subjects, but they are hardly representative of youth in general."[94]

It seems reasonable to expect that in the future efforts will be made to generate theories broad enough to account for empirical facts from a wide range of ethnic groups, social classes, levels of work, and subcultural groups. Implicit in this suggestion is the recognition of the importance of social systems and contingency factors. There are probable limits on a reasonable expectation for generalizability of a theory, and it is probably asking too much to seek a theory that can apply to such diverse cultural groups as the Australian city dweller, the Japanese farmer, and the migrant Mexican worker in the United States, as well as the middle-class American. But at least we must cease to generalize from middle-class, white, Anglo-Americans to blacks (both urban and rural), to American Indians, to Mexican-Americans, and to national groups strongly conscious of their own cultural heritage.

SUGGESTIONS FOR RESEARCH

The purpose of this chapter has been to try to place theories of vocational development in perspective. Such a purpose necessitates broad treatment rather than detailed critical analyses, and so it seems appropriate that suggestions for research also be placed in broad perspective, rather than attempting to develop a long list of specific hypotheses to be tested. Five suggestions are offered.

1. The very concept of vocational development seems to demand longitudinal studies. A few continuing studies got under way by the early 1950s, notably the Career Pattern Study, but it is important that an emphasis on such longitudinal studies be continued on into the 1970s. It would be helpful if some of these studies could be based on subjects from identifiable and different cultural groups, so that eventually it might be possible to compare the patterns of development of such differing groups.

2. There is great need for the use of dynamic rather than static models in the analysis of data. For too long many researchers have seemed to regard prediction of vocational choice as the only really respectable purpose to be achieved. More to the point may be an approach to development in a framework of a chain of events. Some variety of a stochastic model may prove to be an appropriate type of analysis.

3. Currently there is much interest in computer-assisted counseling, and some real breakthroughs have been achieved. But thus far there has been relatively little concern with affective changes which may or may not be associated with the process, and there has been almost no attempt to relate whatever cognitive changes may be found to more subtle personality factors.

4. There is a continuing need for empirical studies but for studies which are carefully designed to test promising hypotheses. The literature is bulging with descriptive studies of characteristics of various groups. Such studies have made contributions but have often added little to theory formulation. We have now reached a stage of sophistication so that what is needed is the testing of hypotheses derived from theories, rather than just more accumulation of data. Important theoretical questions remain unanswered; for example, are there limits to the generalizability of a particular theory of development across age groups, cultural groups, ability groups, and so on? The suggestion offered here is simple to state but very difficult to implement; let the first emphasis be upon getting our theoretical house (or houses) in order, then deriving and testing hypotheses, and so ultimately supporting, revising, or rejecting the theory.

5. Finally, there is need for studies of the meaning of work. It is relatively easy to sketch in broad strokes changes in the concepts of work and career through various historical periods, but it is very difficult to understand in depth what work or career really means to the policeman on the beat, to the man who drives a truck delivering dairy products, to the secretary in a large business office, or to a forest ranger in a national park. It is equally difficult

to understand the meaning of career or work as perceived by the tenth-grade boy or girl in a suburban school whose father is an unskilled worker, or to the high school senior in the inner city whose teachers regard him as promising, but who has never had a father in his home as a masculine model.

Implicit in these suggestions for research are several propositions. First, the particular hypothesis to be tested should be derived from a promising theory, and the hypothesis should become the guide for the selection of the subjects to be studied. For too long the choice of subjects has been determined by the subjects who happen to be available, such as captive groups of high school or college students. Second, longitudinal studies need to be conducted over extended periods of time. This implies a long-range plan for research by continuing research teams, and such teams require continuing financial support. We can no longer depend so exclusively upon shifting groups of graduate students. Even a doctoral student can hardly be expected to delay the completion of his program while he follows his subjects for ten or fifteen years. Third, the idea should take precedence over method. This consideration raises the question of the characteristics and preparation of the investigator himself. He must have a background in the behavioral sciences broad enough so that he can recognize significant theoretical problems. Methods are important, but developing a balance between theoretical perceptions and methods of research is even more important. In our present sophistication about computers, for example, it sometimes seems that the selection of the problem is dictated by what the computer can do. When this occurs the machine has indeed conquered the idea.

NOTES

1. C. G. Wrenn, "Human Values and Work in American Life," *Man in a World at Work,* Henry Borow, ed. (Boston: Houghton Mifflin, 1964).
2. W. L. Slocum, "Occupational Careers in Organizations: A Sociological Perspective," *Personnel and Guidance Journal* XLIII(May 1965):858.
3. Edward Gross, "A Sociological Approach to the Analysis of Preparation for Life Work," *Personnel and Guidance Journal* XLV(January 1967):416–23, quoted from p. 417.
4. H. L. Wilensky, "Orderly Careers and Social Participation: The Impact of Work History in Social Integration in the Middle Masses," *American Sociological Review* XXVI(August 1961):521–39.
5. D. E. Super et al., *Vocational Development: A Framework for Research* (New York: Bureau of Publications, Teachers College, Columbia University, 1957).
6. Gross, *op. cit.,* p. 420.
7. E. L. Herr, *Decision Making and Vocational Development,* Guidance Monograph Series (Boston: Houghton Mifflin, 1970), p. 30.
8. D. E. Super, *Work Values Inventory (Manual)* (Boston: Houghton Mifflin, 1960).
9. A. J. Jones, Buford Stefflre, and N. R. Stewart, *Principles of Guidance,* 6th ed. (New York: McGraw-Hill, 1970), pp. 181–83.
10. R. A. Myers, "Computer-Aided Counseling: Some Issues of Adoption and Use," *Computer Assisted Counseling,* D. E. Super et al. (New York: Teachers College Press, Teachers College, Columbia University, 1970), p. 224.
11. A. A. Brill, *Basic Principles of Psychoanalysis* (New York: Doubleday, 1949).

12. Lloyd Meadow, "Toward a Theory of Vocational Choice," *Journal of Counseling Psychology* II(Summer 1955):108–12.

13. B. R. Forer, "Personality Factors in Occupational Choice," *Educational and Psychological Measurement* XIII(Autumn 1953):361–66; Forer, "Framework for the Use of Clinical Techniques in Vocational Counseling," *Personnel and Guidance Journal* XLIII(May 1965):868–72.

14. E. S. Bordin, Barbara Nachmann, and S. J. Segal, "An Articulated Framework for Vocational Development," *Journal of Counseling Psychology* X(Summer 1963), 107–16.

15. S. H. Osipow, *Theories of Career Development* (New York: Appleton-Century-Crofts, 1968), p. 100.

16. A. H. Maslow, *Motivation and Personality* (New York: Harper and Row, 1954).

17. K. P. Poelling, *A Developmental Study of Abraham H. Maslow's Self-Actualization Theory*, unpublished doctoral dissertation, College of Education, Northern Illinois University, 1971.

18. A. H. Maslow, "Some Educational Implications of the Humanistic Psychologies," paper presented at Brandeis University, 1968, mimeographed.

19. Anne Roe and Marvin Siegelman, *The Origin of Interests* (Washington, D.C.: American Personnel and Guidance Association, 1964), p. 5.

20. Eduard Spranger, *Types of Men,* trans. from 5th German ed. (Halle: Max Niemeyer, 1928).

21. C. H. Miller, *Foundations of Guidance,* 2nd ed. (New York: Harper and Row, 1961), 106–07.

22. Martin Katz, *Decisions and Values* (New York: College Entrance Examination Board, 1963), p. 16.

23. J. O. Crites, *Vocational Psychology* (New York: McGraw-Hill, 1969), p. 97.

24. Osipow, *op. cit.,* pp. 16–37.

25. Joseph Zaccaria, *Theories of Occupational Choice and Vocational Development,* Guidance Monograph Series (Boston: Houghton Mifflin, 1969), pp. 31–33.

26. Anne Roe, "Early Determinants of Vocational Choice," *Journal of Counseling Psychology* IV(Fall 1957):212–17.

27. Anne Roe, "Perspectives on Vocational Development," *Perspectives on Vocational Development,* J. M. Whiteley and Arthur Resnikoff, eds. (Washington, D.C.: American Personnel and Guidance Association, 1972).

28. D. E. Super et al., *Career Development: Self-Concept Theory* (New York: College Entrance Examination Board, 1963), p. 1.

29. Super et al., *Vocational Development: A Framework for Research;* D. E. Super and Phoebe L. Overstreet, *The Vocational Maturity of Ninth Grade Boys* (New York: Bureau of Publications, Teachers College, Columbia University, 1960).

30. D. E. Super, "Vocational Adjustment: Implementing a Self-Concept," *Occupations* XXX(November 1951), p. 92.

31. D. E. Super, "A Theory of Vocational Development," *American Psychologist* VIII(May 1953):185–90.

32. Zaccaria, *op. cit.*

33. Crites, *op. cit.*

34. Osipow, *op. cit.*

35. Zaccaria, *op. cit.*

36. H. D. Carter, "The Development of Vocational Attitudes," *Journal of Consulting Psychology* IV(September-October 1940):185–91.

37. Eli Ginzberg et al., *Occupational Choice: An Approach to a General Theory* (New York: Columbia University Press, 1951).

38. W. S. Dysinger, "Maturation and Vocational Guidance," *Occupations* XXIX (December 1959):198–201.

39. E. H. Erikson, "Identity and the Life Cycle," *Psychological Issues* I, 1(1959): 18–171.

40. R. J. Havighurst, "Youth in Exploration and Man Emergent," *Man in a World at Work* (Boston: Houghton Mifflin, 1964), pp. 221–222.

41. D. V. Tiedeman, "Decision and Vocational Development: A Paradigm and Its Implications," *Personnel and Guidance Journal* XL(September 1961): 15–21.

42. D. V. Tiedeman and R. P. O'Hara, *Career Development: Choice and Adjustment* (New York: College Entrance Examination Board, 1963).

43. R. J. Havighurst, *Developmental Tasks and Education* (New York: Longmans Green, 1950).

44. R. J. Havighurst, "Youth in Exploration and Man Emergent," *Man in a World at Work*, pp. 215–24.

45. Crites, *op. cit.*, p. 60.

46. *Ibid.*, pp. 81–84.

47. D. C. Miller and W. H. Form, *Industrial Sociology* (New York: Harper and Row, 1951), p. 660.

48. Miller and Form, *op. cit.*, pp. 717–38.

49. *Ibid.*, p. 739.

50. Zaccaria, *op. cit.*, p. 27.

51. Ward Edwards, "Behavioral Decision Theory," *Annual Review of Psychology*, Vol. 12, F. R. Farnsworth, ed. (Palo Alto, Calif.: Annual Reviews, Inc., 1961), pp. 473–98, quoted from p. 474.

52. I. D. Bross, *Design for Decision* (New York: Macmillan, 1953), especially Ch. 2, "Nature of Decision."

53. Edwards, *op. cit.*

54. *Ibid.*, pp. 478–79.

55. D. R. Kaldor and D. G. Zytowski, "A Maximizing Model of Occupational Decision-Making," *Personnel and Guidance Journal* XLII(April 1969):782.

56. T. L. Hilton, *Cognitive Processes in Decision-Making*, Cooperative Research Project No. 1046, U.S. Office of Education (Pittsburgh: Carnegie Institute of Technology, 1962), pp. 36–39.

57. Edwards, *op. cit.*, p. 481.

58. W. D. Gribbons and P. R. Lohnes, *Emerging Careers* (New York: Teachers College Press, Teachers College, Columbia University, 1968), p. 100.

59. Edwards, *op. cit.*, pp. 481–85.

60. Jo Ann Harris, "The Computerization of Vocational Information," *Vocational Guidance Quarterly* XVII(September 1968):12–20.

61. Tiedeman and O'Hara, *op. cit.*, p. 24.

62. Tiedeman, "Comprehending Epigenesis in Decision-Making Development," in *Computer Assisted Counseling*, D. E. Super et al. (New York: Teachers College Press, 1970), p. 24.

63. D. V. Tiedeman, "Can a Machine Develop a Career?" *Perspectives on Vocational Development*, pp. 83–104, quoted from p. 84.

64. Super et al., *Career Development: Self-Concept Theory*, pp. 17–20.

65. Ruben Starishevsky and Norman Matlin, "A Model for Translation of Self-Concepts into Vocational Terms," *Career Development: Self-Concept Theory*, p. 33.

66. Herr, *op. cit.*, p. 26.

67. Martin Katz, "A Critical Analysis of the Literature Concerned with the Process

of Occupational Choice in High School Boys," *Harvard Studies in Career Development,* No. 6, August 1954, mimeographed.
68. Katz, *Decisions and Values,* p. 16.
69. *Ibid.,* 15.
70. Harris, *op. cit.*
71. D. V. Tiedeman et al., *Information System for Vocational Decision Making,* annual reports, 1967 and 1968 (Cambridge, Mass.: Harvard University, Graduate School of Education, 1968).
72. R. A. Myers, "Computer-Aided Counseling: Some Issues of Adoption and Use," *Computer Assisted Counseling,* p. 109.
73. Tiedeman, "Comprehending Epigenesis in Decision-Making Development," p. 27.
74. *Ibid.,* pp. 34–36.
75. D. V. Tiedeman, "Decision and Vocational Development: A Paradigm and Its Implications," *Personnel and Guidance Journal* XL(September 1961): 15–21.
76. Tiedeman and O'Hara, *op. cit.*
77. J. L. Holland, "The Present Status of a Theory of Vocational Choice," *Perspectives on Vocational Development,* pp. 35–59.
78. J. L. Holland, "A Theory of Vocational Choice," *Journal of Counseling Psychology* VI(Spring 1959):35–45.
79. J. L. Holland, *The Psychology of Vocational Choice* (Waltham, Mass.: Blaisdell, 1966), p. 10.
80. *Ibid.,* pp. 11–12.
81. *Ibid.,* pp. 39–41.
82. A. W. Astin and J. L. Holland, "The Environmental Assessment Technique: A Way to Measure College Environments," *Journal of Educational Psychology* LII(August 1961):308–16.
83. Holland, "The Present Status of a Theory of Vocational Choice," *op. cit.,* p. 55.
84. *Ibid.*
85. J. A. Mierzwa, "Comparison of Systems of Data for Predicting Career Choice," *Personnel and Guidance Journal* XLII(September 1963):29–34.
86. R. J. Zito and J. L. Bardon, "Negro Adolescents' Success and Failure Imagery Concerning Work and School," *Vocational Guidance Quarterly* XVI(March 1971):181–84.
87. Arthur Cosby and J. S. Picou, "Vocational Expectations of Adolescents in Four Deep-South States," *Vocational Guidance Quarterly* XIX(March 1971): 177–82.
88. Peter Glick, Jr., "Occupational Values and Anticipated Occupational Frustration of Agricultural College Students," *Personnel and Guidance Journal* XLII (March 1964):674–79; Glick, "Anticipated Occupational Frustration," *Vocational Guidance Quarterly* XI(Winter 1963):91–95.
89. J. B. Simons, "An Existential View of Vocational Development," *Personnel and Guidance Journal* XLVI(February 1966):604–10.
90. Katz, *Decisions and Values,* p. 17.
91. *Ibid.,* p. 18.
92. Simons, *op. cit.*
93. D. E. Super, "A Reconceptualization of Vocational Guidance," *Vocational Guidance: A Reconceptualization* (Columbus, Ohio: Division of Guidance and Testing, Ohio Department of Education, 1967), pp. 6–8, and 24, mimeographed.
94. Borow, *op. cit.,* p. 380.

SUGGESTED READING

Crites, J. O., *Vocational Psychology.* New York: McGraw-Hill, 1969.

Edwards, Ward, "Behavioral Decision Theory," in *Annual Review of Psychology,* ed. P. R. Farnsworth. Vol. 12. Palo Alto, Calif.: Annual Reviews, Inc., 1961, pp. 473–498.

Gribbons, W. D., and P. R. Lohnes, *Emerging Careers.* New York: Teachers College Press, Teachers College, Columbia University, 1968.

Herr, E. L., *Decision-Making and Vocational Development.* Guidance Monograph Series. Boston: Houghton Mifflin, 1970.

Holland, J. L., "A Theory of Vocational Choice," *Journal of Counseling Psychology,* XLII(Spring, 1959)52–62.

Katz, Martin, *Decisions and Values.* New York: College Entrance Examination Board, 1963.

Osipow, S. H., *Theories of Career Development.* New York: Appleton-Century-Crofts, 1968.

Roe, Anne, "Early Determinants of Vocational Choice," *Journal of Counseling Psychology,* IV(Fall, 1957)212–217.

Roe, Anne and Marvin Siegelman, *The Origins of Interests.* Washington, D.C.: American Personnel and Guidance Association, 1964.

Super, D. E., "A Theory of Vocational Development," *American Psychologist,* VIII(May, 1953)185–190.

Super, D. E., *et. al., Career Development: Self-Concept Theory.* New York: College Entrance Examination Board, 1963.

Super, D. E., *et al., Computer-Assisted Counseling.* New York: Teachers College Press, Teachers College, Columbia University, 1970.

Tiedeman, D. V., "Decision and Vocational Development: A Paradigm and Its Implications," *Personnel and Guidance Journal* XL(September, 1961) 15–21.

Tiedeman, D. V., and R. P. O'Hara, *Career Development: Choice and Adjustment.* New York: College Entrance Examination Board, 1963.

Whiteley, J. M. and Arthur Resnikoff, eds. *Perspectives on Vocational Development.* Washington, D.C.: American Personnel and Guidance Association, 1972.

Zaccaria, Joseph, *Theories of Occupational Choice and Development.* Guidance Monograph Series. Boston: Houghton Mifflin, 1970.

Life Stages as Organizing Modes of Career Development

11

Jean Pierre Jordaan
Teachers College, Columbia University

ISSUES IN CAREER DEVELOPMENT

Before 1950 the two questions asked most frequently by vocational psychologists were: "How do individuals in one occupation differ from those in another?" and "How do successful people in an occupation differ from those who are less successful?" Answers to these questions, it was hoped, would help to answer two other questions: "Which person for this job?" and "Which job or occupation for this person?" The focus was on matching persons and jobs and on improving methods of selection, placement, and vocational counseling.[1,2]

By 1950 vocational psychologists were asking *other* questions: How do vocational goals develop? How are they modified? How are they implemented? What are the decisions and choices which confront the individual at various points in his or her vocational history? Are some individuals more ready than others to make good decisions and plans? If so, why? What are the factors which facilitate or hinder vocational progress? How should the outcomes of choice be evaluated—in terms of the individual's present status, his original point of departure, or his ultimate destination? In short, what we have witnessed in the past twenty years is a shift away from the study of occupations to the study of careers, and a corresponding shift from the essentially static concept of vocational choice to the more dynamic concept of vocational development.[3]

Propositions

The transition from a psychology of occupations to a psychology of careers is exemplified by the following propositions:
1. Vocational goals, attitudes, decisions, actions, and outcomes are both the result of previous processes and events and the initiators of new processes and events.
2. These goals, attitudes, and decisions are complexly determined, involving such factors, among others, as the individual's biological and social inheritance, family and peer values, social expectations, economic con-

This chapter is based in part on a paper entitled *Vocational Maturity: The Construct, Its Measurement, and Its Validity,* presented at the International Congress of Applied Psychology, Liege, Belgium, July 1971.

ditions, evaluation of himself and his world, previous opportunities for discovering and developing his interests and abilities, access to various educational and vocational opportunities, and the type and amount of education that he or his parents can afford.

3. As he learns from experience (e.g., gains new insights into his interests, abilities, and values), acquires new responsibilities (e.g., a family), and encounters new obstacles or opportunities (e.g., technological changes, an expanding or contracting labor market), the individual may have to revise earlier attitudes, choices, and decisions. Thus choice and adjustment, once accomplished, are seldom final but, rather, are processes which continue throughout life.

4. The study of careers involves the study of lives and especially of the antecedents and outcomes of decisions made and positions occupied and relinquished.

5. These moves or position changes constitute the individual's career, and their defining characteristics constitute his career pattern. While some of the moves or changes may be individual and in that sense idiosyncratic, it is possible to identify common or modal themes, sequences, and patterns. Of particular interest are the nature, determinants, and outcomes of these themes or patterns.

An approach which is limited to predicting future vocational status (e.g. occupational level at age twenty-five from present status (e.g., high school test scores) and which does not enquire into prior and subsequent developments can throw only limited light on the process of choice and adjustment. What is needed, say present day theorists, is a developmental approach which focuses on the evolution of vocationally significant traits and behaviors and on the manner in which successive decisions are approached, clarified, revised, and implemented. The focus should thus be on vocational histories rather than on status at a single point in time, on career criteria rather than occupational criteria, and the approach needs to be longitudinal rather than cross-sectional.[4,5,6,7,8,9,10,11]

Direction of Growth

Development implies growth, evolution, progression, and maturation. A number of researchers and theorists—among them Crites,[12] Ginzberg,[13] Gribbons and Lohnes,[14] Jordaan and Heyde,[15] Tiedeman and O'Hara,[16] and Super[17]—have attempted to delineate the directions in which vocational development might be expected to proceed. These include:

1. Greater familiarity with and more effective use of environmental resources and opportunities.
2. Greater awareness of and concern with impending and eventual choices.
3. More effective and more systematic exploration of one's self and one's environment.
4. More extensive and more specific educational and occupational information.
5. Better understanding of the factors to be considered in making various kinds of choices.

6. Greater awareness of factors which might upset or delay one's plans and of ways of circumventing or coping with these contingencies.
7. Greater willingness to assume personal responsibility for one's decisions.
8. Greater awareness of one's ability to determine the course and outcomes of events through the kinds of decisions one makes.
9. Greater awareness of personal assets and deficits and of their implications for choice.
10. A clearer, more complete, better integrated, and more realistic self-concept.
11. The translation of this self-concept first into general and then into more specific occupational terms.
12. Greater commitment to one's goals and subsequently to one's occupation.
13. More specific, stable, and realistic objectives.
14. More specific plans for achieving these objectives.
15. Goals, and eventually an occupation, which are more in accord with one's interests, abilities, values, personality traits, self-concept, work experience, and job skills.
16. Ability to compromise between desire and reality, between the hoped for and the feasible.
17. The selection of educational and occupational environments which are more compatible with one's personality and life-style.
18. Stable employment offering job security and prospects of a decent livelihood.

Need for A Conceptual Framework

Vocational development can be studied without employing the concepts of life stages, developmental tasks, and vocational maturity. However, observations not guided by theory are likely to be either too narrow or too broad in scope, to overlook or slight promising areas of inquiry, and to yield data which, because of either their diversity or excessive specificity, are difficult to integrate into an internally consistent and meaningful picture. The value of a conceptual framework is that it provides the investigator with a map which, even though it may be lacking in detail, is still a help in identifying the more prominent features of the terrain to be explored. Equally important, a conceptual framework provides the investigator with a coherent basis for organizing and interpreting his observations and findings.

From this vantage point, the concept of stages, which, largely as a result of Ginzberg's[18] and Super's work,[19] has come to play an increasingly important part in vocational development theory, can be said to have considerable utility, even though, as Harris[20] and Beilin[21] have indicated, it has been and continues to be the subject of debate. In Harris' opinion, "even though the concept of stages presents some problems as a scientific concept, it clearly has heuristic value." For Beilin the notion of stages is meaningful if it helps to elucidate related constructs and propositions, suggests new ways of analyzing or interpreting data, or helps to explain what is found or already known. It is within this context that the concept of life stages as applied to vocational development needs to be evaluated.

One cannot get very far with the premise that vocational decisions and outcomes have their roots in the past as well as the present, that they evolve and change as the individual and his circumstances change, and that choice and adjustment are frequently repeated processes without indicating, or at least speculating about, the nature, sequence, significance, and possible determinants of these phenomena. This is why a mere listing of anticipated developments, though useful, is of limited value and why vocational psychologists and counselors have been attracted by the concept of life stages.

Developmental Tasks

The concept of stages and developmental tasks has been, and continues to be, widely used in psychology and psychiatry. Its value as an organizing concept is seen in the work of Freud, Sullivan, Erikson, Piaget, and, more recently, in a chapter by Beilin[22] on developmental stages and processes, in a survey of current approaches and concerns entitled *Developmental Psychology Today*,[23] and in Lidz's *The Person—His Development Throughout the Life Cycle*.[24] The concept of stages and tasks also figures in the thinking of nonpsychologists (e.g., parents, teachers, and peers), although they may not, and in fact usually do not, use these terms. It is reflected in their notions of what a person of a certain age should be like or be able to do. The fact that "across the life span there is a rough correlation between the demand quality of environmental requirements and the potentiality for behavior"[25] serves to reinforce and justify these expectations.

Psychologists and psychiatrists who have written about developmental tasks have sometimes focussed on social norms, sometimes on clinically or objectively derived norms. Their efforts have been most useful when they have attempted to establish by means of clinical and empirical observation the significance of the behavior in question, that is, its importance in terms of facilitating or impeding later developments.

Developmental Tasks as Social Norms

Throughout life the individual encounters expectations and demands which are so widely endorsed that they function as societal norms. These expectations and demands, which are transmitted by peers, reference groups, parents, teachers, and other "significant others," vary with society's evaluation of what might be expected of persons at various stages of their lives and sometimes even at a particular age. But whether these expectations are based on age or stage, they generally involve the mastery of certain skills (e.g., reading), the acquisition of certain attitudes (e.g., toward the opposite sex), and the willingness and ability to assume certain roles and obligations (e.g., of father and provider).

These expectations, based both on what is thought to be typical of persons at a given stage and on what society would like to see happen at that stage, can be conceived of as developmental tasks. The use of such terms as "critical points," "hurdles," and "crises" in discussions of stages and tasks attests to the importance which many writers and theorists attach to them. Failure to deal with a developmental task at the appropriate time, or conspicuous lack of success in dealing with it, is believed to impede or delay the individual's development and to make it difficult for him to proceed to, or deal effectively with, the tasks of the next stage.

Just as developmental psychologists have found it profitable to focus on a particular area of development (e.g., cognitive development), even though the boundary between this and other areas of development is often artificial, so vocational psychologists have suggested that vocational development should constitute a separate area of inquiry. Neglected, for the most part, by personality, social, and developmental theorists, work and vocation should be seen not only as legitimate subjects of inquiry in their own right, but as a "major theatre for the study of personality and society."[26]

From the multiplicity of concerns and developments associated with each stage of development, vocational psychologists have singled out for study those which most clearly have vocational relevance. Other characteristics (e.g., peer relations, personal adjustment, and intelligence) are not ignored but are studied as possible correlates of the vocational behavior being examined. The focus is therefore on *vocational* life stages and *vocational* developmental tasks.

STAGES OF VOCATIONAL DEVELOPMENT

Super has been interested in vocational life stages since 1942,[27] but it was not until he and his associates undertook to develop a comprehensive conceptual framework for their projected twenty-year longitudinal study of a group of fifteen-year-olds[28] that this interest came fully into focus. The ideas developed in that monograph have been revised and extended several times. Table 11.1 summarizes Super's most recent thinking which, like his earlier monograph, draws on Davidson's and Anderson's studies of occupational mobility,[29] on Miller and Form's study of adult work histories,[30] on Havighurst's concept of developmental tasks[31] and, most importantly, on Buehler's life stages[32] and on Ginzberg's study of occupational choice.[33]

Vocational development is conceived of as a life-long process which begins in childhood and usually ends in the period following retirement. It is a developmental process involving progression through a series of more or less clearly discernible stages and substages. The stages are characterized, after Buehler, as growth, exploration, establishment, maintenance, and decline. The labels are intended simply to reflect the important characteristics of each stage, and they do not imply that these characteristics are unique to a particular stage. Attempts to specify the precise age at which a particular stage might be expected to begin and end are open to question, and more general estimates such as "early adolescence" and "young adulthood" are to be preferred since, as Harris[34] has pointed out, "individuals move through developmental sequences at different rates and with different velocities," and they even may manifest more than one type of behavior during the same stage.

Table 11.1 Vocational Life Stages (Adapted from Super, 1957; 1963)

Stage	Period	Vocational Developmental Task	Explanation
A. Growth Stage	Childhood and early adolescence	Forming a picture of the kind of person one is. Developing an orientation to the world of work and an understanding of the meaning of work.	Through role-playing (often as a result of identification with admired adults and peers) and participation in school, leisure, and other activities, the individual learns what he can do well, what he likes, how he differs from other people, and incorporates this knowledge into his picture of himself.
B. Exploratory Stage 1. Tentative substage	Early and middle adolescence	Crystallizing a vocational preference	Possibly appropriate *fields* and *levels* of work are identified (partial specification).
2. Transition substage	Late adolescence and early adulthood	Specifying a vocational preference	Transition is made from school to work or from school to further education and training. Generalized choice is converted into specific choice.
3. Trial (little commitment) substage	Early adulthood	Implementing a vocational preference	A seemingly appropriate occupation having been located or prepared for, a beginning job is found and tried out as a life work. Commitment to the occupation is still provisional and may be strengthened or weakened by experiences encountered on the job or in training. If weakened, the individual may change his goals and repeat the process of crystallizing, specifying, and implementing a vocational preference.

Table 11.1 (Continued)

Stage	Period	Vocational Developmental Task	Explanation
C. Establishment Stage			
1. Trial (with commitment) and stabilization substage	Early adulthood to about age thirty	Settling down, securing a permanent place in the chosen occupation*	Having acquired the necessary skills, training, or work experience, the individual commits himself to the occupation and seeks to establish a place for himself in it. Thereafter, changes which occur are changes of position, job, or employer, not changes of occupation.
2. Advancement substage	Thirties to middle forties	Consolidation and advancement	The individual consolidates and improves his status in the occupation by acquiring seniority, developing a clientele, demonstrating superior performance, improving his qualifications, etc.
D. Maintenance Stage	Middle forties to retirement	Preservation of achieved status and gains	The individual is less concerned with registering new gains than with maintaining present status in the face of competition from younger, more enterprising coworkers who are in the advancement stage.
E. Decline Stage	Age sixty-five on	Deceleration, disengagement, retirement	The individual faces the problems of actual or impending retirement and must plan and find other sources of satisfaction (a part-time job, volunteer work, leisure activities, etc.) to replace those lost through retirement.

*There are individuals who for psychological, personal, or economic reasons do not achieve stable jobs or do so only intermittently. In their case what gets stabilized is an unstable career pattern. For such individuals the vocational developmental task is to recognize, accept, and plan for the inevitability of instability (Super, 1963).

Vocational Developmental Tasks

The task to be accomplished in each stage or substage is called a vocational developmental task. Just as there are points in an individual's life when he or she is expected to be able to feed himself, to stop crawling, to learn to read, etc., so too are there societal expectations in the vocational area. There is a time when the individual is expected to know what kind of work he proposes to do for a living, to settle down if he has been drifting from one job to another, to be able to support his family, to get ahead. These societal expectations may be rejected, but are usually accepted and internalized. They define the tasks he must deal with and the gains he should register at various stages of his life.

The primary task of the *growth stage* is self-definition or self-concept development. Another task is to develop an orientation to the world of work and a conception of the meaning of work. The tasks of the *exploratory stage* are to crystallize, specify, and implement a vocational preference; those of the *establishment stage* to make a place for oneself in the occupation, to commit oneself to it, and to consolidate and improve one's position. The main developmental task of the *maintenance stage* is to preserve one's achievements and gains, and those of the *decline stage* are to decelerate, disengage, and, upon retirement, find other sources of satisfaction.

Vocational Maturity

If, as the theorists referred to earlier assert, vocational development is systematic rather than unsystematic and proceeds in certain identifiable directions, it should be possible to assess not only how much of the road the individual has covered, but also how fast he is travelling in comparison with others who are embarked on the same journey. Super was the first to suggest that rate and progress along this road might be an indication of an individual's vocational maturity.[35] There are, he suggests, two ways of assessing a person's vocational maturity. One is to compare where he is in his development with where a person of his age might be expected to be. The other is to compare his performance with that of others who are in the same stage as he.

Thus a man in his thirties who is still moving from one occupation to another instead of settling might be described as vocationally immature. He is still in the exploratory stage whereas most thirty-year-olds are already in the establishment stage. A sixteen-year-old who is in the tentative substage and has made much greater progress in crystallizing a vocational preference than other boys his age, would be judged more mature than they.

THE GROWTH STAGE

Through maturation and learning the individual's originally limited repertoire of responses is greatly enlarged. In no other period in the individual's life are the changes which occur more rapid than they are in the first fourteen years of life. He enters the world with a limited repertoire of responses, but by the time he enters his teens this repertoire will have been enlarged, if not a thousandfold, then at least to the point where he will be barely recognizable as the infant who once lay virtually helpless in his crib.

His responses become not only more numerous but also more complex. In this process both maturation and learning play a part. As he matures physically and mentally, he is not only capable of doing more but is also expected to do more. His actions are no longer dictated simply by what he would like to do, but also by what others want or expect him to do. Whether through a desire to emulate an admired peer or adult or to conform to the expectations of others, or simply out of curiosity, he tries himself out in a variety of roles. He compares his performance with that of others or hears other people doing so. He becomes aware of his strengths and shortcomings, of the ways in which he is like or unlike other people, and he begins to develop a picture of the kind of person he is or might aspire to become.

If, as Super has suggested, a vocational preference is a reflection of a person's self-concept, then self-definition is perhaps the most important vocational developmental task of the growth stage. Another important task is to develop an orientation to the world of work, including some understanding of the meaning of work and of the different ways in which it is possible to earn a living. To this Havighurst[36] would add two other tasks: learning how to organize one's time in order to get a piece of work done and learning that there are times when work (e.g., chores or a school assignment) must be put ahead of play.

Research on the growth stage is sketchy, although there are some interesting isolated studies. Roe,[37] for example, found some evidence that choice of an occupation which is popularly considered to be more appropriate for a member of the opposite sex is related to early childhood experiences. The women engineers in her study were found to have had particularly good relationships with their fathers and to have identified strongly with them. The male social workers were found to have had stressful and minimally affectionate relationships with their parents, suggesting that their choice of this occupation may stem from a desire to satisfy needs denied in childhood.

The importance of early childhood experiences is also shown by Friend and Haggard's study[38] of well-adjusted and poorly adjusted workers. They found that childhood attitudes to the father were frequently transferred to employers and superiors, that needs not satisfied in childhood tend to persist into adulthood and to affect the worker's adjustment, and that childhood adjustment is predictive of the kind of adjustment a person will achieve as an adult.

Tyler[39] has shown that boys and girls develop different interests very early and that these have important consequences for later development. Twelfth-grade girls who were oriented towards a career rather than towards homemaking were found to have chosen less feminine responses on an interest inventory when they were first graders than the noncareer comparison group. Another indication of the influence and persistence of orientations developed early in childhood is that the twelfth-grade boys who had scientific interests gave more masculine responses than the nonscience comparison group even when they were first graders.

The vocational preferences of young children are generally dismissed as fantasy choices based on daydreams and wish-fulfillment but, as will be seen later, adolescents and young adults also harbor unrealistic and poorly conceived aspirations. Besides, as O'Hara[40] has pointed out, these preferences, which are frequently the result of identification with an admired adult, do provide a basis for exploration. Young people do test these preferences against their interests and values and in so doing learn something from them.

That the career plans of elementary school pupils are not ephemeral has been shown by Cooley and Lohnes[41] who have reported on the stability of the career plans of 141 fifth graders over five years. Classifying the subjects' preferences as science and nonscience, they found that 77 percent of the subjects held the same orientation in sixth grade as in fifth grade. Corresponding figures for the seventh, eighth, and ninth grades are 70 percent, 68 percent, and 52 percent. Thus, half of the subjects exhibited the same orientation in ninth grade as they had in fifth.

Further study of the origins, development, and stability of these and other orientations (e.g., masculinity and femininity of interests, career and homemaking) would seem to be indicated.

THE EXPLORATORY STAGE

Exploration can and does occur in every life stage, but in no period of life is it as sustained and prevalent as it is in adolescence and young adulthood. This is the period in which the individual is expected to translate his self-concept first into general and then into more specific occupational terms. Having done that, he must, usually in late adolescence or early adulthood, convert his choice into reality by taking a job or embarking on a training or educational program which will lead to the desired occupation. He must, in other words, crystallize, specify, and implement a vocational preference.

To do this he needs to clarify his picture of himself and also his picture of the world of work. The ambiguity and uncertainty created by entering a new subculture (that of teenager and budding adult) are the basis for much adolescent exploration. The purpose of such exploration is to reduce ambiguity, uncertainty, and conflict by finding satisfactory roles.

Tiedeman[42] has spoken of the "predicament of tentativeness" in which the individual is torn between a desire for closure on the one hand, and a wish to keep his options open on the other. In more or less the same vein, Super[43] and Jordaan[44] have pointed out that intolerance of ambiguity can lead to premature closure or to what Ginzberg has called "pseudo-crystallization." Exploration stops because the individual finds ambiguity and uncertainty too painful. Conversely, if ambiguity and uncertainty fail to reach a certain threshold, the individual may not be motivated to explore at all. For exploration to occur uncertainty and ambiguity must not be so strong as to be intolerable or so weak as to initiate appropriate tension-reducing behavior.

Other exploratory activities are engaged in, not only for the reasons cited above but also to take advantage of newly conferred freedoms and of social roles for which the individual was not previously eligible. Exploration is characterized by search, experimentation, inquiry, examination, trial and

—in its most advanced form—by hypothesis testing.[45] The individual engages in a wide variety of activities, sometimes of his own accord, sometimes only because it is demanded or expected of him. These include school subjects, part-time and summer jobs, hobbies and pastimes, and home, school, and neighborhood activities. Whether freely chosen, prescribed, or expected, they enable the individual to try himself out in a variety of roles and activities, and to become better acquainted with social expectations and demands and with environmental opportunities and barriers.

When exploration is intended rather than fortuitous, systematic rather than random, self-initiated rather than other-initiated, and is undertaken with the purpose of generating or testing hypotheses, it results in a better understanding of self and environment and facilitates the process of crystallizing, specifying, and implementing a vocational preference. If exploration is inadequate, decisions are likely to be postponed or, if made because they cannot be postponed any longer, to be tentative and provisional.

Much more is known about the exploratory stage than about the growth stage, not only because it has been regarded by researchers as a more fruitful period to investigate but also because a number of investigators have collected longitudinal rather than the more usual cross-sectional data. Research has focused on the direction and amount of change during the high school years, on the bases for choice, on the relationship of aspiration to achievement, and on the construction and validation of measures of vocational maturity.

The Career Pattern Study

The Career Pattern Study, which was initiated by Super and his coworkers in the early 1950s and finally completed in 1973, is a twenty-one year longitudinal study of almost three hundred eighth and ninth graders who have been studied at frequent intervals between the ages of fifteen and thirty-six, but most intensively at ages fifteen, eighteen, twenty-five, and thirty-six. The findings reported here[46] and in other sections of this chapter are limited for the most part to the original ninth-grade group and do not include the age thirty-six follow-up, since those data are still being collected and analyzed.

Crystallization and Specification. The typical twelfth grader or eighteen-year-old has fewer occupations and fields under consideration than he did in the ninth grade, his interests are more adult (as judged by his I-M score on Strong's Blank), his preferences are both more congruent and more specific, and he has more confidence in them. This is what one would expect if the developmental task of this period is, as has been suggested, to crystallize and specify a preference. Further confirmation is provided by a principal components analysis with varimax rotation of sixty-two presumed measures of vocational maturity. Of the nineteen factors extracted, twelve had very similar or quite similar structures at both grade levels, including two which were named "crystallization of interests" and "specificity of vocational preference." A subsequent analysis of the twelfth-grade data, employing a method which yields oblique rather than orthogonal factors, showed that 85 percent of the variance accounted for by the nineteen factors in the twelfth grade can be explained in terms of two factors which are defined by consistency of preferences with respect to field, level, and occupational family.

Direction and Magnitude of Changes.   That the typical eighteen-year-old, though further along in his development than he was four years earlier, still has some distance to go, is shown by the fact that most eighteen-year-olds are still considering several occupations and several fields of work; that about half are considering occupations which are not in the same field or on the same level; that about 40 percent appear to know the field they want to go into but not the level, and vice versa; that only one out of every five has settled on an occupation or a specialty within an occupation; and that two out of three still have little confidence in their expressed vocational goal. These findings suggest that the process of crystallization and specification is still under way rather than completed, so that the first few years after leaving school can be characterized as "trial-little commitment."

While paying special attention to attributes and behaviors which are thought to be indicative of how well an individual is coping with a particular developmental task, the Career Pattern Study has not limited itself to these. It has also been interested in studying those attitudes and behaviors which might be required for, or might result from, the completion of a given developmental task. These have included wisdom of preference, occupational information, work experience, acceptance of responsibility, planning, implementation of preference, use of resources, awareness of contingency factors, and weighing of alternatives.

The more important findings are that twelfth-grade boys are more aware of the significant characteristics of occupations and have more information about occupations which interest them than they did in the ninth grade; that they have more specific plans for obtaining the required training, education, and on-the-job experience; and that they show greater readiness to assume personal responsibility for securing a beginning job or the required education and training. Unexpected and perhaps crucial to an understanding of the events of the post-high school years is the finding that twelfth-grade preferences are *not* more realistic or more appropriate than ninth-grade preferences. At age eighteen about half of the subjects were still entertaining goals which were *not* in keeping with their socioeconomic circumstances, their measured interests, or their level of ability.

The gains registered between the ninth and twelfth grade are significant but not as great as might have been anticipated. While they are better informed about occupations than they were in the ninth grade, most eighteen-years-olds still know relatively little about the occupation they think they might enter. Only about half have well-thought-out plans for preparing for the occupation. Very few have well-thought-out plans for actually *getting* the needed training, education, or beginning job or have done something to implement the plans that they have.

In summary, the Career Pattern Study sheds important light on the direction and magnitude of the changes which take place during the high school years. It suggests that the important questions to ask in assessing a high school student's vocational development are: How much progress has he or she made in crystallizing and specifying a vocational preference? How much does he know about the occupation he is thinking of entering? How specific are his plans for achieving his objective? How much concern with choice (weighing of alternatives) does he evidence? How aware is he of important features of occupations?

The Career Development Study

Like the Career Pattern Study, the Career Development Study by Gribbons and Lohnes is a longitudinal study which has followed a group of subjects through adolescence to adulthood.[47,48] Unlike the Career Pattern Study, it included girls as well as boys. The subjects, fifty-seven males and fifty-four females, were studied at two-year intervals over an eleven-year period beginning in the eighth grade.

Focus in the early part of the study[49] was on assessing "readiness for vocational planning" (RVP) as indicated by eight types of information elicited during a thirty- to forty-minute interview. The subjects' responses were scaled to yield eight RVP scores, each of which was designed to represent a different aspect or dimension of vocational maturity. They are:

1. Factors in curriculum choice
2. Factors in occupational choice
3. Verbalized strengths and weaknesses
4. Accuracy of self-appraisal
5. Evidence for self-ratings
6. Interests (and their relation to occupational choices)
7. Values (and their relation to occupational choices)
8. Independence of choice

Tenth graders scored significantly higher than eighth graders on all eight RVP scales, indicating, as do the CPS data, that older students do differ vocationally from younger students. If they did not, the whole notion of vocational development would, of course, be suspect.

Stability of Preferences. If stability of preferences is evidence of crystallization and specification, then the data collected by Gribbons and Lohnes over a seven-year period (eighth grade to two years after high school) contribute to our understanding of these processes.[50] As in the CPS the subjects' preferences were classified according to field and level and described as similar or different according to whether they were in the same field or on the same level. Examination of eighth-, tenth-, and twelfth-grade preferences showed that 70 percent of the subjects changed fields and 60 percent levels over the five-year period. However, if changing level only once and then only to an adjacent level is regarded as a minor deviation, and the subjects falling in this category are added to those who did not change levels at all over the five-year period, then almost 80 percent of them can be considered to have specified quite early the level at which they intend or hope to be employed one day.

In the Career Pattern Study 40 percent of the subjects did not change fields between the ninth and twelfth grade,[51] a figure not too different from that reported by Gribbons and Lohnes. However, the proportion judged to be undecided about level of occupation in the twelfth grade is about twice as large as in the Gribbons and Lohnes study, no doubt because the CPS subjects' preferences had to be on exactly rather than approximately the same level before they were judged to have specified their anticipated occupational level. Moreover, data on the stability of preferences can be misleading if level of aspiration is not taken into account. In the eighth grade more than 60 percent of Gribbons' and Lohnes' subjects aspired to occupations that required at least a college degree; as late as Spring of the twelfth grade more than half of the subjects were still aspiring to a professionally oriented occupation, including sixteen subjects with IQ's of 105 and below.[52] That these aspirations are not only unrealistic but persistent is shown by data collected on these same subjects two years out of high school, when they were asked what they were currently doing and what they hoped to do in the future. Only 26 percent of the subjects were pursuing educational paths leading to a high level occupation, yet 40 percent were still aspiring to occupations at these levels; more than 40 percent were in unskilled or semiskilled jobs, yet fewer than 16 percent said that this is what they planned or expected to do in the future. Gribbons and Lohnes comment that "fantasy is not a sole possession of children."[53]

It is clear from these data that the stress on upward mobility in our culture leads young people to develop and maintain high level aspirations. If they experience less difficulty in deciding on an occupational level than they do in deciding on an occupational field, it may be because they are limiting themselves to a rather narrow range of possibilities. In other words, specification of level, in and of itself, is not evidence of having coped successfully with the developmental task of crystallizing and specifying a vocational preference. If the preference is unrealistic and persists, it might more properly be described as a fixation and, as such, be expected to inhibit rather than facilitate further development.

Specification, Maturity, and Adjustment. The above possibility also occurred to Gribbons and Lohnes, whose approach to data analysis often displays an unusual degree of creativity. They examined the subjects' eighth-, tenth-, and twelfth-grade preferences and classified them as exhibiting persistent realistic pursuit of the first stated goal (*constant maturity*), passage through the stages and tasks of Super's developmental model (*emerging maturity*), progressive deterioration of aspirations and achievements, accompanied by frustration and loss of status (*degeneration*), and persistent fixation on fantastic, unrealistic goals with no advance in achieved level (*constant immaturity*). They then related these to adjustment two years out of high school or, in Super's terminology, to status in the "trial-little commitment" substage.[54]

Gribbons and Lohnes do not use the terms "crystallization" and "specification," but their findings are nevertheless important for the light they shed on the extent and outcomes of realistic and unrealistic crystallization and specification. Sixteen percent of the subjects were judged to have exhibited constant maturity, 39 percent emerging maturity, 28 percent degeneration, and 17 percent constant immaturity. Thus, about half of the subjects appeared to be proceeding satisfactorily, that is, to have crystallized and specified a preference or to be on the way to doing so. These findings are generally in accord with the CPS findings reviewed earlier.

A subject was judged successful and happy if his current activity (two years out of high school) did not "obviously or seriously contradict his current aspirations." If, on the other hand, what he was doing was seriously out of line with what he hoped to be doing in the future, he was judged to be unhappy and unsuccessful. On this basis half of the subjects were judged to be making poor vocational adjustments. Adjustment two years out of high school was found to be significantly related to the history of the subjects' high school goals, with constant maturity and emerging maturity associated with more successful ratings, and degeneration and constant immaturity with more unsuccessful and neutral ratings.

This is in line with expectation; so is the finding that the subjects who showed greater readiness for vocational planning in the eighth grade were more likely to be contented with what they were doing at H.S.+2 than those with lower RVP scores. Completely unexpected and impossible to explain is the fact that RVP scores failed to discriminate between the subjects exhibiting healthy and unhealthy goal behavior in high school. If, as they were designed to do, the RVP scales assess vocational maturity, then they *should* discriminate between subjects displaying various degrees of maturity in their choice behavior. Equally troublesome is the fact that tenth-grade RVP scores, which, being closer to the criterion, should be an even better predictor of later adjustment than eighth-grade RVP, failed to predict it at all. These shortcomings, however, should not obscure the other findings which indicate a relationship between various kinds of choice behavior in high school and adjustment two years out of high school.

The Concept of Exploration

Though frequently invoked by developmental and vocational psychologists, the concept of exploration has received surprisingly little attention from researchers and theoreticians. Attempts to study it systematically, or even to elucidate it, have been sparse and limited in scope. The focus has generally been on *activities* (work experience, use of resources, and participation in school, neighborhood, and other activities) rather than on the *process* and outcomes of exploration. Such studies indicate what young people do but not why they do it or what they learn from it. In an extensive but still incomplete treatment of the subject, Jordaan[55] defined exploratory vocational behavior as activities undertaken with the more or less conscious purpose of eliciting information about oneself or one's environment which will aid one in choosing, preparing for, entering, adjusting to, or progressing in an occupation. Exploratory behavior is said to be most truly exploratory when it involves the generation and testing of hypotheses about oneself and one's world, particularly the world of work.

The publication of the Jordaan paper was a by-product of the collection of the Career Pattern Study data; consequently, the findings reported below, although based on unusually extensive data, are at this point ground-breaking in only one important respect—they do relate work experience and participation in various kinds of activities to measures of vocational maturity and to later adjustment.

Extent of Participation.   The data show that most CPS subjects participated in several activities in high school and worked after school and during summers. Their participation in out-of-school activities (YMCA, Church Choir, Scouts, etc.) was not as substantial, perhaps because so many of them worked after school. A sizeable number of boys (a quarter or more) did not take part in any school activities, did not work after school, and did not become involved in any out-of-school activities. However, there were very few boys who did not work at least one summer, and at least half worked two summers out of three. About half of the ninth graders (52 percent) and nearly all of the twelfth graders (83 percent) had had two or more part-time jobs, or one or more full-time jobs, during their high school career. Even as early as age fifteen a majority of the boys had already accumulated a considerable amount of work experience.[56]

While the reasons for the subjects' participation in these activities cannot be determined, it is possible to establish whether these activities were in line with the subjects' stated vocational goal. About half of the ninth graders had or were engaged in two or more extracurricular activities which appeared to be vocationally relevant. By contrast, in only a minority of cases (19 percent in the ninth grade and 19 percent in the twelfth grade) were summer and part-time jobs judged to be in line with the subjects' vocational goals.

What benefits, if any, accrue from these experiences and activities or, to be more accurate, since it is impossible to distinguish between cause and effect, how do boys who have these experiences differ from those who do not have them? The benefits are not as great as is commonly believed. The reason may be that they were undertaken for social and economic rather than vocational reasons, with the result that their vocational relevance was not seen by the individual. There are indications that boys who had certain kinds of experiences were likely to be better informed about certain aspects of their preferred occupation, to be weighing more alternatives, and to be further along in crystallizing and specifying a vocational preference than boys who had not had such experiences, but the results are not clear cut and the correlations tend to be small (in the 20s and 30s).

More impressive are data to be cited later which show that involvement in various kinds of activities during the high school years *is* related to a number of important occupational outcomes at age twenty-five.

THE ESTABLISHMENT STAGE

While it may involve some trial, establishment presupposes that the individual either through haphazard or purposeful exploration during the high school and post-high school years, has become committed or resigned to a particular way of earning a living. Typically this happens between the ages of twenty-five and thirty when exploration begun in high school and continued in the labor market, in company-sponsored training programs, in college and in other educational and training institutions, has run its course.

That exploration should continue for so long is not surprising given the data reviewed thus far on the aspirations, vocational readiness, and post-high school experiences of young people.

The Nature of Establishment

For many individuals establishment is preceded by frequent changes of employer, job, and even occupation. The typical CPS subject made six changes between the ages of eighteen and twenty-five. Freedman's subjects (employees of five metropolitan firms) had held on the average between three and four jobs before joining the firm. Three-fourths of the job changes involved a change of occupation, 87 percent a change in industry, and 56 percent a change of employer, occupation, and industry. Voluntary job changing declined sharply after the age of thirty, by which time most workers had either settled down to, or settled for, the occupation they were in.[57]

Establishment is the culmination of earlier processes: partial specification of a vocational objective, followed by more complete specification and, in due course, full specification; minimal commitment to the stated objective, provisional commitment, and deepening commitment or resignation. Trial, stabilization, consolidation, and advancement—this is the expected and desirable sequence of events during the establishment stage. For those who follow this sequence, the years from twenty-five to forty-five constitute a period of planting and reaping, of fulfillment and forward momentum. For those who try to stabilize but are not able to, or who stabilize but fail to consolidate and advance, these are obviously not years of fulfillment, but years of frustration and resignation.

Some individuals, especially those who enter the labor market with fully qualifying training or work experience, encounter relatively little difficulty in settling down and securing a place in the occupation. Others, lacking the necessary qualifications or experience, or possessing the qualifications, but not the commitment, experience much more difficulty. Stabilization is a matter both of qualifications and commitment. If either is lacking, the individual's early work history is likely to be characterized by frequent changes of job, employer, and even occupation. Random trial is likely to outweigh purposeful trial, in which case the individual can be said to be floundering. If, as is true of many who flounder initially, the individual eventually acquires the necessary qualifications, becomes committed to a particular occupation, or acquires responsibilities which make constant or frequent changing impossible or unprofitable, he may develop what Freedman calls "attachment." It may be attachment to an occupation, an employer, an organization, or simply a way of life. But for attachment to qualify as establishment it must involve not only job security but prospects of a decent livelihood.[58]

Research on Establishment Behavior

Data on the establishment stage are sparse or outdated. Buehler's[59] retrospective study appeared in 1933 and Miller and Form's[60] study of adult work histories in 1951. Gribbons and Lohnes followed their subjects only up to about the age of twenty-five; Career Pattern Study data collected in 1973, when the subjects were about thirty-five years old and presumably halfway through the establishment stage, are still being analyzed. But the fact that longitudinal data covering the period from twenty-five to forty-five are not yet available does not mean that the establishment period is completely uncharted territory. Individuals develop at different rates; some of them, the so-called early bloomers, can be expected to reach the establishment stage before the age of twenty-five. Moreover, the boundary between one stage and the next is obviously not as precise as the specified age limits would suggest. It is a broad zone rather than a thinly drawn line. For these reasons, data collected in the years between eighteen and twenty-five, during which most individuals are on their way but not yet fully in the establishment stage, can appropriately be analyzed for evidence of establishment behavior.

The Career Pattern Study: Criteria of Establishment

In the age twenty-five CPS follow-up[61] the focus was on assessing occupational outcomes and progress and on relating these to the ninth- and twelfth-grade vocational maturity measures. Analysis of thirty-three criterion variables showed that they fell into six logically meaningful clusters. Of these the career satisfaction, occupational satisfaction, and early establishment clusters have particular relevance for the present discussion.

The *career satisfaction* cluster includes measures of *career success* (how much progress the subject feels he has made toward his goals); *career establishment* (how desirous S is of continuing in his present occupation); *career satisfaction* (how satisfied S is with the direction his career is taking) and *utilization of assets* (extent to which S is using or expects to use his abilities in his present occupation).

The *early establishment* cluster includes measures of *goal attainment* (S's progress toward achieving his age twenty-five goal) and *number of moves* (position changes since high school).

The *occupational satisfaction* cluster includes *opportunity for self-expression* (extent to which S feels opportunities for self-expression in his present position are great, average, or little) and several measures of *stabilization* and *floundering*.

Status at Age Twenty-Five. A brief discussion of the subjects' status at age twenty-five will help to place the foregoing and following material in context. By age twenty-five four-fifths of the subjects were in possession of a high school diploma or its equivalent, one-fourth had completed two years of post-high school education, and approximately one-fifth had earned a bachelor's degree. The average subject had changed positions six times in seven years and not always for the better. Only about half of the subjects could be said to have engaged in predominantly stabilizing behavior since leaving school. About one-third appeared to be floundering and one-sixth showed equal proportions of floundering and stabilizing behavior. By age twenty-five, however, about four-fifths appeared to be stabilizing or getting established. Five percent were in professional and managerial positions and 25 percent in semiprofessional and lower level managerial positions. About 30 percent were in skilled occupations, another 30 percent in semiskilled occupations, and 10 percent in unskilled occupations. Since leaving high school, less than half (about 40 percent) had actually entered any of the occupations they had specified as students. The great majority of the subjects (90 percent) felt they were doing as well as, or better than, other people of their age in their occupation. While most (about 80 percent) said they were satisfied with their job, many of them also indicated that they were not sure whether they wanted to or would continue in the occupation.

Prediction of Early Adult Behavior.   A stepwise multiple regression analysis[62] utilizing fifteen conventional predictors (for example I.Q. and parental occupational level) and nineteen factorially derived twelfth-grade vocational maturity measures (for example, Occupational Information and Agreement between Ability and Preference) indicated the following to be the best predictors of the age twenty-five criterion measures.

Of the *career satisfaction* criteria: parental occupational level, participation in school activities, after-school employment, high school grades, stability of preferences between the ninth and twelfth grades, information about the preparation involved, supply and demand, hours of work, and, finally, agreement between ability and preference.

Of the *early establishment* criteria: parental occupational level and information about material conditions of work and hours of work.

Of the *occupational satisfaction* criteria: parental occupational level, participation in school activities, after-school employment, participation in out-of-school avocational activities, occupational information about supply and demand and hours of work, agreement between ability and preference, and acceptance of responsibility for implementing career decisions.

The variables which most consistently contribute to the prediction of career satisfaction, early establishment, and occupational satisfaction are seen to be parental occupational level, after-school employment, participation in school activities, certain kinds of occupational information, and agreement between the subject's intellectual ability and the intellectual requirements of the occupation he hoped or intended to enter when he was in the twelfth grade. Two or three measures were usually sufficient to achieve a multiple correlation of between .40 and .50 with the criteria, and four or five to achieve a multiple correlation of between .50 and .60. These correlations can, of course, be raised even further by the use of additional variables.

Whether or not they were conceived of by the subject as exploration, after-school employment and participation in various kinds of activities during the high school years are associated with favorable outcomes at age twenty-five, suggesting that activities which may have been undertaken with other purposes in mind do indeed have exploratory value.

Career Progress.   Floundering is haphazard movement which usually does not serve to take the subject closer to his goal or to improve his status. It therefore delays establishment. By contrast, purposeful moves produce gains and are likely to result in satisfaction and to facilitate establishment.

Career progress in the CPS was judged by improvement in equity (increased benefits, better pay rate, better utilization of training and experience), realism of reasons for moves (moves which remedy or lessen dissatisfying aspects of previous jobs or yield more of the wanted satisfactions), progress toward goals, improvement in socioeconomic status, and improvement in fit between the job and the person's measured interests and abilities.

A stepwise multiple regression analysis showed that career progress, as defined above and expressed as a single score, can be predicted about equally well by the conventional measures and the specially devised vocational maturity measures. It is predicted most economically, however, by high school grades, information about hours of work, and extent of avocational activities. These three measures yield a multiple correlation of .50, suggesting that forward movement between the ages of eighteen and twenty-five can be predicted somewhat better than might have been expected of predictions which cover a seven-year period.

The Career Development Study

Gribbons and Lohnes examined their subjects' post-high school careers in a number of different ways. Most relevant here are the analyses which involve the subjects' coping behavior and placement on the "career tree."

Coping Behaviors. The subjects' educational and occupational placements were examined in relation to their expressed aspirations and, following Super, were characterized as exhibiting floundering, stagnation, trial, instrumentation, and establishment. Floundering and stagnation were considered to be indicative of poor adjustment, whereas trial, instrumentation, and establishment were identified as positive behaviors.

On this basis only 53 percent, or slightly more than half, of the subjects were judged to be making good adjustments four years out of high school.[63] Attempts to differentiate the two groups on the basis of intelligence, socioeconomic status, and their eighth-grade vocational maturity scores proved to be disappointing. These findings with a mixed group of boys and girls are different from those of the Career Pattern Study in which these ninth grade variables were found to be predictive of the success and satisfaction of young males at age twenty-five.[64,65]

Aspirations and Achievements Four and Six Years After High School. Whereas more than half of the subjects aspired to college in the eighth grade, only one-quarter had achieved or were still pursuing a college education four years after high school. However, most (67 percent) had succeeded in obtaining some post-high school education and training.

The discrepancy noted at H.S. + 2 between aspirations and achievement was still very much in evidence two years later. Only one-third of the boys were in professional and managerial occupations, but two-thirds were still aspiring to be. Five times as many girls were in semiskilled occupations as cared to be, and only about half of those who would have liked to be in a skilled occupation had achieved this.[66] The situation was somewhat better at H.S. + 6 (about age twenty-five) but still distressing enough to prompt

Gribbons and Lohnes to conclude that "the majority of adolescents are poorly oriented to career development tasks; fully one-third to almost one-half of young adults at age twenty-five appear to be in career development trouble."[67] The Career Pattern Study findings are not as bleak; most (about 80 percent) of the subjects of that study seemed to have made good progress toward getting established by age twenty-five and were satisfied with, though not necessarily deeply committed to, their current occupation.

It is clear that there are serious discrepancies between the kinds of jobs young people want and the kinds of jobs they hold as young adults entering the establishment stage; while the gulf may narrow somewhat between the ages of eighteen and twenty-five, it is still wide. This suggests that entrenched aspirations do not crumble easily, even when challenged by the realities of the labor market.

Prediction of Field and Level.   Among the more interesting of Gribbons' and Lohnes' analyses are those which have related RVP, sex, I.Q. and Readiness for Career Planning (RCP) to certain career tree variables. RCP is a shortened and purified version of RVP which yields a single score and correlates less highly with intelligence (r = .32) than some of the original scales. A career tree is simply a way of portraying the kinds of educational and vocational choices that a person has made or is thinking of making. The choice points are represented by such questions as, "Shall I go to college or not?" and "Shall I go in the direction of science and technology or in a more people-oriented humanistic direction?"

There are twelve branches in the Cooley and Lohnes Career Development Tree.[68] Twelve are too many to use when there are only one hundred and eight subjects, so Gribbons and Lohnes reduced the number of "career branch tips" from twelve to four as follows:

> College: science
> College: sociocultural and business
> Noncollege: technology
> Noncollege: sociocultural and business

RVP and RCP (the vocational maturity variables) were found to be "robustly related" to the subjects' placement on the career tree at every follow-up point up to H.S. + 4.[69] Sex and RCP were the *best* predictors of tenth- and twelfth-grade choices, and socioeconomic status the best predictor of choices at H.S. + 2. By H.S. + 4 and H.S. + 6 socioeconomic status and intelligence had moved into first place, followed by sex and RCP.[70] Reflecting on these data the authors were moved to comment that "the changes in the direction of increased dependence on adolescent socioeconomic status and I.Q. is sobering, especially as we ponder the well-known interdependence, premised partly on genetic mechanisms, of these two predictors."[71]

How well can career tree choices at age twenty-five be predicted from eighth-grade data? Gribbons and Lohnes report "only a modest shared variance between aspirations at age twenty-five and the eighth-grade predictors"; predictions based on sex, I.Q., and RCP resulted in 53 percent hits and 47 percent misses.[72]

Path Following vs. Path Jumping. From a subject's career tree choices at various points in time (eighth, tenth, and twelfth grade, and two and four years after high school), it can be determined whether he has moved from one branch of the career tree to another. Almost half of the subjects were found to be path jumpers. Path jumping was found to be "moderately predictable" with sex and RCP being the best predictors. Path jumpers tended to be more mature vocationally, to be less conforming, and to have higher levels of aspiration than path followers. This is considered by the authors to indicate that the path jumpers are the "stronger people."[73] Whether path jumping is the result of abandoning unrealistic aspirations or leads to occupational placements which are more in line with the subject's aspirations, cannot be determined from the data presented.

THE MAINTENANCE STAGE

Despite detours and occasional loss of direction, the individual's journey up to this point has generally served to take him forward and upward. But inevitably there comes a time when the opportunities for advancement have been exhausted or are greatly reduced. Realization of this fact may precipitate a period of stock taking in which the individual evaluates his achievements and finds them either good or wanting. If the former, he will not find it unduly hard to relinquish hopes of further gains and to be satisfied with enjoying and preserving past gains. If, on the other hand, he feels that what he has accomplished does not amount to very much or falls far short of what he had hoped to accomplish, he may find it difficult to accommodate to the fact that it may be too late to remedy matters. He may respond by putting forth renewed effort "in order to get more or further before it is too late"[74] or, if it is indeed too late, by reproaching himself and by feeling frustrated, resentful, inferior, and sorry for himself.

The Mid-life Crisis

This kind of stock taking is not limited to the maintenance stage. Levinson's description of the "mid-life crisis" in thirty-five- to forty-five-year-olds resembles that given above, but goes a step further in suggesting that this kind of stock taking can be, and often is, a very painful experience, even for those who seem to have done fairly well for themselves.[75] They may, says Levinson, have done extremely well in achieving their goals and yet find success hollow and bitter sweet. In the process of getting established essential aspects of the self may have been consciously rejected, repressed or left dormant. "It is these excluded components of the self—'other voices in other rooms'—that now seek expression and clamor to be heard." One is reminded of Tyler's statement that potentialities tend to exceed opportunities and that self-actualization may involve slighting and even renouncing certain aspects of the self.[76]

Those who cannot derive much satisfaction from enjoying and preserving past gains, either because the gains, in their eyes, do not amount to much, or because they feel they have potentials and needs which they may still be able to realize, may, in Lidz' words, try to "salvage their lives" by changing occupations, or if that is not possible, by changing jobs.[77] There is a growing interest in persons who seek to invest their lives with new meaning by changing occupations in mid-life, but as yet this interest has not yielded much by way of research.

While maintenance implies preservation of the status quo ("holding on to present gains rather than competing for new gains"),[78] it does not mean resting on one's oars. Challenged by younger, often better prepared co-workers who are consolidating their positions and striving for advancement, the individual who is in the maintenance stage may have to run hard just to stay where he is, particularly if his accomplishments do not give him much of an edge over his challengers.

The terms "preservation" and "status quo" may give the impression that this is a period free of stress, of quiet enjoyment of the fruits of past labors, but enough has been said to suggest that this is not so and that the adjustments which individuals have to make during this period merit serious study.

THE DECLINE STAGE

In the decline stage the road which brought the individual to the plateau of the maintenance stage, begins to slope downward. After the prologue (growth and exploration), climax (establishment), and relative calm (maintenance) comes the epilogue (deceleration, disengagement, retirement, old age, death).

According to Lidz, by 1980 there will be 25 million persons in the U.S. over sixty-five. They will have, on the average, a life expectancy of another twelve years.[79]. For Friedmann and Havighurst the problems of retirement consist of learning how to manage on a reduced income, how to pass the time, and how to find new satisfactions to replace those previously provided by work. Their study of five occupational groups shows that those who view work primarily as a way of earning a living are less reluctant to retire than those for whom work has other meanings.[80]

With retirement come such other problems as loss of influence, authority, or reputation, maintaining a sense of purpose in life, loss of valued associations, and learning to live without the structure provided by work routines. The kind of adjustment the retired worker makes depends on the extent to which the satisfactions previously derived from work can be obtained in other ways and from other sources.[81] Steer's study of retired educators found satisfaction in retirement to be related to the continuation or development of rewarding and meaningful activities, particularly if these resembled preretirement work activities. In addition, the more closely the retirees' concept of self matched their concept of the occupation in middle age, the more likely it was that they would be dissatisfied in retirement. It was those who in their prime implemented their self-concept most fully in their work who suffered the greatest loss upon retirement and who experienced the greatest dissatisfaction.[82]

Old Age

Many of the problems which arise during this period are problems of old age rather than problems of retirement, but they, too, may necessitate drastic changes in self-concept. They include adjusting to failing mental and physical powers, loss of friends and associates through death and infirmity, increasing dependency upon others, feelings of being unwanted and a burden to others, and the first and ultimately final intimations of mortality.

SUMMARY AND CONCLUDING REMARKS

One is impressed by the frequency with which the numbers "50 percent" and "half" appear in the preceding discussion. In the twelfth grade, for example, half of the subjects were considering occupations which were not in the same field or on the same level; about half were aspiring to occupations in the top half of the occupational ladder (Roe levels 1–3); half were entertaining goals which were not in keeping with their interests, abilities, or socioeconomic circumstances; only half had well-thought-out plans for preparing for their prospective occupation (CPS); and about half exhibited constant or emerging maturity between the eighth and twelfth grades (CDS).

Two years out of high school about half were making poor adjustments (were engaged in activities which had little or no relationship to their ultimate goals) (CDS); about half had engaged in predominantly positive or stabilizing behavior between the ages of eighteen and twenty-five; about half of the moves between eighteen and twenty-five can be described as floundering; about half of those whose modal behavior between eighteen and twenty-five was characterized as floundering were stabilizing at age twenty-five; at age twenty-five half were in occupations in the upper half of the occupational ladder; nearly half (40 percent) were in unskilled and semi-skilled occupations (CPS); slightly more than half were making good adjustments (were not floundering or stagnating) four years after high school; half were path jumpers (had changed from one branch of the career tree to another) between the eighth grade and H.S. + 4; and, finally, perhaps as many as half were in "career development trouble" at age twenty-five (CDS).

Stages

If all that is needed to define a stage is that 50 percent or more of the subjects should exhibit the expected behavior, then the existence of an exploratory stage, in which preferences are crystallized, specified, and tried out, and an establishment stage, in which floundering gives way to goal-directed behavior and provisional commitment is followed by deepened commitment and stabilization, would appear to be confirmed.

Present understanding of the growth stage, of the consolidation and advancement substages of the establishment state, and of the maintenance and decline stages is limited. When the data from the age thirty-six CPS follow-up have been analyzed, a more complete picture of the establishment stage will be available, but this will need to be supplemented by other research.

Need for Guided Exploration

It is clear from the foregoing that on a number of counts many if not most eighteen-year-olds are poorly prepared to find and make a place for themselves in the labor market. The persistence of inappropriate and unrealistic aspirations is striking, as is the fact that job and position changes between the ages of eighteen and twenty-five generally do not result in a job which is more in keeping with the individual's interests and abilities than previously held jobs.[83]

One of the reasons why high school students have problems when they leave school and enter "the real world" appears to be that they do not know themselves and the world of work sufficiently well to make good decisions and plans. Why this should be so when the students have access to school counselors, occupational materials and, in some schools, even units which focus on occupations and career planning, is not clear. Much of what passes for trial and exploration in the post-high school years appears to be haphazard rather than purposeful trial. Ways need to be found to get pupils to do their exploring and reality testing while they are still in school and can be helped to plan, obtain, and derive maximum benefit from carefully selected exploratory experiences. CPS data show that boys who are active in school affairs, who have had certain kinds of work experience, and who are actively pursuing hobbies, pastimes, and other activities out of school, fare better in the post-high school years than those who do not. The reason may be that through such activities they learn important things about themselves and the world which, if not learned then, must be learned later through hard experience. But how this learning takes place and how pupils can best be helped to relate their personal characteristics and circumstances to the world of work is, as yet, poorly understood.

Need for Adult Measures of Vocational Maturity

While vocationally relevant traits, attitudes, and behaviors become progressively more evident during the high school years, the gains registered appear to be modest rather than substantial, suggesting that the high school years may be either a prelude or a postlude to a period of more rapid development. This suggests, first, that more attention should be paid to the elementary school years and, second, that the early post-high school years (when aspirations are tested against reality) might provide a better basis for assessing vocational maturity than the high school years. Up to now the post-high school years have been regarded primarily as a source of criterion data, and the focus has been on relating vocational maturity scores obtained in high school to later outcomes. Vocational development obviously does not stop in the twelfth grade. Indeed, the theory of life stages and developmental tasks holds that *each* stage or substage presents new tasks and provides fresh opportunities for assessing the individual's vocational maturity in terms of his awareness of impending tasks and his methods for dealing with them. Post-high school meures of vocational maturity are not only theoretically desirable, but, being closer in time to the behaviors that they are designed to predict, can be expected to result in greatly improved predictions and thus to help at a time at which it is greatly needed, the "floundering period."

Eighth- and ninth-grade vocational maturity measures do have some predictive validity as the CDS and CPS data show, but their correlations with adult occupational outcomes tend to be modest rather than strong, presumably partly because of the effect of intervening events and the length of time separating the predictors and the criteria, and partly because vocational development has not proceeded far enough for the differences between subjects to be very meaningful. In the CPS, which assessed the subjects' vocational maturity in the twelfth grade as well as in the eighth and ninth grades, the twelfth-grade measures were, as expected, clearly superior to the eighth- and ninth-grade measures in predicting later career behavior and outcomes. Adult measures of vocational maturity obtained in the period preceding entry into the next stage or substage and focused on short-range rather than long-range outcomes, are likely to be even more promising and more helpful to practitioners.

Vocational Maturity Measures vs. Conventional Measures

Vocational maturity measures are better for some purposes than conventional measures. In the Career Development Study they predicted path jumping between eighth grade and H.S. + 4 better than the conventional measures. For other purposes (CDS) standard measures (intelligence and socioeconomic status) were clearly better (e.g., in predicting career tree choices at age twenty-five). Sometimes both kinds of predictors were effective (e.g., RCP, RVP, intelligence and socioeconomic status in predicting career tree choices up to about age twenty-two). In some instances neither the conventional nor the vocational maturity measures were effective (e.g., in predicting adjustment at H.S. + 4).

In the Career Pattern Study[84] career and occupational satisfaction were predicted reasonably well by both types of twelfth-grade measures. However, the vocational maturity measures outperformed the standard measures in predicting early establishment (e.g., attainment of the occupational goal set at age twenty-five and, negatively weighted, the number of position changes since leaving high school and stabilization. The standard measures in turn surpassed the vocational maturity measures in predicting self-improvement (moving up the educational and occupational ladder with realistic reasons for each move), economic self sufficiency (months of self-support), and job getting and holding (number of times and number of months unemployed).

Among the *conventional measures,* high school grades, after-school work experience, and the pursuit of avocational activities were found to be most useful predictors. Intelligence, parental occupational level, high school curriculum, summer employment, and stability of occupational preference during the high school years were also useful predictors.

The best *vocational maturity measures* were, in the twelfth grade only, those which assessed the wisdom of the subject's occupational goal (agreement between ability and preference) and his knowledge about the occupation (how to prepare for it, what the hours of work and employment prospects are). Other measures which contributed significantly to the prediction of early adult vocational behavior were crystallization of interests and independence of work experience.

From the foregoing it is possible to construct a tentative picture of the kind of high school senior who is most likely to have achieved success, satisfaction, and a place for himself in the world of work by age 25, as judged by what he says about himself and by how judges evaluate his work history:

He tends to come from a home which is higher rather than lower on the socioeconomic scale, to be a good student, to be active in school activities, to have hobbies and pastimes that he pursues out of school, to have worked after school, to have displayed initiative and independence in finding a part-time or summer job, to have goals which are in keeping with his interests and intellectual ability, and to be informed about the occupation which he thinks he might follow. In short, he is an achiever, a doer; he is active and involved, in school and also out of school, and is not only engaging his environment, but also exploring it.

Several other conclusions can be drawn from the material presented in this chapter:

1. Individuals need help in identifying and developing strategies for dealing with the vocational developmental tasks of the life stage they are in or about to enter.
2. Individuals vary in their readiness and capacity to deal with these tasks.
3. Counselors need to know what developmental tasks the client has completed, how well he has dealt with them, and how ready he is to deal with the tasks of the present and next stage in order to remove past deficits and to help him develop appropriate resources and strategies for dealing with future tasks.

Counselors interested in evaluating, facilitating, and guiding their clients' vocational development have long felt a need for practical instruments to help them accomplish these goals. The vocational maturity measures used in the Career Pattern Study and Career Development Study were based on interview data which are time consuming to collect and difficult to score. Several self-administering tests and inventories are now available which are objective, reliable, and relatively easy to apply and score.

Practical Measures of Vocational Maturity

Of the instruments developed thus far the following are the most adequate conceptually and psychometrically.

The Career Maturity Inventory[85,86] consists of an Attitude Scale and a Competence Test. The Attitude Scale consists of fifty True-False items (e.g. "Parents know better than anybody which occupation you should enter") covering orientation to work, conceptions of the choice process, independence in decision making, preference for vocational choice factors, and involvement in the choice process. The Competence Test consists of five subtests (about one hundred multiple choice items in all) which assess comprehension, problem solving, and the pupils' knowledge of the characteristics and requirements of a wide range of occupations. The subtests are entitled Self-appraisal, Occupational Information, Goal Selection, Planning, and Problem Solving. The Attitude Test takes about twenty minutes to complete and the Competence Tests about thirty minutes each. Normative data are available for grades five or six through twelve.

The Cognitive Vocational Maturity Test[87,88] consists of six subtests, each containing approximately twenty multiple choice items. The first five assess the subjects' occupational knowledge (fields of work, work conditions, duties, and the education and attributes required for various occupations) and the sixth (job selection) the subjects' ability to choose the most realistic occupation for a hypothetical student who is described in terms of his ability, interests, and values. Normative data are available for pupils in grades six through nine. The CVMT takes two class periods for administration.

The Career Development Inventory, Form 1,[89,90] consists of three scales designed to assess three important aspects of vocational maturity: planning orientation (concern with choice, specificity of planning, and self-estimated knowledge of occupations), resources for exploration (knowledge and use of appropriate resources needed in planning), and information and decision-making (actual occupational information and knowledge of vocational decision-making principles). The ninety-one item inventory takes between thirty and forty minutes to complete. Normative data are available for grades eight through twelve.

The Career Development Inventory, Form 9-30,[91] consists of fifty-five behaviors which exemplify or facilitate the completion of the vocational developmental tasks of the following life stages and substages: exploration (crystallization and specification), establishment (implementation, stabilization, consolidation, and advancement), maintenance (holding, updating, innovating) and decline (deceleration and disengagement).

There are five items for each substage. The subject indicates on a five-point scale what his status is with respect to each of the behaviors, for example, "Deciding what I really want to do for a living" and "Finding an area of the country in which to retire." A rating of 5 means "I have already done this," while a rating of 1 means "I have not thought much about it." The subject's responses can be analyzed in two ways: first, to determine how far he has progressed in his development and to compare where he is with where a person of his age might be expected to be and, second, to determine how well he is coping with the tasks compared with others who are in the same stage as he.

The Inventory covers most of the life span and therefore has wider applicability than the other measures discussed. A relatively new instrument, still in the research and development stage, it is among the instruments being used to collect data from the Career Pattern Study subjects at age thirty-six. When the CDI data have been analyzed and related to interview, questionnaire and test data obtained from these same subjects at ages fifteen, eighteen, twenty-five, and thirty-six, its value as a diagnostic and counseling tool will be better understood.

Data on the content, construct, and criterion-related validity of the CMI, CVMT, and CDI can be found in the references which are cited below. They indicate that these instruments are likely to prove useful to counselors in assessing a client's readiness to make certain kinds of decisions, in identifying areas of strength and weakness, in planning remedial steps, in evaluating the outcomes of vocational counseling and of career education and occupational information units, and in helping students and clients to plan experiences which will contribute to their further development.

NOTES

1. L. E. Tyler, "Work and Individual Differences," *Man in a World at Work,* H. Borow, ed. (Boston: Houghton Mifflin, 1964).
2. D. E. Super, "Career Development," *Psychology of the Educational Process,* J. R. Davitz and S. Ball, eds. (New York: McGraw-Hill, 1970).
3. D. E. Super, "Vocational Development Theory: Persons, Positions, and Process," *Perspectives on Vocational Development,* J. M. Whitely and A. Resnikoff, eds. (Washington, D.C.: APGA, 1972).
4. D. E. Super, "Career Development."
5. D. E. Super *et al., Vocational Development: A Framework for Research* (New York: Teachers College Press, 1957).
6. D. E. Super and P. L. Overstreet, *The Vocational Maturity of Ninth Grade Boys* (New York: Teachers College Press, 1960).
7. D. E. Super, R. S. Kowalski, and E. H. Gotkin, *Floundering and Trial After High School* (New York: Teachers College, Columbia University, 1967).
8. D. V. Tiedeman and R. P. O'Hara, *Career Development: Choice and Adjustment* (New York: College Entrance Examination Board, 1963).
9. J. O. Crites, *Vocational Psychology* (New York: McGraw-Hill, 1969).
10. W. D. Gribbons and P. R. Lohnes, *Emerging Careers* (New York: Teachers College Press, 1968).
11. W. D. Gribbons and P. R. Lohnes, *Career Development from Age 13 to Age 25* (Washington, D.C.: U.S. Department of Health, Education, and Welfare, Office of Education Bureau of Research, 1969).
12. J. O. Crites, *The Maturity of Vocational Attitudes in Adolescence* (Washington, D.C.: American Personnel and Guidance Association, APGA Inquiry Series, No. 2, 1971).
13. E. Ginzberg et al., *Occupational Choice* (New York: Columbia University Press, 1951).
14. Gribbons and Lohnes, *Emerging Careers.*
15. J. P. Jordaan and M. B. Heyde, *The High School Years,* Career Pattern Study Monograph III (New York: Teachers College Press, in process).
16. Tiedeman and O'Hara, *op. cit.*
17. Super and Overstreet, *op. cit.*
18. Ginzberg *et al., op. cit.*
19. D. E. Super, *Psychology of Careers* (New York: Harper, 1957).
20. D. B. Harris, "Developmental Psychology Looks at Career Development" (Paper delivered at the meeting of the Eastern Psychological Association, Boston, April, 1972).
21. H. Beilin, "Developmental Stages and Processes," *Measurement and Piaget,* D. R. Green, M. P. Ford, and G. B. Flamer, eds. (New York: McGraw-Hill, 1971).
22. Beilin, *op. cit.*

23. Contributing Consultants, *Developmental Psychology Today* (Del Mar: CRM Books, 1971).

24. T. Lidz, *The Person: His Development Throughout the Life Cycle* (New York: Basic Books, 1968).

25. Harris, *op. cit.*

26. D. E. Super and J. P. Jordaan, "Career Development Theory," *British Journal of Guidance and Counseling* 1, 1(1973).

27. D. E. Super, *The Dynamics of Vocational Adjustment* (New York: Harper, 1942).

28. Super *et al.*, *op. cit.*

29. P. E. Davidson and H. D. Anderson, *Occupational Mobility in an American Community* (Stanford: Stanford University Press, 1937).

30. D. C. Miller and W. H. Form, *Industrial Sociology* (New York: Harper, 1951).

31. R. J. Havighurst, *Human Development and Education* (New York: Longmans, Green, 1953).

32. C. Buehler, *Der menschliche Lebenslauf als psychologisches Problem* (Leipzig: Hirzel, 1933).

33. Ginzberg *et al.*, *op. cit.*

34. Harris, *op. cit.*

35. Super *et al.*, *op. cit.*

36. R. J. Havighurst, "Stages of Vocational Development," *Vocational Behavior: Readings in Theory and Research*, D. G. Zytowski, ed. (New York: Holt, Rinehart and Winston, 1968).

37. A. Roe and M. Siegelman, *Origin of Interests* (Washington, D.C.: American Personnel and Guidance Association, 1964).

38. J. G. Friend and E. A. Haggard, "Work Adjustment in Relation to Family Background," *Applied Psychology Monographs*, No. 16, 1948.

39. L. E. Tyler, *The Psychology of Human Differences* (New York: Appleton-Century-Crofts, 1965), Ch. 8.

40. R. P. O'Hara, "Talk About Self" (Harvard University, Graduate School of Education: Unpublished manuscript, 1959).

41. W. W. Cooley and P. R. Lohnes, *Project Talent: Predicting Development of Young Adults* (Pittsburgh: University of Pittsburgh School of Education and American Institutes for Research, 1968).

42. D. V. Tiedeman and G. A. Dudley, "Recent Developments and Current Prospects in Occupational Fact Mediation," *Implications of Career Development Theory and Research for Counselor Education*, R. A. Myers, ed. (New York: Teachers College, 1967).

43. D. E. Super, "Recent Findings from the Career Pattern Study," *Implications of Career Development Theory and Research for Counselor Education.*

44. J. P. Jordaan, "Exploratory Behavior: The Formation of Self and Occupational Concepts," *Career Development: Self Concept Theory*, D. E. Super *et al.* (New York: College Entrance Examination Board, 1963).

45. *Ibid.*

46. Jordaan and Heyde, *op. cit.*

47. Gribbons and Lohnes, *Emerging Careers.*

48. Gribbons and Lohnes, *Career Development from Age 13 to Age 25.*

49. Gribbons and Lohnes, *Emerging Careers.*

50. *Ibid.*

51. Jordaan and Heyde, *op. cit.*

52. Gribbons and Lohnes, *Emerging Careers.*

53. *Ibid.*

54. *Ibid.*

55. Jordaan, "Exploratory Behavior: The Formation of Self and Occupational Concepts," in D. E. Super et al., *Career Development: Self Concept Theory* (New York: College Entrance Examination Board, 1963).
56. Jordaan and Heyde, *op. cit.*
57. M. Freedman, *The Process of Work Establishment* (New York: Columbia University Press, 1969).
58. *Ibid.*
59. Buehler, *op. cit.*
60. Miller and Form, *op. cit.*
61. Super, Kowalski, and Gotkin, *op. cit.*
62. J. P. Jordaan and D. E. Super, "The Prediction of Early Adult Vocational Behavior," *Life History Research in Psychopathology*, D. F. Ricks, M. Roff, and A. Thomas eds. (Minneapolis: University of Minnesota Press, in process).
63. Gribbons and Lohnes, *Career Development from Age 13 to Age 25*, p. 61.
64. J. P. Jordaan, "Vocational Maturity: The Construct, Its Measurement and Its Validity," Paper presented at the International Congress of Applied Psychology, Liege, Belgium, 1971.
65. Super, Kowalski, and Gotkin, *op. cit.*
66. Gribbons and Lohnes, *Career Development from Age 13 to Age 25*, p. 34.
67. *Ibid.*, p. 119.
68. *Ibid.*, p. 71.
69. *Ibid.*, p. 87.
70. *Ibid.*, p. 111.
71. *Ibid.*, p. 114.
72. *Ibid.*, p. 114.
73. *Ibid.*, p. 87.
74. Lidz, *op. cit.*, p. 460.
75. D. J. Levinson, "A Psychosocial Study of the Male Mid-Life Decade," *Life History Research in Psychopathology*.
76. L. E. Tyler, "Theoretical Principles Underlying the Counseling Process," *Counseling: Readings in Theory and Practice*, J. F. McGowan and L. D. Schmidt, eds. (New York: Holt, Rinehart and Winston, 1962).
77. Lidz, *op. cit.*, p. 418.
78. Super, *Psychology of Careers*, p. 149.
79. Lidz, *op. cit.*, pp. 477, 490.
80. R. A. Friedmann and R. J. Havighurst, *Meaning of Work and Retirement* (Chicago: University of Chicago Press, 1954), p. 188.
81. *Ibid.*, p. 190.
82. R. A. Steer, "The Relationship between Satisfaction with Retirement and Similarity of Self-Ratings for Past Occupation and Present Activity in Educators" (Teachers College, Columbia University: Unpublished Doctoral Dissertation, 1970).
83. Super, Kowalski, and Gotkin, *op. cit.*
84. Jordaan and Super, *op. cit.*
85. J. O. Crites, "The Career Maturity Inventory," *Measuring Vocational Maturity for Counseling and Evaluation*, D. E. Super, ed. (Washington, D.C.: National Vocational Guidance Association, in process).
86. J. O. Crites, *The Maturity of Vocational Attitudes in Adolescence*.
87. B. W. Westbrook and M. M. Mastic, "The Cognitive Vocational Maturity Test," *Measuring Vocational Maturity for Counseling and Evaluation*.
88. B. W. Westbrook, J. W. Parry-Hill, Jr., and R. W. Woodbury, "The Development of a Measure of Vocational Maturity," *Educational and Psychological Measurement* 31(1971):541–543.

89. D. J. Forrest and A. S. Thompson, "The Career Development Inventory," *Measuring Vocational Maturity for Counseling and Evaluation.*

90. D. E. Super and D. J. Forrest, *Career Development Inventory, Form 1: Preliminary Manual for Research and Field Trial* (New York: Teachers College, Columbia University, 1973).

91. D. E. Super and R. Zelkowitz, "Vocational Maturity in the Thirties" (Paper delivered at the American Psychological Association Convention, Montreal, 1972).

SUGGESTED READING

Crites, J. O. *Vocational Psychology.* New York: McGraw-Hill, 1969. A comprehensive (704 pages) and research- and theory-oriented text on vocational behavior. Major topics include the foundations of vocational psychology, theories of vocational choice, the development of vocational choices, vocational adjustment, vocational success and satisfaction, and research and theory construction.

Holland, J. L. *Making Vocational Choices: A Theory of Careers.* New York: Prentice Hall, 1973.

Osipow, S. H. *Theories of Career Development.* New York: Appleton-Century-Crofts, 1973. Description, evaluation, and comparison of current theories of occupational choice and vocational development.

Super, D. E. Career development. In Davitz, J. R. and Ball, S., eds. *Psychology of the Educational Process.* New York: McGraw-Hill, 1970.

Super, D. E. *Psychology of Careers.* New York: Harper, 1957. A developmental approach to the study of careers. Major topics include the nature of work, the course and cycle of the working life, the dynamics of vocational development, and implications and applications.

Super, D. E. and Bohn, M. J., Jr. *Occupational Psychology.* Monterey, California: Brooks-Cole, 1970. A brief (209 pages), clear, and readable overview of major concerns in the field of vocational psychology. Topics include individual differences and their assessment, psychological bases of the division of labor, career development, and applications.

Super, D. E., Starishevsky, R., Matlin, N. and Jordaan, J. P. *Career Development: Self-concept Theory.* Contents include self-concepts in vocational development, making self-concept theory operational, a model for the translation of self-concepts into vocational terms, exploratory behavior, and vocational development in adolescence and early adulthood.

Super, D. E., ed. *Measuring Vocational Maturity For Counseling and Evaluation.* Washington, D.C.: National Vocational Guidance Association, in press. Topics include the nature and importance of vocational maturity, problems of measurement, tests and inventories of vocational maturity and their use in counseling and in planning and evaluating career-oriented programs and courses.

Tiedeman, D. V. and O'Hara, R. P. *Career development: Choice and adjustment.* New York: College Entrance Examination Board, 1963. Topics include a "language" for the analysis of career development, the data of career development, a framework for the study of career development and the mechanisms of career development.

Whiteley, J. M. and Resnikoff, A., eds. *Perspectives on Vocational Development.* Washington: APGA, 1972. Several well-known theorists and researchers, including Tiedeman, Roe, Super, and Holland reflect on the present state of vocational-development theory, practical implications, and future directions and prospects.

Zytowski, D. G., ed. *Vocational behavior: Readings in Theory and Research.* New York: Holt, Rinehart, and Winston, 1968. A compendium of articles and studies on the meaning of work, the nature of occupations, job satisfaction, and the determinants of occupational choice and vocational development.

The following are short monographs (less than 100 pages) in Houghton Mifflin's Guidance Monograph Series: *Career Information and Development.*

Brown, D. Students' Vocational Choices: A Review and Critique. Boston: Houghton Mifflin, 1970.

Herr, E. L. Decision-making and Vocational Development. Boston: Houghton Mifflin, 1970.

Zaccaria, J. Theories of Occupational Choice and Vocational Development. Boston: Houghton Mifflin, 1970.

Zytowski, D. G. Influence of Psychological Factors on Vocational Development. Boston: Houghton Mifflin, 1970.

12 Career Development Processes: A Model of Vocational Maturity

John O. Crites
University of Maryland

Much as the child builds models of the adult world to reduce its infinite complexity to comprehensible proportions, so the vocational psychologist resorts to metaphor and simile to understand the mysteries of career development processes. He constructs an *as if* world of abstraction designed to bring within the reach of his mental grasp the intricate, interacting, ever-changing elements of vocational maturation. Otherwise helpless to conceptually transcend the sheer scope of such phenomena, he subsumes them—literally "gets above the data"—by viewing them from the vantage point of a "model." Far from being just "child's play," model building in vocational psychology has the potential not only for organizing and explicating what is known about career development processes but also for suggesting new lines of inquiry and, ultimately, novel modes of practice. How this enterprise is pursued, however, and how it can be utilized in vocational psychology have not been explicitly articulated.

It is therefore the purpose of this chapter to discuss how a model of vocational maturity can be formulated to describe and explain career development processes as they unfold during the years of late childhood, adolescence, and early adulthood. The discussion has been organized into the following topics: 1) Model Building in Vocational Psychology; 2) Constructing a Model of Vocational Maturity; 3) Testing the Model of Vocational Maturity; 4) Research on the Model of Vocational Maturity; and 5) Implications of the Model of Vocational Maturity.

MODEL BUILDING IN VOCATIONAL PSYCHOLOGY

The word *model* has been given several different meanings in philosophy of science, ranging from its use as a synonym for theory to its use as a collective referent for tentative, unconfirmed hypotheses.[1] Different kinds and levels of models have also been delineated: "theoretical" models, "analogue" models, and "metaphysical" models.[2] In addition, "mathematical" models, in which precise quantitative relationships among nonempirical terms are specified, have been increasingly emphasized in psychology, particularly in the explanation of learning phenomena (e.g., Estes[3]; Rush and Estes[4]). In general, however, when reference is made to a *model* it is usually understood to mean either one of two things: 1) a smaller than full-scale reproduction of some physical object, e.g., a "model" airplane; or 2) a simulation of extant concepts (or terms) and their interrelationships as applied to different subject matter, e.g., society as an organism.[5] It is in the latter sense that theorists and researchers in the behavioral sciences typically employ the term model. They further distinguish a model from a theory, which has been defined in various ways but which is typically thought of as "a deductively connected set of generalizations."[6] The relationship between *model* and *theory* is usually asymmetrical, with one theory being adopted as the model for another.[7] However, depending upon the level of generality at which a model is defined, the converse may obtain; for example, Reese and Overton state that "Any theory presupposes a more general model according to which the theoretical concepts are formulated."[8] Here they have reference to two widely used "world views" or metaphysical models which serve as conceptual frames of reference in psychology: the *mechanistic,* which takes the machine as its analogue, and the *organismic,* which adopts the organism as its prototype.

Given these definitions of model and theory, it is apparent from a review of conceptualization in vocational psychology[9] that much greater attention has been given to theory construction than to model building. What might even broadly be construed as models are not only few in number but informal and intuitive in analogy. Thus, Super has proposed that vocational development is "one aspect of individual development" and has introduced the concept of "vocational maturity," defined in much the same way as mental maturity, to denote "the place reached on the continuum of vocational development from exploration to decline."[10] He has observed that:

> The *vocational maturity quotient* may thus be conceived of as the ratio of vocational maturity to chronological age. It would indicate whether or not the vocational development of an individual is appropriate for his age, and how far below or beyond his chronological age his vocational development is. Such a VMQ will probably never be developed, but the concept is helpful in differentiating two important aspects of the vocational maturity concept, one the status of the individual on a behavioral scale of development, the other his behavior viewed in relation to age.[11]

Similarly, Beilin[12] has extrapolated principles from general developmental psychology and has interpreted them in terms of vocational developmental processes and outcomes. Most of these principles were drawn from Jersild[13] and included such concepts as: developmental preeminence, levels of maturity, developmental pace, development from dependence to independence, differentiation and integration, and the patterning of development. Beilin did not formally incorporate these generalizations into a model of vocational development, although he did note that they are interactive and interdependent.

Still another precursor to systematic model building in vocational psychology, but one which again did not follow generally accepted canons of logic for this type of conceptualization, was the "framework for research" on vocational development formulated by Super, Crites, Hummel, Moser, Overstreet, and Warnath.[14] Following Super,[15] this monograph took "as its principal analogue the process of psychological development" and explicated five dimensions in the process of vocational decision making: 1) orientation to vocational choice, 2) information and planning about preferred occupations, 3) consistency of vocational preferences, 4) crystallization of traits, and 5) wisdom of vocational preferences. This informal "model of vocational maturity" was compared with, although not inferred from, Baldwin's "model of mature behavior." The Baldwin model was based upon the concepts of cognition, goal selection, and goal-directed behavior and upon the general proposition that "The independence of needs and cognition, of goals and the means to goals, of motive and the attempt to satisfy a motive—all constitute evidence for differentiation, and this differentiation is required for behavior to be mature."[16] Translated into vocational terms, Baldwin's model roughly corresponded to the following dimensions of vocational maturity: *cognition*—orientation to vocational choice and information and planning about preferred occupations; *goal selection*—consistency of vocational preferences and crystallization of traits; and, *goal-directed behavior*—wisdom of vocational preferences. Super et al. concluded from this comparison that:

> It seems that our model of vocationally mature behavior is essentially the same as Baldwin's model of mature behavior, with the possible important exception that Baldwin is concerned with the quality of the behavior (e.g., the accuracy of information), whereas our concern is primarily with the occurrence of relevant behavior (e.g., having or seeking information).[17]

In their "framework for research" on vocational development, Super et al. also further specified the operational meaning of Super's earlier definition of the "vocational maturity quotient," differentiating between the changes in vocational behavior which occur from one life stage to another (VMQ I) and the kinds of vocational behavior typical of persons at different age levels within a life stage (VMQ II). Crites[18] subsequently analyzed these separate, and sometimes contradictory, definitions of vocational maturity and proposed instead a "model for the measurement of vocational maturity" based upon a synthesis of the age-scale and point-scale approaches to the assessment of intelligence.

From the age-scale measurement model, as exemplified by the Stanford-Binet, it was proposed that any measure of vocational behavior which was hypothesized as maturing with time (e.g., consistency of wisdom of vocational preferences) should be comprised only of items that had systematic, empirically demonstrated relationships to time. The underlying assumption was that a necessary (although not sufficient) condition for the measurement of a *developmental* variable is that indices of it be either linear or monotonic functions of some unit of time, such as chronological age or school grade. From the point-scale test model (e.g., the WAIS) the practice of constructing norms for each age (or grade) group, rather than using quotients based upon ratios, was suggested to preclude the problems inherent in age-scales of the lack of comparability of items and score dispersions at different levels of maturity. From a combination of the best features of these two assessment methodologies, it was possible to formulate a "model for the measurement of vocational maturity" in which two independent variables could be defined: 1) *degree* of vocational development—"the maturity of an individual's vocational behavior as indicated by the similarity between his behavior and that of the oldest individuals in his vocational life stage"; and 2) *rate* of vocational development—"the maturity of an individual's vocational behavior in comparison with that of his own age [or grade] group."[19]

Elements of model building are implicit in each of these attempts to define and measure vocational maturity, but none of them actually constitutes an explicit model of vocational maturity, patterned after other conceptualizations of behavior and development. Missing from these "provisional tries" at model building is an awareness of and adherence to the rules of correspondence and analogy which are prescribed by philosophers of science and which make possible the self-conscious and rigorous testing of a model once it is constructed. Such formal model building has high priority in the field of vocational psychology, where theory construction has far outstripped empirical research and the necessity for longitudinal data on vocational development has accentuated and widened the gap between explanation and knowledge.[20] Commenting upon the promise of systematically (formally) conceived models, Borow has enumerated two principal purposes they serve:

> First, by offering broadly integrative models, they bring the study of youth in vocational development into the mainstream of behavioral science and allow readier access to the insights and *modus operandi* of related disciplines . . . . Secondly, the newer and broader conceptual systems have suggested a wide-ranging assortment of promising research issues, a condition that has unmistakably revitalized psychological research on occupational behavior.[21]

CONSTRUCTING A MODEL OF VOCATIONAL MATURITY

There are several principles that philosophers of science have specified as essential in constructing a model. Foremost among these is the *isomorphism* which must be established between the model and what has been called the "explicandum," the facts or observations and relationships which have to be explained.[22] Although a one-to-one correspondence might be desirable, it is not necessary. As Hesse[23] has noted, some aspects of the model may be relevant to the explicandum, others contradictory, and a few irrelevant. Similarly, Brodbeck points out that: "An area, either part or all of it, can be a fruitful model for another only if corresponding concepts can be found and if at least some of the laws connecting the concepts of the model also can be shown to connect their corresponding concepts."[24] In other words, to construct a model of vocational maturity according to these principles it must be shown that the dimensions of vocational development and the interrelationships among them correspond, at least generally, to some conceptual schemes which might reasonably serve as a prototype. To explicate this correspondence the logic of analogy is used, the formal expression of which is A:B as C:D.[25] It should be noted, however, as Reese and Overton do, that this type of reasoning is metaphorical: "It is not being asserted that the real world *is* thus and so, only that the real world behaves *as if* it were thus and so" [italics in original].[26] There remains the necessity, therefore, to test the model, once it has been formulated, against empirical truth criteria, not to "prove" or "disprove" it but to determine the extent to which it *fits* reality. The more nearly it corresponds to the data, the more useful it is considered to be for conceptualizing and understanding them.

There are any number of models in the natural and behavioral sciences which might be taken as conceptual schemata for vocational maturity, but those which are dimensional in composition and precept would appear to be most applicable. Among these the factorial models seem to have the greatest descriptive usefulness and potential subsumptive value for conceptualizing vocational maturity.[27] The most prominent of the factorial models are the *spherical* and *hierarchical*, the former representing behavior as the intersect of a given set of variables in *n*-dimensional space and the latter as levels of increasing generality ranging from specific variables to higher-order factors. Experience with the application of these models, particularly with respect to intellectual development, would clearly indicate the advantages of the hierarchical model as a prototype for vocational maturity.

Figure 12.1 depicts this model as it has been used to represent the structure of intelligence.[28] The lowest level is that of the specific factors being measured, i.e., tests of abilities such as verbal reasoning and spatial perception. The intermediate level represents the interrelationships among the tests; it constitutes the group factors in the model. The highest level is the supraordinate factor g, which symbolizes the common variance among the group factors. Not only is such a model more easily comprehended than the spherical, but it appears to fit behavioral data more accurately. Intellectual capacities, like vocational behaviors, are interrelated, not independent,[29] and the hierarchical model allows for such relatedness by solving for oblique factors from data matrices rather than forcing orthogonality upon them. The accumulated data on the structure and dimensions of vocational motivation, success, and satisfaction also support the greater psychological cogency and meaningfulness of the hierarchical model.[30]

The hierarchical model provides a graphic representation of what the formal (i.e., functional) relationships among a set of variables might be, but it does not define or enumerate what the variables are. This facet of the model is a substantive one, extrapolated from the subject matter of a field—in this instance vocational psychology and, more specifically, the so-called "dimensions" of vocational maturity. Some of these, as delineated by Super and Super et al.,[31] have been discussed previously, and, on the basis of empirical findings, they appear to be consistent with a hierarchical model of vocational maturity. Super and Overstreet conducted a factor analysis of eighteen different indices of these dimensions and concluded that vocational maturity in early adolescence (ninth grade) consists of "one general factor, Planning Orientation, and three group factors [Independence of Work Experience, Short-range Planning, Intermediate Planning, and Long-term Planning]."[32] Similarly, Gribbons and Lohnes[33] have proposed eight dimensions of what they call "Readiness for Vocational Planning" but which otherwise might be subsumed by the concept of vocational maturity: 1) Factors in Curriculum Choice, 2) Factors in Occupational Choice, 3) Verbalized Strengths and Weaknesses, 4) Accuracy of Self-appraisal, 5) Evidence for Self-rating, 6) Interests, 7) Values, and 8) Independence of Choice. From principal components analyses of these dimensions, which were scored from semistructured interview protocols, they found, in general, that for both eighth- and tenth-grade data most of the variables loaded on the first com-

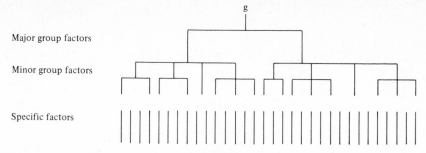

Fig. 12.1 A Hierarchical Model of Intelligence

ponent with the others clustering into groups on subsequent components, thus again suggesting a hierarchical model of vocational maturity.

To synthesize these findings on the factorial composition of vocational maturity and to cast them in terms of the hierarchical model, Crites[34] has proposed the conceptual schema shown in Figure 12.2. The first level of the model has been termed "degree of vocational development," as defined above,[35] and it is comparable to a general or "second-order" factor. As a suprafactor which denotes the individual's overall progress toward vocational maturity within a given period, "degree of vocational development" is hypothesized as being moderately positively related to each of the intermediate-level group or "common" factors. The expectation is that each of these dimensions is, in turn, correlated in the .30s or .40s with the others. For example, it seems reasonable to expect that relatively mature vocational choice attitudes may mediate not only consistent and wise (realistic) vocational choices but also the vocational choice competencies which facilitate mature decision making. Finally, the dimensions are comprised of various specific variables which reflect the same pattern of interrelationships: moderate associations between groups and fairly high ones within groups. These variables are those which have been central in contemporary theories of vocational development and which are presumably the vocational behaviors most subject to maturational processes during adolescence. The theoretical prediction is that they best represent career decision-making processes in this period. Thus, this "model of vocational maturity" is a hierarchical one in which relatively high within-group and moderate between-group positive correlations are predicted. An alternative model, such as that used by Thurstone[36] to define primary mental abilities, would postulate orthogonal group factors with no supraordinate factor interrelating them. Given statistical procedures which allow solutions for both models, it is a matter of empirical testing to determine which fits the data better.

In addition to the hypothesis that the hierarchical model of vocational maturity best describes and corresponds to the interrelationships of the variables and factors in Figure 12.2, there is a second hypothesis which states that the *model is more highly differentiated in late than early adolescence.* More specifically, this means that the loadings of the group factors and variables on "degree of vocational development" will decrease as vocational

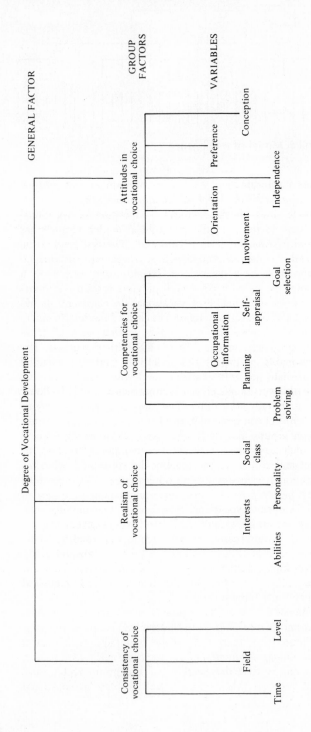

Fig. 12.2 A Model of Vocational Maturity in Adolescence

maturation occurs during the adolescent years (from approximately age eleven or grade five to age eighteen or grade twelve). Extrapolating from Baldwin,[37] Super and Overstreet state the rationale for this hypothesis as follows:

> Through growth and learning, the behavioral repertoire [dimensions of vocational maturity] increases and changes; behavior becomes more complex and also more *differentiated,* and the developing individual becomes more capable of responding to environmental demands in an efficient and independent manner.[38]

According to Super and Overstreet, three principles underlie this process: "1) development proceeds from random, undifferentiated activity to goal-directed, specific activity, 2) development is in the direction of increasing awareness and orientation to reality, and 3) development is from dependence to increasing independence."[39] The prediction that vocationally mature behavior becomes more differentiated over time is analogous to Garrett's "differentiation" hypothesis concerning the growth of intelligence, which, he maintained, "changes in its organization [factorial structure] as age increases from a fairly unified and general ability to a loosely organized group of abilities or factors."[40] The rationale for this expected developmental trend in vocational maturation is that the uniform effects of childhood experience give way to the varied and complex influences of adolescence, the consequence being the increasing specificity of career decision-making processes.

TESTING THE MODEL OF VOCATIONAL MATURITY

Given the model shown in Figure 12.2, the steps required to test it are much like those involved in any empirical investigation. To illustrate this process, procedures and results, primarily from the author's[41] Vocational Development Project but also from studies by other investigators, will be used. First, measurement of the variables in the model of vocational maturity is discussed. How can useful operational definitions be given to the concepts on the "specific factors" level? Second, once appropriate measures have been devised, how can they best be administered to collect the data needed to test the model? At issue here are such considerations as cross-sectional versus longitudinal designs and the effects of repeated measurements. And, third, depending upon the design which is selected, there are decisions which must be made with respect to statistical analyses. Which are the pertinent techniques, and can their assumptions be met? These and related methodological questions are discussed in the following sections.

Measurement of Variables

The variables in Figure 12.2 have been revised slightly from an earlier version of the model[42] in order to make them more consistent logically or to fit them more precisely to research findings. More specifically, Consistency of Vocational Choice by "family" of occupations has been eliminated, and "Activities" as a criterion of "Realism" (formerly "Wisdom") of Vocational Choice has been supplanted by "Personality." In the Vocational Choice

Competencies group "Self-knowledge" has been renamed "Self-appraisal" to more accurately reflect the evaluative nature of the process involved.

Consistency of Vocational Choice. To operationally define this variable, vocational choices must be elicited on two or more occasions and then compared within some system of classification for similarities and differences. A review of the various procedures which have been used to measure choice indicates that the following question, or a close approximation of it, is not only more reliable but also more valid than other methods: "What occupation do you plan to enter? Be as specific as possible. If you have no occupational choice, then put 'Undecided.' "[43] This question is printed on the answer sheet of the Vocational Development Inventory (VDI), which is also used to assess vocational choice attitudes and competencies (see below). Once choices have been declared, they can be classified by field and level in a schema such as that proposed by Roe.[44] Subsequently, they can be compared from year to year, assigning numerical values to represent the degree of consistency in choices over the time span of the study. For example, using this methodology, Hollender[45] determined the choice consistency of 1,648 students in grades six through twelve on test and retest (with a one-year interval) by classifying their choices as consistent by field and level, consistent by field or level, and inconsistent by field and level. The expectation is that, if consistency of vocational choice is a dimension of vocational maturity, then the developmental trend across age and/or grade should be from lesser to greater consistency.

Realism of Vocational Choice. A variety of procedures have been utilized to define choice realism—some applicable only to groups and others to individuals, some derived from judges' ratings, and others based upon discrepancy scores—but none has been comprehensive or methodologically sound enough to measure this variable as conceptualized in the model of vocational maturity.[46] Whether such an operational definition can be achieved remains to be determined, but Crites[47] has proposed a diagnostic system for problems in vocational choice, including realism (or unrealism), which may be a close approximation. Without analyzing the system *in toto*, we can note the general principle upon which it is based: to classify vocational choices according to the fields and levels in Roe's two-dimensional matrix and then to compare them with the abilities and interests requisite for success and satisfaction (i.e., future vocational adjustment) in the chosen occupation. If the choice agrees with both field (interests) *and* level (ability), it is realistic; if it agrees with only field *or* level, it is less realistic; and, if it agrees with *neither* field *nor* level, it is unrealistic. As with consistency of vocational choice, the occupation a student intends to enter can be elicited by the open-ended "choice question" on the VDI answer sheet. Interests can be assessed by a standard inventory, such as the *Strong Vocational Interest Blank* or *Kuder Preference Record* (Form C), and abilities can be measured by a widely used test of scholastic aptitude/achievement, such as the *Iowa Tests of Educational Development*, the scores of which would be available as part of the student's cumulative record. Preliminary evidence that realism of vocational choice increases with age/grade has been reported by Hollender,[48] though he defined realism only by agreement of choice with level of ability and his data were cross-sectional.

Vocational Choice Competencies. One part of the VDI consists of five tests designed to measure the variables in this construct. Test I is "Problems," intended to assess the ability to resolve conflicts among the factors usually involved in vocational decision making. Test II is "Planning," in which the task is to evaluate logical and temporal inconsistencies in the steps leading to various vocational goals. Test III is "Occupational Information," which includes items on job duties and tasks, trends in occupations, and future employment opportunities. Test IV is "Self Appraisal," which involves making judgments of a hypothetical person's assets and liabilities for vocational success and satisfaction. Test V is "Goal Selection," which requires the examinee to choose the "best" (most realistic) occupation for a fictitious individual who is described in terms of his aptitudes, interests, and personality characteristics. The functions or processes which are supposedly involved in taking the competence tests are thus largely what might be designated as comprehension and problem-solving abilities as they pertain to the vocational choice process. Although the psychometric characteristics of this test battery have not as yet been established, it was administered in "open-ended" form to small samples of seventh through twelfth graders in the spring of 1968 in order to gather additional content for item foils, and it will be initially standardized for grades five through twelve with multiple-choice response formats in the near future.

Vocational Choice Attitudes. The second part of the VDI, the Attitude Scale (VDI-Att), was constructed to elicit the conceptual or dispositional response tendencies in vocational maturity which are nonintellective in nature, but which may mediate both choice consistency and realism as well as choice competencies. Approximately two hundred studies of the VDI-Att have been completed,[49] and its psychometric parameters are consequently fairly well-known. However, further longitudinal research is needed on the factorial structure of the scale and the developmental functions, relating its items and total VM score to grade as an index of time. For the factor analysis, the hypothesis is that five oblique group factors will be extracted, corresponding to the following attitude clusters: 1) Involvement in the Choice Process, 2) Orientation Toward Work, 3) Independence in Decision Making, 4) Preference for Choice Factors, and 5) Conceptions of the Choice Process. For the longitudinal study, which spans grades seven through twelve, the expectation is that the developmental functions for the VDI-Att items will be either increasing or decreasing monotonic curves, depending upon whether the stated attitudes are mature or immature, respectively. Data for these investigations have already been collected and are currently being collated for the statistical analyses.

Vocational Maturation. This variable has been deduced from general developmental psychology,[50] where it has been recognized as necessary to an "integrated" theory of development, but its meaning has sometimes been ambiguous. Baldwin notes that "the most important evidence for the maturational process is the appearance of clear chronological age differences. At the same time, however, chronological age differences can stem from a variety of causes."[51] Moreover, it has become increasingly clear that chronological age is *not* an explanatory variable: "though a powerful index, [it] appears to be a rather dull variable (e.g., McCandless and Spiker, 1956) for developmental theorizing."[52] Even if age is viewed simply as "a dimension along which change is to be studied,"[53] it is still not an independent variable and must ultimately be replaced in developmental functions with other substantive variables. It would seem desirable, therefore, to use an index of time which is not subject to these limitations; such a variable, for a school-age population, is grade. Not only would it be theoretically expected that the process of vocational maturation would proceed apace with advancement from one grade level to another due to differential occupational orientation experiences, but there is at least some empirical evidence from the VDI-Att that grade differentiates stages in vocational maturity better than chronological age during the adolescent years.[54] For these reasons, then, grade has been used in the Vocational Development Project to define vocational maturation along the time continuum.

Data Collection

How data are collected for studies of career developmental processes have far-reaching ramifications for the types of analyses which can be made and, ultimately, for the inferences which can be legitimately drawn from the findings. A number of rather complex issues have been identified recently in data collection for developmental investigations,[55] and, although they have not all been satisfactorily resolved, some progress has been made in at least specifying their parameters.

Design. The traditional approach to the collection of developmental data has been the "one-sample" longitudinal design (e.g., Jones[56]; Super et al.[57]), in which repeated measurements are obtained on the same subjects over a given time period. However, it has become increasingly apparent that there are several problems inherent in this methodology, despite the recognition that "Longitudinal analysis is the method par excellence of the developmental psychologist, and, in many cases, the only one that will permit the requisite detailed analysis of developmental functions."[58] One problem is the sheer amount of time required to collect data over any extended period or stage of development. Another problem is the possible reactive effect of repeated measurements, which may modify "the phenomenon under study, which changes the very thing that one is trying to measure."[59] Still another problem is the bias introduced in the sample as subjects are lost on follow-up. Finally, and probably most important, changes in the behavior of the longitudinal sample from one point in time to another are inextricably confounded with whatever environmental (external) changes are taking place concurrently. In other words, it cannot be determined what proportion of the behavioral change is attributable to developmental processes and what to other, extraneous variables.[60] In addition, it might be noted that it is also indeterminate whether the instruments used to assess behavioral change in the "one-sample" longitudinal design actually measure developmental functions until all of the data have been collected. Thus, Gribbons and Lohnes[61] gathered data on Readiness for Vocational Planning at the eighth-, tenth-, and twelfth-grade levels on the same subjects, only to find such inconsistencies in their analyses as correlations between the eight–twelve and ten–twelve scores but not between the eight–ten scores.

The most widely used alternative to the "one-sample" longitudinal design has been the cross-sectional collection of data, in which subjects from different "cohorts," or age/grade groupings, are measured at the same point in time. The great advantage of this approach, of course, is that there are no time lags in the data collection. Moreover, the problems of losing subjects and repeated measurements are obviated, and developmental functions for cohort differences on assessment devices can be derived. The major disadvantage of cross-sectional sampling, however, is that differences among cohorts, as well as environmental conditions, are confounded with differences in the behaviors of interest. The consequence is that definitive conclusions about behavioral changes *per se* cannot be drawn. O'Hara and Tiedeman[62] studied the development of the vocational self-concept, for example, across grades nine through twelve, but, because their data were cross-sectional, they had to qualify their conclusions by such statements as "Setting consideration of sampling variability aside" and "If sampling variations are completely ignored." In short, they were unable to make any unequivocal inferences from their findings concerning developmental phenomena. Cross-sectional data collection precludes some problems, then, but creates others of equal, if not greater, methodological import.

In an effort to conceive a general model for developmental research which would eliminate the shortcomings of the longitudinal and cross-sectional designs, Schaie[63] proposed that there are three parameters which must be taken into consideration in any time-related investigation: age differences, age changes, and cultural changes. He then formulated three presumably independent designs based upon the possible pairwise combinations of these parameters, as shown in Table 12.1. In a critique of this schema, Baltes[64] has pointed out that the age (or grade) of a sample can be directly derived from data on cohorts and times of measurement, thus reducing the number of parameters from three to two. Conceding this criticism, Schaie has nevertheless argued that two parameters are not sufficient:

> . . . one must collect data in such a way that they can be analyzed via two of the three two-factorial sequential strategies deducible from the three-way model [see Table 12.1]. Data analysis limited to any one of the two-way models suffers from the inexorable unidirectional nature of time which must result in the spurious confounding of the third parameter which cannot be directly estimated by a single two-way design.[65]

He then proceeds to derive equations which will provide estimates of two parameters while confounding the third. He points out, however, that there is only one case in which cross-sectional and longitudinal data can be compared: "This is a composite longitudinal gradient which is composed of segments depicting longitudinal change from time k to time l. Each segment in such a gradient is drawn from two observations of the same cohort, but

Table 12.1 Schema for Research Designs Corresponding to Schaie's[66] Trifactorial Model of Developmental Studies[a, b]

Cohort (year of birth)	Time of Measurement														
	'56	'57	'58	'59	'60	'61	'62	'63	'64	'65	'66	'67	'68	'69	'70
1946						15									
1947						14	15								
1948						13	14	15							
1949						12	13	14	15						
1950	6	7	8	9	10	11	12	13	14	15					
1951		6	7	8	9	10	11	12	13	14	15				
1952			6	7	8	9	10	11	12	13	14	15			
1953				6	7	8	9	10	11	12	13	14	15		
1954					6	7	8	9	10	11	12	13	14	15	
1955						6	7	8	9	10	11	12	13	14	15
1956							6	7	8	9					
1957								6	7	8					
1958									6	7					
1959										6					

[a]Entries represent ages corresponding to each combination of cohort and time of measurement.
[b]In this table, *cohort-sequential* design is represented by the cells included within the horizontal parallelogram; *time-sequential* design is represented by the cells included within the vertical parallelogram; *cross-sequential* design is represented by the cells included within the square. The design used in the Vocational Development Project is represented by the triangle.

every successive segment is based on a different cohort."[67] This design is the cross-sequential one shown in Table 12.1. It has been used in the Vocational Development Project, with certain necessary emendations to allow for the loss of one cohort at each successive time of measurement due to graduation from high school, as indicated by the triangle in Table 12.1. It makes provision not only for cross-sectional and longitudinal data but also for comparisons between them.

Sampling Plan. To implement the modified cross-sequential design for data collection outlined in Table 12.1, subjects have been tested in the Vocational Development Project according to the sampling plan depicted in Figure 12.3. The initial administration of the VDI-Att was to the *cross-sectional samples* in grades five through twelve. Approximately 5,000 male and female students participated in this testing. The *core samples* were then followed up each successive year until they graduated from high school. Thus, the original fifth graders were tested eight times, the sixth graders seven times, and so forth. The test administrations were on or about May 1, so that students could be considered as having completed the grade they were in at the time. Included in the testings along with the core samples were all students who had transferred into the school system during the current year and who therefore had not previously taken the VDI-Att. These so-called *non-core* subjects provide data for checking the effects of two uncontrolled variables in the study of the core samples: first, there is the possibility that repeated testings of the core samples with the VDI-Att has enhanced their vocational

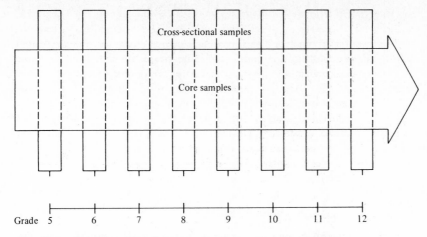

Fig. 12.3 Sampling Plan for Vocational Development Project

maturity over and above what might be attributable to developmental processes.[68] In other words, simply taking the test time and again may significantly contribute to variance in scores from one occasion to another independently of other factors. To determine whether such an effect is present, the core and non-core score means can be compared, and, if they are not reliably different, it can be concluded that the retestings have not introduced a systematic bias into the data. Likewise, the same comparison can be used to establish the effects of attrition in the core sample. Again, if the latter can be assumed to have been drawn from the same population as the non-core samples, it follows that the loss of core subjects is not statistically distorting the data.

Statistical Analyses

In deriving equations to estimate two of the three parameters in his general model for developmental research—*viz.*, age differences, age changes, and cultural changes—Schaie[69] confounded the third parameter. It need not be so treated, however, since the data from a composite cross-sectional/longitudinal design (Table 1) can be analyzed by a standard Lindquist[70] Type I analysis of variance. The main effect of the "between-subjects" factor (cohort) tests for age (or grade) differences; the main effect of the "within-subjects" factor (time of measurement) tests for age (or grade) changes; and the interaction effect tests for cultural changes. If the latter is significant, it indicates that cohorts have not uniformly changed over time, although some of them have changed as a function of intervening extraneous circumstances. The Type I statistical analysis is the appropriate one, then, for modification of Schaie's "cross-sequential" design, which is being used in the Vocational Development Project.

For testing the hierarchical structure of the model of vocational maturity, factorial procedures which provide for both oblique and orthogonal solutions should be followed to allow for the possibility that one may fit the data better than the other.[71] The methodology selected for this purpose in the Vocational Development Project is one used previously by Crites, Bechtoldt, Goodstein, and Heilbrun.[72] It involves the following steps: 1) tests of independence, using the determinants of the population estimates of the variance-covariance and correlational matrices;[73] 2) computation of factors for the various grade levels, applying the complete centroid method;[74] 3) tests for number of significant factors based upon Lawley's maximum-likelihood procedure;[75] and, 4) analytical and graphical rotation of the factors to an oblique (or orthogonal) simple structure.[76] Developmental functions (linear, monotonic, etc.) can then be fitted to whatever the forms of the obtained curves are across the span of age or grade levels used in factor analyzing the model of vocational maturity.

RESEARCH ON THE MODEL OF VOCATIONAL MATURITY

Although studies of various facets of the model of vocational maturity are currently being conducted, many of them having been under way for some time, empirical findings are still scant. There are two principal reasons for this lag between conceptualization of the model, which dates back to Super's 1955 paper on the dimensions of vocational maturity, and research on it. First, most of the variables in the model of vocational maturity are new ones —they had not been previously defined and measured. Consequently, much effort has been expended upon constructing and refining appropriate instruments (tests, inventories, scales, indices, etc.) for giving operational meaning to the concepts (variables) specified in the model. Second, any investigation of a developmental phenomenon, whether vocational, intellectual, social, or physical, takes time—not only to collect the pertinent data but also to collate and analyze them. Thus, a tolerance for delay in obtaining and reporting data on career development processes must be nurtured. Findings are often fragmentary, incomplete, and highly qualified; but, despite their tentative nature, they nevertheless indicate what progress is being made toward filling in the lacunae of the model of vocational maturity. Thus, the results which are reviewed in this section should be considered as preliminary, not definitive. They come from three on-going programs of research on vocational maturity: the Career Pattern Study (CPS), the Vocational Development Project (VDP), and the studies of the Center for Occupational Education.

Career Pattern Study

As mentioned previously, Super and Overstreet have reported a factor analysis of 27 indices of vocational maturity derived from psychometric and interview data on 140 ninth-grade boys in CPS. Indices were constructed to quantify the several dimensions of vocational maturity originally delineated by Super in 1955, and they included such variables as the following: concern with choice; use of resources in orientation; specificity of information; specificity of planning; extent of planning activity; consistency of vocational preferences within fields, levels, and families; degree of patterning of measured interests; interest maturity; liking for work; degree of patterning of work values; orientation toward rewards of work; acceptance of responsibility for choice and planning; independence of work experience; agreement between ability and preference; agreement between measured interests and preferences; agreement between measured interests and fantasy preference; agreement between occupational level of measured interests and level of preference; and socioeconomic accessibility of preferences. Data on the intercorrelations of these and related indices of vocational maturity were factor analyzed, using the principal axes method. Five factors were extracted and rotated to simple structure by the quartimax procedure. This solution yielded essentially the same results as that with four factors, but the fifth factor appeared to be psychologically interpretable and therefore was included in the analysis.

The five factors, however, accounted for only 38 percent of the total variance, a disappointing finding which was difficult to explain. The large percentage of remaining variance may have been due to errors of measurement (unreliability) and specific factors in the indices of vocational maturity, despite efforts made beforehand to reduce these sources of variance to a minimum. Whatever the explanation, there were nevertheless five factors which could be interpreted:[77]

Factor I   Planning Orientation—acceptance of responsibility for choice and planning, specificity of information, and extent of planning activity.

Factor II   Independence of Work Experience—defined by the index of the same name.

Factor III   Long View Ahead—awareness of need for ultimate choices, specificity of information and planning.

Factor IV   Short View Ahead—specificity of high school plans.

Factor V   Intermediate View Ahead—awareness of factors in choice.

Although a "second-order" factor analysis was not conducted, it was apparent from the factor loadings that, with the exception of Independence of Work Experience, the other four factors were interrelated. Super and Overstreet interpreted this communality as follows: "Vocational maturity in the ninth grade thus appears to consist of one general factor, Planning Orientation, and three group factors which contribute differently to the four indices."[78] In other words, their results seem to support a hierarchical model of vocational maturity in early adolescence.

Much the same conclusion, although more tentatively, can be drawn from the work of Gribbons and Lohnes on their Readiness for Vocational Planning (RVP) scales, which were patterned after the CPS indices of vocational maturity. The eight RVP scales were subjected to principal components analyses based upon longitudinal data from 110 male and female subjects tested in the eighth and tenth grades. For both grade levels the findings were complex: all scales except Accuracy of Self-appraisal had high loadings ($\geq .50$) on the first component, but some of them were positively and others negatively loaded on the second component. The latter was, therefore, bipolar in composition, the positive end being defined by Accuracy of Self-Appraisal and the negative by Independence of Choice and Values. From these findings Gribbons and Lohnes concluded that "the eight RVP scales exhibited enough mutual independence to guarantee the multidimensionality of the measurement space."[79] Again a "second-order" factor analysis was not performed, but the data might also be interpreted as indicating a general factor (possibly "degree of vocational development") running through the first component. If such was the case, it would suggest a hierarchical model of vocational maturity.

Vocational Development Project

The most relevant results from VDP on the model of vocational maturity are those from an item analysis of the VDI-Att. From data on 1,254 subjects (approximately equal numbers of males and females) in grades seven through eleven, biserial r's for all fifty items in the scale were calculated from a comparison of the upper- and lower-27 percent of the total score distribution, using Flanagan's[80] procedure and nomograph. Because these correlations are indices of the magnitude and direction of the relationship of each item to the total scale, they can be interpreted as estimates of the first factor loadings on the centroid of the inter-item matrix.[81] Not only the size of these biserial r's but also their sign confirmed the theoretical expectation that the VDI-Att is a factorially complex scale, as it was originally designed to be.[82] In the construction of the prestandardization pool of attitude items, an attempt was made to write items which would represent each of the clusters shown in Figure 12.2. For example, an item intended to measure Involvement in Choice Process is: "I often think about the job I want to enter." Similarly, illustrative of Orientation toward Work is the statement: "Work is dull and unpleasant." A factor analysis of the standardized scale must be conducted, however, and is currently in progress, to determine whether the *a priori* item clusters are supported by their factor loadings. A methodological problem which has delayed this study has been how to treat two-point (True-False) item data when there are extreme splits ($\geqq$ 80–20). A solution has now been found, based upon the use of sub-scale scores, and the preliminary findings appear to be consistent with the hierarchical model of vocational maturity.

Another approach to testing the model of vocational maturity, less desirable than factor analysis but more expeditious, is to simply correlate measures of one presumed group factor with another. This procedure has been followed in several studies, recently summarized by Crites:

> Using the Miller-Haller[83] Occupational Aspiration Scale as a measure of realism of aspiration, Bathory[84] correlated it with the Attitude Scale at the 9th (N = 79) and 12th (N = 58) grade levels. He obtained r's of .39 ($p < .01$) and .31 (ns), respectively, the latter failing to reach significance due to the small sample. In a comprehensive study of VM scores in relation to vocational choice consistency, decision, and realism, Hollender[85] found relationships among each of these "criterion" variables and maturity of vocational attitudes in a sample of 1,648 students in grades 6 through 12, stratified by quartiles on scholastic aptitude. The results of t-tests between high and low groups indicated that those students who were consistent in their choices from one year to the next, who had made choices, and who were realistic in their choices generally had significantly higher mean scores on the Attitude Scale regardless of aptitude level. Likewise, Carek[86] has reported a biserial r of .25 between VM scores and choice decision in a sample of 346 male col-

lege students, which was significant at the .01 level. Finally, some preliminary data have been gathered on the relationship of the Attitude Scale to other measures of vocational maturity. In a small sample ($N = 50$) of Negro ninth graders, Cooter[87] calculated an r of .38 ($p < .01$) between VM and Gribbons and Lohnes' RVP. Wilstach[88] was unable to find a significant correlation between the Attitude Scale and Super's IVM, however, the r being .001 in a group of 104 Mexican-American ninth grade males.[89]

These results, obtained by several different investigators, provide at least tentative support for empirical relationships between the Vocational Choice Attitude group factor and those of Consistency and Realism of Vocational Choice.

The relationship of the Vocational Choice Attitude dimension to Vocational Choice Competencies has not as yet been investigated in VDP, but there are some pertinent data from a recent study by CPS. Super[90] and his associates have constructed what they call the Career Development Inventory (CDI), which is intended to assess both the cognitive and attitudinal aspects of vocational maturity. The CDI is comprised of three scales: Planning Orientation (attitudinal); Resources for Exploration (attitudinal); and Information and Decision Making (cognitive). As part of the initial validation of the CDI, each of these scales was correlated with the VDI-Att in a sample of 110 tenth graders. Only the Information and Decision Making scale of the CDI was related to the VDI-Att ($r = .42$, $p < .01$). From this finding, plus the correlation of the VDI-Att with verbal aptitude (.37) and GPA (.42), Super et al. concluded that: "Crites' VDI-AS thus appears to be in fact, although not in theory, a largely cognitive scale."[91] Reasoning obversely, however, an equally likely inference from the same data is that the CDI Information and Decision Making scale seems to be a largely *attitudinal* scale. Actually, the most meaningful interpretation, pending further study of the instruments involved, is that the obtained relationship between the CDI cognitive and VDI attitudinal scales is what would be expected theoretically from the model of vocational maturity. The r between these two measures may be inflated somewhat due to their common variance on verbal aptitude, but otherwise, as indices of Vocational Choice Competencies and Vocational Choice Attitudes, respectively, they should bear a low to moderate positive relationship with each other.

Center for Occupational Education Studies

Under the direction of Westbrook,[92] a series of studies at North Carolina State University has focused explicitly upon testing the model of vocational maturity. The thrust of the research has been upon constructing a Cognitive Vocational Maturity Test (CVMT) to operationally define variables in the Vocational Choice Competencies group of the model. Items for the CVMT have been written for each of the following areas:

1. Fields of Work—knowledge of the occupations that are available in various fields of work.
2. Job Selection—the ability to choose the most realistic occupation for a hypothetical student who is described in terms of his abilities, interests, values, etc.

3. Work Conditions—knowledge of work schedules, income level, physical conditions, job locations, etc.
4. Education Required—knowledge of the amount of education generally required for a wide range of occupations.
5. Attributes Required—knowledge of the abilities, interests, and values generally required for various occupations.
6. Duties—knowledge of the principal duties performed in a wide range of occupations.

Earlier drafts of these measures were administered to large samples of sixth, seventh, and eighth graders in order to refine the CVMT through extensive analyses of its items. Only those items were selected for final forms which had relatively high correlations with total scores and relatively low *r*'s with a test of mental ability (Otis-Lennon).

The revised form of the CVMT was next administered to 7,367 public school students in grades six through nine. This version of the instrument consisted of a total of 120 items, with 15–25 items in each of the six subscales. Analyses have been conducted of its psychometric characteristics, and, in general, it appears to be a sound test. Kuder-Richardson Formula 20 estimates of its internal consistency range from a few coefficients in the upper .60s to a central tendency in the middle .80s, with two in the .90s. The subscales appear to be homogeneous, and they seem to be rather highly interrelated. Their intercorrelations in grades seven, eight, and nine are in the upper .60s and low .70s, with some as high as .81 and .84. Thus, although the subscales have some unique variance in them, they have a considerable degree of communality. Whether it is more than would be expected in terms of the model of vocational maturity remains to be determined. Part of the high inter-subscale correlations may be attributable to the CVMT's moderate-to-high (.53–.69) relationships with scholastic aptitude, which, if partialled out, might appreciably reduce their common variance. Other data on the CVMT which are relevant to the model of vocational maturity are on its "cross-group" relationship with Realism of Vocational Choice. In a comparison of "adjusted" (realistic) and "maladjusted" (unrealistic) vocational choice groups on the CVMT, it was found that the former had significantly ($p < .05 - .01$) higher means on all subscales. In other words, these findings would support the hypothesized association between the Vocational Choice Competencies and Realism of Vocational Choice dimensions in the model of vocational maturity.

IMPLICATIONS OF THE MODEL OF VOCATIONAL MATURITY

The *theoretical* implications of the model are twofold: first, it has subsumptive value, in that it summarizes and organizes what is known about vocational maturity. It serves as a conceptual point-of-reference for "thinking about" career development processes in adolescence, and it provides a ready schema for relating them to other aspects of development which can be abstracted in similar fashion. Second, it has predictive value in that it generates hypotheses which would not otherwise have been formulated. Reese and Overton observe that:

A good model acts like a pair of binoculars. This function is related to the metaphorical function. Models provide rules of inference through which new relations are discovered, and provide suggestions about how the scope of the theory can be increased. It is this function that makes a good model more than a simple analogy.[93]

Illustrative of this utility of model building is the implied relationship between the increasing differentiation of vocationally mature behaviors over time and discrimination learning processes based upon differential reward and punishment.[94] Theoretically, if not also empirically, an argument can be made that adolescents who are more vocationally mature are those who have learned to discriminate among courses of action which eventuate in more realistic career decision-making. One of the major findings of the Vocational Development Project thus far has been the tendency of younger subjects to be less discriminating in their responses to statements of mature and immature vocational attitudes, and this phenomenon cannot be attributed to test-taking response biases.[95] It can be hypothesized, therefore, that one of the developmental functions which relates the model of vocational maturity to time (either age or grade) may be the process of discrimination learning.

The *research* implications of the model follow from its theoretical utility. Since its formulation, initially by Super[96] and subsequently by Crites,[97] it has had considerable heuristic value in the instigation of research. Not only has it directed the work of the Career Pattern Study and the Vocational Development Project, but it has been adopted by the Center for Occupational Education as the framework for its studies of cognitive vocational maturity. Moreover, many independent investigations—master's theses and doctoral dissertations, surveys of disadvantaged and minority groups, evaluations of guidance programs, etc.—have been prompted by the model of vocational maturity.[98] Any number of research ideas can be deduced from it: measurement of variables, interrelationships of dimensions (group factors), specification of developmental functions, parameters of vocational maturity, relationships to other variables (particularly other aspects of development), the effects of interventive experiences (such as vocational counseling), stages in the structural differentiation of the model, and so on. As findings on the model accumulate, it is expected that it will require revision. A lively intercourse between the data-language and theory-language levels must be carried on, so that the "fit" of the model to reality will be as close as possible. As experience with it is gained, its utility will be evaluated by how well it accounts for and predicts vocational maturity phenomena. At present, it seems justifiable to conclude that what data are available are largely consistent with the model of vocational maturity.

Although it is premature to extrapolate the *practical* implications of the model, a few which are substantiated by current knowledge can be delineated. Super[99] has proposed that once all of the variables in the model have been measured, a vocational maturity profile can be constructed which can be used to describe what Crites[100] has defined as degree and rate of vocational development. From such a VM profile, diagnostic inferences can be drawn concerning an individual's problems in career decision-making. Thus, if he scores high on Occupational Information and Self-Appraisal but low on Goal Selection, it may be that he needs assistance in relating himself to the world of work. Similarly, a measure like the VDI-Att can be used to "checkpoint" vocational development through its use as a screening instrument to identify students who are less vocationally mature than their peers. They can then be invited to contact a guidance counselor, who can provide more intensive counseling for those who need it most. In this manner guidance personnel and facilities can be used more efficiently than they sometimes are when a counselor is expected to see all students for a standard interview—whether they need it or not. Follow-up of clients, as well as entire guidance programs, can be accomplished within the context of the model, and several studies of this type have been conducted.[101] In general, the results from those with appropriate controls and experimental designs indicate that the maturity of vocational attitudes, as assessed by the VDI-Att, can be enhanced by both counseling and didactic experiences. Conceivably, as more research on the model of vocational maturity accumulates and as its theoretical structure is "filled in" with data, it can serve as a general schema within which any number of interventive activities (e.g., traditional vocational counseling, computer-assisted counseling, programmed counseling, etc.) can be implemented with the goal of facilitating career development processes.

NOTES

1. M. Brodbeck, "The Philosophy of Science and Educational Research," *Review of Educational Research* 27(1957):427–40.
2. H. W. Reese and W. F. Overton, "Models of Development and Theories of Development," *Life-span Developmental Psychology*, L. R. Goulet and P. B. Baltes, eds. (New York: Academic Press, 1970), p. 117.
3. W. K. Estes, "Toward a Statistical Theory of Learning," *Psychological Review* 57(1950):94–107.
4. R. R. Rush and W. K. Estes, eds., *Studies in Mathematical Learning* (Palo Alto, Calif.: Stanford University Press, 1959).
5. M. Brodbeck, "Logic and Scientific Method in Research on Teaching," *Handbook of Research on Teaching*, N. L. Gage, ed. (Chicago: Rand McNally, 1963).
6. Brodbeck, "The Philosophy of Science and Educational Research."
7. *Ibid.*; Brodbeck, "Logic and Scientific Method in Research on Teaching."
8. Reese and Overton, *op. cit.*
9. J. O. Crites, *Vocational Psychology* (New York: McGraw-Hill, 1969).
10. D. E. Super, "The Dimensions and Measurement of Vocational Maturity," *Teachers College Record* 57(1955):151–63.
11. *Ibid.*, p. 153.
12. H. Beilin, "The Application of General Developmental Principles to the Vocational Area," *Journal of Counseling Psychology* 2(1955):53–57.
13. A. T. Jersild, *Child Development and the Curriculum* (New York: Teachers College Bureau of Publications, 1946).
14. D. E. Super et al., *Vocational Development: A Framework for Research* (New York: Teachers College Bureau of Publications, 1957), p. 64.
15. Super, *op. cit.*
16. A. L. Baldwin, *Behavior and Development in Childhood* (New York: Dryden Press, 1955).
17. Super, *op. cit.*, p. 64.
18. J. O. Crites, "A Model for the Measurement of Vocational Maturity," *Journal of Counseling Psychology* 8(1961):255–59.

19. *Ibid.*, p. 259.
20. Crites, *Vocational Psychology.*
21. H. Borow, "Development of Occupational Motives and Roles," *Review of Child Development Research,* Vol. 2, L. W. Hoffman and M. L. Hoffman, eds. (New York: Russell Sage, 1966), p. 398.
22. D. B. Bromley, "An Approach to Theory Construction in the Psychology of Development and Aging," *Life-span Developmental Psychology.*
23. M. B. Hesse, *Models and Analogies in Science* (London: Sheed and Ward, 1963).
24. Brodbeck, "The Philosophy of Science and Educational Research."
25. Hesse, *op. cit.*
26. Reese and Overton, *op. cit.*, p. 120.
27. J. P. Guilford, *Personality* (New York: McGraw-Hill, 1959).
28. P. E. Vernon, *The Structure of Human Abilities* (London: Methuen, 1950).
29. D. E. Super and J. O. Crites, *Appraising Vocational Fitness,* revised ed. (New York: Harper and Row, 1962).
30. Crites, *Vocational Psychology.*
31. Super, "The Dimensions and Measurement of Vocational Maturity"; Super et al., *Vocational Development.*
32. D. E. Super and P. L. Overstreet, *The Vocational Maturity of Ninth Grade Boys* (New York: Teachers College Bureau of Publications, 1960).
33. W. D. Gribbons and P. R. Lohnes, *Emerging Careers* (New York: Teachers College Press, 1968).
34. J. O. Crites, "Measurement of Vocational Maturity in Adolescence: I. Attitude Test of the Vocational Development Inventory," *Psychological Monographs* 79(1965):2; *The Maturity of Vocational Attitudes in Adolescence* (Washington, D.C.: American Personnel and Guidance Association, 1971).
35. Crites, "A Model for the Measurement of Vocational Maturity."
36. L. L. Thurstone, "Primary Mental Abilities," *Psychometrika Monograph,* No. 1, 1938.
37. Baldwin, *op. cit.*
38. Super and Overstreet, *op. cit.*, p. 2.
39. *Ibid.*, p. 32.
40. H. E. Garrett, "A Developmental Theory of Intelligence," *American Psychologist* 1(1946):372–78.
41. J. O. Crites, "The Vocational Development Project at the University of Iowa," *Journal of Counseling Psychology* 12(1965):81–86.
42. Crites, "Measurement of Vocational Maturity in Adolescence."
43. Crites, *Vocational Psychology,* p. 139.
44. A. Roe, *The Psychology of Occupations* (New York: John Wiley and Sons, 1956).
45. J. W. Hollender, *Interrelationships of Vocational Maturity, Consistency and Realism of Vocational Choice, School Grade, and Age in Adolescence,* master's thesis, University of Iowa, 1964.
46. Crites, "Measurement of Vocational Maturity in Adolescence."
47. Crites, *Vocational Psychology.*
48. J. W. Hollender, "Development of a Realistic Vocational Choice," *Journal of Counseling Psychology* 14(1967):314–18.
49. Crites, "Measurement of Vocational Maturity in Adolescence."
50. Super, "Dimensions and Measurement of Vocational Maturity."
51. A. L. Baldwin, *Theories of Child Development* (New York: John Wiley and Sons, 1967).
52. P. B. Baltes and L. R. Goulet, "Status and Issues of a Life-span Developmental Psychology," *Life-span Developmental Psychology.*

53. J. F. Wohlwill, "Methodology and Research Strategy in the Study of Developmental Change," *Life-span Developmental Psychology.*

54. Crites, "Measurement of Vocational Maturity in Adolescence."

55. K. W. Schaie, "A General Model for the Study of Developmental Problems," *Psychological Bulletin* 64(1965):92–107; Schaie, "A Reinterpretation of Age Related Changes in Cognitive Structure and Functioning," *Life-span Developmental Psychology.*

56. H. E. Jones, *Development in Adolescence: Approaches to the Study of the Individual* (New York: Appleton-Century-Crofts, 1943).

57. Super et al., *Vocational Development.*

58. Wohlwill, *op. cit.,* p. 151.

59. D. T. Campbell, "Factors Relevant to the Validity of Experiments in Social Settings," *Psychological Bulletin* 54(1957):297–312.

60. Schaie, "A General Model."

61. Gribbons and Lohnes, *op. cit.*

62. R. P. O'Hara and D. V. Tiedeman, "Vocational Self-concept in Adolescence," *Journal of Counseling Psychology* 6(1959):292–301.

63. Schaie, "A General Model."

64. P. B. Baltes, "Longitudinal and Cross-sectional Sequences in the Study of Age and Generation Effects," *Human Development* 11(1968):145–71.

65. Schaie, "A Reinterpretation," p. 487.

66. Wohlwill, *op. cit.;* Schaie, "A General Model."

67. Schaie, "A Reinterpretation."

68. Campbell, *op. cit.*

69. Schaie, "A Reinterpretation."

70. E. F. Lindquist, *Design and Analysis of Experiments in Psychology and Education* (Boston: Houghton Mifflin, 1953).

71. J. R. Nesselroade, "Application of Multivariate Strategies to Problems of Measuring and Structuring Long-term Change," *Life-span Developmental Psychology.*

72. J. O. Crites et al., "A Factor Analysis of the California Psychological Inventory," *Journal of Applied Psychology* 45(1961):408–414.

73. T. W. Anderson, *Introduction to Multivariate Statistical Analysis* (New York: John Wiley and Sons, 1958).

74. L. L. Thurstone, *Multiple-factor Analysis* (Chicago: University of Chicago Press, 1947).

75. G. Thompson, ed., *The Factorial Analysis of Human Ability,* 4th ed. (Boston: Houghton Mifflin, 1951).

76. Thurstone, *Multiple-factor Analysis.*

77. Super and Overstreet, *op. cit.*

78. *Ibid.,* pp. 69–72.

79. Gribbons and Lohnes, *op. cit.*

80. J. C. Flanagan, "General Considerations in the Selection of Test Items and a Short Method of Estimating the Product-moment Coefficient from Data at the Tails of the Distribution," *Journal of Educational Psychology* 30 (1939):674–80.

81. M. W. Richardson, "Notes on the Rationale of Item Analysis," *Psychometrika* 1(1936):69–70.

82. Crites, "Measurement of Vocational Maturity in Adolescence."

83. I. W. Miller and A. O. Haller, "A Measure of Level of Occupational Aspiration," *Personnel and Guidance Journal* 42(1964):448–55.

84. M. J. Bathory, "Occupational Aspirations and Vocational Maturity," paper presented at meeting of the American Vocational Association, Cleveland, Ohio, December 1967.

85. Hollender, "Interrelationships of Vocational Maturity."
86. R. Carek, *The Interrelations between Social Desirability, Vocational Maturity, Vocational Realism, and Vocational Decision,* master's thesis, University of Iowa, 1965.
87. R. D. Cooter, "Occupational Level Preferences among Adolescents," unpublished manuscript, Swarthmore College, 1966.
88. I. M. Wilstach, "Vocational Maturity of Mexican-American Youth," doctoral dissertation, University of Southern California, 1967.
89. Crites, "Measurement of Vocational Maturity in Adolescence."
90. D. E. Super and D. J. Forrest, *Career Development Inventory: Preliminary Manual* (New York: Teachers College, Columbia University, 1972).
91. *Ibid.,* p. 37.
92. B. W. Westbrook, *Toward the Validation of the Construct of Vocational Maturity* (Raleigh, North Carolina: Center for Occupational Education, North Carolina State University, Technical Paper No. 6, 1971).
93. Reese and Overton, *op. cit.,* p. 120.
94. J. O. Crites, "The Maturity of Vocational Attitudes and Learning Processes in Adolescence," paper presented at the 17th Annual Convention of the International Congress of Applied Psychology, Liege, Belgium, 1971.
95. Crites, "Measurement of Vocational Maturity in Adolescence."
96. Super, "Dimensions and Measurement of Vocational Maturity."
97. Crites, "Measurement of Vocational Maturity in Adolescence."
98. *Ibid.*
99. Super, "Dimensions and Measurement of Vocational Maturity."
100. Crites, "A Model for the Measurement of Vocational Maturity."
101. Crites, "Measurement of Vocational Maturity in Adolescence."

SUGGESTED READING

Crites, J. O. *Vocational Psychology.* New York: McGraw-Hill, 1969. A critical survey and synthesis of theory and research on vocational choice and adjustment. Includes chapters on vocational development in adolescence and adulthood. Discusses theoretical issues posed by explanations of vocational behavior and development phenomena.

Crites, J. O. *The Maturity of Vocational Attitudes in Adolescence.* Washington, D.C.: American Personnel and Guidance Association, 1971. A summary and report of the Vocational Development Project, a longitudinal study of vocational behavior in adolescence during its first ten years. Results from over one hundred investigations with the Vocational Development Inventory (VDI) are discussed and implications for future theory, construction, research, and application are extrapolated.

Gribbons, W. D., and Lohnes, P. R. *Emerging Careers.* New York: Teachers College Press, 1968. A description and discussion of the Career Development Study of 110 male and female adolescents from the time they were in eighth grade to follow-ups after their graduation from high school. Extensive data are presented on the Readiness for Vocational Planning (RVP) scales, and the implications of the findings for further research and practice are examined.

Super, D. E., Crites, J. O., Hummel, R. C., Moser, H. P., Overstreet, P. L., and Warnath, C. F. *Vocational Development: A Framework for Research.* New York: Teachers College Bureau of Publications, 1957. The first in a series of monographs on the Career Pattern Study, a pioneer developmental investigation of the careers of 140 males between ages 15 and 35. This monograph articulates the theoretical frame of reference within which CPS has been conducted and serves as the basic document defining such concepts as vocational maturity.

Super, D. E., and Overstreet, P. L. *The Vocational Maturity of Ninth Grade Boys.* New York: Teachers College Bureau of Publications, 1960. The second in the CPS series of monographs, it reports the initial findings on the Indices of Vocational Maturity for the sample at the beginning of the high school years. It also deals with the broader issues of theory and application and sets the stage for subsequent studies over a twenty-year period.

This section does not attempt to capture all of the responses that vocational guidance specialists could conceivably implement in the service of their clients. Indeed, no chapters have been directed specifically to such fundamentals as the processes of counseling, information retrieval, or group approaches. Yet concern for improving the access to the viability of these approaches pervade this section. In essence, this section attempts to highlight, on the one hand, those practices which have been most affected by the conceptual efforts of the past decade and, on the other, the groups of persons least well considered in the literature pertinent to vocational guidance. The section begins with discussions of new foci in practice and ends by placing these against the perspectives found in a growing awareness of the "people" elements which future guidance technologies must address.

Prediger begins by examining individual assessment "in career guidance," a term which he uses to subsume educational and vocational guidance. He identifies the guidance functions of tests in relation to career exploration as it is focused on immediate, intermediate, and distant career pattern segments. As he analyzes major factors in career decision making, he does so in terms of the information which tests yield as one views the individual as the predictor of his own career sequencing. In the latter sense, he contends that only the person can assimilate and combine the objective probabilities based on the experience of others as abstracted through tests with the subjective probabilities based on his own experience. He suggests that perhaps the most important role of the counselor in testing is to help students transform information from tests into experience and into possibilities.

Bergland presents a comprehensive overview of career planning and places it in the context of the importance of decision making in our lives. He reminds the reader that there is no reason to assume that individuals can or will learn to become skilled decisionmakers on their own, the importance of "teaching" decision-making skills becomes evident. In the process he reinforces the heightened activity of counselors in pursuing the development of their clients rather than waiting passively for such development to go awry. In outlining the phases of decision making from defining the problem, through generating alternatives, developing information seeking skills, and processing information, to making plans and selecting goals, he reminds the counselors that people are not closed systems. Thus, he maintains that those searching for a career should be seen as changing organisms engaging in series of career-related developmental tasks. Throughout his analysis of the structure of career planning, Bergland introduces the reader to gaming, simulated activities, and structured practice as methods to facilitate such goals.

Continuing Bergland's application of technology to facilitating particular types of vocational guidance outcomes, Miller and Tiedeman consider the capabilities and characteristics of the various types of computer systems in guidance which are now extant. In view of the contention that students must relate their occupational interests and capabilities to the time consequence they are currently experiencing—speed, instantness, and rapid obsolescence, Miller and Tiedeman argue for the need to devise new forms of guidance to fit this new time and motion framework. In this context, it is contended that guidance must develop ways to help the individual cope with rapid change and to acquire "copeability" skills which facilitate decision making within the rhythm of the motion in time that the individual is experiencing.

Cramer discusses the premise that changes in the environment have the potential either for impeding or for facilitating development. Accepting that notion as a given, he examines the possibilities which lie in conscious, deliberate, and planned uses or changes of environments to achieve effective vocational development. In such strategies the focus of counselor intervention shifts from the individual to the environment and may be comprised of either "thing" changes or "people" changes. Specifically, he considers ways in which the curriculum, cooperative efforts among educational and community personnel, and other elements can be combined in a systems approach to career development.

Matthews takes the reader beyond professional responses *per se* to the contexts through which girls and women develop and to which vocational guidance must attend. After a brief overview of the major trends pertinent to women during the 1950s, 1960s, and the beginning of the 1970s, she details the staging phenomena which affect the development of women from infancy through the adult years. In the process she discusses "concrete possibilities for life-stage specific individualized vocational guidance by parents, teachers, and counselors." Woven into her analyses are identification of the research and conceptual voids in the current literature describing women. Finally, she extends Cramer's concerns for environmental modification to her analyses of discrimination against women in work and in higher education. In so doing, she reinforces the importance of going beyond eliminating discrimination in its tangible forms to the problem of assuring *psychological* freedom of access to all occupations.

Gordon extends the reader's concerns for the characteristics of the consumers of vocational guidance to those of disadvantaged and minority populations. He begins by indicating that the fundamental problems experienced by these populations are not those of vocational guidance but are, rather, those related to the organization, values, and commitments of the society. He addresses the outcomes of a tradition of relative neglect of the development of the intellect that has plagued the educational development of the poor in the twentieth century. He reminds counselors that stereotyping the disadvantaged as a homogeneous population does a disservice to the variability and uniqueness of people. He speaks of the disadvantaged as those more effectively labeled the "opportunity deprived," arguing for a vocational guidance emphasis which nurtures interests and aptitudes and which is aligned with the development and training of capacities and skills. He maintains that guidance has a role in environmental intervention which must attend to foci both in the individual and the field in which he operates. In his view of guidance practitioners as human development specialists, Gordon contends that the individual psychological model is being challenged by the developmental-ecological model. Finally, like Hershenson in the succeeding chapter, he supports the notion that an appropriate approach to vocational guidance for the disadvantaged should reflect those aspects which are suitable to all populations.

Hershenson begins by defining handicap and disability as well as discussing the incidence of different types of disability in America. Carrying forth Gordon's reinforcement of variability among disadvantaged persons, Hershenson indicates that the differences between the handicapped and the nonhandicapped are smaller than the differences within each of these groups. He relates the impact of disability to the emerging concern for second careers and the dysjunctions associated with job displacement in the nonhandicapped populations, drawing the implications which these phenomena hold for elaborating current understandings of career development. Like most of the writers in this section, he speaks to the need for the counselor to assume the stance of an environmental interventionist. Specific to the handicapped, he discusses vocational guidance techniques such as job engineering or placement in facilitating "placeability" and "employability" and the problems encountered in employers' attitudes impinging upon the placement of workers.

This section ends with Hoyt's survey of the professional culture of and preparation for vocational guidance. This chapter is of special importance since, in large measure, the counselor is what he or she is prepared to think he is and to do. Hoyt discusses the historical images to which counselor preparation has given allegiance, and he also examines the impact on counselor preparation of funding expectations and of ambivalence about counselor roles which has characterized professional organizations. Specifically, Hoyt traces his analysis through legislation, conference reports, and the major journals pertinent to the preparation of counselors or to the culture relevant to vocational guidance. In the process he details such future imperatives as are found in the need for new conceptual emphases in preparation, attention to preparing support personnel, greater understandings of vocational education, and improved communication among personnel in industry, labor, business, and education.

The Role of Assessment 13
in Career Guidance

Dale J. Prediger
The American College Testing Program

Inchworm, inchworm
Measuring the marigolds
You and your arithmetic
You'll probably go far.

Inchworm, inchworm
Measuring the marigolds
Seems to me you'd stop and see
How beautiful they are.*

The above lines from a song by Frank Loesser[1] touch on the natural antagonism of mankind in general and counselors in particular toward attempts to quantify human characteristics and experience. Add to this the growing concern among the measurers themselves about whether the products of their efforts really help the marigolds grow, and one has a good perspective on the precarious state of assessment in the career guidance formulations of today. The major purpose of this chapter is to reexamine the role of student assessment in educational and vocational guidance in light of career development theory, career decision-making theory, and the recent emphasis on developmental career guidance programs.

PLACING MARIGOLDS INTO SQUARE HOLES

Critics of student assessment from outside of the guidance and testing movement have been heard for some time. Recently, however, the voices have been getting louder and more familiar. The focus of critical attention has been on the traditional trait and factor applications of student assessment in career guidance. These applications at their worst involve a one-shot, "test 'em, tell 'em," square-peg, square-hole process whereby an individual's characteristics are analyzed in conjunction with the characteristics of occupations in order to find a match indicating the occupation to be

For their helpful suggestions concerning this chapter I am grateful to: JoAnn Harris, Associate Professor of Counselor Education, Northern Illinois University; Fred Brown, Professor of Psychology, Iowa State University; and my colleagues at ACT, Leo Munday and John Roth.
* From "The Inch Worm" by Frank Loesser. © 1951 Frank Music Corp. Used by Permission./Used by permission of Edwin H. Morris & Co., Ltd. & Frank Music Co., Ltd.

entered. From the perspective of career development theory and the resulting view of career guidance as a developmental process, these trait-and-factor applications have been called static, sterile, limiting, directive, and generally unworthy of professional attention.

Serious questions are also being raised about whether traditional trait-and-factor applications in guidance, even if they were desirable, are warranted on the basis of research. In particular, our ability to predict occupational success to a degree useful in career guidance (as opposed to personnel selection) is open to serious question.[2] Compounding the problem, Super[3] maintains the prediction of occupational success at a given point in time is an inappropriate function for guidance assessment. Concern should be focused instead on the prediction of career patterns, an even more difficult task. Finally, Crites[4] documents the generally inconsistent relationship between occupational success and satisfaction.

Because of both the theoretical and research inadequacies in the traditional trait-and-factor approach to career guidance, it is no wonder that the guidance role of assessment is being called into question. When no one was doing much about vocational guidance it did not seem to matter much what was done. Now, however, through the impetus of vocational educators, legislators at the national and state levels, and concerned citizens, career guidance is a high-priority item on the national agenda. Developmental, experientially based career guidance programs are being initiated in all parts of the country. The role of student assessment in these programs is being either vigorously questioned or simply ignored. Primarily for these reasons, the major objective of this chapter is to reexamine the role of student assessment in educational and vocational guidance.

In the discussion that follows the term "career," as in "career guidance" generally refers to both the "educational" and "vocational" aspects of the process. The time-extensive nature of careers is also recognized, and this use of the term is indicated in the appropriate passages. Another term frequently used in this chapter is "developmental career guidance program," generally meaning kindergarten through grade twelve curricular and extracurricular activities organized, articulated, and administered by school personnel for the purpose of providing students with information about the world of work and education, experience (direct or vicarious) with that world, and insight into their potential roles in that world.

As our understanding of the career development process increases, developmental career guidance programs should increasingly be organized around the career-related developmental tasks commonly faced by youth in our society. Activities that might be found in a developmental career guidance program include: a "what-do-you-do" project involving interviews with the fathers and mothers of second graders; a simulated employment service operated and used by fifth graders; tours that provide a firsthand look at workers in a variety of job families; interviews with workers that touch on the psychosocial aspects of their jobs; discussions by teachers of occupations related to their subjects; interpretations of test scores that relate personal characteristics to career possibilities; hands-on, job-related tryout experiences in a junior high industrial arts course; small group discussions of the values and life-styles associated with different occupations; practice in the use of the school's printed and audiovisual materials describing occupations; part-time work experiences relevant to a student's occupational preferences; a "post-high school education night"; exploratory vocational education courses offered in the summer; a cooperative work-study program; and simulation games involving career decisions for fictitious people. Finally, the "personalization" of these experiences through individual counseling would be an integral part of the program. Many of the above activities are especially useful in facilitating the dual exploration of self and careers by providing students with firsthand or vicarious experiences with a variety of occupations and occupational life-styles. As noted later in the chapter, opportunity for these experiences is crucial to the effective use of assessment procedures in career guidance.

In the following discussion the word "student" is generally used in place of the words "counselee, individual, person, youth, or adult." Since the career development stages of major concern to guidance involve the age range typical of students in our society, and since developmental career guidance programs as defined above are mainly found in educational institutions, use of the word "student" appears to be a reasonable compromise. The career guidance of special student groups (e.g., the disadvantaged, the handicapped, and minority populations) is the topic of separate chapters in this volume, and these persons are therefore generally not included in the category of "students."

The word "tests" is used, perhaps more often than appropriate, as a collective term for the wide variety of assessment procedures available to the counselor (e.g., ability measures, interest inventories, rating scales, questionnaires, and grades). Although validities, reliabilities, and measurement techniques may vary, the major principles involved in the guidance use of the various kinds of assessment information are substantially the same. This discussion is also limited to the use of tests *prior* to occupational entry. Readers interested in the measurement of job satisfaction, satisfactoriness, performance, or work adjustment can consult Crites; Weiss et al.; and Boyd and Shimberg.[5] Other recent sources are also suggested for related topics such as: performance tests, e.g., work sampling and gaming (Fitzpatrick and Morrison[6]); nonreading measures of vocational aptitudes (Droege et al.[7]); and the accumulated evidence indicating a circular configuration of basic vocational interest dimensions (Cole and Hanson; Crites[8]). Although the very promising area of career development assessment is considered only in passing here, it is given ample attention in other chapters of this volume.

IN DEFENSE OF TRAITS AND FACTORS

From the previous discussion of trait-and-factor applications in career guidance the reader may have the impression that the assessment of traits and factors should be abandoned. Even if this were desirable, it would not be possible. To see why, it is important to distinguish between traits and factors themselves and the *traditional applications* of traits and factors in vocational guidance. To denigrate trait-and-factor theory in its most basic form is to deny the usefulness, indeed even the possibility, of statements such as "He is strong," "Those children are undernourished," "That team is aggressive," "The class was interested," "She has a capable staff—I'm sure they can handle it." Traits, factors, human characteristics are all abstractions

—concepts, ways of organizing experience, tools for coping with reality. As tools, traits and factors can be put to many uses; hence, the distinction between the tools and their uses is crucial. In career guidance today it is the *manner* in which traits and factors are typically used that is under fire.

Unfortunately, the measurement of psychological traits and the study of group distributions on these traits have, for many, become synonymous with "square-peg" approaches to career guidance. (All too often, trait-and-factor psychologists have contributed to this viewpoint.) It need not be. "Square-peg" approaches to career guidance are not dictated by trait-and-factor theory. The same persons who believe that "marriages are made in heaven" can readily implement a "square-peg, square-hole" approach to career guidance independent of any objective measures or research on the characteristics of occupational groups. The counselor's viewpoint does have a great deal to do with the *effectiveness* of the career guidance he provides, but the existence of trait-and-factor measures does not force any particular viewpoint on him. Blaming trait-and-factor theory for a mechanistic approach to guidance is somewhat like blaming skin color for racial discrimination.

An alternative approach to the use of traits and factors in career guidance is nowhere better illustrated than in the Project Talent research of Cooley and Lohnes.[9] There is none of the simplistic, square-peg use of traits and factors in Cooley and Lohnes' presentation. Instead, trait-and-factor theory is placed firmly in the context of career development theory, and the results of Project Talent research are used in the construction of a career development tree with considerable significance for career guidance and for the study of career patterns.

Others have also suggested alternative roles for traits and factors in career guidance. Katz, for example, after an extensive review of research on educational and vocational prediction, suggests:

> Insofar as trait-and-factor methodology is merely descriptive, it has proven very useful . . . . On the other hand, the implications and practice of trait-and-factor theory often exceed the descriptive and tend toward the imperative . . . . However, if trait-and-factor theory is limited only to the making of predictions and is not extended to the determination of decisions, it is not a theory of occupational choice at all, but only one element that can be worked into a more comprehensive theory of occupational choice. Perhaps it may best be regarded as an expression of the reality element that affects occupational sorting.[10]

Clarke, Gelatt, and Levine,[11] in a discussion of the career decision-making process, emphasize the need for information on the possible outcomes of various courses of action. Career guidance applications of the information from several local validity studies using test scores and grades as predictors are also described. Further contributions of trait-and-factor information to career decision making have been suggested by Gelatt and Clarke, Katz, and Thoresen and Mehrens.[12]

We have certainly passed the era in which the square-peg approach to use of traits and factors could be viewed as the epitome of vocational guidance. Nevertheless, the above-mentioned studies and formulations leave little doubt about the potential contribution of trait-and-factor measures to the process of career development. The nature of the contribution will be the subject of the sections which follow. First, however, it is worth taking a look at a common misconception or feeling about the use of tests in counseling, a feeling that seems to persist independent of whatever use is proposed.

The verses at the beginning of this chapter about measuring marigolds represent something of the attitude of many counselors toward the place of testing in any type of counseling. Somehow tests, with their associated statistics, miss the whole point of counseling—the warm, human relationship between the counselor and the counselee. Test scores are cold and impersonal, and their use will make counseling cold and impersonal. To test is to treat the counselee as a number, to deny the importance of the counselee as a person, and to rule out any possibility of relating to him on a personal level. Maybe so—it can be that way. But it all depends on the training, attitude, and humanity of the counselor. Test scores, by themselves, are no more cold and impersonal than a raised eyebrow. If properly derived, they communicate information—nothing more, nothing less. This information can be used in a cold, impersonal way, or it can be used in a personal, helpful way. It is the counselor, however, who determines how it will be used, just as he determines how information about Johnny's home background, expressed interests, values, and goals will be used. Tests do not manipulate, pigeonhole, provide all the answers, or tell Johnny what to do. They can, however, provide information useful in counseling and guidance. It all depends on what the counselor does with them.

THE GUIDANCE FUNCTIONS OF TESTS

Measurement texts frequently discuss guidance applications of student assessment. Recent books by Goldman and Meyering[13] focus specifically on the use of tests in counseling. The counseling and guidance functions of tests presented in the outline below are among those commonly suggested in the professional literature. The outline is meant to be illustrative rather than exhaustive or definitive, however. It is presented here to provide a point of departure for subsequent discussion.

The following postulate, based on a formulation by Clarke, Gelatt, and Levine,[14] provides the rationale underlying the outline. *Information on personal characteristics as they relate to various career choice options is a necessary but not sufficient condition for optimizing career development.* That is, the information by itself is not sufficient; it is the manner in which the information is used that is crucial.

I. Functions That Make Testing Useful

    A. Organization of existing data or information in a new way. (For example, an interest inventory organizes a number of seemingly discrete activity preferences into a configuration of interest types.)

    B. Provision of more reliable and valid assessments of certain human characteristics than would usually be possible or feasible on the basis of subjective judgment. (For example, a diagnostic reading test is used to identify eighth graders who might profit from remedial or developmental reading programs.)

C. Provision of otherwise unavailable information or perspective on the characteristics of an individual. (For example, a spatial visualization test assesses various aspects of spatial ability and expresses the results on a normative scale based on a national sample of civil engineering students.)

D. Relation of data (scores) on individual characteristics to the world of education and work in a manner that facilitates exploration, planning, and/or decision making. (For example, the high school grades of students attending various colleges are used to develop experience tables showing the relationship of grades in the high school to grades at each of the colleges. The high school counselor uses these tables in discussions with students and parents.)

II. Career Guidance Applications of Testing

  A. Applications directly involving students.

    1. Facilitation of exploration and planning (tentative decision making) over a period of time.

      a. Self-exploration. (For example, a measure of job values is used to help students explore and perhaps reformulate what they want out of a job and out of life.)

      b. Career exploration and planning. (For example, a comprehensive testing program covering interests, abilities, job values, etc., is used to suggest educational programs and/or occupations that a student might want to look into. After an extended period of active exploration, the student tentatively decides to pursue an apprenticeship program in carpentry.)

    2. Provision of information for use in decision making at a specific point in time.

      a. Confirming an existing preference. (For example, a "tailor-made" test battery, together with a wide range of other information, serves to reassure a student about the feasibility of his preferred choice option.)

      b. Choosing from among two or more alternatives of approximately equal saliency. (For example, a reassessment of job values in light of the potential rewards of three different, equally preferred occupations helps a student to resolve the dilemma in favor of one of the occupations.)

  B. Applications indirectly involving students.

    1. Provision of diagnostic information on a student's stage of career development for use by the counselor in planning individually prescribed career development experiences.

    2. Provision of diagnostic information on the stage of career development of a group of students for use by the institution in implementing guidance and/or curricular programs appropriate to the career development needs of the group.

Examples are not provided for the indirect applications listed above because, as of the time of writing, the required measures have not been available for general use. Hence, their specific content and viable applications are still a matter of conjecture. Crites, in the previous chapter, has provided a comprehensive discussion of this area of assessment.

FOUNDATIONS FOR CAREER GUIDANCE TESTING

The role of tests in facilitating career exploration and planning has received relatively little discussion in the guidance and testing literature. By and large, the use of tests in problem solving and decision making has been emphasized. For this reason, attention is focused on exploratory applications of testing in the discussion that follows. Subsequent chapters in this volume provide examples of exploratory activities that can be incorporated into guidance programs. The reader is reminded that career exploration is used primarily as a shorthand term for educational and vocational exploration. In this limited sense of the term, career exploration usually focuses on immediate, intermediate, and distant career pattern segments, in that order.

The Importance of Career Exploration

The term "exploration" is not a recent addition to the field of vocational guidance. On the contrary, Jordaan observes that it ". . . has figured in the vocabularies of counselors and vocational psychologists since 1908 when Parson [sic] wrote the first book on occupational choice."[15] Jordaan also notes that exploratory experiences, job tryouts, and the analysis of past experiences were once the practitioner's chief tools in the guidance process. "As tests and occupational information improved in quality, however, exploratory activities gradually receded into the background . . . ."

Today we are seeing a renewed interest in career exploration, both in career development theory and in guidance practice. Exploratory activities are central to the developmental career guidance programs currently receiving so much attention. An exploratory period, stage, or substage is central to the career choice and development formulations of Ginzberg et al., Super, and Tiedeman and O'Hara.[16] Super suggests that vocational guidance in the ninth grade ". . . should aim to ascertain what alternatives (in the plural, in most instances) might best be explored, to help the pupil define and utilize appropriate explorations."[17] Pritchard[18] directs attention to the relationship between career exploration and self-exploration. Tennyson[19] calls for "directed occupational experiences" as preparatory for decision making. Herr and Cramer[20] describe a systems approach to career development designed to facilitate "vocationalization," and Gysbers and Moore[21] make progressively focused, "hands-on" exploratory activities the central theme of a developmental career guidance program for grades kindergarten through twelve. Career exploration is a concept and a function that has once again come of age.

The current emphasis on career exploration is not surprising if one subscribes to Super's principle that "In choosing an occupation one is, in effect, choosing a means of implementing a self-concept."[22] An occupation gives a person the chance to be the kind of person he wants to be. Thus, the importance of knowing both oneself and the characteristics of occupations is readily apparent. More is involved here than information, however. One's values, goals, and needs (both conscious and unconscious) are relevant, as are the psychosocial reinforcers of occupations. Hence, reasoned vocational choice, alone, may not lead to personally satisfying decisions. Experience, that master teacher, plays a major role in career choice as in everything else. Exploratory activities are designed to provide the experience (direct or vicarious) that leads to the reality testing, clarification, and implementation of the vocational self-concept.

In an excellent article on the role of guidance in career exploration, Pritchard[23] points out that very little attention has been given to the *process* of relating the counselee's self to occupations for purposes of exploration. The mechanical procedures that have been developed (e.g., the Worker Trait Patterns in the *Dictionary of Occupational Titles*[24]) tend to ignore the psychological nature of the process for the individual counselee. Matching persons and job openings is one thing; relating self to occupations for purposes of lifetime career planning is something else. Pritchard suggests that

> *Self-exploration and occupation exploration should become more fully correlative processes.* The strong tendency in counseling to dichotomize *self*-exploration and *occupational* exploration as independent processes—that is, first to build up a picture of the client and only *then* to turn to consideration of occupational information to "find" a "match"—must be overcome.[25]

Could it be that guidance testing can contribute both to self-exploration and to career exploration while at the same time helping relate the two?

The desirability and value of career exploration is widely recognized. The question is, "What can we do to facilitate career exploration?" The ideal answer is, "Provide every child with ample opportunities for intensive, firsthand exploration of every occupation in the world of work." A *sampling* of firsthand and vicarious experiences is more likely to be practical, however. But which experiences? After all, the world of work is large and complex. And what about the student's personal characteristics—interests, abilities, working condition preferences, values, etc.? Are they irrelevant to the exploration, planning, and decision-making processes? If not, then what are some ways of knowing and understanding one's personal characteristics and their career relevance? Through one's experiences? The reactions of others? Tests? But what do tests have to offer? After all, don't tests scores simply reflect the marks the individual makes on paper?

Major Factors in Career Decision Making

Decision making is an integral part of career development. As Katz has pointed out, vocational development may be a continuous process, but ". . . the process is enacted through a sequence of choices."[26] Only recently, however, has career decision making become the subject of scientific inquiry. At the molar level Ginzberg, Super, and Tiedeman have each described a sequence of stages or tasks that are involved in career decisions. For example, Ginzberg et al.[27] talk about exploration, crystallization, and specification. Super[28] speaks of an exploration stage characterized by the developmental tasks of crystallizing, specifying, and implementing a vocational preference. Tiedeman and O'Hara[29] prefer to describe the vocational decision-making process in terms of exploration, crystallization, choice, clarification, and implementation. Each of these formulations suggests a sequence of progressively more specific and definite commitments on the part of the decision maker.

A cursory reading of the three formulations might lead one to believe that each individual, in the process of career choice, travels the decision-making path only once and that exploratory activities, for example, are relevant to only one period or stage of life. Katz[30] points out, however, that career decision making is, in fact, characterized by continuous recycling through the stages of decision making.

> Thus, tentative choice, exploration, crystallization, and specification (to continue to use Ginzberg's nomenclature) slide along from year to year—not however, in one grand consecutive parade as the individual marches through adolescence and into adulthood, but in a number of recurrent series . . . . At the eighth or ninth-grade choice-point, pupils "specify" the most proximate decisions (schedule for next year), "crystallize" those a little more distant (whether to go to college or not), and "explore" even more distant ones (which college or other educational institution . . .).[31]

As implied by Katz and emphasized by Super, society more or less calls the time and sets the pace for the decision-making sequences. However, the process is not an orderly series of unrepeated and unrelated steps.

A final concept useful in describing the decision-making process at the molar level is that of disjointed incrementalism (Braybrooke and Lindblom[32]). As interpreted by Gross, this concept suggests that

> . . . decisions are always made on the basis of very limited knowledge, and typically involve a relatively small change from an existing state of affairs. Further, the choice process is a jagged operation consisting of a series of steps, reversible in many places, and marked often by an adjustment of end to means. . . . often persons do not *first* look at the ends that they seek to attain, and then go about looking for the means.[33]

Instead, a person ". . . *looks for* ends that can be attained by the means that he has."[34]

At the molecular level the components involved in the act of decision making recently have been the subject of considerable attention. (See, for example, Clarke, Gelatt, and Levine; Gelatt and Clarke; Herr; Katz; Thoresen and Mehrens.[35]) Chief among these components are the outcomes associated with different choice options, the desirability (utility) of these outcomes from the standpoint of the individual, and the probability of achieving the outcomes. Clarke, Gelatt, and Levine[36] point out that career decisions are made with a combination of risk and uncertainty and that, one way or another, they involve probabilities—estimates of "what will happen if . . ." In theory the probabilities affecting a decision can be of two kinds: objective (e.g., based on statistical likelihoods) or subjective (e.g., based on personal forecasts). In the realm of career choice, however, the probabilities are always subjective because it is the individual who decides (Gelatt and Clarke; Thoresen and Mehrens[37]). Gelatt and Clarke cite evidence that

... subjective probability estimates play a crucial role in the decision process. Furthermore, the role appears to be sufficiently pervasive to suggest that subjective probability estimates may be an integral part of the educational-vocational decision process *even when the student lacks sufficient objective information upon which to base the estimates.* Thus, if a student is going to make such estimates and use them regardless, it would seem essential that through effective counseling the estimates be based as much as possible on fact rather than on wishful thinking, myth, or "hearsay." [Italics added.][38]

Gelatt and Clarke also cite studies indicating that individuals can incorporate objective data into their personal probability estimates with the result being an increase in realism. Finally, they suggest that ". . . a primary function of an effective guidance program would be the gathering and organizing of a broad base of relevant factual data to be used by students in formulating realistic probability estimates."[39]

Implications for Career Guidance

What are the implications for career guidance of these molar and molecular views of the career decision-making process? We have seen that decision making is an integral part of career development and that information, whether in the form of facts or probabilities, is a necessary component of decisions. According to current formulations, career development involves an overlapping sequence of choice points, each in turn involving a sequence of preparatory decision stages occurring over time. Exploration, whether active or passive, is inescapable as a decision-making stage. Career exploration and self-exploration are part of the same process. Many career decisions, it appears, may be shaped and framed in small increments, and while society does provide one-way gates, the steps leading to these gates are typically small and leisurely. At the same time individuals often travel along career paths largely determined by available means rather than desired ends. Their ability to choose from among the available paths may be seriously hindered by the lack of information enabling them to forecast what lies around the bend.

In summary, it would appear that at least six specific implications for career guidance can be drawn from this view of career decision making.

1. Because of the relative invisibility of occupations in our complex society and because of the natural tendency for means to determine ends in career planning, a major function of guidance is to widen the field of exploration during early stages of the career decision-making process.

2. Career exploration is crucial to career decision making because it can a) provide the student with information about possible choice options including probable outcomes of these choices; b) facilitate the experiencing of career options; and c) focus attention on self in relation to these options.

3. The sequential, incremental, and time-extensive nature of decision making suggests that there is ample opportunity for the provision and the clarification of information needed in career decision making.

4. Because of the sequential, incremental, and time-extensive nature of decision making, information available during the early stages of decision

making is subject to repeated reality testing and undergoes a self-corrective process by means of successive approximation.

5. Since a given individual may be simultaneously involved in several different decision-making problems and stages, his needs for information at a given point in time will vary both in type and content.

6. The need for information of the "what if . . ." variety in career decision making is incontestable. Information on the probable outcomes of different courses of action constitutes a necessary, but not sufficient, condition for making decisions wisely.

THE ROLE OF TESTING IN CAREER GUIDANCE

What, then, do tests have to offer career guidance? The major contribution is information—information that facilitates career exploration and focuses on the "what if's" in career decision making.

Information for Career Exploration and Decision Making

Information for career exploration is not information that forecloses the decision-making process by finding Johnny the occupation he ought to enter or the choice he ought to make. Rather, it is information that suggests to Johnny things about himself and careers that he might want to explore in order to meet the decisions that lie before him. The information is not crucial by itself, but rather, in terms of the exploration it stimulates. Exploration, of course, takes time. Hence, testing for the purpose of stimulating exploration must be introduced early in the decision-making process, and the individual must be provided with encouragement and opportunities for exploration. With respect to career planning and development in the global sense, several factors suggest that tests can make a useful contribution to self-exploration and career exploration as early as the junior high school years. These are the years of puberty for most students, the years when abilities differentiate and interests, values, and other motive attributes begin to crystallize. Whether we like it or not, many students of junior high school age are already making decisions that will have an influence on the direction of their careers. During the junior high school years tests can contribute information relevant to the decisions that must be made while pointing out new avenues to the future that the student may want to explore.

This is not to suggest that tests should or can be the sole means of stimulating career exploration. Instead, it is proposed that tests can best be used in the context of a developmental guidance program, a program that seeks to stimulate student exploration through a wide range of articulated activities. Most frequently, this will be a school-based program. However, developmental guidance and counseling activities readily lend themselves to use with groups in a variety of settings (e.g., colleges, employment services, and youth agencies). Examples of these activities were listed earlier in this chapter, and a comprehensive discussion is provided by the chapter that follows.

The second major contribution of tests to career guidance is the provision of information bearing on the "what if's" of decision making. Decision theory tells us that an essential component of every decision is consideration of the probability of various outcomes. For certain categories of outcomes, which will be discussed later, tests can provide some of the necessary "what if" types of information. However, prior participation by the student in a developmental career guidance program is important because, as every counselor knows, "what if" types of information introduced in the absence of the preparatory stages of decision making can easily be turned into "I should." Counselors may subscribe to the belief that "test scores should be seen in the context of all other available information," but this may be psychologically impossible for a counselee who is provided with a test profile today and feels compelled (internally or externally) to make a choice tomorrow. Under these circumstances test results will often loom large in the decision-making process, and a square-peg interpretation (on the part of the counselee at least) may be unavoidable. A developmental career guidance program should provide the necessary time and the appropriate context for introducing students both to the exploratory and to the predictive types of information from tests.

The Individual as the Predictor

A topic closely related to the one above is the role of tests as predictors in career guidance. Statistical predictions of occupational and educational success are an important part of theory building and theory testing in vocational psychology. Certainly, predictive studies also provide useful background information for career guidance in the form of test validities and the correlates of career development and adjustment. However, in career planning and decision making it is the individual who is the predictor, not the counselor or whatever instruments he may use. Decision theory tells us that the outcome probabilities used by students in making career decisions are always subjective. Only the student can assimilate and combine the objective probabilities based on the experience of others as abstracted through tests, with the subjective probabilities based on his own experience.

Whether or not one holds that it is more accurate to use the formula and the "cookbook" in forecasting the future, the fact of subjective probability remains. Is this necessarily bad? We have repeatedly stated that a major role of tests in career development is to facilitate career exploration. Developmental career guidance programs provide the student with long-term opportunities for exploratory experiences. The accompanying opportunities for individual counseling can help him reflect on, clarify, and perhaps modify his or her value system and preferences in light of these experiences. During the process of exploration new alternatives will come into view and others will recede into the background. The student will also obtain information (perhaps some of it from tests) on his chances of being able to realize each of the alternatives to satisfaction. The resulting subjective probabilities will exist in the context of an evolving value structure related to the same outcomes.

As the student undertakes more intensive exploration of particular alternatives, he or she will receive additional feedback on the likelihood that he can successfully pursue each alternative and that it will yield the valued outcomes.

With counselor monitoring and intervention, the exploratory process can involve a continuous set of assessments and reassessments on the part of the student. As a result, he should have a well-integrated matrix of alternatives, probabilities, and values at the point of decision.

Thus, in the context of a developmental career guidance program, the objective probabilities provided by tests become part of a much larger whole. Tests constitute a vehicle for exploring the self, the outside world, and self in relation to that world. However, the student is the ultimate predictor, and he continually adjusts his predictions on the basis of experience (direct, vicarious, and the experience of others abstracted by tests) and his evaluation of that experience.

Focused Exploration

In previous discussion attention has been directed to the broadening or exploratory uses of tests. However, there comes a stage in the decision-making process when it is necessary to narrow the range of choice options under consideration. Ginzberg, Super, and Tiedeman each speak of crystallizing preferences and specifying or implementing choices. Youth cannot go on forever keeping all possible gates open, for to do so would greatly impair their ability to pass through any but the largest of the gateways. The career development tasks set for youth by society sooner or later force a commitment; a narrowing process eventually has to occur, usually during the late teens in our society. A major task of guidance is to insure that this narrowing does not occur by default—to help youth survey the career world before choosing to take up residence in this or that region.

During the elementary school years the survey is like a plane trip around the world. The major continents of employment become apparent, and the student is helped to identify different climates and features of the workscape. Career awareness is the primary goal. Once the age of puberty is passed, however, the increased consciousness of self, the impending status of adulthood, and the move toward independence and self-direction combine to make more intensive, personalized experience in the world of work desirable. The student now needs to spend some time in different work locales to find out whether they are merely nice places or whether he would really like to live there. At this stage career exploration takes on a new dimension. Whereas during the prepuberty years it could be broad and general, a "once-over-lightly" partly based on transitory fantasies and interests, career exploration during the postpuberty years requires focus and intensity. Exploration of the whole world of work must give way to exploration of the probabilities and the possibilities.

The major task of career guidance at this stage would appear to be broadening the scope of the probabilities and possibilities while helping youth to find *their* way among them. Perhaps the most appropriate term to describe this task is *"focused exploration."* One of the major guidance roles of testing is to help provide focus to career exploration—not a focus that singles out the "right" occupation for Johnny or Sally but, rather, a focus that points to regions of the work world that they may want to visit. Where they will live depends on the climate they are looking for and the opportunities and available resources in the regions with that climate. It is the individual who provides the final focus.

Summary

The role of tests in career guidance is therefore threefold: first, to stimulate, broaden, and provide focus to career exploration; second, to stimulate exploration of self in relation to career; and, third, to provide "what if" information with respect to various career choice options. This role can best be performed in the context of a developmental career guidance program.

IMPLICATIONS FOR COUNSELORS

Initially, it should be emphasized that the chief function of the counselor is *not* testing. Testing constitutes only one of the tools that can be used in a career guidance program. This, of course, is obvious to almost everyone; but, on the other hand, "test 'em, tell 'em" approaches to career guidance are still widespread, and a lot of time *is* spent in test administration, processing, and interpretation. No attention will be given in this section to various types of assessment procedures or to the interpretation of test results since these topics are well covered in many basic measurement texts. For example, Goldman[40] provides an excellent discussion of statistical and clinical approaches to test interpretation along with an analysis of several important problems, including use of tests with the disadvantaged.

Perhaps the most important role of the counselor in testing is to help students transform information from tests into experience, for unless information is experienced and integrated into the self-concept, it can have very little impact on career development. Experience, as used here, refers to both external experience as obtained in career exploration and internal experience as obtained in self-exploration. The former contributes to the latter because of the likelihood of experiencing new aspects of self during the active exploration of careers. This transformation of information into experience is one of a chain of transformations that are necessary if testing is to have impact on career development. First, test data (scores, percentile ranks, stanines, etc.) must be transformed into information relevant to counseling and guidance; next, this information must be transformed into experience; and, finally, the experience must be transformed into career plans and decisions. Test authors have the primary responsibility for data-information transformation, although this responsibility is shared with counselors. Counselors have the primary responsibility for transforming information into experience, although this responsibility is shared with other educators, citizens in the community, and the counselees themselves. Finally, counselees alone have the responsibility of transforming experience into career decisions, although counselors, parents, and other interested individuals can provide help.

The main vehicle for the counselor in meeting his responsibilities is a developmental career guidance program coupled with the periodic opportunity for counseling. The role of counseling in the context of career guidance is to help the student assimilate the information and experience he has attained, to assess its meaning for him, and to plan next steps in the decision-making process. Pritchard[41] points out that a special function of counselors in the transformation of information to experience is to help the student form "occupational hypotheses" concerning those personal and occupational factors and relationships which are of particular significance to him. These may or may not be the factors covered by the normal modes of personal assessment or occupational classification. Pritchard warns against relying too heavily on universal methods for relating information from tests to the career world. While these methods may be useful in general, they should not be used arbitrarily or uniformly. Hence, within the limits of his time and resources, Pritchard suggests that the counselor should tailor the process of "developing trial vocational suggestions"[42] to the characteristics and readiness of his counselees.

Another major role of the counselor in testing, one with special relevance for the disadvantaged, is to help students find ways of transforming possibilities into probabilities. Traditional, prediction-oriented uses of tests in guidance have emphasized the status quo—the probabilities given existing circumstances.[43] On the other hand, exploratory uses of tests focus on possibilities, without ruling out alternatives because of current deficiencies in ability, education, or personal resources. The individual, with the help of exploratory experiences and in the context of his value system, determines his goals. When these goals center on the possible rather than on the probable, the counselor's challenge is to help make the possible a reality. This is a task that cannot be performed by assessment alone, although tests have been faulted for this reason. Tests can point out some of the possibilities and probabilities, and they can provide clues as to how change can be brought about. But they cannot talk with the individual's parents; integrate health, socioeconomic, and classroom performance data into an effective plan of action; help the student weigh the personal costs and directions of change; develop a new school program; obtain financial aid; or arrange for remedial help. The implementation of change requires counseling and guidance of the highest order.

A developmental career guidance program can intervene in the normal course of events by providing an effective context for facilitating change in the student. Strong guidance programs can also be effective in bringing about change in student environments. Both types of change, personal and environmental, can help transform the remotely possible into the highly probable for a given individual.

IMPLICATIONS FOR TESTING PROCEDURES

As noted in a previous section, there is nothing new in the current emphasis on career exploration. Neither is it new to suggest that tests might be used to facilitate exploration. Interest inventories have been used for this purpose for a number of years. In the past, however, attention has been concentrated on the use of tests and other assessment procedures at decision points or in bringing resolution to problems. The nature of assessment appropriate for this purpose differs considerably from that which is needed to facilitate career exploration.

Bandwidth of Testing Instruments

Some years ago Cronbach and Gleser[44] distinguished between what they called wideband and narrowband approaches to measurement. Narrowband instruments focus intensive assessment on a specific, limited area of concern with the objective being highly accurate measures of those personal characteristics most relevant to that concern. Usually only a few measures are involved (e.g., a college placement test covering English, mathematics, and natural science). Wideband instruments, on the other hand, assess a wide variety of personal characteristics relevant to a number of concerns. Thus, many different measures are involved (e.g., ACT's Career Planning Program, which covers eight interests, eight abilities, seven competencies, six job values, four working condition preferences, and a number of educational background items). Since testing time is always limited and since test reliability is a function of testing time, the measures of specific characteristics in wideband instruments will generally be shorter and less reliable than narrowband measures.

Cronbach and Gleser's delineation of the bandwidth dimension in measurement has implications for the types of measures that are used in career guidance. Wideband measurement, it would appear, is especially appropriate to facilitating self-exploration and career exploration. Because of the wide variety of personal characteristics that can be covered, the student is presented with several perspectives from which he can view his "self" in relation to careers. New ways of abstracting experience and focusing it on career plans are added to the information about himself that he already has. Ideally, two kinds of information are added: comprehensive, integrated information on personal characteristics (i.e., information presented in terms of self); and information relating these personal characteristics to career options (i.e., information presented in career terms). Among the major limitations of many tests currently used in guidance are their failure to integrate different kinds of information (e.g., *only* interests or *only* abilities are covered) and their failure to provide information both in self and career terms.

Use of tests in the context of a developmental career guidance program makes wideband measures desirable from another standpoint. Since developmental guidance is for everyone, and since there are wide differences in the information needs of different individuals or of a given individual simultaneously engaged in several decision-making cycles, only wideband measures can provide the variety of information that is needed. As already noted, this cannot be accomplished without the sacrifice of some degree of reliability for any given measure. However, decision making in a developmental program is based on an *accumulation* of information and experience. The weight of any particular piece of information within the whole is therefore minimized. Inaccuracies or inappropriate interpretations tend to wash out over time. The self-corrective process of successive approximation has already been noted. Thus, some degree of reliability loss can be tolerated in wideband measures for the sake of comprehensive assessment.

A second major function of testing mentioned in previous sections is the provision of information for use during the choice or specification stage of decision making. Usually, this information will be in the form of probabilities of success in various endeavors. Since the specification stage of decision making often leads to a commitment of considerable consequence and often involves substantial investments of time, money, and emotion, it is desirable to use the best possible information available. At the same time, information needs are likely to differ radically from one person to another. Hence, the ideal assessment procedure during the specification stage of decision making involves *narrowband* instruments that are *tailored* to the unique circumstances and information needs of the individual. This means tailored testing on an as-needed basis as advocated by Goldman.[45] To summarize, then, one would prefer wideband instruments: for everyone as part of a developmental guidance program, for use in the early stages of career decision making, and to facilitate exploration of self and self in relation to career. One would prefer narrowband instruments: for specific individuals according to unique needs; for the specification and choice stages of decision making; and for information bearing on the "what if" component of decision making.

Models for Data-Information Transformation

Two models for transforming test data to counseling information have been implicit in the discussion thus far: a model suggesting choice options for exploration and a model indicating probable level of success should a particular option be pursued. The model most familiar to readers will undoubtedly be the model used to provide predictions of performance or success, i.e., the correlation and regression model. Less well-known, although by no means new, is the discriminant-centour model (Tiedeman, Rulon, and Bryan[46]). The function of this model is to provide an indication of a student's similarity to the characteristics of persons already pursuing various choice options. Degree of similarity can be expressed statistically via centour scores, two-digit numbers with some of the same properties as percentile ranks. However, there are several nonstatistical versions of this model just as there are nonstatistical versions of the regression model. The Strong Vocational Interest Blank (SVIB) represents a good example. The special test construction procedures used in the SVIB result in standard scores indicating degree of similarity in item responses to the responses of members of various occupational groups.

Most counselors have probably used the discriminant-centour model a number of times without realizing it. The act of test profile interpretation, when conducted for purposes of facilitating career exploration, constitutes a subjective version of what discriminant analysis and centour score procedures accomplish statistically. However, there are well-known difficulties inherent in subjective approaches to profile interpretation. These difficulties result from a variety of problems commonly subsumed under the term "profile problem" (Tiedeman[47]). Rulon, Tiedeman, Tatsuoka, and Langmuir[48] provide an extended discussion of how discriminant analysis and centour score procedures can be used to overcome the profile problem. Prediger discusses[49] and illustrates[50] the potential contribution of these procedures to career guidance.

The goal of the discriminant-centour model, as used in career guidance, is *not* to find a perfect match that leads to choice, to predict membership in some group, or to estimate degree of success in some endeavor, but, rather, to say "Look, here are some occupations (vocational education programs, college majors, etc.) that attract people who are similar to you in several ways. You may want to check into these occupations." A list of regression-based success estimates covering various choice options could also be used to suggest areas for exploration. However, this would invite the counselee to compare his chances for success in the different areas, and unfortunately, such comparisons are fraught with technical problems such as their sensitivity to similarities and differences among regression slopes (Cronbach[51]), differences from area to area in criteria and distributions of success, and possible restriction of range on critical predictors. These problems are surmounted, in part, through use of experience (expectancy) tables. However, for reasons which shall be discussed later in this section, the counseling use of success estimates is best focused on the choice options which the student decides to explore. Thus, these two models for data-information transformation complement each other, with the discriminant model providing information to stimulate exploration and the regression model providing success estimates to be used during the process of exploration.

Similarity as the Interpretive Bridge

Both the statistical and subjective versions of the discriminant-centour model and the regression model extract meaning from test results through the principle of similarity. However, the implications of similarity are different in the two models, and this has relevance for their use. Centour scores, for example, reflect the degree of similarity of a student to typical members in each of several groups. The regression model focuses on one group at a time and tells the student that members of the group with predictor scores similar to his typically perform at such-and-such a level on a criterion variable. (In statistical versions of the regression model, a regression line, plane, etc., is used to represent the trend of the data. Similarity to the subset of group members is exact within the limits of measurement errors only when one predictor is involved.) If the student is also similar to group members in terms of whatever *other* personal characteristics are relevant, he may perform at the same general level.

It is important to note that predictions based on regression equations start with the assumption of *similarity* to members of the group for which predictions are provided. (Some would say that *membership* is assumed [Tatsuoka[52]], a distinction with important practical implications, as noted below.) Regression equations, after all, are based on data from individuals who have been members of a group long enough for some criterion of performance to be obtained. Strictly speaking, predictions from these equations apply only to members of the same group. But we often do not know whether a counselee is or will be a member of a particular group, and this lack of knowledge can lead to some interesting questions. For example, how much credence should Jim give to his success estimates for vocational-technical programs in commercial art, drafting, agri-business, and nursing? He is not similar in important ways to most nursing students, but will his differences affect the accuracy of his success estimate? Suppose that he also differs in many respects from students in drafting. Should his success estimate be adjusted upward, downward, or disregarded completely? Unfortunately, we can never determine empirically the answers to these questions. Jim, after all, will enter one program. Most likely, he and others like him will never receive grades in the other programs. Hence, the necessary validation studies cannot be run.

In a theoretical attack on this problem, Tatsuoka[53] reports the development of a joint index of group membership and success which is obtained by multiplying the probability of membership in a group by the probability of exceeding a specified level on a performance criterion. The general direction of this approach would appear to have promise. However, the multiplicative model for combining membership and success probabilities to obtain the joint index may not be justified by the actual nature of the interaction between group characteristics and individual performance. The use of group membership probabilities rather than similarity estimates is also open to question, especially since the probabilities of membership are affected by relative group size. The key question from a psychological standpoint would appear to be whether similarity of characteristics or probability of membership is the most appropriate conditional consideration for regression predictions. As Prediger[54] has noted, it is possible to have a high probability of group membership with little or no similarity in characteristics. This whole area certainly warrants further investigation.

To review, then, inferences drawn from both the discriminant-centour model and the regression model are based on the principle of similarity. In the latter case similarity of predictor scores to those of a particular subgroup within a group is used to estimate standing on some criterion, usually performance or success. In the former case degree of similarity to typical or average members in various groups is used to indicate potential compatibility with the group members. Success criteria can be used in defining group membership in the discriminant-centour model. However, degree of success is *not* estimated within a specific group. Hence, lack of similarity to a group implies lack of compatibility with the characteristics of group members, not necessarily lack of success.

This difference in function of the two models is possibly reflected by differences in the psychological dimensions usually involved. Multiple discriminant analysis identifies those dimensions of human characteristics which optimally differentiate groups, while multiple regression analysis identifies those predictor dimensions which maximize the associated differences in criterion performance within a group. Past research has generally shown that the discriminant dimensions are more likely to involve subsets of motive variables (such as interests), while regression dimensions are more likely to involve abilities. This finding is in keeping with the different functions of the procedures.

It would appear, then, because of the special emphases and limitations of both the regression and discriminant-centour models, that a two-stage strategy for their use in career guidance is appropriate. The compatibility-oriented discriminant-centour model can be used to survey an entire choice domain in order to identify choice options for possible exploration. The performance-oriented regression model can then be used to focus on probable level of success in those choice options which the student decides to explore. Of course, choice options should not be limited to those suggested by the discriminant-centour model. One must keep in mind, however, that a "reasonable degree of similarity" may well be an appropriate prerequisite for use of the success estimates.

The Viability of Success and Similarity Estimates

We have already discussed some of the serious problems involved in the prediction of occupational success. As noted in the beginning of this chapter, research has shown that the relationship between occupational success and tested characteristics is quite low for guidance (as versus selection) purposes. At best, the data generally support gross estimates of "suitability" or "lack of suitability" rather than estimates of level of success. The picture is brighter, however, with respect to the prediction of educational success. Research has repeatedly shown that there are substantial and useful relationships between tested characteristics and success in educational and job-training programs. Since these programs represent important vehicles for career development, the predictions of success that are possible can make a valuable contribution to career guidance.

While it may never be possible to provide comprehensive predictions of occupational success that are useful in career exploration, the ability to determine the *similarity* of a counselee's characteristics to the characteristics of members of a broad range of occupations is now an actuality. Overlap in the interests, abilities, job values, and other traits of certain occupational groups does not preclude the development of information useful in career exploration. Rather, it is a fact of life which the student should know. Likewise, he should be aware of the degree of diversity within groups as well as the differences that exist among groups—and important differences among occupational (and educational) groups *do* exist.[55] These differences may not be sufficient to allow the accurate prediction of future group membership, but this is not the goal of guidance. Joselyn and Prediger[56] have demonstrated, through use of the discriminant-centour model, that group differences in tested characteristics readily lend themselves to facilitating career exploration. Hence, trait-and-factor research on occupational group differences would appear to hold considerable promise for future guidance applications.

SUMMARY

The following points[57] summarize the main ideas cited or developed in this chapter. In a sense, they represent a set of principles or postulates that might form part of a new foundation for the use of tests in career guidance.

1. The potential contribution of tests and other assessment procedures to career guidance is based on the supposition that information about human attributes, expressed in the form of traits or factors, is a necessary although not a sufficient condition for optimizing career development.

2. Traits are everyday tools for organizing and describing human attributes and experience. Whether assessed by subjective judgment, by tests, or by other procedures, their use in career guidance is inescapable.

3. Theory, research, and common sense tell us that we have passed the era in which square-peg, square-hole uses of tests could be viewed as the epitome of vocational guidance. However, blaming measures of traits and factors for the square-peg approach to career guidance is somewhat like blaming skin color for racial discrimination. It is essential to differentiate between assessments of human attributes and square-peg uses of these assessments.

4. Both career development theory and career decision-making theory suggest that the role of tests in career guidance is threefold; first, to stimulate, broaden, and provide focus to career exploration; second, to stimulate exploration of self in relation to career; and third, to provide "what if" information with respect to various career choice options.

5. Test data must go through a chain of transformations if they are to be useful in career guidance. First, test data must be transformed into information relevant to counseling and guidance; next, this information must be transformed into exploratory activities and self-evaluated experiences; and, finally, these experiences must be transformed into career plans and decisions. Responsibilities for these transformations (in order of presentation) primarily rest with test publishers, counselors, and counselees.

6. Because of the important and active roles of the counselor and counselee in these transformations, tests can best be used in the context of a career guidance program.

7. Two general models for transforming test data to counseling information are available: the regression model and the discriminant-centour model. The compatibility-oriented discriminant-centour model can best be used to survey an entire choice domain in order to identify choice options for possible exploration. The performance-oriented regression model can best be used to provide information on probable levels of success in those choice options which the student decides to explore.

8. Wideband measurement instruments are appropriate for use in career guidance programs to facilitate career exploration during the early stages of decision making. Narrowband instruments, tailored to an individual's unique needs, are preferable for providing "what if" kinds of information during the specification stage of decision making.

9. Research indicates that it will probably never be possible to provide predictions of occupational success that are sufficiently comprehensive and precise to be of general use in career guidance. However, observed differences among occupational and educational groups are of sufficient magnitude to be of use in facilitating career exploration.

10. In career guidance the counselee, not the test or the counselor, makes the ultimate predictions and decisions.

NOTES

1. F. Loesser, *The Inch Worm* (New York: Frank Music Corporation, 1951).
2. E. E. Ghiselli, *The Validity of Occupational Aptitude Tests* (New York: Wiley, 1966); L. Goldman, "Tests and Counseling: The Marriage That Failed," *Measurement and Evaluation in Guidance* 4(1972):213–20; D. J. Pucel, H. F. Nelson, and D. A. Mohamed, "The Ability of Standardized Test Instruments

to Predict Training Success and Employment Success" (Minneapolis: Project MINI-SCORE, Department of Industrial Education, University of Minnesota, 1972); R. L. Thorndike, "The Prediction of Vocational Success," *The Vocational Guidance Quarterly* 11(1963):179–187; United States Department of Labor, *Manual for the USTES General Aptitude Test Battery, section III: Development* (Washington, D.C.: U.S. Department of Labor, Manpower Administration, 1970).

3. D. E. Super, "Vocational Development Theory: Persons, Positions, and Processes," *The Counseling Psychologist* 1, 1(1969):2–9.
4. J. O. Crites, *Vocational Psychology* (New York: McGraw-Hill, 1969).
5. J. L. Boyd, Jr. and B. Shimberg, *Handbook of Performance Testing* (Princeton, N.J.: Educational Testing Service, 1971); Crites, *op. cit.*; D. J. Weiss et al., "Instrumentation for the theory of work adjustment," *Minnesota Studies in Vocational Rehabilitation* 21(1966).
6. R. Fitzpatrick and E. J. Morrison, "Performance and product evaluation," *Educational Measurement*, 2nd ed., R. L. Thorndike, ed. (Washington, D.C.: American Council on Education, 1971).
7. R. C. Droege et al., "Development of a Nonreading Edition of the General Aptitude Test Battery," *Measurement and Evaluation in Guidance* 3(1970): 45–53.
8. N. C. Cole and G. R. Hanson, "An Analysis of the Structure of Vocational Interests," *Journal of Counseling Psychology* 18(1971):478–86; Crites, *op. cit.*
9. W. W. Cooley and P. R. Lohnes, *Predicting Development of Young Adults* (Pittsburgh: American Institutes for Research and School of Education, University of Pittsburgh, 1968).
10. M. Katz, *Decision and Values: A Rationale for Secondary School Guidance* (New York: College Entrance Examination Board, 1963), pp. 12–13.
11. R. Clarke, H. B. Gelatt, and L. Levine, "A Decision-making Paradigm for Local Guidance Research," *Personnel and Guidance Journal* 44(1965):40–51.
12. H. B. Gelatt and R. B. Clarke, "Role of Subjective Probabilities in the Decision Process," *Journal of Counseling Psychology* 14(1967):332–41; M. Katz, "A Model of Guidance for Career Decision-making," *Vocational Guidance Quarterly* 15(1966):2–10; C. E. Thoresen and W. A. Mehrens, "Decision Theory and Vocational Counseling: Important Concepts and Questions," *Personnel and Guidance Journal* 46(1967):165–72.
13. L. Goldman, *Using Tests in Counseling*, 2nd ed. (New York: Appleton-Century-Crofts, 1971); R. A. Meyering, *Uses of Test Data in Counseling* (Boston: Houghton Mifflin, 1968).
14. Clarke, Gelatt, and Levine, *op. cit.*
15. J. P. Jordaan, "Exploratory Behavior: The Formation of Self and Occupational Concepts," *Career Development: Self-Concept Theory*, D. E. Super et al., Research Monograph No. 4. (New York: College Entrance Examination Board, 1963), p. 48.
16. E. Ginzberg et al., *Occupational Choice: An Approach to a General Theory* (New York: Columbia University Press, 1951); Super, "Vocational Development Theory," *op. cit.*; D. V. Tiedeman and R. P. O'Hara, *Career Development: Choice and Adjustment*, Research Monograph No. 3 (New York: College Entrance Examination Board, 1963).
17. D. E. Super, "The Critical Ninth Grade: Vocational Choice or Vocational Exploration," *Personnel and Guidance Journal* 39(1960):106–109, 109.
18. D. H. Pritchard, "The Occupational Exploration Process: Some Operational Implications," *Personnel and Guidance Journal* 40(1962):674–80.
19. W. W. Tennyson, Comment [on Vocational-Technical Education Symposium]. *The Vocational Guidance Quarterly* 18(1970):261–63.

20. E. L. Herr and S. H. Cramer, *Vocational Guidance and Career Development in the Schools: Toward a Systems Approach* (Boston: Houghton Mifflin, 1972).

21. N. C. Gysbers and E. J. Moore, "Career Development in the Schools," *Contemporary Concepts in Vocational Education*, G. F. Law, ed. (Washington, D.C.: American Vocational Association, 1971), pp. 218–29.

22. D. E. Super, *The Psychology of Careers* (New York: Harper and Row, 1957), p. 196.

23. Pritchard, *op. cit.*

24. United States Department of Labor, *Dictionary of Occupational Titles, 1965,* Vol. II. *Occupational classification and industry index.* (3rd ed.) Washington, D.C.: Author, Manpower Administration, 1965.

25. Pritchard, p. 677.

26. Katz, A Model of Guidance for Career Decision-making, p. 8.

27. Ginzberg et al., *op. cit.*

28. D. E. Super, "Vocational Development in Adolescence and Early Adulthood: Tasks and Behaviors," *Career Development: Self-concept Theory.*

29. Tiedeman and O'Hara, *op. cit.*

30. Katz, *Decision and values: A rationale for secondary school guidance.*

31. *Ibid.*, p. 34.

32. D. Braybrooke and C. E. Lindblom, *A Strategy of Decision* (New York: Free Press of Glenco, 1963).

33. E. Gross, "A Sociological Approach to the Analysis of Preparation for Work Life," *Personnel and Guidance Journal* 45(1967):416–23.

34. *Ibid.*, p. 423.

35. Clarke, Gelatt, and Levine, *op. cit.;* Gelatt and Clarke, *op. cit.;* E. L. Herr, *Decision-making and Vocational Development*, Guidance Monograph Series, Series IV (Boston: Houghton Mifflin, 1970). Katz, "A Model of Guidance for Career Decision-making." Thoresen & Mehrens, *op. cit.*

36. Clarke, Gelatt, and Levine, *op. cit.*

37. Gelatt and Clarke, *op. cit.;* Thoresen and Mehrens, *op. cit.*

38. Gelatt and Clarke, *op. cit.*, pp. 338–39.

39. *Ibid.*, p. 340.

40. Goldman, *Using Tests in Counseling.*

41. Pritchard, *op. cit.*

42. *Ibid.*, p. 678.

43. L. Goldman, "The Process of Vocational Assessment," *Man in a World at Work*, H. Borow, ed. (Boston: Houghton Mifflin, 1964).

44. L. J. Cronbach and G. C. Gleser, *Psychological Tests and Personnel Decisions* (Urbana: University of Illinois Press, 1957).

45. Goldman, *Using Tests in Counseling.*

46. D. V. Tiedeman, P. J. Rulon and J. G. Bryan, "The Multiple Discriminant Function—A Symposium," *Harvard Educational Review* 21(1951):71–95.

47. D. V. Tiedeman, "A Model for the Profile Problem," *Proceedings, 1953 Invitational Conference on Testing Problems* (Princeton, N.J.: Educational Testing Service, 1954).

48. P. H. Rulon et al., *Multivariate Statistics for Personnel Classification* (New York: John Wiley and Sons, 1967).

49. D. J. Prediger, "Data-information Conversion in Test Interpretation," *Journal of Counseling Psychology* 18(1971):306–13.

50. D. J. Prediger, "Converting Test Data to Counseling Information: System Trial—with Feedback," *Journal of Educational Measurement* 8(1971):161–69.

51. L. J. Cronbach, "Test Validation," In *Educational Measurement,* 2nd ed.,

R. L. Thorndike, ed. (Washington, D.C.: American Council on Education, 1971).

52. M. M. Tatsuoka, *Multivariate Analysis* (New York: John Wiley and Sons, 1971).

53. *Ibid.*

54. Prediger, "Data-information Conversion in Test Interpretation."

55. The American College Testing Program, *Handbook for the ACT Career Planning Program*, revised ed. (Iowa City: American College Testing Program, 1972); A. R. Baggaley and J. P. Campbell, "Multiple-discriminant Analysis of Academic Curricula by Interest and Aptitude Variables," *Journal of Educational Measurement* 4(1967):143–49; F. H. Borgen et al., "Occupational Reinforcer Patterns," Vol. I, *Minnesota Studies in Vocational Rehabilitation* 24(1968); Cooley and Lohnes, *op. cit.*; A. G. J. E. D'Costa, *The Differentiation of High School Students in Vocational Education Areas by the Ohio Vocational Interest Survey*, doctoral dissertation, Ohio University (Ann Arbor, Mich.: University Microfilms, 1968), No. 68-14, 885; J. J. Doerr and J. L. Ferguson, "The Selection of Vocational-technical Students," *Vocational Guidance Quarterly* 17(1968):27–32; F. E. Dunn, "Two Methods for Predicting the Selection of a College Major," *Journal of Counseling Psychology* 16(1959):15–26; J. C. Flanagan et al., *Five Years after High School*, final report to the U.S. Office of Education (Palo Alto, Calif.: Project Talent Office, American Institutes for Research and University of Pittsburgh, 1971); R. C. Hall, "Occupational Group Contrasts in Terms of the Differential Aptitude Tests: An Application of Multiple Discriminant Analysis," *Educational and Psychological Measurement* 17(1957):556–67; J. L. Holland et al., *A Psychological Classification of Occupations*, Research Report No. 90. (Baltimore: Center for Social Organization of Schools, The Johns Hopkins University, 1970); P. R. Jeanneret and E. J. McCormick, *The Job Dimensions of "Worker-oriented" Job Variables and their Attribute Profiles as Based on Data from the Position Analysis Questionnaire*, Office of Naval Research Contract Nonr-1100 (28), Report No. 2. (Lafayette: Occupational Research Center, Purdue University, 1969); C. E. Lunneborg and P. W. Lunneborg, *Forecasting University Major with the Washington Pre-college Test Using Discriminant Functions* (Seattle: University of Washington, Bureau of Testing, 1970); J. L. Passmore, *Validation of a Discriminant Analysis of Eight Vocational-Technical Curricular Groups*, doctoral dissertation, University of Missouri (Ann Arbor, Mich.: University Microfilms, 1968), No. 69-3271; D. G. Paterson, C. d'A. Gerken, and M. E. Hahn, *Revised Minnesota Occupational Rating Scales* (Minneapolis: University of Minnesota Press, 1953); D. J. Pucel et al., *The Ability of Standardized Test Instruments to Differentiate Membership in Different Vocational-Technical Criteria* (Minneapolis: Project Mini-Score, Department of Industrial Education, University of Minnesota, 1972); H. A. Silver, *A Longitudinal Validation Study of the Minnesota Vocational Interest Inventory Utilizing High School Boys*, doctoral dissertation, State University of New York at Buffalo (Ann Arbor, Mich.: University Microfilms, 1967), No. 67-10, 160; R. F. Stahmann, "Predicting Graduation Major Field from Freshman Entrance Data," *Journal of Counseling Psychology* 16(1969):109–13; L. H. Stewart, "Characteristics of junior college students in occupationally oriented curricula," *Journal of Counseling Psychology* 13 (1966):46–52; L. H. Stewart, *A Study of Certain Characteristics of Students and Graduates of Occupation-centered Curricula*, Contract No. OE-6-85-072, Bureau of Research, USOE (Berkeley: University of California, 1968); R. L. Thorndike and E. Hagen, *Ten Thousand Careers* (New York: John Wiley and Sons, 1959); Tiedeman, Rulon, and Bryan, *op. cit.*; United States

Department of Labor, *Dictionary of occupational titles, 1965,* Vol. II; United States Department of Labor, *Manual for the USTES General Aptitude Test Battery, section III: Development;* D. K. Whitla, *An Evaluation of Differential Prediction for Counseling and Guidance,* doctoral dissertation, University of Nebraska (Ann Arbor, Mich.: University Microfilms, 1957), No. 20-991.

56. G. Joselyn, *School Counselors' Handbook for the Minnesota Statewide Vocational Testing Program* (Minneapolis: Minnesota Statewide Vocational Testing Program, Student Counseling Bureau, University of Minnesota, 1970); Prediger, "Converting Test Data to Counseling Information: System Trial—with Feedback."

57. Many of these points were first presented in D. J. Prediger, "Tests and Developmental Career Guidance: The Untried Relationship," *Measurement and Evaluation in Guidance* 5(1972):426–29.

SUGGESTED READING

Clarke, R., Gelatt, H. B., & Levine, L. "A Decision-making Paradigm for Local Guidance Research," *Personnel and Guidance Journal,* 44(1965): 40–51. Emphasizes the role of information in career decision making and illustrates procedures for obtaining the information needed for effective high school guidance services.

Cooley, W. W., and Lohnes, P. R. *Predicting Development of Young Adults.* Pittsburgh: American Institutes for Research and School of Education, University of Pittsburgh, 1968. An impressive and significant demonstration of the application of multivariate trait and factor procedures to career guidance and research. Places trait-and-factor theory firmly in the context of career development theory. See especially the "career development tree" based on Project TALENT research.

Goldman, L. *Using Tests in Counseling.* 2nd ed. New York: Appleton-Century-Crofts, 1971. Provides a comprehensive discussion of the use of tests with individuals including test selection, administration, scoring, and interpretation. The chapters on "bridges" between test scores and their meaning are especially valuable.

Prediger, D. J., ed. "Symposium—Tests and Counseling: The Marriage That Failed?" *Measurement and Evaluation in Guidance,* 5(October 1972). Papers presented at a 1972 APGA Convention with the same title. The value of tests in counseling is strongly challenged and stoutly defended by experts in the field of guidance assessment.

Thorndike, R. L., ed. *Educational Measurement.* 2nd ed. Washington, D.C.: American Council on Education, 1971. A landmark that presents the best thinking of measurement experts on a variety of theoretical and applied topics.

Thorndike, R. L., and Hagen, E. *Measurement and Evaluation in Psychology and Education.* 3rd ed. New York: Wiley, 1969. A comprehensive and down-to-earth introduction to basic testing concepts (for example, reliability, validity) and a variety of assessment procedures. It includes chapters on guidance applications of tests and on planning a school testing program.

14 Career Planning: The Use of Sequential Evaluated Experience

Bruce W. Bergland
University of Colorado at Denver

Few would argue with the statement that our society is characterized by breathtakingly rapid change, a theme that pervades this book. In *Future Shock* Toffler presents a particularly dramatic description of the breadth, speed, and effects of change.[1] Although, as he points out, change permeates all aspects of our lives, one dimension of particular concern to counselors is that which encompasses the world of work and of career planning. In recognizing the importance of planning for careers, and for life, career development theorists[2] and other investigators of life patterns among American youth[3] have emphasized that individuals need to learn how to adapt to change. These authors have stressed that not only must we be able to set personal goals, but we must also be able to recognize when goal changes are necessary and then make the required changes.

Since decision making is an integral function in the process of setting and changing personal goals, the recent concern with goal setting highlights the importance of decision-making skills in our lives. The difficulty is that many people never learn to solve problems or to make decisions in rational ways.[4] Frequently their decisions are impulsive, based on whim and inadequate information. Although it may be that some decisions in life should be made on impulse, other decisions, particularly those with far reaching consequences, require that the individual spend time and effort engaging in thoughtful and logical decision-making processes.[5]

Since there is no reason to assume that individuals can or will learn to become skilled decisionmakers on their own, the importance of "teaching" decision-making skills becomes evident. Recognition of the importance of teaching decision-making skills is actually by no means new. Decision theorists such as Edwards[6] and Cronbach and Gleser[7] have emphasized the importance of decision making and the use of relevant information in this process. In recent years numerous authors in counseling have repeatedly proposed the development of decision-making ability as a major goal of counseling. Wrenn[8] has stated that the major goal of counseling should be increased self-responsibility and increased maturity in decision making. Similarly, Gelatt[9] has interpreted the counselor's role as that of helping students learn how to make wise decisions. Through "decision-making counseling," he points out, students will be required to learn more about themselves and their environment as this information relates to the decisions facing them. Gelatt also has proposed that through guided participation in the decision-making process students will become increasingly able to make decisions independently and to accept responsibility for those decisions.

Thus counselors and counseling theorists have not been remiss in recognizing the need to help individuals learn how to make wise decisions. However, they seem to have been unable to translate their awareness into effective action plans. This statement is supported by recent studies and surveys of student needs[10] in which young people frequently indicated that during their school years they did not receive adequate assistance in selecting the kinds of occupations and life goals which, if pursued and attained, would have been likely to furnish the personal fulfillment they reported lacking.

The implications of these data for counseling practice are relatively clear. The concern over decision making, so evident in the literature, must be translated into experiences which are effective in helping individuals develop decision-making skills.

In an attempt to stimulate the development of effective strategies for teaching decision-making skills, the remainder of this chapter will be devoted to a description of ways in which individuals can be helped to do so. The ideas and suggestions presented in the chapter have been drawn from literature published during the period from 1963 to 1972. While this literature has focused primarily on adolescents, an attempt has been made in this chapter to develop strategies for teaching decision making, covering the range from preadolescence through adolescence and postadolescence.

DEVELOPING A FOUNDATION FOR DECISION MAKING

Whereas at first glance one might be tempted to assume that there is little need for attention to decision-making skills at the preadolescent level, examination of the relevant data proves otherwise. For example, Creason and Schilson[11] reported that every student in a sample of 121 sixth graders reported having vocational preferences and that only eight indicated that they did not know why they chose their particular preference. Simmons[12] found that elementary school children already exhibited a high degree of awareness of occupational prestige, while Nelson[13] showed that as early as third grade children have well-developed attitudes regarding occupations and that as early as age eight or nine children tend to reject some occupations as of no interest to them. Thus, with or without formal teaching or counseling, preadolescent students begin developing perceptions and preferences which may be either realistic and useful or distorted and counterproductive in their later attempts at decision making. Consequently, if we take the position that it is important for individuals to become skilled in decision making, we must necessarily attend to the importance of early developing a basic structure of accurate perceptions of self, society, and the world of work around which to build these skills. How can this foundation be developed? Herr and Cramer[14] have drawn together a number of interesting ideas related to this question, and their ideas will form the basis for the following sections. These sections will focus on knowledge and awareness of self and environment and the development of an attitude of "planfulness."

Stimulating Self-awareness in Preadolescents

The importance of awareness and knowledge of self in vocational development and choice has received widespread support. According to Cohen,[15] sociologists have found pervasive connections between an individual's career or occupation and his or her entire way of life. O'Hara[16] has reported that self-concept relates to occupational choice and high school achievement, while Galinsky and Fast[17] have stated that identity is clearly expressed in the process of making a vocational choice. In fact, Galinsky and Fast have proposed that the choice of an occupation involves in essence the public declaration: "This is what I am."

Given the importance of self-concept in occupational choice, it becomes obvious that one of the prerequisites to competent decision making is accurate knowledge of self. According to authors such as Blocher,[18] Gross,[19] Gribbons and Lohnes,[20] and Super,[21] students need to be able to differentiate personal values and personal interests as these are related to personal strengths and weaknesses in verbal, quantitative, and scholastic abilities. Students need to assess these elements of self, incorporate their meaning into their self-concept, and relate this self-information to the choices with which they will be confronted. In order to accomplish the development of an accurate, realistic self-concept individuals must become aware of and begin "exploring themselves" during the preadolescent years.

In order to help students in their self-exploration schools and parents will have to exercise intelligence and imagination. Certainly it will be necessary to reinforce any efforts students make to find out about their interests and abilities, but we must not stop with just reinforcement. One of the first steps will have to involve helping students become aware of their individuality. Students must be helped to see how they are both different from and alike each other. This can be accomplished by discussions of stimulus events such as short stories, plays, films, and role-playing sequences. The rationale for these procedures is that the stimulus events will evoke different reactions from different children and that these reactions can be explored through discussion with particular attention to the fact that while the students may be similar in many ways they have unique patterns of likes and dislikes. Needless to say, both teachers and parents will play important roles in stimulating such discussions.

As students begin developing an awareness of self as differentiated from "other," they also can begin exploring the topics of values and abilities. The types of activities to be used in stimulating this exploration are many.[22] In school children can take and discuss interest inventories and value checklists, and they can study short stories and films dealing with different value questions. Naturally, through appraisal of performance in academic areas teachers can help students develop a feel for academic ability, but it is important for them to attend to other abilities as well. For example, Kaback[23] reported a situation in which a first-grade teacher confronted her class with a broken chair, asked them to try to fix it, and in the process prompted them to analyze the activities of a carpenter. Without question, this project helped many students begin thinking about their abilities with respect to tools and carpentry. Parents must also play a significant role in the exploration of abilities and values. One rather simple way in which they can fulfill their role is through appropriately timed conversations in which they stimulate their children to think about their reactions to and their performance in different situations with which they are confronted. If implemented in a nonthreatening and relaxed manner, these discussions can help the child realistically assess his or her abilities in a variety of areas in addition to considering his subjective reactions to the events. Thus, through the use of planned activities and naturally occurring opportunities teachers and parents can stimulate preadolescent students to begin exploring their values, interests, and abilities—a necessary first step in the development of decision-making skills.

Developing Knowledge of the Environment

While knowledge of self is important in decision making, knowledge and understanding of the environment and its contingencies are equally as vital. In order to become skilled in vocational decision making, students need a comprehensive body of information which links their educational activities at various points in time to future educational and work opportunities.[24] Students must understand the availability, composition, and direction of curricular pathways and how these pathways are linked to the occupational world. In addition, knowledge concerning such factors as social roles, the breadth of the world of work, and characteristics of organizations is also necessary for competent decision making.

Although the authors who developed the preceding points did so with no direct reference to grade levels, their statements correspond strikingly to those made by authors writing specifically for elementary students. Smith[25] and Thompson[26] have indicated that elementary school students need to expand their knowledge concerning the occupational world and the characteristics which differentiate the major foci of it. They also have called for increasing awareness of the influence of continuing education on work and on one's life-style, along with a broad experiential background vis-a-vis occupations. Herr and Cramer[27] are among the many authors who have proposed that elementary students should develop a vocabulary of work, a knowledge of the fundamentals of technology, a sex-appropriate social role, and a knowledge of the rudiments of social rules. Thus, the need for initiating activities designed to help preadolescent individuals acquire knowledge of the environment has received ample support in the literature.

The types of activities which have been suggested for stimulating learning about the environment cover a broad range. Hunt[28] has stressed the importance of symbolization in concert with each student's ability to deal with the physical, social, and inner world. Accordingly, he has proposed that whether the activity is a field trip, reading assignment, film or speaker, students should be encouraged to ask questions such as: What is the nature of the problem of living this person routinely solves? What is the nature of this person's competencies? What special tools does this person use for solving problems? What special facilities does this person need? Could I do what this person is doing? Hunt believes that discussion of such questions can help students to acquire the knowledge and skill necessary for further vocational development.

Norris[29] and Bank[30] have presented similar schemes for stimulating elementary students to approach the world of work through ever-broadening radii of interests. Norris, for example, proposed that kindergarten children should learn about the work activities of members of their households while first graders study work in school and neighborhood and second graders expand their attention to the community. However, although this plan seems useful, the authors have not presented any suggestions concerning the content to be included in the learning experiences.

Hackett[31] has called for the introduction of industrial arts activities at the elementary school level. He has proposed the use of pupil-planned and pupil-prepared demonstrations and displays for the purpose of increasing awareness of the relationship between school subject areas and various areas of the world of work. Hackett has also called for the organization of school programs around themes such as construction, transportation, communication, etc. However, while Hackett has presented many good ideas for integrating industrial arts into elementary school curriculums, he has neglected the arts and humanities. The importance of these areas, particularly in the use of leisure time, has been discussed by Gilbert[32] and by Lockwood, Smith, and Trezise.[33]

Moving from general statements concerning program emphases to specific techniques for helping students learn about their environment, Herr and Cramer[34] have described a project in which many different activities were used with elementary age students.[35] These activities included simulation, gaming, short stories, role-played interviews with different workers, filmstrips, evaluation of tools, speakers, and field trips. The purpose of the activities, of course, was to stimulate students to learn about themselves, about educational and occupational opportunities and about social change. Thus, a variety of learning activities have shown potential utility for helping students to learn about their environment and its importance in career decision making.

Planfulness and the Preadolescent Individual

As preadolescent students acquire knowledge concerning themselves and the environment, they must also be stimulated to begin considering the manner in which these factors mutually interact to effect career choice and satisfaction. As Clarke, Gelatt, and Levine[36] have stated, students must become motivated to develop an effective strategy for analyzing, organizing, and synthesizing information. Thus, as is implied in the work of Gribbons and Lohnes[37] and Super,[38] there is a need for an attitude of planfulness in students. This attitude of planfulness involves not only providing the student with knowledge but also presenting him with opportunities to apply the knowledge to his personal characteristics.

If individuals are to develop an attitude of planfulness, the groundwork must be done at the preadolescent age level. As Smith[39] and Thompson[40] have stated, preadolescent age students must be helped to see themselves as value-determining agents capable of affecting their future rather than being victimized by it. This means that these students must learn that by accurately assessing their own interests, values, and abilities along with the relevant environmental factors and by competently judging the interactions among the factors they can be successful in achieving outcomes of importance to them. The problem for schools and parents is designing methods by which elementary age students can develop this attitude of planfulness.

Obviously, a critical factor in an attempt to develop any attitude is favorable experience. In other words, if students achieve outcomes that they desire through the use of planning, they will be more likely to plan in subsequent decision situations. Consequently, reinforcement for competent planning is of prime importance at the elementary level. Teachers and parents, therefore, must be sensitive to students' efforts at being planful and must both reinforce intelligent behavior and provide constructive criticism when appropriate. One procedure which enables students to practice being planful is simulation gaming.[41] Teachers can, with some imagination, make up hypothetical choice situations and then have teams of students compete to see who can plan and choose most skillfully. For example, the students could be asked to plan an afternoon and evening for a hypothetical boy or girl their age such that the hypothetical student would be able to complete his or her homework and discharge household responsibilities while still having time to play with a friend. The various plans could then be discussed and evaluated with some award given to the team which plans most skillfully. Thus, in a gamelike situation the students can practice decision making.

Another possibility for helping students develop an attitude of planfulness involves vicarious learning in the sense that the students are presented with examples of the successful use of planful behavior. Teachers can be effective here in developing stories, plays, and role-playing sequences which illustrate effective planning. In addition, parents and teachers can, when the opportunity arises, call to a child's attention the effective use of planning by someone they know. The critical factor, of course, is that the child be helped to see how planning can bring positive consequences.

To summarize, this section has dealt with the necessity for methods of constructing a basis for the development of decision-making skills at the preadolescent age level. The major elements of this basic framework are self-awareness, knowledge concerning important environmental factors, and an attitude of planfulness. If preadolescent students can acquire knowledge and skills related to these three elements, they will be adequately prepared to develop the more complex decision-making skills required in adolescent and adult life.

TEACHING DECISION MAKING

In order to describe a decision-making strategy for use with adolescent and postadolescent individuals, the obvious first step is to select one framework for presentation. The problem here is not that there is a paucity of possibilities but that the selection from among the variety which exists is likely to be arbitrary. As Thoresen and Mehrens[42] state, it has long been conjectured that there is a rational approach as to how decisions should be made. However, just what this rational approach is and how it operates has been the subject of some debate among decision theorists.[43]

In recent years numerous authors and counselors have proposed different problem-solving and decision-making paradigms for use in vocational decision making. Gelatt[44] proposed a strategy which requires knowing alternatives and outcomes, applying a value scale, and making an evaluation. To exemplify the use of this strategy he considered the problem of a student faced with the prospect of planning his educational future. According to Gelatt, the objective would be to select an appropriate program of courses. In order to accomplish this step, data such as test results, previous course grades, interests, and facts concerning the relation of this decision to future choices would have to be employed. Alternative choices then would have to be identified and their potential outcomes discussed along with the probabilities of occurrence of the different outcomes. In order to carry out these operations questions such as the following would have to be considered: What is the degree of relevance of the data for each alternative? Can success be predicted? Would other data be more suggestive? As these questions are answered, the possible outcomes could be evaluated in terms of their desirability, and a selection could be made or another cycle of the process could be implemented. While Gelatt did not fully explain all of the processes involved in this framework, he did state his opinion that the use of such a framework actually would increase an individual's "freedom of choice." His reasoning was that by using the process the individual would be aware of more alternatives and have an increased understanding of the factors involved in a choice, including his determination of the desirability of the consequences.

Another decision-making paradigm has been presented by Katz.[45] The first step in the Katz strategy focuses on exploration and examination of the individual's own values. This examination should lead to an identification of the relevant value dimensions and a numerical rating of the importance of each dimension (i.e., money income, security, etc.). Once the individual has assessed the importance of the dimensions, he (or she) is ready to begin determination of the degree to which each alternative is capable of satisfying the needs associated with each value dimension. This, of course, requires gathering information about the various alternatives. As this information is gathered, the individual evaluates it and to each alternative assigns a number representing the probability of satisfaction for the respective value dimensions. The probability-of-satisfaction figure for each alternative and each value dimension is then multiplied by the importance rating of the appropriate value dimension, and the products are summed for each alternative. Finally, the individual gathers data relevant to her probability of entry and success in each one of the alternatives and formulates a decimal figure (.00–.99) representing this probability. She then multiplies the probability of success times the sum for each alternative and uses this product to make her choice with the highest number representing the most desirable alternative. Although incompletely developed, this model does have the advantage of emphasizing value questions and attempting to deal with them explicitly and in a systematic manner.

Recently Magoon[46] and Hamilton and Jones[47] have presented more elaborate strategies for decision making. The Hamilton and Jones strategy is of particular interest since it grew out of the authors' efforts to design, develop, and field test a guidance system especially suited to programs of individualized instruction as exemplified by Project Plan.[48] According to Hamilton and Jones, a primary aim of individualized career guidance programs should be to assist each student to formulate educational and vocational goals which will serve to direct his performance both within school and in the environment outside school. To accomplish this purpose the guidance programs must help the student to become skilled in three general types of activities:

1. Assessing himself (herself) on variables such as abilities, aptitudes, interests, job and college preferences, and physical and social characteristics.
2. Obtaining information about educational and occupational alternatives.
3. Employing a strategy for processing this information into personal goals, plans, and actions.

Given this orientation, Hamilton and Jones have designed a decision-making strategy which, like Magoon's formulation, has expanded the general framework to include an initial step focused on problem definition and then additional steps concluding with implementation and evaluation of action plans. Because of the thoroughness with which these strategies cover the entire process from point of indecision to resolution of the decisional conflict, they have been used as a pattern for the approach to be described in this chapter. The present strategy is composed of the following six steps: 1) defining the problem, 2) generating alternatives, 3) gathering information, 4) processing information, 5) making plans and selecting goals, and 6) implementing and evaluating plans. Each of these steps will be discussed in a separate section of the chapter. The discussion will deal with both the rationale for the activity and recommendations concerning its implementation.

In this chapter a good decision will be considered to be one which follows the procedures described rather than one which arrives at any particular outcome. The rationale for this approach stems from the fact that the determination of desirability of outcome is related to each individual's goals and values; consequently, it would be impossible to specify in any general sense what desirable outcomes might be. In fact, even in individual cases, objective specification of desirable outcomes is difficult due to problems arising from factors such as tendencies toward socially desirable responses and the demand characteristics of the assessment situation. Given such difficulties, the process-based definition of a good decision will be used in this section.

It may also prove helpful for the reader to be aware of the fact that a specific set has been maintained in the presentation of this decision-making paradigm. The set is that of *career* decision making. The choice of *career* decision making rather than decision making in other aspects of one's life does not mean that the procedures cannot be used in other decision-making situations. However, since the central focus of this volume is work, *career* decision making will be the focus for this discussion.

Finally, while the first section of this chapter has dealt exclusively with the preadolescent age group, the present section will be developed with both adolescent and postadolescent groups as the target populations. The rationale for this choice of populations stems from the fact that the paradigm to be presented can be used equally effectively by both age groups. Thus, in the description of the paradigm an attempt will be made to present procedures useful in schools and additional ideas for teaching decision making in extraschool settings.

Defining the Problem

The initial step in a decision-making procedure is, as one might expect, crucially important. It is important both to the counselor who is attempting to teach the student how to make decisions and to the student himself. First, consider the counselor and her action. Helping an individual define or clarify the problems which confront him or her derives its importance from the fact that the manner in which problems are stated will have a significant effect on the types of solutions that evolve. Obviously, if one is confronted with a student saying that he or she would like to learn to speak up in class or that he or she wishes to reduce anxiety associated with spiders, there would appear to be little ambiguity as to the nature of the difficulty. However, most individuals do not describe their difficulties in such a simple and straightforward way. In fact, it is often the case that the individual can only state that he or she feels a persistent uneasiness in certain situations. Of course, this is the point at which the counselor's expertise in both listening and empathically understanding clients' feelings and concerns become important. The counselor must behave in such a way that the person becomes willing to express his or her feelings. Thus, a warm, helping relationship is necessary at the problem definition stage. However, the counselor must do more than just listen empathically and clarify the client's perceptions. She must seek answers to questions such as, "What precisely is going on in the client's everyday life? When does he or she feel uneasy? How do these feelings affect his or her behavior in different situations?"[49] The objective here is to help the individual toward a clear delineation of the problems which must be solved.

In the case of vocationally oriented problems with students, it may well be that the student will first evidence the presence of career indecision through problems with school work, such as an inability to concentrate on assignments. Concern about one's future, the possibilities which exist and the choices that need to be made, often result in inability to take positive action in any particular direction while one is involved in course work related to future alternatives. Galinsky and Fast[50] make the point that adolescence is the time of identity formation, and vocational choice is an aspect of that identity. As the adolescent is struggling with his personal identity, he also must face up to the problem of his vocational identity. There are times when these problems become so intertwined that it becomes necessary to deal with and eliminate the personal and psychological difficulties before turning one's attention to the problems of vocational choice.

These parameters of each student's situation are precisely what must be identified and defined before positive action can be taken. Thus, the need for an effective relationship becomes evident.

Problem definition with adults can be more complex than with adolescents. In most cases the adult will be holding a job or at least have job experience. One may be tempted to assume that this fact would make problem identification easier since stated dissatisfaction with a job or inability to hold a position seemingly would indicate inappropriate career choice. While this is certainly true in many cases, the counselor must be aware that inadequate interpersonal skills, for example, could give rise to such aversive situations at work that the individual might decide she does not like the work itself. The point here is that while the identification of a need for career decision making with an adult client may be relatively straightforward, there may be mitigating factors which, unless directly treated, will result in job dissatisfaction no matter what the position.

Let us assume, then, that the counselor and the client have come to the conclusion that one of the client's problems involves decision making related to careers and occupations. What kind of approach should the counselor take at this point? Initially, it is helpful for the counselor to again attempt to understand and listen, this time focusing more specifically on the individual's perception of the world of work. Since these perceptions differ from individual to individual and from group to group,[51] the counselor should attempt to determine the degree of importance that particular client places on the activities associated with work as opposed to those associated with leisure, family life, etc. The counselor's attention to the client's attitudes concerning the importance of work in his or her life will not only aid the counselor in helping the client with his decision but will also help orient the client to considering the variety of factors that must be considered in career choice. This orientation should aid the client in generating realistic alternatives in the next step of the process.

Another topic of importance in the initial stages of counseling in career decision making is consideration of the tentativeness of career choice or, in other words, the degree to which the client sees the choice as final and irrevocable. Both Berger[52] and Tennyson[53] have emphasized the difficulties that arise from the fact that students are pressured to know quite early in life the field in which they will do their life's work. Needless to say, this emphasis completely neglects the fact that an individual's ideas, interests, and occupational maturity develop over time and that becoming locked into a premature choice may result in missed opportunity and dissatisfaction. Thus, if the client is a student, the counselor can, through discussion of tentativeness in career choice, help the student to realize that although a particular alternative may appear perfectly suited to him at the moment, it is possible that his values, interests, and abilities might change enough to bring about dissatisfaction at some future point in time. This awareness will help the student to be receptive to negative data regarding a chosen field rather than purposely ignorant of such data. If the client is an adult, discussion of tentativeness in career choice can frequently help to reduce chagrin and emotional upset over the idea of having supposedly "wasted" a period of time in the wrong job. Obviously, these feelings, if left unattended, can sabotage attempts at further decision making due to the client's anxious desire to "do things right this time."

One method for approaching the topic of tentativeness is through consideration of the concept of "career process" as described by Ivey and Morrill.[54] Career process stresses the continual changes and the varied developmental tasks in occupational life. According to Ivey and Morrill, no final choice point in vocational behavior exists; rather, those searching for a career should be seen as changing organisms engaging in a series of career-related developmental tasks. These developmental tasks include such things as learning new techniques for solving problems, learning new ways of viewing the work environment, developing insights into relationships with coworkers, and changing attitudes concerning work and life. Ivey and Morrill have indicated that if the counselor can help the client develop a "career process" attitude toward his own situation, the client will be better able to both recognize and effect changes in his or her life and in so doing will increase the probability of satisfaction vis-a-vis career development.

In order to stimulate the client to develop a career-process way of thinking, the counselor must help the client both to understand the concept of career development and to assess realistically his own level of development. Obviously, if she is to teach the client about career development, the counselor must have a sound working knowledge of the theories and research related to this topic. Consequently, in order to proceed with a discussion of methods for helping the client, let us assume that the counselor has studied the field and has selected Super's developmental approach.[55] One of the first steps in helping the client, then, will be to explain Super's theory, its stages, substages, and developmental tasks. To supplement the verbal explanation and to help the client conceptualize the stages involved, the counselor might provide either role-played or real audiotapes on which individuals at different levels of development discuss their status, interests, etc. In addition, the client might be encouraged to read selected biographies chosen because they depict in realistic terms the process of career development. As the client develops an understanding of the theory, he can then begin to assess his own level of development. One means of accomplishing this assessment would be through discussions with the counselor of values, interests, and abilities. In some instances these discussions might be supplemented by the results of interest inventories, value questionnaires, and aptitude tests. In addition, it might be helpful to have the client interact with a group of peers having similar concerns. Through such interaction individuals frequently gain valuable insights concerning the reality of their expectations and self-evaluations.

Finally, while a variety of activities may be employed to help the client understand career development theory and begin assessing her own level of development, the counselor must work to integrate these activities so that the desired result is achieved. This result is not merely an assessment of the client's level of development but the formulation of an attitude of career process, i.e., a realization and acceptance of the fact that change and development are occurring continually and that vocational satisfaction will be directly related to the individual's ability to adjust to and profit from changes as they occur.

Generating Alternatives

The first step in a decision-making paradigm is always defining the problem. At this level it is especially important for the counselor to employ expertise in helping the individual move from a state of vague uneasiness about a variety of topics to the point where he or she can state in specific terms those concerns of greatest import at the moment. The nature of the relationship and the questions asked by the counselor are critical at this stage. Once it has been determined that a decision concerning a career is necessary, the counselor can begin helping the client to identify and evaluate her feelings relative to the world of work. This process should help the client develop realistic perceptions of self, improved skills in self-assessment, and an attitude of career process.

Given that the client has clarified the problem to the extent that she realizes a decision must be made, she is faced with the second step in this paradigm, generating alternative courses of action. The activities associated with this step are less complex and therefore may seem less significant than those of problem identification; however, appearances are deceiving in this case. The act of generating alternatives is uniquely significant because it sets the stage for the entire process. The remaining steps all operate on the alternatives identified in this phase. Consequently, if the client does not even consider a particular job as a viable alternative, it will be impossible for her to collect information concerning the job and subsequently decide to enter the occupation. Given the evidence on the difference in perceptions of the world or work,[56] it is entirely possible that many individuals might, in fact, completely neglect entire job families because of their lack of experience with the range of existing possibilities. Hershenson and Roth[57] explain the manner in which such an omission can lead to an ever-narrowing range of experiences and ultimately to unsatisfactory career choices. Consequently, the generation of alternatives has been made a separate step in this decision-making framework in order to emphasize its pivotal position in the process.

If generating alternatives is so important in a decision-making framework, how can a counselor help a client learn to carry out this step in a satisfactory manner? Basically, the question becomes one of how to help individuals learn to consider the entire range of possibilities as they seek to identify those alternatives that they will choose to investigate. Lockwood, Smith, and Trezise[58] have described a process they used to help students become aware of the world in general. This approach involves the systematic consideration of four worlds: the natural world, the technological world, the aesthetic world, and the human world. Discussions of these four worlds were used to help students become aware of the infinitely varied life-work possibilities available to them. For example, in discussion of the natural world, students studied and not only discussed what nature has to offer man but also confronted man's preoccupation with the destruction of nature. They considered the principles of ecology, the problems of air and water pollution, etc. In the process of discussing these topics, the question repeatedly posed to the students was, "What can the individual do?" This question then led to a discussion of the kinds of career areas involved in this particular world.

It is obvious that through a similar kind of discussion on each of the four worlds it would be possible for any individual to become more aware of a wide variety of job possibilities. In fact, this awareness was an important result of the discussions for many of the students in Lockwood's class. The four-worlds approach was implemented in the course of a whole semester of work in a particular school, and therefore it is highly unlikely that it could be used in its full form in a counseling framework. However, the idea of stimulating individuals to come to grips with diverse possibilities through the discussion of the different realms of the world of work seems to have significant potential for helping clients to generate alternatives.

A second method for helping clients to become aware of the variety of opportunities from which to select alternatives has been presented by Leonard.[59] In this project junior high students were shown filmstrips describing job families, after which they selected particular job families for further study. Although the level of sophistication of the presentation may have to be varied for clients of different ages, the use of films or videotapes describing job families could prove most helpful for clients in the "generating alternatives" stage of a decision-making paradigm. Given the availability of the necessary projection equipment, clients could view the films individually or in groups. Viewing of the films could then be followed by structured discussions of job families and finally by selection of specific alternatives for further investigation.

Another means for helping clients consider a variety of types of jobs requires the use of interest inventories. The client (adolescent or adult), attempting to generate alternatives, could take an interest inventory such as the Strong Vocational Interest Blank, Kuder Occupational Survey, or Ohio Vocational Interest Survey. Then, in interpreting the results to the client, the counselor could also emphasize the variety of possibilities described by the profile. Of course, a difficulty with this approach is the fact that as the individual learns about his profile he may quickly exclude certain alternatives because of low scores in those areas. In spite of this limitation, however, the use of an interest inventory frequently results in expanded rather than restricted awareness of career possibilities. A final possibility for helping clients generate alternatives involves the use of counselor-prepared printed descriptions. The counselor who, for whatever reasons, is unable to acquire published descriptions of job categories (e.g., the *Dictionary of Occupational Titles* or the *Occupational Outlook Handbook*[60]) may have to prepare such descriptions or lists of career possibilities. Although such descriptions may not be as polished as films, interest inventories, or other published descriptions, they still should be helpful in stimulating the client to consider a variety of possibilities as he seeks alternatives for further exploration.

Gathering Information

The third step in the decision-making paradigm involves gathering information relative to both the alternatives and to the individual's own likes, dislikes, values, etc. The importance of relevant information cannot be overemphasized. As Clarke, Gelatt, and Levine[61] state, the possession of relevant information is a necessary condition for good educational-vocational decision making. Relevant information cannot guarantee that an adequate decision will be made. However, a good decision cannot be made without it. Thus, the greater degree of relevant information possessed by the decision-maker, the greater the individual's chances of engaging in good decision making. Hoppock and Novick[62] feel so strongly about the importance of adequate vocational information that they have proposed the establishment of the position of "occupational information consultant" in each school in order to insure the presence of relevant and up-to-date information.

How can the client come into contact with useful information? What steps must he take in identifying information which will be important to him in his decision-making process? Initially, the counselor must help the client to consider and recognize the different areas in which information might be gleaned. Magoon[63] has presented one framework which specifies eight different areas relevant for information seeking: 1) the amount of time and efficiency of study, 2) academic ability, 3) academic achievement, 4) work experiences, 5) leisure experiences, 6) interests, 7) the expectations of others, and 8) occupational and educational facts (information about occupations, requirements of different kinds of education, etc.). A list such as Magoon's is obviously designed for the student. He or she is able to attend to each area in turn and to begin thinking in terms of the type of information that is available. For example, with respect to academic achievement, the individual can draw upon previous grades. Work experiences might involve such things as part-time and summer jobs. Information on interest might come from interest inventories such as the Strong or the Kuder. As the student proceeds with his information gathering, he can begin filling in information for each of the eight categories.

A second framework for organizing information gathering has been proposed by Herr and Cramer as an adaptation of the work of Flum.[64] Flum's model, which has applicability for adults as well as adolescent students, groups the factors influencing choice in the following manner:

1. Inner-limiting factors (e.g., intellectual ability, aptitude, skills, experiential history, punctuality, openness, vocational maturity, etc.)
2. Inner-directing factors (e.g., values, interests, life goals, perceived prestige of various occupations, perceived stereotyped attitudes toward occupations, etc.)
3. Outer-limiting factors (e.g., accessibility of occupational and educational opportunities, scope of occupational and educational opportunities, requirements of occupations and curricula, etc.)
4. Outer-directing factors (e.g., social class expectancies, family aspirations, peer influences, community attitudes toward education and work, etc.)

With this model as a guide and with the help of a counselor, any client should be able to identify all of the factors about which she or he needs information in order to make a decision. Thus, both Flum's model and Magoon's categories provide the client with a framework for organizing and directing information seeking.

Is it sufficient, however, to provide only a framework in which to organize information seeking? Will such a framework insure the collection of useful information? The answer to these questions is at best "maybe." In fact, many individuals must be helped to develop the kinds of questions which will elicit useful information. Therefore, a second phase in gathering information is the development of "good" questions.

One approach to the development of "good" questions is presented by Thoresen and Hamilton.[65] These authors specify that "good" questions have three characteristics. 1) The question should elicit *specific* rather than general information. Thus the person should ask, "What are your working hours each day . . . from when to when?" rather than, "Are you happy with your working hours?" 2) The question should be *relevant* to the alternative in mind as opposed to pertaining to a broad category of jobs. If the client is interested in quality control within the electronics industry, her question should be directed at quality control positions rather than at other positions in the electronics industry. 3) Finally, the questions should be asked of reliable sources. If the individual is considering plumbing as an alternative, he should ask his questions of a plumber rather than of Uncle Frank who happens to live next door to a plumber. Obviously, these characteristics cannot be considered as being definitive with respect to the development of good questions and, in fact, some might argue for different criteria. However, the important point is not so much these specific criteria as the emphasis upon the development of questions which will elicit meaningful and useful information.

Developing Information Seeking Skills

At this point it may be helpful to review the position of the decisionmaker. He is at the point where he has defined his problem and has generated alternatives that he plans to investigate. The individual has also been confronted with a model which will direct and organize his information seeking, and he has been helped to learn how to develop questions which will elicit useful information. However, this is frequently not enough, for many clients still will not actively seek information. Some still feel that they don't know how to do what is necessary; others don't see any benefits accruing to them as a result of their efforts; and others have few readily accessible sources of information. Consequently, the counselor must often make efforts to stimulate clients to actually seek information in addition to working to provide facilities that enable clients to accomplish their information seeking effectively and efficiently. In the following paragraphs some of the more promising procedures for stimulating information seeking and for presenting occupational information will be discussed.

In recent years much attention has been paid to helping individuals develop adequate information-seeking skills. A variety of studies have been implemented to investigate the principles of reinforcement and social modeling in promoting career exploration.[66] These studies, in general, have focused on identifying ways to stimulate information-seeking behavior on the part of students. The types of activities involved in these studies include counselors reinforcing students' statements of information-seeking attempts, students viewing video tape student models who explain processes by which they have sought information, and students listening to audio tapes of student models explaining information seeking and being reinforced for the information-seeking behavior. In general, the findings of these studies have shown that students who are reinforced for information-seeking activities do more of these activities than individuals who are not and that listening to models who explain information-seeking activities results in increased information seeking.

Although the use of reinforcement and modeling to stimulate information seeking has received much attention to date, important questions remain at best partially answered. For example, how can counselors provide for the transfer of skills used in counseling sessions to regular use in everyday life? Many students may emit desired behaviors just because the counselor is present, while on their own they quickly revert to old modes of behavior. Thus the problem of transfer must be confronted. With respect to modeling, it is becoming evident that some students learn more from modeling sequences than others and that certain types of models are more effective than others. These factors and their interactions must be studied in order to know how and with whom social modeling can be most effective in developing information-seeking skills and stimulating information seeking itself. A final question of importance concerns the effectiveness of modeling sequences with adults. What types of models and modeling sequences, if any, would be effective in stimulating adults to change old behavior patterns or to develop new behaviors? The answers to these questions certainly will aid counselors in using modeling to help clients develop information-seeking skills.

A related but somewhat different approach to the development of information-seeking skills would involve the use of group projects, similar to those described by Leonard.[67] In this approach clients with basically similar interests vis-a-vis alternatives would be formed into committees, and each committee would be charged with the responsibility of seeking certain kinds of information and then bringing their findings back to the larger group for evaluation and feedback. One advantage of this approach is that through the use of groups the individual who is particularly unskilled at information seeking or who lacks the assertiveness to carry out certain information-seeking activities (e.g., interviews) does not have to shoulder the entire burden of gathering all of the necessary information immediately. Thus, as his skills and confidence develop, he can assume more responsibilities as far as the group is concerned and eventually can begin doing more information seeking relevant to his own alternatives.

While possessing definite strong features, the committee approach does have the disadvantage that it requires numbers of individuals for proper implementation. When the situation involves only one client or at most a small number of clients the counselor may want to employ a structured assignment-based strategy. This would involve careful specification of the steps leading from formulation of questions to identification of information sources to contact with the source and acquisition of information. Depending on the client and his level of skill, this process could vary in sophistication from consideration of only one question at a time to formulation of numerous questions for multiple alternatives. In this process the counselor's major responsibility would be both to provide guidance in terms of development of questions and identification of sources and to provide constructive feedback concerning the information gathered.

Providing Useful Sources of Information

Although helping individuals to develop as competent information seekers is in itself a significant task, the counselor's responsibilities for stimulating information seeking do not stop at this point. The counselor must also confront the problem of providing, whenever possible, useful and usable sources of occupational information. This problem is not always handled adequately. In fact, Magoon[68] claimed that if someone from another planet could visit with a counselor, this visitor would probably regard our occupation materials as classified information. This conclusion would be based on the following facts: 1) there seem to be rather intricate rituals through which an individual must go in order to locate material; 2) the material is generally high in reading difficulty and low in human interest on the whole; and 3) individuals who have read such information rarely report that it has influenced their vocational plans. Needless to say, it would be unreasonable to expect a client to seek information if the information sources were as inaccessible and as useless as those described by Magoon.

In recent years, however, new and innovative ideas have been developed for the presentation of vocational information. Since this chapter is not designed to deal solely with occupational information, no attempt will be made to cover all potentially useful sources in depth. For such treatment one might refer to works such as that of Isaacson.[69] However, although in-depth coverage will not be provided, in the following paragraphs a number of promising delivery systems will be described.

Probably the most effective way of gathering meaningful information about an occupation is to actually experience that occupation, but in most instances this type of information seeking is practically impossible. Consequently, various degrees of fidelity and simulation are present in information sources. In other words, for different sources of information there will be differences in the degree to which the actual experiences are reproduced.[70] Thus, a low level of fidelity might be exemplified by printed material or audio visual experiences, while an experience with a higher level of fidelity would involve direct observation, perhaps moving to simulation and finally to actual work experience. The informational systems to be discussed will range from low to high fidelity in terms of their replication of actual work experience.

Although printed information is low in fidelity and seemingly low in interest value,[71] it is a relatively economical means for conveying facts about occupations. Thus attempts have been made to develop interesting and efficient methods for presenting printed information.

One of the more recent developments in occupational information involves microfilm and microfilm reader-printers. These systems can be most helpful in storing large amounts of information in rather economical packages.[72] With these systems information is stored on either microfilm or microfiche in catalogues according to job type. An individual interested in exploring any particular occupation merely places the appropriate film or card in a reader and then reads the information from the screen of the reader. What makes these systems more economical and useful is the fact that the individual can view information for a number of occupations and select for printing only that information which he finds most helpful. The printing is done by the machine on the spot, and the whole process can be completed in a rather short period of time. The reader-printer and information can be situated in a readily accessible place, such as libraries or possibly the outer offices of counseling departments. Such placement allows immediate access and therefore enables individuals to seek information whenever they so desire with a minimum of red tape. The results of the use of this kind of system have been most positive in terms of student and counselor reactions.[73]

A higher level of fidelity than reading is that involved with listening to audiotapes and viewing films. Magoon[74] has developed a rather interesting device for presenting occupational information. First Magoon synthesized occupational information into five- to ten-minute tape-recorded presentations. Next he added five- to ten-minute interviews with job holders on tape immediately following the information about the particular job. In the next step these tape-recorded segments were pressed into records. These records were then put into jukeboxes, and the machines, with one or two sets of earphones, were placed in areas frequented by students (e.g., library, dormitory lounges, student union, etc.). Any student interested in obtaining information about a particular job could go to the jukebox, select the appropriate record, and at her leisure listen to both information about the job and interviews with job holders. With only minimal changes in procedure, this system certainly could be implemented for adults in non-school settings.

Laramore[75] has carried out similar kinds of operations with film. For example, he has reported making small four-minute films of people performing work in paramedical areas. These films are accompanied by scripts so that students can view individuals working in paramedical professions as well as read relevant information about each occupation. Laramore has also described the development of slide-tape presentations related to various jobs.[76] Thus, Magoon's jukebox and Laramore's films and slides make possible the gathering of information through an experience that has higher fidelity to the actual job than merely reading about the occupation. The benefit here, of course, is that the individual is able to obtain information while participating in an interesting experience.

Rather than reading about occupations or watching films and listening to tapes, the information seeker can also gather data through person-to-person interactions.[77] One possibility in this realm is the frequently employed "career day" and speaker approach.[78] These procedures have the advantage of allowing individuals to interact with people actually employed in jobs of interest, but they also have the limitations of usually allowing only superficial coverage of topics and selective coverage of occupations. Obviously, a more effective procedure is to visit individuals at their place of work and to conduct interviews there. Although in many instances this approach is possible, it does require that the work of interest to the information seeker be performed in a relatively accessible location. When this condition does not exist, one is forced to resort to some other means of information gathering.

Another interesting possibility involving role models has been described by McCourt.[79] In this procedure groups of students were exposed to a role model who, either in person, on film, or through reading, related what he did and the personal meaning of his work for him. Thus the model presented a picture of the kind of person he is while attempting to engage the students in a consideration of real problems faced by him in his job. Afterwards the students discussed the model, his work, and the ways in which they themselves seemed similar to and different from the model. In this way the students could to a degree both explore an occupation and interact with someone engaged in the occupation.

A different approach to job information and one with increased fidelity is conceptualized in the job experience kits of Krumboltz and his associates.[80] These investigators have attempted to develop for individuals actual problem-solving activities related to particular occupations and to present these activities in booklet form. Thus, if a student is interested in accounting, she can, using this system, approach the counselor and obtain an accounting kit. The student then takes the kit with her and works through it at her own pace without outside help or supervision. In working with the kit the student first learns the functions of accountants and a few basic facts about how checks are written and cleared. She is then presented with a problem, a packet of cancelled checks, and a ledger sheet, and she must compare the cancelled checks with the entries on the ledger sheet. If she does this carefully she will discover a number of discrepancies which will identify a certain individual as an embezzler. This procedure provides the student with the opportunity to carry out a few of the actual activities involved in accounting and to solve a problem related to this occupation. The net result is that the student learns something about accounting through involvement in realistic activities.

Related to job experience kits but higher in fidelity are work samples. Herr and Cramer have described three types of work samples.[81] First is the *simulated work sample.* This is a mock-up or close simulation of an actual work activity which does not differ in any significant way from the actual work required in a particular job. Second, the *actual work sample* is a small sample from an actual job involving the use of the same materials and equipment as used on the actual job but differing only in terms of work setting. Finally, the *isolated-trait work sample* assesses a specific trait (e.g., sorting ability) common to a number of different jobs. Needless to say, work samples provide information seekers with important data concerning actual work activities. However, due to the expense, time, and effort frequently required for their production, work samples have not been used as widely as their information-producing possibilities might warrant.

Finally, another method for information seeking and that of highest fidelity involves work experience. Littlefield[82] reports work with boys aged sixteen to seventeen who were school failures and jobless. In this project the boys were actually assigned to jobs and paid for their work. In addition to having supervisors who directed their work activities, the boys had one individual- and two group-counseling sessions per week in which they discussed their experiences and reactions to work. Littlefield reports very positive results in terms of their improved orientation toward work and their reactions to problems with school and school failure. Obviously, then, realistic and real-life experience in a job can be very powerful in altering one's perceptions about work and one's interest. Calvert[83] supports this statement with data indicating that 53 percent of individuals who were involved in Peace Corps activities changed their goals while involved in the Peace Corps. There is little question that realistic experience in actual job positions can be useful in helping one gather information about specific occupations. However, due to the difficulty of arranging such experiences, lower fidelity activities such as those described above hold the greatest potential for helping individuals seek information about career possibilities.

To summarize, once the client determines that a decision is to be made, his next step is to generate alternative possibilities from which to choose. Having developed this list of alternatives, he moves to seeking relevant information about himself and about each career possibility. In order to seek information he must first develop good questions. These questions need to be specific, relevant to particular jobs or topics, and directed to reliable sources. Finally, after formulating the questions the individual may begin seeking answers, and to do this he can use any number of a wide range of informational sources. These sources range in fidelity from reading about jobs to actual work experience. Since work experience is, practically speaking, rarely feasible, lower fidelity sources such as films, tapes, and job experience kits frequently are the most attractive modes of conveying information.

PROCESSING INFORMATION

This step in the decision-making process may be the most difficult for both the counselor and the client. The reason for this difficulty is that the individual must come to grips with the factual information that he has gathered and with his own values and interests. He must weigh these and make a choice reflective of the relative weights of each segment of information.

Thoresen and Mehrens[84] explain that counselors have traditionally operated on the assumption that individuals can see the need to balance their desires and motivation with probabilities for success and that people realize that within limits they have the responsibility for determining what odds they wish to risk. This assumption may be convenient, but it does not necessarily promote wise decision making since it often results in counselors giving clients the facts and then expecting the clients to process the information adequately.

In fact, individuals often need assistance in acquiring an effective strategy for processing the information.[85] An initial step in helping a person process information involves organizing it in such a way that the relative merits of each alternative can be evaluated. These organizational frameworks are relatively easy to develop, and working examples have been presented by Katz,[86] Clarke, Gelatt, and Levine[87] and Magoon.[88] For purposes of discussion Magoon's model will be considered here.

Basically, the framework of Magoon's model involves listing the occupational groups in a column and then placing pluses, zeros, or minuses in a row for each occupational group, depending on the evaluation of the occupation with reference to each of the eight informational categories previously specified. Thus, if the information one has gathered about study time supports the plan for entering the job of electronics technician, a plus is entered in the corresponding box; if the information does not allow the individual to make a decision, a zero is recorded; and if the information is contradictory to entering the occupation of electronics technician, a minus is placed in the box. This rather simple strategy can prove most beneficial in helping clients to organize diverse occupational information.

In order to make accurate judgments regarding alternatives the client must evaluate the adequacy of his information. A number of criteria must be used in evaluating data. First, the client should give some attention to the source of the data. For example, information produced specifically for recruitment is likely to be less accurate than similar information developed for guidance purposes. Next the client should evaluate the currentness of the data.[89] Although recent information is not necessarily accurate, information probably will not be accurate unless it is recent. A third criterion is validity: does the information pertain directly to the job under consideration, and is it subject to distortion arising from the promotional tendencies of job recruiters? Finally, the client should consider the applicability of the data: can the data be utilized by the client, and is the information presented at a level appropriate for the client? Obviously, to the degree that the data meet these criteria the client will be able to use the data to make accurate judgments relative to the alternatives under consideration.

Organizing information and judging factual data, however, is only a first step. A critical point arises as the client begins considering the possible outcomes of various actions and the relationships between the actions and the outcomes. According to Clarke, Gelatt, and Levine,[90] an individual is forced to make particular vocational decisions under a combination of risk and uncertainty. The person in most circumstances cannot be certain that a particular action will lead to a particular outcome, but often he can obtain evidence upon which to base a rough estimate of the probability linking the two. Thus the client need not operate under complete uncertainty. However, by the same token he is unable to operate in his decision making under a condition of certainty. Consequently, the best he can do is to gather data which will provide some evidence of the probability that a particular action will lead to a particular outcome. The more realistic this estimation of probabilities, the more likely it is that the client will achieve his desired outcome.

One method for helping clients to develop realistic estimates of the probabilities of attaining certain desired outcomes is that of experience tables.[91] In developing a decision-making framework for students, Yabroff used data on the post-high school activities of graduates of his particular school to develop charts which give each student the probability of attaining certain outcomes given certain personal characteristics. A commonly used experience table allows an individual to determine the probability that given a particular grade-point in, for example, ninth grade, he will attain another grade-point for his total high school grade-point average. Consequently, the student who in ninth grade has less than a C average is able to see what his chances are of getting a B average for his overall high school grade-point. This is one way in which the decision-making student can use experience tables to estimate the probabilities of certain outcomes.

Experience tables and similar probability estimation devices can be most useful in processing information; however, these devices have certain negative characteristics. First, in order to be maximally useful they must be based upon the experience of persons similar to the decisionmakers who will be using them. This means monitoring the progress of groups of individuals through school and on into post-high school life. This is difficult and time-consuming, especially when one realizes the variety of variables for which such tables could be constructed (e.g., high school GPA, entrance to college, entrance into specific occupations, college GPA, etc.). The second, and possibly more critical, difficulty stems from the perceptions many people have of such tables. When confronted with an experience table and its figures, many individuals interpret the probability estimates as controlling their lives. Such individuals attempt to "live up" to the probabilities presented in experience tables rather than interpreting them as evidence of what has happened to other people with characteristics similar to theirs. The point is that in the use of such tables the counselor must help the decisionmaker to realize that if he maintains the pattern of behavior which has produced his present status, the probabilities of the experience table will be quite accurate. However, the counselor must also impress upon the individual the fact that if he wants a particular outcome enough to change his behavior, he can alter the probabilities in his favor. Thus the counselor plays a significant role in helping the client to use experience tables in processing information.

While the counselor may play an important role in helping the client to process information, it is the client who ultimately formulates the final probability estimates. The counselor can teach the individual organizational strategies, he can develop expectancy tables, and he can even have the client observe models making wise decisions; but, in spite of all this, the person may still allow his preference for an outcome to completely overshadow all objective evidence.[92] These subjective judgments and their determining factors and effects are not yet well understood. Until these subjective elements and their interaction with objective data are more fully analyzed, counselor efforts in the area of information processing will fall short of complete effectiveness.

In summary, many counselors for some time have assumed that clients, possessing factual information, will make adequate decisions because they will see the need to learn how to compare their values and interests with the factual information and to realistically estimate the probability of achieving certain outcomes. Although this is the comfortable assumption to make, there is some evidence that it is not realistic, that there are clients who need to learn how to process information so that they can adequately estimate the probabilities of various outcomes. Important steps in this direction involve the development of organizational frameworks and methods of estimating the probabilities of different outcomes. However, while these strategies are helpful, counselors will not be able to deal with information processing in completely effective ways until more is known about the nature and effect of subjective factors in the decision-making process.

MAKING PLANS AND SELECTING GOALS

The client now has reached the point in the decision-making process where he has gathered and processed the necessary information for enabling him to choose from the alternative possibilities. At this point the counselor might again discuss Ivey and Morrill's statement that career development should be seen as a process,[93] reminding the client that choosing an occupation is not in any way and endpoint and that a great deal remains between making the choice and the attainment of the outcome. In fact, so much may change in the person's life that he or she may turn to a completely different occupation. Consequently, while the client has made a decision and must therefore commit himself to a course of action, he must also maintain a tentativeness that will allow him to adjust to changes as they occur.

The main thrust of a discussion of career process should be to help the client to plan for change. A useful step in this process is to choose one primary plan and one or two alternatives.[94] Choosing an alternative plan or plans makes possible the shift to such alternatives in the eventuality that the client is unable to obtain the primary choice. Having made her choices, the client should turn her attention to the establishment of both long-term and short-term goals. In this sense the short-term goals will describe the small steps leading from the point of decision to the achievement of the long-term goal, which in this case involves entrance into a particular occupation. Finally, as soon as the individual has been able to establish the first sub-objectives she can begin working toward them, and her next steps will involve developing and organizing other objectives in terms of the order in which they are to be pursued and then moving toward their accomplishment.

IMPLEMENTING AND EVALUATING PLANS

On the surface the step of implementing and evaluating plans would seem to be relatively straightforward. After all, the client has done the hard work of distilling information and processing it so that he has chosen between alternatives. Now it would seem that his only task would be to pursue the accomplishment of his goals. However, given the ever-changing process of career development,[95] the problems of tentativeness and commitment arise.[96] The point is that once the decisionmaker has come to a decision concerning a career and has begun to move in a particular direction, a degree of commitment is required; that is, the individual is required to forsake various activities and alternatives for others in order to achieve his goal. However, no matter how firm his commitment, in order to be a wise decisionmaker the individual must be continually involved in evaluation and review of events as they occur and their implications for the appropriateness of the choice he has made. Thus, on the one hand the individual must maintain commitment, while on the other he or she must retain a degree of tentativeness that will allow realistic evaluation of career choice.[97] It is the counselor's responsibility to help the client to see the necessity of maintaining these two conflicting dispositions.

This attitude of tentativeness, coupled with the distinct possibility that changes may occur which will give rise to the necessity for new planning and decision making, highlight the importance of evaluation. Due to these possibilities, the person must maintain an evaluative stance relative to his plans and their implementation, continually evaluating his actions and choices in terms of their effect on the accomplishment of his career goals and objectives. The goals and objectives then can be used as bench marks so that the individual can look back and assess the success with which he has been proceeding toward his ultimate objective. Obviously, this evaluation procedure may lead to the specification of new subgoals which will enable the individual to more effectively pursue his ultimate objective. Then, too, if as a person assesses his position vis-a-vis the accomplishment of his goals, he finds that he is moving in a direction he does not desire or one that is leading to negative consequences for him, he can begin again in the decision-making process and in such a way alter even his final outcome.

TRANSFER OF DECISION-MAKING SKILLS

This chapter has, to this point, focused on the description of a decision-making framework for helping individuals to make career decisions. However, the potential of the paradigm will never be realized in any significant sense if people cannot learn to use the framework on their own. Thus it becomes evident that the counselor must not only attend to helping each client work through his decision-making process, but he must also help the person learn how to apply the procedure himself to new situations which will be occurring in his life. To date there have been very few published reports of efforts both to teach decision-making skills and to evaluate the degree to which the learning transfers to other situations in the person's life. Thoresen and Hamilton[98] report the results of a study in which both video tape social modeling and structured interaction were used to teach eleventh-grade students a decision-making framework. Although the adequacy with which students learned the decision-making framework was evaluated immediately following treatment, there was no attempt made to determine the degree to which the learning transferred to diverse real-life situations.

The only study identified to date in which an attempt was made to determine the degree of transfer of decision-making skills was reported by Evans and Cody.[99] These authors worked with eighth-grade students and, through the use of both guided and nonguided treatment groups, attempted to teach these students how to use a particular decision-making strategy not unlike that which has been described in this chapter. The authors then assessed the degree to which the students learned the decision-making framework immediately following treatment and once again thirteen days later in a situation that was dissimilar to the initial training situation. That is, the training situation was presented to the students as a counseling activity run by counselors, whereas in the follow-up assessment the work was done by a teacher in the usual classroom and the problem used was one more specifically related to classroom work than counseling. Given the results of their study, Evans and Cody concluded that through directed practice it is possible to teach students a decision-making framework and that decision-making skills do transfer to nonexperimental settings. This study, then, supports the claim that it is possible to teach students how to make decisions and to expect them to use the newly learned skills in real-life situations in the absence of direction from the counselor, teacher, or parent.

Simulation Games

Evans and Cody used video-taped social models and group discussion to teach students how to make decisions. While they found some transfer to nonexperimental settings, it may be that additional techniques could stimulate greater transfer. A most promising possibility is simulation as exemplified in the Life Career Game,[100] a decision-making game in which the individuals playing the game are able to span eight to ten years in the future by role-playing the decision-making process for a fictitious person who is presented to them in the form of a profile, a written case history. Individuals playing the game attempt to plan the most satisfying life for the fictitious person by making decisions as to how the fictitious person will allocate certain amounts of time in his or her life. The results of these decisions are fed back to the players in the form of scores or game points which are indications of the relative satisfaction of the life being played. Thus, the decisions for each year in the person's life must take into account the results of the previous year's decisions and the satisfactions gained from them.

The benefits of this type of simulation activity for the decisionmaker are obvious. First, the individual has the opportunity to practice making decisions, to see what types of consequences result, and to determine through discussion how the decision may have been made more appropriately or so that better outcomes would result. The player can do all of this without suffering "real" negative consequences. A second beneficial result is that persons playing the game are forced to clarify their own values. In other words, as they come to the point of having to decide what the fictitious person must do, they must also determine that which they think is most important to them. Consequently, the Life Career Game would seem to have high potential utility for helping individuals learn how to use a decision-making framework in real-life situations.

Structured Practice

Another method for promoting transfer of training involves practicing the use of decision-making skills in real rather than simulated settings. The strategy here is to have the decisionmakers, either individually or in groups, assume the responsibility for planning and implementing actual projects. For example, high school students could be asked to plan either all or part of a career day or occupational information program, while adult decision-makers could be given the responsibility of planning and developing informational brochures for different occupations. As the projects are carried out, the counselor could monitor the adequacy with which decisions and plans are made, and in group feedback sessions the counselor and decisionmakers could discuss ways of improving decision-making skills.

One of the main advantages of this realistic practice is that the decisionmakers are working on an actual project, the adequacy of which will reflect on their expertise. Thus, the individuals in the structured practice situation are likely to be even more involved with the task than those working in a simulated setting. Naturally, the involvement of the decisionmakers will be directly related to the meaningfulness of the task for them. Consequently, the counselor will be required to plan carefully in order to select projects suited to the interests and sophistication level of her clients. Finally, the counselor will play her most important role in monitoring and evaluating the client's decision-making efforts. This will require attention to every step in the process from identifying problems to making and implementing plans. However, the counselor will have to do more than just monitor events as they happen; she will also be required to provide the decisionmakers with feedback concerning the adequacy of their activities and suggestions for more effective techniques. To the degree that the counselor can accomplish these tasks, the structured practice technique will be an effective strategy for promoting transfer of training to real life settings.

SUMMARY

This chapter has dealt with decision making and its importance in career planning. The necessity for wise decision making is obvious. There are a variety of possible paradigms for this purpose, and techniques related to teaching decision-making skills have been described here. However, the fact remains that no matter how important we as professionals see a procedure to be for other individuals, those individuals will make little use of the procedure unless it is seen as meaningful to them. Bruner[101] states that students, when given an opportunity to do so, will learn what is meaningful to them and what appeals to them as significant. However, when experiences seem irrelevant, students pay little attention and, in fact, avoid even making an effort to learn. Thus, unless we can help clients see the utility of decision making in their lives, there is no reason to expect that they will make use of such decision-making strategies. Simulation and structured practice experiences provide the opportunity for students to practice the use of decision-making skills in a manner which is meaningful to them.

NOTES

1. A. Toffler, *Future Shock* (New York: Random House, 1970).
2. D. E. Super, "The Changing Nature of Vocational Guidance," *Issues in American Education*, A. M. Kroll, ed. (New York: Oxford University Press, 1970), pp. 139–55.
3. H. Janne, "Teaching People to Adapt to Change," *The Futurist* IV (1970); Carnegie Commission on Higher Education, *Less Time, More Options: Education Beyond the High School* (New York: McGraw-Hill, 1971).
4. J. D. Krumboltz and C. E. Thoresen, "Planning," *Behavioral Counseling:*

Cases and Techniques, J. D. Krumboltz and C. E. Thoresen, eds. (New York: Holt, Rinehart, and Winston, 1969), pp. 328–29.

5. *Ibid.*

6. W. Edwards, "Behavioral Decision Theory," *Annual Revue of Psychology* XIII(1961):473–99.

7. L. J. Cronbach and G. C. Glaser, *Psychological Tests and Personnel Decisions,* 2nd ed. (Urbana, Ill.: University of Illinois Press, 1965).

8. C. G. Wrenn, *The Counselor in a Changing World* (Washington, D.C.: American Personnel and Guidance Association, 1962).

9. H. B. Gelatt, "Decision making: A Conceptual Frame of Reference for Counseling," Journal of Counseling Psychology IX(1962):240–45.

10. D. L. Bay, P. P. Preising, and Dejong, *Santa Clara County 1968 Needs Assessment* (San Jose, California: Supplementary Education Center, 1968); E. Donaldson, "Project Search Four-Year Follow-Up Study" (San Mateo, Calif.: Sequoia Union High School District, 1968); J. Flanagan, "The Project Talent One-Year Follow-Up Studies," Bulletin No. 5 (Pittsburgh: Project Talent Office, University of Pittsburgh, 1966).

11. F. Creason and D. L. Schilson, "Occupational Concerns of Sixth Grade Children," *Vocational Guidance Quarterly* 18(1970):219–24.

12. D. Simmons, "Children's Ranking of Occupational Prestige," *Personnel and Guidance Journal* 41(1962):332–336.

13. R. Nelson, "Knowledge and Interest Concerning Sixteen Occupations Among Elementary and Secondary Students," *Educational and Psychological Measurement* 23(1963):741–754.

14. E. L. Herr and S. H. Cramer, *Vocational Guidance and Career Development in the Schools: Toward a Systems Approach* (Boston: Houghton Mifflin, 1972).

15. A. Cohen, "Sociological Studies of Occupations as a Way of Life," *Personnel and Guidance Journal* 43(1964):267–272.

16. R. P. O'Hara, "A Theoretical Foundation for the Use of Occupational Information in Guidance," *Personnel and Guidance Journal* 46(1968):636–640.

17. M. D. Galinsky and Irene Fast, "Vocational Choice as a Focus of the Identity Search," *Journal of Counseling Psychology* 13(1966):89–92.

18. D. H. Blocher, "Wanted: A Science of Human Effectiveness," *Personnel and Guidance Journal* 44(1966):729–733.

19. E. Gross, "A Sociological Approach to the Analysis of Preparation for Work Life," *Personnel and Guidance Journal* 45(1967):416–423.

20. W. D. Gribbons and P. R. Lohnes, *Emerging Careers* (New York: Teachers College Press, 1968).

21. D. E. Super, "Vocational Development Theory: Persons, Positions and Processes," *The Counseling Psychologist* 1(1969):2–9.

22. Herr and Cramer, *op. cit.*

23. Goldie R. Kaback, "Occupational Information in Elementary Education," *Vocational Guidance Quarterly* 9(1960):55–59.

24. Blocher, *op. cit.*
    Gross, *op. cit.*
    Gribbons and Lohnes, *op. cit.*
    Super, *op. cit.*

25. D. E. Smith, "The Vocational Aspects of Guidance in the Elementary School" (Harrisburg: Pennsylvania Department of Education, 1968), mimeographed.

26. J. M. Thompson, "Career Development in the Elementary School: Rationale and Implications for Elementary School Counselors," *The School Counselor* 16(1969):208–209.

27. Herr and Cramer, *op. cit.*
28. E. E. Hunt, "Career Development K-6: A Background Paper of Initial Suggestions," Program Development Committee of the Cobb County, Ga., Schools, 1970, mimeographed.
29. W. Norris, *Occupational Information in the Elementary School* (Chicago: Science Research Associates, 1962).
30. I. M. Bank, "Children Explore Careerland Through Vocational Role Models," *Vocational Guidance Quarterly* 17(1969):284–289.
31. D. F. Hackett, "Industrial Element for the Elementary School," *School Shop* 25(1966):58–62.
32. H. G. Gilbert, *Children Study American Industry* (Dubuque, Iowa: Wm. C. Brown, 1966).
33. O. Lockwood, D. B. Smith and R. Trezise, "Four Worlds: An Approach to Occupational Guidance," *Personnel and Guidance Journal* XLVI(1968):641–643.
34. Herr and Cramer, *op. cit.*
35. Abbington School District, *Career Development Activities, Grades V, VI, VII* (Abbington, Pennsylvania: Abbington School District, 1967–68).
36. R. Clarke, H. B. Gelatt, and L. Levine, "A Decision-making Paradigm for Local Guidance Research," *Personnel and Guidance Journal* XLIV(1965):40–51.
37. Gribbons and Lohnes, *op. cit.*
38. Super, *op. cit.*
39. Smith, *op. cit.*
40. Thompson, *op. cit.*
41. S. S. Boocock, "The Life Career Game," *Personnel and Guidance Journal* 46(1967):328–334; Herr and Cramer, *op. cit.*
42. C. E. Thoresen and W. A. Mehrens, "Decision Theory and Vocational Counseling: Important Concepts and Questions," *Personnel and Guidance Journal* XLVI(1967):165–72.
43. Edwards, *op. cit.*
44. Gelatt, *op. cit.*
45. M. Katz, "A Model of Guidance for Career Decision-Making," *Vocational Guidance Quarterly* XV(1966):2–10.
46. T. M. Magoon, "Developing Skills for Solving Educational and Vocational Problems," *Behavioral Counseling: Cases and Techniques*, J. D. Krumboltz and C. E. Thoresen, eds. (New York: Holt, Rinehart, and Winston, 1969).
47. J. A. Hamilton and G. B. Jones, "Individualizing Educational and Vocational Guidance," *Vocational Guidance Quarterly* XIX(1971):293–99.
48. J. C. Flanagan, "The Plan System for Individualizing Education," *NCME Measurement in Education* 2(1971):1–8.
49. J. D. Krumboltz and C. E. Thoresen, "Problem Identification in Behavioral Counseling," *Behavioral Counseling: Cases and Techniques.*
50. Galinsky and Fast, *op. cit.*
51. D. L. Shappell, L. G. Hall, and R. B. Torrier, "Perceptions of the World of Work: Inner City versus Suburbia," *Journal of Counseling Psychology* XVIII(1971):55–59.
52. E. M. Berger, "Vocational Choices in College," *Personnel and Guidance Journal* XLV(1967):888–94.
53. W. W. Tennyson, "Comment," *Vocational Guidance Quarterly* XVIII(1970):261–63.
54. A. E. Ivey and W. H. Morrill, "Career Process: A New Concept for Vocational Behavior," *Personnel and Guidance Journal* XLVI(1968):644–49.

55. S. H. Osipow, *Theories of Career Development* (New York: Appleton Century Crofts, 1968).
56. Shappell and Hall, *op. cit.*
57. D. B. Hershenson and R. M. Roth, "A Decisional Process Model of Vocational Development," *Journal of Counseling Psychology* XIII(1966):368–379.
58. Lockwood, Smith and Trezise, *op. cit.*
59. R. S. Leonard, "Vocational Guidance in Junior High: One School's Answer," *Vocational Guidance Quarterly* XVII(1969):221–22.
60. R. S. Leonard, *ibid.*
61. Clarke, Gelatt and Levine, *op. cit.*
62. R. Hoppock and B. Novick, "The Occupational Information Consultant: A New Profession?" *Personnel and Guidance Journal* XLIX(1971):555–58.
63. Magoon, *op. cit.*
64. Herr and Cramer *op. cit.* in an adaptation of work reported in Y. Flum, "Hatsac Lesivvg Hegoremim Lakoveim et Behirat Hamiktsoa (Proposal to Classify Factors in Determining Occupational Choice)," *Megamot* 14(1966):225–228.
65. C. E. Thoresen and J. A. Hamilton, "Peer Social Modeling and Structural Materials in Promoting Career Relevant Behaviors," paper presented at the annual meeting of the American Educational Research Association, Los Angeles, California, April, 1969.
66. J. D. Krumboltz and W. W. Schroeder, "Promoting Career Planning Through Reinforcement," *Personnel and Guidance Journal* XLIV(1965):19–26; J. D. Krumboltz and C. E. Thoresen, "The Effect of Behavioral Counseling in Group and Individual Settings on Information-Seeking Behavior," *Journal of Counseling Psychology* XI(1964):324–33; J. D. Krumboltz, B. B. Varenhorst, and C. E. Thoresen, "Nonverbal Factors in the Effectiveness of Models in Counseling," *Journal of Counseling Psychology* XIV(1967):412–18; M. Q. Lewis and R. D. Baker, "Model Reinforcement of Verbalizations versus Actions," *Journal of Counseling Psychology* XVIII(1971):283–84; J. B. Meyer, W. Stronig, and R. E. Hosford, "Behavioral-Reinforcement Counseling with Rural High School Youth," *Journal of Counseling Psychology* XVII(1970):127–32; T. A. Ryan and J. D. Krumboltz, "Effect of Planned Reinforcement Counseling on Client Decision-Making Behavior," *Journal of Counseling Psychology* II(1964):315–323; C. E. Thoresen and J. D. Krumboltz, "Relationship of Counselor Reinforcement of Selected Responses to External Behavior," *Journal of Counseling Psychology* XIV(1967):140–44; C. E. Thoresen and J. D. Krumboltz, "Similarity of Social Models and Clients in Behavioral Counseling," *Journal of Counseling Psychology* XV(1968):393–401; C. E. Thoresen, R. E. Hosford, and J. D. Krumboltz, "Determining Effective Models for Counseling Clients of Varying Competencies," *Journal of Counseling Psychology* XVII(1970):369–75; C. E. Thoresen, J. E. Krumboltz, and B. B. Varenhorst, "Sex of Counselors and Models: Effect on Client Career Exploration," *Journal of Counseling Psychology* XIV(1967):503–08.
67. Leonard, *op. cit.*
68. T. Magoon, "Innovations in Counseling," *Journal of Counseling Psychology* XI(1964):342–47.
69. L. E. Isaacson, *Career Information in Counseling and Teaching* (Boston: Allyn and Bacon, 1971).
70. R. A. Ehrle, "Vocational Maturity, Vocational Evaluation and Occupational Information," *Vocational Guidance Quarterly* XIX(1970):41–45.
71. Magoon, *op. cit.*
72. E. A. Whitfield and G. A. Glaeser, "The Microfilm Approach to Disseminat-

ing Vocational Information: An Evaluation," *Vocational Guidance Quarterly* XVIII(1969):82–86.

73. G. S. Dubato, "VOGUE: A Demonstration System of Occupational Information for Career Guidance," *Vocational Guidance Quarterly* XVII(1968): 117–19.
74. Magoon, *op. cit.*
75. D. Laramore, "Jobs on Film," *Vocational Guidance Quarterly* XVII(1967): 87–90.
76. D. Laramore, "Counselors Make Occupational Information Packages," *Vocational Guidance Quarterly* XIX(1971):220–24.
77. Herr and Cramer, *op. cit.*
78. C. Avent, "Studies in Teaching Occupations in Great Britain," *Vocational Guidance Quarterly* XIV(1965):97–102.
79. H. McCourt, "The Vocational Development Lesson," unpublished Ed. D. thesis, Teachers College, Columbia University, 1965, mimeographed.
80. G. B. Jones and J. D. Krumboltz, "Stimulating Vocational Exploration Through Film-Mediated Problems," *Journal of Counseling Psychology* XVII (1967):107–14.
81. Herr and Cramer, *op. cit.*
82. P. G. Littlefield, "School Dropout Demonstration Project," *Vocational Guidance Quarterly* XIV(1966):183–86.
83. R. Calvert, Jr., "Peace Corps Service and Career Choice," *Vocational Guidance Quarterly* XIV(1966):236–40.
84. Thoresen and Mehrens, *op. cit.*
85. Clarke, Gelatt and Levine, *op. cit.*
86. Katz, *op. cit.*
87. Clarke, Gelatt and Levine, *op. cit.*
88. Magoon, *op. cit.*
89. Herr and Cramer, *op. cit.*
90. Clarke, Gelatt and Levine, *op. cit.*
91. W. Yabroff, "Learning Decision-Making," *Behavioral Counseling: Cases and Techniques.*
92. H. B. Gelatt and R. B. Clarke, "Role of Subjective Probabilities in the Decision Process," *Journal of Counseling Psychology* XIV(1967):332–41; Thoresen and Mehrens, *op. cit.*
93. Ivey and Morrill, *op. cit.*
94. Magoon, *op. cit.*
95. Ivey and Morrill, *op. cit.*
96. D. V. Tiedeman, "Predicament, Problem and Psychology: The Case for Paradox in Life and Counseling Psychology," *Journal of Counseling Psychology* XIV(1967):1–8.
97. Tiedeman, *op. cit.*
98. Thoresen and Hamilton, *op. cit.*
99. J. R. Evans and J. J. Cody, "Transfer of Decision-Making Skills Learned in a Counseling-Like Setting to Similar and Dissimilar Situations," *Journal of Counseling Psychology* XVI(1969):427–32.
100. Boocock, *op. cit.*
101. J. S. Bruner, *The Process of Education* (Cambridge, Mass.: Harvard University Press, 1960).

SUGGESTED READING

Clarke, R., H. B. Gelatt, and L. Levine. "A Decision-making Paradigm for Local Guidance Research." *Personnel and Guidance Journal* 44(1965): 40–51. Presents and discusses a decision-making paradigm for use in schools. A major point in the discussion is the importance of relevant information in decision making. Types of relevant information are considered, and applications of the paradigm to guidance research in schools are presented.

Herr, E. L., and S. H. Cramer. *Vocational Guidance and Career Development in the Schools: Toward a Systems Approach.* Boston: Houghton Mifflin, 1972. A complete, well-researched volume dealing with vocational guidance in elementary, junior high, and high schools. Topics considered include the American occupational structure, formulation of objectives for vocational guidance, strategies for vocational guidance in elementary schools, junior high schools and secondary schools, and strategies for effecting change in schools.

Krumboltz, J. D., and C. E. Thoresen. *Behavioral Counseling: Cases and Techniques.* New York: Holt, Rinehart and Winston, 1969. An edited text describing a variety of behavioral counseling techniques. Applications of the techniques are presented through the use of numerous case reports. Major sections of the volume are focused on problem identification, reinforcement, social modeling, counterconditioning, and cognitive and multiple techniques. A useful text for stimulating the development and implementation of new counseling techniques.

Thoresen, C. E., and W. A. Mehrens. "Decision Theory and Vocational Counseling: Important Concepts and Problems." *Personnel and Guidance Journal* 46(1967):165–72. A thorough treatment of the topic of subjective probabilities and their influence on decisions. The concepts of subjective probability and utility are discussed; relevant research is reviewed, and questions for further study are presented.

Tiedeman, D. V. "Predicament, Problem, and Psychology: The Case for Paradox in Life and Counseling Psychology. *Journal of Counseling Psychology* 14(1967):1–8. An insightful discussion of goal and choice predicaments in life. The article defines requirements for developing the capacity to hear both predicaments; proposes an organization of teaching and counseling in education within which awareness of both predicaments can be cultivated; and proposes that counseling psychologists expect problem solution rather than awareness of predicament.

Technology and Guidance: The Challenge to More Elastic Existence amid Accelerating Obsolescence

15

Anna L. Miller
Behaviordyne, Inc.

David V. Tiedeman
American Institutes for Research

THE CHALLENGE

The survival of guidance as a vital and useful activity depends upon the recognition that a new day has dawned, a new individual has emerged, and a new way of life is upon us—that, consequently, the old methods and pre-technological ways of thinking are no longer viable.

We in vocational guidance have posited the obvious future needs of youngsters—to work—but we have too often neglected the effects of technology on efforts to fulfill that need. We have not educated students to relate their occupational interests and capabilities to the speed and instantness of change and obsolescence in our era. Our one-dimensional thinking is evidenced in the types of guidance we now provide our young people, guidance which matches individuals' interests and capabilities but does not anticipate the realities that trigger change in every facet of one's life as well. This change must be confronted if counselors are to guide their clients in the process of growth and "cope-ability."[1]

We need to alert students not only to the fact that occupations as we now know them are changing but also, and more importantly and specifically, to the fact that the individual's way of looking at a career is changing as well. As technology evolves an environment with more leisure and new kinds of jobs, it is imperative that we more frequently consider our present situation in view of future possibilities. We are now faced with the need to consider "multiple careers" in order to adapt our personal position and capacity to deal with the new environment.

A panoramic view of society will show us the obsolescence of our present conceptual framework for education and guidance. First, we will survey the changed societal conditions produced by technological developments. Second, we will develop the argument that our own conceptual framework can be updated if we see ourselves as moving with time. Third, we will argue that we must involve technology in guidance so that it facilitates such updating in the conceptual frameworks of our students (clients) as well. We take this final step after reviewing the status of present computer systems in guidance and criticizing them for having put "old guidance" into the computer instead of devising new forms of guidance to fit the new time-and-motion framework in which we now must operate.

OUR CURRENT FAST PACE

We live today at a rapid pace unequaled since the beginning of time. Cognitively and technologically, though not emotionally, we are propelling ourselves through time at amazing speed, and the "action and the reaction occur almost at the same time."[2] We can look, for example, at the following table showing the technological advances in the field of transportation and the rate of acceleration from the beginning to the present day.

Number of years to accomplish	Year	Means	Speed
millions	Prehistory	Walking	3 m.p.h.
	6000 B.C.	Camel	8 m.p.h.
	1784 A.D.	Horse-drawn coach	10 m.p.h.
65 years	1825 A.D.	Steam locomotive	13 m.p.h.
58 years	1880 A.D.	Advanced steam locomotive	100 m.p.h.
	1938 A.D.	Airplane	400 m.p.h.
22 years	1960s	Rocket plane	4,000 m.p.h.
	1960s	Space capsules	18,000 m.p.h.

Notice that it took us millions of years to increase the speed of travel from 3 to 13 miles per hour; about 60 years to accelerate the rate to 100 miles per hour and then another 60 years to quadruple that speed; but a mere 30 years to increase that speed over 400 times.[3]

"Things are moving too fast," "I've just had too much to respond to this week," "I've got to get away from it all"—these comments reflect the intuitive knowing that something is happening, something is different. Our emotions know it, but our minds don't; change is going too fast for the intellect to comprehend it because the mind is not educated to rapid movement. Very little time and effort have been devoted to educating the person about his technologically oriented environment. He is basically unprepared to cope with an ephemeral system in which things and relationships enter and leave one's life at a phenomenal rate of speed without adequate simultaneous development of man's cognitive system.

The problem of coping with present day pace is therefore one of the factors reflected in the fact that incidence of mental illness has risen one and one-half times in the past ten years.[4] These statistics show, among other things, that the current societal framework has not provided for the development of motion-coping mechanisms which would, in turn, sift down into our educational system and, more specifically, into our guidance programs. It is no surprise, then, that we in guidance have not built the needed motion framework into our programs.

Our Cradling in Technology

In the past man has been more or less able to isolate himself from change. However, technological advances have given rise to external structures which surround man and are impossible to avoid. These external structures have emerged in many forms, one of them television, which put man in direct contact with the entire world and continually inform him in ways never before thought possible. History is no longer impacted by a communication lag, for sophisticated communications systems have brought the world into the front room and have been the implosive factor in changing the "world view" of all exposed to it. Television has forced us to be different people, aspiring to higher levels of awareness, toward more humanness and whole-ness. "The aspiration of our time for wholeness, empathy and depth of awareness is a natural adjunct of electric technology."[5]

Another major external structure which has emerged is systems technology. Perhaps the single greatest accomplishment in this area was the placing of a man on the moon, a feat that intrigued and staggered the imaginations of men and proved one of the most outstanding examples of the adjuvant capability of the human mind. One example of the creative capacity of systems technology is the computer-assisted instruction now available to children in a remote Pueblo community of New Mexico via satellite from Stanford University. An Applications Technology Satellite (ATS-3) beams the courses from Stanford to Islee Pueblo each morning from 8:30 to 10:00 a.m.[6] It is believed that by 1975 equipment and experience will be available to broadcast similar programs to other remote areas in the country.

Our Social Ineptness

Technically, then, we have exhibited giant capabilities, but socially we have not done so well. We have discovered that engineering a man to the moon was easier than quelling riots in the street and allaying poverty in the ghetto. We have found the technical capability to leave this planet and return safely, but we lack the ability to marshall our resources in regard to current social problems. Perhaps the greatest social fiasco in the last decade has been the "War on Poverty," which was initiated to integrate the underprivileged minorities of the United States into the mainstream of America. It also has become painfully apparent that we have blazed through space with great accuracy but have erred on earth. Part of the problem has been the failure to consider the effect of technology on the people as it catapulted them through time, bringing change too quickly for the people to assimilate it. Not enough time has been allowed to build "stability zones."[7] When a population is subjected to drastic change, a society of misfits is created, "unbalanced, explosive, and hungry for action."[8] Evidence of this can be seen in the following list of social concerns which, though they have been with man for ages, still continue to pervade the mass media today: war, racism, sexism, aging, community control, poverty, economic instability, crowding, technology, and ecology.

Pervading these concerns today are the fear of insecurity and the desire for personal value and participation. The themes of territorialism and the superiority of man over man, themes inherent in war, racism, sexism, and age discrimination, point to the worldwide fear of presumed scarcity signaled by poverty and by a shaky economy. Today these perpetually present con-cerns occur with dawning understanding that crowding and technology can exhaust usable matter on earth precipitously, almost momentarily. The desire for personal worth and control is central to the desire for community control, to the call for decentralization that would enable the individual to participate effectively in government and education. That desire finds extension in the current pressure to tear down our system of public education and to erect one based on individual choice.

INCIPIENT RESPONSES TO ACCELERATING OBSOLESCENCE

Our response to accelerating obsolescence is for the most part merely pre-conscious. We sense the increased speed and press of technology and seek its reward for our society. In the meantime, we engage in personal responses that we see only murkily and need to bring into sharper focus. Let us, therefore, consider mobility, occupational change, and information technology as emerging responses to the new life speed inherent in technology.

Mobility

Man's new relationship to time and motion is at this moment only visible "through a glass darkly," but a part of what we see is reflected in our new understanding of motility and mobility in life. Our society and its culture now supports the imperative of "change or die." We can now live in several different locations on the globe during our lifetime, for we have moved the radius of a day's travel from the 25 miles it is on foot, to the 500 miles it is by automobile, to several thousand miles by airplane. For example, "in 1967 108,000,000 Americans took 360,000,000 trips involving an overnight stay more than 100 miles from home. These trips alone accounted for 312,000,000,000 passenger miles."[9] In fact, mobility is so commonplace that the important differences between people are no longer place-related to a great extent.[10] Technological change permits corporate decentralization which, in turn, accelerates both geographic mobility and the demise of place-relatedness associated with the extended kinship family. Today, there-fore, we seem to be moving from stationary lives to a kind of "nomadic" existence.

Occupational Change

As one aspect of increased motility and mobility, it is becoming more usual for a person to experience several occupational changes during his or her lifetime. Progress in career is closely related to the imperative of occupational change. Today existence itself demands that same imperative. That which I seek and do today will not necessarily be that which is needed tomorrow. In 1972 U. S. Commissioner of Education Marland staked a good deal of the Federal educational dollar on the bet that liberal education, which used to be the privilege of the elite, needed to become, through career education, the imperative for all. A skill for immediate employment plus understanding of job movement and self-development become the new imperative in education. This imperative is supported by the realities of the work world —jobs becoming obsolete, more people than jobs available, shifting markets, differing area demands, changing economic conditions, and seasonal differences. These considerations are crucial to our students who move from school to work.

The new relationship of man to time and motion appears in information technology. Man continues to lend his mind to the library to cause in his interaction with those weldings into new wholes or synergistic reactions which are his intuitions of dawning comprehensions. Conversationalists put their minds into splint-like or adjuvant relation with the telephone in order to bridge the gaps of space and time so that they can secure what is needed but not yet recorded. Man also puts himself into adjuvant relations both with the same telephone and with messages (data) of others through the functional means of computer programs to get at library-like material faster, more flexibly and more comprehensively, as the output of such material is now of such staggering magnitude. For example, the United States Government alone generates 100,000 reports each year, plus 450,000 articles, books and papers. On a worldwide basis the production of scientific and technical literature rises at a rate of some 60,000,000 pages a year. In addition, books published internationally have increased from 1,000 a year pre-Gutenberg to 365,000 a year by the middle of 1960.[11] Since, therefore, we are being inundated by words, a new strategy or way of thinking with words is imperative.

TOWARD A NEW CONSCIOUSNESS OF SELF IN TIME AND MOTION

The question now becomes: what is the solution to all these societal conditions and responses brought about by technological advances which have outdated our current conceptual framework in education and, more particularly, in guidance? The solution lies in admitting our need to relate to energy rather than matter and, as we do so, to move from mono-converging thinking to multi-converging thinking. In multi-converging thinking we can think synergistically and thereby understand our synergistic nature and our synergistic relationship to time more fully. But let us look more closely at each of these areas to understand what we are doing now and what we have to do to get quicker and deeper insight so that we can be more effective as we seek to guide young people.

Although we are living faster and more extensively than heretofore, we still lack those solutions which are required to move our nutritional dependence from matter to energy. For instance, we must learn to take energy more directly from the sun or from tides for one thing. In starting reconstruction of the missing *Operating Manual for Spaceship Earth*,[12] Buckminster Fuller points out that energy is inexhaustible; only matter is not. Since the time required for the reconversion of energy to matter is so long, we have little time left to live off matter—the nutriment needed to sustain us between being and disappearing—unless we adapt ourselves to our environment or our environment to us. But Fuller's message is a hopeful one, not a pessimistic one; it indicates that our problem is merely to learn how to live off energy more directly, not to remain as bodies and beings relying solely on matter as our sources of energy. Since the body adapts only slowly, it remains for the mind to adapt if we are to solve the riddle of direct-energy living before exhausting the usable matter on which we presently exist.

The biological solution of this dilemma is an evolutionary one. The species which persists is that which is most adaptive to its environment. However, man has progressed to the stage where he adapts by mind rather than body.[13] He has divested himself of special structural forms external but still accessible to himself. But the structure that man needs to live the faster life of more direct relation to energy, instead of the slow life of direct relation to matter, requires that he comprehend the possibility of being in different relation to time and motion. The needed new comprehension of self in motion requires the differentiation of multi- from mono-converging thinking as foundation to the needed synergistic thinking.

Solution for Change: Multi-Converging Thinking

If we are to achieve the equivalent of an evolutionary change in the concept of our relation to time and motion, we need to abandon "one-way" or mono-converging thinking and to espouse "interactive" or multi-converging thinking. "One-way thinking" is the habit of separating events into causes and effects and of accepting explanations which consistently relate causes to single effects while rejecting other explanations. These logical habits of separating the independent from the dependent help us to organize our experience. Through such habits we differentiate those experiences which permit us to affect our environment from those which do not, and we come to understand somewhat better the condition that those events and principles of control seemingly produce. While all this is acceptable, it is neither the model nor a good model of thinking. One-way thinking has the effect of creating a relatively stable system, of freezing values as once and for all determined, and of preventing revision of thought patterning. For all practical purposes thinking about something thereby ends.

"Interactive" or multi-converging thinking is a more encompassing process than one-way thinking. It allows for some seeming "disorder" in otherwise ordered thought. Explanations, while enlightening, engulf thinking if we let them. The forms in which explanations are offered paradoxically both empower what one understands and limit what one can understand. Realization of this process probably most importantly defines the feeling of *being* educated. In order to understand that one's thought is partial and limited by the way in which one thinks, it is necessary to have understanding and appreciation of the phenomena which a person seeks to encompass in his explanations and of the conceptions in which those phenomena are being encapsulated. Understanding and appreciation are achieved by interacting with differentiated, systematic circumstances sufficiently long and intensively to permit their *re*integration as new forms into other continuities of one's psychic energy.

What we call "new" technology enhances man's potential for interactive multi-converging thinking in two principal ways. First, technology puts more powerful systems at man's command, thereby giving him new possibilities with which to interact. A part of such interaction results in understanding that more powerful systems are achieved at the risk of obtaining potentially more powerful destructive effects as well. Technology also drives man's explanatory systems into realms and magnitudes of detail heretofore unimagined. Additionally, it creates computers in which that detail can be recorded, processed, and quickly acted upon so that the analyses can have reliable effects; e.g., directing men safely to the moon and back. Finally, technology markedly reduces the time scale in which effects can be noted, analyzed, integrated into action systems, and acted upon. If we change our relation to time and motion through multi-converging thinking, we can advance our living on energy and retard our living on matter. But we need to acknowledge synergistic thinking in the change process.

Synergistic Thinking

Buckminster Fuller suggests that man can live comprehensively and synergistically with his environment if he will capitulate to and live in harmony with it; accordingly, it has been "experimentally proven by physics that 'unity is plural and at a minimum two' the complementary but not mirror-imaged proton and neutron. You and I are inherently different and complementary. Together we average as zero—that is as eternity."[14] Man and technology are inherently different and complementary; they average as zero—that is as eternity. This principle needs incorporation into our thinking: "unity is plural and at a minimum two." Thought is never ended; it's always ongoing. There is another and variable side to that which we hold to be invariable; man must believe in himself enough to relate himself to the duality of himself and "the other" in that unity which is synergy—wholes which are more than the sum of their parts.

In order fully to comprehend self in relationship to time and motion one must gain insight into the complementary nature of technology and man. We must understand man as a physiological system, existing in an environmental system and relating to other physiological and environmental systems, all continually in motion. For example, physiologically the body operates on certain interactions which must take place for man to maintain health; that is, the cooperation of the different parts with the whole. Man must recognize that he is an internal system which is physiological, psychological, social, and emotional, and is continually finding ways to maintain these internal systems in interaction with social and environmental systems. Thus, there is continual physiological, psychological, emotional, and social movement in time. An individual needs to comprehend himself as a system (continually in motion) existing in a system (continually in motion) and relating to various subsystems (continually in motion). For optimum functioning an individual must get the first two systems interacting smoothly with the many external subsystems. To further clarify, think of yourself as a teacher and/or counselor, i.e., as a system existing in a system (your environment and its maintainers), interacting with a student (a separate system, existing in a system and trying to understand you and the teacher and/or counselor which is his external system). For the interaction to be synergistic, one must embrace those four systems within teacher, student, and/or counselor and client, first attempting to make sense of self, then each other, and then trying to gain understanding and comprehension. While in this state of flux, man is also experiencing himself in time, trying to center himself in time while living the experience of time in motion.

Man's Synergistic Relationship to Time

The full significance of time in motion is analogous to the movement of a clock. A clock gives approximate time because of its ability to continue to flow forward in motion with the parts behind its face. If the hands of a clock did not move and time were stationary, then many things would go awry. The person is similar in that he must keep moving forward in the "now" and synchronize with the process of movement in order to experience his ultimate self and potential. It is the realizing and coming into awareness of the self as a system in relation to time and motion in the environment that allows one to gain control of his environment, to feel as if he is both in relation to this environment as well as comprehending that relationship to his environment.

But in order for an individual to comprehend time he must understand that it has three parts: a location, an interval, and a sequence. Location means that one identifies a particular clock time, which refers to a specific point in time. The time interval, on the other hand, encompasses a block or string of time points set aside for a particular task or activity. Finally, the time sequence consists of an arrangement of time intervals put together to obtain the desired goal. An individual moves toward a sense of motion by being able to differentiate these three properties of time in such a way that he comes into control of each part, knows each one, what each one contains, how they fit together to make a whole. As he comprehends how time loci, intervals, and sequences adhere in their wholeness, he comes into harmony with time and is able to understand the power available to him through planned events in each interval of time, which leads to a sequence in which he has mastered the task of bringing time into his awareness within his control; therefore, he becomes master of himself in time and motion. He ultimately experiences himself in the ebb and flow of life processes. "The universe is a mammoth perpetual motion process,"[15] and man is a part of that universe and is continually trying to garner past experiences in order to stabilize and to sustain himself in the Now, which is perpetually moving toward the future. Man must gain a sense of himself in motion in the Now in order to intercept and redirect energies which sharpen his insight into the power hidden in discovery of himself in perpetual forward motion. He must perceive himself as free to create his future as living and contemplating change. Once an individual is able to conceptualize himself as a being in motion, physiologically, psychologically, emotionally, and socially, then he is in a better position to understand and use the available technology to further his own self-development. He is able to see these structures as externalizations of what was once manually performed but which time and technology have outmoded. For example, man is no longer capable of storing in his mind all the information needed for decision making in this rapid paced society, so he begins to depend on the computer for assistance; he finds, for example, that instead of spending time in the library handwriting notes, he can use a copy machine to speed up his task and have "more time." Once the individual begins to realize this dynamic society, he realizes his chances of being able to dream about what heretofore seemed impossible goals. Let us, therefore, look at the present guidance systems and determine their capability for "impossible dreams."

PRESENT TECHNOLOGY AND GUIDANCE

Educators tend to think of technology in guidance in terms of hardware (equipment and machines) and software (data, directions, and operations). More specifically, they usually think of computerized information systems, individually operated audio and video reproductions, and reader-printers with copy devices. Such technology has come into guidance in a piecemeal and mechanistic way without adequate explanation of its place within our society and its adjuvant capability to assist man in making sense of the millions of words coming into print daily. In the midst of such staid and proper change, we are experiencing a revolution in guidance[16] and a questioning of our purposes, perhaps because what the planners in the field think is necessary is not consistent with the forces moving our society. If we do not recognize these structures as potentially helping us to organize and make sense of the vast array of information in this society, we will never reach the stage of technological development where we can dream beyond what we are now presently experiencing and be in a position to carry out that dream. This would be bad for us. Pierce[17] suggests that ". . . an educator must never lose sight of the fact that he is preparing citizens for the future. He must feel that there is nothing more urgent than the proper accomplishment of this mission, and he must dare to hope for things that he can only begin to glimpse or that lie beyond both his comprehension and imagination."[18] If we as educators live in that spirit and trust the capability of technology to chart our course to an ever-evolving stated goal, we can begin to show progress akin to the natural sciences.

Present Guidance Systems

The computer-based guidance systems which are currently available to help us begin charting the recommended new course are of two basic kinds: test reporting and inquiry. Mark-reading and aggregating machines became available for test scoring just before World War II. During and after the war this machine reading and aggregating system was united with score tabulating, statistics computing, and score translations systems. Answer sheets can now be fed into a system and within a very short period of time rosters of raw and converted scores can be printed out for various minor, intermediate, and major groupings of the individual answer sheets.

In the past ten years programming for narrative test interpretation has been added to the basic systems for mark reading and aggregating and score translation. Behaviordyne, Inc., is one example of such service at the present time. This firm commercially offers narrative interpretation of the California Psychological Inventory (CPI) and the Minnesota Multiphasic Personality Inventory (MMPI). The interpretation for these tests is based on the interaction of 166 scales transformed into four different sets of T scores. Still the printed interpretation is much more idiographic than nomothetic; it speaks to psychological conditions based upon interaction and patterning in the many scores rather than displaying mere numbers. Different interpretations are available for clients, counselors, caseworkers, psychologists, psychiatrists and other doctors, and penal institutions. In essence it simulates the clinician, and as such presents information in a manner that we are used to and are therefore better able to utilize.

Inquiry systems on the other hand are of four kinds: indirect inquiry systems; direct inquiry systems without system monitoring; direct inquiry systems involving system monitoring; and direct inquiry systems involving both system and personal monitoring. The purpose of all these types is to permit inquiry concerning choices in colleges, vocational-technical schools, financial aid, and occupations. However, we will begin by explaining each type of system, then we will indicate projects that typify each type, and remark upon the current status of each.

In *indirect inquiry systems* an individual's request is held until a large group of requests is received. Such queueing of requests may involve a delay of hours, days, or sometimes weeks, depending upon how volume and price are used in buying the needed computer time. Because of queueing and its usual delays and since a charge is made for each use, indirect inquiry systems are ordinarily used only once by students. Therefore, the student seldom examines the results of his first inquiry and changes specifications for a second or later round of facts. The data received also ordinarily do not directly correspond with the student's desires because, if his specification list is overly long, the system has to compromise original specifications to keep at least some options on the report. In addition, the student is not usually apprised of all possible options and compromises. However, the system thereby usually allows the student to get at least one alternative reported to him. Finally, the system does not provide counseling but serves more as a dictionary and/or encyclopedia.

Indicative of this type are several college selector systems which furnish applicants with the names of colleges most suited to their interests, aptitudes, and abilities. For example, SELECT is a program that in 1969 cost the student $15, recommended 10 to 15 colleges, had 3,000 colleges to select from, processed the questionnaire in approximately 5 days. Another system is MATCH, which in 1969 cost the student $15, recommended 5 to 10 colleges, had 500 colleges to choose from, and processed the questionnaire in approximately two weeks. EDU-DATA in 1969 cost the student $15, recommended 20 to 25 colleges, had a data base for 3,000+ colleges, and processed questionnaires in approximately one week.[19]

None of the indirect inquiry guidance systems has so far proven very successful financially, However, the College Entrance Examination Board recently announced availability of its college selector system. Since this system will be operated in the public interest through a representative advisory system characteristic of Board programs, it holds greater chance of continuation.

The second type of system is the *direct-inquiry system without monitoring,* which gives the student direct access to a data file as he uses a terminal connected to a computer. These systems are usually arranged so that a student must reduce the number of available alternatives (i.e., the colleges and/or occupations on the list satisfying his exact specifications) to at least twenty-five before the program will print the list. The direct-inquiry system is characterized by speed as the student's request receives almost immediate attention. The student can use the system repeatedly at each sitting or at a later time and can receive a rather complete list of educational institutions or occupations which fit his criteria. He is thereby continually aware of his own cognitive filters which expand or reduce his list. This system is not designed to promote counselor participation as it merely lists items and does not collect and store data from prior use.

Typical of this type is the College Guidance System of the Interactive Learning Systems, which costs the student between $3 and $7 to use, recommends up to 20 colleges and contains a data base of 2,500 colleges. With this system the student learns what he sought the same time he makes the request.[20] Interactive Learning Systems, Inc., has proven able to provide service continually on a commercial basis since its founding in 1968.

The third type of computer-based guidance system is the *direct inquiry system with monitoring.* This system occasionally provides some visual capabilities, such as a cathode ray tube or filmstrip projection potential in addition to, or instead of, the teletype or printer device, characteristic of direct inquiry systems. The counselee request is processed almost immediately and the use can be multiple or sequential. A variety of scripts, approaches, modes, and branching opportunities are available to the counselee and allow him flexibility in his approach. The data files can be accessed directly or by means of scripts from a previous response of filed data about the user. The computer often stores data obtained through the interactive process or previously stored data which can be integrated into the interaction. In the monitoring system the computer program oversees, keeps a record of the alternatives chosen by the user, relates it to the chosen alternative, comments on consistency in accordance with a decision table determined by the system designer, states probabilities of successes, and reviews paths of decision making. In essence, the student experiences a counseling situation in interacting with the system. In some cases counselors may also obtain these data so they can use them in talking with the student. The direct inquiry system with monitoring is ostensibly the most popular type of which the following are examples.

The Computer-assisted Career Exploration System

The Computer-assisted Career Exploration (CACE) System was designed for ninth-grade boys interested in pursuing vocational and technical courses in high school. It is an information system which provides on-line use and helps the boys match their attributes with occupational requirements. This function is entirely computer-based, and the computer stores the program controlling the sequence of system operations, information about student users, and the information about forty selected occupations. Student information includes: a General Aptitude Test Battery (GATB) profile for each user and a student preference profile.[21] This system was developed at the Pennsylvania State University and is currently inoperative because of a lack of market, as are most of yesterday's promising computer-involved guidance systems.

Educational Career Exploration System

Educational Career Exploration System (ECES) was developed by the International Business Machines Corporation and invites a confluence of the person and the stages of vocational development on which the student behavioral changes expected from the system are predicated. The system frees the counselors from repetitive informing about jobs, giving them more counseling time with students. The system will familiarize the student with problems of educational and vocational planning, provide the counselor with information about student progress, and free the counselor from having to maintain a general educational-occupational information library.

The system's programs (1) broaden the student's knowledge of work and inform him of its many opportunities, (2) permit college-bound students to explore curriculum and then relate it to their occupational potential, and (3) help the student narrow his search for post-high school training institutions which meet his career goals and personal preferences.[22] Students who use this system need to have on file a gradepoint average from the previous year and complete scores from an interest inventory and a vocational planning inventory. Both such instruments are currently used in producing a "search strategy" to help students use ECES.[23] The system is currently in operation at Genesee County School District. At the moment it is entering its fifth year of overall operation.

Vocational Counseling System

The Vocational Counseling System was developed by the Systems Development Corporation (SDC) and like other direct-inquiry systems with monitoring automates the information processing and guidance functions which machines can perform in order to free the counselor to perform on a much more personal level with the students. The system is designed to (1) provide vocational and educational information, (2) provide probability statements estimating student success in various educational and occupational fields from follow-up data on previous students, and (3) perform clerical functions such as preparing report cards, progress reports, and lists of failing students. A function unique to this and the following system is that the counselor may determine what operation is to be performed, with what data, and for what population, without possessing extraordinary computer programming skills. One of the important facts about this particular system is that the counselors were involved in the design and development of the system.[24] Although the system has been tried and found very useful, it no longer operates because it lacks a market.

The Computerized Vocational Information System

The Computerized Vocational Information System (CVIS) is a computer-based guidance and administrative system which makes individualized educational and vocational information more readily available to students and counselors. The system serves as an automated library for vocational and student cumulative record information. Students and counselors alike have on-line access to the vocational information and specific student information. Counselors receive off-line reports of student interaction with the computer as well. The system is a growing one whose main original function was to provide individualized vocational information to students according to the Roe classification by level and field. In the beginning the cumulative class rank, composite score on an aptitude and achievement test battery, and scores on the Kuder Preference Record are stored in the computer. "The computer will compare individual student attributes with occupational requirements by relating the student's rank in class and composite test battery score to the six Roe level categories and by relating the Kuder scores to the eight Roe interest categories."[25]

Examples of the counseling functions in CVIS are the feedback to the student about his achieved grades, measured abilities, and stated interests at various choice points; the reviewing of past exploration on the system; pointing out of discrepancies; and the "remembering" of a large number of student choices in order to produce a list of occupations or colleges which fit the characteristics stated by the user."[26] CVIS is located at Willowbrook (Illinois) High School and is currently operative with support from local school district, community college, and State Department funds. The system is now being used in more than twenty locations.

The System for Interactive Guidance and Information

The System for Interactive Guidance and Information (SIGI) is also computer-based. The main object is to "enhance the student's freedom of choice, to develop his understanding of elements involved in choice, and to increase his competence in the process of making informed and rational career decisions."[27] SIGI is an adjuvant choice system designed to make the student ". . . a conscious artist of his own career."[28]

SIGI is comprised of four major sections: values, information, prediction, and planning. It is estimated that completion of each section takes about one hour of the student's time. The values section is the core of the SIGI system and involves the same computer functions with respect to information retrieval and matching as do abilities or worker traits matching in other vocational guidance systems.[29] But in SIGI the student does the matching himself and is thereby helped to comprehend his values as he does so.

The information section consists of two parts: locate and compare. The former allows the student to retrieve occupations that agree with his values, while the later allows the student to ask questions and receive answers about any three occupations simultaneously.[30] The Planning and Prediction sections are both in process of development. They are also based upon student values; that is, both Planning and Prediction are descriptive rather than prescriptive. The Planning section begins with a student tentatively selecting an occupation. Then, in reverse order, it takes the student through the steps he will have to follow to enter the occupation.[31]

The Prediction section will inform the student that X number of students out of ten at his local junior college have received a grade of C or better in a certain curriculum when they entered with test scores and previous marks like his. Thus the Prediction section is actually an experience statement derived from local data. The Prediction System will be available to the student at all times after the initial run through all four sections.[32]

The SIGI system is located at Educational Testing Service, and, as of October 1971, the Values section has been completed in a form suitable for formative evaluation.

There is no currently operating example of a *direct inquiry system involving both system and personal monitoring*. The Information System for Vocational Decisions was programmed with several examples of personal monitoring, that is, of comparison with criteria which the subject set into the system rather than the original programmers.[33] The system and its documentation are presently filed in ERIC but are not in use.

Now that we know some of the systems available to chart our course, what is their potential for Guidance and what are their adjuvant capabilities in relationship to the individual user?

NEEDED TECHNOLOGY IN GUIDANCE

When we think about the potential of guidance systems, we must consider what needs exist and how well those needs are being met by present systems. We are experiencing occupational changes as jobs are changing to meet new technological outputs. As a result of this burgeoning technology, we are being inundated by words. So what we are presently experiencing is a technical capability unmatched by any society or civilization to date, and a human relations incapability that almost all societies have experienced, but the implications for guidance are these:

1. Guidance must recognize and realize the world is different today and will be different tomorrow—it is in continual flux.
2. People are different today and will be different tomorrow—they too are in flux.
3. Guidance must be different today and should be different tomorrow—it too has to be in continual flux to survive.

So what does this say about present guidance systems? It says first that we are using technology to do old guidance, rather than using technology to get the new forms of guidance enabled by its use. Super supports this "all's well with new technology" in guidance notion when he suggests ". . . that a computer is really just another library, that a terminal is just another book with a good table of contents, a good index and programmed interaction to insure good personal use of the data. . . ."[34] As our review of computer guidance systems has shown, this is more than true. The fact that these systems are largely only libraries hooked to the person via computer indicates that our present conceptual framework is immediately obsolete in relation to existing computer guidance systems as soon as it comes into being.

Secondly, "new" systems must be purged of the old guidance and programmed for a truly new guidance if we are going to continue to experience any success. This means that guidance is going to have to give up old ways and admit that once valid structures and ideas meet with obsolescence as time and motion ebb and flow. Thus, the new guidance requires (1) the centering of self in time and motion in a way that cannot be done when computer technology is used for today's routine guidance jobs only and (2) the use of a new guidance computer technology to structure both new situations which have come about due to the rise of technology and a new relationship of self to those changed circumstances. Therefore, a different thinking is required, one that allows us to get a panoramic view of the changes that have occurred in our society as a result of technology. We need to understand how these changes bear upon the individuals we seek to guide. We must come to understand the dissonance experienced by our young people who have "cut their teeth" on the "ring" of technology and are trying desperately to find a continuity in self compatible with what they are experiencing in time and motion so that they may launch and live their lives in an effective way. Therefore, effective guidance means developing a curriculum with one basic objective—learning to cope with rapid change.

If you are tuned in to the forces of our society, you know it is not only a "mix and match" game; it is a "mix and match" game within the framework of comprehended motion in change. The new age calls for an understanding of transiency and the centering of one's self in this process, the individual coming into control of the processes affecting his life, not being victimized by this motion, i.e. preparing for a particular career and finding it no longer exists as he graduates. Therefore, if the individual can experience his experience and know that he is experiencing it, he can learn to anticipate shifts in time and events and he can synchronize with as well as live in the change that is occurring. "There is absolutely no inevitability as long as there is a willingness to contemplate what is happening."[35] The acceleration of pace is a function of the growth of technology which makes more time frames available to man in his lifetime because technology has both broken up and compressed the several long developmental tasks and created many short bursts of tasks. Therefore, the individual finds himself in need of confidence in a new capacity to exercise the "cope-ability" skills required to make sense of all the short intervals caused by accelerating technological developments.

Pierce echoes this imperative as he suggests that today's toddler must be educated so that he can adjust gracefully to the twenty-first century world. "The sheer number of times that he may have to be recycled vocationally demands that he have a certain flexibility of mind as well as elastic attitudes toward obsolescence."[36] In short, we must teach students from the very beginning that knowing facts is not as important as knowing the transiency of all facts—that facts may be true today and false tomorrow. We must teach students to cope with change and build tolerance levels high enough to exist with a fair degree of psychological continuity in their lives.

The student must be ". . . able to unlearn and relearn many things ranging from vocational skills to attitudes toward other human beings."[37] Pierce also notes that futurology is gaining strength as a legitimate curriculum offering on the university level, but he strongly suggests that futurology should be taught to grade school students. Coleman goes even farther in suggesting that the traditional role of the schools as the teacher of cognitive skills and imparter of factual information is being usurped by a suddenly "information rich" society where media provide the information about the outside world once transmitted only by schools.[38] Coleman's concept of a future school incorporates in it the time and motion elements inherent in the life-cycle framework. He suggests that "the school, from the upper elementary grades on, would become a productive community in which the young would carry out responsible activities in service to the larger community," thus coming more into rhythm with the natural structure of life. His second suggestion was to modify workplaces to incorporate the young. The U. S. Office of Education (USOE) is currently trying out this idea in its employer-based career education model, which is an attempt to allow the student to earn and learn within the boundaries of his own stated feelings about what he needs. What Coleman is suggesting, plus what USOE is at present trying to implement, is an implicit if not explicit move to structure activities more within the natural evolution of life.

However, inherent in this time and motion framework we are developing is the fact that more decisions are possible and faster decisions about a choice naturally follow as time and motion have compacted the period when you are presented with the choice and when you have to act upon that choice. Decision making must come more within the rhythm of the motion in time that the individual is experiencing.

Part of this will have been accomplished when a student can experience decision making at a computer terminal which moves at the rate of speed he is experiencing. Eber suggests:

> Let the terminal show Johnny the odds against his becoming an astronaut; let it show why—because he has done so poorly in freshman algebra. Then regardless of whether or not the system was designed to explore simulation of "false" data some Johnny will find a way to ask the computer "What if . . . ?" and having that answer, some or many Johnnys will find ways to translate "What if . . ." into reality, will find them even though the school curriculum does not yet offer them.[39]

At this point, a new day will have dawned for guidance. Obsolescence will still occur, but it won't be quite as frustrating because we will be expecting it in all phases of life. We will have come into harmony with the life cycle, that of being born, living, serving purposes, then dying. So it is with technologies that continually evolve into better and more efficient forms; so it ought to be with the thoughts of a student using a revised new technology in guidance. We have a great challenge. There is no turning back. There is only going forward as a new "What if . . ." comes to mind. We must press forward into the era of indirect inquiry systems involving both system *and* personal monitoring. The flux of the world and people make this the new imperative for technology in guidance.

NOTES

1. Alvin Toffler, *Future Shock* (New York: Random House, 1970).
2. Marshall McLuhan, *The Medium is the Message* (New York: Bantam Books, 1967), p. 20.

3. Toffler, *op. cit.*, p. 26.
4. *Statistical Abstracts of the United States,* 1970, p. 73.
5. McLuhan, *op cit.*, p. 21.
6. *San Jose Mercury News,* 1972.
7. Toffler, *op. cit.*, p. 378.
8. Eric Hoffer, *The Ordeal of Change* (New York: Harper & Row, 1963).
9. Toffler, *op. cit.*, p. 76.
10. *Ibid.*
11. *Ibid.*, p. 3.
12. R. B. Fuller, *Operating Manual for Spaceship Earth* (New York: Simon and Schuster, 1969).
13. J. D. Bernal, *The World, The Flesh, and The Devil* (Bloomington, Ind.: Indiana University Press, 1969).
14. Fuller, *op. cit.*, p. 125.
15. *Ibid.*, p. 90.
16. D. V. Tiedeman and A. L. Miller, *Guidance-in-Learning: An Examination of Roles in Self-Centering during Thinking* (Palo Alto, Calif.: American Institutes for Research, 1972), xerox.
17. C. M. Pierce, "The Pre-Schooler and the Future," *The Futurist* 6(1972):13–15.
18. *Ibid.*, p. 13.
19. D. S. Rosser, "What you should know about new computer based college selection services," *Nation's Schools* 84(1969):47–49.
20. *Ibid.*
21. J. T. Impelletteri, "Implementation Problems: Counselor Acceptance of Systems," *Computer-Based Vocational Guidance Systems,* Alice Scates, ed. (Washington, D.C.: U.S. Department of Health, Education and Welfare, Office of Education, 1969), p. 151.
22. F. J. Minor, "The IBM Experimental Educational and Career Exploration System," *Ibid.*, p. 130.
23. R. A. Myers et al., *Preliminary Report: Assessment of the First Year of Use of the EDUCATIONAL AND CAREER EXPLORATION SYSTEM in Secondary Schools of Genesee County, Michigan* (New York: Teachers College, Columbia University, September 30, 1971).
24. H. F. Silberman, "The SDC Vocational Counseling System," Computer-Based Vocational Guidance Systems, *Ibid.* p. 139.
25. J. A. Harris, "The Willowbrook Computerized Vocational Information System," *Ibid.*, p. 160.
26. J. A. Harris, "Status Report: Computerized Vocational Information System (CVIS)," *Eighth Annual Invitational Conference on Systems under Construction in Career Education and Development* (Palo Alto, Calif.: American Institutes for Research, October, 1971), p. 2.
27. Warren Chapman, "Present Status of SIGI," *Ibid.*, p. 1.
28. *Ibid.*
29. *Ibid.*
30. *Ibid.*
31. *Ibid.*
32. *Ibid.*
33. D. V. Tiedeman, ed., *First and Second Annual and Third Reports, Harvard-NEEDS-Newton Information System for Vocational Decisions* (Cambridge, Mass.: Harvard Graduate School of Education, 1967, 1968, 1969).
34. D. E. Super, ed., *Computer-assisted Counseling* (New York: Teachers College Press, 1970), pp. 105–06.
35. Marshall McLuhan, *op. cit.*, p. 25.
36. Pierce, *op. cit.*, p. 13.

37. *Ibid.,* p. 13.
38. James Coleman, "Future Schools Should Not Teach, Coleman Says," *Report on Education Research,* March 1, 1972, p. 5.
39. H. W. Eber, "Computer as Library," *Contemporary Psychology* 17(1972): 49–50.

SUGGESTED READING

Holtzman, Wayne, ed. *Computer-Assisted Instruction, Testing, and Guidance.* New York: Harper and Row, 1968.

Super, Donald E., *Computer-Assisted Counseling.* New York: Teachers College Press, 1970.

The Futurist. Washington, D.C.: World Future Society, P. O. Box 30369, Bethesda Branch. A journal of forecasts, trends, and ideas about the future.

Tiedeman, David V., and Willis, Mary B., eds., *Career Education and the Technology of Career Development.* Palo Alto, Calif.: American Institutes for Research, 1972.

Planned Utilization and Change of Environments 16

Stanley H. Cramer
State University of New York at Buffalo

Career development is an offspring whose progenitor is human development in the generic sense. As such, career development is subject to the same assumptions as its parent theory. Among these assumptions are the following:[1]

1. The developmental process is the result of the interaction of both heredity and environment.
2. Development is continuous, regular, and orderly.
3. The rate of development varies for individuals.
4. The developmental process is a complicated, interrelated procedure.

Thus, human development is, to some currently unknown extent, an innate series of phenomena. However, it is also apparent that certain changes in the environment have the potential for either impeding or facilitating development. If an individual's environment is such that especially exciting and germane incentives are present, then one assumes that these stimuli will effect or encourage positive development in that person. Conversely, the absence of these stimuli are presumed to produce a negative effect on human development.

About a decade ago Burton[2] demonstrated that a number of different "ages" could form appropriate bases for the planning of educational experiences. Among these ages he included: chronological, mental, educational, anatomical, physiological, social, moral, and emotional. To this list, one might add *vocational age*, a term analogous to the contemporary usage of *vocational maturity*. If one can build educational experiences based upon the concept of vocational age, then there are obviously certain vocationally relevant tasks which arise at specific vocational ages and which must be mastered in order to insure adequate future vocational development. The concept of vocational tasks, like the concept of vocational development, is the progeny of Havighurst's[3] comprehensive formulation of developmental tasks.

Cultural pressures and the values and aspirations of an individual will largely determine what constitutes a vocational task. Therefore, if one wishes to intervene in the process of an individual's vocational development, one method that will likely be effective is to utilize existing environments or to change those environments in order to achieve a more vocationally healthy milieu. By "environment" is meant any structured setting which has the potential for acting upon an individual in either a positive or a negative manner—the family constellation, peer groups, neighborhoods, schools, and various agencies, among other structured settings. Further, if one seeks to alter such environments toward vocationally beneficial ends, he must proceed in a planful way. To leave such a potentially important variable to the whims of circumstance is to invite a diseased vocational development. Planned utilization and change of environments denotes change that is "conscious, deliberate, and intended."[4] Matheny[5] has suggested that the counselor should arrange growth-inducing experiences for clients by means of making better use of the existing school and community environments. By arranging appropriate experiences within the school or community and by identifying necessary and available resources, the counselor can more effectively assist the client to realize the major goals of guidance—self-exploration, the assuming of responsibility for one's life, and the development of satisfactory interpersonal relationships.

Translating the preceding into a specific illustration may be helpful at this point. There has been a great deal of evidence which clearly demonstrates that there are substantial differences in the habits, attitudes, and values of students in different educational settings (environments) and that such discrepancies subsequently give rise to corresponding differences in educational achievement and aspirations.[6] In other words, it is evident that school cultures differ, that they differ because of student characteristics, school characteristics, and peer mores, and that these differences affect student development. Similarly, studies have shown that students in various types of school environments differ markedly in degree of vocational maturity at the same age and grade level. Maynard and Hansen[7] have reported that students from socially, culturally, and/or economically disadvantaged schools have a pattern of vocational development different from that of their more advantaged suburban neighbors. Ansell and Hansen[8] have refined that conclusion to state that disadvantaged youth, regardless of race, are approximately two years slower in vocational development when compared to middle-class whites.

It is obvious that the variable factor operating in these cases is that of environmental differences, and it is equally apparent that planfully changing or utilizing the school environment can produce an equalizing effect in terms of vocational development. This chapter, then, will discuss ways in which the professional practitioner of vocational guidance can utilize or change various environments in order to facilitate vocational development.

THE INDIVIDUAL, THE ENVIRONMENT, AND CAREER DEVELOPMENT

Environmental Design, Environmental Control, Individual Differences

Since the time of Francis Galton and through the more recent work of J. P. Guilford, psychology has taught us the concept of individual differences. It is a concept to which virtually every professional practitioner of vocational guidance pays at least lip service. As is well-known, the idea of individual differences means that while all individuals pass through the same developmental stages, the time necessary for each to accomplish his or her goal will vary according to individual perceptions. Hence, individuals will differ relative to a wide spectrum of traits or of patterns of traits. For example, individuals will vary appreciably in terms of their measured intelligence and in the development of that trait. These differences will obviously have a profound effect on an individual's capacity to learn, since readiness for an experience to a great extent determines whether the learning experience will be mastered.

For the practice of vocational guidance the lesson of the concept of individual differences is the reminder it presents of the need for flexibility in responding to individual clients. It suggests that a planful effort must be made in order to insure that individuals are provided the necessary experiences that will give them a readiness to cope with vocationally relevant tasks that should be mastered at various developmental stages. It further suggests that individuals must be taken from where they are vocationally and brought to where they ought to be in order to best help the individual accomplish his or her goal. And it suggests that since all individuals do not respond in the same way to a variety of stimuli, the professional practitioner of vocational guidance must employ a wide range of materials, techniques, as skills as he intervenes in the vocational lives of individuals.

Career Development through the School Curriculum

One environment which offers especially high potential for the enhancement of vocational development is the school. As a result of the impetus provided by U.S. Commissioner of Education Sidney P. Marland, the concept of career education has emerged to provide a framework for the stimulation of vocational development within the parameters of the school environment. As defined by the federal government, career education advocates "that all educational experiences, curriculum, instruction, and counseling should be geared to preparation for economic independence and an appreciation for the dignity of work."[9]

Four current attempts of a massive nature have been seeking to accomplish what Herr[10] has termed the "institutionalization of career development," by means of the evolution of models pertaining to various settings. These models, described in detail by Herr in Chapter 2, are school-based, employee-based, home/community-based, and residential-based. Although each of these four models is envisioned as a discrete entity, there are, in fact, complementary and symbiotic relationships among them.[11] It is true that the residential-based model seems to be an island unto itself and that its goals are both more ambitious and less concrete than those of the other three. But the remaining three are not mutually exclusive, and one would not be surprised to see an ultimate melding of them in the course of time. For example, there is a great deal of sense in the idea that all school children can serve mini-apprenticeships in business, industry, public institutions, and the professions as an integral part of their formal schooling. One can also imagine that home-based, media focused education will simply become an extension of career education once it is adopted in the schools or will be utilized in the schools, much as in the English system of wedding education and the media. The school-based model offers the greatest promise in terms of already available delivery systems, ease and low cost of implementation, client availability, and comprehensiveness. It presents the opportunity for students to gain an awareness of self, to acquire an understanding of the vocational environment, and to develop decision-making skills within the context of the existing environmental structure. For these reasons, this chapter will concentrate on changing the existing formal educational environment.

The idea of career education is still so new that the concept has not crystallized. While most educators agree that the ultimate goal of career education in the school-based model is the enhancement of vocational development by means of the curriculum, there is some discrepancy regarding what tangible behaviors can be construed as representing adequate vocational development. There are some who view ultimate success in terms of a relative specificity of vocational choice by the termination of an individual's secondary school years. Thus Wykle[12] can state that "if a student does not have a career direction at the end of twelfth grade, we as educators have failed." The National Advisory Council on Vocational Education[13] is even more specific and has recommended that "every secondary school should be an employment agency." In more general terms, Herr and Cramer[14] advocate the use of the concept of vocational maturity as the broad criterion toward which efforts at career education should be directed, thus subsuming specificity of vocational choice as only one aspect of full vocational maturity.

Neatly summarizing some of the current thinking about principles relating to vocational development by means of school curriculum, Moullette[15] cites eight career preparation assumptions:

1. Education, training, and skill development ought to prepare students for initial employment and continued education and for advancement in either or both.
2. Experiences provided, courses offered, and subjects taught to students in an education, training, and skill development program ought to be related to a major field of study in an occupational cluster.
3. Education, training, and skill development ought to be organized into a substantial block of time.
4. Students ought to be academically employed in realistic education, training, and skill development experiences.
5. Learning and training stations, facilities, materials, and equipment ought to be realistic and conducive to learning.
6. Students ought to be explicitly informed, instructed, and trained. Their progress should be followed and evaluated in sufficient periods of time.
7. Work experience and educational experience ought to be part of every skill subject teacher's background.
8. Education, training, and skill development ought to be on-going and accessible to students at any level or stage in the career development process.

It is becoming increasingly clear that career development through the curriculum can mean many different things to many different populations. In an excellent review of the precepts and concepts which underlie a variety of on-going career education programs, Herr[16] suggests that such programs can denote or connote the following *minima:*

1. An effort to diminish the separateness of academic and vocational education.
2. An area of concern which has some operational implications for every educational level or grade from kindergarten through graduate school.
3. A process of insuring that every person exiting from the formal educational structure has job employability skills of some type.
4. A direct response to the importance of facilitating individual choice making so that occupational preparation and the acquisition of basic academic skills can be coordinated with developing individual preference.
5. A way of increasing the relevance or meaningfulness of education for greater numbers of students than is currently true.
6. A design to make education an open system in that school leavers, school dropouts, adults can reaffiliate with it when their personal circumstances or job requirements make this feasible.
7. A structure whose desired outcomes necessitate cooperation among all elements of education as well as among the school, industry, and community.
8. An enterprise requiring new technologies and materials of education (i.e., individualized programming, simulations).
9. A form of education for all students.

Thus the concept of career education as an approach to enhancing vocational development via the school curriculum represents one alternative for structuring environments toward vocationally beneficial ends. There are, as might be expected, divergencies in terms of the thinking as to what specific form such structuring might take. In one attempt to redesign the curriculum to assist students in coping with career development tasks, Bottoms and O'Kelley[17] have proposed an overlapping program which progresses from long-range orientational goals in the elementary school to concrete and immediately relevant goals in adulthood (outlined in broad terms in Table 16.1). They view such a curriculum as sequential and consonant with the other objectives of the school and, hence, integrated with all other curricular foci. Specifically, all general and academic courses would be taught in a manner which highlights their occupational implications.

Other approaches are also possible. For example, working on the developmental principle that individual readiness is variable, Oakland Community College has developed a system of personalized educational sequences which utilizes a variety of teaching media, instructional techniques, and flexible time blocks geared to the strengths and weaknesses of individual learners.[18] These sequences are determined after diagnostic testing. The U.S. Office of Education[19] envisions career education as proceeding along lines related to fifteen occupational fields or clusters which can describe the world of work. These fifteen clusters would be taught by means of refocusing the curriculum for grades 1-8 and by relating subject matter to careers in grades nine through twelve.

These examples are merely illustrative, and there are many other possible approaches to effecting vocational development via the curriculum. The preceding brief examples of approaches to career education are cited to point up the need for sequential, integrated, and articulated curriculum planning, a need which is mandated by what is currently known about

Table 16.1 Intent of a Developmental Vocational Curriculum

Intent	Level	Desirable outcome
Orientational	Grades K–6	Student acquires positive attitude toward work, school and increased knowledge of self in relationship to work
Exploration and Employability	Grade 7	Student makes tentative choice of broad occupational areas or of several occupational clusters for further exploration
Exploration, Employability, and Job Preparation	Grade 8	Student makes specific choice of occupational cluster for in-depth exploration and for acquiring employability skills
Exploration, Employability, and Job Preparation	Grade 9	Student makes choice of occupational cluster for entry-level job preparation and for further exploration
Job Preparation, Employability, Exploration, Job Entry, and Job Adjustment	Grades 10–12	Student prepares for and satisfactorily enters an entry-level job, or seeks further education and/or job preparation
Job Preparation, Job Entry, Adjustment, and Exploration	Post-Secondary	Student prepares and satisfactorily enters a specific technical or skilled occupation
Job Preparation, Upgrading, Job Entry, Adjustment, Progression, and Exploration	Adult	Student prepares for and satisfactorily enters a new occupation or updates and upgrades competence in existing occupational field

SOURCE: Bottoms, G., and O'Kelley, G. L. Vocational Education as a Developmental Process. *American Vocational Journal* (October 1971), pp. 36–39.

vocational development as a process. To some extent, it does not matter which specific theory of vocational choice and development forms the theoretical basis for a career education program; but, obviously, if one builds a developmental curriculum, it makes sense then to utilize a developmental theory. Thus, while trait-and-factor analysis, decision theory, and sociological and psychological approaches all have something to contribute as groundwork theories, it is those approaches which emphasize developmental principles that hold the most salience for the construction of a career education program. Clearly, the most comprehensive of such theories is that developed, refined, and tested by Donald Super and his associates. If one combines Supers' emphases with those of other theoreticians, one emerges with a synthesis of inputs to vocational development as in Table 16.2.

Translating these theoretically evolved inputs into operational modes constitutes one goal of career education. An environment, specifically the school, is being employed in such a manner that the inputs to vocational development are influenced. For example, Table 16.2 suggests that some time between the preschool years and the onset of pubescence, students need to develop a vocabulary of work. One can leave this task to the caprices of

Table 16.2 Synthesis of Inputs to Vocationalization

Approximate Ages ——→

Preschool	5–9	10–14	15	18	19–25

Formation of self-concept ——→ Translation of self-concept into vocational terms ——→ Implementation of self-concept

Developing preference or anticipation ——→ choice ——→ induction ——→ reformation ——→ integration

Fantasy ——→ Tentative ——→ Realistic

Trial (with little more commitment) ——→ Trial (more commitment) ——→ stabilization ——→ advancement

Awareness of the need to crystallize (orienting) ——→ Use of resources (exploring) ——→

——→ Formulating Interests ——→ Relating interests and capacities Relating interests and capacities to values

——→ Developing a vocabulary of self ——→ Awareness of factors to consider in formulating a Preparing for marriage selecting a mate
vocational preference

——→ Developing a vocabulary of work ——→ Awareness of contingencies which affect vocational Developing capability for intimacy
goals   starting a family

——→ Rudiments of basic trust in self and others ——→ Differentiation of interests and values Becoming a productive person

——→ Rudiments of initiative ——→ Awareness of present-future relationships

——→ Rudiments of industry ——→ Accepting oneself as in process Mastering the skills of one's occupation

——→ Knowledge of fundamentals of technology ——→ Relating changes in the self to changes in the world Moving up the ladder within one's occupation

——→ Differentiating self from environment ——→ Acquiring basic habits of industry

——→ Identification with a worker ——→ Learning to organize one's time and energy to get work done

——→ Developing sex social role ——→ Learning to defer gratification, to set priorities

——→ Learning rudiments of social rules ——→ Achieving personal identity

——→ Learning fundamental intellectual, physical and motor skills ——→ Acquiring knowledge of life in organizations

Preparation for role relationships

Preparation for level and kind of consumption

Preparation for an occupational career
Formulation of generalized preference
Possession of information concerning the preferred occupation
Planning for the preferred occupation

Choosing and preparing for occupation
Achieving more mature relations with peers of both sexes
Achieving emotional independence of parents and other adults

Independence of choice

Developing planfulness
Developing decision-making strategies

Role-playing ⎫
Identification ⎭ ⟶ Role-playing, curricula exposure ⟶ reality-testing ⟶ work-study
　　　　　　　　　attitudes of others ⟶ identification ⟶ self-appraisal

SOURCE: Herr, E. L. and Cramer, S. H. *Vocational Guidance and Career Development in the Schools: Toward a Systems Approach.* Boston: Houghton Mifflin, 1972, p. 119.

chance, as has been typically done in the past, or one can attempt to structure the school environment in such a way that this goal is achieved by means of planfully utilizing the school curriculum.

Attitudes of Those Who Monitor Career Development

It has been observed that those innovations which become absorbed into school curricula are largely "thing" oriented. They require no great change in the attitudes of administrators, teachers, and other school personnel; rather, they are simply changes in work practices or in technology, such as programmed-learning hardware, grouping practices, new procedures for scheduling electronic data-processing, and well-packaged curriculum materials.[20] On the other hand, those changes which are less readily adopted might be described as "people" oriented—that is, innovations which require changes in the basic attitudes of school personnel and/or the community. Examples of this type of change include busing to the basic manner of organizing teaching practices in a classroom.

The inauguration of a career education program within an existing institutional environment represents a change problem that is approximately equidistant between these two extremes. New curricular materials and specific technological aids are certainly a part of career education (e.g., gaming and simulation, syllabi, multimedia packaging, etc.). These types of "thing" changes are relatively easy to accomplish.[21] However, career education also requires "people" change—that is, an alteration of the basic attitudes of all school personnel, students, and parents. This task is relatively difficult.

However difficult the task may be, if the attitudes of those who monitor career development as aspects of environments are not "right," then the notion of environmental intervention for career education will likely fail. What is the right attitude? It is a predisposition to respond to students with a respect for their individuality. It is the manifestation of a positive stance toward the idea of career education. It is the recognition of the potential worth and dignity that people bring to all types of work. It is the cognizance that students may be vocationally naive and that something can be done to reduce that naiveté. It is the development of a classroom atmosphere or climate which is conducive to self-examination and group involvement.[22] It is a belief in the cooperative and multidisciplinary functioning of all school personnel. And it is an awareness of the importance of community involvement in the planning, implementation, and evaluation of career education programs.

Such attitudes do not come about as though sprung from the head of Medusa. They are consciously and deliberately planned for; they are incubated and nurtured. Pruitt[23] has suggested, for example, that teachers must be carefully assisted to participate in career education programs. She notes that teachers are frequently unaware that their subjects are foundations for a variety of occupations and that they do not have easy access to information about the jobs in which their subjects are primary. In short, they do not view their subject matters in any vocationally relevant sense. To build the attitude in teachers that their subject matters are vocationally relevant is thus a major task. Teachers are also typically ignorant of the idea of vocational development and the importance of individual self-awareness to the vocational development process, and they need to be made aware of the important part they can play in developing the emerging self of a student and directing that self toward vocationally beneficial ends. The development, enhancement, or alteration of attitudes is not an easy task. Yet, unless those who monitor career development possess healthy attitudes toward that function, it is unlikely that intervention efforts will succeed.

Partnership of General and Vocational Education

Historically, vocational aspects of education have received considerable attention, at least theoretically if less in the implementation. It is currently fashionable to perceive career education as a totally new phenomenon. In fact, there are clear-cut historical antecedents for the role of education in preparing young people for a vocational life. A sampling of such antecedents might prove instructive.

As long ago as 1914, the Commission on National Aid to Vocational Education[24] urged both training for a vocation and the development of "civic or vocational intelligence" as goals of the schools. Four years later in 1918 the NEA's Commission on the Reorganization of Secondary Education[25] cited *vocation* as one of the seven primary objectives of American secondary education. Similar statements continued through the 1920s and 1930s. In 1946 the U.S. Office of Education sponsored a series of conferences dealing with "Vocational Education in the Years Ahead." As reported by Cremin,[26] the consensus of these meetings was that secondary education should become more vocationally germane. These concerns persisted throughout the 1950s and into the 1960s, highlighted by the Vocational Education Act of 1963 and its Amendments in 1968. These acts foster vocational education as an integral part of general education and something that is of value for all students. The type of insight contained in these Acts is reflected in the *General Report of the Advisory Council on Vocational Education* (outlined in Chapter 2).[27]

What has emerged is a view of vocational education that transcends the confining notion of a school child simply learning a manipulative skill—the ability to use some set of tools or piece of knowledge to accomplish a specific task—largely by a "hands on" procedure. Rather, vocational education is viewed as the acquisition by all students of a set of skills beyond simple task skills. These broader skills include an examination and clarification of personal habits, attitudes, and values; the development of a vocabulary of work; an understanding of the occupational structure and its relationship to education; and the ability to engage in meaningful decision-making. These skills require a knowledge of self, a knowledge of vocationally relevant environmental options, and the ability to process these two types of information so that an individual will be better able to choose from among available vocational options.

As the previous historical overview has demonstrated, these broader skills have been paid lip service throughout this century as goals for general education. The assumption has been made that—as though by osmosis—

these goals woud be achieved and that no deliberate or specific efforts to define sequential experiences necessary for their attainment was required. To the contrary, it is now clear that if vocational education is to achieve full partnership with general education, then there must be a conscious, indeed strenuous, effort at "interrelating, articulating, sequencing, individualizing, differentiating, and integrating the deluge of experiences which constitute growth, learning, and the attainment of personal competence."[28]

General education, then, has traditionally been concerned with at least some aspects of career education, tangential and undifferentiated though that concern may have been. What is now required is a conscious vocational focus that systematically addresses the ultimate goal of vocational maturity. What is needed is a series of vocational activities geared to the developmental needs and levels of students. What must emerge is an integrated and articulated focus on career development to replace what is now largely a compartmentalized *potpourri* of isolated experiences.

A *bona fide* partnership of general and vocational education recognizes the uniqueness of individuals and the need for many different types of degrees of talent. It emphasizes the positive strengths and characteristics that each student brings to the educational environment. In place of occupational illiteracy it promises occupational fluency; in place of a lack of goals it promises goal-directedness; and in place of nonemployability it promises saleable skills.

COOPERATION FOR CAREER DEVELOPMENT

If environments are to be structured in such a manner that career development is enhanced, then the cooperative efforts of a number of "publics" and personnel are necessary. To be sure, counselors and/or vocational educators cannot produce the desired outcomes by themselves; they must draw upon all aspects of the school and the community. Toward the culmination of adequate career development for all youngsters, counselors and/or vocational educators must assume an advocacy role, in the sense that they must create and use a greater diversity of school personnel and community resources than are currently being utilized.

Structuring the school environment in order to implement career development concepts generates problems of resources, structure, and personnel. If the personnel involved can achieve cooperation, then the problems are at least assuaged. If parents, teachers, counselors, administrators, employers, and workers can be marshaled in the cause of career education, the objectives of vocational guidance can be achieved. The coordination of cooperative efforts by personnel in the schools, in community agencies, and in business and industry is therefore essential.

In one sense, such cooperation is mandated by legislation which makes "parity" or some less potent joint effort a condition of receiving funds. Beyond legislation, however, the need for cooperation possesses its own "face validity," its own logic. Finally, given the relatively small number of guidance and vocational education specialists, and given the complexity of vocational development, logistical concerns alone justify cooperative efforts. These cooperative efforts can come about in at least two ways.[29] First, one can identify the unique contributions that specific people (e.g., counselors, teachers, employers, and agency personnel) can make and then assist them, through training or administrative arrangement, to acquire the attitudes, knowledge, and strategies to accomplish these goals within their own baili-wicks. Second, one can create overriding goals and strategies, and specific resource contributions can then be "plugged into" the master system. Clearly, the latter alternative is superior to the former since it requires the planning of overall objectives and specifies the resources necessary to accomplish these aims.

Teachers

For example, teachers can be employed as a vital resource for transmitting the required knowledge, for developing the necessary attitudes, and for imparting the mandatory skills that lead to vocational maturity. By means of demonstrating the vocational salience of their subject matter, of intro-ducing students at all levels to pertinent vocational development concepts, of expanding student awareness of alternatives, and of actively encouraging vocational exploration, teachers can assist students to gain an understanding of the vibrance of the occupational world and of their potential places in that structure. The classic "spiral curriculum" defines the parameters within which can be addressed the developmental learning phases variously termed "perceptualization, conceptualization, and generalization";[30] "fantasy, tenta-tive, realistic";[31] and "exploration, crystallization, choice, and clarification."[32]

As has been previously noted, the attitudes of teachers will have a deep influence on the vocationalization of students. In effect, teachers serve as behavioral models for students, and the manner in which they act can either extinguish or reinforce a pupil's vocational aspirations.[33] Thus teachers can provide not only a series of structured experiences designed to enhance vocational development; they also can create a psychological climate which draws out students and nurtures their best vocational capacities and aspirations.

School Counselors

Since teachers lack much of the "know-how" involved in career develop-ment, the counselor must work in collaboration with teachers, individually and through in-service programs, to design sets of educational experiences that respond to the individual differences of students. To do this the counselor must monitor, diagnose, and prescribe in relation to student vocational development needs. He must suggest appropriate experiential and informational resources for the use of classroom teachers. In short, the counselor must bring to bear his unique "expertise" in vocational develop-ment in order to assist the classroom teachers to integrate career develop-ment concepts within the curriculum.

In addition to this collaborative function, the counselor also performs a role for which he has primary and often sole responsibility. For instance, he still engages in individual and group counseling, in both a stimulus and a treatment mode. He still has a placement role, in the sense of assisting in transitional processes at various points in time (e.g., junior high school to high school, high school to further education, or high school to work). And he still has a research function which allows him to plan career development experiences on the basis of knowledge gained from, for example, follow-up studies on graduates and drop-outs, data on the aspirations and characteristics of the student population, and data on students who succeed or fail in various curricula rather than on the basis of "hunch" or purely subjective impulses.[34]

In order to accomplish this role, at once one of leadership and collaboration, the counselor must be adequately prepared. There is some evidence that he is not. In their sixth report on counseling and guidance, the National Advisory Council on Vocational Education[35] presents a scathing, although frequently hyperbolic, condemnation of the state of vocational guidance in the schools. Among their recommendations for improvement are the following.

1. Counselor education institutions should require at least one introductory course in career education and at least one practicum devoted to on-site study of the business-industry-labor community.
2. Responsible decisionmakers should embark on an immediate major campaign designed to upgrade the vocational knowledge and career guidance skills of currently employed counselors.
3. Job placement and follow-up services should be considered major parts of counseling and guidance programs.
4. Career development programs should be considered a major component in career education, both in legislation and in operating systems.
5. The United States Congress should create categorical funding for counseling and guidance in all legislation calling for these services.

It is clear that a change is required of counselors, a change which would move them from what is now essentially a treatment mode to a manner of operation which is largely stimulus oriented. Rather than identify problems that have emerged and try to correct those problems, counselors must work to prevent the emergence of future problems by concentrating on building a developmental set of experiences which will assure the vocational maturity of the students with whom they work.

Employment Service Counselors

Responsible for a clientele much more heterogeneous than that with which his school counterpart works, the employment service counselor has traditionally had as his goal the optimal and quick placement of clients. This facile matching of persons and jobs has been broadened recently to include the identification, recruitment, and provision of appropriate training experiences for a wide variety of people and through an emphasis that can be more accurately described as professional counseling rather than job advising.[36] The accomplishment of this goal requires greater articulation and cooperation among school counselors, employment service counselors, teachers, rehabilitation personnel, and representatives of business and industry.

The 1968 Amendments to the Vocational Education Act of 1963 suggest areas of cooperation between school counselors and employment service counselors. These amendments urge that schools provide to the employment service information regarding both graduates and drop-outs of vocational education courses or schools and, in turn, that the employment service make information regarding occupational openings available to schools and engage in the practice of vocational guidance and counseling with students. In fact, in a few schools, largely urban, counselors of the employment service are actually housed in the schools.

Cooperation between school and employment service can extend along many dimensions as both institutions seek to alter environmental input in order to facilitate vocational development. Among these dimensions are providing aptitude testing, employment counseling, placement, proficiency testing, information on local employment trends by industry and by occupation, information on MDTA classes, speakers at career days or in classes, local wage rate information, consultation on work-bound students, information on shortage occupations, and consultation on potential drop-outs.[37] Particularly, the General Aptitude Test Battery, the most carefully and extensively validated and developed multifactor aptitude battery in existence, could be used in the schools at earlier grade levels for guidance purposes. In addition to counseling uses, the information thus gained could greatly influence school counselors and educators in assessing student proficiency, planning vocational programs, designing curricula, and placing students.

Rehabilitation Counselors

Historically, the rehabilitation counselor differed from his counterparts in schools and in employment services by virtue of the fact that his clientele was limited to persons with physical disability. In recent years such disability has been broadened to include not only the physically but also the emotionally, mentally, and culturally disabled. As a result, the historically clear lines of demarcation among counselors in various settings have been obfuscated. In any case, to the degree that whatever disabilities exist are modifiable, the rehabilitation counselor coordinates those services that will modify them (e.g., prosthetics, training, etc.). When they are not susceptible to modification, he assists the client to circumvent them and to find employment within the limits prescribed by the disability.

Because of her broadened clientele, the rehabilitation counselor now has goals of vocational habilitation as well as vocational rehabilitation.[38] Rehabilitation, of course, is the restoring or reeducating of individuals to productive lives, while vocational habilitation is the educational process of developing the vocationally naive, those individuals who have little or no previous contact with the world of work. Vocational habilitation thus is evident in job training programs for the handicapped and the disadvantaged and in state cooperative programs between special education and vocational rehabilitation. As vocational rehabilitation moves closer to vocational habilitation, the functions of rehabilitation counselors, school counselors, and employment service counselors become less differentiated. What will be required ultimately is a less fragmented approach and greater articulation of services by all counseling specialists. If vocational habilitation is to be effective, coordinated effort is necessary by means of fully utilizing all institutional and agency settings.

Communication among persons in the world of work and rehabilitation, employment service, and school counselors can take two forms:[39] "those that serve primarily the counselor's client (the student or postschool adult) and those intended to inform or update the counselor." This relationship can also be reciprocal. When such interaction takes place one outcome will likely be the increased employability of certain segments of the population. Carr and Young[40] point out that cooperative efforts by industry and business have already taken such directions as leadership in stay-in-school campaigns to raise the occupational sights of minority youth, in earn-and-learn programs, in faculty summer internships, in industry-education seminars, and in vocational training for the unemployed.

Section 553 of the Vocational Education Amendments of 1968 provides for funding of various forms of industry-education exchange programs, institutes, and in-service education to provide personnel in vocational education. Since legislative support already exists to facilitate cooperative efforts, educators, counselors, and representatives from the work world must bring their energies and ingenuity to bear in creating sound and exciting experiences that will provide an extension of an individual's vocational environment. What clearly emerges is the need to prepare existing personnel to adapt to changing expectations of their roles in the process of enhancing the vocational development of their clients. Hoyt et al.[41] have postulated several of the changes that will be required if environmental intervention is successfully to affect career development. Classroom teachers will need to devote greater time to their tasks, to acquire new knowledge and expertise, to develop and use more appropriate teaching materials, to learn to work with paraprofessionals, and to change their current attitudes about the world of work. Vocational educators will need to learn to work at the elementary school level, to broaden their emphases at the junior high school level, and to become more flexible at the senior high school level. Further, they will need to incorporate college preparatory students into vocational education and, in general, to expand the opportunities they offer to students and the modes through which these opportunities are transmitted. School counselors will also need to change their attitudes, to increase their numbers, to make greater use of available technology, to develop better occupational assessment devices, and to become more familiar with the work world.

These needed changes in teachers, vocational educators, and counselors can come about only through a massive, carefully planned and implemented in-service education program for those currently practicing and through a new emphasis on career education in pre-service college and university preparation programs. Concomitant changes must also occur in the business-labor-industrial community. Representatives from the work world must get into the schools, opportunities for work experience and work-study must be expanded—not only for students but also for educational personnel—and the notion of "parity," of an equal partnership in education, must be realized. Again, what is required is education and reeducation in proportions that are unprecedented in the history of American education—not an impossible task but certainly a challenging one.

IMPLICATIONS OF SYSTEMS APPROACHES

Herr[42] has observed that research and theory relating to career development primarily deal with what happens if there is no planned intervention in the vocational development process, if there is no conscious and deliberate attempt to utilize or to change the vocational environment. The preceding discussion in these pages, however, has indicated that career development is capable of being acted upon by modifying influences in the environment. Hence, a whole new body of research knowledge leading to theory must evolve regarding what aspects of career development are modifiable, at what points in time, and by what means. In short, research must give us answers to questions of what, when, and how.

A priori, the most promising avenue for exploring possible responses to these questions is that represented by what has been termed a systems approach or, at the very least, a systematic approach to intervention. Although educators have long incorporated aspects of a systems approach in their pedagogy,[43] it is only in relatively recent times that the concept of a systems approach has been applied totally to the entire educational enterprise. There are many possible definitions of a systems approach, at least partly because of the great variety of disciplines which utilize the method. However, common to all definitions is the idea that such an approach determines what needs exist and then relates those needs to goals and objectives. Bushnell[44] has outlined the basic components of a systems approach as follows: "diagnosing the problem, searching for alternative solutions, testing these solutions, implementing the alternatives selected, and providing for subsequent evaluation and feedback." The key features of a systems approach appear to be a primary concern for inputs and subsequent outputs as determined by performance assessment.

What is proposed, then, is that in order to utilize the school environment in the service of vocational development one must: 1) state in behavioral terms the student outcomes desired at various age, grade, or developmental levels;[45] 2) provide treatments (e.g., activities, experiences, resources, etc.) directed toward the accomplishment of the objectives; and 3) evaluate to insure that the objectives have been achieved at the desired level of competency.

Objectives for vocational development must include both a cognitive dimension (i.e., knowledge, understanding, and skills) and an affective dimension (i.e., habits, attitudes, appreciations, and values). These objectives are developed with due regard for various inputs, including learner characteristics, resource characteristics in school and community, teacher characteristics, counselor characteristics, utility of teaching methods, administrative characteristics or management requirements, and community expectations. Treatments will come in a variety of modes, ranging from didactic instruction to field trips, from work experience to counseling, from test interpretation to gaming and simulation, from man-machine interaction systems to discussion groups—in short, ranging through the entire gamut of educational methodologies. Evaluation, too, will demonstrate a variety of methodologies.

Jones[46] has expanded this three-step process into a five-step program and sees the following sequence as paramount.

1. Identification of youth development needs and translation of these into behavioral objectives which state desired youth outcomes.
2. Classification of objectives by similarities and priorities which will serve as guidelines for the design of guidance and counseling programs.
3. Specification of alternative strategies which could be used in guidance and counseling programs and selection of those strategies which seem most appropriate for particular groups of objectives.
4. Design, scheduling, and implementation of the selected strategy or strategies through the organization of instructional and counseling materials and procedures into individualized guidance-related learning units.
5. Evaluation of the efficiency and effectiveness of such units in helping students achieve the desired terminal outcomes specified in each unit's behavioral objectives.

In summary, a systems approach to utilizing the school environment to promote adequate vocational development for all students appears to offer greater promise than does any other methodology.

SUMMARY

This chapter has argued that in the process of progressing from childhood to adulthood individuals must master certain vocationally relevant tasks at various developmental levels. If this vocationalization is left to chance, it is likely that the required mastery will not be achieved. One method of insuring that vocational development is adequately nurtured is to utilize or to change existing environments, the good use of which can facilitate the desired vocational maturity of young people. Hence, this chapter has discussed ways in which vocational development can be enhanced through the curriculum and through the cooperative efforts of diverse personnel. Lastly, this chapter has proposed that a systems approach is the best method available for accomplishing this purpose.

NOTES

1. J. F. Travers, *Fundamentals of Educational Psychology* (Scranton, Pa.: International Textbook Company, 1970), p. 83.
2. W. H. Burton, *The Guidance of Learning Activities,* 3rd ed. (New York: Appleton-Century Crofts, 1962).
3. R. J. Havighurst, *Developmental Tasks and Education* (New York: McKay, 1948);
4. R. Chin and K. D. Benne, "General Strategies for Effecting Changes in Human Systems," in W. G. Bennis, K. D. Beanne, and R. Chin (eds.), *The Planning of Change* (2nd edition), New York: Holt, Rinehart, and Winston, 1969, pp. 32–59.

5. K. Matheny, "Counselors As Environmental Engineers," *Personnel and Guidance Journal*, Volume 49, February 1971, pp. 439–444.

6. C. W. Bachman and P. F. Secord, *A Social Psychological View of Education* (New York: Harcourt Brace Jovanovich, 1968); R. P. Boyle, "The Effect of the High School on Student Aspirations," *American Journal of Sociology* 71(1966):628–39; J. S. Coleman, *The Adolescent Society* (New York: Macmillan, 1961); R. A. Dentler, "Equality of Educational Opportunity: A Special Review," *Urban Review* 1(April 1966):27–29.

7. P. E. Maynard and J. C. Hansen, "Vocational Maturity Among Inner-City Youths," *Journal of Counseling Psychology* 17(September 1970):400–05.

8. E. M. Ansell and J. C. Hansen, "Patterns in Vocational Development of Urban Youth," *Journal of Counseling Psychology* 18,6(1971):505–08.

9. *Career Education* DHEW Publication No. (DE) 72-39 (Washington, D.C.: Office of Education, U.S. Department of Health, Education, and Welfare, 1971).

10. E. L. Herr, "What Is Career Education?" paper presented at Career Education Conference for Cochise County School Administrators, Casa Grande, Arizona, August 1971.

11. The following discussion is drawn largely from Career Education Development Task Force, especially *The Career Education Program: Status Report* (Washington, D.C.: U.S. Office of Education, July 30, 1971).

12. J. H. Wykle, "Career Education: Facts and Expectations," *American Vocational Journal*, February 1972, pp. 50–56.

13. National Advisory Council on Vocational Education, "Career Preparation for Everyone," *Vocational Guidance Quartely* 20(March 1972):183–87.

14. E. L. Herr and S. H. Cramer, *Vocational Guidance and Career Development in the Schools: Toward a Systems Approach* (Boston: Houghton Mifflin, 1972).

15. J. B. Moullette, *Career Preparation in the Integrated Curriculum of Comprehensive Career Education*, paper presented at the LEA Curriculum-Career Preparation Workshop, Jefferson County, Colorado, January 12, 1972.

16. E. L. Herr, *Review and Synthesis of Foundations for Career Education* (Columbus, Ohio: Center for Vocational and Technical Education, Ohio State University, March 1972), p. 10.

17. G. Bottoms and G. L. O'Kelley, "Vocational Education as a Developmental Process," *American Vocational Journal*, March 1971, pp. 21–24.

18. J. E. Hill and D. N. Nunnery, "Career Mobility Through Personalized Occupational Education," *American Vocational Journal*, October 1971, pp. 36–39.

19. Wykle, *op. cit.*

20. B. A. Benedict et al., "The Clinical-Experimental Approach to Assessing Organizational Change Efforts," *Journal of Applied Behavioral Science* 3(1967):347–80; North Central Association, special issue of *Today* 11 (1967).

21. K. B. Hoyt, R. N. Evans, E. F. Mackin, and G. L. Mangum, *Career Education: What Is It and How To Do It* (Salt Lake City, Utah: Olympus Publishing, 1972).

22. E. Swain, "A Training Program for Career Exploration Teachers," *American Vocational Journal*, November 1971, pp. 81–82.

23. A. S. Pruitt, "Teacher Involvement in the Curriculum and Career Guidance," *Vocational Guidance Quarterly* 17(March 1969):189–93.

24. House of Representatives, *Report of the Commission on National Aid to Vocational Education*, 63rd Congress, 2nd Session, Document, No. 1004, 1914.

25. U.S. Bureau of Education, *Cardinal Principles of Secondary Education* (Washington, D.C.: The Bureau, 1918).
26. L. A. Cremin, *The Transformation of the School* (New York: Alfred A. Knopf, 1961).
27. National Advisory Council on Vocational Education, *The Bridge Between Man and His Work: Highlights and Recommendations from the General Report* (Washington, D.C.: U.S. Office of Education, 1968).
28. Herr and Cramer, *op. cit.*
29. *Ibid.*
30. N. C. Gysbers, *Elements of a Model for Promoting Career Development in Elementary and Junior High School,* paper presented at the National Conference of Exemplary Programs and Projects Section of the 1968 Amendments to the Vocational Education Act, Atlanta, Georgia, March 1969.
31. E. Ginsberg et al., *Occupational Choice: An Approach to a General Theory* (New York: Columbia University Press, 1951).
32. D. V. Tiedeman and R. P. O'Hara, *Career Development: Choice and Adjustment* (New York: College Entrance Examination Board, 1963).
33. S. R. Day, "Testing Influence on the Occupational Preference of High School Students," *Vocational Guidance Quarterly* 14(1966):215–19.
34. S. H. Cramer et al., *Research and the School Counselor* (Boston: Houghton Mifflin, 1970).
35. National Advisory Council on Vocational Education, *Counseling and Guidance: A Call for Change,* 6th Report, June 1, 1972.
36. L. Schantz and J. F. McGowan, "Upgrading Employment Service Counselors in Missouri," *Vocational Guidance Quarterly* 13(1965):169–72.
37. J. E. Rossman and E. M. Prebonich, "School Counselor-Employment Service Counselors in Missouri," *Vocational Guidance Quarterly* 13(1965):169–72.
38. J. A. Bitter, "The Training Counselor: An Emerging Professional," *Vocational Guidance Quarterly* 15(1967):294–96.
39. K. R. Kunze, "Industry Resources Available to Counselors," *Vocational Guidance Quarterly* 16(1967):137–42.
40. H. C. Carr and N. A. Young, "Industry-Education Cooperation," *Vocational Guidance Quarterly* 15(1967):203–04.
41. Hoyt et al., *op. cit.*
42. E. L. Herr, "Contributions of Career Development to Career Education," *Journal of Industrial Teacher Education* 9(Spring 1972):5–14.
43. B. S. Bloom et al., *Taxonomy of Educational Goals, Handbook I: Cognitive Domain* (New York: Longmans, Green, 1956); D. R. Krathwohl, B. S. Bloom, and B. B. Masia, *Taxonomy of Educational Objectives, Handbook II: The Affective Domain* (New York: David McKay, 1964).
44. D. S. Bushnell, "A Systematic Strategy for School Renewal," *Planned Change in Education: A Systems Approach,* D. S. Bushnell and D. Rappaport, eds. (New York: Harcourt-Brace Jovanovich, 1971), pp. 3–17.
45. J. D. Krumboltz, "Behavioral Goals for Counseling," *Journal of Counseling Psychology* 13(1966):153–59; H. B. McDaniel, *Youth Guidance Systems* (Palo Alto, Calif.: College Entrance Examination Board, 1970).
46. G. B. Jones, "Individualized Guidance and Counseling," *Planned Change in Education,* pp. 142–167.

SUGGESTED READING

Hansen, L. S. *Career Guidance Practices in School and Community.* Washington, D.C.: National Vocational Guidance Association, 1970. A compendium of some of the better vocational guidance programs in schools.

Herr, E. L., and Cramer, S. H. *Vocational Guidance and Career Development in the Schools: Toward a Systems Approach.* Boston: Houghton Mifflin Company, 1972. Reviews the appropriate literature of vocational guidance and suggests how principles of career development can be implemented in the schools in a systematic manner.

Hoyt, K. B., Evans, R. N., Mackin, E. F., and Magnum, G. L. *Career Education: What It is and How To Do It.* Salt Lake City, Utah: Olympus Publishing Company, 1972. A practical, down-to-earth discussion of how career education programs can be planned, carried out, and evaluated.

Krause, E. A. *The Sociology of Occupations.* Boston: Little, Brown, and Company, 1971. Contains excellent discussions of ten occupational fields from which guidance practitioners can infer practical applications.

Watson, G. "Resistance to Change," in G. Watson, ed. *Concepts for Social Change.* Washington, D.C.: National Training Laboratories, 1966. A primer of obstacles to be avoided by school personnel who wish to utilize the educational environment in the service of career development.

Willingham, W. W., Ferrin, R. I., and Begle, E. P. *Career Guidance in Secondary Education.* New York: College Entrance Examination Board, 1972. A collation of descriptions of many current vocational guidance programs which utilize the school environment.

The Vocational Guidance of Girls and Women in the United States

17

Esther E. Matthews
University of Oregon

Vocational guidance for all people over the entire life span is a national priority of the decade of the seventies. In this chapter the particular needs of the female population will be studied, but many of the statements could also be applied to the needs of the male population as well for humane, comprehensive, and expert vocational guidance.

Used in a broad sense, the term "vocation" is partially synonymous with life-style, particularly related to that portion of life-style characterized by the expression of time, energy, and ability in the form of job, occupation, or career—paid or unpaid, full-time or part-time, stable or changing. A broad definition like this enables us to look at the "occupation" of growing and experiencing in childhood, of being a student in adolescence, a worker in adulthood, or a productive retired citizen in later life. In order to practice effective "vocational guidance" for this broad population we need to understand the needs and problems in depth, as well as the possibilities and impediments for growth and development *throughout* life. Then, perhaps, we can move toward creating an evolving, growth-paced, individualized response to the needs of people. Vocational counselors must learn to depend upon many disciplines for help in continuing to try to unravel the intricate mysteries of the human career.

The vocational guidance of girls and women has its roots in the total fabric of society. Parents, relatives, teachers, counselors, and employers respond to women in modes defined by the dominant mores of the time, and the vocational guidance deemed appropriate for females in the seventies is not the kind of guidance given to many girls and women during the fifties and sixties. The vocational guidance provided for girls during that period can be described as lukewarm, indifferent, unfocused, negative, or even nonexistent. Some counselors, as agents of society rather than agents of change for individuals, acquiesced to cultural norms specifying "proper," "happy" roles for girls that did not include the possibility of strong career commitment as a viable individual option.

During the late sixties and the seventies we have been witnessing marked and rapid changes in attitudes toward women—and men, too—and their roles in the society. In order to understand the remarkable educational, legal, and social changes that are upon us we need to look back over the last few decades; to study some of the research that supported constricted views of the potentiality of women; to find out how women viewed themselves and how they were seen by important others; to understand how families reared their daughters and how women fared in the work places of the country. We need to raise questions about the occupations they entered, the vocational preferences they expressed, and the factors that delimited their participation across the spectrum of occupations. Then we may be able to understand the type and caliber of vocational guidance given to or withheld from girls and women in the past and contemplate the changes needed in the future.

It is possible that there have been more changes in custom, practice, and law during the early years of the 1970s than in the prior centuries. It is inordinately difficult to write, with any perspective, about history while it is happening, since each subsequent generation, retrospectively, can clarify the trends and outcomes of the past with greater objectivity. However, a glimpse of some of the major trends of the decades of the 1950s and 1960s can give us a valuable perspective on the early years of the 1970s. With this framework in mind, we will then study each stage of a woman's life, report relevant research, raise questions and suggest concrete possibilities for individualized vocational guidance by parents, teachers, and counselors specific to the life-stages of women.

PERSPECTIVES FROM THREE DECADES

The Ambivalent Fifties

The spirit of each decade of history is reflected in its popular and professional books, articles, documents, research, and conferences. The 1950s could be characterized as a period of marked ambivalence. On the one hand, it was a period of observation and reaffirmation of the status quo with respect to the position of women. It was a decade when observed and recorded "facts" supported the dominant views of society that woman's "real" place was in the home and that advanced career education would be largely wasted on women. On the other hand, there were definite stirrings of concern and questioning on the part of some who wondered why such a small proportion of educated women showed interest in seriously considering careers.

A few *selective* references, arranged chronologically, will demonstrate the tenor of the times and foreshadow the developments of the 1960s. The year 1953 saw three publications by Mueller,[1] Komarovsky,[2] and Bragdon[3] depicting the conflicts and frustrations of the educated woman and emphasizing the need for women to adapt to a changing world in urgent need of their skills and talents. No doubt these books were read by educated women and scholars interested in women's education, but the great majority of people were probably unaware of their contributions. Mead's *Male and Female: A Study of Sexes in a Changing World*,[4] published in 1955, did receive widespread attention, even from the general public, though it is difficult to say whether the subject matter or the real significance of the book was the focus of attention. In any case, this contribution helped to prepare the way for intensive study of *changing* sex roles and helped to dilute the conviction that sex roles are immutable and ordained.

That same year a major report of the American Council on Education

(ACE) was authored by Hottel.[5] The report summarized the status quo of American women in terms of their education and employment and made suggestions for changes. In 1956 an historic study[6] of all women receiving the Ph.D. from Harvard over a fifty-year period showed that these women had not fulfilled the promise of their unusual preparation for professional accomplishment. The study noted that few had achieved leadership positions or produced scholarly research, though some were characterized as devoted and competent teachers, but it did not recognize a lack of societal support and lesser opportunity for achievement as important factors to consider. Indeed, some used the report as further proof of the incapacity of women for contribution to knowledge.

It is therefore remarkable that in 1957 *Womanpower*[7] presented the following suggestions for the integration of women into the labor force: expansion of counseling at every age; increasing educational opportunity and financial support; legislation guaranteeing equal pay; provision of part-time work arrangements; and accelerating research on women. Moreover, in 1958 the National Manpower Council[8] presented a comprehensive and definitive study of work in the lives of married women. Many working women would have been relieved of their burden of guilt by learning that the negative consequences (delinquency, school drop-out, etc.) in the lives of children, often attributed to maternal employment, actually related more to the *quality* of the child's relationship to the mother than to the quantity of direct contact.

In that same year the ACE reported a major conference (held in 1957) on *The Education of Women: Signs for the Future*.[9] The rising interest in the subject of educated women was indicated by the Carnegie Corporation's financial support of the conference. Invitational papers were contributed by leaders in higher education on such topics as motivation of women for higher education; pressures and opportunities facing educated women; current trends and patterns in higher education; and the career development of women.

The Fact-finding Sixties

It is impossible to do justice to the vast outpouring of important contributions regarding women during the sixties. Perhaps carefully selected highlights may convey some feeling for the rising tide of excitement. The 1960s were a decade of fact finding, of documentation of discrimination, of intense concern and of definite legal, political, social, and educational action encompassing women of all classes and races. The late sixties saw establishment of the *right* of women to work; the *legal* abolition of at least certain forms of discrimination; a marked decrease in women's feelings of powerlessness and isolation; a rise in radical protest; and a widening of the proportion of men and women opening their minds to the possibility of mutually designed and shared patterns of home, family, and occupational life.

The need for close attention to the lives of little girls and of adolescents was widely recognized, but, with some exceptions, it seems to have been tangential to the powerful focus of reports and conferences on the needs of adult women. Research studies, to be presented later on as we look at each stage of life, still largely continued to confirm preconceived, traditional ideas about females with little awareness that the growing edge of social change might be gleaned from studying the *unusual* instead of the usual. The discarded findings concerning this minority of subjects would have generated new concepts and reduced the cultural lag between research and the changing world. The fundamental flaws in research on women would not be apparent until the social climate had changed sufficiently to mandate different designs, methods, instruments, approaches, and values. Meanwhile, researchers were lulled by the false security of producing results that confirmed generations of studies showing that women, *in general,* selected a narrow set of occupations and demonstrated lukewarm or nil career commitment. While the small proportion of women demonstrating career commitment were previously written off as "unusual" or more likely aberrant, the late 1960s began to show that such patterns were probably normal choices deserving support and acceptance. As each life-stage is inspected, detailed studies will be reported to reinforce the concepts presented thus far.

The decade opened with the conference commemorating the fortieth anniversary of the Women's Bureau, resulting in a publication on *Today's Woman in Tomorrow's World.*[10] Conference participants heard reports on the work of the United Nations Commission on Women that had been established in 1946 by the Human Rights Commission of the United Nations. Since our emphasis is on vocational guidance in the United States, we will not detail the international reports here, but it is important for counselors to realize that such a commission had been in existence for this length of time and that women the world over were stirring toward new awareness of themselves as human beings.

When the history of women during this decade is recorded, the report of President Kennedy's Commission on the Status of Women[11] may be deemed the most influential event. That report elevated to national consciousness the condition of American women as persons, parents, and workers. One major emphasis of the report was the need for more creative and innovative educational and vocational counseling for girls and women at every stage of life. The ongoing task of the Kennedy Commission was assigned in the Johnson Administration to the United States Interdepartmental Committee on the Status of Women. In 1968 this group produced a progress report titled *American Women 1963–1968.*[12] Again the urgent need for expert counseling was stressed. The ratio of full-time public secondary counselors had improved somewhat (one for every 450 high school students); elementary schools were only beginning to hire counselors (one for every 7,000 elementary students); and the junior or community colleges were also beginning to hire counselors (one for about every 500 students in public junior colleges). This report also summarized federal government programs designed to help disadvantaged groups—including women—move toward educational and vocational equality (Job Corps, Neighborhood Youth Corps, etc.). Yet the conclusion was that the needs of the disadvantaged remained a major challenge and continued to be inadequately met.

Continued education programs for adult women were one of the definitive signs of the decade. The small numbers of women seeking a return to educational institutions in the early 1960s swelled into the thousands by the time the decade ended. This quiet revolution in life pattern may be the foundation of the inevitable change in the position of women within the society. At first the women returning for further education seemed to be members of the economically and educationally favored groups, but by the time the revised edition of a national directory of *Continuing Education Programs and Services for Women*[13] was published by the Department of Labor in 1971, women in every segment of the society were involved.

A few notable events in women's continuing education will exemplify the evolution of this phase of history. In 1960 the Radcliffe Institute was established by Dr. Mary I. Bunting, the President of Radcliffe College. According to Smith's[14] historical account, the purpose of the Institute was to enable educated women to continue their intellectual, professional, and creative development on a part-time basis; to establish seminars; and to provide counseling for women wishing to return to careers or to plan educational and occupational changes in their lives. Senders' 1961[15] landmark report on the Minnesota Plan for Women's Continuing Education stimulated the interest and concern of a number of other institutions. Only a year later, at the American Council on Education's Itasca Conference, pilot programs at Rutgers and Sarah Lawrence were described by Dennis.[16]

The transition toward widespread interest in the reality of women's position in the society is also reflected in the themes of change, choice, and challenge that characterized conferences, books, and journals of the era. A few examples will illustrate the chronological development of consciousness into the seventies, when it became clear that the challenges are for both men and women and that talk without action is fruitless.

Examples of emphasis on change included Cassara's[17] *American Women: The Changing Image* and special issues of journals by groups such as AAUW[18] and NAWDC.[19] The American Academy of Arts and Sciences devoted one issue of their journal *Daedalus*[20] to "The Woman In America." Lifton's[21] book version of that issue served a wider public. Focus upon both change and choice were exemplified by the important collections edited by Farber and Wilson,[22, 23] and Harbeson[24] epitomized the emerging shift in the social climate from powerlessness to responsibility. Sounding the challenge for national debate, Friedan's *Feminine Mystique*[25] became a controversial bestseller, obviously touching some readiness for change within many women. As the general public began to hear more about women, some counselors began to express a need for more help in understanding how to counsel them. The Women's Bureau responded to that need by organizing regional workshops,[26] and the AAUW sponsored an intensive summer-long workshop on "Counseling Mature Women."[27]

The Action-packed Early Seventies

Although we are only in the early years of this decade, many significant events have already happened in this period of widespread affirmative action. The decade opened with the 1970 Report of the President's Task Force on Women's Rights and Responsibilities.[28] The report, entitled "A Matter of Simple Justice," contained five major recommendations to the President: 1) establishment of an office of Women's Rights and Responsibilities; 2) a White House Conference on that topic; 3) a message to Congress citing the widespread discrimination against women, proposing legislation to remedy the inequity, and recommending corollary action in the states and by the private sector; 4) taking Cabinet level action to implement policy regarding sex, race, and poverty discrimination; 5) appointing more women to top-level executive positions in all branches of the federal government.

In 1970 the Citizen's Advisory Council on the Status of Women[29] reported to the President actions and recommendations regarding American women that were similar to those of past commissions and task forces: the passage of an Equal Rights Amendment; provision for maternity leaves; improved retirement and pension plans; more child care centers (now called child development centers); occupational counseling of women at every stage of life; and increased opportunities for continuing education. Additionally, the report of the subcommittee on counseling and continuing education maintained that much of the vocational counseling which girls and women receive is inadequate and obsolete, and it presented specific recommendations aimed at updating, expanding, and strengthening the counseling of females.

The fiftieth anniversary (1970) of the Women's Bureau was commemorated by a conference on "American Women at the Crossroads: Directions for the Future."[30] Representatives from over 300 agencies, institutions, and organizations met to work, to study, and to strongly suggest changes and actions. The recommendations of the final session covered a wide range of areas including legislation, employment, and education. Counselors were encouraged to plan comprehensive, multilingual, life-span counseling.

Scholarly journals continued to produce valuable special to women issues,[31] and popular magazines also reflected the controversy. *Life*[32] emphasized woman as timeless sex object, historical militant feminist, and uneasy liberationist, while one business magazine[33] seemed to capture the deeper essence of social change in a special issue on "Revolution II: Thinking Female." The early 1970s also saw a proliferation of newsletters on women's concerns, representing every type of group from the most conservative to the most radical. *Women Today,*[34] summarizing progress and action in all areas—political, economic, legal, educational and occupational, soon established its usefulness. Finally, of course, is the vast literature[35] of the Women's Liberation Movement, a major historical phenomenon of the late sixties and early seventies.

Since females of every age have been influenced by this vigorous movement, every counselor has an obligation to study and understand the history, evolution, and goals. Many counselors were heavily influenced by the attitude of the press and television during the early 1970s when many newscasters tended to sensationalize the movement and to convey ridicule, disgust, and rejection. For a time this highly negative treatment spilled over into all aspects of the struggle for human rights, but that phase is already passing at this point.

One aspect of the women's movement was the appearance of women's studies courses in colleges and universities.[36] By 1972 courses and scholarly work had proliferated to the extent that a *Women Studies Abstract*[37] became available. The history, sociology, and psychology of women moved into university studies throughout the world, as attested to by the foundation of the *Journal of the International Institute of Women's Studies.*[38] Colleges and universities also were forced to look at the employment, promotion, and financial situation of women. The AAUW exemplified the action trend by producing a practical guide[39] for assisting academia in achieving sexual equality.

Our brief review of some of the highlights of the 1950s, 1960s, and the first two years of the 1970s should provide a base of knowledge for our study of girls and women during their life stages.

THE EARLY YEARS OF LIFE

Infancy and Early Childhood

It may seem strange to even think of vocational guidance in the early years of life. Yet we know that fundamental developments in the formation of identity occur at that time. It is far too late to begin attending to vocational development in early adolescence. Vocational guidance, in some form and to some degree, is a necessary component of life from beginning to end. In its broadest sense, it is an effort to assist each person to evolve a self-selected life-style which, at every stage of life, incorporates values and capacities in some visible form of energy utilization.

What are little girls like? How do their values, beliefs, abilities, and role perceptions develop and how do all of these complex aspects of their early days affect their life-long vocational development? Is it conceivable that we can identify aspects of infancy and early childhood relevant to vocational guidance? It is certain that many people would reject such an idea, partly because this period of life has had but slight attention from vocational psychology and partly because the term vocational guidance has been narrowly construed to mean direction into a job choice. In any case, we can discern important roots of later vocational behavior beginning to be shaped even in infancy through the attitudes and beliefs of parents and families. The perception of what a girl *should* be like has an effect upon every aspect of her early conditioning.

For most girl infants, as for boys, persistent sex-role training is very likely, except in the most unusual of families, to supersede highly individualistic upbringing. Strong sex-role training is based partly upon the need of generations of families to protect their children through insuring their "adjustment" to the world. Consequently, little girls may learn that passivity, docility, and low levels of curiosity and activity are more rewarded than their opposites. Such concepts of behavior extend unknowingly to restricted or channelized cognitive development and to proneness to over-reactivity and sensitivity to social adaptability. The learned behaviors engraved upon the mind, character, and personality have direct significance for later vocational foreclosure. Much research is based upon the belief that what we can easily observe, test, and repeat must be innate rather than basically acquired. Another most unfortunate trend in research—one that will appear frequently as we study vocational development in later periods of life—is the tendency to discount, to label as abnormal, or to derogate as masculine, the behavior, personality, and learning styles of girls reared in an individualistic manner as persons in their own right. Interviewers and testers almost invariably characterize them as bold, aggressive, and unfeminine. Even before entry into kindergarten girls learn that they are less free to roam the neighborhood and to seek out experiences away from adults. That kind of adventuring is for boys or for tomboys. Yet in the past a few girls among thousands did manage to develop and sustain strong vocational choices.

Even in the first stages of life it is possible to suggest ways of building toward a society of open, natural choice that captures the varied potentiality of each new human being. The "vocational" guidance of early life consists of careful fostering of any direction in play or personality that a young child may show. This, in turn, necessitates early exposure to varied choice in toys and activities and long, patient, loving observation of trends, dispositions, and tendencies. It involves a sensitive awareness of the need for encouragement, reinforcement, support, and approval for tentative exploratory overtures into the world of thought and action. It is *listening* and *hearing*.

Early School Years

When the little girl enters school she has already become predisposed to involve herself in some activities and to exclude others—to seek approval for certain kinds of behavior and learning and to avoid disapproval or even punishment for other kinds. She may have learned that she is "supposed" to be better in reading than in numbers, afraid of bugs and animals, and timid about risktaking.

Occupational preferences of the adult years will be markedly affected by the kinds of personal skills and vocational attitudes built in the early school years. Clark[40] found that both black and white children in grades three through six expressed definite vocational preferences. His study adds the dimensions of race and socioeconomic class to the complex influences upon early vocational preferences. While all girls selected female stereotyped occupations, those in the lower economic class showed greater interest in occupations than did middle class girls. The presence of marked occupational interest in lower class girls is an important clue for elementary school counselors. Since the base of class mobility is still heavily related to the level of educational and occupational status attained, support and encouragement of these early interests can make a great difference in the lives of all children.

Our understanding of the vocational development of girls depends heavily upon the work of Tyler,[41] whose studies have contributed vital knowledge. So far, however, her work does not seem to be utilized by counselors, partly because there are so few in the elementary school and partly because, until recently, vocational counseling or prevocational counseling was either unheard of or actually rejected as premature, inappropriate, or damaging. Yet Tyler's work demonstrated that much had already occurred in the lives of little girls. For example, interests and abilities did not correlate in first-grade girls as they did in boys of that age, and by the age of ten all the children manifested sexually differentiated patterns of career interests. Thus, Tyler's work certainly confirms the futility of waiting until junior or senior high school to begin prevocational counseling.

Vocational Guidance and the Elementary School

Occupations have long been used as focal points of interest in the elementary school curriculum. Children read about jobs in their textbooks, and they go on trips to occupational settings. Yet why have former approaches had dismal results in arousing and maintaining strong vocational interests in young girls? The fact is that, since occupational life has been segmented into role stereotypes, until recently an elementary school girl rarely heard about *women* occupying any roles except homemaker, nurse, teacher, or secretary. Another important problem has been the fact that job visitations were merely school exercises. Adults selected the jobs and settings, managed the trips, suggested the points for observation and reviewed the "lesson" back in the classroom. Under such conditions the strong relationship between occupation and identity formation did not become explicit, at any level of awareness, in children's minds. Girls gave especially polite and uninvolved attention to any occupation that was "masculine."

There is a marked increase in vocational guidance in the elementary school. Textbooks are changing, open classrooms are encouraging boys and girls to think broadly about their lives and responsibilities, and children are being encouraged to react spontaneously to what *they* see, how *they* feel, and what is important *to them*. One current trend emphasizes "career awareness." When this concept is strongly linked with personal awareness and the growth and development of identity, children will have a strong base for later vocational choices. The personal integration of self and experience challenges all of the skills of every elementary teacher and counselor. Teachers alone cannot be responsible for the kind of total vocational guidance program needed in the elementary school. Developmental counselors working with all children are also necessary.

Sylwester and Matthews[42] suggested a broad, flexible framework for vocational guidance in the elementary school based upon four basic questions: 1) What am I like? 2) How am I changing? 3) What will I be like? 4) How will I affect others, and how will they affect me? This kind of a framework can serve the children and the staff as a kind of rough, but personally meaningful, filtering device for sifting through the rich, multiple experiences of daily life.

SECONDARY SCHOOL YEARS

Girls in Junior and Senior High

There has been little more attention to the vocational development of girls during the junior high school years than during the prior life stages. Some of the studies to be reported here overlap the junior and senior high school period. Life during junior high school is an important and often overlooked time in the lives of girls. For many the early interests and enthusiasms of preadolescence are submerged by the pressures of peer conformity and by interest, curiosity, and anxiety about sex role expectations. For some girls this stage of life means an almost complete lack of thoughtful attention to any vocational aspects of education that are not concerned with homemaking or "feminine" occupations. To think otherwise may actually induce guilt and shame in girls who see themselves defying the role society has decreed for them.

Junior high schools have elaborate prevocational education programs, but they are still strongly sex-typed. Few girls dare to risk the social exclusion by peers and the veiled or open disapproval of adults that could result from taking a course in mechanics or woodworking. Girls also sense subtle pressure to achieve high grades but, at the same time, to inhibit curiosity, avoid contradiction, and limit individualized learning. In this way the development of career commitment may be deflected or extinguished, though it should be clear that a minority of girls have maintained both personal and occupational goals even in the face of opposition.

Parents, teachers, and counselors of junior high students need to continue to support and affirm diversity of interests while they meet the urgent needs of this age group for understanding of personal, social, and sexual development. In fact, involvement in a personally meaningful spectrum of interests and activities might relieve a great deal of the tension of life at this age. The sincere recognition of skills, talents, abilities, and characteristics in classes and in small life-development groups would bring a sense of security and competence to boys and girls. Girls urgently need to meet with their counselor in small groups as well as to participate in mixed-sex groups. The fact that boys and girls mature at different rates means that individuals of different ages may interact more effectively. Counselors should depend heavily upon the wisdom of students to form compatible groups.

A rare example of the use of vocational counseling with young girls is found in an experiment by Anderson and Heiman.[43] Thirty junior high girls met with a counselor once a week for six weeks to examine needs and feelings, acquire occupational information, and understand cultural stereotypes. Even in that brief time girls in the experimental group showed significant positive change in vocational maturity.

As the girl moves into senior high school all of the trends previously noted are accentuated. In the lives of many girls the emphasis on sex role as the predominant expression of identity assumes clear and stylized behavior that meets with strong peer approval by both sexes. This point will be strikingly demonstrated in some of the research to be reported, but it is important to caution the reader that we do not know what comparable studies of high school girls in the seventies will illustrate. There is some foreshadowing that societal changes toward women will affect role concepts and vocational values at large. At this time, however, societal changes seem to be reflected most powerfully in the attitudes, beliefs, and behaviors of mature women returning to work or to occupational preparation.

Predominant Themes

Some of the identifiable themes in the research on high school girls include: job values and desires; sex-role concept; attitudes regarding marriage and career; career development; and the special situation of the creative and gifted girl.

The famous study of sex differences and job values by Singer and Stefflre[44] has been used to support the lack of interest in counseling girls vocationally. The findings themselves probably reflected the societal values and child-rearing practices of the era. Therefore, the authors found male high school seniors desiring jobs that offered power, profit, and independence, while the senior girls were drawn toward jobs characterized by interesting experiences and social service. In 1964, a decade later, Turner[45] showed the price of unitary career interest in terms of peer acceptance. Of 1,441 high school senior girls studied, the most popular planned to combine homemaking and a career; those next in popularity planned on being housewives only; and the least popular contemplated careers only.

An interesting cross-cultural study by Tyler and Sundberg[46] compared fourteen-year-old Dutch and American adolescents and found that American girls were more similar to one another and more different from boys than the Dutch subjects. The authors felt that American girls had a restricted concept of femininity that resulted in inadequate life planning. With their cross-cultural perspective, they suggest that social norms rather than something inherent in human nature may be involved. We are reminded of Tyler's earlier work findings that attitudes toward many occupations are formed at an early stage of development and may persist in an immature form unless a person repeatedly rethinks them. Tyler and Sundberg remind us that "a girl who at the age of ten has ruled out almost all occupations because she considers them unsuitable for girls . . . . may never really think about any of them again, and thus she never applies to them the conceptualization processes she develops as she matures."

A major national study by Douvan and Adelson in 1966[47] confirmed the stereotype of the adolescent girl held by a majority of the society. Patterns of female identity were described along an apparent value continuum: unambivalent feminine, ambivalent or omnipotent feminine, neutral, boyish, achievement oriented, and unfeminine. The findings indicated that feminine girls were generally described in the most positive terms.

Marriage-career Attitudes. In 1964 Matthews and Tiedeman[48] reported a study of attitudes toward marriage, career, and life-style among 1,237 young women ranging in age from eleven through twenty-six. The major attitudinal theme affecting the life planning of every age group centered around their expectation of negative male reaction to the use of female intelligence.

In 1969 Kuvlesky et al.[49] studied racial differences in orientation toward marriage among black and white girls living in east Texas. Although a large majority of both groups expected to work after marriage, both black and white girls desired and expected to marry and have children, and black girls wished to marry significantly later.

The predominance of marriage over career is, of course, intimately related to strong and exclusive sex-role training. Moreover, many girls expressing career interest seem to really mean job employment. Career and job really are not separated in their minds, although there may be some vague sense of difference in the terms. A job may be seen as a way to earn money, perhaps only from time to time, with minimum involvement and often little training; while a career involves long-term training, serious commitment, and permanent employment. Girls need to think about these differences.

Maladjustment Hypothesis.   Another theme reflected in the research literature could be characterized as the "maladjustment hypothesis" of career
interest in high school girls. When we study college girls this theme will
appear again labeled as a "deviance" hypothesis.

Although Lewis[50] feels that counselors should help girls make occupational
decisions, he also observes that career-oriented girls are atypical, perhaps
maladjusted, and likely to be frustrated and dissatisfied with themselves. He
feels that the girl who wants to avoid the typical role must overcome many
cultural roadblocks, and this may take its toll in her personal adjustment. It
is hard to imagine a counselor who begins with reservations such as this not
conveying, at least subtly, the gloom of atypicality, maladjustment, and
frustration when confronted with a career-oriented high school girl.

Career Development During High School.   There has been some serious
study of girls' career development during the high school years, and, in part,
it seems to parallel the research that explains career-saliency as an
"enrichment" phenomenon during college. The Project Talent data bank has
been a major source for this type of research. For example, Astin[51] studied
the career development of high school girls in order to identify the characteristics of ninth-grade girls that would predict their twelfth-grade vocational
choices. Expressed and measured interests at the earlier age were the *only*
important predictors of senior plans. Counselors need to know that girls
who recalled having "job" counseling or "college" counseling planned
accordingly. Girls in large high schools were more likely to aspire to careers.
It is a sobering thought that *ninth*-grade counseling and high school size can
so affect a person's life.

Kuvlesky and Lever[52] studied the occupational goals and expectations
of rural and urban Negro girls. Both groups had similar occupational goals,
but both expected to be deflected from their goals by the society. These
girls did not want to become housewives or unskilled workers, and they were
urgently in need of practical, informed, and supportive vocational guidance.
A high school counselor might initially concentrate effort on understanding
and helping these career-oriented girls, described by Rezler[53] as "pioneers."
These girls did not seek traditional vocations but preferred to explore complex male-dominated occupations. They are still in particular need of the
counselor's support in order to resist cultural standards and handle uncertainties over the consequences of their decisions.

Pioneer girls and gifted, creative girls share much in common. Drews[54]
has encouraged counselors to see their role as helping these young girls to
actualize their potentiality. She feels that gifted girls are more highly
"growth-motivated" than average girls but that their development is stifled
by social sanctions. Torrance[55] provided counselors with insights about the
special needs of gifted girls. Their intellectual and personal independence
may be interpreted by the counselor as indifference to the need for a counseling relationship, but he feels that these girls need a refuge and a sponsor
to help them cope with life.

The work of Anastasi and Schaefer[56] typifies the "enrichment" hypothesis.
In a large sample of high school girls those identified as creative and

academically superior recalled strong, supportive early life experiences of approval from their well-educated parents. Similarly, in his study of 100,000 National Merit Scholarship students Wertz[57] found that 50 percent more boys than girls attended college, but that very able girls in all social classes and girls with highly educated fathers were as likely to attend college as boys. Another important factor is shown in a recent study by Entwisle and Greenberger,[58] which indicated the strong peer pressure that boys may exert on the attitudes of girls. In seven Baltimore schools ninth graders of varied economic and racial groups expressed strong opinions on women working: girls said "yes" and boys said "no." Early childhood experiences are therefore crucial in providing a base of personal power and competence sufficient to withstand the peer pressures of adolescence toward conformity and sex-role stereotyping.

Vocational Guidance for High School Girls

The intent, substance, and direction of vocational guidance in high school must derive directly from the tangible world of the high school student's experience. Vocational guidance cannot be segmented out from life in general. How, then, does one begin to assure at least the opportunity for personal vocational exploration and experimentation?

Perhaps the beginning is to select counselors who have a high probability of being able to interact successfully with high school students. In a major study of the impact of guidance services in Minnesota, Tamminen and Miller[59] found that the *one* guidance input that had an effect upon hoped for guidance outcomes was the personality of the counselor as seen by the students and others. The effective counselor was perceived as being warm, accepting, open and having interest in and respect for others.

How would a counselor like this begin to help students untangle the complex threads of their experience in some way that could help them to make sequential decisions about their lives? The model proposed here is the small developmental group led at first by the counselor but eventually by students themselves. A definitive philosophy of group process is fundamental to understanding how such groups can form the strong base for the whole life development process at any particular stage.

The major philosophical tenet involves a shift in the mind of the counselor from *doing for*—helping, teaching, providing the structured input for the group—to the very different stance of *receiving*, as an important member of the group, the enormous variety of living, everyday experiences that the students are trying to sort out and manage. The group gradually moves toward understanding more about how individuals learn to pick out themes, threads, values and hopes. They begin to see how, out of the confused and confusing bombardment of experiential stimuli a human being can learn to plan for the nearby and long-range future. Attention to the translation of values, attitudes, interests and goals into some variety of vocational planning is a natural result of this style of developmental group process. The process cannot be rushed by adult-dominated, rational planning and structure. As one high school girl expressed it, "You really have to know something about who you are before you can plan your future."

The small group serves as a living filter for experience. It serves as a haven, a stabilizer, and as a source of strength and courage. In the initial stages the natural development of the group is toward the establishment of trust and the improvement of communication. As the early anxiety subsides group members begin to share everyday life experiences. Gradually there is a natural movement toward trying to understand and frame tentative answers on a more complex level to the very questions raised by Sylwester and Matthews[60] with young children—What am I like? How am I changing? What will I be like? How will I affect others and how will they affect me?

This stage of group development is reached earlier each succeeding year in high school. For example, one counselor found girls thinking and planning over the summer what they wanted to do in *their* group in the fall. All of the usual explorations, interviews, visits, trips eventually occur but what a difference in involvement and impact! The search for vocational knowledge and experience is pursued with relentless energy because it represents a natural outgrowth of strong small-group interest and support. Parts of life fall into some kind of understandable pattern. Areas of study are selected more from a base of personal knowledge. Activities are recognized as related to needs and interests. Part-time and summer jobs confirm or negate vocational directions. High school classes and labs, both general and vocationally specific, are recognized as giving valuable information about each person. Vocational films, books, and tapes are put to enthusiastic use.

The use of small, exploratory, developmental groups in vocational guidance in high school requires time, energy, patience, and caring. The outcomes are sometimes astonishing and usually highly positive. Students generally express increased confidence in their capacity to understand others, to cope with the unexpected events of life and to make more personally meaningful decisions.

THE COLLEGE YEARS

A Perspective on Research

Research on young women between the ages of eighteen and twenty-two is almost exclusively limited to the college-based group. There is a pressing need for careful research on young women who work and/or who are home-based. A triadic research emphasis (work, home, college) would bring us nearer to understanding this large age group. There is a vast amount of research on college women. Until fairly recently it was heavily directed toward proving that the majority of women do *not* have serious career commitment. As we look at the trends and findings about college women we will study such themes as: the homemaking-career dichotomy, research on man's "ideal" woman, the career development of college women, gifted and creative college women, and role innovations among women who have recently graduated college. We will conclude our study of this period of life with suggestions for vocational counseling of college women.

For decades studies have been reiterating the personality differences between homemaking-oriented and career-oriented women. Although the studies appear to be objective, the instruments used and the interpretations of the results do not seem objective. As in the studies of high school girls, career orientation is often given a negative connotation or actually equated with maladjustment, or even neurosis. Assessment is often made through time-honored tests that favor the majority of respondents and assign minority respondents to negative categories. What is "true" of the majority seems to be interpreted as the standard of normality. This phenomenon is not limited to our topic of discussion but is common throughout psychology. The era of the seventies will probably see great changes in test construction to accommodate more varied models of societally acceptable life-styles and behaviors.

In the meantime, the entire research literature on masculinity-femininity must be reevaluated in terms of current attitudes, knowledge, and beliefs. Much of the literature was based upon frequency of sex-appropriate traits or behaviors. Thus, women infrequently demonstrating feminine interests, behavior, or personality traits were labelled masculine with a subtle or even overt negative implication. The massive evidence built upon this shaky theoretical foundation helped to lock women into narrow occupational channels and into restrictive personality patterns. Of course, after many years research of this type reached into child-rearing practices and became a part of accepted folklore even for professional counselors, psychologists, and psychiatrists. The attitudes of teachers, college and graduate school admissions boards, professors and employers were shaped in the direction of rejecting the plausibility, suitability, or even normality of career commitment in women. Research designs based upon a marriage-or-career dichotomy helped to perpetuate the myth, even in the face of growing evidence to the contrary. The stereotypes of man-aggressive-career and woman-passive-home were repeatedly confirmed through research approaches that narrowly and virtually exclusively sought such evidence.

A few selected studies will exemplify the situation. Even as late as 1968 Rand[61] thoroughly investigated the hypothesis that career-oriented women are more masculine than homemaking-oriented women. She found evidence to support her hypothesis and concluded that the existence and validity of the masculine-feminine dichotomy between the groups was valid. She does suggest a semantic search for a more objective term, because of the negative connotation of the term masculine. In the same year Gysbers and Johnson[62] found career-oriented women to be more intellectual and enterprising and homemaking women to be more social and conventional.

Role Expectations

College mores of the sixties certainly perpetuated the conviction of an either/or world for most women. Their lives were molded by the role expectations they had been trained in since birth. The vast majority planned on marriage and perhaps a few years of work prior to the arrival of children. It is clear that for most "work" did not involve commitment to a career, for, in general, these women expected to direct their energies toward commitment to marriage and family. The personal needs for individualized achievement that would probably emerge in the third and fourth decades of their lives remained either unacknowledged, unimagined, or unacceptable.

Freedman[63] studied role expectancy of women in elite eastern colleges. During their four years of college they showed little interest in even discussing woman's role. They evidenced little dedication to careers and yet expressed the conviction that they could combine marriage and a career without difficulty. They may, of course, have interpreted employment as career, particularly in view of their expressed inclination to be subordinate to their husbands and to avoid competition with men.

In the same decade Hewer and Neubeck[64] found freshmen at a large midwestern university accepting the traditional nurturant role of women and the belief that the men should support the family economically. This study exemplifies how certain patterns of life move toward becoming beliefs. When this happens a whole set of behaviors related to investment in perpetuation, assumption of finality, and inability or unwillingness to reexamine beliefs becomes apparent. Beliefs come to be looked at as true and immutable— beyond reassessment. A reinforcement cycle between cultural beliefs, attitudes, practices, and research helps to support this self-perpetuating situation, as we will see when we look at the research on man's "ideal" woman.

A major contributor to the research on man's "ideal" woman, Steinmann[65] found that mothers and daughters were inhibited in the pursuit of work interests because they were convinced that men prefer women who are traditional homemakers. Women were sensing male ambivalence, expressed as intellectual approval but emotional rejection of women working. A decade later, in 1970, Steinmann[66] found women were still guided by the image of homemaker as ideal woman. However, Steinmann and Fox[67] found that black college women felt that men wanted women to be *both* family-oriented and self-actualizing, while white college women in that study still felt that man's ideal woman was family-oriented. It is encouraging that men of both races shared the perceptions of black women.

Career Development During College

The career development of women, at least in the recent past, has been overshadowed by female role considerations. Comparing homemaking-oriented and career-oriented college women, Cook[68] found that the former were likely to be married, majoring in liberal arts, influenced by men in decision making, high in need for security and less committed to working. Career-oriented women were mostly single, less conforming in religious beliefs, more committed to using their ability and high in independence and confidence.

Harmon[69] found that college women had expressed more varied and sophisticated occupational preferences in preadolescence. By the time they reached college their choices were mostly in typical feminine fields, and they seemed to avoid occupations requiring talent and extended training. In another study Harmon[70] noted that women who persisted in careers and those who did not often stated similar plans at the time of college entrance. The difference in outcome caused her to consider career development as motivational not circumstantial. She felt that motivation to actually pursue a career occurred after college entrance. Another explanation might be that many girls feel obligated to state a career plan regardless of their intent. It seems likely that career commitment is a generalized value embedded into some lives in childhood.

The work of Almquist and Angrist[71] supports this contention. Career-salient women were likely to have had working mothers, a variety of work experience prior to college, and strong occupational role models. These women were strongly influenced by college professors and selected careers dominated by men. Again it seems that positive early childhood experience must enable these women to accept and utilize the stimulus of complex role models.

Almquist and Angrist have made a significant contribution of knowledge in proposing an "enrichment" hypothesis to counteract the "deviance" explanation of career development in women, which linked disruptive family experience and low dating frequency to career interest in girls. These authors have helped to untangle the old controversy about the presumed arbitrary relationship between career commitment and masculinity. Almquist and Angrist studied over one hundred college women for four years and found that women planning careers in male-dominated fields did not differ from women selecting traditional feminine careers in terms of dating, level of participation in activities, and relationships to parents. These women apparently sought to enrich their lives through complex development— personally as women and occupationally as competent workers.

A study by Wilson[72] recorded the strong expectation of marriage and career in black college women. A persistent trend through all research is their hope for significant career involvement. In Wilson's study of eastern college women black women planned academic and professional careers to a greater extent than their white classmates.

Although we have some fragmentary research on career development of college women, it is impossible to state with any confidence that we have any substantial theory to help us out. The few attempts in the literature cannot yet qualify as theories. Research of the past twenty years has, amazingly enough, concentrated on why women, in general, do *not* evolve careers. The careers of successful women have been largely ignored as a source for generating theory.

Creative, Gifted College Women

For some reason it has been considered most acceptable to study the development of creative, gifted college women. However, these studies, like those of ordinary college girls, also seem to be based more upon interest in personality development than in studying career development.

Faunce,[73] for example, studied the relationship between personality characteristics, vocational interests, and college persistence among academically gifted women. Her results showed that nongraduates had less insight into their own personality structure, greater difficulty in interpersonal relationships, more problems with impulse control, and greater inner tensions, while graduates were more insightful, conventional, temperate, modest, and self-confident, had better ego strength and psychological integration, and were relatively free from inner tension. The SVIB-W scores of graduates seemed to reflect feminine career interests, and the scores of nongraduates indicated mostly business occupations.

Apparently, academically gifted women have not been inclined to or encouraged to seek varied vocational outlets for their abilities. The problem of limited or absent career motivation in bright women has been clarified by the work of Horner,[74] who observed sex difference between university students participating in interpersonal competitive situations. Even the *anticipation* of success by a female in competition with a male produced fear and anxieties concerning loss of femininity and self-esteem. In this way achievement is inhibited and occupational commitment is diluted.

Helson[75] has also made a significant contribution to our understanding of creative women. She followed two groups of Mills College graduates —the "creatives" and the "controls"—at two-year and five-year intervals. Creative women resembled creative men in personality, and in childhood they had higher levels of aspiration than the "controls." The impact of society upon some creative women was indicated by the fact that four-fifths of the creative women (in contrast to one-third of the control group) expressed feelings of emptiness, desolation, and aloneness. Preoccupation with thoughts of death and suicide were common in the creative group. Helson will continue to study these women over their life-span, but at this point we can only regret the past devaluation of such a precious talent resource and hope that these women will find a place for themselves as society changes.

Studies of college women in the seventies are likely to reveal more varied patterns of life planning. As subgroups become larger more women may develop the courage to create flexible, compatible individualized life plans. In a random sample of college women Tangri[76] found three approximately equal groups—the "role innovators," the "traditionalists," and the "in-betweens." The study confirmed others reported herein. Role innovators were likely to have had working mothers as role models, and they had high aspirations and both romantic and nonromantic friendships with men. Traditionalists planned to enter predominantly female occupations and tended to project achievement values upon present or future husbands.

Counseling College Women

College counselors have found women of this age reluctant to enter into sustained vocational development counseling. The minority of women who decided to pursue advanced training for a profession felt no need for rethinking their career plans in relationship to their total life-style, while the large number of women who planned on a temporary job before marriage avoided vocational counseling because they had no intention of reevaluating their powerful desire to establish their identity as married women.

But, when reached, both of these groups of women could have profited from expert vocational counseling as a part of total life planning. Counselors must therefore move out from the medical and psychological service units into the dormitories and student unions. Counseling is still too often linked with illness, confusion, and deviancy. A life planning center in a student union could develop, under student direction, services sought and used by students. Consultants from the university and the community could supply needed services. The power, energy, and organizational ability of college students could be set in service to the felt needs of that population. In the process it would become clear that there are many options to consider, and the creating of an individualized life-style would involve conscious decision making rather than drifting into chance situations.

Vocational counseling is in need of far greater emphasis. How can a person select a likely career to suit her interests, temperament, and life-style if she has never even heard of the new career options, or in fact of many of the old careers? College counseling presents a great challenge to all counselors: to work *with* young adults while they think, plan, work, experience, travel, and create their individual life-styles. They are not interested in being told by experts what they should do with their lives. They want and need interactors, strong model adults of purpose, involvement, and courage.

POST-COLLEGE YEARS

Follow-up and Longitudinal Studies

There have been some informative follow-up studies of college graduates and a few longitudinal studies, a one-time check on college graduates being a follow-up study and long-term, repeated studies being longitudinal. The work to be scanned has been aimed at understanding such factors as achievement motivation, educational levels attained over time, and work patterns.

Two studies of achievement motivation in women resulted in different conclusions. Studying of the achievement motive in Radcliffe alumnae in 1966, Baruch[77] found a dramatic decrease in the achievement motive in women five to ten years out of college and a return to regnancy of this motive after fifteen or more years out of college. It would seem likely that women merely shift the focus of their achievement drive to their husbands and families in the period following college and pick up their own personal goals in a later life-stage.

In a study that contrasts with Baruch's, Eyde[78] studied work motivation in women five and ten years after graduation from Jackson College of Tufts University and found that work values remained fairly stable for her subjects. Similarly, Harmon[79] did a follow-up on 98 women from the University of Minnesota classes of 1933 through 1936 twenty-five years later. Women were classified according to the amount of time they had worked in the intervening years. Those who worked consistently or who didn't work at all scored no differently on work patterns on the Strong. Thus, the validity of the SVIB-W remained neither proven nor disproven.

Harmon's study reminds the counselor that results on an interest test and actual entry into an occupation are two different matters. Vocational counseling needs to promote the synthesis within a person's life-style of career expectancy and career commitment. That is why vocational counseling alone is inadequate to meet people's needs. Ideally, vocational counseling should be set within the framework of the individual's personality traits, character structure, and philosophical value system.

In 1966 the Women's Bureau[80] reported the results of a seven-year follow-up of a representative sample of the college graduating class of 1957 (5,846 surveyed as a representative sample of the 88,000 graduating in 1957). The results indicated that 51 percent were working; that the average had worked 5.5 years out of that 7 years; that most wanted to continue their education for career purposes or for personal development; that about one-half had taken one university course; that 15 percent had earned a master's degree and 1 percent, the doctorate. Women involved in graduate study reported encountering difficulties regarding age requirements, financial aid restrictions, and limited course offerings. The majority of the women were or had been married and over one-half had children under eighteen. Four-fifths of them had jobs they wanted, and the majority of women with children under six were not working. More than one-half reported that their husbands favored their working, but a screening of these results would probably show differences between job holders and career committed women: while there is much less resistance by men to women holding a job and bringing home money, there is considerable resistance to deep involvement and concern with work brought into the home at night.

Nationwide data on the educational and occupational development of college graduates over a ten-year period (1959–1969) was reported by Sharp[81] in 1970. One interesting finding was that more women than men terminate their education with the bachelor's degree and take graduate courses for academic and intellectual reasons rather than for job advancement. The majority of women with master's degrees earned them in education, Sharp found, and only in the field of education are women fully satisfied with their status and opportunities for advancement. Three years after college 75 percent of both men and women are employed, but the figure for women drops to 56 percent after five years. This report urges colleges and universities to develop more innovative programs for meeting the needs of women.

In 1962 the Women's Bureau[82] reported on 580 alumnae from the class of 1945. These women aspired to develop means other than marriage and child-rearing "to assert their individuality, attain personal recognition, and serve society." They expressed strong interest in future employment, though at that time only one-half were employed. Eighty-three percent of the group had married and 90 percent had children.

The results of follow-up studies need to be placed in life-stage perspective. As we amass much more longitudinal information we may be able to draw out commonalities and differences in the development of women. We will be more aware of what forces women see shaping their lives, how they cope with these forces, and what skills and decision-making powers they develop. In short, we will be able to build a more comprehensive psychology of adulthood.

Watley[83] assessed the career progress of a large sample of National Merit Scholars (1,014 males and 368 females) seven to eight years after they had entered college. The findings are not attributable to unequal ability or to differential achievement during high school but, rather, to family background and personality characteristics. The results regarding female scholars are of interest for our purposes: the bachelor's degree was not obtained by 7 percent of the capable women (6 percent of the men); the bachelor's degree was obtained but no further study completed by 25 percent of the women (13 percent of the men); and so few women received the doctorate that those figures were lumped with the master's degree, the combined percent for women being 68 (72 percent of the men scholars completed the master's degree, and 10 percent had already achieved the doctorate). At the time of this follow-up most of the women were raising children, and 90 percent of that group indicated that they still planned a career.

ADULTHOOD

Early Stages

Most women spend the early stages of adulthood in all the time-consuming tasks of caring for the home and raising children. Except for a small percentage, work outside of the home is generally characterized by the need for money or to fill in time until marriage. For those few seriously involved in a career this can be a time of graduate study often combined with marriage and a family.

The vocational guidance needs of this period of life are not well defined or even in operation in institutions. There is an immediate need for complex life-stage counseling in graduate schools and in early career placements. Time, energy and money invested in the lives of young adults would result in incalculable benefits for the whole society. Women would not drift out of college and become overwhelmed by trying to manage a career, home, and family simultaneously. Men would be drawn into this type of counseling, and new and effective cooperative arrangements would make it possible for both husband and wife to develop in every dimension of life, if they so desired.

The young woman who freely selects the home and family role is given little or no attention and support from any kind of counseling until trouble develops. Yet there are many kinds of adjustments and problems that occur. Tyler[84] pointed out that the unrest of women is related to *identity* and the need for each person to utilize their own capacities. Therefore, Tyler feels, counseling must become less problem-centered and counselors must open up channels of communication with people who at a certain point in time or stage in life see no real need for counseling.

In order to try to understand the vocational guidance needs of the *adult* period of life we need to study what happens to adult women in the society. This should help us forge some type of meaningful base for vocational guidance during adulthood. We need to develop a context or framework about adult women in order to attend to their needs. Vital areas of attention include patterns of education and work, attitudes of important others, evidences of discrimination, and suggestions for its elimination. Suggestions for improving the vocational guidance of women will conclude the chapter.

Education and Work Patterns

Educational attainment is directly related to level and position within the occupational structure. The *1969 Handbook for Women Workers*[85] is our basic source of information on this topic. According to the *Handbook*, many more women than men had graduated from high school: 38.2 percent of women, 30.6 percent of men. A substantial proportion of women spent some time in college: 11.3 percent of women, 12.4 percent of men in two-year institutions and 5.7 percent of women, 6.9 percent of men in four-year colleges. The graduate statistics were markedly different: persons having five years or more of college included 1.9 percent of women and 5.3 percent of men. In addition to influencing position and occupational level, educational level also affected *rate* of participation in the labor force; thus, women with four or more years of college showed the highest rate of participation and women with less than eight years of schooling the lowest rate.

Although the *number* of women in the work force had increased significantly over past decades, the *proportion* of women in certain occupations had not changed markedly. Selected examples from the 1969 *Handbook* will show the contrast between 1940 and 1968 with respect to the percentage of women employed. The percentages represent women as a part of the total employed group. In most occupational categories they increased their participation from 1940 to 1968: professional and technical workers, 25.9 percent to 36.6 percent; clerical workers, 52.6 percent to 72.6 percent; sales workers, 27.9 percent to 39.7 percent; private household workers, 93.8 percent to 97.6 percent; service workers, 40.1 percent to 57.0 percent. A marked exception was the drop in woman managers, officials, and proprietors from 45.4 percent to 38.6 percent.

It is apparent that women dominated the lower-paid fields. At all levels they earned less than men for comparable work. In 1968 Hahn[86] noted that 60 percent of women earned less than $5,000, in contrast to 28 percent of men; 3 percent of women earned $10,000, but 20 percent of men were in that bracket. Women continue to make up a small proportion of the membership of select professions. In 1971[87] the figures were: scientists, 9 percent; physicians, 7 percent; lawyers, 3 percent; and engineers, 1 percent. Surely during the seventies the representation of women in select careers will increase due to changes in law and social custom. The participation of black women will make a particularly strong contribution toward increased proportions of women in high level professions. As shown by a 1967 HEW study,[88] black college women, as compared with their white counterparts, were twice as likely to express the wish to combine work and marriage.

There is a need to reduce the sex-typed and psychological constraints which inhibit the free and informed choices of women so that within a few decades women will be distributed across the occupational spectrum according to interest and ability. Present constraints will be apparent as we turn to the attitudes of important others.

Attitudes of Important Others

Women go to work for many reasons: they may need the money to support themselves and/or their families; or they may want to use specific training and talents, just as men do. Each woman has a variety of reasons for her decision. Although careful research has shown that working per se is not the critical variable, each woman with a family worries over the effect her employment will have upon her children. The *quality*, not the quantity, of the relationship is the important factor. In fact, there is some evidence that employed mothers have more favorable attitudes toward children. Stolz'[89] review of the research on maternal employment is a useful and comprehensive aid in evaluating this question.

The views of husbands toward the employment of their wives are critical. The collision of values takes place if the husband holds an exclusive "bread-winner" male image and if, at the same time, the wife's salary is absolutely essential for family survival. The actual fact of a woman working tells little in itself because it is embedded in an individual family and social class context. Whitehurst,[90] for example, reported that lower class husbands expressed open hostility toward their wives working, while middle class men are more hesitant to express open condemnation of women working. Thus they frequently indicate intellectual approval of work, or even of career, but they can also send out powerful signals of ambivalence, cues which can be the source of a woman's continued confusion when she talks with counselors about returning to work or embarking upon a career. Farmer and Bohn[91] found they could demonstrate in a testing situation that a woman's interest in work would rise if home-career conflict were even hypothetically reduced.

Still another facet of the situation is revealed by how women see other women who work. There is no doubt that some women have negative and antagonistic feelings about women who defy convention and become involved in absorbing, complex careers. On the opposite side, there are some women involved in careers who find an exclusive emphasis upon home and family to be a limiting concept. Until fairly recently, these two groups of people were so different in proportion that nonworking women had little chance of understanding the need that some women felt for different life-styles. Social patterning in adult life has revolved around couples of similar life-style giving each other support and friendship and excluding persons that do not fit that model.

Goldberg[92] performed a study to find out whether or not women were prejudiced against other women. Women rated women authors inferior to men, even when they wrote in traditional women's fields. Goldberg, therefore, concluded that women were prejudiced against intellectual attainment by women and that they accepted the dominant view of society. The results are discouraging because, since college girls are not researchers, the name of an author would be given only casual notice—yet even in that second a sex discriminant operated.

A final view of women as seen by important others is expressed in a 1970 article by Broverman et al.[93] According to that study, women are seen by clinicians as less healthy than men. Forty-six clinically trained and practicing psychiatrists, psychologists, and social workers responded to a Sex Role Stereotype questionnaire. They agreed upon particular attributes of mental health, and they held different standards for the sexes that parallel current sex role stereotypes. This discrepancy shows how the prejudices of sexism exist in a professional realm.

Dual-career Families

In future decades the dual-career family can be expected to become a natural way of life for increasing numbers of people. The term dual career means more than the *fact* of employment: it means that both husband and wife are seriously committed to an occupation; that they both have invested in a long period of training; and that they expect to continue with their careers for much of their lives.

Research on dual-career families seems to be of recent origin. We do not yet know much about how some people are able to sustain such a demanding pattern of life while others find it impossible to do so. Research seems to be directed toward family structure and attitudes. Poloma[94] studied fifty-three professional couples in law, medicine, or higher education. The family structures and the number of families in each category were: traditional patriarchy (1), neotraditional (20), egalitarian (27), and matriarchy (5).

Dual-career families certainly have complex problems. Men often appear to be negative or resigned, to have trouble separating marital and professional roles, and to object if their wives earn more money.[95] In many cases the women seem to be in the position of being *allowed* to engage in a career, provided all home and family responsibilities are carefully fulfilled. In a study of men and women lawyers married to each other, Epstein[96] observed that the professional partnership facilitated the successful combination of work and family life. However, the wives were still subsidiary to the husbands with respect to division of labor and prestige. The strains and complexities of dual-career families seem to rest heavily upon women, and undoubtedly they discourage many women from continuing serious careers. The great need for study, understanding, and counseling is apparent. In the past the solution of nonmarriage was unacceptable to most women, but the present decrease in the proportion of people married[97] may reflect unwillingness to accept previous limitations.

Work Discrimination and Women

It is impossible to understand the vocational guidance needs of women at every level without understanding the realities of work discrimination. The conditions reported herein could change, at least on the surface, in the time between writing and publication, but the lingering doubts and anxieties about full and open acceptance of women in all levels of business and the professions will be around for a long time to come.

There is a substantial body of research on work discrimination centered upon business and the professions, and the situation of women in blue-collar jobs should also be publicized. Dependence upon unions, legal aid, and governmental protection is insufficient to provoke change. In this brief summary only a few comprehensive studies will be reported, but the research amply demonstrates that the barriers against women are real and substantial; that the patterns of discrimination are similar across the board; that the results are comparable; and that the remedies suggested are specific and reasonable. Suggestions for change will be summarized at the end of this section.

Discrimination in Business.   Two examples will convey some sense of the attitudes and conditions women have faced in trying to achieve executive status. Five hundred presidents of large corporations responded to Bennett's[98] questionnaire about utilization of women in top management. The respondents demonstrated prejudices deriving from attitudes regarding marriage, education, and religion. In brief, they believed that woman's role is defined by family and church.

Dolson[99] studied responses from over 4,000 top hospital administrators in the United States. About 800 of the respondents were women. Although women constituted the majority of the work force, they occupied only 21 percent of the administrative positions. They were paid less for the same work and took longer to achieve executive status. Administrators attributed the low number of women in top posts to their lack of technical knowledge and the demands for travel and entertaining involved in the job. However, for a long time women in religious orders have capably demonstrated their ability to administer hospitals.

Discrimination in Higher Education.   Long before women even sought positions in higher education barriers were in force that reduced the likelihood of their subsequent involvement. Roby[100] noted conditions such as discrimination in admission and in receipt of financial aid, negative attitudes of faculty, discouragement by counselors, and absence of sufficient role models.

Women successful in gaining employment in universities have faced a complex power structure operating on subtle, venerated customs. Epstein[101] maintained that prestigious male-dominated professions supported career development *systems* that controlled and limited women's achievement through the use of the protege system, the sex-typing of occupations, and the use of peer-group relationships to establish performance criteria. Oltman[102] polled 750 institutions of higher education, and the responses received from 450 revealed that women were underrepresented at every position level. In addition, the mean percentage of department headships held by women was extremely low (3 percent).

The report by Harris[103] summarized the conditions in 1970. There was widespread discrimination at all levels of higher education. Men discouraged women from intellectual pursuits despite evidence of high ability, low attrition, and high-level career commitment demonstrated by women completing the doctorate. Discriminatory practices included lower salaries, antinepotism rules, exploitation of part-time faculty women and nonappointment of women to top level positions.

Discrimination in the Professions.   There is little doubt that women have faced discriminatory practices in male-dominated professions. Even in professions where the majority of workers are women, such as librarianship, top level positions have usually gone to men. As examples of discrimination against women in all professions, we will look briefly at conditions in medicine, law and engineering.

Medicine has long ranked as one of the most difficult professions for women. In 1970 Kaplan[104] completed a seven-year study of the recruitment and utilization of women in medicine, concluding that prejudice on the part of American medical educators was a significant factor in the low number of women doctors in the United States (9 percent). Kaplan based his conclusion on the responses received from 95 percent of American and Canadian medical schools and from Ministers of Health in foreign countries. In 1966 Bowers[105] found discrimination against women in medicine in the United States to be more pronounced than in most European countries, in Asia, in Africa, or in Latin America. He suggested that medical schools actively seek women to offset the view that medicine presents insurmountable barriers for women.

Studies in the field of law compared men and women lawyers after completion of training. In 1967 White[106] reported his study of a large sample of men and women lawyers graduating from law school between 1956 and 1965. Men earned about $1,500 more on their first job than women, and after ten years of legal practice 9 percent of men were earning over $20,000 in contrast to 1 percent of women. White's conclusion—that women lawyers were discriminated against—was based on the fact that income differences were not related to class rank, law review experience, school attended, type of employer, type of work, or rate of turnover.

In the field of engineering conditions also have been difficult for women. Perucci[107] studied over 3,000 recipients of engineering degrees in a large midwestern university over the years 1947 to 1964. She found that men and women attained similar initial jobs, though women were paid less for the same technical and supervisory responsibilities. Salary differential between the sexes increased over time. Although work values of the sexes did not differ, the disparities were explained by the "fact" that women, single or married, did not need or value income and prestige as much as married men do. In his survey of 182 engineering firms Parrish[108] found that women were more likely to be employed by large firms. Companies said they did not hire more women because of lack of applicants, unsuitability of the field of specialization for women, requirements of traveling and irregular hours, lifting of heavy equipment, and female lack of career orientation.

The Elimination of Discrimination.   There are two main aspects in the elimination of discrimination against women—legal and psychological. The legal structure is partially available in the Equal Pay Act of 1963 and in the Equal Opportunity Act of 1972. The ratification by the states of the Equal Rights Amendment (passed by Congress in 1972) is the next priority. The passage of laws does not insure their application. Each law is tested through lengthy and costly legal battles. Sanctions are imposed upon violators to make it unprofitable to continue to oppose laws. Once laws are enforced for a time, they eventually become traditions. Even after every form of educational, economic, and occupational discrimination is eliminated, we will still need to address the problem of assuring *psychological* freedom of access to all occupations. The difficult implementation of the "spirit" of the new laws will require widespread changes in societal attitudes. Women—and men, too— need more than grudging legal consent; they need strong affirmation, support, and respect in order to free their energies for building careers of significance that will contribute to world civilization.

Discrimination begins in the cradle when each sex begins to be shaped toward a particular future regardless of innate temperament. As we have indicated in this chapter, each life-stage experience in home, school, and work carries opportunities for reducing or eliminating discrimination and for fostering growth and responsibility. Human beings at every stage are entitled to the kind of vocational counseling that incorporates the understanding of career within the total structure of evolving life-style. Adult women have some specialized needs for vocational guidance.

Vocational Guidance and Women

The vocational guidance of adult women is a difficult but compelling challenge for counselors, and there are several kinds of vocational decisions at issue. The woman who has worked all, or most of her life and is seeking advancement or a new occupation may be ready for vocational information, experimentation, or new training. Counselors see few people like this because they have a base of experience, skill, independence, and just plain "know-how."

The challenge for the counselor comes from the ever-increasing numbers of educated and uneducated women who want to begin or reenter occupations, after a long lapse of time. These women may seek counseling after decades of life experiences that have often operated as a powerful brake on individual choice and occupational decision-making. Moving directly and prematurely into vocational choice is bound to create difficulties later on. Actual vocational choice and preparation occupy a later priority in the counseling process for adult women. Ideally, that process[109] should proceed through interrelated and overlapping phases of inner preparation, intensive family involvement, vocational experimentation, vocational planning, vocational implementation, vocational analysis, and vocational resynthesis. In the final stage, termed "vocational development resource," many women could become skilled and empathic counselors for new women entering the early stages of the process.

Where do we find counselors for adult women? At present our resource includes secondary, community college and college counselors. Adult vocational counseling, as a distinct specialization in counselor education programs, currently seems embedded in rehabilitation counseling. The increasing mid-career changes of men and the career ferment among adult women will gradually be felt and responded to by the universities. Studies of counselors' attitudes toward women by Engelhard,[110] Cline-Naffziger,[111] and Naffziger[112] revealed that counselors, like the general public, have conflicting views. In general, the higher the counselors' level of education the more liberal the stated views. However, even at the highest levels of education, intellectual acceptance of changing patterns in womens' lives was sometimes contradicted when priorities involving husbands were at stake. We need intensive training programs for counselors of adults, programs which emphasize the unrecognized resources and the power of commitment that many adults bring to a counseling experience.

NOTES

1. K. H. Mueller, *Educating Women for a Changing World* (Minneapolis: University of Minnesota Press, 1954).
2. M. Komarovsky, *Women in the Modern World—Their Education and Their Dilemmas* (Boston: Little, Brown and Co., 1953).

3. E. Bragdon, *Women Today: Their Conflicts, Their Frustrations, and Their Fulfillments* (Indianapolis: Bobbs Merrill, 1953).

4. M. Mead, *Male and Female: A Study of Sexes in a Changing World* (New York: William Morrow and Co., 1953).

5. A. Hottel, *How Fare American Women? A Report of the Commission on the Education of Women of the American Council on Education* (Washington, D.C.: American Council on Education, 1955).

6. Radcliffe Committee on Graduate Education for Women, *Graduate Education for Women: The Radcliffe Ph.D.* (Cambridge, Mass.: Harvard University Press, 1956).

7. National Manpower Council, *Womanpower* (New York: Columbia University Press, 1957).

8. National Manpower Council, *Work in the Lives of Married Women* (New York: Columbia University Press, 1958).

9. O. David, ed., *The Education of Women: Signs for the Future. A Report of the Commission on the Education of Women of the American Council on Education* (Washington, D.C.: American Council on Education, 1957).

10. U.S. Department of Labor, Women's Bureau, *Today's Woman in Tomorrow's World* (Washington, D.C.: U.S. Government Printing Office, 1960).

11. U.S. President's Commission on the Status of Women 1963, *American Women* (Washington, D.C.: U.S. Government Printing Office, 1963).

12. U.S. Interdepartmental Committee on the Status of Women 1968, *American Women 1963–1968* (Washington, D.C.: U.S. Government Printing Office, 1968).

13. U.S. Department of Labor, Women's Bureau, *Continuing Education Programs and Services for Women* (Washington, D.C.: U.S. Government Printing Office, 1971).

14. C. Smith, "The Radcliffe Institute, Cambridge, Mass., U.S.A.," *Convergence: An International Journal of Education* 2,2(1969):56–60.

15. V. L. Senders, "The Minnesota Plan for Women's Continuing Education: A Program Report," *The Educational Record* 42,4(1961):270–78.

16. L. E. Dennis, ed., *Education and a Woman's Life* (Washington, D.C.: American Council on Education, 1963).

17. B. B. Cassara, ed., *American Women: The Changing Image* (Boston: Beacon Press, 1962).

18. "Change and Choice for the College Woman," *Journal of the American Association of University Women* 55,4(1962):276–282.

19. "Women 16 to 60: Education for Full Maturity," *Journal of the National Association of Women Deans and Counselors* 29,4(1966).

20. "The Woman in America," *Daedalus* 93,2(Spring 1964).

21. R. J. Lifton, *The Woman in America* (Boston: Houghton Mifflin, 1965).

22. S. M. Farber and R. H. L. Wilson, eds., *The Potential of Women* (New York: McGraw-Hill Book Co., 1963).

23. S. M. Farber and R. H. L. Wilson, eds., *The Challenge to Women* (New York: Basic Books, 1966).

24. G. E. Harbeson, *Choice and Challenge for the American Woman* (Cambridge, Mass.: Shenkman, 1967).

25. B. Friedan, *The Feminine Mystique* (New York: W. W. Norton, 1963).

26. U.S. Department of Labor, Women's Bureau, *New Approaches to Counseling Girls in the 1960's,* Report of the Midwest Regional Pilot Conference, Chicago, 1965 (Washington, D.C.: U.S. Government Printing Office, 1966); U.S. Department of Labor, Women's Bureau, *Counseling Girls Toward New Perspectives,* Report of the Middle Atlantic Regional Pilot Conference,

Philadelphia, 1965 (Washington, D.C.: U.S. Government Printing Office, 1966).

27. E. Dolan, *Counseling Techniques for Mature Women* (Washington, D.C.: American Association of University Women, 1966).

28. President's Task Force on Women's Rights and Responsibilities, *A Matter of Simple Justice* (Washington, D.C.: U.S. Government Printing Office, 1970).

29. Citizen's Advisory Council on the Status of Women, *Women in 1970* (Washington, D.C.: U.S. Government Printing Office, 1971).

30. U.S. Department of Labor, Women's Bureau, *American Women at the Cross-roads* (Washington, D.C.: U.S. Government Printing Office, 1971).

31. "Women Today," *Journal of the National Association of Women Deans and Counselors* (*JNAWDC*) 34,1(1970); "Women's Roles, Labels, and Stereotypes," *JNAWDC* 34,3(1971).

32. "Woman," *Life*, August 1971.

33. "Revolution II: Thinking Female," *College and University Business*, February 1970.

34. *Women Today* Newsletter (Washington, D.C.: Today Publications and News Service).

35. The vast amount of women's liberation literature published in the early 1970s will one day be judged for its quality and historical significance. A few important references are cited in "Selected Readings" at the end of this chapter.

36. J. Osofsky and H. Feldman, "Evaluation of Female Personality," course developed and taught at Cornell University, 1970.

37. *Women's Studies Abstract*, P.O. Box 1, Rush, New York 14543.

38. *Journal of International Institute of Women's Studies*, 1615 Myrtle St., N.W., Washington, D.C. 20012.

39. American Association of University Women, "Standard for Women in Higher Education" (Washington, D.C.: AAUW, 1971).

40. E. T. Clark, "Influence of Sex and Social Class on Occupational Preference and Perception," *Personnel and Guidance Journal* 45,5(1967):440–44.

41. L. E. Tyler, "The Relationship of Interests to Abilities and Reputation Among First Grade Children," *Educational Psychology Measurement* 11,2 (1951):255–64; L. E. Tyler, "The Development of Vocational Interests: I. The Organization of Likes and Dislikes in Ten Year Old Children," *Journal of Genetic Psychology* 86(1955):33–34; L. E. Tyler, "The Development of Career Interest in Girls," *Genetic Psychology Monographs* 70(1964):203–12.

42. R. L. Sylwester and E. Matthews, "Peacemaker, Plumber, Poet, Drummer? Why Children Must Explore the World of Work and How You Can Help Them," *Instructor Magazine* 81,6(February 1972):45–52.

43. D. G. Anderson and R. H. Heiman, "Vocational Maturity of Junior High School Girls," *Vocational Guidance Quarterly* 15,3(1967):191–95.

44. S. L. Singer and B. Stefflre, "Sex Differences in Job Values and Desires," *Personnel and Guidance Journal* 32,8(1954):483–84.

45. R. H. Turner, "Some Aspects of Women's Ambition," *American Journal of Sociology* 70,3(1964):271–85.

46. L. E. Tyler and N. D. Sundberg, "Factors Affecting Career Choices of Adolescents," Cooperative Research Project No. 2455, 1964.

47. E. Douvan and J. Adelson, *The Adolescent Experience* (New York: John Wiley and Sons, 1966).

48. E. Matthews and D. V. Tiedeman, "Attitudes Toward Career and Marriage and the Development of Life Style in Young Women," *Journal of Counseling Psychology* 11,4(1964):375–84.

49. W. P. Kuvlesky et al., "Racial Differences in Teen-Age Girls, Orientations Toward Marriage: A Study of Youth Living in an Economically Depressed Area of the South," paper presented at Annual Meeting of Southern Sociological Society, 1969.

50. E. C. Lewis, *Developing Woman's Potential* (Ames, Iowa: Iowa State University Press, 1968).

51. H. S. Astin, "Career Development of Girls During the High School Years," *Journal of Counseling Psychology* 15,6(1968):536–40.

52. W. P. Kuvlesky and M. Lever, "Occupational Goals, Expectations, and Anticipatory Goal Deflection Experienced by Negro Girls Residing in Low-Income Rural and Urban Places," paper presented at Southwestern Sociological Society Meeting, Dallas, Texas, 1967.

53. A. Rezler, "Characteristics of High School Girls Choosing Traditional or Pioneer Vocations," *Personnel and Guidance Journal* 45,7(1967):659–65.

54. E. M. Drews, "Counseling for Self-Actualization in Gifted Girls and Young Women," *Journal of Counseling Psychology* 12,2(1965):167–75.

55. E. P. Torrance, "Helping the Creatively Gifted Girl Achieve Her Potentiality," *Journal of the National Association of Women Deans and Counselors* 29,1 (1965):28–33.

56. A. Anastasi and C. Schaefer, "Biographical Correlates of Artistic and Literary Creativity in Adolescent Girls," *Journal of Applied Psychology* 53,4 (1969):267–78.

57. C. E. Werts, "Sex Differences in College Attendance," National Merit Scholarship Corporation, 1966.

58. D. R. Entwisle and E. A. Greenberger, "A Survey of Cognitive Styles in Maryland Ninth Graders: 4 Views of Women's Roles," Report #89, Johns Hopkins University Center for the Study of Social Organization of Schools (Baltimore, Maryland: Johns Hopkins University Press, 1970).

59. A. W. Tamminen and G. D. Miller, *Guidance Programs and Their Impact on Students: A Search for Relationships Between Aspects of Guidance and Selected Personal-Social Variables* (St. Paul, Minn.: U.S. Department of Health, Education and Welfare and Minnesota Department of Education, 1968).

60. Sylwester and Matthews, *op. cit.*

61. L. Rand, "Masculinity or Femininity? Differentiating Career-Oriented and Homemaking Oriented College Freshmen Women," *Journal of Counseling Psychology* 15,3(1968):284–86.

62. N. C. Gysbers, et al., "Characteristics of Homemaker- and Career-Oriented Women," *Journal of Counseling Psychology* 15,6(1968):541–46.

63. M. B. Freedman, "The Role of the Educated Woman: An Empirical Study of the Attitudes of a Group of College Women," *Journal of College Student Personnel,* March 1965, 145–55.

64. V. H. Hewer and G. Neubeck, "Attitudes of College Students Toward Employment Among Married Women," *Personnel and Guidance Journal* 42,6 (1964):587–92.

65. A. Steinmann, "Women's Attitudes Towards Careers," *Vocational Guidance Quarterly* 8,1(1959):15–18.

66. A. Steinmann, "Female Role Perception as a Factor in Counseling," *Journal of the National Association of Women Deans and Counselors* 34,1(1970): 27–32.

67. A. Steinmann and D. J. Fox, "Attitudes Toward Women's Family Role Among Black and White Undergraduates," *The Family Coordinator,* October 1970, 363–68.

68. B. I. W. Cook, "Role Aspirations as Evidenced in Senior Women," unpublished doctoral dissertation, Purdue University, 1967.

69. L. W. Harmon, "The Childhood and Adolescent Career Plans of College Women," *Journal of Vocational Behavior* 1,1(1971):45–56.

70. L. W. Harmon, "Anatomy of Career Commitment in Women," *Journal of Counseling Psychology* 17,1(1970):77–80.

71. E. Almquist and S. Angrist, "Role Model Influences on College Women's Career Aspirations," paper presented at American Sociological Association Meeting, 1970 (to be published in *Merrill-Palmer Quarterly*); E. Almquist and S. Angrist, "Career Salience and Atypicality of Occupational Choice Among College Women," *Journal of Marriage and the Family* 32,2(1970): 242–49.

72. K. M. Wilson, "Black Students Entering College Research Center Colleges: Their Characteristics and Their First-Year Academic Performance," Research Memorandum 69-1, College Research Center, Vassar College, 1969.

73. P. S. Faunce, "Personality Characteristics and Vocational Interests Related to the College Persistence of Academically Gifted Women," *Journal of Counseling Psychology* 15,1(1968):31–40.

74. M. Horner, "Sex Differences in Achievement Motivation and Performance in Competitive and Non-Competitive Situations," unpublished doctoral dissertation, University of Michigan, 1968.

75. R. Helson, "Personality Characteristics and Developmental History of Creative College Women," *Genetic Psychology Monographs* 76(1967):205–56.

76. S. Tangri, "Role Innovation in Occupational Choice Among College Women," unpublished doctoral dissertation, University of Michigan, 1966.

77. R. W. Baruch, "The Achievement Motive in Women: A Study of the Implications for Career Development," unpublished doctoral dissertation, Harvard University, 1966.

78. L. D. Eyde, "Work Motivation of Women College Graduates: A Five Year Follow-up," *Journal of Counseling Psychology* 15,2(1968):199–202.

79. L. W. Harmon, "Women's Working Patterns Related to their SVIB Housewife and 'Own' Occupational Scores," *Journal of Counseling Psychology* 14,4(1967):299–301.

80. U.S. Department of Labor, Women's Bureau, "College Women Seven Years After Graduation (A Re-Survey of Women Graduates—Class of 1957)" (Washington, D.C.: U.S. Government Printing Office, 1966).

81. L. M. Sharp, *Education and Employment: The Early Careers of College Graduates* (Baltimore: Johns Hopkins Press, 1970).

82. U.S. Department of Labor, Women's Bureau, "15 Years After College: A Study of Alumnae of the Class of 1945" (Washington, D.C.: U.S. Government Printing Office, 1962).

83. D. J. Watley, "Career or Marriage?: A Longitudinal Study of Able Young Women," *National Merit Scholarship Corporation Research Reports* 5,7 (1969):1–16.

84. L. E. Tyler, "The Problem That Has No Name," *Journal of Counseling Psychology* 10,3(1963):210.

85. *1969 Handbook on Women Workers,* Women's Bureau, U.S. Department of Labor, Washington, D.C.

86. M. C. Hahn, "Equal Rights for Women in Career Development," *Personnel* 47,4(1970):55–59.

87. YWCA, "Feminine Figures, 1971" (New York: National Board YWCA).

88. U.S. Department of Health, Education, and Welfare, Public Health Service,

"Graduates of Predominantly Negro Colleges: Class of 1964" (Washington, D.C.: U.S. Government Printing Office, 1967).

89. L. M. Stolz, "Effects of Maternal Employment on Children: Evidence from Research," *Child Development* 31,4(1960):749–82.

90. R. N. Whitehurst, "Employed Mothers' Influences on Working Class Structure," unpublished doctoral dissertation, Purdue University, 1963.

91. H. S. Farmer and M. J. Bohn, Jr., "Home-Career Conflict Reduction and the Level of Career Interest in Women," *Journal of Counseling Psychology* 17,3(1970):228–32.

92. P. Goldberg, "Are Women Prejudiced Against Women?" *Trans-action* 5,5(1968):28–30.

93. I. K. Broverman et al., "Sex Role Stereotypes and Clinical Judgments of Mental Health," *Journal of Consulting and Clinical Psychology* 34,1(1970): 1–7.

94. M. M. Poloma, "The Myth of the Egalitarian Family: Familial Roles and the Professionally Employed Wife," paper presented at American Sociological Annual Meeting, 1970.

95. M. M. Kaley, "Attitudes Toward the Dual Role of the Married Professional Woman," *The American Psychologist* 26,3(1971):301–06; N. T. Garland, "The Better Half: The Male in the Dual Professional Family," paper presented at American Sociological Association Annual Meeting, 1970.

96. C. F. Epstein, "Law Partners and Marital Partners: Strains and Solutions in the Dual-Career Family Enterprise," paper presented at the 11th International Family Research Seminar, Tavistock Institute of Human Relations, London, 1970.

97. "Census Study Shows Increase in Single Men and Women," *Women Today* 2(1972):1,3.

98. W. W. Bennett, "Institutional Barriers to the Utilization of Women in Top Management," unpublished doctoral dissertation, University of Florida, 1964.

99. M. T. Dolson, "Where Women Stand in Administration," *The Modern Hospital* 108,5(1967):100–05.

100. P. Roby, "Structuralized and Internalized Barriers to Women in Higher Education," *Sociology of Women*, C. S. Rothschild, ed. (Boston: Ginn-Blaisdell, 1971).

101. C. F. Epstein, "Encountering the Male Establishment: Sex-status Limits on Women's Careers in the Professions," *American Journal of Sociology* 75, 3(1970):965–982.

102. R. M. Oltman, "Campus 1970—Where Do Women Stand? Research Report of a Survey on Women in Academe," Washington, D.C.: American Association of University Women, 1970.

103. A. S. Harris, "The Second Sex in Academe," *American Association of University Professors Bulletin*, Fall 1970, pp. 283–95.

104. H. I. Kaplan, "Women Physicians: The More Effective Recruitment and Utilization of Their Talents and the Resistance to It—The Final Conclusions of a Seven Year Study," *The Woman Physician* 25,9(1970):561–70.

105. J. Z. Bowers, "Women in Medicine: An International Study," *New England Journal of Medicine* 275(1966):362–65.

106. J. J. White, "Women in the Law," *Michigan Law Review* 65,6(1967): 1051–1122.

107. C. C. Perucci, "Minority Status and the Pursuit of Professional Careers of Women in Science and Engineering," *Social Forces* 49,2(1970):245–58.

108. J. B. Parrish, "Are There Women in Engineering's Future?" *Journal of the American Association of University Women* 59,1(1965):29–31.

109. E. Matthews, "The Counselor and the Adult Woman," *Journal of the National Association of Women Deans and Counselors* 32,3(1969):115–22.
110. P. Engelhard, "A Survey of Counselor Attitudes Toward Women," *Minnesota Counselor* 9,1(1969):14–28.
111. C. Cline-Naffziger, "A Survey of Counselors' and Other Selected Professionals' Attitudes Towards Women's Roles," unpublished doctoral dissertation, University of Oregon, 1971.
112. K. Naffziger, "A Survey of Counselor-Educators' and Other Selected Professionals' Attitudes Towards Women's Roles," unpublished doctoral dissertation, University of Oregon, 1971.

SUGGESTED READING

Astin, H. S., Suniewick, N., and Dweck, S. *Women: A Bibliography on Their Education and Careers.* Washington, D.C.: Human Services Press, 1971. An indispensable research tool. Contains a topical, carefully annotated bibliography of over 350 key references.

Gornick, V., and Moran, B., eds. *Women in Sexist Society: Studies in Power and Powerlessness.* New York: Basic Books, 1971. A comprehensive selection of basic contributions on the topic from diverse fields (anthropology, sociology, psychology, etc.).

Maccoby, E. E., ed. *The Development of Sex Differences.* Stanford, Calif.: Stanford University Press, 1966. The most comprehensive reference on this complex subject (includes an annotated and topical bibliography by Oetzel of hundreds of references).

Matthews, E., et al. *Counseling Girls and Women Over the Life Span,* NVGA Monograph. Washington, D.C., American Personnel and Guidance Association, 1972. This monograph examines the special career needs of girls and women as well as presenting an analysis of current problems in utilizing their potentiality in the world of work.

Neugarten, B. L., ed. *Middle Age and Aging: A Reader in Social Psychology.* Chicago: University of Chicago Press, 1968. An important reference book on a vital and heretofore neglected phase of the life cycle.

Women Today. Washington, D.C.: Today Publications and News Service. A comprehensive newsletter concisely reporting on major events, legal decisions, conferences, etc., regarding all major aspects of women's lives. (National Press Building, Washington, D.C., 20004.)

18 Vocational Guidance: Disadvantaged and Minority Populations

Edmund W. Gordon
Teachers College, Columbia University

In this country the 1960s have abounded with pleas for improved civil rights and greater human rights, generating increased concern for the problems of those handicapped by disadvantaged economic, ethnic, and social status. Such concern has emerged as an urgent national problem because of changes both in the requirements for social competence in a highly technical society and in the awareness and political demands of disadvantaged populations. Vocational guidance of the socially disadvantaged and minority populations can best be discussed with the understanding that it is those conditions related to low social, ethnic, or economic status which primarily hinder the individual's functioning in the society in a respected, productive, and satisfying manner. Limited opportunities and prejudicial attitudes, rather than the characteristics of the poverty/minority populations themselves, can be viewed as significant determinants of social disability.

Those populations which experience the highest incidence of social disadvantage include the blacks, Puerto Ricans, Cubans, Eskimos, native Americans, Chicanos, the Orientals to some extent, and the white members of the lowest economic class, who actually comprise the largest number of socially handicapped. The problem of limited employment opportunities confronting members of the various ethnic and minority groups at the ages of twenty through twenty-four, when some vocational stability might be assumed, is illustrated by the fact that, according to the 1970 census, only 1,261,000 of this total national population of 2,089,194 were actually employed in January 1972. Bureau of Labor statistics also reveal that approximately 40 percent of the ethnic minority populations in this country were unemployed in January of that year. This very high percentage seems indicative of the large amount of human resources that are not utilized because of various social handicaps and environmentally imposed barriers.

In considering social disadvantage a distinction must be made between the ethnic or socioeconomic status and other factors associated with members of groups who are socially disabled. Although there are conditions related to social disadvantage which contribute to *absolute* physical or mental disability, we are primarily concerned with *relative* social disability, that which makes the individual unable to function effectively, even in the absence of any clearly definable physical or mental handicap. Regardless of the kind of socially determined disability, whether it be a behaviorally discernible handicap or the result of discriminatory practices of the environment, the individual experiences the feeling of powerlessness, and that itself may well be the chief handicapping factor. Because of the disproportionate distribution of resources and socially created barriers to opportunity, those of low status, sometimes further burdened by geographic isolation, are left with this feeling of powerlessness which exacerbates even minor handicaps and leads to an inability to function effectively within the society. Such incapacitating behavior might be corrected if these poverty/minority members were given a strong enough feeling of power and equal access to economic opportunity.

THE DISADVANTAGED AND THE MINORITIES: DOMESTIC, ECONOMIC, SOCIAL AND POLITICAL FACTORS

It is difficult to embark upon a serious discussion of low economic and social status persons without realizing that their position in our society's hierarchy is not accidental. These people are held back, in part, because of the nature of the economic and political structure of our society which has maintained segments of its population at differing levels of reward and participation, both as a function of the competitive traditions and as a device for controlling the demands of wage earners. Unfortunately, the major socialist models which are available also have not yet succeeded in abolishing lower status groups, even though they have made more progress in reducing the gaps between the various levels of material wealth.

In the United States, where free enterprise and competition have prevailed, the opportunities for democratic participation on the part of the ethnic minorities have been severely limited. As a result, ethnic minorities are heavily represented in the lower class. Because they are readily identifiable, their class status has become equivalent to caste status and operates as a greater hindrance to their egalitarian participation in the society. Despite the unique disadvantages of their lower caste status, the ethnic minorities are not alone; often overlooked in our discussions of the ways in which political and economic conditions in the United States limit opportunity are those native white U.S. nationals who are poor, often geographically isolated, and bypassed by our rapidly advancing technology. These whites were displaced from productive agricultural work by their inability to compete with the large slave-holding plantations. Later they were displaced from productive industrial labor by their inability to compete for work with masses of recently freed slaves whose wage demands were low. Since that time they have been handicapped by their geographic isolation and their general exclusion from national politics and economic life. The southern political block remains in the control of the affluent bourgeoisie, and even the heralded farm subsidies have been designed with little regard for the small dirt farmer or his urban-dwelling counterparts who have been displaced from the farms. Further, these whites and their black neighbors have been encouraged to view one another as threats to each other's respective employment security. Both have been held down in exploited and powerless positions, and their efforts at changing these conditions have often been diffused by intergroup conflict.

The rural whites, particularly those in some of our southern mountain and delta regions, have only a slightly better plight than their black neighbors.

Education

The nation's concern for the education of the disadvantaged population grew along with burgeoning demands for skilled labor. For the major part of the twentieth century and the latter part of the nineteenth century a larger and larger literate labor force has been required for industrial and commercial expansion. In one of the important debates of the nineteenth century, Booker T. Washington and W. E. DuBois tackled the issue of whether education for blacks should focus upon the training of skilled labor or on the development of intellectuals. Washington's stance on the subject prevailed: society would favor the development of manual skills for its black population. This decision, however, was not limited to the education of blacks, for a heavy emphasis on technical-vocational skills came to permeate education for all in the United States. Therefore, through-out the post-World War I period general education and the study of the liberal arts were thought to be purposeless, while greater attention was devoted to the technical-vocational, preprofessional, and professional educa-tion. While these developments modestly contributed to increased oppor-tunity for poor whites and some blacks to be absorbed in the labor market, the relative neglect of the development of the intellect—of attention to the liberal arts and sciences—has plagued the educational development of the poor in the mid-twentieth century.

Following the launch of the first Russian satellite, the development of the intellect became a prominent concern as part of the country's political investment in keeping up with the technological development of the U.S.S.R. The more privileged segments of the population were able to more quickly recover from the nation's previously narrow orientation. The less advantaged, having fewer resources, less flexibility, and few options, found this turn-around process considerably more difficult to cope with.

What emerged in the fifties, then, was a shift of educational focus and purpose toward the "talented" segment of our population. In the present period, however, that shift in purpose has become a shift in demand for high-level conceptual and technical skills. The society's vastly more com-plex political and social organization, with its demand for higher levels of general sophistication, have not only rendered disadvantaged or socially handicapped populations more visible, but also have exacerbated the problem of assimilation and, for many, have precluded opportunity for even minimal participation in the affairs of the society. With the disparity in the distribu-tion of benefits, resources, and preparation, along with qualitatively richer requirements for participation and advancement, it seems evident that it is even more difficult today for the socially disabled to make it in the system than it was for these people in the early part of this century.

International Politics and the Disadvantaged

Not only have the qualitative changes in society's demands on its members greatly influenced the status and conditions of the disadvantaged popula-tions, but the external political concerns of the nation have determined to a large extent the nation's internal concern with its socially disabled members. Following World War II, as Third-World nations reemerged and sought to throw off traditional colonial yokes, it was thought desirable that the United States win the respect and friendship of these countries. However, the treatment of minority groups at home (particularly blacks) was inconsistent with this purpose. Thus, the shift in concern for increased advancement of civil rights and improved conditions for minority and poverty-stricken members is thought by some to be linked with the nation's international aspirations. Greater participation of minority groups in the democratic process was considered to be advantageous in our relations with African and Asian nations. Consequently legal and federal policy decisions were made to the benefit of the socially handicapped; these did not, however, change the conditions of the disadvantaged quickly enough to satisfy changing expectations or to prevent frustration. Essentially, a shrouded problem emerged to the forefront as poverty/minority populations demanded more from society, while the society demanded more of them even as it claimed to be giving them more. As a partial consequence the frustration and anger of disadvantaged peoples erupted violently in some of our cities.

Further domestic and international considerations have made both the constructive but inadequate efforts of the United States and the destructive and inadequate reactions of the disadvantaged counterproductive to the best hopes of either. An extended and unpopular war contributed to the security-threatening escalation of inflation. This condition was most threatening to the working class and the lower-middle class, which had, in the past twenty-five years, come to believe that they had begun to command a bigger share of the benefits of democratic capitalism. The accelerated rates of inflation and the expanding of civil rights combined with increasingly heavy tax burdens to create a sharp reversal of political support for what had been anticipated as a domestic human rights revolution. At the same time, the failure of the United Nations to quickly emerge as an effective world federation reduced this country's dependence upon its forums as a major political instrument. Moreover, the military strength of the U.S.A. and the U.S.S.R. has given each of these nations the capacity to dominate the political economies of the world and/or to destroy the world, thus freeing both to abandon post-World War II policies of winning allies abroad and turn to political and economic imperialist policies in international relations.

In the United States, and, some claim, in the U.S.S.R. as well, these conditions have resulted in a return to reactionary and racist policies at home. Under such conditions civil rights, antipoverty, and other programs designed to advance human welfare, particularly for the disadvantaged, were first subjected to benign neglect and later to open attack. The position of the socially handicapped is an increasingly perilous one because there is little in the national or international political policies which is operating in their favor. With the growing complexities of our society and demands for increased competencies, these people are experiencing the debilitating effects of pervasive feelings of frustration and powerlessness.

An understanding of the way in which economic, political, and social factors interact to contribute to and maintain the state of disadvantage provides a background against which we can now examine various aspects of the problem of the socially disabled and implications for change. Fundamental to an adequate understanding is the fact that while a number of things can be done to make the adjustment of the disadvantaged individual easier and more fruitful through vocational guidance and other services, the fundamental problems are not the concerns of vocational guidance but, rather, relate to the organization, values, and commitments of the society in which poverty and minority populations exist.

RESEARCH ON SOCIAL DISADVANTAGE: THE STUDY OF POPULATION CHARACTERISTICS

As the complexity of the problem of social disadvantage becomes increasingly evident to educators, the concern is no longer simply pedagogical but is one which includes the community at large. The application of pedagogical concern to the teaching of the underdeveloped or handicapped learner is forcing the field of education to examine more closely the mechanisms of learning facility and dysfunction and to utilize this knowledge in an effort to facilitate optimum development of heterogeneous populations, characterized by differential backgrounds, patterns of opportunities, and modes of intellectual and social function. Sensitivity to this differentiation has been the result of a growing body of research data and program experience.

Gordon has covered a wide variety of issues and approaches involved in the research related to the education and guidance of the socially disadvantaged.[1] This work can be divided, essentially, into two basic categories: the study of population characteristics and the description and evaluation of programs and practices. Within the first category is the prevalence of a perspective which holds the characteristics of minority/poverty populations responsible for their dysfunctions in educational, social, and vocational development and views these characteristics as "deficits" to be overcome. The research in this area can be broken down further into those studies dealing with performance and those concerned with life conditions.

Intellectual Function

Intellectual function is the primary focus of most of the studies dealing with performance. It is the usual contention that high economic, ethnic, and social status are related to high intellectual status. However, although recent investigators in the field tend to interpret the data as reflective of a complex interaction between environmental and hereditary forces in the determination of the quality of intellect, the nature-nurture conflict continues to rage.

Although much attention has been directed toward quantitative evaluations of intellectual status among target populations, very little analysis of the qualitative aspects of intellectual function has been undertaken. Attempts have been made to factor-analyze standardized tests and to identify differential strengths and weaknesses in the functioning of socially disabled populations. Typical of this work is that of Lesser and associates, who tried to match patterns of intellectual function with various ethnic groups.[2] Their work stands as a pioneering effort in the move towards qualitative rather than quantitative evaluation.

Another area of study concerned with intellectual function is the research covering plasticity of intellectual development. Based upon the work of Binet and Montessori,[3] who dealt with the trainability of the intellect, investigators worked with mildly or severely retarded children as well as with normal and below-average children. Although no definitive conclusions have emerged from these studies, the best available data suggests that the quality of intellectual function is more likely to be significantly changed if radical positive changes in environmental interactions occur before the consolidation of adolescence. There is very little evidence to support the notion that basic cognitive processes are significantly malleable in the late-adolescent and adult periods of life. A worthy contribution to this area of investigation is the work of Zigler, who has concluded that the affective processes (motivation, task involvement, etc.) are more malleable than the cognitive processes.[4] Zigler's view of the stable nature of basic cognitive function reflects the position of Bloom,[5] who argues that intellectual functions lose their plasticity after the third year of life.

The stability of the cognitive aspect of intellectual function is further attested to by Jensen, who argues that intelligence is, for the most part, genetically determined.[6] Relying upon hereditary rather than environmental forces as an explanation for the failure of education to significantly modify academic achievement in minority and low-income groups, this view is considered by many to be highly questionable. Thus far the technology of genetic research has not been sufficiently developed for us to be able to determine the extent of hereditary influence on the quality of intellect. However, since we are as yet unable to change the genetic constitution of learners but can manipulate environmental encounters in ways which seem to facilitate development, our best option is to use environmental change to influence the quality of interactions, even though the complex nature of these interactions is not fully understood.

Performance Characteristics

A great quantity of data on performance characteristics is available, reflecting school achievement and a more limited body of data referrable to school inefficiency and neglect in poverty/minority populations. Regardless of the population under examination, socially disadvantaged youths rate high when attrition rate is used as an index to school efficiency and educational neglect. The characteristics which most readily distinguish these young persons are the low-income status of their families, the disorganization of their home and family life, and their low academic achievement.

However, at least one encouraging observation has arisen from this pessimistic data, the observation that achievement levels of lower status groups are not independent of the circumstances relating to their school attendance. The data reveal that in the 1930s and 1940s the achievement levels of blacks educated in southern schools were lower than those of the blacks educated in northern schools; but as the blacks moved north and west their achievement levels rose.[7] In such cases researchers have been unable to determine whether selective migration, a change in the quality of the schools, or both were the contributing factors to this phenomenon. Nevertheless, in the 1950s conflicting data emerged which attributed higher achievement levels to southern urban blacks than to children in northern urban schools which were increasingly populated by blacks.[8] The factors responsible for this observation are undetermined. It is worthy of note, however, that in the late 1940s and early 1950s, funds were being directed toward southern black schools in order to improve these schools and to avoid desegregation, while the quality of education in the northern urban ghetto schools was rapidly on the decline as black enrollment in these schools sharply rose. These data and the findings of Coleman,[9] which indicate that quality of schooling is an important factor for low-income and ethnic minority groups, tend to support the position of those who argue for the power of environmental influences.

Life Conditions: Their Influence on School Performance

A large body of research which is complementary to the study of performance characteristics is that which deals with life conditions and the influence of these factors on school performance. Much of this research is concerned with those children who have been separated from the mainstream because of their ethnic origin, socioeconomic status, or both. Most of the evidence reflects the disadvantageous results of such a separation or segregation. In studies of school desegregation and integration the desegregation process has been correlated with a rise in achievement levels, although the interplay of reactions has not been clearly defined.[10] Improved teacher morale may be a significant factor, for example. At the same time, integration according to racial-group and status-group criteria has produced improved achievement levels for members of lower ethnic and socioeconomic groups who are placed in schools with a majority of higher status children, while the latter show no significant decline in achievement.[11] On the other hand, when children of higher status are in the minority in the school, a rise in achievement level is not demonstrated in the lower status group.[12] Such findings must be regarded with caution because studies of minority-group performance under experimental conditions of ethnic mix suggest that the subjects' awareness of the norm against which they are being evaluated creates highly varied patterns of performance on the part of the children in the lower-status group.

Very little educational research has been directed toward the investigation of the relationship between school performance and the health and nutritional status of the socially disabled child. This may be partly due to the obviousness of the relationship between a child's suffering from poor health and nutrition and his inadequate school performance. Health disadvantage is thought to impair school efficiency rather than actual mental function. Although the distribution of health care is inequitable and detrimental to the relatively poor in this country, ill health and inadequate nutrition usually are probably not sufficiently severe to cause organic changes in the nervous system.

However, in the area of the health status of the pregnant mother researchers have found a possible significant relationship between health and nutrition and the development of the child's intellectual function. Many mothers from lower socioeconomic groups receive poor prenatal care and do not provide themselves and their unborn children with adequate nourishment. These factors are linked with a significantly higher incidence of premature births and mental retardation among these groups, the former resulting in an increased risk of congenital abnormality and abnormal postnatal development.[13] Inadequate nutrition and prematurity have also been associated with inadequate height and weight development, which are in turn correlated with low school achievement.[14]

Greater attention has been directed toward examination of the family life of the socially handicapped, and three major trends in this area have emerged: the collection of a variety of demographic data, the documentation of coping patterns and life-styles within this segment of the population, and the study of patterns of child rearing with attention to such aspects as language modeling, task orientation, cognitive stimulation, and value orientation. Demographic studies have fallen into several categories. One concerns economic, employment, and educational levels of the family; another covers various aspects of family disorganization such as consensual marriage, divorce rates, and broken homes; and a third type of demographic study deals with the matriarchal or female-dominated household.

The Moynihan monograph on the black family provides the most important summary of this last type of material.[15] Concentrating on the problems and deficiencies of the black family in an effort to win federal government intervention, the report concluded that the strengthening of the role of the black male and thus the black family unit are essential to the optimal development of blacks in general throughout the country. Moynihan's work, however, has been sharply criticized because of its heavy emphasis on negative family and other characteristics, which he implies are associated with ethnic characteristics. He does not take into account the similarities between poor black and poor white populations; nor does he make use of the work of other investigators such as Hylan Lewis,[16] who calls attention to, for example, the contributions of the extended family and the impact of welfare laws and regulations on the incidence of reported paternal absence from the home.

Comparisons between child-rearing patterns of advantaged families and less advantaged families have been developed in the research devoted to understanding the relationship between these patterns and the process of development. Associations have been made between the quality and style of intellectual function in the mother and work habits and skill achievement of the children[17]; between familial styles in decision-making and language usage in the child[18]; and between attitudes toward school, encouragement of learning activities, and actual school achievement.[19] These research efforts are not limited to the identification of atypical patterns and speculation about possible consequences but are intended to *demonstrate* the relationships between these patterns and the development patterns in the behavior of the child.

DESCRIPTIONS AND EVALUATIONS OF EDUCATIONAL PROGRAMS AND PRACTICES

The examination of educational programs and practices for socially disadvantaged children stands in contrast to the detailed and varied studies dealing with population characteristics. Research on school programs and practices has been characterized by superficial description and evaluation. Unfortunately, little effort has been made to relate the findings concerning population characteristics to new treatments for these children; instead, treatments have emerged from particular biases or dominant models in the field with little attention being paid to the quality or nature of the intervention but, rather, to the fact of intervention or the magnitude of manipulation. This may account for the superficiality of the reporting on these programs. Research literature in this field of program description usually identifies major program elements or the central features of the practice used. These reports cover a wide range of levels from preschool through adult and community-centered activities. The emphasis in these descriptions is placed upon the mounting of demonstration projects rather than controlled experimentation.

Especially in the early 1960s, considerable support from private grants and the federal government was provided in order to launch demonstration projects for target populations. The contribution of such projects was the development of valuable models, some of which progressed from the stage of demonstration, to exemplary program, to technique dissemination. This concern with demonstration and model programs resulted in an increased interest in evaluation, but the simplistic question which prevailed was, "Did the treatment work?" While the classical experimental model of comparing treated groups with untreated control or comparison groups was often utilized, much of the data collection heavily relied upon subjective impressions of those administering the service or those receiving the treatment.

Despite the large numbers of programs and expenditures, there have been very few significant positive findings, leading many investigators to conclude that compensatory education has failed. Furthermore, when positive findings are reported, it is difficult to establish which treatment effects are responsible for the results; attribution of cause and effect is complicated by the possibility of the Hawthorne effects (brought about by possible impact of a changed situation) or the Rosenthal effects (the result of the impact of changed expectations).

These efforts at demonstration and evaluation reflect the search for a generic treatment which will work for large numbers of people. The tendency to want to find one answer to the problems of many is similarly reflected in the research on population characteristics. The underlying assumption is that we are dealing with a large, homogeneous group with common problems of development. Very little of this research has explored the relationships between differential-learner characteristics and differential-treatment characteristics through carefully controlled experimentation or qualitative analysis of large samples in naturally occurring programs. Questions as to what works for which children under what specific conditions are not adequately dealt with in the research available to date.

EFFECTS OF RACIAL OR CLASS SEPARATION IN THE SCHOOL SETTING

One issue of particular interest to educators has been the effects of racial or class separation in the school setting. This concern led to a good deal of research, encompassing the outcomes of racial segregation and desegregation as well as examining equality of access to and opportunity in a variety of educational programs. Studies along these lines can be categorized by several methods and subject areas. Some are designed to show varying levels of academic achievement among schools consisting predominately of one or another ethnic group. Others center around the quality of resources available in the ethnic school, the characteristics of the staffs of such schools, the actual or predicted performance of pupils subject to differing patterns of opportunity, and the sociopolitical processes influencing access to equal educational opportunities. This latter group of studies is headed by the Coleman report, *Equality of Educational Opportunity,*[20] and the Civil Rights Commission report, *Racial Isolation in the Schools.*[21]

Findings in this area are not very definitive, although Coleman reported no significant relationship between the quality of school facilities and achievement levels. In general, he found little difference in the quality of facilities for rich and poor, black and white, although other previous studies had indicated that the quality of educational facilities and opportunity is influenced by the level of family income. This conflict in conclusions may be the result of temporal factors, the earlier studies being conducted at a time when greater differences between schools were obvious, or a result of the heavy emphasis Coleman placed upon static as opposed to dynamic qualitative aspects of the school situations.

The Coleman report, as well as a number of other studies, points to home conditions and general life conditions as the most important variables in predicting school achievement. Although it is possible that an individual child may overcome the limitations set by his background in response to an improved school setting, the majority of the population do not respond so positively to better quality schools. It must be noted, however, that Coleman did find quality of school to have a greater impact on school achievement for poor and minority group children than for the more advantaged pupils. More important than the quality of the school, and second only to family background as a factor closely related to school achievement, is what may be termed sense of environmental control. Regardless of ethnic or economic level, school achievement tends to be high when pupils rate high in this variable. It is as yet unclear, however, whether access to better school and living conditions are in themselves linked with a high sense of environmental control.

While the data concerning access to and opportunity in elementary and secondary school is inconclusive, the available research with respect to higher education provides more definite information. The data reveal that participation of minority and lower-status groups in post-high school institutions is considerably less than that of the more advantaged segments of the population. In addition, the quality of institutions attended by the minority-group youth is very much inferior to those available to the more privileged students. The literature does, however, report rapid changes in this regard, though the changes are not equal to the demands of socially handicapped youth for access to and development in institutions of higher education. Aside from the efforts of many senior colleges to be more responsive to the disadvantaged post-secondary population, the major development at this level has been the enormous expansion of community colleges. All across the country state and local governments have created postsecondary institutions which provide a wide variety of pre-senior college, terminal, and continuing education programs. Although these institutions are not limited to poor or minority groups, their low cost, accessibility, and nonselective nature of their admissions policies has resulted in their heavy use by disadvantaged students seeking college admission.

VIEWS OF SOCIAL DISADVANTAGE

The "Deficit" Perspective

The problem of social disadvantage has been discussed from several different perspectives. For a long time we were concerned with those who were considered atypical, our focus being on their weaknesses or deficits, which were often viewed as inherent, predetermined characteristics, largely discussed in terms of school performance. These deficits—or differences from the white and middle-class populations—could be categorized as high rates of social maladjustment, behavioral disturbance, physical disabilities, and mental abnormality. Dominance of this deficit perspective has in the past led to strategies which were directed at compensating for the weaknesses of the deprived. Enrichment programs, remedial and compensatory programs, and the War on Poverty number among those efforts designed to compensate for what was considered to be essential lacks among the socially disabled (see Herr, chapter 2). Closely associated with this view was the focus on deficits in motivation, a problem heavily represented in the guidance effort by programs for remotivation to inspire a rise in aspiration by exposing these students to new possibilities for which they could aim.

The deficit perspective has prevailed throughout the 1960s and is represented in the research work of two leading spokesmen on disadvantaged children, Martin Deutsch and Frank Reissman. Deutsch conducted a number of studies which singled out the home environment as the primary influence on the school performance and I.Q. of deprived elementary school students. Deutsch's work pointed to specific environmental factors involved in the child's development, such as parental encouragement of academic achievement and language development, as well as poverty conditions which result in cognitive and learning deficits. These factors in turn contribute to a lower self-image of the child, thereby compounding his poor performance and hindering his sense of competence. Certain areas of poor scholastic performance were correlated specifically with race: abstraction, verbalization, and experientially dependent enumeration. Deutsch concluded that a combination of poor home environment, years of poor school experience, and minority-group status render the student less capable of dealing with standard intellectual and linguistic tasks. (The black child's awareness of his caste status increases the handicap.) Deutsch also argued that social advantage can reverse the cumulative deficits of these youngsters; therefore, intervention attempts such as enrichment programs and compensatory programs were positively viewed.[22]

Reissman's work also focused upon the deficits of the "culturally deprived" child, although strengths of the black culture were discussed as well. Reissman's findings stressed the idea that the deprived culture is built upon attitudes, mores, and traditions which are not functional in a middle-class milieu but which must be understood, nevertheless, in order to eliminate the subtle discrimination prevalent among many teachers and other educators. In calling attention to differences and stereotypes associated with the "culturally deprived," Reissman's analysis emphasizes the compensatory or correctional aspect of educational intervention. Along the lines of this deficit perspective, he suggests revised teacher education, careful use of testing, programmed learning which is culturally geared, and further research on testing materials.[23]

The views of both Deutsch and Reissman form the contemporary conceptualization of an approach to social disadvantage, a view which, sympathetic but patronizing, sees the deprived child primarily as a poor academic performer whose deficits must be overcome. The deficit perspective is reflected as well in the other major research efforts dealing with this population. In Gordon's review of the leading research investigations concerned with the socially disabled up through 1965, the following breakdowns of characteristics were identified as the principal areas of focus: home environment and family status; language, cognition, and intelligence; perceptual styles and patterns of intellectual function; and motivation and aspiration.[24]

Effects of Home and Family.   Among the studies concerned with the effects of the home and family is the work of Keller,[25] which cites some statistics relevant to black family life and parental attitudes toward their children's education. Her findings reveal that one-sixth of the black families' breadwinners were unemployed, one-half of the children ate a meal regularly with their parents, and 50 percent of the black parents and all of the white parents from the same socioeconomic status were satisfied with their children's progress in school. According to the work of a number of researchers, lower-class parents were found to be highly concerned with their children's education, although they shared society's general leaning toward anti-intellectualism.[26] Bronfenbrenner[27] noted greater overprotection of girls and a lack of discipline with boys in lower-class homes as compared to middle-class homes.

Other research in the realm of home and family influence includes the work of Gill and Spilka,[28] which correlated underachieving children with mother-dominated environments. Dave[29] found parental behavior to outweigh status as the chief influence on academic achievement. The work of Kohn and Carroll[30] revealed that working-class parents tended to clearly divide parental roles by sex, the mother being responsible for child rearing and the father serving as disciplinarian. Middle-class families demonstrated greater equality in parental sex-role assignment.

Language, Cognition and Intelligence.   Under the second category of deficit studies—language, cognition, and intelligence—Gordon included several examples. When studying the cognitive and motivational effects of lower socioeconomic status in the acquisition of certain formal language forms, Ausubel[31] found that such conditions associated with this status lead to difficulty in the transition from concrete to abstract modes of thought. Jensen[32] and John[33] each reported that lower-class children made inadequate use of language as a cognitive tool and that the more abstract forms of expression are hampered by living conditions. Gordon[34] found that content-centered, inductive tendencies of socially disabled children limited their ability to generalize from specifics to universals and to transfer previously learned knowledge to present problems. A cross-cultural study performed by Montague,[35] measured the acquisition of arithmetic concepts by kindergarten children and revealed significant differences among social class groups, with lower-class children experiencing greater difficulty. The majority of research in the area of cognitive abilities report a relationship between intelligence and socioeconomic status in which low status in one is associated with low status in the other.[36] Other studies suggest that this effect is not invariable but is related to quality of developmental experience. In his definitive research review on the question of race, environment, and I.Q. Klineberg[37] concludes that there is no scientifically acceptable evidence in support of the theory that ethnic groups differ in innate ability, despite the high correlations between low ethnic groups and low functional intelligence.

Perceptual Styles and Patterns of Intellectual Function.   The third category of research on characteristics of the socially handicapped—perceptual styles and patterns of intellectual function—is represented by several important studies. Jensen[38] and others have concluded that these children fail to learn the verbal mediators which are facilitative of school learning. Reissman[39] identified slowness as a feature of their cognitive functioning. Carson and Rabin[40] found northern blacks to demonstrate a higher level of meaningful communication than southern blacks, and white children were shown to communicate more effectively than the black children. In the realm of concentration and persistence, Deutsch[41] found lower-class children to be inferior to middle-class children. Among other aspects of perceptual style discussed in the research literature are differences in temporal orientation and in the degree of internal vs. external control.

With regard to affective function, some dynamics of the socially disadvantaged child's personality have been the subject of much research. These concerns include behavioral disturbances, low self-esteem, impaired interpersonal relationships, ego deflation, difficulty accepting personal responsibility, and self-depreciation.[42]

Motivation and Aspiration.   Theoretical discussions concerning motivation and aspiration suggest that the goals of socially disadvantaged children tend to be more immediate and utilitarian and that there exists less postponement in obtaining gratification and fewer symbolic rewards among them than among the middle and upper classes. In addition, it has been concluded that there is no concern for aesthetics of knowledge, symbolization as an art form, introspection, and competition with self. The drive may be present, but the goals toward which it is directed are not complementary to academic achievement. Edwards and Webster[43] have stated that favorable self-concepts are related to higher aspiration and academic achievement. Wylie[44] has found that blacks and lower-class children set estimates of their ability to do school work lower than do white and upper-class children.

Bernstein[45] found that parental demands for success played a more crucial role in determining achievement strivings for middle-class students than for their lower-class peers. Essentially, the research in this area indicates that attitudinal factors are closely related to the level of motivation and aspiration of children, and such attitudes or values are largely dependent upon socioeconomic status.

Limitations of the "Deficit" Perspective. There are evident limitations to the deficit perspective exemplified by the above research efforts. The majority of investigators who have developed the core of knowledge dealing with the characteristics of the socially disabled child have a background of experience in working, for the most part, with children from the homes of middle-class white Americans. Researchers have set this group up as the norm against which to evaluate and measure the characteristics of the socially handicapped, the resulting behavioral and environmental deviances from the standard being described as deficits. These behaviors and conditions have not been considered as given information to be utilized by educators for the design of appropriate and meaningful learning experiences. Instead, these studies imply that their language, styles, and values are drawbacks to be overcome. Certainly, upward mobility may not be possible without such an emphasis; however, immobility on the part of the child may well be the outcome of the denigration of all that with which he or she identifies. Such a concern is seldom mentioned in the research literature.

Moreover, even if the characteristics and environmental conditions of this population were essentially negative and unwholesome, the research effort to support these observations would still be basically inadequate. In the first place, researchers have generalized from the "typical socially disadvantaged child" to the entire population. This is an unsound generalization because no allowance is made for the variety of such children with widely varying characteristics; differential psychology is equally important in the realm of the socially handicapped. Furthermore, the *correlation* between poor school adjustment and certain conditions or characteristics does not necessarily imply *causation*. The research dealing with the identification of characteristics has not yet pinpointed the cause, nor a plan for remedial action. Research has yet to determine the nature of learning facility and disability in this population by determining what conditions in the learning situation result in success or failure and how these can best be manipulated to the advantage of the handicapped learner. More accurate and sensitive assessment procedures are also needed to determine developmental potential and behavioral change. The appropriate developmental conditions might then replace existing pedagogical principles and technology, which are ineffective when applied to the wide variety of underdeveloped learners.

The "Opportunity Deprivation" Perspective

A second view of social disadvantage also regards the characteristics of the socially disabled as deficits; however, the major factor which sets this view apart from the deficit perspective is its treatment of the genesis of the condition. The characteristics of this population are said to exist because these people are deprived of certain opportunities. The concept of *opportunity denial* leads some to refer to this population not as "disadvantaged" but as "opportunity-deprived." According to this view, the conditions derived from the state of opportunity deprivation not only result in intellectual under-development but also alienation, disengagement, frustration, and a variety of other negative characteristics often viewed as innate in disadvantaged populations.

Investigators adhering to this view placed greatest emphasis upon such intervention strategies as the development of opportunities for work and education in an effort to replace or compensate for poor education, health, jobs, etc. Opportunities for participation in decision making were also developed through community organization and community action pro-grams. In addition, the subsidization of schooling was encouraged in order to enhance the quality of educational exposure.

The strategies proposed are appropriate regardless of the viewpoint from which they stem, since it is evident that opportunity deprivation is a major component of the problem of disadvantagement. However, although the socially disabled may be functioning with a significant handicap imposed by their environment, the provision of opportunities is not enough to en-compass all of the complexities of the problem. Therefore, the broadening of opportunities is helpful but not sufficient in itself as a solution to the condition of social disadvantage.

The "Different But Not Inferior" Perspective

A third approach has been supported by those persons who view the socially disabled as different but not inferior to their white or higher socioeconomic group counterparts. The characteristics of this population are said to reflect differences rather than functional deficits. Instead of focusing upon the need to overcome the intrinsic characteristics of the disadvantaged, the proponents of this viewpoint center upon the utilization of those traits to their best advantage. It is recognized, however, that the characteristics of the socially handicapped may be inferior for specific purposes and that a change in behavior may be necessary for the attainment of certain goals; but, at the same time, these characteristics and behaviors are respected and considered viable for other purposes.

A challenge lies in the implementation of this concept of differences. Two major implications for education emerge. The first is a change in the attitudes of teachers and other educators who may begin to relate to the minority child with more understanding and respect, and the second involves a change in curriculum design and in the learning experience. Although a radical change in the educational process may not occur, it is likely that the differences prevalent among these children can be utilized and respected in the curriculum rather than excluded. Greater attention and effort might be directed toward the development of materials and experiences which will be meaningful, rather than foreign, to these children.

The respect for the differences found in these populations leads to a serious concern for the nature of the learner and those specific features of his or her learning behavior which may be dealt with in the process of development. In this approach we have moved away from the characteristics of the learner toward a concern for the meaning of the learning experience and the extent to which that experience reflects the purposes which are expressed by the learner. This new focus is reflected in the growing concern for community control, participation in decision making, relevance, assisting young people in the definition of the meanings of their own experiences, and in the utilization of materials and persons more representative of the life patterns to which they have been exposed. Further evidence of the implementation of this view can be seen in the rising concern for ethnic studies, the utilization of paraprofessionals, and the introduction of indigenous models. It is from this perspective that the problem of disadvantagement becomes a pedagogical issue of relevance to all populations as well as to the entire field of education. All of education is concerned with meeting the demands created by the characteristics of the learner. An analysis of the learning experience in general, regardless of what population is being considered, is of primary importance in designing and refining an effective learning experience.

The process of individual development may not emerge naturally following the reorganization of the child's educational environment because of a distorted self-concept and distorted perception of his life field, both of which stem from a negative life experience and self-defeating attitudes. In such cases it is important to provide the kinds of psychological support and opportunities for the development of insight that counseling and other therapeutic procedures encourage. The researchers and practitioners who approach the problem of disadvantage from this counseling perspective are more concerned with strengthening and working with individual attitudes and behavioral change than with conceptualizing or focusing upon the environmental causation of the problem. A Rogerian orientation has been espoused by some in the past decade as a nondirective technique which may lead the counselee to greater self-exploration as the result of the communication of warmth and unconditional positive regard on the part of the therapist. More recently, however, with a growing emphasis on action-oriented, behavioral techniques, some therapists and counselors advocate not only a directive and didactic approach toward changing the child's attitudes and behavior, but active intervention by the counselor in an effort to manipulate hindering environmental conditions.

This cognitive-behavioral approach, which seeks to teach the counselee not only how to minimize his self-defeating attitudes but also how to deal effectively with adverse conditions in his environment, has been purported by such experts in the field of psychotherapy as Arnold Lazarus and Joseph Wolpe, William Glasser,[46] Albert Ellis,[47] and Robert Carkhuff,[48] a leading researcher in the fields of psychology and sociology. Although most of the cognitive-behavioral theorists concentrate on improving reality appraisal, self-concept, and attitudinal change, a greater emphasis is being placed upon effecting changes in the behavior of the counselee, encouraging him to try out new behaviors in order to gain greater control over the course of his life. Fundamental to their position is the view that a change in behavior brings about a change in attitudes; therefore, the behavioral component of therapy is emphasized.

Other views emphasize behavioral change but also hypothesize that the counselee will be moved toward such action as a result of a supportive relationship with a counselor whose approval the counselee will be striving to obtain. The counselee could then generalize his successful behavior patterns to other situations, after gaining the confidence that follows supported experimentation with more effective behavior. Regardless of whether the focus is placed on cognitive or behavioral processes, counseling efforts directed at encouraging active behavioral change and effecting environmental intervention on behalf of the counselee, seem to be the most promising techniques for dealing with the socially disadvantaged if the individual counseling approach is to be utilized.

Discussion of the Various Perspectives on Disadvantagement

Each of the several approaches mentioned above has its merits. The way in which the problem is conceptualized depends in part upon the context in which the person being helped lives and works. For example, the disadvantaged youth who wishes to compete in the mainstream of society's opportunity structure can be considered to have functional deficits in relation to the demands of society. He requires certain skills, such as the mastery of standard English, in order to attain his goals. Unless we radically change the educational system, there is no alternative to viewing the child's weaknesses as deficits. On the other hand, if we begin with the assumption that the mastery of skills is not as important as a positive attitude toward oneself as a learner and as a participant in society, then the problem might better be viewed as a political and social issue with the emphasis upon helping the young to become involved and skilled in the manipulation of those processes which control their lives. This perspective is supported by some investigators who argue that it is from the experience of exercising control and influencing one's destiny that a sense of power is derived, and it is this sense of power that generalizes to other behaviors, including academic learning.

FUNCTIONS OF PRESENT GUIDANCE PRACTICE: THEIR RELATION TO THE ENVIRONMENT OF THE SOCIALLY DISADVANTAGED

With so much attention having been directed toward singling out characteristics of ethnic and minority populations (as outlined earlier), the question of the importance of focusing on such traits for guidance purposes requires consideration. It seems that the significance of the disadvantageous characteristics lies in the fact that they appear with a higher incidence in the disadvantaged populations, and their seriousness is accentuated by the lack of opportunities afforded these people to compensate for such behaviors. However, the characteristics of the individuals themselves are not of primary importance for the guidance specialist, except for the need to be concerned with attitudes regarding discrimination and the growing cultural nationalism among some ethnic minorities, both of which contribute to a hypersensitivity and a higher degree of alienation among some members of these populations. The question, then, of the guidance function is, rather, a more generic one involving the relation of this function to the environment in which the socially disabled individual is situated.

A contemporary purpose of guidance is to aid the individual to identify his or her abilities, aptitudes, and interests and to develop these optimally. The issue here is not merely one of assessment but of identifying the nature of the behavior and the conditions under which it is manifested. In what ways can the individual's characteristics best be developed and nurtured? If the traditional instruments of assessment are employed, they will produce a static measurement of the child's current status, whereas the use of a qualitative analysis would be more descriptive of his functioning and would provide clues to his potential. "Potential" might best be defined not as present ability or capacity but as an estimate of what the individual can become, given an appropriate match between his existing patterns of functioning and optimal opportunities for their development. Rather than viewing the child as a combination of static, predetermined characteristics, he or she might better be viewed as a person in the process of change and growth, to be cultivated through a creative exchange between the educator or counselor and the individual.

The static and quantitative emphasis in assessment of abilities, aptitudes, and interests is a result of the long-standing dominance of the field of measurement by the projective view of the genesis of behavior.[49] This bias has also been reflected in the neglect of the training and development of intelligence. A stimulating approach to academic and social readiness has been bypassed as well in favor of a monitoring of these processes. Furthermore, an exaggerated emphasis has been placed upon the predictive value of the classification and quantification of psychological appraisal data at the expense of a qualitative appraisal, which would provide a basis for planning and intervention. Another distinctly deleterious result has been the distortion of aspiration and expectation levels of these underdeveloped youth based upon unjustified ceilings on their potential for growth and adaptation. Not only do children suffer from underestimates of their abilities, but the burden of proof for such assumptions is placed upon the examinee rather than the appraiser or method of appraisal, on the learner rather than on the teacher or the method of teaching, and on the counselee rather than on the counselor or method of counseling. Yet another drawback to present assumptions regarding the static nature of human development is the emphasis placed upon adjustment or acceptance of assumed realities rather than on the modification of the environment and the individual's interaction with this environment. Overemphasis has also been placed upon selection and placement (both educational and vocational) rather than on the nurturing of interests and aptitudes and the development and training of capacities and skills.

In addition to the concern with identification and assessment of abilities and interests are those functions which are directed at aiding the individual to understand, accept, and utilize those traits which have been identified through quantitative testing and to help him adapt his aspirations accordingly. This function is clearly of limited value for those individuals whose abilities and interests have been underestimated or incorrectly identified. Moreover, it is evident that if the child has not been given the opportunity to cultivate or explore his potential, his aspirations will be limited within the confines of his supposed interests and aptitudes rather than expanding to suit his potential.

Nature of Career Guidance

A second function of the present guidance practice is that of providing the individual with opportunities for learning about areas of occupational and educational endeavors. This function may decrease in importance or may be altered significantly as the term "career" is coming to be more broadly defined to mean the course by which one makes a productive and satisfying place for himself in the society. Since "career" is no longer synonymous with "vocation," vocational guidance for the future may be more concerned with decisions relating to the development of the total human being—how he lives his life, rather than how he earns a living. Of greater importance than choice of an occupation are the biological and social roles which the individual must deal with or select—selection of friends and mate, family living, aesthetics and self-expression, political participation, cultural identification, consumer orientation, and urban versus rural living.

Changes in the nature of our economy as well as attitudinal changes with regard to traditional biosocial role adoption require that vocational guidance expand to meet the demands and challenges of today's society. The political economy is much more fluid and open to individual effort than it was two or three decades ago, so that few of us and none of our children are likely to spend a lifetime in the same occupation. In addition, sustained employment and advancement require more than simple training; a generic competence and continuing trainability are required. Along with these changing occupational demands, changing sex roles must also be taken into account in vocational guidance since biology is no longer automatically equated with destiny. The implication that women may be considered as another socially disadvantaged or minority population opens up another issue for guidance specialists to investigate and act upon.

Another current function of guidance is to aid the individual in the development of values. In minority or other low socioeconomic groups the selection of values is particularly relevant. The poverty/minority group member is faced with the question of which values and cultural traditions and mores are beneficial to him. It is important that he or she be exposed to all that is available in order to freely choose which aspects of his own culture or of the society at large he wishes to maintain or utilize.

The present guidance practice also encompasses the function of helping the individual to obtain those experiences which will assist him in making free and wise choices. This valuable function involves two important aspects. First, the opportunity structure should be changed. Active intervention and environmental manipulation on the part of the counselor is of crucial importance, for it is a responsibility of the guidance specialist to open up the possibilities that will enable the counselee to truly experience self-direction and free choice. With the opening up of opportunities, it is then possible to expose the individual to the existing possibilities for the free choice of pursuable goals, thereby fulfilling the ultimate goal of guidance practice as it has been and most likely will continue to be conceptualized—that of aiding the individual to become as independent and self-directive as possible.

Although some of the present guidance functions are appropriate to the changing demands of our society and to the increasingly recognized need for environmental intervention, they do not, for the most part, adequately control and modify the organizational system in the environment, the system which is crucial to the development of the individual. An appropriate reconceptualization of a model for the professional tasks of guidance would include the following goals.

1. To make available to human subjects expanded alternatives for choice referrable to their development.
2. To optimize decision behavior in these expanded situations of choice.
3. To facilitate development and movement toward the objectives specified by these choices.

Each of these points focuses both on the individual and on the field in which the individual operates. So far counseling has directed its attention toward the individual in order to predict behavioral function and to determine how to effect behavioral change. At present, however, the individual psychological model is being challenged by a developmental-ecological model which recognizes that the nature of the choices that an individual makes, as well as the quality with which these choices and his total development are implemented, are primarily dependent upon the interaction between that which is given or possible in the individual and that which is given or possible in the system in which he functions.

A FUTURE-ORIENTED FRAMEWORK FOR VOCATIONAL GUIDANCE

Thus far we have been speaking of a vast body of research and literature which points to the crucial role of the home and school environments as well as economic and political trends in determining, to a large extent, the development of the individual who is exposed to these conditions. If the problem of social disadvantage is truly a reflection more of the environment in which the poverty/minority populations exist rather than the result of predetermined and inherent characteristics, then the principal function of the counselor or guidance specialist should be that of environmental manipulation—the design and provision of environmental encounters calculated to best complement individual human potential and need. The counselor or guidance specialist should be prepared for such intervention by training to understand individual variance and to organize the learning experience in such a way as to accommodate this variation. In addition, these members of the helping professions should become actively involved in the actual experiences of the counselee and with those persons who influence and determine his experiences. This would entail political and economic influence, family and community involvement, and curriculum planning. Essentially, the potential counselor or guidance person can be thought of as a kind of ombudsman and developmental specialist who recognizes that low achievement and mental and behavioral disturbance are chiefly the result of society's failure to provide those learning experiences, environmental supports, and access to opportunities necessary for optimum growth of the individual.

With this framework Gordon has identified several implications for the reformation of guidance, and they show equal relevance for vocational guidance specifically. The logical first step is a shift from appraisal of individuals to appraisal of environments or individuals *in* environments, with attention to such issues as the nature of the conditions of learning and development and the reciprocal relationship between this individual and her developmental-learning environment. The new focus calls for a shift to the study of systems—the family as a social system, the school as a social system, the plant or office as a social system, education and development as social processes.

Also required is a shift from the assessment of behavioral product to the assessment of behavioral process. With less emphasis on quantitative summary and classification, the guidance specialist will examine the nature of intellectual and social functioning for the individual and describe those functions qualitatively. This shift in focus of appraisal will result in a movement away from prediction to prescription; the more sophisticated and sensitive appraisal process will provide information making possible the prescription or design of learning experiences and learning environments. This should be followed by a shift from identification of and placement in available opportunities to the creation of and placement in appropriate opportunity situations.

The guidance function should be vastly broadened from our traditional concern for the discovery of the talented few to the development of talent in all. This entails a fundamental commitment to those policies and practices which ensure universal optimal development. We will also need a shift in method from didactic exhortation to discovery and modeling as vehicles for learning, with more attention given to use of naturally occurring or contrived environments to provide interactions supportive of learning and development in specified directions.

The ecological model implies a shift from interpretation to environmental orientation as the principal focus in counseling and in other forms of directed learning. The skills that the behavior specialist helps to develop in young people should come to include the use of environmental clues and relationships to analyze and interpret behavior and experiences, to manage information, and to bring order to confusion and chaos. Emphasis on consultation should be greater than emphasis on counseling, and the focus in consultation should include active efforts to influence persons and groups who have the power to make necessary and relevant changes in the conditions which determine the course of the student's life.

In addition to these changes in focus and method, a significant consideration is *style*, for what is needed is a shift from diplomacy to advocacy. Our clients do not need to be apologized for and to have their troubles explained away; they need to be more actively involved in the decision-making processes that control their lives. Their rights need to be more appropriately defended, and opportunities for meaningful involvement need to be more vigorously advanced. Equally important, the role of the guidance specialist should not be that of ambassador for the establishment—but that of ombudsman for students—protecting the individual and collective students from accidental, incidental, or intentional abuse by the establishment or its representatives.

Finally, we will need to bring about a shift from a primary concern with socialization to a major concern with politicalization. Probably one of the most important contributions we can make to the optimal development of young people is to help them to learn not only what is expected of them by the social order—the traditional concern of socialization—but, most importantly, how they can effectively use themselves in relation to other people to cope with the systems which in large measure control their lives. Systems-management or systems-maneuvering skills are not only important for building a strong concept of self but also for future survival. This means that participation of the behavior specialist with students in the politicalization process is raised to the level of urgency.

There are serious questions as to whether there is a special approach to vocational guidance which reflects the needs of disadvantaged populations. A careful reading of this paper should reveal the bias that an appropriate approach to vocational guidance or guidance of any type should be one which is suitable to all populations but flexible enough to speak to the special needs of the person or persons being served. With this individualized approach the basic dimensions of the field gain their specificity from the study of the client. People who have been subjected to special experiences, advantaged or disadvantaged, may require that services directed at them reflect these experiences and derivative needs. It is in this sense that vocational guidance of disadvantaged and minority populations cannot be divorced from the problems of social disadvantage in general.

SUMMARY

Cogent arguments have been made for the relationships between conditions of life, progress in life, and sense of power to influence one's life. Consistently we find deleterious life conditions, slow progress, and powerlessness closely associated. Since mounting evidence points to environmental encounters as crucial influences on human behavior, including academic and vocational performance, educators and guidance specialists alike must be concerned with tackling or helping the youngster to tackle the socially imposed handicaps impeding the development of some segments of our nation's population.

But it is not only to help youth deal with socially imposed handicaps that the guidance function exists; it should be more generally concerned with the analysis, design, and management of environmental encounters in ways which facilitate the optimal development of the client. With such a charge, the guidance specialist becomes sensitive to and concerned with positive and negative factors which influence human development. He will then increasingly define his role as that of human development specialist with a primary responsibility for assisting young people to acquire the competencies, skills, and understanding necessary to gain increasing control over themselves and their environment, and to thus exercise greater influence over the course of their lives. This is the essential task of guidance for the disadvantaged and advantaged as well.

NOTES

1. E. W. Gordon, "Introduction" to *Review of Educational Research* 40(1970): 1–12.
2. G. S. Lesser, G. Fifer, and D. H. Clark, *Mental Abilities of Children from Different Social-Class and Cultural Groups,* monographs of the Society for Research in Child Development, Serial No. 102, Vol. 30, Whole No. 4 (Chicago, Ill.: Society for Research in Child Development, 1965).
3. A. Binet, *The Development of Intelligence in Children* (Baltimore, Md.: Williams and Wilkins, 1916); M. Montessori, *The Discovery of the Child,* 3rd ed., trans. by Mary A. Johnstone (Madras, India: Kalakshetra Publications, The Vasanta Press, 1962).
4. E. Zigler, "Mental Retardation: Current Issues and Approaches," *Review of Child Development Research,* Vol. I, M. Hoffman and L. W. Hoffman, eds. (New York: Russell Sage Foundation, 1964), pp. 107–68.
5. Benjamin S. Bloom, *Stability and Change in Human Characteristics* (New York: John Wiley and Sons, 1965).
6. A. R. Jensen, "How Much Can We Boost I.Q. and Scholastic Achievement?," *Harvard Educational Review* 39(1969):1–123.
7. A. Anastasi, *Differential Psychology; Individual and Group Differences in Behavior* (New York: The Macmillan Company, 1958), pp. 584–88.
8. *The Status of Public School Education of Negro and Puerto Rican Children in New York City* (New York: Public Education Association of New York City, October 1955).
9. J. S. Coleman, *Equality of Educational Opportunity* (Washington, D.C.: U.S. Office of Education, Department of Health, Education and Welfare, 1966).
10. N. H. St. John, "Minority Group Performance under Various Conditions of School Ethnic and Economic Integration," *IRCD Bulletin* 4,3(May 1968) (New York: ERIC Information Retrieval Center on the Disadvantaged, Yeshiva University).
11. J. S. Coleman, *op. cit.*; U.S. Commission on Civil Rights, *Racial Isolation in the Public Schools,* Volume I (Washington, D.C.: Government Printing Office, 1967), pp. 91–100.
12. *Ibid.*
13. H. Birch and J. D. Gussow, *Disadvantaged Children: Health, Nutrition and School Failure* (New York: Harcourt, Brace and World, 1970), pp. 46–80.
14. *Ibid.*
15. Office of Policy Planning and Research and the U.S. Department of Labor, *The Negro Family—the Case for National Action* (Washington, D.C.: Government Printing Office, 1965), commonly referred to as the Moynihan Report.
16. H. Lewis, "Culture, Class, and the Behavior of Low Income Families," report prepared for Conference on Lower Class Culture, New York, June 27–29, 1963.
17. R. D. Hess and V. C. Shipman, *Cognitive Elements in Maternal Behavior* (Chicago, Ill.: University of Chicago Press, 1966).
18. F. L. Strodtbeck, "The Hidden Curriculum of the Middle-Class Home," *Education of the Disadvantaged* A. Harry Passow et al., eds. (New York: Holt, Rinehart and Winston, 1967), pp. 244–60.
19. E. W. Gordon, "Characteristics of Socially Disadvantaged Children," *Review of Educational Research,* 35(1965):377–88.

20. Coleman, *op. cit.*
21. U.S. Commission on Civil Rights, *op. cit.*
22. Martin Deutsch et al., *The Disadvantaged Child* (New York: Basic Books, Inc., 1967).
23. F. Reissman, *The Culturally Deprived Child* (New York: Harper and Row, 1962).
24. Gordon, "The Characteristics of Socially Disadvantaged Children," *op. cit.*
25. S. Keller, "The Social World of the Urban Slum Child: Some Early Findings," *American Journal of Orthopsychiatry* 33(1963):823–31.
26. D. Durkin, "Children Who Read before Grade One," *Reading Teacher* 14 (1961):163–266; R. A. Cloward and J. A. Jones, "Social Class: Educational Attitudes and Participation," *Education in Depressed Areas,* H. A. Passow, ed. (New York: Bureau of Publications, Teachers College, Columbia University, 1963), pp. 190–216; H. Lewis, "Culture, Class and the Behavior of Low Income Families," paper presented at the Conference on Lower Class Cultures, Washington, D.C., Howard University, 1963, mimeo.; *Youth in the Ghetto* (New York: Harlem Youth Opportunities Unlimited, 1964).
27. U. Brofenbrenner, "The Changing American Child—A Speculative Analysis," *Merrill-Palmer Quarterly,* April 1961, pp. 73–84.
28. L. J. Gill and B. Spilka, "Some Non-Intellectual Correlates of Academic Achievement among Mexican-American Secondary Students," *Journal of Educational Psychology* 53(1962):144–49.
29. R. H. Dave, *The Identification and Measurement of Environment Process Variables That Are Related to Educational Achievement,* unpublished doctorate thesis, University of Chicago, 1963.
30. M. L. Kohn and E. E. Carroll, "Social Class and the Allocation of Parental Responsibilities," *Sociometry* 23(1960):372–92.
31. D. P. Ausubel, "How Reversible Are the Cognitive and Motivational Effects of Deprivation? Implications for Teaching the Culturally Deprived Child," *Urban Education* 1(1964):16–35.
32. A. R. Jensen, "Learning Ability in Retarded, Average, and Gifted Children," *Merrill-Palmer Quarterly* 9(1963):123–40.
33. V. P. John, "The Intellectual Development of Slum Children: Some Preliminary Findings," *The American Journal of Orthopsychiatry* 33(1963):813–22.
34. E. W. Gordon, "Counseling Socially Disadvantaged Children," *Mental Health of the Poor,* F. Reissman, J. Cohen, and A. Pearl, eds. (New York: Free Press of Glencoe, 1964), pp. 275–82.
35. D. O. Montague, "Arithmetic Concepts of Kindergarten Children in Contrasting Socioeconomic Areas," *Elementary School Journal* 64(1964):393–97.
36. A. D. B. Clarke and A. M. Clarke, "How Constant is the I.Q.?," *Lancet* 216(1953):877–80; M. Deutsch and B. Brown, "Social Influences in Negro-White Intelligence Differences," *Journal of Social Issues* 20(1964):24–25; R. M. Dreger and K. S. Miller, "Comparative Psychological Studies of Negroes and Whites in the U.S.," *Psychological Bulletin* 57(1960):361–402; K. Eells, "Some Implications for School Practices of the Chicago Studies of Cultural Bias in Intelligence Tests," *Harvard Educational Review* 23(1953):284–97; C. Higgins and C. H. Sivers, "A Comparison of Stanford-Binet and Colored Raven Progressive Matrices I.Q.'s for Children with Low Socioeconomic Status," *Journal of Consulting Psychology* 22(1958):465–68; Montague, *op. cit.*; R. T. Osborne, "Racial Differences in Mental Growth and School Achievement: A Longitudinal Study," *Psychological Reports* 7(1960):233–39.
37. O. Klineberg, "Negro-White Differences in Intelligence Test Performance: A New Look at an Old Problem," *American Psychologist,* 18(1963):198–203.
38. A. R. Jensen, *op. cit.*

39. F. Reissman, "The Culturally Deprived Child: A New View," *Programs for the Educationally Disadvantaged,* Bulletin 1963, No. 17, U.S. Department of Health, Education and Welfare, Office of Education (Washington, D.C.: Government Printing Office, 1963).

40. A. S. Carson and A. I. Rabin, "Verbal Comprehension and Communication in Negro and White Children," *Journal of Educational Psychology* 51(1960): 47–51.

41. M. Deutsch, "Minority Group and Class Status as Related to Social and Personality Factors in Scholastic Achievement," monograph No. 2 (Ithaca, New York: Society for Applied Anthropology, Cornell University, 1960).

42. D. P. Ausubel and P. Ausubel, "Ego Development Among Segregated Negro Children," *Education in Depressed Areas, op. cit.;* E. S. Battle and J. B. Rotter, "Children's Feelings of Personal Control as Related to Social Class and Ethnic Group," *Journal of Personality* 31(1963):482–90; R. M. Goff, "Some Educational Implications of the Influence of Rejection on Aspiration Levels of Minority Group Children," *Journal of Experimental Education* 23(1954): 179–83; S. Keller, *op. cit.;* Dreger and Miller, *op. cit.*

43. T. B. Edwards and S. W. Webster, "Correlates and Effects of Ethnic Group Identification," *Research Relating to Children,* Bulletin No. 17, U.S. Department of Health, Education and Welfare, Welfare Administration, Children's Bureau (Washington: Government Printing Office, 1963), p. 85.

44. R. C. Wylie, "Children's Estimates of Their Schoolwork. Ability as a Function of Sex, Race, and Socioeconomic Level," *Journal of Personality* 31(1963): 203–24.

45. B. Bernstein, "Language and Social Class," *British Journal of Sociology* 11 (1960):271–76.

46. W. Glasser, *Reality Therapy* (New York: Harper and Row, 1965).

47. A. Ellis, *Reason and Emotion in Psychotherapy* (New York: Lyle Stuart, 1967).

48. R. R. Carkhuff, *The Development of Human Resources: Education, Psychology and Social Change* (New York: Holt, Rinehart, and Winston, 1971).

49. E. W. Gordon and D. Wilkerson, *Compensatory Education for the Disadvantaged: Programs and Practices, Preschool through College* (New York: College Entrance Examination Board, 1966), pp. 25–26.

SUGGESTED READING

Coleman, J. L. *Resources for Social Change. Race in the United States.* New York: John Wiley and Sons, Inc., 1971. "The problem to which this essay is addressed is a very general one in all societies, though more acute in some than others. It is the problem of how a distinct subgroup in society, with little power and without direct resources for gaining more power, can nevertheless come to gain those resources" (p. 1).

Ginzberg, E. *Career Guidance: Who Needs It, Who Provides It, Who Can Improve It.* New York: McGraw-Hill Book Company, 1971. Ginzberg and his research group, the Conservation of Human Resources Project, Columbia University, have investigated the socioeconomic factors determining the opportunities and constraints that people encounter when establishing and implementing their career plans, as well as the effects of the processes of psychological growth and development on the activity of the individual and his planning for the future with regard to his career.

Through the assessment of the present guidance function and guidance personnel, associated problems and inadequacies are presented along with a strong statement of recommendations for the future, which focus upon community, institutional, and governmental reform with respect to the functions and goals of career guidance.

Ginzberg, E., and Hiestand, D. L. "The Guidance of Negro Youth," *Employment, Race, and Poverty,* A. M. Ross, and H. Hill, eds., New York: Harcourt, Brace and World, 1967, pp. 435–59. This essay considers the conditions and circumstances in which black youngsters grow up in terms of family background, income, education, location, and occupational trends. It then discusses the kinds of assistance which are likely to prove most effective in finding and taking advantage of better employment opportunities.

Katz, I. and Gurin, P. *Race and the Social Sciences.* New York: Basic Books, 1969. The authors present an inventory of what research in the various social sciences reveals about the current state of knowledge on the problem of racial inequality. An interdisciplinary effort is made to develop coordinated research strategies that take into account the interaction of psychological, social, political, and economic factors. Hypotheses for public policy are suggested, and a wide range of methodologies for testing them are discussed.

Lewis, H. "Culture, Class, Poverty, and Urban Schooling," *Reaching the Disadvantaged Learner,* A. H. Passow, ed. New York: Teachers College Press, 1970. Educational planning must be based on more valid information about the poor and their behaviors, as well as about school personnel and their behaviors toward low-income families. The article argues for understanding the differences which exist among poor families, the bases and significance of these differences, and the collective life which evolves around such differences.

Mink, O. G., and Kaplan, B. A. *America's Problem Youth. Education and Guidance of the Disadvantaged.* Scranton, Pa.: International Textbook Co., 1970. Based on a series of workshops designed for school personnel desiring to improve educational programs for disadvantaged youth, this publication addresses itself to the questions of severity and dimension of deprivation and to strategies and approaches for alleviating this deprivation. Included chapters are "Difficulties in 'Helping' the 'Disadvantaged,'" "Innovating Educational Practice for Disadvantaged Youth," and "Behavioral Counseling and the Total Educational Environment."

19 Vocational Guidance and the Handicapped

David B. Hershenson
Illinois Institute of Technology

Lofquist and Dawis[1] observed that American society makes special provision for free, public vocational guidance services for only two groups, the handicapped and the poor. By recent (1969) estimates, the handicapped constitute approximately 9 percent of the working-age population,[2] and those living at or below the poverty level constitute approximately 8 percent of that population.[3] Since there is considerable overlap between the conditions of poverty and being handicapped, we are probably talking about a group which constitutes some 12 percent or less of the working-age population. There appear to be two rationales on which the decision to provide vocational guidance to this relatively small proportion of the population has been based: the economic and the humanitarian.

The economic rationale asserts that it is cheaper for society to spend money making these groups financially self-sufficient than to continue to support them at public expense. Further, the program can even be considered self-supporting through the taxes paid by those who are served by it and consequently enter or are restored to gainful employment. Conley[4] presented evidence relevant to this argument and concluded that the money expended in rehabilitating the handicapped through the state-federal vocational rehabilitation program is recouped through reductions in welfare payments and taxes paid by rehabilitants in two to five years, so that the program yields a return of somewhere between one and a half and five times its cost, depending on the basis for figuring certain items. It may be pointed out, however, that the economic argument loses some cogency in an economy in which a high rate of unemployment exists, for there is little financial benefit to be derived for the society through spending money to turn unemployables into unemployed.

The humanitarian rationale is based on the belief that being economically self-supporting is necessary for individual self-respect. The view is particularly cogent in a democratic society, wherein the dignity of the individual is a basic tenet. Although some elements of American society are today calling this value orientation into question, there is little doubt that the dominant majority still relate personal worth to economic self-sufficiency. An interesting but unanswered question exists as to whether the poor and the handicapped share this belief in the same proportions as the general population or whether, having been systematically excluded from employment, they have found other bases on which to establish their identities.

Prior to the rationales developed by any given society to justify offering vocational guidance services to its handicapped members, Jaques and Hershenson[5] suggest that certain conditions must exist in the society to create a climate that allows for such services. These conditions are sufficient affluence to allow the society to tolerate and sustain potentially nonproductive members, and sufficient division of labor to offer jobs in which the disabled can function and to provide a discrete work role for counselors.

WHAT IS DISABILITY?

Two sets of terms which have suffered from confusion and inexactitude of definition are "handicap"/"handicapped" and "disability"/"disabled." To arrive at a working definition of these terms it is necessary to review both the concepts and the categories employed in talking about people who are generally characterized by these terms. Nagi[6] offers one useful frame of reference in suggesting a set of five concepts for research purposes: "active pathology" for the disease process resulting from infection, trauma, metabolic imbalance, or other causes; "impairments" for anatomical or physiological abnormalities and losses; "functional limitations" for impairments which affect an individual's ability to perform his or her usual or expected roles; "sickness" or "illness" as the behavioral response to the presence of pathology (the former being the response to acute, short-term conditions and the latter being the response to chronic, long-term conditions); and "disability" for the behavioral response to long-term functional limitations. For the vocational counselor, however, probably three concepts should suffice to describe the handicapped clients with whom he will work: "chronic condition" may refer to the long-term impact of the disease process on the individual's physical and/or mental integrity (for example, an amputated foot); "functional limitation" may refer to the consequent reduction in capacity to carry out activities of living; and "adjustment" may refer to the individual's mode of coping physically and emotionally with his "chronic condition" and its resultant "functional limitation." Thus, a person who suffers a mild heart attack may have to make almost no adjustment to physical functional limitations but may be extremely worried about the exacerbation of his chronic condition, while an amputee whose amputation resulted from an accident would usually have more concern about his functional limitations than he would have about further amputations. Moreover, the quality of the individual's adjustment may affect both his chronic condition (worrying about ulcers makes them worse) and his functional limitations (concerns about "doing too much in the light of his condition" may restrict the individual's activities more than need be the case).

Chronic conditions may be categorized along a number of parameters. In the first place, they may be physical, intellectual (e.g., mental retardation), emotional, or sociocultural (which are particularly dealt with in Chapter 18). Typically, chronic conditions are divided into those which are congenital and those which are acquired after birth. From the standpoint of vocational counseling, probably a more significant distinction could be made between those which occur before an individual seriously approaches a career decision and those which occur after that time. Thus, it generally makes less difference whether an individual was born deaf or became deaf in early childhood than it does whether she was deaf before deciding to become a musician or became deaf after she had already entered that career. Chronic conditions also may be divided into self-limiting ones and progressive ones. Thus, a traumatic amputation presents a fairly stable prognosis, and there is usually no reason to anticipate further deterioration. Multiple sclerosis or muscular dystrophy, however, are conditions in which further deterioration may almost always be expected. Therefore, an attempt to aid a client with such conditions must take this prognosis into account. Chronic conditions also may be classified as visible or covert. Being restricted to a wheelchair as a result of quadriplegia constitutes a visible condition that an outside observer will notice and react to in certain ways (some helpful and some disconcerting). However, diabetes, heart disease, or any of a wide range of other chronic conditions affecting internal organs are covert and present a different variety of reactions by the afflicted individual and others. For example, the man with a heart condition which prevents him from climbing stairs may encounter conflict and negative reactions from those around him when he enters an elevator containing a sign saying, "If you are only going one flight, please walk," and he presses the button for the adjacent floor. Functional limitations may be similarly divided into those which are vocationally relevant and those which are not. Thus, loss of a leg may well be vocationally irrelevant to an accountant or other sedentary worker but may be vocationally highly relevant to an athlete, dancer, or mailman. The vocational relevance of a functional limitation may be indirect, rather than direct, as in the case of a salesman who suffers a facial disfigurement. He may still do his job in exactly the same way as before, but customers may react to him differently.

THE INCIDENCE OF DISABILITY

The set of concepts which has just been presented is an extremely complex, interrelated one which creates all sorts of problems in approaching the issue of disability. It may be argued that even the most perfect specimen of mankind is functionally limited because he cannot fly like a bird, swim like a fish, or run like a deer (or, for that matter, bear a child like a woman), but this argument may be turned around to the position that no one except a total "basket case" should be qualified as "disabled" since the individual still possesses some residual capacities. One place where these apparently spurious extreme positions influence significant practices is in reporting statistics on the prevalence of the disabled. Thus, figures reported by no two sources correspond exactly with each other, since each source employs a different definition, the choice of which is frequently influenced by whether the purposes of the reporting agency would be best served by maximizing or minimizing the incidence of that disability group.

One current source[7] reports the total number of people in this country afflicted in some degree by disabling conditions as follows (only categories including a million or more persons are listed here in descending order of magnitude): heart and circulatory disorders, 26,200,000 (of whom 12,670,000 suffer from hypertensive heart disease, 8,370,000 from hypertension without heart disease, 3,650,000 from coronary heart disease, 2,000,000 from strokes, and 1,510,000 from rheumatic heart disease); mental and emotional disorders, 20,000,000; arthritis and rheumatic diseases, 16,000,000 to 17,000,000; alcoholism, 9,000,000; hearing impairments, 8,549,000 (of whom 236,000 are totally deaf); mental retardation, 6,000,000; visual impairments, 5,390,000 (of whom 421,250 are legally blind); diabetes mellitus, 4,000,000; neurological disorders, between 3.3 and 4.3 million (of whom between 1,000,000 and 2,000,000 suffer from epilepsy, 1,000,000 from Parkinsonism, 600,000 from cerebral palsy, 500,000 from multiple sclerosis and related diseases, and 200,000 from muscular dystrophy); and cancer (now under treatment), 940,000. This same source reports that half the population of the United States has digestive complaints, which are the leading cause of hospitalization and loss of work time; and in 1967 and 1968 there were 249,037,000 episodes of infectious diseases, of which over 132,092,000 required medical attention and which caused 130,404,000 days lost from work. It should be noted that the figures cited above are drawn from a variety of governmental and voluntary agency sources which may have different motives (e.g., raising funds, getting attention, etc.) and bases for determining their estimates. Further, these figures are based on the total population of the country and not just those of working age. The same individuals also may appear in more than one category.

In 1966 the Social Security Administration[8] surveyed 17,753,000 disabled adults between the ages of 18 and 64, that is, of working age. In this study the incidence of major disabling conditions, in descending order of magnitude, is as follows. (Only categories involving 300,000 or more are given here. It should also be noted that in these figures each individual is counted only once under his principal disability. However, some individuals may actually suffer from several of these conditions, none of which alone might have been sufficient to have rendered him "disabled.") The number disabled by arthritis, rheumatism, and back and spine impairments was 5,492,000; cardiovascular disorders (heart trouble, hypertension, etc.), 4,408,000; respiratory and related disorders (asthma, allergies, chronic bronchitis, TB, emphysema, etc.), 1,986,000; digestive disorders (stomach ulcer, hernia, etc.), 1,284,000; mental disorders, 1,114,000; nervous system disorders, 922,000; endocrine-metabolic disorders (diabetes, thyroid, etc.), 690,000; visual impairments and deafness, 620,000; urogenital disorders, 451,000; and cancer, 301,000.

Finally, one may look at the distribution of disabilities among those who were habilitated or rehabilitated for work. In the fiscal year 1964 119,708 such individuals were officially reported.[9] Of that number the following (again presented in descending order of magnitude) constituted the categories including over 1,000 cases: orthopedic deformities or impairments, 33,241 (of which 3,854 involved upper extremities, 12,151 involved lower extremities, 12,074 involved both upper and lower extremities and the trunk, and 5,162 others); mental and emotional problems, 13,863 (of which 9,769 were psychotic and neurotic and 4,094 were personality or behavior disorders); visual impairments, 11,919 (of which 5,013 were total blindness); amputation or absence of extremities, 9,187 (of which 2,471 involved upper extremities, 6,640 involved lower extremities, and 76 involved both); hearing impairments, 7,376 (of which 2,243 were deaf and two-thirds unable to talk); mental retardation, 7,206; cardiac diseases, 5,215; TB and pulmonary problems, 4,581; epilepsy, 2,363; and speech impairments, 1,422. It should be pointed out that in these figures, again, any one individual may appear in only one category.

Despite the evident problems attendant on comparing data based on different assumptions, it is of interest to examine the differences in ranking of magnitude of disabilities reported by the three sources discussed above. As may be seen in Table 19.1, there is a considerable difference among the rankings based on incidence in the total population, incidence in the working-age population, and incidence in the successfully treated working-age population.

Table 19.1   Rank Order of Top Ten Disabling Conditions in United States by Reporting Category

Afflicted in general population (compiled 1971; most data from 1969)[7]	Incidence in disabled of working age (1966)[8]	Incidence among habilitated and rehabilitated (1964)[9]
1. Cardiovascular disorders	Arthritic, rheumatic and orthopedic diseases	Orthopedic impairments
2. Mental & emotional disorders	Cardiovascular disorders	Mental and emotional disorders
3. Arthritis & rheumatic diseases	Respiratory disorders	Visual impairments
4. Alcoholism	Digestive disorders	Amputation or absence of limbs
5. Hearing impairments	Mental disorders	Hearing impairments
6. Mental retardation	Neurological disorders	Mental retardation
7. Visual impairments	Diabetes and other endocrine metabolic disorders	Cardiac diseases
8. Diabetes	Visual impairments	Respiratory disorders
9. Neurological disorders	Urogenital disorders	Epilepsy
10. Cancer	Cancer	Speech impairments

SOURCES: National Health Education Committee *Facts on the Major Killing and Crippling Diseases in the United States Today* (New York: National Health Education Committee, 1971). L. D. Haber, "Epidemiological Factors in Disability: I. Major Disabling Conditions," *Social Security Survey of the Disabled, 1966—* Report No. 6 (Washington: U.S. Department of Health, Education, and Welfare, 1969). J. S. Felton, D. C. Perkins, and M. Lewin, *A Survey of Medicine and Medical Practice for the Rehabilitation Counselor* (Washington, D.C.: U.S. Department of Health, Education, and Welfare, Vocational Rehabilitation Administration, 1966).

DIFFERENCES BETWEEN THE DISABLED POPULATION AND THE GENERAL POPULATION

Some of the differences between the general population and the working-age disabled may be accounted for by the greater incidence of certain conditions in individuals below the age of eighteen or over the age of sixty-four. Other differences between these two groups may be accounted for by the fact that certain chronic conditions existing in the general population are not specifically vocationally disabling; that is, in the terms discussed earlier in this section, they may represent chronic conditions which do not produce very many functional limitations or, conversely, they may represent less generally prevalent chronic conditions which produce a high incidence of functional limitations. Thus, many individuals with emotional problems are able to continue to work, which may in part account for such problems being second in prevalence in the general population but only fifth in prevalence among the disabled of working age.

Of possibly greater interest are the differences between the incidence of chronic conditions among those listed as "disabled" and those listed as "restored." In part, these differences may reflect the ease with which individuals with certain conditions may be restored to ability to work. This may work in two ways. In the first place, certain chronic conditions may not require the specialized professional services on which the reported incidence of rehabilitation is based. For example, many cardiac patients are able to return to their former jobs once their chronic condition has stabilized itself. Thus, the fact that cardiovascular conditions rank second in incidence but seventh in successful restoration may reflect the fact that many cardiac patients did not even need the treatment services that would put them in the "successfully treated" category. A similar phenomenon may exist for those with respiratory disorders who follow cardiac cases in both incidence and restoration. On the other hand, these differences in ranking may reflect the unique difficulties in treating or placing into employment individuals with certain chronic conditions.

The very prevalent prejudice against the hiring of epileptics by employers may well contribute to the fact that neurological disorders were sixth in incidence among those of working age, but epileptics were ninth in being successfully treated.

Another factor which influences differences between incidence and successful rehabilitation is the amount of attention and effort expended on behalf of the persons with different conditions. For example, the blind and visually handicapped have long constituted an active, vocal group which has produced special attention and services directed to their needs. This may contribute to the fact that visual impairments were eighth in incidence but third in successful treatment among those of working age. The same phenomenon may be occurring among those with mental disorders. Similarly, the existence of trained, effective speech pathologists may account for the fact that the speech-impaired, who are not present as one of the top ten groups of disabled, are nonetheless among the ten most successfully treated. Likewise, the presence of audiologists may account for the appearance of the hearing-impaired among those successfully treated but not among those most frequently disabled. Finally, economic pressures may contribute to rates of restoration, as in the case of amputees. About 75 percent of all new amputees are men, and among younger men the most frequent cause is trauma resulting from contact with high speed transportation or mechanized equipment.[10] As such, insurers press for the restoration of such individuals in order to reduce accident and workmen's compensation claims. In addition, of course, many amputees are easily restored to work.

World of Vocational Guidance

SOCIAL DEFINITION FOR TREATMENT

There is good reason to believe that political and economic considerations contribute as much to determining which groups get treated as does the prevalence of the disabling condition in the population or the likelihood of successful outcome with that group. Thus, as may be seen in Table 19.2, both the number and percentage of mentally ill and of retarded who were successfully treated rose steadily from 1945 to 1968.[11]

Table 19.2 Change over Time in Percentage of Total Successfully Rehabilitated in Certain Selected Disability Categories[11]

Disability Category	Fiscal Year		
	1945	1957	1968
Amputation and orthopedic	50%	39.5%	24%
Blind and other visual	12%	11%	9%
Deaf and other aural	7.5%	7%	6%
Mental illness	3%	4.5%	19.5%
Mental retardation	0.5%	2%	10.5%
Total number rehabilitated	41,925	70,940	207,918

SOURCE: Division of Statistics and Studies, Rehabilitation Services Administration, *Statistical History: Federal-State Program of Vocational Rehabilitation, 1920–1969* (Washington, D.C.: U.S. Department of Health, Education, and Welfare, Social and Rehabilitation Service, 1970), pp. 38 and 45.

These changes reflect changing legal definitions of what constitutes a handicap, which in turn reflect changing societal views. Jaques and Hershenson[12] pointed out that the terms "handicap" and "disability" are a special case of the concept of deviance and that deviance as a concept exists in all cultures and is a culture-relative phenomenon. Thus, among the ancient Romans and American Indians epilepsy was a divine gift, while in mechanized societies it is a disabling condition. In American society the general trend has been to widen the definition of "illness" and "disability" to include progressively more conditions. Thus, while the initial definition of disability concerned just the physically impaired, this was expanded progressively to include the emotionally disturbed, the retarded, alcoholics and addicts, the socially, economically, and educationally disadvantaged and legal offenders.

The reasons for this trend are many, among them a movement away from a fundamentalist belief that certain conditions are the stigmata one bears for one's evil nature or conduct toward a belief in environmentally caused problems and a need to legitimize the treatment of such conditions by existing interest groups. Thus, as long as doctors were fully occupied with the treatment of cases of mumps and measles, there was no reason for the medical profession to seek other concerns; however, once vaccines eliminated much of these conditions, the physicians required new foci of activity.[13] For these various reasons alcoholism was discovered to be an "illness" rather than the "curse" it had been accepted as before. This was required if the condition was to be brought within the domain of the medical profession, as physicians are only ethically and legally entitled to treat "illnesses." Similarly, vocational and rehabilitation counselors have sought to legitimize their role in working with a progressively wider scope of clients by expanding, in the directions outlined above, the definition of "the disabled"—that is, those with whom they are professionally entitled to work. Indeed, it requires no great powers of clairvoyance to predict that the retired and those with avocational concerns will be among the next groups to be legitimized for service by being declared "disabled," "handicapped," or the like.

At this point we are left with several options in defining "the disabled" or "the handicapped." One operational definition would be that a "disabled person" is anyone who is serviced or is entitled to be serviced by supportive, habilitative, or rehabilitative professionals. While this definition is probably the most accurate one in terms of an individual's initiation into the rolls of this formally recognized category and while it best reflects the changes in who is entitled to call himself "disabled," this definition lacks a certain amount of internal consistency. Thus, until the mid-1950s most individuals with emotional problems were "unfortunates" and most alcoholics were "derelicts," but thereafter, by legislative fiat, they became "disabled." An alternative definition would involve anyone afflicted with a chronic condition which creates functional limitations and/or adjustment problems in activities which he or she has performed or might reasonably expect to perform if free of that condition. This definition, while somewhat more internally consistent, allows for less accuracy of specification. For instance, the man who reaches age sixty-five (a chronic condition which can be expected to last at least a year) and is therefore forced to retire (a functional limitation in an activity which he has performed, possibly accompanied by adjustment problems) would qualify as "disabled" by this definition. Society and its agents, however, are not yet ready to classify such an individual as disabled. Recognizing these limitations, we must nonetheless arrive at a working definition. Since this chapter appears in a book concerned with vocational guidance, perhaps our definition should involve the insertion of the word "work" before the word "activities" in our last approximation, acknowledging that other words would have to be used if the topic of this book were physical education, psychopathology, or social adjustment.

THE IMPACT OF DISABILITY

In the light of the problems in defining concepts, it is not surprising that, despite considerable work in the field, few solid conclusions have been reached. In 1960 Wright[14] reviewed these studies and concluded that there was no substantial indication that persons with an impaired physique differ *as a group* from the rest of the population in their general adjustment, in personality patterns, or in attitudes toward disability; that is, the range of these characteristics is as great among the disabled as among the nondisabled. Further, she found no evidence of a consistent relationship between types of physical disability and personality characteristics. Virtually her only affirmative conclusion was that physical disability has a profound effect on a person's life, but that effect is not of any consistent kind. A decade later

Shontz[15] reviewed over 150 more recent studies and arrived at substantially the same conclusion—that neither the type nor the severity of physical disability relates systematically to the personality or adjustment of the disabled.

Acknowledging this apparently well-documented conclusion presents some interesting problems in attempting to formulate a consistent approach to vocational counseling with the handicapped. These problems become even more complex when one recognizes that there has been very little evidence found to support the hypothesis of occupationally specific personalities. The realities of the world of work appear to allow for a wide range of personality types within most occupations. Thus, a person-oriented individual may succeed as a research team leader in an ostensibly thing-oriented field such as engineering, or a thing-oriented person may find a place as an agency budget director in an ostensibly person-oriented field such as social work. The failure of most personality-specific vocational choice theories to produce supportive empirical findings (or at least findings that account for more than a few percent of the variance) is probably related to this fact. The question therefore arises that if the handicapped constitute such a diverse, internally heterogeneous group as to functional limitations and personality types, and if the world of work allows for a wide range of abilities and temperaments in most jobs, are there any unique considerations in vocational guidance with the handicapped? The conclusion of the writer is that there are probably very few unique considerations, and most of these could profitably be applied to nonhandicapped clients in working with them. There are, however, certain differences in emphasis which have traditionally existed, although whether these differences actually are relevant to the presence or absence of a handicap is another matter. Let us now look at these particular foci and then consider how they apply in the vocational guidance process.

VOCATIONAL DEVELOPMENT OF THE HANDICAPPED

For a topic of such major concern in terms of availability of services, relatively little has been written on the vocational development of the handicapped. It is of interest that the final report of a two-week workshop on the "Implications of Career Development Theory and Research for Counselor Education,"[16] held in 1967, indicates that those in elementary school counseling and those in rehabilitation counseling could find little in the far-ranging readings and presentations on career development of relevance to their concerns, while those in high school and college counseling could. However, a few directly relevant studies do exist. At the career choice stage Allen[17] found that when matched for cumulative grade-point average and father's occupational level, physically disabled high school seniors did not differ significantly from their nondisabled classmates in the amount of discrepancy between their occupational aspirations and expectations. (Without matching, the disabled were lower in grades and in level of father's occupation and higher in aspiration-expectation discrepancy than the nondisabled.)

Concerning those who experience the onset of disability in mid-career, McDaniel[18] reviewed the applicability of the vocational development theories of Roe, Ginzberg, Super, and Tiedeman and concluded that the last of these had the greatest relevance. He identified four considerations which should be particularly emphasized in employing Tiedeman's theory to conceptualize the rate and direction of vocational redevelopment of the mid-career disabled. These were the individual's premorbid vocational, personal, and social experiences, the nature of the disabling factors, the number and kinds of concepts and decisions which the individual had to modify, and the types of assistance and information which were available to him. Finally, looking at the late career stages (ages fifty-five and over) of disabled workers, Rusalem[19] found that many held a series of short-term jobs, which he hypothesized to be analogous to the "floundering period" of youth who enter the labor market because it educates the person to his new vocational status.

In suggesting a framework for viewing alternatives in vocational development, Lo Cascio[20] proposed three patterns: continuous (or essentially unimpeded), delayed, and impaired. Super[21] suggested the relevance of this conceptualization to the disabled but reduced the distinction to one between continuous and discontinuous developmental patterns. The onset of a disability generally creates a discontinuity in career development, particularly if it occurs in mid-career. Allen's[22] data, however, based on a group who experienced disability at a precareer stage, suggests the absence of significantly greater incidence of discontinuities among the precareer disabled as compared to nondisabled individuals at the same level of vocational development.

At this point the writer would like to suggest a model for vocational behavior which, while developed with reference to the general population, appears to have particular applicability to the handicapped. This model utilizes five constructs: the individual's background (physical and psychosocial), his work personality (his constellation of psychological traits and attitudes which mediate adaptation to work), his work competences, his work choice, and his work adjustment (the satisfaction with his working behavior by himself and others). Thus, at any given time, his background partly determines his work personality, work competences, and work choice. These three also influence each other, and the output of this system is his work adjustment. A diagrammatic representation of this model is presented in Figure 19.1. Each of these constructs involves several elements. The work personality involves the person's self-concept as a worker and his work motivation. Work competences include work-adaptive behaviors, job-related skills, and interpersonal abilities in the work setting. Work choice concerns the appropriateness and degree of formulation of the person's career plans, particularly as represented in his current job. Finally, adopting the terminology of the Minnesota Studies in Vocational Rehabilitation,[23] the individual's work adjustment consists of his satisfaction and satisfactoriness as a worker.

If the person's career is conceptualized as a three-dimensional column, the third dimension being time, then the model shown in Figure 19.1 represents the slice out of this column at any point in time. To relate this to our prior discussion, functional limitations would most directly affect work competences, and adjustment to disability would relate most directly to work personality. There is rarely, if ever, a total discontinuity, although the extent of a discontinuity depends on the number and magnitude of readjustments which must be made in the elements within the square. The considerations suggested above by McDaniel as relevant to Tiedeman's theory apply here

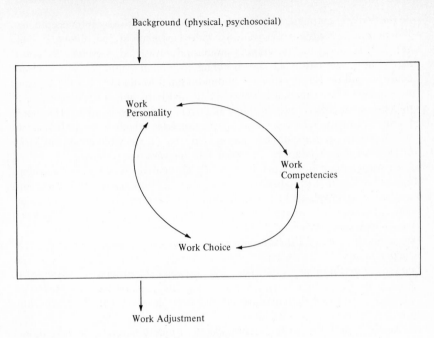

Figure 19.1 A Model of Work Behavior

as well. On the basis of available evidence, these readjustments are idiosyncratic and involve the prior nature of the elements and their interrelationships, how far down the career-time column the event of disability is introduced, and its specific impact on the elements in the system. It should be noted that the event of disability is merely one of a number of possible events which can be treated in essentially the same way. Forced retirement, work layoffs, and technological changes in jobs all can produce similar effects in the system, as can a sudden or matured decision to alter one's career. Indeed, within this model the experiences of the handicapped and nonhandicapped should shed light on each other to contribute to an overall theory of career development.

This chapter has consistently presented the view that no specific effect of particular disabilities on adjustment can be assumed to exist. There are, however, certain fairly consistent functional limitations associated with particular chronic conditions. These generally affect work competence, and if they are of sufficient magnitude, they may spread in effect to work personality and/or work choice. For instance, lower-limb amputees should avoid jobs which require climbing ladders; individuals confined to wheelchairs must work in locations with appropriate access and toilet facilities; those with degenerative diseases must assume a decreasing supply of energy and range of activity in planning their vocational future; and those whose conditions may be worsened by stress (for example, some tubercular cases, ulcer and colitis cases, certain epileptics, and emotional problems) should seek job roles which minimize this factor; those with cardiac conditions must adjust their jobs to their work classification status, and so on. A number of books exist which provide information and standards relevant to these considerations. (See the suggested readings at the end of this chapter.) The other side of this coin, however, is equally important, for there are relatively few occupations which are totally closed to all individuals with any given chronic condition. For instance, the blind can be found in most fields, including law and proof reading (of braille). Where specific exclusions exist, they are as often the result of limitations imposed by workmen's compensation insurers as they are the result of limitations imposed by the individual's condition. Essentially, the area of vocational development of the handicapped is as much a psychology of individual differences as is the vocational development of the nonhandicapped.

It is of interest that through the period from 1945 to 1968 the percentage of the total annual number of rehabilitants entering professional, technical, and managerial occupations remained stable at about 9 to 10 percent; those entering clerical and sales fields dropped from about 20 to 15 percent; those entering industrial occupations fell from 55 to 30 percent, and those entering service occupations rose from 8 to 24 percent.[24] These figures follow the general trends of the national labor market, indicating further that the differences between the handicapped and nonhandicapped are smaller than the differences within each of these groups.

To carry this point further, a recent review of the 139 job placements made by one New York agency between 1965 and 1970[25] demonstrates the range of occupations within which the handicapped have been successfully placed. In this report quadriplegics were placed in positions such as management, rate clerk, and programmer; paraplegics were placed as estimators, purchasing agents, personnel assistants, clerks, and diamond cutters; cerebral palsy cases as varitypists, record clerks, case investigators, and college instructors; amputees as construction foremen, occupational therapy aides, and distribution specialists; left hemiplegics as accountants, collection clerks, and manuscript readers; right hemiplegics as draftsmen and bookkeepers; multiple sclerosis cases as precision technicians, architects, and economics research assistants; muscular dystrophy cases as loan clerks, claims examiners, and medical records clerks; and others (including arthritis, neurological, and plastic surgery cases) as film editors, scale makers, switchboard operators and adjudication clerks.

There is, of course, another side to the coin of work performance by the handicapped, and that is the willingness of employers to hire them. McDaniel[26] has reviewed the studies on this issue, and several conclusions clearly emerge. First, employers show different degrees of willingness to hire individuals with different sorts of disabilities. These differences in willingness are in part related to notions about the relationship between the functional limitations typically associated with a given chronic condition and the tasks required in the performance of a given job. They are also in part related to preconceptions about and prejudice against the handicapped. Thus, McDaniel reported a survey made in New York City, in which firms in a range of industries were both willing to hire and had hired significantly more individuals with orthopedic or cardiac conditions than epileptics, visually impaired, or cerebral palsy cases. It was subsequently pointed out by several reviewers of this survey that these findings correspond with those on general public attitudes toward the disabled, in which stronger negative reactions are expressed toward more highly visible functional limitations. Of further interest in this study was the finding that employers who had past experience with disabled workers were more favorably inclined toward hiring them in the future. Of course, this finding may say as much about initial predisposition as it does about the effects of experience on attitude change. McDaniel also reviewed a series of six studies on employer attitude toward hiring individuals with cardiac conditions. These studies were done between 1955 and 1965 and involved samples in Boston, New York, Chicago, Minneapolis-St. Paul, Los Angeles, and a national sample. Sample size ranged from 18 to 436 employers, with a median of 100. In all six studies only two reasons were uniformly given for not hiring workers with cardiac conditions: workmen's compensation limitations and the cost of benefits for such individuals. In only half the samples were concerns about productivity given as a major reason for discriminating against such workers.

Thus, one may conclude, at best, that the handicapped as a group of workers represent a wide range of capacities and adaptations which must face an equally wide range of employer responses toward allowing them to work. Hence, it falls upon the vocational counselor to assist the individual from this group to recognize his uniqueness by identifying capacities, achieving adaptation, and mobilizing the opportunity structure. For any counselor these tasks should be familiar.

VOCATIONAL GUIDANCE FOR THE HANDICAPPED: TRADITIONAL ELEMENTS

One of the great difficulties which pervades the field of vocational guidance is the wide gap between most theories of vocational development and their applicability to vocational guidance practice. The majority of vocational development theories make no attempt to relate themselves to guidance applications but stand as clear of such considerations as many personality theories do of counseling in general. It is the the admittedly biased conclusion of the writer that this gap has impeded the development of a coherent approach to vocational guidance or counseling (at least since the work of Frank Parsons), but, rather what exists is a *potpourri* of principles and techniques drawn largely from the general field of counseling and indiscriminately applied to individuals with vocational problems. If this is true and if our prior conclusion that the handicapped are not systematically different from other persons is true, there is no need to be surprised at the lack of any systematic vocational guidance approach in their case. There have been, however, a number of specific techniques which were developed or selectively applied to assist the handicapped in their career development. The greatest value of these may well lie in their applicability to the population as a whole, rather than merely to that segment whose particular deviance has been declared a handicap. Traditionally, vocational guidance contains at least three elements: evaluation, occupational information, and counseling. Sometimes the fourth element of job placement is added, and more rarely the fifth element of adjustment to the job on which the client has been placed. Vocational guidance with the handicapped has utilized all of these and added certain special services which are unique to this group, such as sheltered workshops and work adjustment programs.

The evaluation process with handicapped clients has followed two lines. The first is the traditional psychometric measures of abilities, aptitudes, interests and personality. One review[27] of such studies with a classical instrument, the Strong Vocational Interest Blank, indicated little work and fewer conclusions in its use with the physically handicapped. These findings were attributed largely to the heterogeneous nature of the physically handicapped as a group. With the emotionally disordered the major consideration found to limit the validity of this instrument was the lack of self-awareness of many having this condition. (There was generally sufficient reality contact to allow these individuals to carry out the test task.) A perusal of the psychometric literature indicates an almost total absence of standardized tests which provide norms for the disabled as a group or for specific types of disability. This state of affairs may well suggest that the conclusions drawn concerning the Strong apply equally to other instruments. An alternative approach, which was developed initially with reference to the handicapped, is that of work samples. Starting with the "TOWER" system developed by the Institute for the Crippled and Disabled in 1959, a variety of work-sample batteries have been constructed which abstract the evaluation process less from actual job performance than do paper-and-pencil tests. Thus, work performance can be evaluated in context, and the subject's attitude toward a real-world work task (for example, typing a paragraph, assembling a ladder, totaling an invoice, etc.) can be seen. Moreover, these tasks can be presented in a simulated work environment (established working-time periods, using a timer, allowing coffee breaks, etc.) through which work elements such as dependability and relations with supervisors and coworkers can be evaluated. In this way, the capacity of functionally limited individuals to compensate for their limitation can particularly be assessed. Several recent systems of this sort are the work-sample battery developed by the Philadelphia Jewish Vocational Service and the M.O.V.E. battery developed by the Chicago Goodwill Industries. The applications of these approaches have already been extended beyond the physically, intellectually, and emotionally handicapped to economically and educationally disadvantaged individuals, and there is every reason to foresee their eventual use with all individuals seeking vocational guidance (for example, in counseling for the selection of a vocational education program).

Another element traditionally associated with the practice of vocational guidance is the use of occupational information. It is of interest to note that the N.V.G.A. guidelines for the preparation and evaluation of occupational information make no mention of including information on the appropriateness or employment opportunities in the occupation for individuals with specific functional limitations. Thus, it rests upon the counselor to interpolate these considerations when presenting occupational information to disabled clients. It is further incumbent upon the counselor to be aware of opportunities specifically reserved for certain groups of disabled, such as the jobs as newsstand operators in most federal buildings, which are reserved for the blind, or the special program for placing the retarded in civil service jobs. Disabled clients should also receive information about the availability of services through public or voluntary organizations specifically concerned with their particular chronic condition, such as the Epilepsy Foundation, the National Association for Mental Health, organizations for the blind, deaf, and neurologically impaired (cerebral palsy, multiple sclerosis, etc.), and so on. Many of these agencies provide information on jobs for individuals who are victims of the condition with which the organization is concerned.

The third generally accepted element in the vocational guidance process is the counseling relationship. It is of interest how little has been written which differentiates the counseling process in vocational guidance from counseling to any other end. Many of the authors who acknowledge the unique existence of a vocational counseling function (for example, Bordin, Brammer and Shostom, and Krumboltz and Thoreson,[28] who represent such diverse orientations as developmental, actualization, and behavioral counseling) assert that it is merely a particular case to which their general orientation is applicable. There have been few writers since Parsons who have been brash enough to assert that vocational guidance is a sufficiently unique process to require its own formulation of the counseling relationship. Among these few are Samler, Thoroman, and the writer of this chapter.[29] However, the weight of opinion has clearly been to the contrary, so that most vocational counselors operate as adherents to a general school of counseling (be it client-centered, psychoanalytic, Adlerian, behavioral, eclectic, or any other). Consequently, the self-fulfilling prophecy has been established which denies the uniqueness of vocational counseling or the need to investigate it as an independent entity.

Since there is little that is specifically relevant to vocational counseling as an independent process in the counseling literature, it is not surprising that relatively little exists on its applicability to the handicapped. Probably the one issue which has received the most attention in this area is whether vocational counselors working with the handicapped (particularly those employed in state-federal rehabilitation programs) should devote more attention to coordinating adjunctive services or to developing a supportive or therapeutic relationship with the client. In the view of many in the field,[30] this is a spurious issue because it is in practice partially predetermined by the aims, structure, and size of caseload of the agency in which the counselor is employed, and it should ultimately be determined within this context by an evaluation of the needs of the particular client. In any case, it would appear that the counseling process in vocational guidance with the handicapped, regardless of its composition or orientation, must focus largely on the question of *adjustment* to chronic condition and/or functional limitation, particularly as related to work. Toward this aim, all the elements usually present in vocational counseling must be brought into consideration (personality, abilities, interests, available options, goals, etc.) as influenced by the issue of adjustment to handicap. The influence of this latter issue varies from client to client, more on the basis of the nature of the client than on the basis of the nature of the chronic condition or the functional limitations it imposes. To date, probably slightly more attention has been paid in the literature to differences between vocational counseling with handicapped and nonhandicapped clients than has been paid to differences between vocational and other forms of counseling. If our prior conclusions concerning the equality of range of adjustment by handicapped and nonhandicapped is valid, it may be concluded that the emphasis of the literature has been misplaced.

VOCATIONAL GUIDANCE FOR THE HANDICAPPED: NEW DIMENSIONS

In addition to the three traditional areas of evaluation, information, and counseling, vocational guidance for the handicapped has more frequently extended to placement and after-care than has been the case with other clients. Vocational counselors have frequently sought to shy away from these areas, both out of the conviction that they should focus on intrapsychic problems and out of their discomfort with the salesmanship aspects of the placement role. Aside from the usual practices of locating jobs or job-producing resources and convincing employers of the work potential of their clients, vocational guidance with the handicapped has promoted the development of several original placement strategies. Among these are the techniques of job engineering or structuring jobs to the capacities of workers. These involve the analysis of jobs into their component activities or tasks and the reassembly of these components into jobs which an individual with a particular functional limitation can perform. Thus, two jobs, both of which require sitting, inspecting, lifting, and carrying, might be restructured into one job requiring sitting and complex inspecting, which would be open to an individual in a wheelchair, and another job requiring lifting and carrying, which would be open to a retarded person. However, without the job restructuring, both jobs would have been closed to both these people.

To gain acceptance of this approach by employers it is frequently incumbent on the counselor to demonstrate that the jobs as restructured lead to greater economy or productivity. A major proponent of this approach is Sidney Fine,[31] whose work on task analysis is seminal to this area. Closely related to this is the need for the counselor to keep abreast of the rapidly changing nature of jobs even when their occupational titles remain static. Thus, as automation is introduced into an industry, certain jobs are so altered that a particular functional limitation is no longer a bar to performing the job. Further, equipment used on a job can frequently be modified at small cost to compensate for an individual's functional limitation. Thus, machine tools can be equipped with jigs in which an individual with a perceptual-motor impairment may place the part to be machined, and he may consequently be able to turn out the finished product with equal or better speed and less spoilage than a nonhandicapped worker. Finally, the unique functional advantage of certain disabilities can be capitalized on, such as the value of using deaf workers in noisy areas, where they will neither be distracted nor injured by the noise.

In evaluating a handicapped client for entry into the labor market two concepts are useful: "placeability" and "employability." These refer, respectively, to the ease with which a client can successfully negotiate the hiring process and his ability to keep the job once he is hired. A client with a facial disfigurement may have problems with placeability but once placed may have few problems with employability. To a large extent, placeability reflects the attitudes of the personnel manager toward the client's disability, while employability reflects the attitudes of the client's supervisor and coworkers. It may well be incumbent on the counselor to try to modify these individuals' attitudes in order to get and maintain a job for a handicapped client.

Certain specialized techniques have been employed to help handicapped clients adjust to their jobs once they have been hired. One of these is a "buddy system" by which an experienced coworker with a similar functional limitation is assigned to a new employee to aid him in his adaptation. For example, a deaf worker who has performed a particular job may be better able to instruct a new deaf employee through signing than could any set of detailed written instructions or miming by a hearing person, as there is some evidence that the linguistic and thought structure underlying signing differs from speech. The use of follow-up group counseling for handicapped workers may assist them in making adjustments to their jobs by letting them see that the reactions to their presence on a job is not unique to themselves but is to some extent shared by other disabled workers in other settings. The group may provide both support and suggestions to help them cope with the adjustment to the job and to the reactions of coworkers. Several agencies working with physically or mentally or intellectually handicapped clients have adopted the use of "job coaches" from the manpower programs developed to assist disadvantaged persons. The "coaches" assist the client in such things as learning how to get to work, learning to be prompt and reliable, learning how to do the job tasks, and learning how to budget their wages.

Because of the special problems in learning to perform certain job tasks associated with certain functional limitations, special services have been developed to assist the handicapped. The most common of these are sheltered workshops[32] and vestibule training programs. Sheltered workshops may be divided into transitional and terminal shops. Transitional shops evaluate and prepare handicapped clients for entry into competitive employment, while terminal shops provide job opportunities for individuals whose functional limitations are too great to allow much hope for their becoming employable through the open labor market. It is of interest that two principal orientations tend to exist in transitional workshops. Some workshops (more frequently those on the East Coast) view their role as developing employability by concentrating on the client's self-concept as a worker. Their view is that if the client develops a positive self-concept as a worker, his productivity will increase. The other orientation (more commonly found in West Coast workshops) involves a focus on productivity, with the underlying theory being that if the worker can achieve industrial norms of productivity, his self-concept as a worker will improve. In both instances, however, the aim of the workshop is to improve both the client's self-image as a worker and his work productivity. There is a lack of adequate studies comparing the relative effectiveness of the two approaches with clients of different types, although it seems reasonable to hypothesize that for clients with different sorts of functional limitations and adjustments these two approaches will be differentially effective.

Recently an alternative type of work adaptation procedure has evolved. This is known as "vestibule training," in which the client is evaluated and made work-ready right in the job setting that he will eventually occupy. The arguments in favor of this approach are that it allows a more realistic evaluation than is possible in the simulated environment of the workshop, it allows the handicapped worker and his eventual coworkers to adjust to each other earlier and under supervised control, and it requires only one adaptation for the client instead of two (first to the workshop and then to the job). This technique appears to have potential for use with nonhandicapped clients as well.

THE FUTURE OF VOCATIONAL GUIDANCE FOR THE HANDICAPPED

As was pointed out at the start of this chapter, more than 90 percent of the working-age population in this country have no vocationally relevant functional limitation. Nonetheless, a huge superstructure of laws, state-federal rehabilitation programs, government and private agencies, and professional organizations has been constructed to assist the handicapped in their vocational adjustment. The profession of rehabilitation counseling established its identity on this mission, and every year several thousand counselors are trained in this field at the graduate level. If one seeks the motivation behind this massive effort, at least four reasons come to mind. First, for many handicapped individuals work is an economic necessity. For many, special help is required to allow them to compensate for their particular functional limitation, which may affect their ability to perform activities of daily living, even if it does not necessarily limit their working. This help is often expensive. Second, in our society working is viewed as an appropriate behavior for adults and not working is not (regardless of the difficulty or lack of economic compulsion). In our social context work is an accepted way of structuring time, of providing social interactions, and of gaining an identity. To keep an individual away from work is tantamount to subjecting him to sensory deprivation. Third, because of the functions of work in our society, it has been a personal requisite for attaining a sense of adequacy. Individuals (or at least those with a middle-class value orientation) feel compelled to work or, if not working, to offer rationales for their deviant behavior. Finally, in addition to its economic, social, and personal compulsions, work may be therapeutic. By providing structure, work may reduce or bind anxiety; by giving the worker a sense of purpose, it may reduce anomie; by demonstrating accomplishment, it may promote self-esteem; by proving his effectiveness as a worker, an individual may gain a sense of worth. Naturally, like any other adaptive process, it can be carried to a negative extreme and reduce itself to compulsive work or to a "marketing orientation" in which the individual's worth is based only on his productivity and the price that commands in money or esteem. Nonetheless, to the extent that an individual can demonstrate his adequacy in the work area, functional limitations in other areas may become more tolerable.

In looking to the future, three elements are worthy of consideration: the techniques of vocational guidance developed specifically for the handicapped which may be profitably applied to other clients, the implications of the experience of the handicapped for career development theory, and the implications for societal change. Throughout the prior section the general relevance of vocational guidance techniques developed particularly for use with handicapped clients has been noted. Work-sample evaluation procedures and vestibule training are two major examples. It would not appear to be overstating the case to assert that there has been no technique developed for use with the handicapped which does not have relevance to at least some other groups of vocational guidance clients, and all such techniques have at least some potential with most clients.

The experience of the handicapped has at least four major implications for career development theory. In the first place, it focuses attention on career development as a life-long process rather than a single event. An individual who incurs a disability in mid-career must continue his vocational development. He cannot retreat to a prevocational stage and start over but must incorporate his prior adjustment into his new one. Increasing attention is being given to the phenomenon of second careers, and there is every reason to look to the vocational adaptation of the mid-career disabled as a source for approaching this phenomenon. This concern is of relevance both to the individual who seeks to change careers in the middle of his working years and to the individual who is forced by retirement policies to change his career.

In addition to focusing on career development as a lifelong process, the experience of the handicapped is of general value in bringing attention to the phenomenon of disjunctions in career development. A disability incurred in mid-career is only one of a number of types of disjunctions which may occur. Changes in technology or economic conditions may remove an individual from an established, satisfactory career course, as may changes in a person's own personality or values. A study of the effects of career disjunctions in the mid-career disabled may well shed light on the phenomenon which would be applicable to all who experience disjunctions. Indeed, such typical events as promotions, changes in job duties, and transfers within a company all constitute disjunctions to some degree. Research directed at examining the effects of predisjunction adjustment on postdisjunction adjustment is badly needed.

A third area in which the experience of the handicapped is of general relevance is in approaching the issue of nonmodal career patterns. The particular influence of factors other than the intrapsychic ones stressed by Roe, Holland, Super, and other vocational development theorists can be particularly seen in the handicapped. It is of interest to observe that many theories of personality were generalized from observations on deviants to the population as a whole (e.g., Freud, Adler, Jung, Fromm, Rogers, etc.). However, most theories of vocational development evolved from observations made on nondeviant, modally or better functioning samples of subjects (e.g., Ginzberg, Roe, Holland, Super, Tiedeman, etc.). Consequently, just as many personality theories end up defining normality by an absence of psychopathology, so that many vocational development theories neglect the range of adaptive approaches in favor of a focus on a modal pattern. If the field of vocational development is to attain a breadth of conceptualization which is congruent with reality, it must take account of the validity and integrity of nonmodal patterns. Only by examining the impact of a range of functional limitations can the process of defining the parameters of vocational development be achieved.

A fourth phenomenon to which the experience of the handicapped adds insight is that of compensation in vocational adjustment. If work behavior is conceived of as the purposive expenditure of time, effort, and attention, then the observation of how functionally limited individuals redistribute these elements to attain a work goal is vital to an understanding of how all workers distribute their in-puts. Career-related behavior has been associated with the concepts of mastery[33] and of competence.[34] It seems fairly safe to hypothesize that the attainment of competence and a sense of mastery in a career require a particular deployment of the resources which the individual brings to his work. To the extent that functional limitations require compensatory redistributions (for example, the sacrifice of speed for accuracy in individuals with certain neurological conditions), the process of attaining mastery by compensation in all workers is made more available for study.

In addition to these contributions of the experience of the handicapped to the study of vocational development processes, their experience has several implications for the social structure within which vocational development occurs. In the first place, the techniques of job restructuring and job engineering may contribute to a redistribution of options within the world of work which may affect all workers. If jobs come to be seen more as opportunities for self-expression, personal contribution and growth, and optimizing one's unique pattern of assets (rather than as rigidly defined, externally imposed sets of limitations and requirements), then all workers should benefit. To the extent that the democratic ideal values the integrity of the individual, the contribution of the handicapped in furthering the individualization of work furthers the goals our system espouses.

A further social impact of the handicapped may be in modifying the long-standing orientation of equating personal worth with work productivity. As members of a group which has often been excluded from job opportunities on irrelevant bases, many of the handicapped have demonstrated that an individual may attain a sense of personal dignity in spite of discriminatory treatment. This lesson, of course, was also learned by members of various ethnic groups who faced similar conditions. As the nature of jobs changes, there is reason to expect further vocational displacements and an increased number of people who will have to find bases other than a no longer required productive capacity on which to found or maintain an identity. Thus, work may become *a* value, rather than *the* value in establishing personal worth. The experience of the handicapped and other deviants may then provide alternative models for adjustment for larger segments of the general society.

Perhaps the most cogent contribution of the handicapped to changing the social context was best summarized by Booker T. Washington, a man whose most limiting chronic condition was the color of his skin: "I have learned that success is to be measured not so much by the position that one has reached in life as by the obstacles which he has overcome."[35]

NOTES

1. L. H. Lofquist and R. V. Dawis, *Adjustment to Work* (New York: Appleton-Century Crofts, 1969), p. 17.
2. Estimate derived from figures provided in National Health Education Committee, *Facts on the Major Killing and Crippling Diseases in the United States Today* (New York: National Health Education Committee, 1971) and Bureau of the Census, *Statistical Abstract of the United States* (Washington, D.C.: U.S. Department of Commerce, 1971).

3. Bureau of the Census, *Pocket Data Book, U.S.A., 1971* (Washington, D.C.: U.S. Department of Commerce, 1971), pp. 202–03.

4. R. W. Conley, *The Economics of Vocational Rehabilitation* (Baltimore: Johns Hopkins Press, 1965), pp. 92–93.

5. M. E. Jaques and D. B. Hershenson, "Culture, Work, and Deviance: Implications for Rehabilitation Counseling," *Rehabilitation Counseling Bulletin* 14(1970):49–56.

6. S. Z. Nagi, "Some Conceptual Issues in Disability and Rehabilitation,"*Sociology and Rehabilitation*, M. E. Sussman, ed. (Washington, D.C.: American Sociological Association, 1966), pp. 100–13.

7. National Health Education Committee, *op. cit.*

8. L. D. Haber, "Epidemiological Factors in Disability: I. Major Disabling Conditions," *Social Security Survey of the Disabled, 1966—Report No. 6* (Washington, D.C.: U.S. Department of Health, Education and Welfare, Social Security Administration, 1969).

9. J. S. Felton, D. C. Perkins, and M. Lewin. *A Survey of Medicine and Medical Practice for the Rehabilitation Counselor* (Washington, D.C.: U.S. Department of Health, Education and Welfare, Vocational Rehabilitation Administration, 1966), p. 170.

10. R. E. Jooms, "Amputations" *Campbell's Operative Orthopaedics*, Vol. I., A. H. Crenshaw, ed. (St. Louis: C. V. Mosby, 1971), pp. 838–39.

11. Based on data provided in Division of Statistics and Studies, Rehabilitation Services Administration, *Statistical History: Federal-State Program of Vocational Rehabilitation, 1920–1969* (Washington, D.C.: U.S. Department of Health, Education and Welfare, Social and Rehabilitation Service, 1970), pp. 38 and 45.

12. Jaques and Hershenson, *op. cit.*

13. For example, see T. S. Szasz, *The Myth of Mental Illness* (New York: Hoeber-Harper, 1961).

14. B. A. Wright, *Physical Disability–A Psychological Approach* (New York: Harper and Row, 1960), pp. 373–77.

15. F. C. Shontz, "Physical Disability and Personality: Theory and Recent Research," *Psychological Aspects of Disability* 17(1970):51–69.

16. R. A. Myers, *Implications of Career Development Theory and Research for Counselor Education*, Workshop Report (New York: Teachers College, Columbia University, 1967), p. 182.

17. G. H. Allen, "Aspirations and Expectations of Physically Impaired High School Seniors," *Personnel and Guidance Journal* 46(1967):59–62.

18. J. W. McDaniel, "Disability and Vocational Redevelopment," *Journal of Rehabilitation* 29(1963):16–18.

19. H. Rusalem, "The Floundering Period in the Late Careers of Older Disabled Workers," *Rehabilitation Literature* 24(1963):34–40.

20. R. LoCascio, "Delayed and Impaired Development: A Neglected Aspect of Vocational Development Theory," *Personnel and Guidance Journal* 42(1964): 885–87.

21. D. E. Super, "The Development of Vocational Potential," *Vocational Rehabilitation of the Disabled: An Overview*, D. Malikin and H. Rusalem, eds. (New York: New York University Press, 1969), pp. 84–88.

22. Allen, *op. cit.*

23. Lofquist and Dawis, *op. cit.*

24. Division of Statistics and Studies, Rehabilitation Services Administration, *Statistical History*, p. 44.

25. R. R. Zuger, "To Place the Unplaceable," *Journal of Rehabilitation* 37(1971): 22–23.

26. J. W. McDaniel, *Physical Disability and Human Behavior* (New York: Pergamon Press, 1969), pp. 33–38.
27. D. B. Hershenson and C. M. Sloan, "Recent Studies Using the SVIB with the Physically, Emotionally, and Culturally Handicapped," *Rehabilitation Counseling Bulletin* 12(1968):23–28.
28. E. S. Bordin, *Psychological Counseling*, 2nd Ed. (New York: Appleton-Century Crofts, 1968), Ch. 14.; L. M. Brammer and E. L. Shostrom, *Therapeutic Psychology*, 2nd Ed. (Englewood Cliffs, N.J.: Prentice-Hall, 1968), Ch. 14.; J. D. Krumboltz and C. E. Thoresen, *Behavioral Counseling* (New York: Holt, Rinehart, and Winston, 1969), pp. 70–73, 213–34, 293–306, 343–96.
29. J. Samler, *The Counselor in Our Time* (Madison, Wisc.: University of Wisconsin, 1966), especially pp. 37–54; E. C. Thoroman, *The Vocational Counseling of Adults and Young Adults* (Boston: Houghton Mifflin, 1968); D. B. Hershenson, "Techniques for Assisting Life-Stage Vocational Development," *Personnel and Guidance Journal* 47(1969):776–80.
30. For example, D. L. Angell, G. T. DeSau, and A. A. Havrilla, "Rehabilitation Counselor versus Coordinator . . . One of Rehabilitation's Great Straw Men," *NRCA Professional Bulletin* 9,1(1969).
31. J. Boling, C. McDaniels, and S. Fine, *The World of Work: Counseling for Career Development* (New York: Appleton-Century Crofts, in press).
32. W. Gellman and S. B. Friedman, "The Workshop as a Clinical Rehabilitation Tool," *Rehabilitation Literature* 26(1965):34–38.
33. I. Hendricks, "Work and the Pleasure Principle," *Psychoanalytic Quarterly*, 12(1943):311–29.
34. R. W. White, "Competence and the Psychosexual Stages of Development," *Nebraska Symposium on Motivation: 1960*, M. R. Jones, ed. (Lincoln, Neb.: University of Nebraska Press, 1960), pp. 97–141.
35. Quoted in *Fortune* 85,1(1972):32.

SUGGESTED READING

Felton, J. S., Perkins, D. C., and Lewin, M. *A Survey of Medicine and Medical Practice for the Rehabilitation Counselor*. Washington, D.C.: U.S. Department of Health, Education and Welfare, Vocational Rehabilitation Administration, 1966. A concise overview of chronic conditions, the functional limitations typically associated with them, treatment procedures, and implications for vocational adjustment and counseling. This should be an adequate reference source for most of the problems one encounters in vocational counseling with the handicapped.

Jacques, M. E. *Rehabilitation Counseling: Scope and Services*. Boston: Houghton Mifflin, 1970. A concise, thorough overview and statement of direction for rehabilitation counseling as a field and as a profession. This treatment of the field uniquely relates rehabilitation to the needs of handicapped school children, as well as to the usual adult client population.

Lamb, H. R., et al. *Rehabilitation in Community Mental Health*. San Francisco: Jossey-Bass, 1971. A review of vocational rehabilitation procedures for emotionally disturbed clients, with an emphasis on their reintegration into the community. While this book derives from the authors' experiences with one particular program, it provides useful information on the vocational rehabilitation of all mental patients and has implications for other disability groups, as well.

Malikin, D., and Rusalem, H., eds. *Vocational Rehabilitation of the Disabled: An Overview.* New York: New York University Press, 1969. A collection of pieces especially written for this book by luminaries in the field and focusing on the philosophical and theoretical bases for vocational counseling with the handicapped. This book is more oriented toward theory than toward applied techniques.

McDaniel, J. W. *Physical Disability and Human Behavior.* New York: Pergamon Press, 1969. A review of findings on psychological factors associated with physical disability, including attitudes, emotions, sensation and perception, motivation, and learning. This short book provides much information of value in counseling the handicapped, including information on the attitudes of professionals toward the handicapped.

McGowan, J. F., and Porter, T. L. *An Introduction to the Vocational Rehabilitation Process.* Washington, D.C.: U.S. Department of Health, Education and Welfare, Social and Rehabilitation Service, Rehabilitation Services Administration, 1967. An up-dated revision of the most comprehensive practically oriented training manual in the field. This manual is concerned with how to do it, whereas Jaques (*op. cit*) and Malikin and Rusalem (q.v.) are more concerned with why it should be done. Thus, these books should be read in balance with each other.

Moses, H. A., and Patterson, C. H., eds. *Readings in Rehabilitation Counseling,* 2nd Ed. Champaign, Ill.: Stipes, 1971. An up-to-date collection of readings on the theory and practice of rehabilitation counseling which covers material published since the first edition appeared in 1960 (for which Patterson was the sole editor). Taken together, the two editions provide significant material related to many of the major concerns in the field, including adjustment to disability, counseling techniques, counselor role, vocational evaluation, job placement, and sheltered workshops.

Myers, J. S., ed. *An Orientation to Chronic Disease and Disability.* New York: MacMillan, 1965. A longer and more intensive treatment of most of the same topics touched on in Felton (*op. cit.*). This book is valuable in gaining a deeper and broader understanding of the nature, etiology and effects of various chronic conditions, although relatively little attention is paid to their vocational implications.

Obermann, C. E. *A History of Vocational Rehabilitation in America,* Minneapolis: T. S. Denison, 1965. A history of the development of federal vocational rehabilitation legislation, of the emergence of rehabilitation as an organized movement, and of the relationship between the two. This material provides insight into the context within which the vocational counselor of the handicapped currently functions.

Safilios-Rothschild, C. *The Sociology and Social Psychology of Disability and Rehabilitation.* New York: Random House, 1970. A sociological approach to the study of disability. This book essentially does for the study of disability what Sussman's book (*op. cit.*) does for the study of rehabilitation, that is, it provides a different viewpoint which enriches the range of approaches to this topic.

Sankovsky, R., Arthur, G., and J. Mann, eds. *Vocational Evaluation and Work Adjustment (A Book of Readings).* Auburn, Ala.: Alabama Rehabilitation Media Service, 1970. A collection of readings on psychometric and job-sample evaluation techniques and their application to handicapped clients. This book provides many useful concepts and approaches for vocational counseling with all clients.

Simmons, O. G. *Work and Mental Illness*. New York: John Wiley and Sons, 1965. A case-study approach to the impact of mental illness and hospitalization on vocational adjustment, using individuals covering a range of career patterns and stages. The insights and considerations developed by the author have relevance for vocational counseling with clients at all levels of adjustment.

Sussman, M. B., ed. *Sociology and Rehabilitation*. Washington, D.C.: American Sociological Association, 1966. A sociological approach to the study of the rehabilitation process and its professional structure. This orientation provides a different perspective than the usual focus on intrapsychic phenomena.

Wright, G. N., and Butler, A. J., eds. *Rehabilitation Counselor Functions: Annotated References*. Madison, Wisc.: University of Wisconsin Regional Rehabilitation Research Institute, 1968. A comprehensive index, with summaries, of articles in the rehabilitation literature concerning counselor role, relationships with agency and with clients, and counseling practices with the handicapped.

Wright, G. N., and Trotter, A. B., eds. *Rehabilitation Research*. Madison, Wisc.: University of Wisconsin Regional Rehabilitation Research Institute, 1968. A thorough collection of abstracts of government funded research studies on the rehabilitation process. This book provides a good overview of topics and findings which should be of concern to those doing vocational counseling with the handicapped.

20 Professional Preparation for Vocational Guidance

Kenneth B. Hoyt
University of Maryland

The availability of funds has been perhaps the major determinant of change and evolution in the counseling and guidance movement in general and vocational guidance in particular. Although it is true that such funds have represented outgrowths of various kinds of societal concerns, the fact is, nevertheless, that the responses of the guidance movement can be more correctly pictured as related to availability of funds than to any long-range, systematic attempt to develop this field as an effective part of the larger society. Those who wish to understand the professional culture of the personnel and guidance movement must therefore study, in detail, the major federal legislation that provides funds for counseling and guidance services. Herr has reviewed this legislation in Chapter 2, and his discussion should be read carefully as a basis for this one.

The literature related to professional preparation of counselors has been voluminous during the last decade. No attempt will be made here to provide a comprehensive review of that literature, but, rather, references included in this chapter have been selected for the purpose of illustrating the dynamics of the professional culture of counselor preparation in American society. The goal is one of trying to understand the forces that have interacted so as to bring us to where we are today in hopes that such understanding may lead this movement to exert a greater degree of professional autonomy over its long-run future.

This chapter has been organized in three major parts. First, a short, subjective summary of the dynamics of change in counselor preparation is presented. Second, an attempt will be made to review illustrative literature related to: a) professional association activities; b) major national conferences related to counselor preparation; c) support personnel in the counseling and guidance movement; and d) counselor certification. Finally, some comments will be made regarding possible future directions for counselor preparation in vocational guidance.

THE DYNAMICS OF CHANGE: A SUBJECTIVE VIEW

Two compelling reasons for this section exist. First of all, to simply review major events one at a time leaves the reader with no systematic way of relating these events to each other; both the nature and the timing of the various events must be related if the dynamics are to be understood. The second reason is the right of the reader to know the biases of the writer. Such biases and personal value systems substantially influence the ways in which any writer selects and interprets literature to be reviewed. Because they can be neither proven nor disproven in an absolute sense, they are bound to anger those whose own biases are of a different nature. This makes it more, not less, important to make the writer's viewpoint as explicit as possible.

Those of us who have lived through and been active combatants in the dynamics of change in the counselor preparation movement know that much of importance has never been recorded in the professional literature. It would seem, then, that there is some responsibility to refer to completely undocumented and undocumentable happenings in the past.

Historical Perspective: Pre-NDEA Period

Prior to 1938 the counseling and guidance movement grew slowly, based primarily on locally perceived needs for guidance services. With passage of the George-Dean Act of 1938, there was created in the Vocational Education Division of the U.S. Office of Education an Occupational Information and Guidance Service headed by Harry A. Jager, a former high school principal. This, in turn, led to creation of the position of State Supervisor of Guidance in state departments of education throughout the nation; these supervisors, like Jager, were funded with vocational education funds and operated within divisions of vocational education. With passage of the George-Barden Act of 1946 it became possible to use vocational education funds to reimburse counselor training institutions. Only then could Jager move to encourage state supervisors of guidance across the land to initiate state certification provisions for school counselors. That is, there was no nationwide way of requiring counselors to take academic work until provision was present for assuring that such academic work would be available.

Thus, counselor education became graduate education essentially by the edict of Jager, who was encouraged by Clifford P. Froelich, then serving as Specialist for the Training of Guidance Personnel in Jager's USOE unit. At that time there were eighty colleges and universities purporting to train secondary school counselors. Half were operating undergraduate programs and half operated graduate programs of counselor preparation. Jager's objective was to increase both the number of counselors and counselor status as rapidly as possible. He reasoned that the best strategy to use in getting school boards to hire full-time counselors was the one that had worked for the high school principalship movement twenty years earlier—namely, to picture this new specialist as a "teacher plus." Since most teacher education programs were at that time seen as leading to the baccalaureate degree, Jager decided that school counselors should be prepared at the graduate level and should come from the ranks of successfully employed secondary school teachers. When he put USOE funds into those colleges and universities preparing school counselors at the graduate level, those who had been operating undergraduate counselor education programs either ceased operation or converted to a graduate program. True, a few resisted for several years, but they, too, are gone now.

Between 1949 and 1952 Jager's unit issued a total of eight reports on counselor preparation, six in various course-content areas and two on in-service education, the last of these entitled "Supervised Practice in Counselor Preparation." Each of the six course documents was viewed both as a basis for judging a "reimbursable counselor training course" and as a course requirement for counselor certification. The reports themselves were prepared, under USOE leadership, by state supervisors of guidance and "reimbursed counselor trainers" who attended one or more of a series of conferences dedicated to this purpose.

These USOE bulletins set the pattern for school counselor education and heavily influenced other forms of counselor education during the 1946–1958 period. By the time six courses had been identified, it was easy to see why both counselor educators and their students wanted to have an M.A. degree with a major in counseling and guidance. After all, it gave status to the counselor educators and higher pay to their students who, after completing the master's degree, found themselves at a different point on the salary schedule.

It was during the 1946–1952 period that the Veterans Administration initiated doctoral programs in counseling psychology. These had little influence on the school counselor education movement because: a) they were typically housed in departments of psychology rather than colleges of education; b) they were typically staffed by noneducators; and c) they were at such a high level of preparation as to be impractical for school counselor education. When federal legislation made possible counselor education programs for vocational rehabilitation counselors in 1955, it was judged by those responsible to be more appropriate to train vocational rehabilitation counselors at the same level and in ways analogous to the way school counselors were being trained. Thus, most vocational rehabilitation counselor education programs were placed in colleges of education, rather than psychology departments, and they were designed to lead to the master's degree. They became graduate education primarily because of Jager's earlier actions with respect to school counselors. The training of employment service counselors followed a similar direction, although, because funds were not available, not to the same degree as was true for vocational rehabilitation.

In 1949, when the USOE bulletins on counselor competencies began to appear, APGA had, of course, not yet been formed. The National Vocational Guidance Association did publish a monograph on counselor preparation in 1949. That monograph largely reflected the philosophy and substance of the counselor-competency bulletins. We did have a great deal of uniformity during that period, but, in terms of what we now know, it can only be described as uniform mediocrity. Those who today are again calling for uniformity in counselor certification standards would do well to review the history on this matter.

The Impact of NDEA

The National Defense Education Act of 1958, particularly in Title V-B: Counseling and Guidance Institutes, has had a greater impact on counselor education than any other single force in the history of the guidance movement. Many of the documents to be reviewed later in this chapter sprang directly from the influence of Title V-B of NDEA. Thus, a closer view of this influence is called for here.

The basic force behind the strength of Title V-B was that, by creating this title along with Title V-A calling for state guidance supervision and support of local school guidance programs, it was possible for the first time for counselor educators to determine the nature and content of counselor education programs independent of the influence of state supervisors of guidance. Many counselor educators were greatly dissatisfied with the "course" and "techniques" approach to counselor education that had previously existed. They were eager to expand their total counselor education programs independent of such restrictions. Our history would have been quite different had Title V of NDEA been written in only one part. By writing it in two parts, two different sets of guidance specialists were created in the U.S. Office of Education, one headed by Dr. Frank Sievers and concerned with Title V-A and the other headed by Dr. Ralph Bedell and concerned with Title V-B. While they tried, and to some extent succeeded, in working together, it was inevitable that programs supporting guidance services in state departments of education and local school systems (Title V-A) and programs supporting special counseling and guidance institutes (Title V-B) would vary somewhat in their emphases and in the directions they took.

Title V-B called for using up to 7.5 million dollars per year in support of short-term (usually summer) and long-term (usually academic-year) counseling and guidance institutes. When funds first became available in the fall of 1958 a call was put out for institute proposals. A flood of proposals resulted and fifty short-term institutes were funded for summer 1959. Selection of those fifty institutes was necessarily made on the basis of professional judgments made by panels of consultants employed by Title V-B in the U.S. Office of Education on a part-time basis. These consultants were themselves counselor educators who were running programs thought to be respectable by the USOE officials who picked them as consultants. Consequently, there was no valid, objective way by which the consultants could make judgments regarding other institute proposals; they were forced to simply use their best professional judgments and to draw on such knowledge as they possessed regarding other institutions. The Title-V-B USOE professional staff adopted an initial strategy of developing individual contracts in joint consultation with participating institutions, which, in view of our lack of accepted standards, was probably the wisest possible approach to take. An evaluation completed in 1960 by Dr. Leona Tyler contains much evidence that worthwhile activities took place even in the first fifty institutes.[1]

The operational problem was that of distinguishing good counselor education programs from poor ones. The USOE wanted to help the good programs and discourage those of questionable quality. However, no set of standards for judging the quality of a counselor education program existed. Thus, in 1959 a small group of USOE Title V-B consultants initiated action through the National Association of Guidance Supervisors and Counselor Trainers (which became the Association for Counselor Education and Supervision in 1961) to undertake a five-year project aimed at building a set of standards for education in the preparation of secondary school counselors. The ACES study was officially launched in April 1960. At that time the American School Counselor Association (ASCA) was formally invited to send representatives to the "grass-roots" discussion groups which hopefully were to develop content for the ACES standards statement.

From the standpoint of the dynamics involved, several important points need to be made here. First, it must be recognized that the impetus for counselor education standards came from the USOE's need to justify awarding NDEA Title V-B institutes to some institutions and not to others. Second, with its limited funds, the USOE had to have standards sufficiently high so that relatively few institutions could meet them. With most counselor education institutions submitting proposals, it was essential that some justifiable means of turning down a majority of them be found. Third, NDEA institute enrollees were, by law, either counselors or teachers preparing to become counselors. This made for a heavy emphasis on the counseling function and was seen as a viable means of emphasizing the importance of the supervised counseling practicum. The emphasis was on counseling and counselors, not on guidance and guidance programs, which is clearly evident in the eventual standards that resulted from this effort. Finally, it must be remembered that NDEA Title V was directed at the intellectually able student as a primary target, not at the entire school population. It was inevitable that the resulting set of standards should reflect the kinds of counselor education programs that were thought to best meet needs of the intellectually able student who, after leaving high school, would enter college. The heavy emphasis on the one-to-one counseling relationship was certainly appropriate for use with this portion of the high school student population.

In terms of implications, it is equally important to note the large number of enrollees in Title V-B NDEA institutes, most of whom either were or later were to become school counselors. In 1967 McDaniels published figures for the first eight years of Title V-B, indicating $58,380,830 spent in training 14,630 enrollees in short-term NDEA institutes and 4,769 in academic-year institutes.[2] This same article reviews several other publications, most of which drew favorable conclusions regarding the Title V-B program. For purposes of our discussion, it seems sufficient to speculate that to a great many of today's practicing school counselors the content of counselor preparation must be what is taught in NDEA Title V-B institutes—an emphasis on the great importance of the counseling relationship.

The implications of splitting Title V of NDEA into two parts cannot be overemphasized in terms of counselor preparation. This can perhaps be most dramatically seen by recognizing that, underlying the movement towards picturing two full years of graduate preparation as minimal for school counselors, was the need for limiting the number of counselor education institutions eligible to participate under Title V-B of NDEA. (The fact that this statement is certain to be vehemently denied by those who championed the two-year minimal requirement makes the statement itself no less true.) In spite of the "two-year minimal" syndrome, as of 1971 there was still no state in which school counselor certification standards were at this level, and only a minority of states in which certification at this level was even possible.[3]

Next to NDEA Title V-B, Project CAUSE (Counselor-Advisor University Summer Education Program), initiated by the Bureau of Employment Security of the U.S. Department of Labor in 1964 and continued as CAUSE II in the summer of 1965, has probably influenced counselor preparation in the United States the most.[4] Project CAUSE provided training to only about 1,900 persons in 62 institutions at a cost of approximately 6.8 million dollars.[5] Yet, with this minimal input, it has had very great implications for counselor preparation over the last eight years. The content of this program will be discussed in the section of this chapter dealing with support personnel, but here only the implications of CAUSE, in terms of dynamics for counselor preparation, will be the focus of concern. Three major kinds of changes, each having multiple ramifications and implications, resulted from this effort.

One such result was a general emphasis on the importance of preparing support personnel for the personnel and guidance movement. The timing here was most crucial. In March 1964, when, at its national convention in San Francisco, APGA adopted its policy statement which described adequate counselor-preparation programs as those that "consist of a minimum of two years of graduate study, a substantial portion of which should be in full-time graduate study."[6] Two months later CAUSE I was announced, calling for both counselor aides and youth advisors to be fully trained in a period of eight to nine weeks,[7] making clear that graduates were to be regarded as subprofessionals. This announcement, while causing great initial consternation among guidance leaders responsible for adoption of the APGA policy statement referred to above, was followed by a whole series of movements within the counselor-preparation community to recognize and accommodate the preparation of subprofessionals in the guidance movement. Had it not been for the initial action establishing CAUSE I, there is no good way of telling how long it might have taken the guidance movement to recognize and act on this concept.

The second major change resulting from the impact of CAUSE I was recognition of the potential importance of using the guidance function as a direct agent of environmental change. In *The Effect of Cause* document referred to above, the following description of potential job duties of CAUSE I graduates appears:

> Workers in the Youth Opportunity Centers will have to exercise understanding and ingenuity in coping with disadvantaged and other youth on a person-to-person basis. These young people may be difficult to reach, requiring the Youth Opportunity Center to go out into the community and to create the conditions which will make it possible for disadvantaged and other youths . . . to use the services of the Center.[8]

Both the emphasis on going out into the community and that of acting as a direct agent of environmental change were quite contrary to the professional counseling emphasis being utilized in the NDEA Title V-B counseling and guidance institutes of that period. Both of these emphases are being rather dramatically felt in the current guidance scene and seem sure to continue for some time into the future of this movement.

The third major directional change implied in the CAUSE I approach was the presence of selection criteria which, while requiring applicants to be at least twenty-one years old, did not require them to meet graduate school admission standards—or even to possess a baccalaureate degree. Thus, the stage was set for a return to the earlier period when some counselors were educated at the undergraduate level. This, too, can be seen as the forerunner of current movements, particularly in the case of vocational rehabilitation counselors, to prepare some counselors at the undergraduate level.

Perhaps the biggest contribution growing out of Project CAUSE was that of helping the personnel and guidance movement recognize that there is no single best approach possible for meeting the counseling and guidance needs of all individuals. The general need to explore new and varied approaches to meeting the guidance needs of the disadvantaged grew, of course, out of the Economic Opportunity Act of 1964 in general, but it was the CAUSE I program which first made these needs clear to the counselor-preparation community.

Impact of the Vocational Education Act of 1963 and the 1968 Amendments

Passage of the Vocational Education Act of 1963, and especially passage of the 1968 Amendments to that Act, should theoretically have had a great impact on counselor-preparation programs for vocational guidance personnel; that is, in both pieces of legislation the crucial importance of the guidance function was recognized in terms of the need to help persons decide whether or not they wished to enroll in vocational education.

Both of these pieces of legislation have influenced the personnel and guidance movement in general and, to some extent, the counselor-preparation programs in particular. The prime ways in which this impact has been seen consist of: a) a number of national conferences on vocational guidance (to be reviewed later); b) a very large number of state and local conferences designed to improve relationships between guidance and vocational education personnel; c) a significant number of innovative projects in career guidance, counseling, and placement implemented through Part D funds from the 1968 Amendments; and d) the formation of the Guidance Division of the American Vocational Association. The influence of such activities is definitely being felt within the personnel and guidance movement at the present time.

However, in terms of specific impact on counselor preparation programs, it seems safe to say that neither of these major pieces of vocational education legislation has as yet made a major impact. This will be seen more clearly when results of some of the major conferences on this subject are reviewed. Here it seems appropriate to simply note the lack of impact and to comment briefly on possible reasons for this. The biggest reason, it would seem, is lack of provision for subsidizing counselor education programs. While a long list of other reasons could be formulated, it seems reasonable to conclude that this one is of major operational importance. As such, it simply illustrates the general statement with which this chapter began. There seems to be little doubt that counselor preparation programs would change rapidly and dramatically in attempts to respond to challenges of vocational education programs if financial incentives of sufficient magnitude were made available to them. In the absence of such financial incentives, no great nationwide movement towards substantial change in counselor-preparation programs can be said to have resulted from vocational education legislation. In viewing the culture of counselor preparation, this may be a significant observation.

TOWARDS STANDARDS FOR COUNSELOR PREPARATION

No systematic national movement towards development of counselor-preparation standards occurred until after the National Defense Education Act of 1958 became law. Effective movement began with action of the National Association of Guidance Supervisors and Counselor Trainers (NAGSCT). In 1960 that organization established the "Cooperative Study of Counselor Education Standards."[9] All members of the NAGSCT national committee for that project were at the time actively involved in NDEA Title V-B counseling and guidance institutes. In a 1961 article the co-chairman of the committee stated:

> Accreditation of counselor education is not presently considered as an ultimate objective of NAGSCT. However, the specification of acceptable standards might well serve other professional accrediting organizations, federal and state agencies as a basis for evaluation of institutional programs seeking approval for counselor preparation or for subsidies in the operation of their programs.[10]

From the beginning the NAGSCT study was pictured as a long-term project extending over several years that would involve "grass-roots" participation of counselor educators, guidance supervisors, and practicing school counselors. Hints with respect to some of the eventual goals of committee members can be seen from another 1961 article discussing this project: "Perhaps, not all counselors *need* to rise from teaching ranks . . . Support for a two-year professional program of graduate preparation in counseling is growing . . ."[11]

In August 1960 an invitational Conference on Counselor Education was held in Chicago, sponsored by the Guidance, Counseling, and Testing Section (Title V-A, NDEA) of the U.S. Office of Education. Key staff members from Title V-B, all members of the NAGSCT study committee, and a few additional individuals were invited to be present. The consensus report of that conference did not lend direct support to either elimination of the teaching requirement nor the notion of a two-year minimum period of graduate preparation for school counselors.[12] While that report was to be discussed by NAGSCT members at their 1961 convention, NAGSCT essentially viewed it as only one more input into the total Cooperative Study of Counselor Education Standards. The history of counselor preparation standards would have been quite different had that conference report been adopted by NAGSCT in 1961. It is emphasized here because of a subjective impression that there might, even today, be more national consensus on the contents of that report than on the eventual standards that were to be adopted in 1967. At any rate, for those who can obtain copies, that document would be well worth serious study.

Attainment of Counselor-education Standards for Secondary School Counselors

With the change in name in 1961 from NAGSCT to Association for Counselor Education and Supervision (ACES), the Cooperative Study of Secondary School Counselor Education Standards continued. A great number of "grassroots" discussions on the topic were held, and the active involvement of the American School Counselors Association was sought. At the APGA Chicago Convention in April 1962 six position papers, each dealing with a different area of standards, were presented and reacted to by representatives of ASCA and by selected state supervisors of guidance. Much controversy was evident in the reactions. Both the six position papers and the invited reactions to them were subsequently published by the American Personnel and Guidance Association.[13] A great deal of criticism and controversy resulted during 1962 and 1963 as the ACES Cooperative Study continued its activities. Members of the national committee continued their practice of seeking input from all possible sources and trying to resolve these in the further development of standards.

In March 1964 the national committee presented its recommendations for standards, and, after much discussion at the ACES business meeting, they were tentatively approved with recommendations that they be used for three years on an experimental basis and that a new committee be appointed to recommend revisions at the conclusion of that period. It was felt that, with an entirely new committee, perhaps consensus could finally be obtained. The 1964 version of the standards clearly supported the concept of the two-year program of counselor preparation with the following statement:

> The institution provides a two-year graduate program in counselor education, based primarily on the program of studies and supervised practice outlined in B and C below.[14]

The new ACES Committee on Standards for Counselor Education, created by the 1964 action, worked diligently during the 1964–1967 period in encouraging 105 counselor education institutions to try out the 1964 standards on a voluntary basis and in seeking consensus for the finished standards to be voted on in 1967.[15] The revised standards were adopted by a mail vote of ACES members in 1967, and they were published by the American Personnel and Guidance Association. That some revision resulted is evident from the following quote with reference to length of the program:

> The institution provides a minimum of one year of graduate counselor education . . . (and) . . . at least one additional year of graduate study in counselor education either through its own staff and facilities or through cooperative working relationships with other institutions which do have at least a two year program of counselor education.[16]

There are, of course, other ways in which the 1967 standards differed from the tentative version first adopted in 1964. As Hill pointed out,[17] it is expected that in future years other revisions will also be made. However, no revisions have been made to date beyond the 1967 version.

Evolvement of APGA Policies on Counselor Preparation

For reasons that can be known fully only to those who participated directly in the decision, the American Personnel and Guidance Association issued an APGA statement of policy entitled "Standards for the Preparation of School Counselors" in the December 1961 issue of the *Personnel and Guidance Journal*.[18] This was only a year and a half after initiation of the ACES Cooperative Study and four years prior to the time the ACES study was scheduled to be completed. Most of the members of the APGA Special Committee for the Preparation of the APGA Policy Statement on Counselor Education were also members of the ACES Cooperative Study Committee. This first APGA policy statement on preparation of school counselors contained the recommendation for a minimum of two years of graduate education as a standard, provisions for selecting candidates with no teaching experience, and a heavy emphasis on supervised practice in counseling.

As an APGA policy formulated without approval of the APGA Senate, this policy found many dissenters. At the 1962 APGA Convention the APGA Professional Preparation and Standards Committee was charged with formulating a tentative statement of policy for APGA on counselor preparation for discussion among the APGA membership and having an official policy statement ready for adoption by the 1964 APGA Senate. Two significant changes are important to note from the 1961 APGA policy statement: a) the new charge was to develop an APGA policy statement on the professional preparation and role of the counselor, *not* to develop *standards* for counselor education; and b) the new charge spoke to *all* professional counselors, regardless of the setting in which they were employed, not just to school counselors.

After preparing an interim report during 1962–1963, the final report of the APGA Professional Preparation and Standards Committee was presented to and adopted by the APGA Senate at its 1964 national convention. As was true of its earlier version, this final version also supported the notion that counselor preparation should require a minimum of two years of graduate study and a heavy emphasis on developing competencies in counseling *per se* through supervised practice in counseling.[19] This general APGA policy was viewed as a "framework for more specific standards and criteria by each Division." It was, of course, consistent with the ACES Standards for Secondary School Counselors. This official APGA policy is still in effect. Current actions reported by Thorsen appear to be placing two divisions of APGA— ARCA and NECA—in danger of running into conflict with this official APGA policy.[20]

The Accreditation Problem

While originally announced as having goals independent of those related to accreditation, it was logically inevitable that once standards were promulgated someone would express interest in seeing them applied in ways that would lead to either accreditation or the loss of accreditation on the part of counselor education programs. In 1966 the APGA Professional Preparations and Standards Committee established a special subcommittee on accreditation charged with making proposals relative to this matter. That subcommittee, chaired by Dr. Robert Callis, prepared a special report, along with a suggested series of steps for attainment of accreditation, for presentation to the APGA Executive Council in 1966.[21] The proposals were rejected by the APGA Executive Council in November 1966 and directions given to involve professional groups, other than APGA and its divisions, in moving towards accreditation for programs of preparation in the personnel and guidance field.

The issue of accreditation for counselor education programs is bound to come up again and again, for it is an issue that must eventually be settled. Those who are charged with accomplishing accreditation could gain much from observance of four basic principles contained in the Callis report of 1966. First, accreditation must be sanctioned by the National Commission on Accrediting (or its successors), an organization that was created for purposes of, in effect, "accrediting" the accrediting commissions. Second, NCA operates under a general philosophy that discourages the proliferation of many accrediting commissions and encourages its currently approved accrediting commissions to expand so as to accommodate demands for accreditation on the part of new groups, such as APGA. Third, if NCA is to act favorably on accreditation, it seeks to have accreditation standards sent to it by institutional groups, not by professional associations. Finally, NCA has consistently made clear that it would regard implementation of accreditation standards for the personnel and guidance movement as a logical undertaking for the National Commission on Accreditation for Teacher Education (NCATE). It seems clear that NCA does not look with favor on establishment of a new accrediting body solely concerned with the personnel and guidance movement. These principles seem as applicable today as they were in 1966 when the APGA Executive Council failed to adopt the Callis report. The Callis report did make clear provision for taking each of the NCA principles into account, and it seems unfortunate that this report was never widely circulated nor allowed to be presented to the APGA Senate for action.

Support Personnel

As indicated earlier, concern for support personnel in guidance came about primarily because of Project CAUSE of the U.S. Department of Labor in 1964—the same year in which the APGA policy statement on professional preparation and role of the counselor was released and the first tentative edition of the ACES standards for counselor education was adopted. These things occurred between March and June of 1964, with the first official APGA reaction being a statement dated June 4, 1964.[22] That statement was, essentially, a plea for unity in counselor preparation programs along with acknowledgment that "it is recognized that there may be job situations requiring only certain technical skills and it would be possible to train individuals for these specific skills in limited periods of time."

In 1965 APGA did voice official concern relative to CAUSE to the Department of Labor and, as a result, became officially represented on the Interagency Task Force on Counseling operating out of the Office of Manpower, Automation, and Training. A special subcommittee on support personnel was established within the APGA Committee on Professional Preparation and Standards and produced a statement on support personnel officially adopted as an APGA Policy Statement in 1967.[23] That APGA Policy Statement was identical to the position on support personnel contained in the official Department of Labor report of its Interagency Task Force on Counseling,[24] a direct result of cooperative efforts. The APGA Policy Statement placed heavy emphasis on the importance of support personnel working directly under the supervision of the professional counselor. Additionally, it reserves counseling *per se* as a service to be provided by the professional counselor, not by support personnel.

There are two additional important documents on this subject to be studied by those concerned with the concept of support personnel for guidance. The first is a paper by Hansen,[25] in which he attempts to differentiate the "professional" from the "subprofessional," not in terms of types of duties performed (for example, he contends that counseling will be done by both) but, rather, in terms of the degree of autonomy afforded the practitioner. In effect, he views the subprofessional as one who may be trained to know *how* to perform a function if directed to do so, but will not know *why* he is doing it or how far he should carry it. The professional, on the other hand, is seen as one with sufficient autonomy to make subjective judgments regarding what is appropriate for him to do at any particular point. This paper is a very important document.

The second important document is one published by ACES in 1970 and coauthored by David Zimpfer, Ronald Fredrickson, Mitchell Salim, and Alpheus Sanford.[26] While directed towards the school setting, this monograph contains the most extensive review of the literature on the topic yet available in any single publication. Here three levels of support personnel are identified in a career-ladder concept with the levels distinguished according to their relationships to data, people, knowledge, and autonomy. The basic rationale contends that the subprofessionals work directly under counselor supervision and that, by employing such personnel, professional counselors can be more free to engage in higher level professional activities. The ACES statement does not absolutely prohibit support personnel from engaging in counseling, but lists actual counseling at the bottom of their functions. (Interestingly enough, "placement" is listed at the top as a function of support personnel—a concept that has very many implications at the present.)

In general, the literature clearly pictures the length of preparation time for the subprofessional to be considerably less than that for the professional. There is no clear-cut agreement apparent with respect to who should train the support personnel, the kinds of training settings that should be utilized, or whether routine provision should be made to view support personnel training as one step on a career ladder towards becoming a professional counselor. On all of these points disagreement continues.

PREPARATION FOR VOCATIONAL GUIDANCE: MAJOR CONFERENCE REPORTS

It should not be necessary here to review the standard journals with respect to preparation for vocational guidance. That literature is easily accessible to any who find themselves interested in this topic. However, there exists, at the current time, a fairly sizeable amount of "fugitive" literature related to this topic that is not easily accessible to the typical student—nor to most practitioners in the field. This literature is primarily in the form of conference reports containing proceedings of several national conferences that have been held during the last eight years. It is the purpose of this section to review selected portions of those conference reports that deal directly with the professional culture of and preparation for vocational guidance.

It will be difficult, and in some instances impossible, to focus this review strictly on preparation for vocational guidance. This is because wide disagreement exists within the counselor education field regarding the desirability of this level of specialization with respect to counselor preparation. The APGA policy statement on the professional preparation and role of the counselor clearly states its concern for a general statement applicable to all counselors in all settings.[27] The American Vocational Association's Policy Statement on Vocational Aspects of Guidance also clearly pleads for the unity of guidance services as opposed to the preparation of vocational counselors as a special "breed."[28] Whether this position is a currently viable one is another matter to be discussed later in this chapter.

Counselor Development in American Society: 1965 Invitational Conference

One of the most historic and significant conferences bearing on counselor preparation for vocational guidance was the invitational Conference on Government-university Relations in the Professional Preparation and Employment of Counselors, held in Washington, D.C., June 2–3, 1965, administered by Dr. John F. McGowan, University of Missouri, and jointly sponsored by the U.S. Department of Labor and the U.S. Office of Education.[29] This conference, involving key counselor educators and government officials responsible for employing counselors, was a direct outgrowth of the great consternation caused by the many and varied kinds of government programs that sprang up between 1958 and 1964 calling for counselors. The conference papers (including the reaction papers) serve as a rich resource for those concerned with the culture of counselor preparation. This review must limit itself to comments dealing directly with that topic.

One example is found in the reaction of Louis Levine, then Director of the U.S. Employment Service, to a major conference paper presented by Darley.[30] The following quotes from that paper are directly related to both the culture of counselor preparation and its current problems.

> The traditional curriculum for counselor preparation may be seriously deficient in providing the information, analytical insights, and understanding of the environment and forces which most influence the outlook of the poor to whom the anti-poverty program is directed."
> That the curriculum for the training of counselors involves preparation in interviewing and guidance . . . is a *sine qua non*. However . . . that is not enough . . . Much more needs to be done, probably on a graduate level, with those branches of economics and sociology which are most directly concerned with manpower and human resources and their relationship to employability and job markets.

The constellation of dynamics of change for counselor preparation programs contained in the total conference report is, of course, much broader than the single quotation cited above. Rather than attempting even a brief review of the many significant papers which form the main body of the conference report, only a brief capsule of the perceived dynamics of change involved will be presented here.

The conference began with a paper by Darley summarizing historical relationships between universities and government in the area of counselor preparation.[31] Darley emphasized, as did several others in this conference, the problems created for universities when special government funds are made available for the preparation of one "kind" of counselor versus another. Stripling gave further emphasis to the dynamics involved with the following statement:

> There is general agreement on the undesirability of preparing "academic counselors" and "vocational counselors," but there is also recognition of the fact that most counselors have not been prepared sufficiently to help the early potential school leaver, the out-of-school youth, or the student who does not plan to continue formal education after high school.[32]

The dilemma is seen as involving preparation for working with specific segments of the population clearly in need of remedial help versus professionally educated counselors who are equipped to deal, in a helpful fashion, with the guidance needs of the entire population. The dilemma is stated in a very thoughtful paper by Tiedeman and Field,[33] who make a strong argument for simultaneous concern for improving both the quantity of counselors needed for specific problems and the quality of the profession of counseling. The differences between training guidance counselors in techniques which may be helpful to meeting immediate guidance needs of only a portion of the population versus educating professional counselors and providing them with professional autonomy required for dealing with people of all ages in all parts of society are obviously great. Tiedeman and Field argue strongly for professionalizing guidance as a prerequisite to protecting real freedom of choice for the individual. At the same time, they clearly recognize current inadequacies in counselor preparation programs in terms of their ability to prepare counselors for the rapidly growing need for guidance on the part of the total society. This paper, along with Woods' very thoughtful paper on the dynamics of social change and curriculum development in education,[34] made clear the general directions for change called for in counselor preparation. Unfortunately, one can see little that has been done to implement such needed changes since that time.

There were many other very thoughtful papers included in this conference report. Taken as a whole, these papers appear to be making the following generalizations: a) potential for conflict exists between governmental programs calling for counselors to work with specific portions of the population and the desires of counselor educators to have uniform programs of counselor preparation; b) current counselor education programs are inadequate for preparing counselors to work in vocational counseling, particularly with the disadvantaged and the out-of-school youth and adults; c) the need for support personnel in guidance is clear, but the need for professional autonomy of the counselor is equally clear; and d) the need for increasing both the quantity and the quality of counselor preparation, while holding potential for conflict, must be attacked simultaneously.

Vocational Aspects of Counselor Education: 1965 Airlie House Conference

One of the first major benefits for counselor education coming from enactment of the Vocational Education Act of 1963 was a grant to Dr. Carl McDaniels of the George Washington University to conduct a national conference on vocational aspects of counselor education, held in December 1965 in Warrenton, Virginia. Papers presented at that conference and the general conference recommendations hold great implications for vocational guidance aspects of counselor education.

The first paper, presented by K. B. Hoyt, addressed itself to needed counselor competencies in vocational aspects of counseling and guidance,[35] relating counselor competencies to counselor *attitude* and to counselor *activities*. Such competencies were pictured as best being intertwined throughout a total counselor education program rather than concentrated in one or two courses. Work values were stressed as part of a total human value system, and the importance of recognizing differences in personal value systems among persons from varying cultural backgrounds was emphasized. In general, this paper called for an increased input into counselor education from the fields of sociology, labor economics, and vocational education.

A second paper, by Strowig and Perrone, reported on a national study of the current emphasis on vocational aspects of counseling and guidance in current counselor education programs.[36] Their survey revealed that most programs for educating school counselors included only one course in the area with that course concentrating on comparing various systems for classifying occupations and various theories of vocational development. Counselor educators, city supervisors of guidance, and state supervisors of guidance were included in this study. While they disagreed on many recommendations, they agreed, in terms of suggestions for improvement, that much greater emphasis should be placed on the use of field experiences in increasing both counselor knowledge and the skill development of counselors. While agreeing with a need for more field experience in counselor education, Strowig and Perrone raise serious questions about the apparent lack of confidence in building counselor competencies through didactic instruction:

> We are inclined to applaud the trend (towards field experience) . . . but we are also disposed to wonder and regret that didactic learning may shrivel and dessicate from neglect. Frankly, it could hardly afford such a fate. Is there no body of knowledge and theory that is worthy of learning? Are we being forced to resort more and more exclusively to the patent inefficiency of field experiences as the primary mode of professional training?[37]

This issue that Strowig and Perrone raised so clearly in 1965 has apparently not been substantially resolved—nor, in general, even carefully studied—even now.

A third paper, presented by Henry Borow, emphasized implications of research in vocational development for changes in vocational aspects of counselor education.[38] In this paper Borow argues persuasively for *lengthening* the counselor education program well beyond its traditional one-year period with a much increased emphasis in the behavioral and social sciences. His review of the literature on career development stands in marked contrast to the relatively simple kinds of information that the Strowig and Perrone paper found to exist in practice.

The three discussion groups that operated during this conference came up with suggestions for forty specific changes for vocational aspects of counselor education programs, along with twelve specific vocationally relevant behaviors desired for youth and twenty research studies that needed to be done in order to provide necessary input into vocational aspects of counselor education. Certainly, it could be said that general consensus was reached that major change should occur in vocational aspects of counselor education programs. We do not need another conference aimed at specifying what should be done; rather, we are today in need of some clear indication that recommendations, such as were made in that conference, are, in fact, being carried out.

National Seminar on Vocational Guidance: Marquette, Michigan, 1966

In August 1966, under a grant using funds from the Vocational Education Act of 1963, a national seminar on vocational guidance was held at Marquette, Michigan, to which state supervisors of guidance, counselor educators, vocational educators, and representatives of the business-labor-industry community were invited. The conference, jointly sponsored by AVA and APGA, resulted in a report edited by Norman Gysbers.[39] The seminar director was John G. Odgers, Ohio State Department of Education, under whose direction the seminar was conducted and the report published.

The general conclusions of the conference emphasized the need for improved communication among personnel in industry, labor, business, and education; the need for counselors to accept responsibilities for vocational placement and follow-up activities; the need to make greater use of community resources; and the need to know and communicate more effectively to students and to parents the wide variety of education, training, and occupational opportunities available to persons who do not seek a college degree. The conference report itself is replete with specific examples of ways in which these things could be accomplished and isolated communities in which they are now being done.

Only one work group made specific recommendations for changes in vocational aspects of counselor education programs. Their seven recommendations included:

1. Study of economics, the labor movement, and the free enterprise system.
2. Study of the sociology of subcultures related to the meaning of work.
3. Work experience outside of education for counselors.
4. Accumulation of knowledge regarding all possible educational opportunities, not just those regarding colleges.
5. Knowledge of community and school resources for vocational guidance.
6. Knowledge regarding how best to collect and use information.
7. Knowledge regarding manpower trends, including collection of local knowledge.

As with the Warrenton conference, strong agreement was present that there should be a much greater emphasis on vocational aspects of counselor education programs than currently exists. The emphasis on the desirability of work experience outside of formal education for practicing school counselors stands in contrast to the Thorsen study, reported earlier, showing a trend towards eliminating this requirement from counselor certification standards, while the Sixth Report of the National Advisory Council on Vocational Education strongly recommends that such work experience be required.[40]

National Seminar on Vocational Guidance: Columbia, Missouri, 1967

In August 1967 a second national seminar on vocational guidance, designed as a logical counterpart of the 1966 Marquette, Michigan, seminar, was held in Columbia, Missouri. Whereas the Marquette seminar had involved relatively large numbers of state guidance supervisors, the Columbia seminar was designed to involve relatively large numbers of counselor educators. As with the Marquette seminar, there were also representatives from business, labor, and industry, as well as some selected practicing school counselors. Like the Marquette seminar, this one was jointly sponsored by AVA and APGA using funds from the Vocational Education Act of 1963. Proceedings editor was Leeman C. Joslin, University of Alabama, and seminar director was Norman C. Gysbers, University of Missouri.[41]

This seminar approached the problem of preparing counselors for vocational guidance in three basic ways. First, three major papers dealing with new content having perceived relevance for counselor preparation were delivered. One of these was presented by Herbert Striner, an eminent economist who spoke about counseling from the standpoint of the changing economy of the country and the role of the counselor primarily as a change agent in the social forces affecting the economy.[42] A second paper, by eminent sociologist Edward Gross, addressed the topic of work and society by discussing ways in which manpower problems and policies are influenced by the social structure.[43] The third paper, also by a sociologist, was devoted to the general topic of work and the individual and concentrated on the variety of meanings work holds and could hold for various members of society.[44] Each of these papers contains much content that is not now typically found in counselor education programs, though they hold great implications for directional changes.

A second focus of the seminar was directed at helping guidance personnel in attendance gain a greater understanding of vocational education, the obvious implication being that this, too, is a topic that should be given serious consideration as a part of preparing counselors for vocational guidance. The third focus of the seminar was on resources available for vocational guidance outside the counselor himself. This included an emphasis on resources in the school, in community service agencies, and in the business-labor-industrial community itself. The general emphasis, holding great implications for counselor preparation programs, was on guidance services outside the school other than counseling itself and on the necessary willingness of the business-labor-industrial community to help counselors become more knowledgeable regarding the world of work outside of education.

The general sessions were followed by a series of discussion sessions for task groups. Recommendations from the task groups included such specifics as: a) planned practicum in the world of work as part of counselor preparation; b) programs of paid work experience during summer months for counselors; c) greater concentration on culturally different populations in counselor preparation programs; and d) greater concentration on helping counselors develop more positive understanding regarding the many meanings of work. Task group reports related to current efforts to change counselor preparation programs were devoted primarily to reports of workshops, short courses, and various in-service activities of counselor education institutions and state departments of education, rather than basic changes in the nature of counselor preparation programs themselves.

The entire set of proceedings from this seminar is fascinating reading, for it seems to illustrate very well the need for change in counselor preparation programs, the awareness of general directions such change should take, and the relative slowness with which it is coming about. In terms of the culture of counselor preparation, it would be especially revealing to compare the conference recommendations with the ACES standards for the preparation of secondary school counselors, which were finalized in the same year. There are a host of differences.

PREPARATION FOR VOCATIONAL GUIDANCE: THE PROFESSIONAL LITERATURE

Those reading the preceding section will hopefully have obtained an impression that, as a result of these several significant national conferences held during the last several years, a considerable number of thoughtful recommendations for change in counselor preparation programs have been advanced. It would seem reasonable to assume that if, in fact, counselor education programs are being changed so as to reflect significantly greater emphasis on vocational guidance, those responsible for such changes would report them in the professional literature. Thus, a systematic search was made covering the period beginning in 1964 and going through spring 1972 in an effort to find reports of changes in counselor preparation programs related to vocational guidance. Journals studied included *Counselor Education and Supervision*, the *Vocational Guidance Quarterly*, and the *Personnel and Guidance Journal*. While this, admittedly, is a most limited search, it does include those journals in which it seems logical that those making such changes would choose to report them.

Changes Reported in Counselor Education and Supervision

The journal *Counselor Education and Supervision* is the official journal of the Association for Counselor Education and Supervision. As such, it appears to be the single most logical source of articles reporting changes in counselor preparation programs related to vocational guidance. A total of 411 articles published in that journal between 1964 and 1972 were examined. Of these a total of six related to changes in vocational aspects of counselor preparation, and of the six, two were regular articles while four were in the form of comments appearing in "ACES Corner," a special part of the journal reserved for short comments rather than regular articles.

Pruitt reported on results of nine vocational guidance institutes sponsored by Plans for Progress during the summer of 1965.[45] These institutes, typically three weeks in length, were aimed at providing practicing school counselors, teachers, and administrators with a better understanding of the disadvantaged minority student. The largest amount of time was spent in actual visits to business and industry. Pruitt recommended that counselor educators become actively involved in this kind of program as an adjunct to the regular counselor education program. A follow-up progress report on this kind of activity was reported by Leonard, who indicated that the program expanded to seventeen cities in 1966, to twenty-three cities in 1967, and to thirty-four cities in 1968.[46] Leonard emphasized the positive evaluations of these institutes, which have been carried out through the initiative of private business and industry without the benefit of support from either APGA or the Office of Education. It *is* a vocational guidance activity of counselor educators, but obviously not an integral part of change in regular counselor education programs.

Two short articles by Robert Hoppock appeared during this period in the "ACES Corner" portion of the journal. One described an assignment given counselor education students to search occupational information files being used for purposes of discovering the extent to which such files contained obsolete occupational information.[47] The second describes a new course at New York University entitled "Independent Study: Occupational Field Visits," which may be taken for anywhere from one to six semester hours of credit. In this course students are required to visit various business-industrial establishments and receive detailed directions for conducting and reporting on their visits.[48] Although this is the kind of practice strongly recommended in several of the national conferences reported earlier, this article represents the only time that it has been reported in the ACES journal as having been put into effect in a regular counselor education program.

An article by Paul Payne and Robert Mills reports on a practicum being conducted in an employment agency aimed at making prospective counselors more competent in meeting the counseling needs of disadvantaged youth.[49] This practicum was part of a clinical and counseling psychology program at the University of Cincinnati. The authors reported results such as less time spent in interviewing students and greater inefficiency in operation than in the regular practicum, and so they recommended that this kind of practicum be used as a supplement, rather than a replacement, for the regular practicum.

The final article summarizes a survey report on school counselor preparation in California.[50] This survey sought opinions of counselor educators, counselors in secondary schools, and counselors in junior colleges with respect to adequacy of emphasis given to vocational aspects of school counselor preparation programs. General agreement seemed to exist that improvement was needed in this area, although the counselor educators did not feel as strongly about this need as did the practicing counselors. McCreary reported that of eight counselor education institutions all but one offered only one course in the area of educational and career planning, but all claimed that attention was given to this area in other courses. In view of the set of national conference recommendations reported earlier, McCreary's results are clear indication of differences between recommendations and practice.

Changes Reported in Vocational Guidance Quarterly

For purposes of emphasizing differences between recommendations and practice, it may be significant to note that a review of all issues of the *Vocational Guidance Quarterly* published between 1964 and 1972 failed to reveal a single account of reported change in vocational aspects of counselor preparation programs. There were, of course, many articles appearing in this journal during that period that have direct application to the content of counselor preparation materials, but no reported examples of institutions changing their counselor preparation programs were found.

Changes Reported in Personnel and Guidance Journal

All issues of the *Personnel and Guidance Journal,* the official journal of the American Personnel and Guidance Association, were examined covering the period from January 1964 through May 1972. No single article was found dealing directly with actual changes being made in any counselor education institution with respect to vocational aspects of counselor preparation. True, a great many articles pertaining to counselor role changes having implications for counselor education were found, but there was not one article dealing with such changes in actual counselor education programs. Eight special issues, each dealing with what is pictured as a major problem for the profession, were found. No special issue of this journal has yet been devoted to career development, to career education, or to needed changes in vocational aspects of counselor education.

PROJECTIONS: COUNSELOR PREPARATION FOR CAREER GUIDANCE

To conclude this discussion with only a review of the *status quo* would seem to be a most negative thing to do. The current picture with respect to vocational aspects of counselor preparation can in no real way be said to appear bright. Yet there are forces on the horizon that make it apparent that this phase of counselor preparation simply must be given high priority. Among those forces a very powerful one is almost certain to be the sixth Report of the National Advisory Council on Vocational Education entitled "Counseling and Guidance: A Call for Change."[51] Among sixteen recommended changes contained in this report, the following have direct implications for vocational aspects of counselor preparation.

- State departments of education require work experience outside of education for all school counselors who work with students and prospective students of vocational education.
- Individuals with rich backgrounds of experience in business, industry, and labor, but with no teaching experience, be infused into the counseling system.
- Counselor education institutions require at least one introductory course in career education and at least one practicum devoted to an onsite study of the business-labor-industry community.
- Decisionmakers in education make extensive provision for the training and employment of a wide variety of paraprofessional personnel to work in guidance under supervision of professionally qualified counselors.

- Increased efforts be made to improve sound counseling and guidance services to members of minority populations and other disadvantaged persons.
- Special efforts be made to mount and maintain effective counseling and guidance programs for handicapped persons, for adults, for correctional institution inmates, and for veterans.
- Community service counseling programs be established and operated throughout the United States.
- Job placement and follow-up services be considered major parts of counseling and guidance programs.
- Career development programs be considered a major component in career education, both in legislation and in operating systems.

To the extent the NACVE is successful in influencing others to implement these recommendations, major changes are sure to come to counselor education programs. The nature of such change is fairly obvious from the specific wording of the recommendations. Some comments regarding certain of these changes, especially in light of the picture presented earlier in this chapter, would seem to be in order here.

A requirement that counselors possess work experience outside of formal education would certainly meet with great resistance from many of today's practicing counselors. Yet, in terms of counselor competency in understanding the nature of the occupational world and, more importantly, in understanding and appreciating various forms of work values, the common sense behind this recommendation cannot be ignored. It seems important to note that the NACVE made this recommendation only for "school counselors who work with students and prospective students of vocational education." The counselor education field is going to have to shortly resolve the issue of unity in counselor education.

The basic point to be recognized is that in the years just ahead there will be a major emphasis given to the career guidance function—and that function is going to be assumed by some group. If the unity of counselor preparation is to be retained, it appears that one price to be paid will be an emphasis on preparation for career guidance on the part of all counselors. Unless this is done, we surely face a period where separate "vocational counselors" are sure to emerge despite the philosophical pleas of counselor educators. This is already happening in states such as Florida and Texas.

The prerequisite of a teaching certificate and demonstrated successful teaching experience has already been removed in several states. With the advent of career education calling for a total educational program extending into the community as well as within the walls of the school, it seems inevitable that the teaching credential as a prerequisite for entry into school counselor education programs will quickly disappear. It is now both logical and sensible that this be accomplished. This means, of course, that counselor education will have to seek other basic means of justifying itself as graduate education. This too should now be done. As this is accomplished, it seems reasonable to believe that a major part of that justification will be found in providing counselors with competence in career guidance.

The counselor, viewed as an agent of social change, as well as one who provides direct assistance to clients in psychological adjustment, seems likely to form a significant part of the new justification for counselor education as

graduate education. Helping the society adjust to the client as well as helping the client adjust to society calls, in the case of career guidance, for
counselor knowledge in sociology and labor economics that is not now a
common part of counselor preparation programs. When the NACVE recommendations for at least one course in career education and at least one
practicum in the industry-business setting are added, we can see significant
changes in total patterns for counselor education.

It would seem that counselor education has effectively ignored the question of support personnel for guidance long enough. In spite of the rather
profuse amount of literature on the problem, the Zimpfer report made it
clear that relatively few school systems are employing support personnel in
guidance at the present time.[52] Perhaps it is time for our field to recognize
that if effective vocational guidance is to be provided for those from a wide
variety of cultural backgrounds, this can be effectively done only if we do
include support personnel who are able to relate effectively with those from
cultural backgrounds that may be different from the background of most of
today's practicing counselors. That is, it seems reasonable to project that
support personnel may be viewed not as a means of freeing the professional
counselor to perform higher level tasks but actually as a means of accomplishing certain parts of the career guidance job that the professional counselor
is incapable of performing herself. This possibility must be faced.

Certainly, the longitudinal nature of career development is going to call
for a vocational guidance emphasis beginning in the preschool years and
continuing through the retirement years. It seems highly unlikely that most
counselors will continue to exist in the school setting. While more counselors
will undoubtedly be needed in the schools than currently exist, even more
will be needed in community agencies and other settings outside of formal
education. Counselor education programs must gear up to preparing counselors for such settings who are competent in career guidance.

The advent of career education holds greater promise for furthering the
personnel and guidance movement than any other new educational emphasis
that has yet existed. As part of career education, the counselor will certainly
be expected to be competent in performing the career guidance function.
This will call for much more than the one or two courses that now typically
exist in counselor education programs. Again, the career guidance function
in career education is a vital task that will surely be performed by some set
of individuals. If counselor education can change fast enough, it can provide
the counselors needed for career education. If it cannot, then some other
form of individual will be invented and prepared for this task. This seems
very certain.

The counselor education field must shortly face very squarely the large
discrepancy existing between standards that call for a minimum of two years
of graduate work with a heavy concentration on developing competency in
the counseling relationship and the realities of career guidance. While, to be
sure, we would have no trouble finding meaningful learning experiences that
could take at least two full years of graduate study to master, the concept
of the two-year minimum is not viable today and does not appear to be one
that will be viable in the near future. Similarly, it should be clear now that
the development of counselor competency in the counseling relationship

per se is grossly overemphasized in the current counselor education standards developed by the profession. Counselors are going to need a great many additional competencies if they are to meet the career guidance needs of their clients. We must further face the fact that placement and follow-up are once again being pictured as important tasks for the counselor. These functions cannot continue to be ignored or pictured as tasks that are to be accomplished by paraprofessionals but are not legitimate concerns of the professional counselor. Competency in performing these functions must become a routine and important part of counselor education.

It seems reasonable to assume that at some time during the next ten years accreditation must come to the counselor education movement. If this is to occur, the kinds of petty bickering and false status needs that have prevented accreditation in the past must cease to operate. The basic rationale that the Callis committee developed in 1966, referred to earlier in this chapter, contains many elements that must be considered if the goal of accreditation for counselor education is to be attained.

Finally, there exists considerable doubt whether the kinds of major changes now clearly seen to be needed in counselor education can be accomplished in the absence of specific government funds allocated for this purpose. The personnel and guidance movement has never yet demonstrated sufficient internal strength and determination so as to control its own destiny; rather, it has always reacted to governmental pressures to change whenever those pressures have been accompanied by federal dollars. Within the culture of the personnel and guidance movement itself there is no significant sign to indicate that this condition is different now than it has been in the past. At the present time there is every indication that a greatly renewed emphasis on career guidance, counseling, and placement exists within the federal government structure. To meet the challenges called for in this emphasis, significant changes must occur in the counselor education movement. It is already late.

NOTES

1. Leona E. Tyler, *The National Defense Counseling and Guidance Training Institutes Program: A Report of the First 50 Institutes* (Washington: Government Printing Office, OE-25011, 1960).
2. Carl McDaniels, "The Impact of Federal Aid on Counselor Education," *Counselor Education and Supervision* 6 (Spring 1967):263–74.
3. Jack Thorsen, *Counselor Certification, 1971* (Washington, D.C.: American Personnel and Guidance Association, 1972, mimeo.
4. Harry Kranz, "A Crash Program to Aid Disadvantaged Youth," *APGA Guidepost*, 6(1964):3–6.
5. McDaniels, *op. cit.*
6. American Personnel and Guidance Association, *The Counselor: Professional Preparation and Role: A Statement of Policy* (Washington, D.C.: American Personnel and Guidance Association, 1964).
7. U.S. Department of Labor, *The Effect of Cause* (Washington, D.C.: Bureau of Employment Security, Manpower Administration, 1965).
8. *Ibid.*
9. Robert O. Stripling and W. E. Dugan, "The Cooperative Study of Counselor Education Standards," *Counselor Education and Supervision*, 0(1961):34–35.

10. *Ibid.*
11. Willis E. Dugan, "Critical Concerns of Counselor Education," *Counselor Education and Supervision,* 0(1961):5–11.
12. Carroll H. Miller, *Report of the Conference on Counselor Education* (Washington, D.C.: Guidance, Counseling and Testing Section, U.S. Office of Education, 1961), mimeo.
13. American Personnel and Guidance Association, *Counselor Education: A Progress Report on Standards* (Washington, D.C.: American Personnel Guidance Association, 1962).
14. American Personnel and Guidance Association, *Standards for Counselor Education in the Preparation of Secondary School Counselors* (Washington, D.C.: American Personnel and Guidance Association, 1964b).
15. George E. Hill, "The Profession and Standards for Counselor Education," *Counselor Education and Supervision* 6(1967):130–36.
16. American Personnel and Guidance Association, *Standards for the Preparation of Secondary School Counselors–1967* (Washington, D.C.: American Personnel and Guidance Association, 1967).
17. Hill, *op. cit.*
18. American Personnel and Guidance Association, "A Statement of Policy: Standards for the Preparation of School Counselors," *Personnel and Guidance Journal* 40(1961):402–07.
19. APGA, *The Counselor.*
20. Thorsen, *op. cit.*
21. Professional Preparation and Standards Committee, *A Proposal to Improve and Expand Accreditation of Programs of Graduate Preparation in Personnel and Guidance* (Washington, D.C.: American Personnel Guidance Association, 1966).
22. American Personnel and Guidance Association, *The Relationship of Short Term and Specialized Programs to the APGA Policy Statement, The Counselor: Professional Preparation and Role* (Washington, D.C.: American Personnel and Guidance Association, June 4, 1964c) 2 page mimeo.
23. American Personnel and Guidance Association, "Support Personnel for the Counselor: Their Technical and Non-Technical Roles and Preparation," *Personnel and Guidance Journal* 45(1967):857–61.
24. U.S. Department of Labor, *Report of the Interagency Task Force on Counseling* (Washington, D.C.: The Department, 1967).
25. D. A. Hansen, "Functions and Effects of Subprofessional Personnel in Counseling," *Counselor Development in American Society,* John McGowan, ed. (Columbia, Mo.: University of Missouri, 1965), pp. 211–33.
26. David Zimpfer, Ronald Fredrickson, Mitchell Salim, and Alpheus Sanford, *Support Personnel in School Guidance Programs* (Washington, D.C.: Association for Counselor Education and Supervision, March 1970).
27. APGA, "A Statement of Policy."
28. American Vocational Association, *Vocational Aspects of Guidance: A Statement of Policy* (Washington, D.C.: American Vocational Association, 1967).
29. John F. McGowan, ed., *Counselor Development in American Society* (Columbia, Mo.: University of Missouri, 1965).
30. Louis Levine, "Reactions to 'Some Aspects of History': A Paper by John G. Darley," *Counselor Development in American Society.*
31. John G. Darley, "Some Aspects of History," *Counselor Development in American Society.*
32. Robert O. Stripling, "Training Institutions: Standards and Resources," *Counselor Development in American Society.*

33. David V. Tiedeman and Frank L. Field, "From a Technology of Guidance in Schools to the Profession of Guidance in Society: A Challenge to Democratic Government," *Counselor Development in American Society.*

34. Bob G. Woods, "Social Change and Curriculum Development," *Counselor Development in American Society.*

35. K. B. Hoyt, "Needed Counselor Competencies in Vocational Aspects of Counseling and Guidance," *Vocational Aspects of Counselor Education,* Carl McDaniels, ed. (Washington, D.C.: George Washington University, 1965).

36. Wray Strowig and Phillip Perrone, "Survey of Current Training Approaches, Format Materials, and Curriculum Content in Vocational Aspects of Counselor Education," *Vocational Aspects of Counselor Education.*

37. *Ibid.,* p. 59.

38. Henry Borow, "Research in Vocational Development: Implications for the Vocational Aspects of Counselor Education," *Vocational Aspects of Counselor Education.*

39. Norman Gysbers, ed., *Proceedings: National Seminar on Vocational Guidance* (Columbus, Ohio: Ohio State Department of Education, 1967).

40. National Advisory Council on Vocational Education, *6th Report—Counseling and Guidance: A Call for Change* (Washington, D.C.: The Council, June 1972).

41. Leeman C. Joslin, ed., *Preparing Counselors for Vocational Guidance,* Proceedings of the National Seminar on Vocational Guidance (Columbia, Mo.: University of Missouri, 1967).

42. Herbert E. Striner, "Counseling: A New Process in a Dynamic Economy," *Preparing Counselors for Vocational Guidance.*

43. Edward Gross, "Work and Society: Social Structure and Manpower in the United States," *Preparing Counselors for Vocational Guidance*

44. Donald Hansen, "Work and the Individual: Autonomy, Alienation and Work Orientations," *Preparing Counselors for Vocational Guidance.*

45. Anne S. Pruitt, "Plans for Progress: Vocational Guidance Institutes," *Counselor Education and Supervision* 7(1968):292–98.

46. George E. Leonard, "Vocational Guidance Institutes: A Progress Report," *Counselor Education and Supervision* 8(1969):237–38.

47. Robert Hoppock, "Assignment: Obsolete Occupational Pamphlets," *Counselor Education and Supervision* 10(1970):95–96.

48. Robert Hoppock, "Occupational Field Visits," *Counselor Education and Supervision* 8(1968):396–97.

49. Paul A. Payne and Robert B. Mills, "Practicum Placement in a Counseling-Employment Agency for Disadvantaged Youth," *Counselor Education and Supervision* 9(1970):189–93.

50. William McCreary, "Counselor Preparation in California," *Counselor Education and Supervision* 8(1969):143–45.

51. National Advisory Council on Vocational Education, *op. cit.*

52. Zimpfer et al., *op. cit.*

SUGGESTED READING

American Personnel and Guidance Association. *The Counselor: Professional Preparation and Role: A Statement of Policy.* Washington, D.C.: American Personnel and Guidance Association, 1964. Details the image, the responsibilities, and the functions of counselors as seen by the major professional organization representing their interests.

American Vocational Association. *Vocational Aspects of Guidance: A State-*

ment of Policy. Washington, D.C.: American Vocational Association, 1967. Identifies the perspective of guidance services held by the major professional group representing vocational education.

National Advisory Council on Vocational Education. *Sixth Report—Counseling and Guidance: A Call for Change.* Washington, D.C.: The Council, June 1972. A perspective on counselor functions and preparation with regard to responsibilities in the vocational aspects of guidance which synthesizes many current issues.

Zimpfer, D., et al. *Support Personnel in School Guidance Programs.* Washington, D.C.: Association for Counselor Education and Supervision, March 1970. The most comprehensive treatment available of the research and conceptual literature pertinent to support personnel in guidance.

PART FIVE

The Future of Vocational Guidance

It is a truism that man guides his present behavior both by what he remembers and what he imagines. Knowing whether a given individual emphasizes his memories or his dreams gives one insight into his status-maintaining behavior or his risk-taking behavior; his propensities to react or to initiate. So it is with a profession.

Vocational guidance has a distinguished heritage and an exciting future. Extending Hansen's observations in Chapter 6 that America is a transforming society which may become a planned society or even an international society, the two chapters in this section attempt to address planning, internationalism, and the implications they appear to hold for vocational guidance in the future.

Wolfbein begins Part Five by analyzing the commonalities among the nations of the world in terms of such dimensions as economic growth, work and employment opportunity, technological change, the occupational-industrial-education shift, and mobility. He contends that the interactive effects of these factors on a worldwide basis portend revolutionary prospects for the characteristics and importance of work. Addressing specifically the matter of planning for work around the world, he identifies the combined importance of educational and manpower development. In analyzing the requirements for educational development, he particularly notes the importance to be ascribed to raising educational levels, to an expansion of vocational education, and to continuous education. In deliberating about manpower development, he discusses the matter of providing for economical ways to attain the prerequisites for employment and to coming to terms with goals for manpower utilization. Throughout his presentation he draws implications for vocational guidance.

Herr discusses the characteristics of the developed, developing, and least developed nations of the world as they provide the contexts for vocational guidance. He addresses the political, social, and industrial issues which shape the questions asked by persons in different countries, and which in turn shape the foci to which vocational guidance responds. He identifies the possibilities that reside in current attempts to apply systems thinking to defining vocational guidance objectives, the expansion of technology in guidance, and the changing theoretical bases to which preparation and practice respond.

Planning for Work in a World Community **21**

Seymour L. Wolfbein
Temple University

In the winter of 1970 I spent two months going around the world for the Bureau of Cultural Affairs of the U.S. Department of State lecturing on the inter-relationships between manpower and education. Once, after a lecture in Kathmandu, Nepal, a young man asked for a demonstration of how the principles of input-output analysis might be used in generating manpower estimates to which educational planning might be related in his country. Even with our cornucopia of statistical information, this relatively complicated, mathematically based technique has not yet been fully developed in the United States. Yet there in Nepal, still overwhelmingly agricultural and with about four out of every five persons still illiterate, a young man with a brand new Ph.D. in economic theory and economic development from a major American university was striving to help his country to achieve a balance of needs and supply in its initial stages of development by using the most "up-to-date" techniques.

The answer given was in a cautious vein and hopefully did not dampen his zeal too much—especially since judging by such advances as the sizzling traffic jams in downtown Kathmandu, Nepal may very well again leap-frog several centuries and come up with a great input-output study.

Thus I learned again and again that in the world of work, as in many other spheres, it is the same the world over, despite what are often large differences in tradition, culture, economic, and educational development among nations. The differences must be perceived, understood, and respected. Yet there is an enormous arena of commonality among us all, built not only on the nature of the human condition but on the fact that knowledge has a way of surmounting countless impediments and making itself known and felt around the globe.

INTERNATIONAL CONCERNS AND TRENDS

It is therefore worthwhile and instructive to review briefly some of these areas of commonality. There are five fundamentally important areas which are economically and vocationally related and which carry overriding portents for the education and guidance process from a world point of view.

Economic Growth

Throughout the world, in countries of every economic and political persuasion, the quest is for growth, for development in order to obtain the economic vantage point for achieving national goals. The rhetoric is often

531

different, but the substance of the strategies (policies) and tactics (programs) for achieving economic growth are much the same everywhere, involving a wide variety of fiscal and monetary measures as well as international economic policies such as tariffs, common markets, and wage-price stabilization efforts. The reasons for pursuing the goal of economic growth and development are quite clear. Without that goal it becomes very difficult, if not impossible, to satisfy rising expectations and aspirations; with it, there comes change, mobility, and an expansion of options.

In the 1970s spurring economic growth and then watching the Gross National Product (GNP) scorecard has taken on a significantly different cast from much of the previous quarter of a century following the end of World War II. Two factors are particularly important in this regard and both are intimately related to the goals and interests of those in the field of human development.

The first is represented by the ongoing debate concerning economic growth and ecology, that is, the environmental limitations of "Spaceship Earth."[1] We have come a long way from the simplistic arguments which inveighed against economic growth and the GNP as the culprits in this matter. Anyone who wants to see some classic examples of environmental pollution, both physical and human, ought to visit a few areas of the world characterized by a no-growth economy. What has emerged is the view that it is important to assess how we achieve economic growth and what we do with its consequences. Economic growth involves a variety of costs, including impacts on the environment which, in turn, can be avoided if there is a willingness to pay the attention and the price needed. As Barry Commoner has indicated, "there is no such thing as a free lunch,"[2] and in this case the piper has to be paid to prevent pollution. There is an overriding significance in this point to all practitioners in the field of human resource development in general and in vocational guidance in particular: *economic* growth and development itself has now demonstrably become a worldwide policy matter which in turn affects *human* growth and development as well.

The second factor is the recent recognition that the investment in human capital goes a long way toward explaining and generating the very economic growth that all nations are attempting to achieve. Looking at the problem from a world perspective, Theodore Shultz, a leading American innovator in this field, has remarked:

> My last policy comment is on assistance to low-income countries to help them achieve economic growth. Here, even more than in domestic affairs, investment in human beings is likely to be underrated and neglected—Some growth, of course, results from the increase in more conventional capital even though the labor that is available is lacking both in skill and knowledge. But the rate of growth will be seriously limited. It simply is not possible to have the fruits of a modern agriculture and the abundance of modern industry without making large investments in human beings.[3]

A growing body of documentation evidences the fact that even (and perhaps especially) in the more developed nations such as the United States the biggest component of economic growth stems from investment in human capital, particularly in education and training.[4] Throughout the world community the education and guidance process has become a force overtly recognized as one to be accounted for and encountered with in all considerations of economic growth. Krueger notes that "the differences in human resources between the United States and the less developed countries accounts for more of the difference in *per capita* income than all other factors combined."[5]

Work and Employment Opportunity

The goals of economic growth and development can be complex and their side effects equally diverse, but the prime objective is to generate an adequate supply of job opportunities for a nation's labor force. What has characterized the post-World War II era and differentiated it from past periods of time is affirmative, assertive, active, and even aggressive public policy and action in promoting full employment, to the point where governments have risen and fallen in relation to their ability to consummate such policies and programs. In the United States the groundwork was laid in the Employment Act of 1946 with its commitment of national policy to bring about "conditions under which there will be afforded useful employment opportunities, including self-employment, for those able, willing, and seeking to work." Again, while the rhetoric varies, this is the crux of the matter throughout the world.

Commitments of this sort are not guarantees of success, of course, and at the beginning of the 1970s the picture was spotty at best. Unemployment and underemployment were very high in many parts of the world, particularly in the developing nations of Asia and Africa. The Soviet Union complained of technological displacement and Italy reported more than one million men and women out of work. The United Kingdom's rate of joblessness equaled the record set in the early years of the 1930s, and in the United States an overall unemployment rate of about 6 percent persisted, despite a variety of economic policy actions.

A philosophy of spurring economic growth and full employment involves the education and guidance process in a wide variety of ways, some of which will be underlined later on. At this stage the point to be made is that a good part of the economic malaise of the early 1970s is *worldwide*, reflecting the role of such international factors as floating currencies, devaluation and the price of gold on such national issues as jobs and cost of living.

Technological Change

In the field of work technological change is perhaps the most common of the common denominators in the world community, and no nation is immune to its results. In fact, the challenges and promises of economic growth and opportunities for work and employment originate in good part from this phenomenon. In the United States output per manhour has risen by about 100 percent in the past twenty-five years; that is, there has been a doubling of the amount of goods and services produced for every hour of work put in. Other countries such as Japan and parts of Western Europe have exceeded that figure, while others have fallen far short of it.

Increasing productivity is, of course, also fundamental to rising standards of living. Like everything else, however, it also has its costs and side effects and, as in the case of economic growth generally, these have to be recognized and taken into account—not necessarily to constrain or restrict the process but to avoid or mitigate whatever effects are considered inimical to national goals. Table 21.1 presents some related data on this subject for the United States, Canada, Japan, and some of the key countries of Western Europe. The information underscores how a country's position in this arena can change in a relatively brief span of time, and it also illustrates the relationship of productivity to such key factors as the compensation of workers and the net result on labor costs, which play a critical role in trade relationships among nations.

In the period 1960–1970 every country listed in Table 21.1 experienced a larger increase than the United States in output per manhour in the manufacturing sector. At 107.8 the United States index for 1970 compared with 152.2 for Japan and even lagged behind that of the United Kingdom, which has not been considered a leader in technological change. Hourly compensation for employees (which includes all payments made by employers directly to their workers, plus all employer contributions to legally required insurance programs and other benefit plans for employees) went up more than output per manhour, with the result that unit labor costs, which reflect the relationships between what employees receive as compensation and their productivity, rose in most countries. The United States index of unit labor costs in 1970, at 112.8, was above most of the countries listed in Table 21.1, as indeed it had been for most of the latter part of the 1960s. A substantial turnaround occurred in 1971 because of the much higher increases in hourly compensation abroad. As a result, unit labor costs were generally higher outside of the United States, generating an improvement in the relative cost position of this country in the arena of foreign trade, which, in turn, is related to the two preceding factors of economic growth and work and employment opportunity.

Throughout the world, then, in countries with significantly different social and economic systems, one indicator which gets the closest scrutiny is technological change, particularly as it is reflected in labor productivity and in its impact on worldwide shifts in competitive costs.

The Occupational-industrial-educational Shift

Technological change also has up-ended the job structure of the world of work. As Table 21.2 documents, a prime example of this can be drawn from agriculture. In the United States fewer than 4 million workers produce all the food, feed, and fiber for a nation of more than 200 million people, plus the very large amounts exported—and millions of dollars are still paid out to farm owners for not adding to production. That the United States is no exception in relation to other industrialized nations is shown by the detail in Table 21.2.

Even in the much less developed and much more agriculturally based economies of such continents as Asia, the shift from farming has gained momentum. The results are not confined to the economic sector alone, of course. They have generated, in this country and abroad, enormous shifts to

Table 21.1 Indexes of Output per Manhour, Hourly Compensation and Unit Labor Costs in Manufacturing; Selected Countries 1960–1971 (1967 = 100)

Country	1960			1970			1971		
	Output Per Manhour	Hourly Compensation	Unit Labor Costs	Output Per Manhour	Hourly Compensation	Unit Labor Costs	Output Per Manhour	Hourly Compensation	Unit Labor Costs
United States	80.5	76.6	95.2	107.8	121.6	112.8	111.5	129.1	115.8
Canada	76.0	71.1	104.1	114.6	128.2	115.7	118.3	139.3	125.7
Japan	52.6	43.3	82.8	152.2	164.7	109.4	162.9	190.6	121.9
Belgium	68.1	54.7	80.1	122.0	126.9	104.1	126.8	143.0	115.5
France	69.6	56.4	81.4	119.0	132.9	99.4	125.7	147.7	104.9
Germany	66.4	54.2	78.1	116.8	134.9	126.2	123.7	154.8	143.5
Italy	65.1	49.6	76.3	118.3	141.0	118.6	121.8	159.2	132.0
Netherlands	67.2	45.9	65.2	133.7	143.4	106.8	142.9	163.7	118.2
Sweden	62.5	52.7	84.2	125.6	136.9	108.5	133.6	152.8	115.6
Switzerland	80.5	60.9	75.8	125.5	124.5	99.6	129.8	140.9	114.2
United Kingdom	77.7	65.0	85.3	111.5	134.3	104.9	116.5	151.0	115.3

SOURCE: *Monthly Labor Review*, 95, 7 (July 1972): 6.

Table 21.2   Percentage Decline in Agricultural Employment 1950–1970

Country	% Decline in Agricultural Employment
U.S.A.	51
Belgium	56
Canada	46
France	43
Germany	51
Italy	57
Japan	43
Netherlands	41
Sweden	60
United Kingdom	42

SOURCE: Calculated from *Monthly Labor Review,* 94, 10 (October 1971) Table 1, p. 4.

the urban scene, major alterations in family structure and relationships and, indeed, a general ambience of change and uncertainty which is bound to be the hallmark of this generation if not of many generations to come. What had become a cliche among vocational guidance workers in describing the American scene—the emergence of a dominant white-collar, service-producing economy—had by the early 1970s begun to overtake most economies of the western world and was beginning to emerge with some force in many of the less developed nations as well.[6]

In six of the ten economically advanced nations listed in Table 2 more than one-half of all civilian employment was in the service sector of the economy in 1970 (United States, Belgium, Canada, Netherlands, Sweden, and the United Kingdom). This occurred even in Japan, which experienced enormous industrial growth in the post-World War II period and where, in fact, industrial employment grew from one-fourth of all workers in 1950 to one-third of all workers in 1970. In Japan services accounted for a shade below one-half of all workers (47½ percent) in 1970, as agricultural employment declined significantly.

Similar trends permeated the occupational structure with huge advances in the proportion of the labor force engaged in white-collar work, led again by the United States where, in the beginning of the 1970s, almost one out of every three workers was a professional person or employed in a clerical position. There has also been a sharp upward thrust in the schooling of the world's population, including the labor forces of most countries, with a large expansion in college and university enrollments. The changing industrial-occupational mix has required a good part of this, and increasing education has in turn generated increasing demands for services, not only for more and more but for better and better quality of health care, recreation and leisure time activities, and so forth.

The portents of these shifts go well beyond such obvious (although extremely important) factors as job guidance, and they affect the size and distribution of everything from income to trade union membership. Here again, however, one of the most important impacts lies in the changes they are causing in attitudes, motivations, and aspirations of the world community in the arena of work.

One of the most important examples, and one which appears in most countries of the world, no matter what their current stage of economic development, is the so-called "emerging worker" phenomenon.[7] Briefly, the evidence seems to indicate that all of the trends described so far have produced a labor force which is significantly better educated, better placed in terms of employment, better off in terms of income, yet restive because they do not participate in the decision-making, management process as much as they think they have a right to. Another way of putting this is that the line between management and labor gets increasingly blurred, at least as far as potential for assuming responsibility for affecting the destiny of the enterprise is concerned, as differences in education, training, standards of living between the two diminish. A frequently mentioned analogue is academia where much of the decision-making responsibility lies with the workers (faculty) and where, in fact, there is a substantial amount of rotation in and out of "administration." These are hardly models of administrative efficiency, of course, and it will be interesting to see how far this thrust goes and what it will bring. The restiveness is there and if some of the current trends in collective bargaining continue, particularly in the service side of the economy, this part of the scenario of work is going to be quite different at the end of this decade from what it is now.

There is another side to this coin, however. The rising number and proportions of the population experiencing substantial amounts of schooling have emphasized economic growth and employment development even more than at any other time, and they will continue to do so in the years ahead. Thus, from the United States and its unemployed engineers and Ph.D.s to India and Ceylon with their jobless university graduates, there is restlessness stemming from a total lack of employment opportunity and the creation of the group known as "the educated unemployed."

In India, for example, even before the beginning of this decade the number of unemployed university graduates began to move into the hundreds of thousands, and the Education Commission of that country estimated that even on the basis of a 6 percent rate of economic growth there would be by the middle of the 1980s around 1½ million jobless college graduates, even if there was no increase in the rate of expansion in education.[8] At a 1971 intergovernmental conference called by the Organization for Economic Development and Cooperation (OECD) made up of the countries of Western Europe plus Turkey, Japan, Australia, Canada, and the United States, the first conclusion reached read as follows:

> Participants noted that, since the first Conference on this subject, held in Paris in September, 1966, important changes had taken place in the employment situation as well as that of education in the Member countries. These changes, resulting, among other factors, from the rapid expansion of education, have led, in a number of countries, to a paradoxical situation of a surplus in the overall number of people with higher education qualifications available in the labor market and, at the same time, shortages in the supply of specific qualifications required by a rapidly evolving economy and society.[9]

From both the employment and unemployment side, therefore, these shifts underscore not only the interacting effects of the trends described so far but also focus the spotlight more and more on problems of the relationship of the individual to the work place as reflected in his education, training, placement, utilization, and career development generally.

Mobility

As has already been indicated, the agricultural revolution and its accompanying industrial and occupational changes have generated a substantial geographic shift, especially to the urban centers. In the United States this has resulted in a situation where 70 percent of the population lives on 1 percent of the land area, where two out of every three people are concentrated in the major metropolitan areas characterized in large part by the phenomena of an inner city with a suburban ring and all the remaining problems of housing, transportation, social services and the like. In most of the countries of the world this pattern is being replicated as the diminution in job opportunities in the rural areas exerts a powerful push, while the often relatively few employment opportunities in the cities and the greater availability of social services, entertainment and other elements of urban life-style act as an equally powerful pull for population movement.

Employment opportunity itself has become much more mobile for two major reasons, both of which already have been touched upon. The first is the growing composition of employment opportunity in the service sector which, by definition, is people oriented and therefore is bound to move to where the people are. The other is the growing technology of fuel, power, light, and transport which frees industry from previously rigid locational factors such as having to be near a coal seam or water power.

In this new freedom, enterprise can now independently respond in determining its location more and more to where the supply of manpower is, not only in terms of numbers but in terms of quality as well. Where the hands, the talents, the skills are is increasingly becoming the major force determining the geography of employment opportunity. Thus, throughout the world mobility involves a one-two punch as both people and jobs are on the move.

The major forces of mobility should not mask the fact that considerable portions of national populations do stay put. Even in a place like the United States, which is usually portrayed as having a practically nomadic population, continuous surveys indicate that large groups in the labor force hold on to their jobs for a long number of years. One survey taken close to the beginning of the current decade showed that almost one out of every five workers in this country had been in the same job or business continuously for fifteen years or longer, a period covering the enormous dynamism described so far in this chapter.[10] This point is cited particularly to stress the fact that long term attachments to place and job are not uncommon and may, in fact, develop problems of their own if and when those specific places become depressed areas and the jobs begin to go.

Another point, however, is involved as well. Migration and mobility may be extensive, but just as important throughout the world is the fact that the highest rates of movement are exhibited by those population groups which are at the cutting edge of national problems—the young and the educated, as well as the poor and dispossessed.

One other feature of the mobility problem warrants mention at this point.

The factors which have generated increasing mobility within nations have also brought about movement of people and jobs across national borders. The so-called "brain drain" of the past two decades sent hundreds of thousands of well-trained and educated personnel to the United States, which reaped the advantage of a significant manpower pool for meeting some of its major talent shortages in areas such as medicine. But in the early 1970s there was some evidence not only of a lessening of this drain, but of a turnaround in its movement, as some American engineers, scientists, and teachers moved abroad.

Cutting across all of the five points reviewed so far and reinforcing their worldwide impact is the change they are bringing about in the "comparative advantage" that each nation has in the field of international trade. For a long time the importance of different natural resources in different countries has been emphasized as the vantage point for engaging in international trade, and almost without exception natural resources were described and analyzed in terms of coal, iron ore, forest products, and the like.

However, as has already been said, technology has a tendency to even all of this out. Japan, for example, can afford to buy out a substantial proportion of West Virginia's coal production, cart it all the way back to their country and use it to help manufacture goods which are then sold competitively in the United States. Moreover, more and more of a country's production turns out to be services which are not quite as neatly exportable as those goods. More and more, therefore, a nation's comparative advantage may have to be based on another natural resource which was always there but never fully recognized as such—the people and their skills. It is not surprising in this context to note that in the midst of huge unfavorable balances of trade for the United States in the early 1970s the items still showing an advantage for us were those representing the products of what has come to be known as the "knowledge industry," e.g., computers and their associated programs.

It appears, therefore, that the 1970s has *potentially* revolutionary prospects for the world of work, using the term "revolutionary" in its etymological sense as a really primary turn of events. In the continuing quest for economic and employment development throughout the world, the dynamic turn of the technological wheel has moved nations in the direction of services which by definition are people-oriented. Under these circumstances, the chances are that more and more countries will move to the point where the primary consideration and emphasis will be on production of services rather than things.

The word "potentially" has been emphasized for at least two reasons. The first is that these forces require an extended period of peace for their development, and as of the beginning of the 1970s there was no solid evidence that peace and amicability, even in the economic sphere among nations, was anywhere near being a reality. As a matter of fact in a significant number of countries, including the so-called developing ones, huge proportions of budgets and expenditures were going for the production of the goods of war.

The second is that there is still a long way to go in providing some of the most elementary items in a population's level of living in many nations. As has already been indicated, unemployment and underemployment are still rampant in major areas of the world. Ernst Michanek of Sweden, a world authority on international economic development, has pointed out that in the developing countries about 75 million workers out of a labor force of about 1 billion were unemployed at the beginning of the 1970s, that "underemployment can be set in the hundreds of millions," and that it would require the creation of about 300 million new jobs during this decade just to keep the problem from getting worse.[11] Michanek offers the following concrete illustration.

> An example may shed some light on the problem. The number of people born in India between 1955 and 1965 (who will thus turn 15 years of age during the 1970s) is 170 million. I repeat this figure—170 million 15 year-olds in a single country during a 10-year period! The net increase in the Indian labor force has, using this figure, been calculated at 63 million persons for the decade of the 1970s. This means 100,000 new people seeking work during just the first *week* of the 1970s, and then a larger increase every week thereafter, until the number of new job-seekers exceeds 140,000 per week at the end of the decade. Nothing in the five-year plan India is currently trying to fulfill indicates a belief that all these people can be given employment.[12]

The clincher, perhaps, is represented by the estimate that even a 6 percent rate of economic growth in the Indian subcontinent right through the end of this century would still permit only a $200 annual per capita income by the year 2000. All of which points the finger right at what may very well be the biggest people problem of all—population growth itself.

Finally, these few statistics serve as a reminder of both the similarities and differences in the world economic scene. They emphasize the enormous gulf in standards of living among different parts of the world and the problems generated by that very fact itself. They also emphasize the relative nature of much of what is being discussed here. The United States also has a serious problem of poverty. In fact, by the terms of the classification system used by the Federal government itself, there were about 25 million persons living in poverty in the early 1970s. Without derogating the problem at all, however, it is also important to indicate (in relation to the figures on income in India just cited, for example) that a nonfarm family of four was classified as living in poverty if it had money income of $4000 a year as compared with $50 or $200 per year in some of the nations of the world.

These, then, are some of the promises and pitfalls, some of the opportunities and perplexities emerging from a brief review of the forces affecting the world of work from an international point of view. Against this background, what can be said of planning for work in a world community? Here again, it is impressive to note the significantly common cores, common issues, and common programs and policies which prevail throughout the world. This is particularly so in the general area of human resource development, and the following discussion will therefore focus on the twin pathways involved: educational and manpower development.

EDUCATIONAL DEVELOPMENT

Before moving on to the discussion under this heading it will be helpful to make clear the use of the terms "education" and "training." This is not to propound any new set of definitions in a field which already abounds with definitional problems, but only to help make explicit how they are used in the context of this chapter.

Education refers to the formal, institutional instruction involved in an individual's first round of learning experience. For some this will be a relatively brief encounter before exiting from school; for others it will be an extensive period running through a graduate university curriculum. By *training* (or retraining) is meant all later transactions with learning, most often more vocationally oriented and which take place, for example, while one is employed, after loss of a job and entry into a manpower training program, or after marriage and childbearing.

One other prefatory note: since it is impossible to be at all inclusive in the matter of educational development, this section focuses on three items which already show substantial evidence of significant action in the 1970s. These are the problems of putting together a coherent educational system with adequate resources for tackling problems faced by the various population groups in a country, the forces affecting vocational education, and the explosive growth of the retraining area.

Raising Educational Levels

Every country in the world is witnessing the need for developing a rationale for deploying the limited resources available in order to increase educational and training opportunities. In every nation of the world that problem is exacerbated by the almost savage decisions which have to be made on which groups in the population get those resources and, of course, which do not. The implications for the role of the various population groups in the world of work are obvious. The problem is particularly difficult in those developing nations which at the start of this decade had very close to one billion illiterates in their populations, with the number going up every year. Aside from human needs, economic development is minimized if indeed it occurs at all under these circumstances; therefore, most of these countries have engaged in large programs to make a dent in this problem. While success has varied, in general the numbers have simply been too large up to now; teachers, classrooms, and curricula have been quite inadequate.

At the same time, nearly every developing country has tried to put a substantial share of competitive resources into higher education in order to obtain needed talent in medicine, natural sciences, agricultural and industrial economics, administrative and legal personnel and the like. As it has already been indicated, in many countries this has resulted in a supply which has outpaced economic development and the demand for such people, resulting in the "educated unemployed."

How to keep educational and economic development in some kind of phase is therefore a paramount problem. Five-year plans are very common in the developing world; every one of them budgets education in the context of projected economic growth, and in every one of them many very hard decisions have to be made.

In commenting on the often felt need to limit educational resources to selected groups, Alden Miller, a seasoned observer of the Asian scene, holds to a hard (if defensive) line:

> As for selectivity, it mainly means in this context that, if cruel economic facts force you to concentrate your campaign on a limited front, then it

would be more profitable to leave Grandma in her happy state of analphabetism and to concentrate on the twenties and thirties, who are going to be the key men and women in industrialization, in the reform of agriculture—and in "family planning." To make these literate, and to build their literacy into their life and work, is the aim of "functional literacy"—It may sound rather sordid, this linking of adult education strictly to economic (for the real emphasis is here) development. But it is necessary.[13]

These problems have analogues in the western world, although they may not be as overwhelming in magnitude or as stark in the dilemmas they pose. Yet the deployment of resources for educational development in the United States, for example, involves some very hard decisions, too, as is witnessed by the actual (though temporary) closings of public school systems in a number of major cities, the arguments about resource allocation for low-income groups all the way from Head Start at the nursery school level to Upward Bound at the college level and the size and composition of federal aid to education at the state and local level.

Since economic development in general and the problem of planning for the world of work in particular, begins at the education level, this section begins with that subject. What the pattern of response to the problems of educational development will be, through acts of commission as well as omission, remains to be seen as the 1970s move along. One major kind of response seems to be emerging, however. It is moving with enough force to warrant the possibility that it will become an important step forward during this decade.

We refer to the worldwide drive for new formats, new institutions, new systems for the provision of opportunities for learning. One now growing in countries such as England and the United States is the "university without walls" such as Thomas A. Edison College in New Jersey, an institution without buildings or campus which offers "external degrees." At the secondary school level there is a similar movement, illustrated by the Parkway School in Philadelphia, where schooling takes place in the various art museums, scientific institutes, and the like which line the Benjamin Franklin Parkway near the center of the city. Scheduled for India are television and satellite relays to cover the more than one quarter of a million villages of that nation. UNESCO is giving more and more support to such efforts, and, significantly enough, the World Bank is not only financing many educational ventures for reasons already developed in this chapter but is also actually providing staff for educational planning by bringing together experts from various countries.

It ought to be pointed out that many other decades have started out with great hopes for new breakthroughs in this arena but have ended up with comparatively little to show for their efforts. What may (hopefully) differentiate this decade from some of the others is the staggeringly large pent up demand, which may at last refuse to be denied, and the more aggressive entry into the field of such organizations as the World Bank with a monetary, proprietary interest in getting something on. We may know soon enough.

Vocational Education

Cutting across a good part of this problem is the course of events in the general area of vocational education. It has become clear that an improvement in the quality and pertinence of this field of education would result in a discernible dent in the problem of educational development generally. Whether one stays with the term "vocational education," broadens it to the idea of "functional education,"[14] or uses the more encompassing term "career education" now in vogue in the United States, the idea is the same, i.e., the provision of occupationally related learning opportunities, preferably from the elementary grades on through a setting and with curricula which are paced to individual needs and realistically related to the working world.

The current worldwide thrust in vocational education comes at a time when it could play a pivotal role in moving critical sectors of the population in countries at all stages of development into gainful employment. Even in the United States, manpower projections for the current decade show a need for as many workers with manual skills and training as for those with academic training.[15] So far the supply has not been forthcoming, despite specific shortages and rising wage rates in these fields.

Similar factors, including unresponsive curricula and restrictions to entry into various occupations, are causing this phenomenon throughout the world. And not to be omitted from these worldwide phenomena is the matter of status, the frequent derogation of manual skill in favor of concentration on university training. Thus, surveys among students asking them to rank various job fields always result in the same pattern of response in this country: occupations such as judge, engineer, scientist, and cabinet official come out first, while janitor, garbage collector, waiter, and the like appear at the bottom of the list. A recent survey among secondary school students in Zambia, Africa, gave almost exactly similar results: heading the prestige list were scientist, engineer, cabinet minister, and doctor, while down toward the bottom were laborers, domestic servants, dancers, and the like.[16]

Thus, another common denominator in planning for work in the world community revolves around the field of vocational education. Although it is too early to make any reasonable predictions regarding how all of this will come out in the 1970s, there are some favorable signs. Excellent technical training centers have been established in, for example, Asia and South America by and with American help. In fact, these centers are some of the most successful examples of international cooperation in planning and actual execution of programs in the field of work. This includes the training of indigenous personnel to be teachers, some of whom are brought to this country for part of their training, and in the United States it is possible to discern the beginnings of programs for our own country which are involving strategies which promise some successful breakthroughs.[17]

Continuous Education

One of the more rapidly growing fields in the general area of educational development has involved the accelerating acceptance of the concept of continuous or recurrent education and training. Shortly after the end of World War II, this took the form of extensive programs of manpower training and retraining, particularly for industrial personnel disemployed because of technological advances or the changing industrial demands due to alterations in foreign trade and so forth. The United States was the last country of the western world to adopt this format, but with the passage of the Manpower

Development and Training Act of 1962, this country went on to surpass most of the others in the number of trainees and in the variety of training programs afforded. All of these programs, both here and abroad, have brought extensive government, labor, and industry involvement, illustrated by the JOBS program in this country and by the industrial training programs in Great Britain, which are financed by levies on industry.

At the same time accelerating technology in the scientific and other professional fields has caused an enormous increase in the number and variety of programs for updating and refreshing substantive knowledge in these areas. Scores of American universities provide programs in these areas and many universities provide software and personnel for similar programs abroad. Included under this rubric are numerous programs in the field of administration and management, including many business fields such as accounting, operations research, and marketing—programs which are in very short manpower supply in developing nations. Private American foundations such as the Ford Foundation and the Salzburg Seminar in American Studies (which runs programs such as an annual seminar on management) have supported such efforts in Europe. International groups such as the O.E.C.D. have also sponsored work in this area.

These specific programs have been cited to indicate that the idea of continuous education and training and retraining has been made concrete in a variety of ways in many places in the world. There is, however, another point involved which is significantly more important in terms of the theme of this chapter. The development of these programs and many more (such as sabbaticals for steel workers under the labor-management contract in this industry) has led to the blurring of what for a long time have been the classic three stages of life in most countries: the progression in lockstep sequence through a number of years spent in getting an "education," followed by a block of years spent in "work," followed by a block of years spent in "retirement."

For reasons already cited, technological change not only makes this kind of arrangement unresponsive to changing needs; it actually provides a vantage point for breaking that sequence. Already hundreds of thousands of persons in many countries go to school, then work, then go back to school (and often both work and go to school), then return to full-time work, then take retraining, then work, then retire, then go back to part-time work, etc. Even as far back as 1960, a man beginning his work career at age twenty in this country could expect to spend 10 percent of his working life in part-time employment.[18] Although the 1970 data are not available at this writing, the trends of the past decade make it certain that this proportion has since risen.

This section closes at full circle with its beginning discussion of the differences between education and training. The evidence is at hand that there is a strong current running through many countries of the world which is eroding these differences and melding them into a more general mosaic of educational development. In the more industrialized nations the pressure in this direction has come from the sophisticated needs of changing technology, but more recently the needs of those at the lower ends of the living scale have come to the fore. Conversely, in the less industrialized nations the pressure has historically been immense from the emerging populations, but recently the needs of a changing technology in the context of economic development have been prominent. The result is a concurrent worldwide drive for programs to initiate and concretize new patterns of educational development which will correspondingly alter the patterns of our working lives.

MANPOWER DEVELOPMENT

Manpower development traditionally has a fourfold goal. The *first* goal involves the provision of the maximum amount of opportunities for training and retraining, for "second chance" institutions of learning—a matter which already has been reviewed in the previous section. The *second* goal, literally referred to as "manpower matching," focuses on perfecting the "fit" between supply and demand through programs ranging from aids to migration and mobility to the redesign of prerequisites for jobs to fit the characteristics of the available labor supply more closely.

The *third* goal involves manpower information, including research and study on current and anticipated developments affecting the working scene and the dissemination of the results in the most effective manner for purposes of guidance and counseling. The *fourth* goal calls for programs of manpower utilization, emphasizing standards of recruitment, promotion, and general career development of the individual, with particular reference to the provision of adequate working conditions, the avoidance of discrimination, and other human affairs concerns.

From the large array of program and policy issues in this context, the following three have been selected to illustrate some of the problems facing the planning process for work internationally.

Prerequisites for Employment

One of the key questions which has come to the fore in the 1970s, especially in view of the changing supply-demand relationships all over the world, relates to the educational prerequisites for different occupations. The question can perhaps better be put as follows: what are the best educational pathways for entry into a given job? For some careers, such as medicine, that road may be relatively clear, but for most the answer really lies in what is being done now and not in what could be more efficient and economical for the individual as well as for the nation. In fact, in just such a field as medicine, there has been a great deal of malaise concerning the length and composition of the curriculum. Similarly, through a program begun in 1967 the Ford Foundation is helping ten leading universities change their doctoral programs in the social sciences and humanities, by reducing to four years the time it takes to get the Ph.D., now averaging about seven and one-half years.

This is an area which still needs a great deal of research and experimentation as well as demonstration. Crossnational study in just this field alone would promise enormous dividends and payoffs in the crucial arena of manpower and education. Although this problem was illustrated with professional personnel, it is one which pervades the entire occupational structure.

The Learning Force

Even in such a highly developed country as ours, very little is known about a country's total educational thrust in relation to the work place. As a leading student of this matter points out, just about all of our information relates to the core of our educational and training efforts—"that sequential ladder of formal educational activity ranging from kindergarten through graduate schools." What we overlook is the "Educational Periphery—the variety of formally organized educational activities ranging from vocationally oriented programs in business, government, the military, proprietary schools, and anti-poverty programs, to culture and leisure-oriented programs in regular core institutions, religious education, television, correspondence courses, and private associations."[19] The educational core plus the educational periphery equals the learning force, and some idea of the enrollments involved under this concept can be seen from Table 21.3.

It is difficult to make a judgment about some of these figures since the sources for the data are not revealed, but there is little doubt that the message has substantial validity: there are enormous numbers of people having some learning encounters and transactions outside of the regular formal system. The popular television program "Sesame Street" is one well-known example of such an experience.

Very little is known about the "educational periphery" both here and abroad, and studies of its characteristics and the potentialities of harnessing it more deliberately in aid of educational development in various countries would be a most useful effort.

Table 21.3   The Learning Force 1940–70 (in millions)

		1940	1950	1960	1970
I.	The Educational Core				
	1. Pre-primary	.7	1.3	2.7	4.4
	2. Elementary	20.5	21.0	29.1	32.3
	3. Secondary	7.1	6.5	13.0	19.8
	4. Undergraduate	1.4	2.4	3.2	6.5
	5. Graduate	.1	.2	.4	.8
	Sub total	29.8	31.4	48.8	63.8
II.	The Educational Periphery				
	1. Organizational	8.2	10.2	13.0	21.7
	2. Proprietary	2.5	3.5	4.0	9.6
	3. Anti-poverty	—	—	—	5.1
	4. Correspondence	2.7	3.4	4.5	5.7
	5. TV	—	—	0.1	7.5
	6. Other adult	3.9	4.8	6.8	10.7
	Sub total	17.3	21.9	28.3	60.3
III.	The Learning Force (I + II)	47.1	53.3	76.7	124.1

SOURCE: S. Moses, "The 'New' Domain of Post-Secondary Education," *Notes on the Future of Education*, Vol. II, Issue 3 (Syracuse, N.Y.: Educational Policy Research Center, 1971).

Practitioners in the field of making manpower projections related to education and guidance have learned of the many pitfalls which beset their efforts. Even those who have the authority to design five-year plans and corresponding budget allocations for their countries have learned how events exogenous to their exercises, such as changes in international monetary rules, can affect the outlook.

What all of them have been learning recently, too, is that projections carry with them self-fulfilling prophecies. The problem has been, however, that these side effects were rarely recognized, anticipated, or made overt until very recently. Thus, many of the job effects of the multi-billion dollar interstate highway system generated by the American Congress two decades ago have been built into manpower projections for this country. What was not built in were such phenomena as Ralph Nader, huge increases in pollution, and significant expansion of employment in the production of antipollution devices.

As the society becomes more conscious of the side effects of economic development and begins to make clear what its goals in general are, the projected utilization of that society's hands, skills, and talents, can become clearer, too. In fact, as alternative goals are debated and adopted or not, it is quite possible to clarify what their manpower impacts will be.

This matter has been made clear in concrete and specific fashion by recent research in this field, particularly by the National Planning Association in this country. Table 21.4 illustrates the significantly different occupational composition of the American labor force prevailing in 1975, depending on where we put our resources in terms of our goals. Thus, in the years during which this volume is being prepared, if more resources are devoted to urban development and social welfare gets less, not only will the overall employment impact differ, but the kinds of manpower needed would be radically different. It would require, for example, a 67 percent increase in white-collar workers as against a 104 percent increase under the social welfare goal.

Table 21.4 illustrates two things, both sides of the same coin. It shows,

Table 21.4 Estimated Manpower Requirements Associated with Different U.S. Goals 1962–1975

	Social Welfare Goal			*Urban Development Goal*		
Occupation Group	*Employed in 1962 (000)*	*Employed in 1975 (000)*	*Percent Increase 1962–75*	*Employed in 1962 (000)*	*Employed in 1975 (000)*	*Percent Increase 1962–75*
Total	4,592	8,395	83%	6,336	10,160	60%
White Collar Workers	2,081	4,252	104	2,264	3,778	67
Blue Collar Workers	1,421	2,194	54	3,691	5,855	59
Service Workers	674	1,423	111	245	408	67
Farm Workers	416	526	26	136	119	−13

SOURCE: L. Lecht, *Manpower Requirements for National Objectives in the 1970s* (Washington, D.C.: National Planning Association, 1968).

first, that it is quite possible to document the manpower implications of different national goals, different sets of priorities, and different patterns of resource allocation. It shows, too, that manpower consequences may then point to desirable changes in the goals themselves in order to effect different manpower impacts. The possibilities of such an exercise are enormous, and in a free and democratic society could be the basis of much fruitful debate on national goals. The potentialities for such an exercise on an international basis, even on a bilateral basis in only a few economic sectors, are incalculable. Such would be the nature of planning for work in a world community!

THE FUTURE

As we look ahead to the coming decade, therefore, two major phenomena emerge. The *first* is that as man continues to transact with the environment throughout the world and mold it so that it yields him the goods and services he needs and wants, he will continue to confront an enormous amount of dynamism, generated particularly by an accelerating technology. This will also continue to alter the nature of work performed as well as the places where that work will be performed. More and more emphasis will be put on the human values involved in the work process; national goals will highlight work as opportunity for more than just the accumulation of goods; workers will ask for more of a chance to determine those very national goals. The *second* important phenomena is that these changes will enhance the services which have to be performed by the educational processes and its related activities such as guidance and counseling. What changes of the recent past already have uncovered, however, is a great need to know more about these processes, even in such an elementary but fundamental arena as what are the most meaningful pathways between education and work. New modes, new answers are already being demanded and those demands are going to increase even more.

From a world point of view these two developments suggest both a need and an opportunity. In an interdependent world, research, planning, and actual conduct of cooperative programs on a cross-national basis is a sheer necessity. By that same token, of course, it represents a great opportunity for cooperative efforts, increasing the chances for the production of new knowledge, its more rapid dissemination and the redress of some of the intractably large differences in levels of living among the various nations of the world.

NOTES

1. Cf., e.g., Ezra Mishan, *Costs of Economic Growth* (New York: Praeger, 1967) and the more popular exposition of his views in "The Ludites Were Not All Wrong," *The New York Times Magazine*, November 21, 1971. A good balanced summary of the matter can be found in "Economic Growth and Ecology," *Monthly Labor Review* 94,11 (November 1971):3–21, giving the views of a biologist (Professor Barry Commoner) and an economist (Professor Walter Heller).
2. Barry Commoner, *The Closing Circle: Nature, Man, and Technology* (New York: Alfred A. Knopf, 1971).

3. Theodore W. Shultz, *Investment in Human Capital* (New York: The Free Press, 1971), p. 47.
4. Cf. Edward F. Denison, *The Sources of Growth in the United States and the Alternatives Before Us* (New York: Committee for Economic Development, 1962) and such papers as Gary S. Becker "Underinvestment in College Education?" *American Economic Review* 50 (May 1960); Jacob Mincer, "Investment in Human Capital and Personal Income Distribution" *Journal of Political Economy* 66 (August 1958); and Zvi Greliches, "Research Expenditures, Education and the Aggregate Agricultural Production Function" *American Economic Review* 54 (December 1964).
5. Anne O. Krueger, "Factor Endowments and *Per Capita* Income Differences Among Countries," *The Economic Journal* 78(September 1968):658.
6. Some of these trends are detailed in C. Sorrentino, "Comparing Employment Shifts in 10 Industrialized Countries," *Monthly Labor Review* 94,10(October 1971):3–11.
7. Cf. W. A. Westley and M. W. Westley, *The Emerging Worker: Equality and Conflict in the Mass Consumption Society* (Montreal: McGill-Queen's University Press, 1971).
8. The problems of this group are eloquently described in a special issue of the Indian journal *Seminar* for August 1969, entitled "The Educated Unemployed" (Malhotra Building, Janpath, New Delhi, India).
9. O.E.C.D., Directorate For Scientific Affairs *Intergovernmental Conference on The Utilization of Highly Qualified Personnel: Conclusions* (Paris: O.E.C.D., November 1971), ED (71) 24, p. 1.
10. *Job Tenure of American Workers*, Special Labor Force Report 112 (Washington, D.C.: U.S. Department of Labor, September 1969).
11. Ernst Michanek, *The World Development Plan* (Stockholm: The Dag Hammarskjold Foundation, 1971), p. 45.
12. *Ibid.*, 46.
13. Alden Miller, "First Things First" *Lifelong Learning*, F. W. Jessup, ed. (New York: Pergamon Press, 1969), pp. 162–63.
14. Cf. Ralph W. Tyler, "The Concept of Functional Education" in Sterling M. McMurrin, ed. *Functional Education for Disadvantaged Youth* (New York: Committee for Economic Development, 1971), Chapter 1.
15. Cf., e.g., *Occupational Employment Patterns 1960 and 1975*, Bulletin 1599, and *Tomorrow's Manpower Needs*, Bulletin 1606, Vols. 1–IV (Washington, D.C.: Bureau of Labor Statistics, U.S. Department of Labor, 1968 and 1969, respectively).
16. R. E. Hicks, "The Relationship of Sex to Occupational Prestige in an African Country" *The Personnel and Guidance Journal* 47 (March 1969).
17. Cf. S. L. Wolfbein, "Seven Strategies for Success in Vocational Education," *Functional Education for Disadvantaged Youth*, Chapter 3.
18. S. L. Wolfbein, "On the Nature and Conditions of Working Life," *The American Statistician* 19 (April 1965).
19. Stanley Moses, "The 'New' Domain of Post-Secondary Education," *Notes on the Future of Education*, Vol. II, Issue 3 (Syracuse: Educational Policy Research Center, 1971).

SUGGESTED READING

Ginzberg, E. and Smith, H. A. *Manpower Strategy for Developing Countries.* New York: Columbia University Press, 1967. A case study of the various forces affecting the relationships among education, manpower, and economic development with lessons learned that are applicable to most parts of the developing world.

Organization For Economic Cooperation and Development (O.E.C.D.). *Policy Conference on Higher Qualified Manpower,* 26–28 September 1966. Paris: O.E.C.D., 1967. Discusses some of the major issues in educational development along cross-national levels, with particular emphasis on the relationships between education and manpower development in the context of economic growth. Raises the program and policy issues of planning for work in an international setting.

Manpower Report of the President, 1972. Washington, D.C.: Government Printing Office, April 1972. An annual report, required by congressional statute, which brings together a discussion of some of the major problems affecting manpower development and work in the United States and their relationships to education and training. Also contains substantial section giving current statistical intelligence on these matters.

Wolfbein, S. L. *Work in American Society.* Glenview, Ill.: Scott, Foresman, 1971. Analyzes the major forces affecting work on the American scene, with emphasis on the social and economic factors impinging on current and anticipated patterns of education, work, leisure, and retirement under conditions of technological change and future trends in jobs, education, and mobility.

The Decade in Prospect: Some Implications for Vocational Guidance

22

Edwin L. Herr
The Pennsylvania State University

Each of the previous twenty-one chapters is markedly oriented to the future. They reflect many alternative possibilities in the human environment and in the institutional forms which respond to such possibilities. In various ways the preceding chapters have addressed the many faces of change and identified its pervasive effects upon individuals, groups, and nations. They have suggested that change has the potential to give rise to many negative conditions in human existence—withdrawal, alienation, depersonalization, ennui, lack of the familiar, disruption of the traditional and the orthodox—as well as to many positive ones—universal discourse, interpersonal sensitivity, freedom from want, latitude for choice, and impetus to individual responsibility. It has been suggested that accelerating change can be seen as an outcome of historical and technological evolution as well as a vehicle to move a greater number of individuals from the bondage of want, reactivism, and personal unimportance to the greater freedom found in the gratification of physiological need, the formulation of personal identity, and the possibility of imposing oneself upon an evolving opportunity structure so that one's personal characteristics can be used as choice factors.

It is not the intent of this chapter to summarize systematically what has gone before in this volume; rather, its focus will be upon sharpening some transcendent points which have been identified here and in other pertinent places as they seem to bear upon the immediate future.

THE FUTURE AND THE FUTURISTS

To speculate about a future decade is at once optimistic and also involves a large margin of error. To do so at all with an eye on implications for vocational guidance assumes that man will not destroy himself during the period being forecast, that man will continue to wrestle with identity questions and ponder his options, and that a growing number of national governments will provide their citizens with comprehensive occupational and educational alternatives and the freedom to choose among them.

There are serious threats to taking on such an optimistic stance about the future. Former Prime Minister of Canada Pearson has recently noted that we face five major threats to peace, progress, and even to human survival.

1. Nuclear war in which one single mechanism can explode more destructive power in one blast than all the guns and bombs of all the wars of the past.

2. The population explosion which at the present unprecedented rate will soon require a sign on our planet "Standing Room Only."
3. The pollution and poisoning of our environment, to the point that man can now go into outer space in triumph, but breathes his own atmosphere in danger.
4. The depletion and eventual disappearance of the resources needed to keep our technological world from collapsing.
5. And, to many the most important of all, the division of our one world into a small residential area surrounded by slums.[1]

These problems or some combination of them have become a familiar litany to the world's consumers of the mass media. Each of these threats and its ramifications casts a sobering pall across virtually any discipline or institution in the process of contemplating what will be required in the years immediately ahead. However, neither the threats nor the pessimistic outcomes projected for them are inevitable. They can be averted by planning and by using available resources in new ways.

It is worth noting that responses to the five threats cited by Pearson are embedded in a generation of changes in occupations, in learning, in uses of technology, and in thinking about people. Each of these represents arenas to which vocational guidance in some form or another has a contribution. As the governments of the world become increasingly aware that the major questions regarding technology are not technical but human questions,[2] the role of vocational guidance processes is likely to become increasingly prominent in world affairs. We will take up this issue later in the chapter.

A growing belief that the future can be planned has been stimulated by persons in different academic disciplines as well as in a number of public and private panels, task forces, editorial boards, and seminars who have in common a concern for "futuristics"—the application of an array of scientific methodology designed to anticipate social and technological developments before they happen. Indeed, legislation has been introduced to provide federal funds for planning and the data bases which must support such activity.[3]

While it is probably accurate to suggest that each generation has had its peculiar breed of futurist—whether prophet, seer, medicine man, revelator—the current emphasis seems not to be focused alone on anticipating the future but, rather, and more importantly, on considering how different futures can be brought about. In essence, the futurist attempts to define the most plausible among many possible alternative futures, to describe in depth the probable characteristics of these alternatives, and to specify the events, processes, and materials which are required to convert the various plausible alternatives into reality. They "dream of using social science instead of pressure politics to solve the nation's problems."[4]

Planning for the future may evoke fears of Skinner's *Walden Two,* Huxley's *Brave New World,* or Orwell's *1984.*[5] Certainly, the language of systems analysis—PPBS, input-output, social and economic indicators—does little to allay such concerns. However, the responses by "future-planners" would likely be that such fears are only valid where technology is the master and not the servant, that the lack of information and not the conflict of interests is at the bottom of society's problems. Such a point may be moot, but the need to identify in a dynamic era the dimensions of the emerging blueprint of which vocational guidance is a part seems to be beyond controversy.

Futurists are not agreed about whether the future will be revolutionary in its differences from the present or evolutionary, an extrapolation from yesterday and today. Although each of these positions has strength, it will be assumed here for purposes of analysis that the seeds of the future are apparent in the problems of the present and that they presage the years immediately ahead. The remainder of this chapter will be devoted to an examination of some of the factors likely to define the contexts in and the methods by which practitioners of vocational guidance will function in the next ten years.

AN INTERNATIONAL CONTEXT FOR VOCATIONAL GUIDANCE

Super's discussion of American trends in vocational guidance in world perspective (Chapter 3) gives credence to the hypothesis that the form and substance of vocational guidance are not independent of political, social, and economic contexts. In America much of the impetus for the proliferation of vocational guidance at the beginning of the twentieth century came from a rise in industrialism and a growing reform movement concerned with the plight of the individual caught up in the web of the economic, educational, personal, and social factors which accompanied industrialism.[6] It was clear that there were dynamic connections between industrialism and the social order. Now, as Wolfbein notes in Chapter 21, the ramifications of industrialism are affecting the peoples of all the nations in the world in one form or another. In this context, Burns has contended that:

> Industry is the characteristic institution of modern advanced societies. So much so, indeed, that the old distinction between 'civilized' and 'primitive,' 'literate' and 'pre-literate' societies is nowadays preserved and given relevance in the terms 'industrial' and 'non-industrial' (or, 'developing,' which preserves the former invidiousness in the guise of a kindlier world). It has become as central because it is seen as the prime mover of economic, political and social change in Europe and America during the past two centuries and, because of this, as in large measure the 'substructure' of the present social and cultural order. In this belief, newly independent nations of whatever political complexion have adopted industrialization as a major political goal.[7]

In addition to the movement of industrialism noted by Burns, Wolfbein indicates in Chapter 21 that there is evidence of a growing international "people orientation." Evidence for the rise in people orientation can be seen in many of the activities fostered by the various agencies of the United Nations. For example, in a study for the United Nations of the importance of children in the process of economic and social development, Singer has emphasized that children are "the people of the future." He observes that perhaps the most powerful and universal motive in the world today is the desire by parents to provide a decent life for their children, preferably a better life than they themselves are having. It is appropriate and necessary, he says, that top priority be accorded to the formulation of a strategy of investment in human resources. In his perspective "expenditures on children is the most important part of human investment."[8]

International concerns about a people orientation are not confined to children, for it is also becoming clearer that the poor and the jobless exist throughout the world and that the solutions to their ills must transcend national boundaries. The United Nations Committee for Development Planning has stated that "employment and mass poverty must be moved from the periphery to the centre of all development planning."[9] A recent United Nations report has called for special measures for twenty-five "least developed" countries. These countries qualify as the poverty-stricken of the developing nations on the basis of the following criteria: per capita income of less than $100 a year; less than 10 percent of the gross domestic product derived from manufacturing; and a less than 20 percent literacy rate for persons aged fifteen and over.[10] It is difficult for a person raised and living in an industrialized country to place the implications of such criteria into perspective in terms of the quality of life which they represent. However, it is evident that responses to these conditions require a reorientation of policies by the governments of the developing nations and the agencies which bridge these two worlds. Jobs for the unemployed, minimum incomes to assure decent living standards, as well as wider distribution of income go beyond the need for simple economic growth which may affect very few of a given nation's population. If new but unemployable elites are to be avoided, education in these areas must be focused upon basic literacy and vocational training for adults rather than simply upon university education.

It is expected that by 1974 the developing world will have 200 million people needing work, and by 1980 the figure will be 300 million.[11] In order to respond to this matter governments will need to interrelate many factors and, perhaps more importantly, to redirect their patterns of production to meet the needs of the poor majority, not the affluent minority. They will need to revitalize their rural sectors in order to expand their agricultural productivity and reduce the mobility to the urban areas. This mobility takes on particular significance in view of the trends to more and larger cities which point up mankind's growing migration from the countryside to the cities. In 1970 there were 1,784 cities with population larger than 100,000—an increase of 20 percent in ten years. Of these 133 have more than one millon inhabitants, as compared with 104 a decade ago.[12]

In addition to the general spatial implications they hold for people, these numbers are also important to worldwide concerns for energy consumption (which was up 12 percent around the world between 1966 to 1969),[13] the search for new energy sources,[14] increasing forms and magnitude of pollution,[15] nutrition,[16] social welfare,[17] potential new sources of water,[18] expanded forms of economic activity,[19] and educational reforms.[20]

To a large extent solutions of the problems of mass unemployment and poverty must occur as a function of the developed (the industrialized) nations entering into new and different relations with the developing (the nonindustrialized) nations. At one level it is unlikely that the developed nations will overlook for much longer the plentiful supplies of labor in

Third World countries which can, if used effectively, preclude the purchase of expensive machinery. At another level the most developed nations (the so-called postindustrial nations) must find outlets for their "knowledge economies."[21] Their rising abilities to apply knowledge of all kinds to problems of creating productivity, delivery, transportation, and communication systems are precisely what many of the developing nations must "buy" in order to make quantum leaps in human or economic development over short periods of time.

In order for some of the cooperative activities just cited to occur, new forms of economic relations must be accomplished in the next decade. Recent crises in world monetary matters have accentuated the fact that what happens in one country affects others and that the future can no longer be viewed in simple national terms. Thus, it is likely that the poorest or least industrialized nations of the Third World will be more effectively integrated into international negotiations on monetary and trade problems.

There is evidence to suggest that other economic relations are on the threshold of development. For example, the agenda of the third annual session of the International Chamber of Commerce—United Nations and General Agreement on Tariffs and Trade Economic Consultative Committee[22] included the transfer of technology to developing countries, foreign investment in developing countries, and improvement of the human environment. Suggesting the emergence of the developing nations as a potentially growing and viable economic force is also seen in the fact that one hundred manufacturers from sixteen developing countries met in New York from October 2–13, 1972, with representatives of the World Trade Institutes, the United Nations Industrial Development Organization and other agencies to learn how to adapt their products for export to the developed countries.[23] Simultaneously, the United Nations is undertaking studies dealing with such topics as the impact of foreign investment on developing countries in the context of national developmental priorities[24] and the impact of multinational corporations on development and international relations.[25]

Economic interests weave among all countries. As of 1971 corporations in the United States had direct investments abroad (in terms of acquired or held equities in businesses) of over 80 billion dollars; foreign investment in the United States represents approximately 15 or 20 percent of that amount.[26] These latter factors have prompted the AFL-CIO, among other organizations, to express considerable concern about the deteriorating United States position in world trade and the adverse impact on American workers, communities, and industries. They have cited the emergence of trading blocs like the European Common Market, the internationalization of technology, which often permits the manufacture of high quality goods with labor costing 50–90 percent under U.S. rates in many countries of the Third World, and the proliferation of multinational corporations. They cite the need for the establishment of international fair labor standards.[27] Obviously, the impact of the Third World and a growing internationalism is not smooth and without reverberations. The problems are massive, and they require vision of the most comprehensive form. The point here is not to provide an exhaustive analysis of these matters but to cite them as the conditions or preconditions in which vocational guidance will manifest its contributions during the next decade.

VOCATIONAL GUIDANCE MODELS IN WORLD PERSPECTIVE

Neither counselors nor other practitioners of vocational guidance are distributed throughout the world. They are concentrated principally in industrialized nations; the so-called "developed" countries or "postindustrial societies." The ways they discharge their responsibilities vary from nation to nation with different emphases upon their role in facilitating human development or in acting as an agent for manpower distribution. Indeed, nations with quite different political systems may agree on a summary list of goals for vocational guidance but some may interpret them in terms of the individual's responsibility to his government while others may see them in terms of the governments' responsibilities to the individual.[28]

Underlying such differences are matters of freedom of choice for the individual. To the degree that such a principle operates, the choices to be made are unique to each individual and, consequently, far more complex than in situations where many constraints or imperatives operate to limit the individual's field of alternatives or his freedom to sort among them. Indeed, in some of the "least developed" nations choices are primitive or nonexistent, as is the individual's awareness that such human luxury is even possible.

It seems clear that as societies grow in occupational diversity or in their recognition of the importance of human development as an economic and-or a social resource, the climate for vocational guidance begins to flourish. However, the brief analysis of the Third World and the earlier perspectives on the most developed nations (or postindustrial societies) indicate several important things for vocational guidance. Perhaps the chief one is that the focus of vocational guidance will differ in the least developed, the developing, and the most developed countries because questions facing these governments and their populations differ.

Vocational Guidance in the Least Developed Nations

In simplistic terms, the least developed nations operate from a standpoint of economic insufficiency and a constant requirement to meet the basic needs of their population. The "have not's" are the majority, and the "have's" are the minority. In these instances needs are defined as the basic physiological requirements for survival. Work, to the degree that it is available, is visible. It is likely to be accomplished as a family enterprise whether it entails begging, farming, or craft activities. One's place in the social strata dictates to a large extent whatever possibilities for work there are and defines the field of alternatives which it is appropriate for one to consider.

In these situations vocational guidance is delivered by the family as the information center. Rarely are specialists available to perform such roles. Where they exist their activities are likely to be devoted to delivering fairly primitive types of information by which some segments of labor supply can be meshed with the inadequate opportunities for labor requirements. In these situations vocational guidance is concerned with sorting and distributing labor within existing forms of work. It is unlikely that "counseling" will be the treatment of choice or that philosophical discourses on the meaning of work or the solutions to questions such as "Who am I?" will be dominant. These latter are luxuries reserved for those societies where energies can be used in pondering such issues. When people who have had virtually no formal education must work from dawn to dusk to eke out survival for themselves and their families, questions like "Who am I?" "What do I want to be?" "In what ways can I exploit society's opportunities in terms of my personal characteristics?" are questions which surface rarely; and the state rarely provides resources to help the individual resolve them.

It is important to recognize that many of the nations of the world, including the least developed, are undergoing social change. The dimensions of this change are equally applicable in the rise of industrialism or of a people orientation. They include, first, psychological and sociological changes in the beliefs, values, or motives which prevail in a society and are internalized by man. They also involve external technological changes which directly affect the economic structure of society. And, finally, there is the continual emergence, dominance, and sometimes decline of institutional or organizational forms with which man must deal on both an internal and an external basis.[29] Vocational guidance will be required increasingly to focus its responses on these dimensions if its fullest potential is to be realized in the future.

In addressing mechanisms of change and adjustment to change, Smelser has described "structural differentiation" in periods of development. He has employed this concept to analyze the "marked break in established patterns of social and economic life" during periods of development. By definition, "differentiation is the evolution from a multifunctional role structure to several more specialized structures (i.e. during a society's transition from domestic to factory industry the division of labor increases and the economic activities previously lodged in the family move to the firm; the school emerges to perform the educational functions previously accomplished by the family and church)."[30] Thus, as social change and industrialization occur, differentiation causes changes in role structures, the integration of newly differentiated roles produces new social units with norms of behavior, and new organizational forms also emerge. Vocational guidance practitioners have roles to play in response to each of these transitions in role structure and in helping individuals come to terms with their culture in its dynamic form as social change occurs. It is very likely that the "least developed nations" will be among the world's most voracious in their needs for such assistance in the next decade.

Vocational Guidance in the Developing Nations

In the developing nations where an economic base which can permit occupational diversity exists, vocational guidance is more likely to address questions which deal with identifying the underemployed and the unemployable and in helping such individuals sort out available choices or consider training opportunities, whether formal or on the job. In countries which verge on the periphery of marginal economics between insufficiency and scarcity questions of acquired psychological needs found in rising consumerism and economic and social mobility provide the context for vocational guidance. In such a context vocational guidance can be seen as an active process for identifying and facilitating the attainment of skills and aptitudes, preferences, and other individual differences which are related to differences in requirements for manpower development. In this context such approaches as trait-and-factor analysis and information dissemination are more likely to have support than in the least developed nations. However, it is important to recognize a movement here to the psychological from the logistical. As technology is available in the developing nations, it unleashes a rising tide of expectations among the people it touches. Thus, vocational guidance is likely to be asked to respond to the emergence of hopes and fears related to achievement, livelihood, and career as these concepts become viable in the growth and efficiency of industrial organizations.

Vocational Guidance in the Developed Nations

In the developed nations or the postindustrial societies some small groups within the society may experience conditions analogous to the vast majorities in the least developed or the developing nations. However, they are the exceptions, and they are likely to be the focus of crash programs of a variety of kinds designed to wipe out the perceived deficits they encounter which have caused them to be "disadvantaged" relative to their majority contemporaries. It is of little consequence that the poorest among them may be richer than most of the people in the world. Social disadvantage may be an absolute in one society but highly relative in other societies. In the postindustrial societies the economy is likely to be one of abundance rather than of insufficiency or scarcity. Here the "have's" rather than the "have not's" are the majority. The problem is a distributive one in relation to the "wants" of the population rather than the "basic needs."

Practitioners of vocational guidance are likely to be specialists who are highly prepared for their tasks. This is so in part because the complexity of opportunity is such that the choice problem can be uniquely and individually defined. More importantly, perhaps, the individual is both provided the opportunity and indeed the encouragement to choose in response to how he answered the question "Who am I?" Choice becomes increasingly psychological, persons are educated for choice making as well as for productivity, and they are faced with the burden of decision rather than the burden of physical survival. Work becomes a subject for constant redefinition.[31] Education and work tend to be symbiotically and longitudinally related. One's family heritage becomes less important for social mobility than do levels of education and of responsibility attained. The individual is encouraged to relate himself to the psychological or affective dimensions of work rather than the work activity *per se*. Because these dimensions of work are walled off from the individual, particularly the young, in the process of choice work activity of a variety of types must be simulated in order for the individual to relate its meaning to himself.

While this discussion has suggested a linear relationship between vocational guidance, the phase of industrialism in which a particular country finds itself, and the characteristics of the political and social order, such a suggestion is highly simplistic. Models of vocational guidance differ markedly in their locus, organization, operation, and focus, even among the developed nations in Western Europe and the United States. These are the countries which have similar levels of industrial development, gross commonalities in the social order, and political goals. However, extending from Super's discussion in Chapter 3, some of the differences in vocational guidance models in these countries include:

1. Occupational information in the United States tends to be treated in the abstract and as nice-to-know; in Europe such information is treated much more concretely and as "must-know" information.
2. In the United States, the role of the schools and of employment agencies have been rather independent of each other with the former serving students and the latter serving out-of-school youth and adults. In other nations, one agency or the other has a virtual monopoly on vocational guidance (e.g., in Germany, it is the National Employment Service; in France, it is the Ministry of National Education).
3. In the United States, counselors are the principal specialists in vocational guidance. In England, careers teachers and careers officers are major specialists. Sweden, too, has specially designated teachers for vocational guidance purposes.
4. Some nations have extensive programs of prevocational education (Switzerland, Sweden, Denmark); others do not (France and Germany). In one nation (the Netherlands) it is elective rather than compulsory.
5. In the United States, "the counselor is prepared for and is expected to provide assistance to the student with all aspects of his development including social, personal and vocational, while his foreign counterpart tends to be solely concerned with the vocational. As a result, vocational guidance *is* guidance in Europe and available to and welcomed by a large proportion of the population, while it is only a part and, in some cases, a small part of the guidance program in this country."[32]

In essence the availability of vocational guidance is likely to expand as more nations enter their own industrial era during the next decade. However, the models and assumptions which characterize vocational guidance in America or in specific countries of Europe will be modified in their translation to the political ethos or degree of industrial sophistication in the developing nations of Africa and Asia. The decade ahead is likely to involve many vocational guidance practitioners from the developed nations in advisory roles with developing nations considering the assumptions and the methods by which their vocational guidance systems should take shape. In order to respond to such advisory roles effectively the persons involved in such activity are very likely to participate in efforts that will be generated by the systems approach.

THE SYSTEMS APPROACH

It seems highly probable that in the next decade we will see increased application of the systems approach to the problem of unemployment, poverty, and social welfare at national and international levels as well as in terms of institutions or processes such as vocational guidance which represent subsystems within a larger whole. The systems approach views activities and processes formerly considered unrelated as, indeed, parts of a larger integrated whole. It emphasizes interaction; the idea of parts all changing as they act on other parts and as they are acted upon in the whole.

The perception of systems has historic antecedents in the ecological thinking of the biologist, the notions of gestalt psychology, and the anthropological concepts of culture.[33] But the systems approach as we have come to consider it in the recent past is, according to Drucker, actually a measure of our newly found technological capacity. He maintains that "earlier ages could visualize systems but they lacked the technological means to realize such visions."[34] Inherent in the power of technology available in the developed nations is a potential for man to increasingly decide what end he wants and to fashion the means to arrive at such a goal. In essence, systems thinking requires one to attempt to understand a whole and to account for the effects of different actions you might take to achieve it.

In application to such a massive problem as poverty in the Third World countries or one country among them, systems thinking would necessitate consideration not only of the matter of poverty and its effects but of such related factors as the characteristics of the education system available, raw resources—such as materials for mining, food stuffs, the climate or scenery as a spur to tourism—the assumptions of the political structure in power, the types of occupations which can be developed, information dissemination networks, foreign markets, and many other pertinent factors. A systems approach gives credence to the point that if you correct or respond to only one of these aspects, needed changes in other related pieces of the problem will tend to absorb whatever change is made without permitting much affect upon the larger problem at issue. An analogue is found in group dynamics: if you change the composition of the group, the climate and focus of the group will change. A different leadership style may be required, and new content may need to be introduced.

While the application of the systems approach to the problems of warfare and the development of weaponry, to the sending of man to the moon, or to the development of mass production has become fairly common—even if we have not used the term "systems approach" to describe these things—such an application to the delivery of human services has been less common. This approach suggests that if you wish to attain some outcome—e.g., a student who possesses vocational maturity, an adult who is employable, an institution which provides a psychological climate that is mentally healthy—it is first necessary to determine what behavior comprises such goals and then to build strategies to attain them by taking into consideration the functional relations between parts, elements, and components which make it up.[35]

Basically, a systems approach to educational or to psychological problems requires such steps as the following:

1. Convert the goals to be attained into specific objectives which can be made explicit and operational.
2. Identify the individual behavior which will result if the objectives are attained.

3. Construct the procedures which are intended to accomplish the objectives.
4. Implement the resulting model and evaluate the results of it in terms of the operationally stated objectives.[36]

In such a context one can view the vocational aspects of guidance or vocational guidance as a subsystem of a larger system—education. This seems of particular consequence when vocational guidance is viewed developmentally as a stimulus variable or as an integral component of education. In this sense, if education and vocational guidance share the goal of developing students who possess the characteristics which collectively result in effective vocational behavior, then one is forced to examine the interdependent effects of vocational guidance and education. One cannot examine or treat vocational guidance as an isolated phenomenon; nor can one restrict oneself to what counselors alone do to produce effective career vocational behavior.

The Specificity of Vocational Guidance Objectives

Given such premises, it is likely that the systems approach will significantly affect the specificity with which the objectives of vocational guidance are defined during the next decade. Vocational guidance has historically experienced some difficulty in articulating what its purposes are in an operational way. Shaw,[37] for example, has argued that descriptions of guidance services are frequently simple inventories of what will be done—e.g., individual counseling and testing—rather than an explanation of why anything is to be done or the behavioral changes in students or clients which are expected as a function of guidance intervention. Rising pressure seems to be developing against the alleged fact that guidance objectives are stated typically in such gross terms as "to facilitate happiness or satisfaction," which do not lend themselves to being operationalized or measured. Relevant here is the observation of Krumboltz that "it is crucial that we conceptualize human problems in ways that suggest possible steps that we can take to help solve them." Further, "they must be translated into specific kinds of behavior appropriate to each client's problems so that everyone concerned with the counseling relationship knows exactly what is to be accomplished."[38]

Several attempts to identify the specifics of the counselor role, the parameters of counselor behavior, the modes and context of interaction, and the types of information to be exchanged between counselor and client (student) are underway. One of the most complete is that conducted by the State of Washington. In this plan school counselor certification rests upon behaviorally stated performance standards related to client outcomes. Some examples of the types of elements included in the plan include:

1.0 The counselor facilitates goal achievement of specific clients or client populations. . . Included among the counselor's clients are:
   1.1 Students
   1.2 Teachers
   1.3 Administrators
   1.4 Colleagues
   1.5 Parents

1.6 Community Representatives

1.7 Employers

. . . . .

3.0 As appropriate, the counselor is able to elicit responses from clients and goal facilitators (1.1–1.2) which include one or more of the following:

3.1 Specific informational responses

. . . . .

3.2 General informational responses

. . . . .

3.3 Affective responses

. . . . .

3.4 Cognitive responses

. . . . .

3.5 Commitment responses

. . . . .

4.0 Together with a specific client or specific client population or goal facilitators, the counselor realistically (4.1 vs 4.2) identifies the contributions *he* can make toward the achievement or approximation of specific goals:

4.1 Ideal goals

4.2 Realistic goals within a estimated time limit

4.3 Immediate goals

. . . . .

9.0 From within the framework of a selected rationale (8.9), the counselor interacts with specific clients or specific client populations and with significant elements in the client's life space in a manner which enables the client to achieve or approximate the goals (4.0) toward which both have agreed to work.[39]

It is likely that the proliferation of attempts to specify precisely the characteristics of counselor behavior in terms of the vocational aspects of guidance or in other contexts will spawn a variety of alternative functional approaches to the delivery of human services. As the conditions requiring different forms of intervention become increasingly known, it is likely that the use of differentiated staffing, career ladders, and other structural modifications in vocational guidance will expand and the need for the systematic management of how these subsystems can be tailored to individual needs will escalate.[40]

VOCATIONAL GUIDANCE AND SOCIAL ENGINEERING OR SOCIAL TECHNOLOGY

Facing the challenges of developing vocational guidance for the people of the Third World or for those of the postindustrial societies will likely mean the deliberate application of systematically accumulated knowledge and theory about the nature of man and his institutions for the purpose of influencing the behavior of man and his institutions. This will require much research on what produces and what can change the circumstances being attacked. It will also proliferate the use by the social scientist of the computer to combine in complex models data about the variables necessary to understand and predict human behavior or the institutional and social processes which can foster change.[41]

The understandings which result will constantly raise the spectre of who is to decide who is to be manipulated and for what ends. As indicated earlier, Skinner's *Walden Two*, Huxley's *Brave New World*, and Orwell's *1984* will each be cited as prophetic of the impact of technology upon us when, in fact, it is not so much a question of the impact of technology in the next decade but rather the accumulated impact of not assigning priorities to the social tasks which must be accomplished if we are to realize our ideals. To an increasing degree persons in every country of the world will be facing the insistence of value questions.

In order to respond to the pressures for social manipulation within value questions across varying economic and political contexts, the practitioner of vocational guidance in the next decade is likely to become increasingly eclectic and increasingly empirical in the discharge and in the appraisal of his or her professional behavior. Thoresen[42] and, more recently, Berdie[43] have argued that the counselor needs to become an applied behavioral scientist. Thoresen has contended that the rigidities of theoretical dogma or the obscurity of complex abstractions to describe human problems or counseling methods need to give way to the systematic evaluation of a variety of techniques applied to a wide range of human problems. Berdie recommends abandoning counseling in its traditional sense and replacing it with a discipline called applied behavioral science. While Thoresen seems to support the evolution of counselors into applied behavioral scientists, Berdie suggests essentially beginning again with new training programs, expectations, and emphases.

To suggest a movement toward applied behavioral science is not to suggest that other perceptions no longer persist. Certainly, the skepticism about the effects of technology on man's "humaneness" and the counselor's response to it will continue to occupy a place in the professional literature. Gamboa, Kelly, and Koltveit, for example, have addressed their perception of the humanistic counselor in a technocratic society.[44] They have argued the case for accepting technology and at the same time dealing with the dehumanization that is its byproduct. They view the counselor as one whose task is to assist others in developing humane educational environments within the school and other institutions or in conceiving related experiences that will enhance the humanization process.

The concerns expressed in the recent past under the rubric of humanistic psychology[45] for helping the individual to become more empathic, more aware, and more sensitive to himself and to others are likely to blend increasingly with the emphases subsumed by applied behavioral science. The dissonance between humanistic psychology and applied behavioral science will be reduced in the next decade; they will be viewed less as polarities than as differences in emphasis. Even now Thoresen[46] has begun to speak of "behavioral humanism" as a means of translating the goals of humanistic psychology into terms susceptible to systematic and scientific inquiry.

THE COUNSELOR AS AGENT OF CHANGE[47]

The forces which are pushing the counselor toward becoming an applied behavioral scientist are also heightening the pressure for him or her to individualize or tailor responses to students or clients. Counselors are increasingly being encouraged to depart from strict adherence to the traditional one-to-one relationship with clients and, instead, to adopt and use any ethical technique which will result in the appropriate altered behavior. In addition, counselors are being encouraged to look outside of the person for resolution of certain types of problems and in so doing to treat the environment rather than the person. This latter conception of the vocational guidance person as a change agent relative to institutional expectations may become exceedingly important in the developing nations.

In gross terms treating the environment can mean "environmental modification" or "environmental manipulation." The former may mean assisting others—teachers, parents, employers—in changing the reinforcement schedules provided in a job situation or in a classroom, becoming more encouraging or supportive of a given student or worker, and developing diverse learning experiences attuned to a wider range of individual needs than was previously available. Some observers[48] believe that treating the environment requires intensive action in the community in behalf of clients: e.g., actively seeking job placements for minorities, working with employers in facilitating the acceptance of minority workers, encouraging the recruitment and training of minority group members, encouraging employers to reexamine job entry requirements and dropping those which are unrealistic (See Cramer, Chapter 16). Environmental manipulation, on the other hand, may mean literally moving a person from one environment to another more congenial to his or her needs. Thus, in some instances the counselor will serve as a resource person, in others as a collaborator with other professionals, or perhaps as a political activist in the community. Regardless of the specific role emphasis required, environmental modification and manipulation affirm the need for teamwork among counselors in schools and agencies with teachers, parents, representatives of industry and other community agencies.[49]

Whether or not one practices actual environmental modification or manipulation, these techniques give rise to the counselor being described as a change agent,[50] environmental engineer, manipulator, or behavioral engineer.[51] In addition to providing a focus on the environment as the object of concern, these roles also suggest that the counselor of the future might have minimal personal involvement with his or her clients; in essence, since the counselor's energies will be expended on making the psychological climate more positive, he or she will proffer his skills indirectly rather than directly in behalf of those he serves.

CHANGING THEORETICAL MODELS FOR COUNSELING AND GUIDANCE

Addressing the subject of preparing the counselor of the future (the applied behavioral scientist), Berdie has suggested that the present counselor's difficulty is "not that he has too much theory, but rather too little. This is particularly true of vocational guidance practitioners in those nations which have supported virtually no research or development effort. He does not have enough ideas and concepts to understand the problems that face him or to develop approaches and solutions to these problems."[52] Thus, Berdie recommends that in the future counselors should be well acquainted with theories of the following types: social influence, reinforcement and learning, cognitive development, field, psychoanalytic, trait and factor, role, decision, organizational, and vocational development. Further, he maintains that counselor insights from anthropology, economics, and sociology will need to have increased attention.

Tyler seems to echo awareness that the conceptual background for counseling and guidance efforts is less than complete when she states: "Perhaps more than it needs answers, at this juncture counseling research needs new questions—questions not about what counselors do but about the developmental process they are attempting to promote." She argues that the dominant personality theories "give us useful conceptual tools with which to think about what is wrong with a person and how it might be set right, but not to consider the question: What might this person do?"[53]

In response to Tyler's concerns are the implications radiating from knowledge and theory about career development (See Miller, Chapter 10; Jordaan, Chapter 11; Crites, Chapter 12). One of the axioms which has gained wide agreement in the theoretical approaches describing career development is that decision making is a process which has a longitudinal character, finding its roots in early childhood and extending throughout one's life. Indeed, it appears that the process of career development is intimately associated with the process of personality development more broadly conceived. In essence, every individual has a cumulative history which continues to express itself in present choicemaking behavior and in one's orientations to the future. Decision-making, then, involves translations of how one has come to view himself and his orientation to the past, present, and future as this is expressed in what he thinks he can do, what he chooses to do, and what he does.

Collectively, these views of career development and of choice behavior indicate that the way in which man views himself and his choice possibilities is a learned characteristic based upon the accuracy and scope of the information one has about the self, about environmental opportunities, planning, ways of preparing oneself for what he chooses and ways of executing what one has planned. In other words, career development does not unfold unerringly from some chromosomal or genetic mechanism but is primarily a function of learned responses, whether negative or positive in their results.

The current state of career development theory is such that a variety of developmental tasks,[54] elements, or themes[55] can be identified which can be used to answer tentatively such questions as "What can man do?" "What behaviors do individuals need to acquire an information processing strategy?" or "What knowledge, attitudes, values, or skills comprise decision-making?" as related to middle-class people in Western society (See Crites, Chapter 12).[56] Thus, career development theory as presently constituted provides a powerful stimulus to considering counseling and guidance as having two functional roles: stimulation or treatment.[57] Stimulation is essentially synonymous with development. In this role, counselors can create experiences by which students will develop the attitudes, knowledge, and skills conducive to personal competence in decision-making. There is a strong thrust in this view that guidance should be viewed as a major educational function paralleling and complementing the teaching function from elementary school through college.[58] On the other hand, career development provides the structure for a cognitive map of potential conflicts by which counselors can serve in a treatment capacity for certain students or for other clients.[59]

In a more global conceptual sense than is presently found in career development theory, Foa and Turner[60] argue that by the year 2000 we can expect to experience an integration of behaviorism and psychophysiology; a movement from the study of single behavioral variables to organized behavioral wholes; a greater knowledge of structural dynamics—how behavioral patterns become progressively differentiated as one matures; more attention to the notion that cultures are complex learning programs which have different structures and emphases among them and that these are important to the understanding of persons from various ethnic, racial, or social groups.

Such a perspective validates the growing importance of a developmental theory or structure such as career development theory (See Miller, Chapter 10; Jordaan, Chapter 11) to guide the stimulative efforts of counseling and guidance. In addition, it also adds credence to the growing perspective that many problems experienced by counselees are indeed problems of learning. Thus, insights into operant and classical conditioning, reinforcement, contingency management, as well as social learning, modeling, and vicarious reinforcement will receive growing attention as conceptual structures for counseling and guidance efforts.

It is important to note that current concerns for development are not confined to decision-making, choice behavior, or information processing. Mosher and Sprinthall,[61] for example, have promoted the importance of developing personal or psychological maturity of the self. This requires, of course, not only theories about abnormal behavior but, more importantly, models of human effectiveness. It imputes increasing vitality to questions like "What is self-actualized behavior?" "What are the constellation of traits which comprise psychological maturity?" "How did persons so described acquire such characteristics?" "What are the possibilities of man and his nature?" "How can human fulfillment be described and assessed as well as facilitated by changes in psychological climates?"[62]

The sum of these theoretical perspectives seem to be that vocational guidance will likely emphasize preventative approaches during the next ten years rather than operating principally as a remedial or *ex post facto* approach to counseling individuals with problems. In this sense, vocational guidance practitioners will become active rather than reactive in the discharge of their professional responsibilities. Long-term guidance efforts are likely to begin in the preschool period and continue throughout adult life. It is likely that there will be incremental increases in vocational guidance (in the broadest sense of this term) in the elementary school and a significant increase in outreach activities as counselors in the schools and other agencies attempt to make contact with the unemployed dropout, the floundering young adult, and the disoriented or displaced older worker.

THE USE OF TECHNOLOGY IN THE PREPARATION FOR OR PRACTICE OF VOCATIONAL GUIDANCE

Walz has suggested that "The future of guidance could well depend on the capacity of the counseling profession to utilize technology effectively."[63] This would seem not to be a problem since the future is likely to see an escalation of the use of such forms of technology as microcounseling and stimulation. These approaches already influence both counselor training and practice. In the former instance, microcounseling is an approach in which trainees work with volunteer "clients" in brief counseling interviews in order to acquire specific behaviors.[64]

The assumption on which both microcounseling and simulation are based is that "realistic" samples of expected professional behavior can be developed so that trainees can rehearse professional competencies under supervision without posing difficulties for "real" clients. Obviously, the analysis of counselor behaviors, modes of interaction, and types of information which counselors use with different clients, as these were cited above, represent a large repertoire of specific behaviors which a counselor needs and which can be learned in separate "packages." A number of current applications of such packages exist. For example, Wittmer and Lister[65] and Panther[66] have trained counselors in consultation skills through the use of videotaping. Fredrickson and Popken[67] have used similar simulation techniques in training directors of guidance to deal with such problems as guidance staffing, budgeting and program development. Hackney[68] developed a prepracticum model of counseling skills which included specific training in such skills as learning to tolerate and use silence as a tool, learning to listen and learning to identify feelings through verbal and nonverbal communication channels. Danish has developed a film-simulated counselor training model which uses a series of filmed emotional vignettes: a) to increase trainee self-awareness and b) to provide the trainee with a basic repertoire of counseling behaviors.[69] Higgins, Ivey and Uhlemann[70] have developed a programmed approach to teaching behavioral skills emphasized in mutual communication which they have entitled media therapy. Ivey, Normington, Miller, and Haase have developed a set of instructional materials designed to facilitate the learning of the following counseling skills:

1. Attending behavior.
   a. Eye contact
   b. Postural position, movement, gestures
   c. Verbal following (counselor's responding to a client's comment without introducing new data)
2. Reflection of feeling.
3. Summarization of feeling.[71]

Such approaches to the preparation of counseling and guidance personnel have moved from separate packages dealing with specific techniques to the structure for total programs of counselor preparation in such places as Stanford University and Michigan State University.[72] One can only expect that such approaches to counselor preparation will grow in numbers and status in the future.

The microcounseling and simulation approaches just identified, which are used to train counselors in some set of skills rely on such devices as films, videotaping, and programmed manuals to illustrate or reinforce the behaviors to be acquired. But these devices are not confined to preparing counselors. They are being used in a variety of ways to assist clients in altering their behavior. Games, work samples, films, film strips, problem solving kits, computers used for information retrieval or as interactive systems with which clients can have a dialogue are examples of forms of technology which can help counselors to facilitate the development of exploratory behavior, information-seeking skills, awareness of alternatives or contingency factors, decision-making strategies, and a host of other possibilities for client activity (See Bergland, Chapter 14; Miller and Tiedman, Chapter 15). While these forms of technology make it possible for counselors to do old things in new ways or even to do things which were never possible before, they also introduce new problems of confidentiality, privacy, and management of personal data. They further require that the counselor become familiar with the capabilities, the limitations, and the procedures for use of a wide range of technological concepts or devices. Beyond that, however, they tear at the historical images of the counselor and stimulate the need for sharpening them and for moving in new directions. Role and function questions are not answered by the availability of man-machine systems or counselors and technology coming into new symbiotic relationships; they are simply reordered and changed.

SUMMARY

This chapter has been an attempt to identify some major points of emphasis which are pertinent to vocational guidance in the next decade. In particular, the nations of the world have been classified as the "least developed," the "developing," and the "developed" in terms of their status with regard to industrialism. The relationship of vocational guidance to these various classifications has been discussed with the general notion that models of vocational guidance are interactive with political, economic, and social characteristics.

The systems approach has been described in terms of its applicability to understanding the economic and manpower problems at national levels as well as to refining the characteristics of vocational guidance. Various positions pertinent to the counselor as a change agent or an applied behavioral scientist have been explored relative to their likely impact upon the future. The expanding role of vocational guidance in a stimulative, preventive, developmental mode as contrasted to a remedial mode has been explored in relationship to the evolution of theory. Finally, the use of technology for counselor preparation and as an extension of the movement toward eclectic behavior with clients has been considered. Among these approaches, microcounseling and simulation seem most likely to be powerful influences in the decade ahead.

NOTES

1. Centre for Economic and Social Information, United Nations, "Text of Keynote Address by Lester Pearson at Boston Symposium on Second U.N. Development Decade," *CESI Note*, May 28, 1971.
2. P. Drucker, *Technology, Management and Society* (New York: Harper and Row, 1970), p. 84.
3. A. Kopkind, "The Future-Planners," *American Psychologist* 22(November 1967):1036–41.
4. *Ibid.*

5. B. F. Skinner, *Walden Two* (New York: The Macmillan Company, 1960); A. Huxley, *Brave New World* (New York: Bantam Books, 1960); G. Orwell, *1984* (New York: Harcourt and Brace, 1949).

6. W. R. Stephens, *Social Reform and the Origins of Vocational Guidance* Washington, D.C.: The National Vocational Guidance Association, 1970).

7. Tom Burns, ed., *Industrial Man* (Baltimore, Maryland: Penguin Books Inc., 1969), p. 7.

8. P. Singer, "Study of Children and Economic and Social Development Published by United Nations," *CESI Note,* September 12, 1972.

9. Centre for Economic and Social Information, United Nations, "Changes Needed in Third World Development Strategy to Stop Rising Tide of Poor and Jobless," *CESI Features,* May 22, 1972.

10. Centre for Economic and Social Information, United Nations, "U.N. Report Calls for Special Measures for 25 'Least Developed' Countries," *CESI Features,* June 2, 1971.

11. Centre for Economic and Social Information, United Nations, "Third World's Left-Over People Loom as Major Challenge in Mass-Poverty Fight," *CESI Features,* April 7, 1972.

12. Centre for Economic and Social Information, United Nations, "1970 Demographic Yearbook issued Today," *CESI Features,* November 12, 1971.

13. Centre for Economic and Social Information, United Nations, "World Energy Consumption up 12 percent from 1966 to 1969," *CESI Features,* November 19, 1971.

14. Centre for Economic and Social Information, United Nations, "Ethiopia's Hot Rocks Promise Power for Development," *CESI Features,* April 13, 1972; ———, "Sea-bed Mineral Riches under United Nations Scrutiny," *CESI Features,* November 24, 1971.

15. Centre for Economic and Social Information, United Nations, "Encouraging Progress on Marine Pollution Agreements for 1972 U.N. Conference on the Human Environment," *CESI Features,* December 3, 1971; ———, "Major Sources of Marine Pollution identified in Report to be considered by 51st Session of Economic and Social Council," *CESI Features,* July 8, 1971.

16. Centre for Economic and Social Information, United Nations, "High-Level U.N. Panel to work out Global Action Programme for Combatting Protein Deficiency," *CESI Note,* May 1, 1971.

17. Centre for Economic and Social Information, United Nations, "Statement of U.N. Under-Secretary-General for Economic and Social Affairs to Conference of European Ministers Responsible for Social Welfare," *CESI Note,* August 22, 1972.

18. Centre for Economic and Social Information, United Nations, "Controlling River Basins and Digging Village Wells, U.N. Search for Water in a Thirsty World," *CESI Features,* March 31, 1972.

19. Centre for Economic and Social Information, United Nations, "Better Bathtubs and Preserving the South Pacific—U.N.'s Little Known Role in Tourism," *CESI Features,* March 30, 1972.

20. Centre for Economic and Social Information, United Nations, "UNESCO Report says I.Q. Not the Only Factor in Educational Performance," *CESI Note,* September 20, 1971.

21. P. Drucker, *The Age of Discontinuity: Guidelines to Our Changing Society* (New York: Harper and Row, 1969).

22. Centre for Economic and Social Information, United Nations, "World Business Leaders to Third Annual Meeting with U.N. and Other International Experts," *CESI Note,* December 2, 1971.

23. Centre for Economic and Social Information, United Nations, "100 Manufacturers from 16 Developing Countries to attend Programme on How to Adopt their Products for Export to Developed Nations," *CESI Note,* July 17, 1972.

24. Centre for Economic and Social Information, United Nations, "Statement on the U.N. Panel on Foreign Investment in Developing Countries," *CESI Note,* December 7, 1971.

25. Centre for Economic and Social Information, United Nations, "U.N. to study Impact of Multinational Corporations on Development and International Relations," *CESI Features,* September 14, 1972.

26. The Conference Board, "Foreign Direct Investment in the Last Decade," *Road Maps of Industry,* July 1, 1972.

27. U.S. House of Representatives, "The Export of American Jobs. An AFL-CIO Analysis," Statement of Andrew J. Biemiller, Director, Department of Legislation, American Federation of Labor and Congress of Industrial Organization before the Committee on Ways and Means, House of Representatives on Pending Foreign Trade Proposals, May 19, 1970.

28. E. L. Herr and S. H. Cramer, *Vocational Guidance and Career Development in the Schools: Toward a Systems Approach* (Boston: Houghton Mifflin, 1972), pp. 221–222.

29. Tom Burns, ed., *Industrial Man* (Baltimore, Maryland: Penguin Books Inc., 1969), pp. 11–12.

30. N. J. Smelser, "Mechanisms of Change and Adjustment to Change," *Industrialization and Society,* B. Haselitz and W. E. Moore, eds. (New York: UNESCO, 1962), pp. 32–54.

31. Robert L. Cunningham, "The Redefinition of Work," *Modern Age* 9(Summer 1965):279–94.

32. Theodore J. Cote, "Vocational Guidance: European Style," *Contemporary Concepts in Vocational Education,* Gordon F. Law, ed. (Washington, D.C.: American Vocational Association, 1971).

33. Drucker, *The Age of Discontinuity,* p. 252.

34. Drucker, *Technology, Management and Society.*

35. E. L. Herr and S. H. Cramer, *op. cit.*

36. See L. C. Silvern, "Systems Analysis and Synthesis in Training and Education," *Automated Education Letter,* November 1965, pp. IC1–IC25.

37. M. C. Shaw, *The Function of Theory in Guidance Programs,* Guidance Monograph Series 1: Organization and Administration (Boston: Houghton Mifflin, 1968).

38. J. D. Krumboltz, ed., *Revolution in Counseling* (Boston: Houghton Mifflin Company, 1966).

39. H. C. Springer and L. M. Brammer, "A Tentative Model to Identify Elements of the Counseling Process and Parameters of Counselor Behavior," *Counselor Education and Supervision* 11(1971):8–16; See also L. M. Brammer and H. C. Springer, "A Radical Change in Counselor Education and Certification," *Personnel and Guidance Journal* 49(1971):803–08.

40. R. A. Ehrle, "Managing Human Service Subsystems in the 70's," *Journal of Employment Counseling* 9(1972):24–33.

41. D. N. Michael, "Social Engineering and the Future Environment," *American Psychologist* 22(November 1967)888–92.

42. C. E. Thoresen, "The Counselor as an Applied Behavioral Scientist," *Personnel and Guidance Journal* 48(1969):841–74.

43. R. F. Berdie, "The 1980 Counselor: Applied Behavioral Scientist," *Personnel and Guidance Journal* 50(1970):451–56.

44. A. M. Gamboa, Jr., W. F. Kelly and T. H. Koltveit, "The Humanistic Counselor in a Technocratic Society," *The School Counselor* 19(1972):160–66.

45. See, for example, V. E. Frankl, *Man's Search for Meaning* (New York: Washington Square Press, 1959); A. H. Maslow, "Towards a Humanistic Biology," *American Psychologist* 24(1965):724–35; R. E. May, *Existential Psychology* (New York: Random House, 1961); C. R. Rogers, *On Becoming a Person: A Therapist's View of Psychotherapy* (Boston: Houghton Mifflin, 1961).

46. C. E. Thoresen, *Behavioral Humanism*, Research and Development Memorandum No. 88 (Stanford, California: School of Education, Stanford University, April 1972).

47. Some of the analyses in this section and in the remainder of the chapter have previously appeared in altered form in E. L. Herr, "Counseling and Guidance: What Will They Become in the Remaining Years of the Twentieth Century," *Revista InterAmericana de Psicologica*, June 1973.

48. C. C. Healy, "Manpower Trends: Counseling or Political Solutions," *Personnel and Guidance Journal* 51(1972):39–44.

49. See, for example, W. E. Dugan, "Guidance in the 1970's," *The School Counselor* 10(1963):96–100; P. R. Harris, "Guidance and Counseling in the Year 2000," *The School Guidance Worker* 24(1969):22–28.

50. S. B. Baker and S. H. Cramer, "Counselor or Change Agent: Support from the Profession," *Personnel and Guidance Journal* 50(1972):661–66.

51. Among others D. S. Arbuckle, "Educating Who for What?" *Counselor Education and Supervision* 11(1971):41–48; K. Matheny, "Counselors as Environmental Engineers," *Personnel and Guidance Journal* 49(1971):439–44.

52. R. F. Berdie, "The 1980 Counselor: Applied Behavioral Scientist," *Personnel and Guidance Journal* 50(1970):451–56.

53. L. E. Tyler, *The Work of the Counselor* 3rd ed. (New York: Appleton-Century-Crofts, 1969).

54. D. E. Super et al., *Career Development: Self-Concept Theory* (New York: College Entrance Examination Board, 1963); E. L. Herr and S. H. Cramer, *op. cit.*

55. E. L. Herr, "Contributions of Career Development to Career Education," *Journal of Industrial Teacher Education* 9(1972):5–14.

56. B. W. Westbrook and Margorie M. Mastie, "On Pathfinding: Some Suggestions for Increasing our Understanding of the Construct of Vocational Maturity," *Journal of Industrial Teacher Education* 9(1972):39–46.

57. E. L. Herr and S. H. Cramer, *op. cit.*

58. N. A. Sprinthall, *Guidance for Human Growth* (New York: Van Nostrand Reinhold, 1971).

59. R. H. Mathewson has indicated that since 1950 the development of the individual's ability to make his own choices and to direct his own affairs has become an overriding concern; recurrent needs and problems are seen as opportunities to foster individual capacity for self-determination. Thus, to a growing degree in the future counseling and guidance shall "employ educative (not impositional) processes aimed at fostering, on a developmentally graduated scale, the capabilities of the individual for self-direction. . . In these educative forms of guidance, the guidee will be looked upon as a learner and the counselor as an educator who provides—or helps to provide —special forms of learning experience, who aids the learner to interpret and evaluate his experiences and his approaches to experiences, and who accompanies the learner as he shapes his autobiographical pattern among many subject matters, over many years of schooling, and through many types of

personal and social experiences." R. H. Mathewson, "The Status and Prospects of Guidance," *Counseling and Guidance in the Twentieth Century, Reflections and Reformulations*. W. H. Vanhoose and John J. Pietrofesa, eds. (Boston: Houghton Mifflin Company, 1970), p. 141.

60. U. G. Foa and J. C. Turner, "Psychology in the Year 2000: Going Structural," *American Psychologist*, 1970, 25:244–47.

61. R. L. Mosher and N. A. Sprinthall, "Psychological Education: A Means to Promote Personal Development during Adolescence," *The Counseling Psychologist* 2(1971):3–84.

62. C. R. Walker, ed., *Modern Technology and Civilization* (New York: McGraw-Hill, 1967).

63. G. R. Walz, "Technology in Guidance: A Conceptual Overview," *Personnel and Guidance Journal* 49(1970):175–84.

64. J. D. Kelly, "Reinforcement in Counseling," *Journal of Counseling Psychology* 18(1971):268–72.

65. J. Wittmer and J. L. Lister, "Microcounseling and Microcounseling Consultation via Videotape," *Counselor Education and Supervision* 11(1972): 238–40.

66. E. E. Panther, "Simulated Consulting Experiences in Counselor Participation," *Counselor Education and Supervision* 11(1971):17–23.

67. R. H. Fredrickson and C. F. Popken, "SARGO: A Training Program for Directors of Guidance Services," *Counselor Education and Supervision* 11 (1972):302–08.

68. H. L. Hackney, "Development of a Pre-Practicum Counseling Skills Model," *Counselor Education and Supervision* 11(1971):102–09.

69. S. J. Danish, "Film-Simulated Counselor Training," *Counselor Education and Supervision* 11(1971):29–35.

70. W. H. Higgins, A. E. Ivey, and M. R. Uhlemann, "Media Therapy: A Programmed Approach to Teaching Behavioral Skills," *Journal of Counseling Psychology* 17(1970):20–25.

71. A. E. Ivey et al., "Microcounseling and Attending Behavior: An Approach to Pre-Practicum Counselor Training," *Journal of Counseling Psychology* 15(1968):1–12, pt. 2.

72. J. J. Horan, "Behavioral Goals in Systematic Counselor Education," *Counselor Education and Supervision* 11(1972):162–70.

SUGGESTED READING

Drucker, P. *The Age of Discontinuity: Guidelines to Our Changing Society.* New York: Harper and Row, 1969. A comprehensive analysis of the meaning of shifting forms of technology for knowledge economies. Discusses emerging industries, changes in corporate forms, and implications of a knowledge economy for education. Addresses the characteristics of and needed assistance in developing nations.

Herr, E. L. and Cramer, S. H. *Vocational Guidance and Career Development in the Schools: Toward a Systems Approach.* Boston: Houghton Mifflin, 1972. Discusses the stimulus role of vocational guidance in the service of vocationalization as an educational goal. Describes various forms of technology in guidance in relation to the characteristics of planned programs of vocational guidance. Identifies the contributions of various specialists to career development as well as the components of change which need to be considered in program implementation.

Vanhoose, W. H. and Pietrofesa, J. J., eds. *Counseling and Guidance in the Twentieth Century, Reflections and Reformulations.* Boston: Houghton Mifflin, 1970. Presents the autobiographical statements of twenty-two distinguished theorists and researchers in counseling and guidance. Many of the statements deal with predictions about the future of these services.

About the Authors

Bruce W. Bergland, Associate Professor of Education at the University of Colorado (Denver), was formerly Assistant Professor of Education and Psychology at Northwestern University. Concerned particularly with behavioral counseling and its diverse ramifications, he has presented several papers at national conventions and authored articles in various national journals.

Henry Borow, Professor of Psychological Studies in the General College of the University of Minnesota, has held positions as a personnel technician, vocational appraiser, and as a member of the faculty at the Pennsylvania State University. He has served as consultant to several government agencies, including the U.S. Army, the Veterans Administration, and the Social Security Administration. A former president of the National Vocational Guidance Association, he has published approximately one hundred articles, chapters, and tests. Among his books are *Vocational Planning for College Students; Career Guidance for a New Age;* and *Man in a World at Work,* the first volume in the decennial series of which the present volume is a part. Professor Borow has served as consulting editor of the *Personnel and Guidance Journal* and the *Journal of Counseling Psychology* as well as co-editor of the "Research Frontier" department of the latter journal.

Stanley H. Cramer is Professor and former Acting Provost, Faculty of Education Studies, State University of New York at Buffalo, where he has been since 1965. Previously he was a part-time instructor in guidance and counseling at Columbia, Hofstra, and St. John's Universities, as well as a school counselor, English department chairman, and a coordinator of language arts in two suburban New York high schools. During a sabbatical in 1971–72 he was associated with the Career Research and Advisory Centre at Cambridge University in England as a Winston Churchill Traveling Fellow. He is the author or co-author of approximately thirty articles and four books, *Guidance of the College Bound: Problems, Practices and Perspectives; Research and the School Counselor; Group Guidance and Counseling in the Schools; Vocational Guidance and Career Development in the Schools: Toward a Systems Approach.*

John O. Crites has been Professor of Psychology at the University of Maryland since 1971. He served at the University of Iowa from 1958 until 1971, holding positions as Professor of Psychology, Professor of Education, Director of Counselor Training, and Director of University Counseling Service. In addition to service as an Air Force officer concerned with career guidance, he has been a lecturer at Columbia University, a counseling psychologist at the University of Texas, and a Research Associate at Harvard. He has authored or co-authored three books (*Vocational De-*

575

velopment: A Framework for Research; Appraising Vocational Fitness; Vocational Psychology: The Study of Vocational Behavior and Development) and more than forty articles, book chapters, reviews, and tests. Since 1961 he has been co-editor of test reviews for the *Journal of Counseling Psychology*. From 1965–1967 he was a member of the Editorial Board of the *Vocational Guidance Quarterly,* and he has also served as a counsulting editor, *APGA Inquiry Series, Journal of Counseling Psychology, Journal of Vocational Behavior, Psychological Monographs,* and *APGA Counseling Monographs.* He received the APGA Research Award in 1966.

Robert L. Darcy, Professor of Economics and Director, Center for Economic Education, Colorado State University, formerly taught at Ohio University, Kansas State University, Oregon State University, and the University of Colorado. From 1961 to 1966 he was Executive Director, Ohio Council on Economic Education. He has authored more than thirty articles, book chapters, reviews, and books. Among the latter are *Manpower and Economic Education* and *Primer on Social Economics.* He has served or is now serving as a consultant to such organizations as U.S. Department of Labor, U.S. Office of Education, Joint Council on Economic Education, Committee for Economic Development and numerous educational institutions.

Edmund W. Gordon is currently at Teachers College, Columbia University, where he holds the positions of Director, Division of Health Services, Sciences, and Education; Professor of Education and Chairman, Department of Guidance; Director, ERIC Information Retrieval Center on the Disadvantaged; Director, National Center for Research and Information on Equal Educational Opportunity. In addition, he serves as Research Assistant Professor of Pediatrics, Albert Einstein College of Medicine. Among his many professional positions have been those of Presbyterian minister; clinical associate in psychiatry; counseling, clinical, consulting, and supervising psychologist; Chairman, Department of Educational Psychology and Guidance, Ferkauf Graduate School, Yeshiva University. He is co-author of *Compensatory Education for the Disadvantaged: Programs and Practices—Preschool Through College,* and he has authored numerous articles in professional publications. In addition, he has served as consulting editor for both the *American Educational Research Journal* and the *Personnel and Guidance Journal.*

Donald A. Hansen is Associate Professor of Education, University of California at Berkeley. He formerly served on the faculties of the University of California, Santa Barbara; Purdue University; and University of Otago, New Zealand. With a Ph.D. in sociology and a Ph.D. in educational psychology, Dr. Hansen has consulted and written extensively in counseling, sociology, and education. He has been consulting editor for *Social Science Quarterly, Sociology of Education,* and *American Sociological Review.* He edited *Explorations in Sociology and Counseling* as well as *On Education—Sociological Perspectives* and co-authored *Mass Communication: A Research Bibliography.*

Edwin L. Herr is at The Pennsylvania State University, where he holds the positions of Professor and Head, Department of Counselor Education;

University Director, Vocational Teacher Education; and Acting Assistant Dean for Graduate Studies, College of Education. He formerly served on the faculty of the State University of New York at Buffalo, as Visiting Professor at the University of Reading, England, and as Director, Bureau, of Guidance Services, Pennsylvania Department of Education. Prior to completing the doctorate he served in several school systems as a business teacher, school counselor, and director of guidance, and he has been a consultant to numerous government and educational organizations. Currently the Editor of the *Journal of Counselor Education and Supervision,* he formerly was a member of the editorial boards of the *Vocational Guidance Quarterly* and the *School Counselor.* He has published over seventy-five articles, book chapters, and reviews in addition to seven monographs and books. The latter include *Decision-Making and Vocational Development; Vocational Guidance and Career Development in the Schools: Toward a Systems Approach; Research and the School Counselor; Guidance of the College Bound: Problems, Practices, Perspectives; Group Techniques of Guidance.* He is currently president-elect of the Association for Counselor Education and Supervision.

David B. Hershenson is Professor of Psychology, Coordinator of Programs in Counseling Psychology, Rehabilitation Counseling, Counseling and Guidance, and the University Counseling Center, Illinois Institute of Technology. A consultant to many governmental and health organizations, he formerly served as a counseling psychologist, research fellow or lecturer at State University of New York at Buffalo, Peter Bent Brigham Hospital, Boston University, and several Veterans Administration hospitals. Author of numerous articles in professional journals, he has co-authored *The Psychology of Vocational Development: Readings in Theory and Research.* He is currently Associate Editor of *Rehabilitation Counseling Bulletin* and a consulting editor of the *Journal of Vocational Behavior.*

Kenneth B. Hoyt is Professor of Education and Director of the Specialty Oriented Student Research Project, University of Maryland. He formerly served as Professor of Education and Head, Division of Counselor Education, University of Iowa. In addition, he has occupied positions as an Instructor at the University of Minnesota and as a teacher, teacher-counselor, and director of guidance in several public school systems. He is past president of the American Personnel and Guidance Association, Founding Editor of *Counselor Education and Supervision* and on the Editorial Board of the *Personnel and Guidance Journal.* He has served or is now serving in such roles as Chairman, American Delegation, International Association for Educational and Vocational Guidance, Vienna; Chairman, National Advisory Board, Control Data Corporation Education Institutes; Consultant, National Advisory Council on Vocational Education; Consultant, ERIC Center for Counseling and Guidance; Consultant, Office of Manpower Policy; and many others. He has been honored with such awards as the First Distinguished Service Award, Association for Counselor Education and Supervision, 1965; Professional Recognition Award, Iowa Personnel and Guidance Association, 1967; Iowa Vocational Association, 1969; and the Outstanding Service Award, American Vocational Association, 1972. He is the author of more than one hundred monographs, articles, and books, and among the latter are *Career Education: What It Is and How to Do It; Career Education and the Elementary Teacher;* and *Guidance Testing*.

Jean Pierre Jordaan is Professor of Psychology and Education, Teachers College, Columbia University. A native of South Africa, he served as a high school teacher of English, Latin, and history, as a Housemaster, South African College High School, and as Vocational Psychologist and Inspector of Schools, Natal Education Department, prior to serving on the faculties of George Peabody College and Teachers College, Columbia University. From 1954 he has been associated with D. E. Super in the Horace Mann-Lincoln Institute Career Pattern Study, in the evaluation of computer-based educational and career exploration systems, and in the construction of various career development instruments spawned by these projects. Author of many articles in professional journals, he has also co-edited or co-authored *Counseling in the Rehabilitation Process; Career Development: Self-Concept Theory; The Counseling Psychologist;* and *The High School Years*.

Robert L. Lathrop is Research Professor of Vocational Education, The Florida State University. Immediately prior to his current position, he served as Professor of Psychology and Education and Associate Dean for Resident Instruction, College of Education, The Pennsylvania State University. Formerly he served on the faculties of Iowa State University and the University of Minnesota. Principally concerned with measurement theory, he has published articles pertinent to the latter and has served as a consultant to a number of governmental and educational institutions.

Eleanore Braun Luckey is Professor and Head, Department of Child Development and Family Relations, The University of Connecticut. Formerly on the faculties of the University of Minnesota, State University of Iowa, and Ohio University, she served from 1967 to 1970 as Director, Institute on Family Life Education (University of Connecticut) in the Virgin Islands. Currently President of the National Council on Family Relations, she served as President of the Connecticut Council on Family Relations from 1964–1966. In addition to publication of over eighty articles, she has co-authored *Guidance for Children in Elementary Schools*.

Esther E. Matthews is Professor of Education, Department of Counseling, University of Oregon. In addition to public school teaching and counseling, she has served on the faculties of Harvard, Columbia, Boston University, and the University of Toronto. Among her professional leadership positions are Secretary, Trustee, and Chairman, Commission on the Occupational Status of Women for the National Vocational Guidance Association. She has also served on the editorial board of the *Vocational Guidance Quarterly*. Author of numerous articles, she also co-authored *Counseling Girls and Women over the Life Span*. She is currently president-elect of National Vocational Guidance Association.

Anna Louise Miller is Counseling Specialist with Behaviordyne, Inc., in Palo Alto, California, and a counselor in the San Mateo City School District. She formerly served as Associate Educational Development Specialist,

Appalachia Educational Laboratory; Human Relations Specialist, Institute for Regional Development; and, Resident Hall Director, Ohio University. Her major interests are in individual development and the facilitation of hierarchical restructuring through self-understanding. She has written a number of reports, articles, and book chapters on vocational psychology and guidance.

Carroll H. Miller, Professor of Education emeritus at Northern Illinois University, has been a high school teacher and principal, a personnel technician, and a program specialist in the U.S. Office of Education. In addition, he has served on the faculties of Wittenberg University and Colorado State University, where he was Professor and Head, Department of Psychology and Education. He has been awarded certificates of recognition from the National Vocational Guidance Association and the Northern Illinois University chapter of Phi Delta Kappa. The author of many articles, he has authored *Foundations of Guidance* and *Guidance Practices: An Introduction.*

Walter S. Neff is currently Professor of Psychology, New York University, and Director, Community Research Unit, New York State Department of Mental Hygiene. From 1960 to 1964, he was Director of Research with the Institute for the Crippled and Disabled of New York City and served as Research Consultant since that time. Serving intermittently as a clinical psychologist and a professor, he has been on the faculty or staff of Cornell University, the University of Maine, C.C.N.Y., the Jewish Vocational Service, the Illinois Institute of Technology, and the University of Chicago. In addition to numerous articles, he has published *Adjusting People to Work; The Success of a Rehabilitation Program: A Follow-up Study; Work and Human Behavior; Reliability and Improvement: A Research Monograph.* He is currently completing preparation of *Society and Mental Disorder.*

Dale J. Prediger is currently Director, Development Research Department, The American College Testing Program. Prior to this assignment he served as Professor of Education, University of Toledo; as a research assistant with the University of Missouri Testing and Counseling Bureau; and as a teacher-counselor. He has directed numerous significant research projects dealing with measurement theory or application and has served as an editor of special features dealing with such topics. He has published more than twenty-five articles and monographs.

Donald E. Super is Professor and Director, Division of Psychology and Education, as well as Director of the Career Pattern Study, Teachers College, Columbia University, where he has served as a member of the faculty since 1945. He has served also as Assistant Employment Secretary, YMCA, and Director, Cleveland Guidance Clinic, and he has been on the faculties of Clark University, the University of Buffalo, Harvard, and the University of California. During World War II he served as an Aviation Psychologist and Major in the Air Force. Among his innumerable consultancies are the American Institutes for Research, USAF, AID, IBM, Young Presidents Organization, the U.S. Office of Education and the U.S. Civil Service Commission. Professor Super has been a Fulbright Lecturer at the University of Paris; Ford Foundation Fellow to Poland; American Specialist for the State Department in Japan; and a Visiting Professor, University of Keele, England. The recipient of many research and professional honors, he has been President of both the Division of Consulting Psychology and the Division of Counseling Psychology, American Psychological Association; President, the National Vocational Guidance Association; President, American Personnel and Guidance Association; Vice-president, International Vocational Guidance Association, and Director, International Association of Applied Psychology. The author of innumerable articles and twelve books, the latter include such works as *Computer-assisted Counseling; Occupational Psychology; La Psychologie des Interets; Appraising Vocational Fitness; The Psychology of Careers; The Dynamics of Vocational Adjustment;* and *The Vocational Maturity of Ninth Grade Boys.*

David V. Tiedeman is Principal Research Scientist and Director, Project TALENT, American Institutes for Research, Palo Alto, California. His earlier career involved positions as Head, Test Construction Department, College Entrance Examination Board; Associate Head, Statistics Division, Manhattan Project, University of Rochester; Professor and Head, Program in Guidance, Harvard University. In addition, he has occupied such roles as Fellow, Center for Advanced Study in the Behavioral Sciences: Special Fellow, National Institute for Mental Health; Associate Director, Center for Research in Careers, Harvard University. He has held national offices as President, National Vocational Guidance Association; President, Division of Counseling Psychology, American Psychological Association; and, President, the National Council on Measurement in Education. Involved in numerous consultantships, his affiliations include the National Manpower Advisory Committee Panel on Counseling and Selection and the Commission on Tests, College Entrance Examination Board. Author of more than one hundred articles, book chapters, test reviews, and books, the latter include *Career Development: Choice and Adjustment; Multivariate Statistics in Personnel Classification; Thought, Choice and Action: Exploration and Commitment in Career Development.*

Seymour L. Wolfbein is Professor of Economics and Dean, School of Business Administration, Temple University. From 1943–1966 he served with the U.S. Department of Labor in such roles as Chief, Occupational Outlook Service; Chief, Division of Manpower and Employment; Deputy Assistant Secretary of Labor; Director, Office of Manpower, Automation, and Training; and Economic Advisor to the Secretary of Labor. He has also served as a Visiting Professor in several American and European Universities. Honored by his alma mater, Columbia University, and by the U.S. Department of Labor with distinguished service awards, he has served in many important consultantships and has authored innumerable articles and papers. Among his many books are *Our World of Work; The Decline of a Cotton Textile City; Employment and Unemployment in the United States; Employment, Unemployment, and Public Policy; Education and Training for Full Employment; Occupational Information; Work in American Society.*

Kaoru Yamamoto is currently Professor of Education, Arizona State University. He previously was on the faculties of the Pennsylvania State University, the University of Iowa, Kent State University, and the University of Minnesota. He has authored more than seventy-five articles in educational and psychological journals, several book chapters, and such books as *Experimental Scoring Manuals for Minnesota Tests of Creative Thinking and Writing; The College Student and His Culture: An Analysis; Teaching: Essays and Readings;* and *The Child and His Image: Self-Concept in the Early Years.* Professor Yamamoto is the current editor of the *American Educational Research Journal.*

Index